Entrepreneurship

Entrepreneurship
Context, vision and planning

John M. Legge
Kevin G. Hindle

palgrave
macmillan

First published 1997 as *Entrepreneurship: How Innovators Create the Future* by Macmillan Education, Australia Pty Ltd
This edition published 2004 by
PALGRAVE MACMILLAN
Houndmills, Basingstoke, Hampshire RG21 6XS and
175 Fifth Avenue, New York, N.Y. 10010
Companies and representatives throughout the world

PALGRAVE MACMILLAN is the global academic imprint of the Palgrave Macmillan division of St. Martin's Press, LLC and of Palgrave Macmillan Ltd. Macmillan® is a registered trademark in the United States, United Kingdom and other countries. Palgrave is a registered trademark in the European Union and other countries.

ISBN 1–4039–0160–0

This book is printed on paper suitable for recycling and made from fully managed and sustained forest sources.

A catalogue record for this book is available from the British Library.

10 9 8 7 6 5 4 3 2 1
13 12 11 10 09 08 07 06 05 04

Printed in China

To the memory of Sir John Monash GCMG;
entrepreneur, soldier and public servant

Contents

List of figures

List of tables

Preface

This book is primarily intended for use on final year undergraduate business programmes and later year postgraduate business programmes as the text for a capstone subject, success in which will force students to call on most or all of their previous business studies. The book should also prove useful to professionals who need to prepare a business plan to exploit an innovative concept that they or their colleagues have developed.

Those who complete such a subject (or read and understand the book without undertaking a structured study programme) will be able to:

■ screen proposals for a new enterprise or initiative to be undertaken within an established enterprise rapidly and effectively
■ estimate the resources that will be needed to establish and grow an enterprise, and estimate their cost and the dates at which they must be made available
■ prepare a convincing and compelling business plan in support of any proposed innovation, including the most sophisticated and complex ones
■ understand in general terms the process by which a new venture raises the money it needs to commence and grow its operations

Readers will, along the journey, gain an insight into why innovation and entrepreneurship are important in a modern economy and get a chance to practise two desperately undervalued skills: concept and opportunity-screening; and revenue-forecasting, given a marketing budget, or setting a marketing budget, given a revenue forecast.

Our approach

The past 15 years have seen a veritable explosion in the number of tertiary institutions offering entrepreneurship subjects, sub-majors and programmes; as well as an equally explosive increase in the amount of research conducted into all aspects of entrepreneurship and the economic significance of entrepreneurial activity. Many textbooks on entrepreneurship were published over this period; but in our view, too many of these have taken too little account of contemporary research in entrepreneurship, economics, management and marketing.

This book, to the best of its authors' ability, does reflect such contemporary research. We expect our readers to learn about the 'why', 'when' and 'where' as well as the 'how' of entrepreneurship. We also expect at least some of our readers to plan and lead the most complex and demanding of innovative projects. For this reason we have not attempted to write a book about 'entrepreneurship' but rather we have focused on the development and production of business plans that will command the attention of potential investors seeking to take a stake in high-growth markets. To make room for such a focus, we have provided no more than a brief overview of the topic of entrepreneurial finance and have assumed our readers' knowledge of the marketing, finance and management subjects normally taught in the first two years of an undergraduate business programme or the first year of an MBA.

This is not an introductory text and neither is it the last word on the subject of entrepreneurship. At the very least a complete programme of study for entrepreneurs should include a full semester subject on entrepreneurial finance and a further full semester subject on the particular problems of managing rapidly growing businesses.

The focus of this book is both narrower and wider than that of many similarly named texts. It is narrower because of its focus on a limited number of entrepreneurial skills: opportunity-screening; revenue-forecasting; and the preparation of a logical, convincing business plan. It is narrower because we pay little explicit attention to new small business formation. It is wider because we embrace all forms of innovation, whether undertaken in new commercial ventures, as projects within established enterprises or pro bono. The common factor is innovation, an irreversible change in social and economic structures and relationships, and the men and women who assemble and direct the resources needed to carry them out.

There are limits to the applicability of military analogy to entrepreneurship, but if one wishes to learn from the military one should start with the best. To English readers the archetypical successful general is probably still Arthur Wellesley, first Duke of Wellington; and anyone involved in any aspect of management and entrepreneurship could learn a lot from reading a biography of the Iron Duke. Our particular hero is General Sir John Monash, who certainly didn't win the First World War on his own, as some overblown Australian patriots and anti-British Americans have suggested; but he had the honour of planning and commanding the offensive that convinced Ludendorff, the chief of the German general staff, that Germany had lost it.

Wellington and Monash were remarkably successful in their military activities. One of the key factors in that success was their ability to define precise objectives and the resources needed to achieve them. Neither general commenced offensive operations before those required resources were under their command. Once one objective was achieved, they developed a new plan before moving towards the next one. When Wellington and Monash encountered difficulties, they were less the result of bad planning than the consequence of subordinates failing to obey their orders. Lord Uxbridge's failure to halt the heavy cavalry's charge after completing the task that Wellington had ordered at the Battle of Waterloo put the entire British position at risk. The heroism of the Guards saved the day for Wellington and the Allies, but the price was heavy and paid in blood. Uxbridge's subsequent sangfroid has distracted attention from his incompetence. Monash was embarrassed on two occasions when he had American troops temporarily under his command and their officers failed, like Uxbridge, to observe Monash's stop lines and so lost the protection of his preplanned artillery strikes. No one has any right to challenge Uxbridge's bravery or that of the American officers and men who fought alongside Monash; but bravery can easily topple into folly.

In facile discussions of entrepreneurship, entrepreneurs are too often described as 'risk-takers', displaying the same reckless indifference to circumstances as Lord

Uxbridge, or his even more notorious successor, Lord Cardigan of the Charge of the Light Brigade. We prefer Monash's approach:

> I had formed the theory that the true role of the infantry was not to expend itself upon heroic physical effort, nor to wither away under merciless machine-gun fire, nor to impale itself on hostile bayonets, nor to tear itself to pieces in hostile entanglements ... but, on the contrary to advance under the maximum possible array of mechanical resources, in the form of guns, machine-guns, tanks, mortars and aeroplanes; to advance with as little impediment as possible; to be relieved as far as possible of the obligation to fight their way forward; to march, resolutely, regardless of the din and tumult of battle, to the appointed goal; and there to hold and defend the territory gained; and to gather in the form of prisoners, guns and stores, the fruits of victory. (Serle 1982)

Planning does not eliminate risk but it minimises it, and a well-planned venture, like a well-planned battle, often succeeds so completely that the effort that went into prior planning gets ignored: in the glare of 20:20 hindsight, it just looks easy – or the result of incredible luck.

This book is about how to be a lucky entrepreneur; not necessarily a glamorous or a famous one but certainly a successful one.

Structure

- Chapters 1 to 3 set the context: who becomes an entrepreneur; why they are important, socially and economically; how they should behave; and why entrepreneurial opportunities are unlimited. We devote some attention to the economics of entrepreneurship and the basis of entrepreneurial ethics. We emphasise that entrepreneurship is a social as well as an economic activity and certain institutions must be present and functional before significant entrepreneurial activity is possible.
- Chapter 4 summarises the process of opportunity screening and introduces a sophisticated revenue-forecasting model; an appendix to this chapter summarises the mathematical basis of the forecasting model and the hurdle rate table. The body of the chapter contains tables and methodologies that can be used by people not willing or able to tangle with the mathematics to arrive at soundly based conclusions under most circumstances.
- Chapter 5 discusses the strategic context envisaged for a new enterprise and discusses the issues surrounding the personnel structure and the creation of an asset register. While the work described in Chapter 4 will have established staff budgets, this chapter discusses the completion of the organisational design and the creation of a business model.
- Chapter 6 is our alternative to the list of lists found in books for the less ambitious: rather than providing a business plan and letting you fill in the blanks, we explain what a business plan is and what its crucial attributes are. We draw on recent research that establishes the critically important features of successful business plans.
- Chapter 7 provides a high level view of the law as it affects entrepreneurs, focused on issues that should be dealt with in a business plan. It is necessarily superficial,

and business law is worth at least a full semester subject on its own; but students should learn enough from this chapter to be able to complete a business plan that is not actually dependant on breaches of the law.

■ Chapter 8 discusses the impact of government policy on entrepreneurs, in both the neoclassical economic view and the more relevant view arising from system and complexity theories. Government policy is simply too fickle and varies too much from country to country for this to be a useful list of schemes, with tips for making a successful application; rather, we explain why governments might, on occasion, offer help to entrepreneurs. We hope that entrepreneurs who understand the reasoning of those who develop such schemes will be able to focus their applications on the issues that the schemes' authors will consider important.

■ Chapter 9 discusses the opportunities and difficulties facing innovative employees of corporations and makes some practical suggestions for corporate entrepreneurs seeking to enlist the resources of a corporation in support of their proposed innovation. While we nowhere exclude corporate innovation as a legitimate entrepreneurial activity, there are sufficient differences in the decision-making process to justify a chapter explaining them. Leading corporations are already replacing their traditional capital budgeting documents with a requirement for a properly prepared business plan and this trend will become general.

■ Chapters 10 and 11 deal with the entrepreneurial business plan. Chapter 10 discusses the financial model and explains the construction of a complete set of financial and management accounts for a new venture; this chapter will be critically important for students whose instructor elects not to use 'ExampleCo' or a similar model and useful in explaining the 'ExampleCo' model to those students who will be using it.

■ Chapter 11 makes some suggestions for laying out a convincing and compelling plan. We can't claim any great novelty in this chapter; the proposed table of contents and plan structure won't be very different from that recommended in other texts but we provide this chapter for the sake of completeness.

■ Chapters 12 and 13 look beyond the completion of the plan: Chapter 12 discusses the sources of finance for entrepreneurial ventures, necessarily limited to an overview of a topic that can easily justify at least a full semester subject.

■ Chapter 13 provides a broad overview of entrepreneurial research and the problems and opportunities of encouraging entrepreneurship in societies and cultures where capitalism has barely taken hold.

Using this book

Students

Students will find that we have assumed that they have acquired a basic knowledge of marketing, accounting and other subjects from a standard business curriculum. They will find that this book is very readable, which we hope will compensate them to some extent for the difficulty of some of the concepts and, if their instructor follows our suggestions, an extremely arduous assignment.

There are subjects where students at every level are aware that there is still more to learn and even those at the top of their discipline know that there are still unsolved problems to work on. Entrepreneurial business planning, as described in this book, is not such a subject, and while there will always be more to learn about business planning and entrepreneurs generally, the successful use of entrepreneurial business planning depends on your skills at collecting information, processing it using all the skills that you will have learned during your business studies, and a few more besides, and presenting it as a coherent, convincing plan and argument for undertaking a particular set of actions with a particular set of objectives. Planning requires the integration of many skills and is meaningless in their absence.

You will not learn how to 'get rich', although entrepreneurial business planning skills can certainly be applied to the gaining of personal wealth. By and large you will learn, from experience if not from this book, that most of those entrepreneurs who do get rich do so as a result of achieving a personal objective that has little to do with money as anything more than an essential resource for those who wish to create new enterprises and as a scorecard at the end of the process. John Kay, writing before Al 'Chainsaw' Dunlap's full contribution to the accounting scandals that marked the start of the twenty-first century became public knowledge, wrote:

> I do not recommend that you read Bill Gates's recent book any more than I recommend Al Dunlap's. But if you do read them both, you should notice the contrast: Gates's is entitled *The Road Ahead*; Dunlap's is called *Mean Business*. Gates is enthused by what businesses he might set up; Dunlap by those he might close down. Above all, you learn that while Dunlap's primary concern is money, Gates is primarily interested in computers. Yet Gates, not Dunlap, is America's richest man. (Kay 1998)

Gates has already given away far more in charitable donations and endowments than Dunlap has earned in his life.

Some readers may care even less for money than Gates appears to and seek to create pro bono enterprises or take an active role in one of them, perhaps as a country programme manager for Oxfam or an equivalent role in some other philanthropic organisation. All the skills needed to construct an entrepreneurial business plan for a profit-seeking enterprise are still needed when planning to create a pro bono one: objectives must be determined, the required resources must still be identified and assembled, finance raised and the enterprise staffed and equipped. An entrepreneur's extreme desire for personal wealth won't make a misconceived or ill-planned project profitable; but neither will an aid worker's sincerest desire to deliver benefits to those in need compensate for a failure to define the objectives of a mission properly or assemble the resources it needs.

You will also find that, while we provide numerous examples and anecdotes, there are no extended case studies or narratives. Our reason is that a successful entrepreneurial endeavour must, in some essential respect, be original and so must a sound entrepreneurial business plan. You won't succeed as an entrepreneur by merely copying what someone else has already done, and a plan that merely fills a few blanks in a predefined template is hardly a platform from which to launch a genuinely innovative enterprise.

Instructors

Obviously we are pleased that you have adopted our text. We will not be offended if you ignore our suggestions for teaching entrepreneurial business planning or a similarly named subject, but we are happy to offer them.

We have structured the book to support a course of 12 lectures over a single semester, assuming a two-hour lecture and a one-hour tutorial in each week. The text should be useful for courses taught in other formats or other sequences: having emphasised that students should not treat anyone else's ideas as scripture, we certainly don't claim to have produced a work of scripture ourselves.

We suggest that the lectures should not follow the text strictly. Conceptually, Chapters 10 and 11 should follow Chapter 6, and a lecture series should cover the financial model (Chapter 10) and writing the plan (Chapter 11) immediately after dealing with the theory of the plan in Chapter 6. Students whose assignment consists of a complete business plan will, however, be a long way short of either building their financial model or writing the plan body in week 6, and until they have completed at least a first draft of their plan, Chapters 10 and 11 will lack the immediacy that the practical problems of completing a plan present. Students should therefore be expected to read Chapters 10 and 11, notionally for the second time, as they prepare their assignments for submission and assessment,

Our experience has been that this subject is best taught in parallel with a major business planning assignment, with students expected to produce and present a plan of 30–40 pages for a genuinely innovative project. Most students will propose a plan for a new venture, but we believe plans for an innovation in either the corporate or pro bono sectors should be acceptable. Students can be asked to work as individuals or in teams of up to five members: teams may spread the workload or make it more bearable; a good business plan may take 200 hours or more to research and write.

Some students may find the selection of an appropriate subject for their business plan difficult but most won't. When teaching a class of new engineering graduates undertaking a management diploma full time, we required each team to go into the world and find someone who needed their help. On the first occasion we worried about a backlash, but there wasn't one and the subjects all seemed very grateful for the plan the students prepared for them and other advice they were able to give. Such an approach might not work so well with part-time students. Many part-time (and relatively mature) students will start this subject with a clear idea for a plan and should be encouraged to use it; those without such an idea can be prompted to ask their employer for suggestions; most companies have a backlog of ideas that they would like to see properly investigated.

We have recently allowed students to use a prewritten Excel® model to perform the calculations described in Chapter 4 and Chapter 10, and the 'ExampleCo' model is available in the instructors' section of the Palgrave website (http://www.palgrave.com/business/legge) for your use as an educational tool. Note that neither the authors nor Palgrave accept any responsibility for the consequences of the use of this model commercially. If students on a course for which this book is the prescribed text discover errors in the model, they may be referred to John Legge, who will respond as and when time becomes available. The model does not appear to reduce the time spent by students much, if at all, but for the majority of students being relieved from a substantial volume of Excel® programming appears to allow them to concentrate on other planning issues and generally produce better plans, judged overall.

Because of the workload, students should be encouraged to commence work on their plans from the end of the first lecture, and each tutorial should include time for reviewing progress and resolving issues. To offset the workload inflicted by the assignment, we suggest running a short exam only, possibly using the test bank available in the instructors' section of the Palgrave website, or even deleting the exam and substituting an individual assignment, such as writing and presenting a report on an innovation.

If time, timetables and resources permit, students should present their business plans to the class. When possible the instructor should be assisted in the assessment by someone from the business world; we have used senior accountants, venture capitalists and successful entrepreneurs in this role, generally successfully.

Instructional aids

We have 'topped and tailed' each chapter with an introduction and a summary, and added a number of questions that could be used to stimulate class discussion or private study. We provide, on the instructors' section of the Palgrave website (http://www.palgrave.com/business/legge), an instructor's manual, the 'ExampleCo' Excel® model, a substantial test bank in 'ExamView' format, and a set of PowerPoint slides. Palgrave representatives can make the instructor's manual available in hard copy. The website also includes a downloadable student workbook, which aids independent study and enables the students to work at their own pace. In addition, the website highlights the changes which differentiate this text from the previous Australian edition, giving it greater global appeal.

Professionals

Some of the readers of this book will not be current students in a business programme but they will wish to launch an enterprise of some form; possibly a new venture, but more probably an initiative within a corporation. Traditionally, corporations allocated money to internal projects through a capital budgeting process where those proposals that passed divisional scrutiny were referred to the controller's office. The controller's staff ranked them before a senior committee selected those that would be allowed to proceed. The process placed a premium on the ability to fill in forms correctly but has often failed to select good projects or reject bad ones.

The business planning process, if carried out thoroughly as described in this book, stops a lot of bad projects simply by exposing their dependence on unrealistic assumptions; it also means that top executives can make far better decisions when choosing between competing proposals because the information they need to inform such decisions is presented to them in a systematic and readily appreciated manner. Some corporations have already replaced the capital budgeting process with a business planning one; but the executives of those who have not yet done so are likely to respond far more favourably to a capital requisition backed up by a high-quality business plan than they will to a similar document where the same forms are supported by an undocumented and unfocused stream of optimistic verbiage. Most senior executives of major corporations take their duties seriously and really do wish to act in 'the interests of the company'. A well-written business plan is one of the best ways of explaining to them how to do their job properly.

JOHN M. LEGGE
KEVIN G. HINDLE

Acknowledgements

The authors and publishers would like to thank the following for permission to use their copyright material:

ACADEMY OF MANAGEMENT: for Figure 13.5, 'Moore's framework of the influences on entrepreneurial process through time,' adapted from C.F. Moore, 'Understanding Entrepreneurial Behaviour', in J.A. Pearce and R.P. Robinson (eds) *Academy of Management Best Papers Proceeding*, Forty-Sixth Annual Meeting of the Academy of Management (Chicago, 1986); and for Figure 13.1, 'The four core attributes of entrepreneurial opportunities: flow-charting the argument of Shane and Venkataraman', adapted from Shane and Venkataraman (2000) 'The promise of entrepreneurship as a field of research', *The Academy of Management Review*, **25**(1): 217–26.

ALLEN & UNWIN (Sydney) for Table 12.2 'Golis's ratios', based on Golis (1998) *Enterprise and Venture Capital: a business builders' and investors' handbook*, 3rd edn.

BLACKWELL PUBLISHING for Figure 13.6, 'Forbes' cognitive stages in the development of new ventures', adapted from Forbes (1999) 'Cognitive approaches to new venture creation', *International Journal of Management Reviews*, **1**(4): 415ff.

GLOBAL ENTREPRENEURSHIP MONITOR for Figure 13.4, 'Total entrepreneurial activity (TEA) by global region, 2002', and Table 13.1, 'Total entrepreneurial activity (TEA) index and estimated counts by country', from Reynolds et al. (2002), and Figure 13.3 'The GEM theoretical model' – all from the *GEM 2002 Global Report*.

THE *GUARDIAN* for 'It's All Over The Shop', Catherine Bennett, 16/11/2000, © Guardian.

INSTITUTE OF MANAGEMENT SCIENCES for Figure 13.2, 'Walsh's model of knowledge structure research: an organising framework', adapted from Walsh (1995) 'Managerial and Organization Cognition: Notes from a Trip down Memory Lane', *Organisation Science: A Journal of the Institute of Management Sciences*, May, **6**(3): 280ff.

THE FREE PRESS for Figure 6.1, 'Mintzberg's model', from Mintzberg (1994) *The Rise and Fall of Strategic Planning* (New York).

ROUTLEDGE for an extract from *Capitalism, Socialism, Democracy*, by J.A. Schumpeter (1942), pp. 83–4.

SALON.COM for 'Save The Earth – Dump Bush', David Talbot, 19 November 2003. This article first appeared in Salon.com, at http://www.Salon.com. An online version remains in the Salon archives. Reprinted with permission.

Every effort has been made to trace all the copyright holders but if any have been inadvertently overlooked the publishers will be pleased to make the necessary arrangements at the first opportunity.

We would like to thank Anna Faherty and Annika Knight of Palgrave Macmillan, all at Aardvark Editorial, Ann Copeland of Swinburne, and Robyn Legge for their invaluable help with this book.

1 Perspectives on entrepreneurship

This chapter

- In this chapter we set entrepreneurship in context. We explain that entrepreneurs are a critical force for change in developed capitalist economies; and that capitalism, as we now experience it, would be impossible without them. We explain how, in other times and under other circumstances, entrepreneurship, as we now understand the term, could be impossible.

- We then discuss, in relatively abstract terms, what entrepreneurs 'do' and who they are; we show that they create enterprises by drawing together new combinations of people and resources in order to do something that has not been done before. When an entrepreneur's task is completed, society and the economy have been irreversibly changed.

- We conclude with a brief overview of entrepreneurship as members of various economic traditions see it; not so much in the expectation of learning much that can be applied in practice, but in order to appreciate the context in which public discussion of entrepreneurship and innovation takes place.

Looking backwards

A young person who celebrated her 21st birthday in 2001 was born into a world that now seems impossibly remote. In 1980 the Internet was no more than a plaything of a few academics and the personal computer was a hobbyist's toy – IBM and its main-frame computers dominated the computer industry; Microsoft was a few pizza-eating young enthusiasts catering to the hobby market from nondescript premises in a place few people outside the Pacific northwest of the USA had heard of. A few people had home video recording systems, nobody had CD players and mobile telephones were rare, expensive and so heavy that they had to be installed in a car or truck. Rapid changes were not concentrated in the last few years: someone whose 70th birthday and possible retirement occurred in 2001 was born into a world without television or jet aircraft, where short distance travel was by bus or electric tram and longer distances were covered in steam trains or boats. In the USA car ownership was widespread in 1930, although far short of one car per household; in the rest of the world car ownership was limited to people of considerable wealth and their indulged children. Our retiree would have been lucky enough in childhood to avoid poliomyelitis and the other infectious diseases that regularly killed or crippled millions of children while doctors wrung their hands helplessly or mouthed useless plat-itudes. Our 21-year-old would have been immunised against the same diseases or, if infected, treated with a dose of pills and a couple of days in bed.

Fifteen generations earlier and change on this scale and of this speed would have been inconceivable. Even in today's developed countries, the great majority of the population 350 years ago were peasants or rural labourers working, living and dying as their parents and grandparents had. Change, when it occurred, was seldom for the good: wars, famines and plagues came, wreaked havoc and went. One historical milestone stands out: in 1688 the English revolted against the attempt by James II to institute autocracy and invited William of Orange from Holland to become the con-stitutional King William III of England. With the rule of law elevated above the rule of kings, property became relatively secure and private enterprise on a significant scale became possible. Many historians describe the ensuing century and a half as the Age of Improvement, the creation of a legal, monetary, fiscal and ideological structure which supported the Industrial Revolution.

The Industrial Revolution in England was dramatic from a historical perspective, although, as far as most people were concerned, changes came less frequently than they did in the late twentieth century. The processes that started with the Glorious Revolution of 1688 culminated in the Second Reform Act of 1867, the Education Act of 1870, and the Trade Union Act of 1871. In less than 200 years England turned from an aristocratically run confessional state superimposed on a subsistence-level rural economy to an industrial power with an electorate embracing the 'respectable' working classes, a general system of religious tolerance and real living standards unprecedented in European history.

The modern process of industrialisation started in England, but certainly didn't end there. During the nineteenth century industrial revolutions occurred in Germany, France and several other countries in Western Europe as well as in the United States and Japan. Between 1960 and 2000 Korea, Taiwan and Singapore underwent industrial revolutions while China, Malaysia, Thailand and Indonesia made gigantic strides in their transition from rurally based subsistence economies to industrially based affluent ones. Not every country that attempted to join the devel-oped world succeeded. Between 1945 and 1989 the countries of Eastern Europe became, with various degrees of willingness, the subject of a socialist experiment that produced 15 years of growth, 30 of stagnation and, in most cases, 10 of deep recession as they attempted to join the capitalist mainstream. By the end of the Second World War, Argentina appeared to have become part of the developed world but it then entered a long period of going, economically, nowhere. Mexico spent most of the twentieth century with periods of startling growth interspersed by longer ones of recession and stagnation.

The economic system that carried England through the Industrial Revolution was entrepreneurial capitalism; entrepreneurial capitalism was succeeded, initially in the USA and Germany, by corporate capitalism and, at the end of the twentieth century, by the system of network capitalism originally developed in Japan (Lazonick 1991). The process of succession did not involve replacement as much as augmentation; Soichiro Honda and Akio Morita were entrepreneurs no less than Josiah Wedgwood or Matthew Boulton;[1] more advanced forms of capitalism increase the possibilities open to entrepreneurs, they don't displace them.

Few human urges are as strong as the urge to reproduce; not necessarily to conceive as many children as possible, but to raise children, and nephews and nieces, who will themselves become successful parents. Money can't buy everything, but it can overcome defects of appearance or personality in the search for a suitable partner, and it can enable parents, uncles and aunts to provide their descendants with adequate food, care and education. In an entrepreneurial capitalist society, and its successors, creating a profitable business is one way, by no means the only way, to acquire wealth and admiration. Profitable new businesses are built upon innovations, advantages that allow them to become established and build a customer base before their rivals can pre-empt them, and in consequence the search for wealth and status will encourage at least some people to innovate. Innovations drive economic growth, but they also displace older innovations; so the wealth and status gained from a successful act of entrepreneurship is temporary and entrepreneurial growth proceeds without any implicit limit.

Comparative studies, such as the GEM project (see Chapter 13), reinforce the view that a common set of conditions is necessary for entrepreneurship to flourish and entrepreneurs' host societies to enjoy rapid economic development.

Preconditions for entrepreneurship

The monetary system

The creation of a new enterprise implies the assembly of resources: people, equipment and money. In the general sense an entrepreneur cannot assume that any of these resources are currently unemployed, so the entrepreneur must bid them away from their current uses. To do so the entrepreneur needs money, but money is one of the resources that the entrepreneur starts without or without enough of. The solution provided in an entrepreneurial capitalist society is a banking system, which can create the money required by entrepreneurs as it is needed. In 1694 the Bank of England was established by royal charter and England had the key ingredient of a modern banking system, a central clearing bank that could smooth out the monetary fluctuations to which an unregulated banking system is liable. (Money lent by any bank in the banking system will be deposited, as it is received in payment, in the banking system, but not necessarily in the original bank. The central bank takes deposits from banks in surplus, and makes loans to those in deficit, when there is a temporary imbalance between the amount any bank lends and the amount deposited with it.)

A monetary system needs an agreed unit of money, yet for most of history there have been few agreed standards, none lasting very long. Coinage in particular was subject to clipping and forgery so good money rapidly became bad. In 1699 Sir Isaac Newton became Master of the Royal Mint. As Master, Newton supervised a great recoinage, recalling and reissuing the entire circulating currency of England, this time with milled edges to suppress clipping and machine-struck coins to inhibit forgers. Newton decreed that five English shillings would contain one ounce of silver, and that twenty-one English shillings, or one guinea, would be worth a quarter of an ounce of gold. Twenty shillings became one pound, and a golden sovereign containing five twenty-firsts of an ounce of gold allowed the rich to use small purses. Newton's currency, and the relationship between the price of gold and silver, lasted until the First World War of 1914–18.

Stabilising the value of money meant stabilising the rate of interest, since lenders no longer demanded a premium to protect them against likely inflation. It also meant that relatively long-term loans did not involve the lender in taking the risk of lending good money and being repaid in bad.

Many historians praise the foundation of the Bank of England and the stabilisation of the currency for the increased military clout it gave the English government: the Napoleonic wars cost the English government a quarter of a billion pounds more than it took in revenue over the period, but the money was raised effortlessly. War is the antithesis of entrepreneurship, and more economically minded historians might consider that the development of Wedgwood's factory at Etruria, Boulton and Watt's plant at Soho and cotton factories based on Arkwright's and Crompton's innovations across Lancashire as conferring a more lasting benefit on England than the suppression of Napoleon. Even Wellington's victories over the French depended as much on the artillery supplied by Carron's ironworks as the bottomless credit of the Bank of England.

No major country uses a metallic currency today; instead we have fiat currencies, whose value depends on their status as the lawful means of contract settlement, their use by governments as payments for the goods and services that governments purchase and because sums in the national currency are required to pay taxes. Governments and their central banks attempt to control the amount of money available, both as circulating coins and notes and, far more importantly, as bank credit, in order to prevent excessive inflation or fluctuations in purchasing power. Experience suggests that modest rates of inflation, up to ten per cent per year, are not incompatible with an entrepreneurial economy, while attempts to keep inflation at very low levels involve restricting credit to the point that entrepreneurs are starved of the bank finance they require.

Actually measuring the rate of inflation in an entrepreneurial economy is surprisingly difficult. With new products appearing all the time and the quality of existing ones rising, it is impossible to define a single 'basket' of goods and services that measures purchasing power accurately at two different times. In the nineteenth century a person might have gone to their doctor and paid a guinea (£1.05) and been told to go home, put their affairs in order and make their peace with God. In the twenty-first century a patient (or her insurer) might be asked to pay 15 or more times as much for a medical consultation but the patient will leave with a pill that will lead to a complete cure. How much inflation has there been in the interval between these outcomes?

Contract law

Time is of the essence to an entrepreneurial venture; investors put money in now, expecting returns later and buyers place orders for a future supply and an even later payment date. Even ordinary workers labour today in the expectation of a pay cheque on Friday. Each of these time shifts is an opportunity for fraud and deception, and even when there is a general expectation that contracts will be honoured, some ultimate sanction is needed to punish actual defaulters and deter or coerce potential ones. In traditional economies ostracism often took the place of law: our word 'bank-rupt' (broken bench) comes from the ceremonial destruction of the bench (banco) from which a defaulting trader had operated in medieval Genoa or Venice. Throughout the eighteenth and nineteenth centuries and for most of the twentieth, the London financial markets still operated on the honour (and ostracism) principle; the New York diamond market does so to this day.

In a growing economy with free entry to trades and professions, such internal disciplines have repeatedly been proved inadequate, while (see below) the professional discipline that made ostracism an effective punishment may itself be seen as a barrier to the development of an entrepreneurial economy. Only the state has the power needed to enforce performance or punish wilful fraud, and during much of the eighteenth and early nineteenth centuries the High Court of England evolved a doctrine favourable to the enforcement of contracts. Atiyah (1979) describes how several centuries of precedent were overthrown as the court chose to base its rulings, not on the justice of a particular arrangement, but on the formal circumstances under which the parties had undertaken it. If neither force nor fraud was present and the contract did not embrace an unlawful purpose, contracts were held to be generally enforceable, irrespective of the justice or fairness of the probable or actual outcome.

The presumption in favour of enforcement of contracts involved two breaks with the past: the excessive formality that may have been required to make a contract binding; and the right that the courts claimed, in the name of the king (who spoke in the name of God), to prevent injustice. Imagine a venturer who negotiated a contract with a wealthy man, under which the venturer would undertake a long and difficult journey to buy a valuable artefact for the wealthy purchaser. On the venturer's return, a wealthy man who regretted the contract had two main unprincipled options. One was to challenge the contract on the grounds that it had been drawn up or executed defectively; with hundreds of years of pettifogging precedents on record, a good lawyer was bound to find something. The other was to use the 'glare of 20:20 hindsight' to challenge the price: the wealthy man's lawyer might argue that the seas had been mild and the natives friendly and therefore the venturer's prospective profit was wildly excessive, and so the wealthy man should only be obliged to pay a much smaller price than that originally agreed.

When the court rejected both pettifogging procedural arguments and those based on economic justice, they swept away a major barrier to the growth of an economy based on contracts rather than on traditional obligations and duties. That was not, however, all that the High Court did. In order to assert the primacy of the contract, the court assumed that both parties had consented to the conditions under which it was carried out. If a merchant entrusted a cargo to a shipper, who in turn engaged the drunken master of an unseaworthy boat to carry it, the court rejected the merchant's claim against the shipper on the grounds that drunken seamen and unseaworthy boats were part of the ordinary risks of transport and as such had been implicitly accepted by the merchant. If a labourer, with no alternative but starvation, accepted a job in an unsafe mine and was crippled in an accident, the mine owner could successfully defend a claim from the labourer on the grounds that the worker accepted the hazards when he accepted the job.

When the parties to a contract were equally well informed and both had alternatives short of starvation, the main response to the court's construction of implicit conditions was ever-longer lists of explicit ones. This was of little help to the poor and the defenceless, so Parliament stepped into the breach. Today laws and regulations define the limits of contractual relationships and impose numerous duties on entrepreneurs and businesspersons whenever they employ people, construct buildings, operate processes and offer goods and services for sale. 'Freedom of contract' may be a libertarian slogan, but does not describe the actual business environment. Irksome regulations may be removed or relaxed, but complete deregulation is neither politically acceptable nor economically necessary for entrepreneurial capitalism to flourish.

What has survived is the freedom to decline an offer: no one in an entrepreneurial economy can be legally obliged to enter into any contract, whether to work, buy or sell, because of who they are or who their parents were, or even what they have previously done. Laws and regulations hedge in those who make offers, but those to whom the offers are made enjoy nearly complete freedom to accept or decline them.

An intellectual property regime

Entrepreneurs create considerable amounts of intellectual property: novel designs, trademarks, trade dress, trade secrets, patentable and unpatentable inventions, operating manuals, promotional materials and more. Once the entrepreneur has done this work, a copyist can generally reproduce it at a considerably lower cost and may be able to seize a share of the entrepreneur's market or, in extreme cases, take it over entirely. If an entrepreneur thought that such piracy was certain, or even highly probable, then there will be very little economic incentive to proceed with an innovation and society may be worse off than it might have been.

Intellectual property law in England emerged by the innovative reinvention of the royal prerogative. Kings everywhere had created monopolies to raise cash and reward favourites, but when Parliament moved to suppress monopolies in the early seventeenth century, it specifically left a loophole for monopolies in 'new methods of manufacture'. A prerogative that had been stripped from the king was granted to entrepreneurs. The other major form of intellectual property law, copyright, emerged from the practice of enforcing censorship by licensing printers; censorship was eventually abolished, but the privilege stripped from the king was now vested in the creator of a work.

Many economists have pointed out that the grant of a monopoly, whether a patent, a copyright or one of their modern derivatives, will tend to result in higher prices and smaller quantities than might prevail in an unconstrained market. Most such economists recognise that the social benefits of innovation offset the cost of the associated competitive imperfections. A few economists argue that society will be better off if an entrepreneur's intellectual property is stolen as long as the thief sells the resulting copies at a low enough price. This argument is irrefutable, as long as society is satisfied that it has all the innovations it will ever want. A number of economists have felt sufficiently strongly about the need for market perfection to make proposals for rewarding innovators that do not involve the grant of monopoly rights, such as grants and prizes. These have their place, but there are serious problems involved in designing, much less operating, a system of prizes and rewards sufficiently effective to replace the patent and copyright systems at no net social cost.

One consequence of the widespread concern among economists about the impact of patent and copyright monopolies has been the care taken by lawmakers to limit the use of patents and other intellectual property by numerous conditions and restrictions. A side effect of these complications has been to reward successful manipulators of the intellectual property system far more generously than the system rewards most inventors. The US patent system is rather more subject to such manipulation than the patent law in most of the rest of the world, with its subjective test of 'first to invent' rather than the objective 'first to file', the secrecy surrounding applications and the possibility of long delays between filing and publication. At best the opportunity of making a fortune from a 'submarine' patent or other exploitation of the system distracts genuine entrepreneurs from wealth-creating into wealth-shifting activities; but it is possible that large companies, the usual targets of submarine patents and other devices, divert their internal resources from innovation into defensive stratagems. If someone takes Microsoft or Ford down for a few hundred million dollars, a first reaction may be to think that they can easily afford it; but if the effect is to reduce those companies' innovation budgets and increase the size of their legal departments, the social cost may be considerable.

An intellectual property regime serves a 'signalling' as well as an enforcement role; by publicly acknowledging inventors' and creators' rights, the law discourages infringements even where the infringer faces little risk of being detected and punished. Schumpeter ([1942] 1967) pointed out that economic competition had to be suspended by one means or another in order to permit innovation to occur and economies and societies to progress. An effective intellectual property regime provides an orderly mechanism for such a suspension.

Economic freedom

Democracy, with one vote per person and representative government, is a fine form of social organisation, but it is neither a necessary nor a sufficient condition for successful entrepreneurial capitalism. Setting contemporary examples aside, the Industrial Revolution was led by men like the dissenting (from the Church of England) Josiah Wedgwood, who were prohibited under the Test and Corporation Acts from becoming MPs or participating in local government. The Glorious Revolution established a Bill of Rights, including freedom from arbitrary seizure and any liability for taxation except as established by act of Parliament, but it did not institute democracy. In fact, the word 'democracy', when used throughout the eighteenth and much of the nineteenth century, carried much the same connotations as the word 'communism' did at the height of the recent Cold War.

The economic rights conceded during the Glorious Revolution gave entrepreneurs confidence that they could keep their profits and their businesses, and to the extent that they were concerned with political rights, their rapidly rising wealth ensured that they could not be ignored. Those whose principles did not prevent them occasionally attending a Church of England service could, by such 'occasional conformity', take part in local government. Three other major reforms completed most of the work of the Glorious Revolution. There was the adoption of a presumption in favour of freedom of contract by the High Court as discussed above and, early in the nineteenth century, the repeal of the Statue of Apprentices and the reform of the

Poor Law. Catholics, Dissenters and Jews were freed from practically all legal disabilities during the nineteenth century.

The medieval Statute of Apprentices required that every person who wished to enter a trade had to serve a seven-year apprenticeship with an established master. For many trades this was a wholly excessive period, serving mainly to give existing masters a supply of cheap labour and suppress competition from potential entrants. The apprenticeship system also deterred innovation and restricted labour mobility, in that it was difficult for either masters or men in declining trades to move their employment or businesses to expanding ones. The force of the statute was greatly weakened in the eighteenth century by judicial rulings that limited its application to ancient trades, before it was repealed completely early in the nineteenth century.

The Poor Law gave everyone the right to relief if they were unable to work or there was no work available, but only in the parish in which they had been born or a parish in which they had lived for a year and a day. Since most parishes felt that their own poor were a heavy enough burden on the rates, they made it exceedingly difficult for any new poor person to 'settle' by living there for more than a year. The Poor Law became a very serious barrier to labour mobility at a time when agricultural improvement was reducing rural employment and the Industrial Revolution was creating new jobs in the cities. In 1834 the Poor Law was radically reformed to remove the residential qualification and permit the free movement of labour in England.

The economic freedoms created in England after 1688 permitted the Industrial Revolution to occur and entrepreneurship to flourish, leading to an unprecedented rate of innovation. This in turn led to rising living standards, especially in the cities, increased literacy and raised the pressure for a widened franchise. In 1867 the franchise was extended to all (adult male) householders and boarders (but excluding women, the homeless, live-in domestic servants and factory hands). Democracy, of a sort, was eventually conceded in England, but a hundred and eighty years after the concession of those economic reforms that allowed entrepreneurs to drive economic growth at unprecedented rates.

'Social capital'

The widely differing rates of economic and social development in northern and southern Italy, even after unification in 1870, led the sociologist David Putnam to develop his concept of 'social capital' (1993a, 1993b). Flourishing entrepreneurship, Putnam believed, required more than an effective monetary system, enforceable contract law and economic freedom. It also needed a social environment in which people had a sufficient disposition to cooperate with each other to make the ordinary conduct of business, both within and between firms, possible without minutely detailed contracts and incessant supervision. Putnam's research was clearly original and so were some aspects of his description of social capital; but the underlying concept has a long history.

Adam Smith wrote his *Theory of Moral Sentiments* ([1759]1853) before his *Wealth of Nations* ([1776]1835) and certainly believed that economic freedom only made sense within an accepted moral framework. The 'invisible hand' of market forces might push economic actors into doing good where they had intended none, but the moral system provided the tram tracks that kept the majority of economic actors from actually intending social harm.

Intensive supervision of workers and the negotiation of detailed performance contracts drain economic resources as well as suppressing innovation. A simple idea for an improvement in products or processes may be neglected if its adoption requires the renegotiation of a long and detailed contract or the rewriting of a thick and detailed procedure manual. Other things being equal, a society in which businesspersons generally honour the spirit rather than the letter of contracts, and employees work intelligently and conscientiously even when the foreman is not breathing down their necks, will have more resources to spare for productive uses and, even more importantly, the improvement of production and delivery techniques, than one in which such levels of trust do not obtain.

Dawkins (1989: 184–8) cites research showing, by the use of a simple game theory model, that selfish individualism is an 'environmentally stable strategy', in that altruists cannot survive in a population dominated by selfish individuals; those who might be inclined to repay a favour never get the chance. Once the mafia takes over, there may be no natural mechanism, short of dispersion of the host population, which can get them out again. A population with a sufficient proportion of individuals who will return favours without being forced to is also environmentally stable, in that selfish individuals get marginalised. There is no automatic mechanism that can change a society in which entrepreneurial behaviour flourishes to degenerate into one in which force and fraud dominate normal social interactions or vice versa.

More recently, Guttman (2003) has revisited the tendency for cooperation to emerge in spite of the presence of potential defectors. While Dawkins and his successors saw cooperation or defection as a genetically determined behaviour, and looked to evolution over several generations to establish a balance, Guttman considered a society of relatively rational agents, some of whom believed in 'every man for himself and the devil take the hindmost', while others preferred win–win outcomes even if their personal gain from a particular transaction was lower than it might otherwise have been. Guttman added the assumption that any person who actually did defect became notorious for doing so, such that no one, whatever their preference, would offer cooperation to that person again. Guttman showed that, as long as the proportion of those predisposed to defect was below a critical level, even those who preferred defection would cooperate in every transaction before the last one.

Putnam pointed out that, for many generations before 1861, southern Italy was part of the kingdom of Naples, a greedy, corrupt, autocratic police state where every gathering that extended beyond the host's immediate family was suspected of being a conspiracy and every stranger was quite reasonably suspected of being a police informer. By contrast, northern Italy had been home to the merchant republics of Milan, Genoa, Florence and Venice, many of whose cooperative civic institutions survived their rule by France and Austria from the sixteenth century until the Risorgimento of 1861–70. In southern Italy the church choirs were professionals, supported out of church taxes and property income, while in the north each merchant guild took responsibility for a number of cathedral services each year. While the members competed with each other to be chosen for the choir, the guilds competed among themselves to put on the best performance. From the south emerged the Mafia, from the north, Benneton. In the south there was stagnation and poverty, in the north, innovation and prosperity.

Putnam offered neither the first nor the last word on the subject of social capital. While the remarkable culture of northern Italy may have its roots in the eleventh century, other centres of innovation, such as Silicon Valley, have different antecedents. Cohen and Fields (1999, 2000) discuss the development of Silicon Valley and note that it is remarkably deficient in even the modern equivalent of eleventh-century cathedral choirs. Cohen and Fields demonstrate that the initial evolution of Silicon Valley was the result of some quite deliberate decisions by Stanford University, supported by the University of California at Berkeley. Silicon Valley has evolved a dense network of technologists, venture capitalists, accountants and lawyers who have established rapid and effective links between performance and reputation: workers and merchants are trustworthy in Silicon Valley because of the 'old' sanctions of exposure and ostracism, not the new habits bred of social interaction.

Cohen and Fields suggest that the Silicon Valley model could be recreated elsewhere by similar policies, but they do so without reviewing the economic implications of their own research. In Silicon Valley, they report, there is one lawyer, accountant, venture capitalist or head-hunter for every four technologists, effectively a 20 per cent plus supervision overhead. Even Caesar's legions had a broader span of control. Silicon Valley may be truly unique: a community built around an epochal industrial innovation, generating investment rates and profit levels that can carry the costs of a superstructure to enforce trustworthy behaviour in a community that contributed none of it. Cohen and Fields suggest that, for every industrial cluster, the host communities will take on characteristics that reflect both the community and the nature of the industry it is supporting. Silicon Valley happened, but there can be no confidence that the circumstances can be reproduced elsewhere, or even that they could have coalesced in San Jose county at a different time or around a different industry. The conscious design of a community that can become the world centre of a major industry is still beyond us. It is, however, clear that 'social capital', either embedded habits of trust and cooperation or an infrastructure that can detect and sanction untrustworthy behaviour, or both in some combination, is an essential precondition for vigorous entrepreneurial capitalism. Societies that are fortunate enough to have ample social capital, for whatever reason and created by whatever historical process, need to take care not to lose or destroy it.

The American author Francis Fukuyama, made famous by his book *The End of History* (1992), has written an extensive cross-national study of social capital *Trust: the Social Virtues and the Creation of Prosperity* (1995), only modestly marred by his insistence on the validity, indeed the perfection, of neoclassical economics. He points out that social capital is multidimensional and takes different forms in different countries; he further established that the size and management structure of an enterprise will be dependent on the form that the social capital takes in a particular cultural setting. Entrepreneurial activity will be largely stifled in cultures with no social capital, but the form that the social capital takes will constrain the way an enterprise can develop. As a good American, Fukuyama praises the American pattern of weak family ties combined with a remarkable willingness to form voluntary associations; but he is a sufficiently honest scholar to point out that Japan and Germany have a broadly similar basis for building trust between unrelated parties, without the rhetoric of individualism that is so often used in the US to justify exploitation and the neglect of social responsibilities.

Explaining growth and recession

Firms in a market economy are always under pressure from other firms, most directly from those other firms that make similar products or offer similar services. When a reasonably large number of firms or traders compete to sell similar products, none of them will have much influence over the market price and the only way to make a good profit is to have below-average costs. As soon as one trader is seen to be making a good profit, the others will try to cut their own costs, wiping out the first trader's advantage. The pressure to keep reducing costs is very strong.

One of the most obvious ways to reduce the costs of each product made or service delivered is to make or deliver more of them with the same number of workers, by using better machinery or reorganising the way the work is done. Once most of the firms in an industry have found ways to cut unit costs by making larger quantities of their product, they will have to lower the price in order to encourage buyers to take the extra supply. Soon they will reach the point where lowering the price does not attract any more buyers and only those firms with the lowest costs will survive.

The sellers in one market are, however, the buyers in another. When the less efficient firms are driven to the wall, their workers lose their jobs and their owners lose their profits; they can no longer afford to buy the things they did before. This will put more pressure on the surviving firms to cut their costs and boost their share of the market, and another round of less efficient firms will go to the wall and another bit of demand will be drained from the economy.

From the time modern capitalism started to emerge in England in the 1770s, this downward spiral started quite frequently. Until the 1890s periods when the world economy ran backwards were called 'crises'; the 1891–92 crisis was so bad that the next time the economy got stuck in reverse the powers that be called it a 'depression', then thought of as a less alarming term. The Great Depression of 1930–33 gave that word a bad name, and so when the United States economy started going backwards again in 1937 President Franklin D. Roosevelt called it a 'recession', and that is the word we use today for economic bad times.[2]

Capitalist economies get into trouble quite regularly, but they have always got out of trouble again and returned to growth and fairly full employment. The history of capitalism has been a story of long-run growth, not crisis. From the end of the Roman Empire until 1830 a labourer in Europe had to work for between 100 and 400 days to earn the price of a tonne of grain. This was just enough to keep an average family at bare subsistence level for a year. The typical labourer worked for about 200 days a year; few of them had paid work in the winter months. Living standards only rose above bare subsistence level when the price of a tonne of grain fell to less than the wages of 200 days of labour. Half the time half the population lived below subsistence level. In one out of every seven years, bodies could be found starved to death in the streets of Europe's towns and cities.

A hundred and sixty years of capitalism has seen the real price of a tonne of grain fall to the money equivalent of one to four day's labour. The average person in a modern western country lives better, and longer, than most eighteenth-century aristocrats. Capitalism creates unemployment, as machines replace workers and more efficient processes replace less efficient ones, but it also soaks it up. The displaced workers are employed in new forms of economic activity and demand and output continue to grow.[3]

A capitalist economy grows when new products enter the market and new services are offered: while competition is driving down the cost of supplying well-known products and flooding the markets with them, new products have no direct competitors. Innovation offers firms an escape from price-based competition and an opportunity to earn substantial profits – until imitators follow the innovator and the price-competitive cycle begins in the market for the new product.[4] Two processes are at work simultaneously:

- in established markets, price competition is forcing costs and prices down and quantities up, squeezing profits and displacing workers
- at the same time innovators are creating new markets by introducing new products, both goods and services, earning substantial margins and taking on workers to satisfy growing demand.

In normal times sufficient new firms arise, and sufficient new divisions are created inside existing ones, to absorb the workers displaced by progress. This is a continuing process: the workers employed last year to make new products and deliver new services are displacing workers this year; the new jobs that these workers find will start displacing other workers next year. Not all the new jobs are in new firms: some firms will grow, and employ more people, and other firms will reassign staff to new duties rather than retrench one lot and hire another.

A modern economy is perpetually changing. Old products get replaced by newer ones, old ways of doing things get replaced by better ones. Some firms are wound up and some divisions of large firms close, while new firms are formed and new divisions are opened. On a short time frame, a year or so, this does not amount to an overwhelming amount of change: most firms and divisions that were operating last year are still operating; most products that were on the market last year are still available.

Put in numbers, 3–6 per cent of the firms and company divisions that are operating today won't be operating in a year's time: about one person in forty will find that their work, in the form that they have been used to performing it, is no longer required. About the same number will have to change jobs if they want to go on using their existing skills. For the level of unemployment to stand still at a time when the workforce is not growing, the work of producing new goods and delivering new services must add at least 2 per cent to the total stock of jobs each year. When the workforce is growing, either through birth or immigration, the required economic growth rate is 2 per cent plus the workforce growth rate. The truly amazing fact is that the capitalist system has managed to keep unemployment below the sort of levels that trigger revolutions for two centuries.

Economists study economies and various economists have been trying to explain how a capitalist system works for well over 200 years: the attempt started before capitalism got properly going.[5] The standard undergraduate syllabus focuses on the 95 per cent of the economy that will not cease to operate over the course of a year, the steady state, or equilibrium, part of the economy. Even many advanced researchers in economics limit their analyses to a state of 'general equilibrium' which will occur when all innovations lie in the distant past and from which all change is impossible.

Two of the greatest names in twentieth-century economics focused on the 5 per cent, the new activities that keep the economy from collapsing into an equilibrium state. The English economist John Maynard Keynes looked at ways in which demand was stimulated so as to generate employment for those displaced by the increasing efficiency of the established economy. He identified two major sources of new demand: one was entrepreneurial activity (which Keynes called the result of 'animal spirits'), because entrepreneurs place orders for new materials, buildings, machines and services in order to make or deliver their new products, pushing up demand and employment right through the economy; and the other was intervention by governments, whose orders for public works and defence equipment would generate immediate demand for contractors to fill these orders and provide flow-on opportunities for workers and subcontractors.[6]

Innovation

The Austrian-American economist Joseph Schumpeter focused on innovation rather than animal spirits as the guiding force behind entrepreneurs. Schumpeter emphasised the importance of non-price competition between differentiated products where orthodox economists, then and now, focus on price competition between perfectly interchangeable ones. Schumpeter emphasised the importance of the large firm while most teaching of economics deals with an imaginary world in which all firms are small.[7]

Adam Smith and Alfred Marshall, two of the most famous authors on economics, are claimed by both the orthodox and the entrepreneurial schools. Smith introduced the concept of economic progress, which he saw almost entirely in terms of process and supply improvements. He did not give any serious consideration to product innovation. Smith did, however, emphasise the role of the individual entrepreneur in creating new businesses and opening up new avenues of trade. Marshall was one of the founders of the modern orthodox school, but his writing shows him to have been deeply dissatisfied with the timeless picture of the economy that emerged from mathematical models.

The majority of academic economists rely on general equilibrium theory, with an implicit assumption that the only interesting states of the world are those where all change has ended and the noise of all disturbances has died away. They study change by creating a new picture with the world in a different equilibrium state. Users of general equilibrium theory make the deep assumption that the state of an economy is determined by economic conditions and does not depend on the way the economy developed. The equilibrium state of an economy is analogous to the steady state of a physical system. Imagine a mountainous part of the countryside just after a rainstorm: water will be cascading over every surface, splashing and falling. After a while all the water will have gathered in the lowest places, while the higher areas are dry again. This is the equilibrium state of the water-mountain system. As long as there is no erosion and no earth movement, the water will wind up in the same place after a storm or a shower: the equilibrium state depends on the shape of the hills, not the nature of the rainfall. If general equilibrium theory reflected the real world, then entrepreneurship would be quite irrelevant to the economy; market forces would be the only driver of change and individuals would have no role to play beyond assisting or retarding the economy's journey along a predefined path to a predetermined end.

Modern mathematics has provided conclusive proof that the state of a system as complex as an economy must reflect its history as well as its past states: individual acts do make a lasting difference. Going back to the mountain: rain does cause erosion and the mountains are shaped by the rain just as much as the shape of the mountains determines the destiny of the water. The outcome of any attempt to change the world is never going to be entirely predictable: entrepreneurs know that they are agents of change, but when they look back over their achievements, they usually find out that neither the journey nor the destination was what they expected when they started.

Many, although by no means a majority of, leading economists have studied the forces behind change and development in more realistic economic models. Paul M. Romer (1986, 1994) created endogenous growth theory, setting out the macroeconomic conditions necessary for sustained economic growth to become possible. Paul Krugman (1996) has applied dazzling mathematical skills to the study of differential growth. W. Brian Arthur (1989, 1994) is widely credited with being one of the first economists to make a systematic exploration of the consequences of frequent innovation.[8]

Products and processes

In this book we will use the term 'product' as a package of goods and services offered to users in return for money, and a process as a clearly defined subset of the activities need to produce a product. Innovations can involve new products, new processes, or sometimes both. Sometimes a process innovation may become a product, or be an important part of a product, when it is offered for sale to firms that will use it to make products of their own. Many industrial products are hybrids; there may be a physical deliverable, such as a new etching machine for a semiconductor plant, but its value will not be in the nuts and bolts, but in the improvements it offers to its users' manufacturing processes, which in turn may be rendered possible by innovations in the way the machine operates.

Sometimes the distinction between 'product' and 'process' depends purely on perspective. Federal Express, the widely praised and discussed entrepreneurial firm, offered a product that was nearly as old as humanity, the transport of goods. The firm is successful because of the processes it employs, enabling it to make a useful profit while offering a less expensive, easier to use express delivery service than had been previously available. South West Airlines held, at the start of 2003, about 10 per cent of the US air travel market but its value on the stock exchange exceeded that of all other US airlines put together. At the time of a major downturn in air travel, South West remained profitable because its internal processes, tailored to a well-defined segment of the market, enabled it to offer lower average fares than its rivals while remaining profitable. The product, passenger air transport between two airports, was hardly a novelty when South West commenced operations in 1971. Firms such as Ryanair in Europe or Virgin Blue in Australia imitate South West but must be considered innovative because they have introduced a concept proven in the USA to other markets.

We will return to this issue in Chapters 3 and 6; but in brief, we find that large firms in relatively mature markets tend to devote the majority of their innovation funding to process innovations, while the more glamorous start-up entrepreneurs tend to be associated with new products. Please think of this as a tendency, not an iron rule.

Entrepreneurs and leaders

We discuss entrepreneurs and entrepreneurship in Chapter 2, where we will define the entrepreneur as an enterprise creator and agent of change, a builder of teams and organisations. Builders of human structures need to be able to do many things, and one of them is provide leadership. Very few projects can be completed by one person acting on their own, most rely on the extensive cooperation of suppliers and workers to anticipate problems and expedite the work. When the project is intended to bring a new product to market, the timing of the product's introduction may be crucial to its success. Equally, many modern products are complex and a minor defect in a component can mean the failure of the whole. An entrepreneur who can create a cohesive team, one where the members anticipate problems and eliminate them before they can damage the project, has an enormous advantage over the one who must rely on bribes or threats.

> As for the best leaders, the people do not notice their existence. The next best, the people honour and praise. The next, the people fear, and the next, the people hate …
> When the best leaders' work is done the people say: 'We did it ourselves.'
>
> *Townsend 1970 (adapting Lao-Tse)*

Corporate rejuvenation

The enterprises that exist today all have a starting point in time: there must, once, have been an entrepreneur or entrepreneurial team who turned a concept into an enterprise. Time, however, brings change and the needs that the enterprise was created to address may become less urgent, or other enterprises may appear to address them. When established enterprises ignore these external changes, their revenues decline, their profits erode and their shareholders see the value of their investment fall. There are three broad strategies open to medium and large firms seeking to remain profitable and valuable in a turbulent economy:

- They can concentrate on cutting their costs and getting better at making their products, growing their markets by cutting their prices. The price cuts will attract new consumers to their product and will force their less efficient competitors to withdraw from the market, giving them still more scope for growth.
- They can practice 'downsizing', abandoning their least profitable product lines and their least profitable customers, and retrenching the workers who used to service them. These firms tend to grow more slowly than their competitors, but they often report very attractive profits in the year following a major downsizing activity.

■ They can innovate, launching new products to replace those whose sales growth is slowing down and whose profitability is threatened by competition.

The first strategy, that of flooding the market with more and more of a cheaper and cheaper product, is sometimes referred to as the 'Model-T' strategy, recalling Henry Ford's success with that car and that strategy between 1908 and 1923.[9] Other textbooks may call it an 'experience curve' strategy. More recently the companies making semiconductors in Taiwan have applied this strategy to their overseas markets if not to each other, leading to their global dominance of the merchant semiconductor industry. Many companies find that their markets do not respond strongly enough to falling prices to make the experience curve strategy viable. Others have found that counter-strategies based upon product differentiation can defeat the experience curve approach.

Downsizing, delayering, flattening and other organisational tricks became extremely popular in the late 1980s and stayed popular well into the 1990s. Many companies underwent dramatic divestment and downsizing, and in nearly every case the immediate result was a surge in profits and a lift in the share price. When the longer term results of downsizing are reviewed, the picture is less clear. Approximately two-thirds of major US corporations that downsized were worse off two years later than they had been before the process started. In review, it appears that quite a lot of downsizing was just the conversion of assets into income. Before the downsizing, the typical firm had enjoyed the goodwill of its customers and staff, and both sets of goodwill had a positive effect on the firm's performance. The customers trusted the firm to provide quality products and services, and so they placed orders with the firm without squeezing the last cent out of the quoted prices. The staff worked hard and loyally for rather lower wages than they might have got elsewhere in the expectation of career opportunities and job security.

Neither market share nor staff loyalty and dedication appear in the certified accounts of a public company and so degrading them does not have to be mentioned in a firm's annual report. The combination of demotivated staff and dissatisfied customers leads to falling sales and a higher cost for each sale, so as the effects of a downsizing work through the firm and become apparent to its customers, the initial profit boost is replaced by a long-term decline in revenue and profit. Even when the downsized firm continues to grow, it seldom achieves its previous growth rate.

The remaining way to preserve a firm's value is to innovate, introduce new and improved products faster than the old ones lose their market appeal. New products add most value to a firm in the first few years they are on the market. The most innovative major corporations launch new products long before sales of their existing products have plateaued out and sometimes while the previous product is still showing strong sales growth.

The problems and opportunities facing an innovative corporation are the reverse of those facing a downsizing one. The costs of new product development and marketing are not shown as a capital item in the accounts, so they reduce the firm's current profit even as they guarantee its long-term value. The innovative firm relies on high staff commitment to keep its product launches on track and overcome any minor hitches in their launch or development. New products need enthusiastic customers who gain their enthusiasm from committed sales and other staff.

The innovative company has one problem all of its own: how to keep its highly motivated staff from 'leaping on their horses and galloping off madly in all directions'. There will always be more ideas than prototypes and more prototypes than marketed products in an innovative company. Once marketed there will be some products that must be withdrawn in order to release resources for other ones. Deliberately or accidentally, most medium and large corporations have built organisational barriers to innovation; committees that must assess projects, tight budgetary controls, demanding performance targets based on the current product line and even deliberate overload policies.

Whatever the particular bureaucratic procedure and whatever the ostensible reason behind each of them, they create a set of hurdles which only a highly motivated person, with a committed team behind them, can hope to surmount. The products that do survive this obstacle course are those with a product champion or 'intrapreneur' driving them. Relatively few products are successfully championed by their inventor or initiator: good research scientists and development engineers tend to have too high a regard for literal accuracy, and too much faith in the power of reason, to carry a project through the bureaucratic minefield. A relative outsider can also find it easier to see a new idea in the wider market context, while the developer may act as if even discussing a rival product is a criticism of their own.

The stakeholders

An entrepreneur makes the important decisions about the initiation and conduct of a project and accepts the praise and rewards for success along with the blame and punishment for failure. While the final measure of success is often financial, personal financial success for the entrepreneur is usually impossible without satisfying all the principal stakeholders. These are the customers, the financiers and the community. In the usual case where the entrepreneur leads a team in order to bring a product to a successful conclusion, the members of the team are stakeholders to some extent, but managing and motivating them is usually treated as an aspect of leadership rather than entrepreneurship.

The customers show that the enterprise is a success by using the services it provides or buying the goods that it markets at a price that enables the entrepreneur to pay all the bills and have a fair profit left over. In most cases the customers survived before the new firm put its products on the market and they don't have to buy them anyway. Achieving or exceeding the planned unit volumes, sales revenue and profit are good indicators that the enterprise was successful at identifying and satisfying its customers' requirements.

Some entrepreneurs become involved in public benefit enterprises, providing services to people who cannot pay the full commercial cost, if they can afford to pay anything at all. Such enterprises serve two constituencies, the people who rely on their services and the donors whose contributions pay the bills. Successful public benefit enterprises must satisfy both their clients and their donors. Their entrepreneurs must set out their success criteria and get their donors' agreement to it fairly early in the project, because if they don't they will find themselves chasing a perpetually moving target. Would-be public benefit entrepreneurs often make the mistake of thinking that, since their objectives are admirable and their motives are impeccable, donors are morally obliged to support them. Donors are likely to limit their support to enterprises with excellent objectives and realistic plans for achieving them: purity of motive is seldom enough.

The financiers often declare their measures of success before they commit any money to a project. Different financiers may enter a project at different stages of its life and their success criteria will differ. In each case, however, the financiers' success criteria come in two parts: there is the return they expect on their funds and the associated schedule of interest, dividend and capital repayment dates; and there is the maximum level of risk they will permit their investment to be exposed to. Many financiers control their risks by setting apparently arbitrary rules concerning the sort of projects they will support and the security they will require.

Would-be entrepreneurs often get a shock when they discover that their potential finance providers are interested in much more than the promised interest payments. At one end of the scale there are the major commercial banks, who charge relatively low interest and in return look for extremely strong security, such as a guarantee backed up by a cash deposit or a first mortgage security over a valuable property. The major banks strengthen their own position even further by the rules they impose, for example the bank's loan agreement may allow it to demand its funds back within 30 days for any reason or none and seize the security if the advance is not repaid in full on the newly specified day.

Equity investors share the entrepreneur's risks; if the business fails, their money is usually lost and so they expect higher returns than the banks. The earlier in a project's life that equity is sought, the higher the promised returns must be. Few investors are prepared to invest in start-up enterprises, but when they do they will look to get 15–20 times their initial investment back when they sell their interest in seven or so years from the date they put up the first money. Even with this level of return such venture capitalists demand much more than promises. The new enterprise's plans will be scrutinised intensively, its market research tested and its key staff interviewed and their references checked. The money will then be advanced under the terms of an agreement that may not be as onerous as the ones the banks impose, but which will, for example, allow the venture capitalist to sack the entrepreneur and appoint a new chief executive if certain financial and other targets are not met.

The government represents the community in a democratic country, and while it does not define entrepreneurial success, it has a vast number of laws and regulations. Entrepreneurs who breach these may face fines or worse personally, but more often they will be denied the permits and planning authorities that their enterprise needs. In general terms the laws and regulations are intended to protect the community from the acts of reckless, immoral or incompetent individuals. While many regulations appear ridiculous, most of them are there because, at some time, an individual caused harm to her neighbours, employees or customers in a way now prohibited by law.

The governments of different countries attempt to protect their citizens from harm in different ways. Sometimes there is merely a law against doing or threatening harm, such as the law against dangerous driving, but often there are prescriptive regulations, such as speed limits. Many entrepreneurs get their enterprises into serious trouble when they start to export or do business in other countries by assuming, naively, that the regulations are the same as those with which they are familiar at home. In 1991 a US delegation, led by the president, complained that 'unfair' Japanese regulations blocked the import of US motorcars. The Japanese explained, as tactfully as possible, that their motorists drove on the left and therefore preferred right-hand drive cars: no US manufacturer, at that time, had right-hand drive vehicles in production. Working in the other direction, many Japanese bought land in California in 1990 and 1991 expecting to develop it immediately. Only when they had paid for it did they discover that the US has local, county, state and federal governments, all of whom need to be satisfied before a sod is turned or a brick is laid. The prices the Japanese investors paid were appropriate for development sites where work could commence immediately, but were far too high for sites where, as for many of these purchases, development was years or decades into the future.

Governments don't merely prescribe laws and regulations; they provide for remedies and punishments when these laws are broken. In most cases the law looks for a person to hold responsible for any damage an enterprise causes to its neighbours, employees or customers, and that person is the entrepreneur. The costs and delays caused by trials and investigations can doom an enterprise. Entrepreneurs do not want to be found innocent but broke at the end of a long and expensive trial: they want to stay out of court altogether. Like Caesar's wife, they should be above suspicion.

Staying out of court and avoiding disputes generally are signs that a new enterprise has been a good neighbour and a good local citizen.

Avoiding risk, managing uncertainty

'Risk' and 'uncertainty' are simple words for a very complex set of concepts. The statistics of risk are based on 'random' events, such as tossing dice or spinning a coin. A new business venture is not really like spinning a coin: the people who will make the new enterprise a success by buying its products are mostly alive and set in their ways. There are very few totally random events in the modern world, so when some event occurs it is usually possible to find out what caused it, what caused the causes and so on for as long as the investigator wishes to keep looking and the people that the investigator must interview will go on answering questions.

Business risk is more a matter of uncertainty than chance: an entrepreneur might start a casino but would be unlikely to place more than a social bet in one. Business proposals are seldom set out as win–lose gambles. A proposal may require some investment in product development and the new firm may need a certain number of customers prepared to pay at least a minimum price if it is to survive. If it starts and fails, it may be because product development took too long or cost too much or too few customers were prepared to pay the minimum feasible price. Some projects fail absolutely, by attempting the impossible or producing a product which generates no sales at all, but these are rare.

The term 'risk' comes from insurance, where it refers to the probability that an insurance company will be forced to pay a claim before the insured party has paid enough in premiums to cover it. Insurance is possible because the risks accepted by the insurance company are statistically distributed with a constant or slowly moving mean and a known, bounded standard deviation. One precondition of this is independence: the occurrence of an insured incident is not affected by any previous occurrences. On a true roulette wheel the odds on any number, or either colour, turning up are the same for every spin of the wheel. Individual events in the life of a business may be assigned a probability of success (or conversely, a risk of failure) but the outcome of successive events is linked, not just because if an event leads to the failure of a business no further favourable events can occur.

In business, success feeds on success and failure breeds failure. A salesperson might, as a matter of pure luck, chance upon an eager buyer on her first call. This will boost her self-confidence, and her increased enthusiasm and greater conviction will both encourage her to persevere after less successful calls, and may secure additional sales from borderline prospects. It is well known among sales managers that a few of the salespersons will secure the bulk of the orders but, equally, there is no way of predicting which members of a sales team will be the successful ones in advance. The realm of risk and probability has been left behind, and we are dealing with uncertainty: 'all we know is that we do not know'.[10]

The geometric random walk provides one of the simplest models with an uncertain outcome, and although such a model has a non-stationary mean and an unbounded standard deviation, the standard deviation per unit of time is well defined and can be used as a measure of uncertainty. For planning purposes, a standard deviation is the difference between the expected outcome, with a 50:50 chance of being achieved, and the one-in-six worst case. If, for example, an entrepreneur plans to sell a new venture in seven years for a million dollars, with a one-in-six chance that it will fail and be worth nothing before the seven years are up, the uncertainty is 100 per cent. If the one-in-six worst case is that the business will only fetch half a million dollars, the uncertainty is 50 per cent. If the one-in-six chance leaves the entrepreneur with a worthless firm and an enforceable debt of a million dollars, the uncertainty is 200 per cent.

The economist Avinash Dixit (1992) has developed a quite simple formula for converting uncertainty into hurdle rates. We reproduce Dixit's formula in Chapter 4, where we explain how to put a provisional value on a proposal. The hurdle rate as defined by Dixit (1992) is the expected rate of return on a project below which an investor would be better off leaving her money in government bonds. It is the minimum return a thoughtful investor would demand before supporting a proposal. This will be explained in more detail in the chapter on finance; but Dixit's work has shown that venture capitalists who demand returns of 60 per cent or more or who will only put up $40,000 against a promise of a million dollars in seven years' time are not greedy or risk-averse, just rational.

In the case of a successful new enterprise, the risks often vanish entirely with hindsight; one of the facts about great enterprises is that, when they are completed, practically everybody is able to find fault with the way they were carried out, and many people are likely to comment on how obvious it all was and how little the entrepreneur really did or how lucky she was. In practice successful entrepreneurs create their own luck: often either of two possible courses of action will succeed if the decision is made quickly and the necessary actions put in place vigorously. Timidity, delay and trying to 'put an each-way bet on a two-horse race' may seem like caution or prudence. In fact these ways of behaving increase the probability of ultimate failure.

The degree of uncertainty facing a new enterprise is primarily a measure of the defects in the current state of generally available knowledge about the forces for and against the project. At one extreme major western governments announce from time to time that they are selling ten year bonds, the selling price is such an amount, the interest will be so much, paid according to a clearly set out schedule, and the bonds will be redeemed for their face value on such and such a date. The government usually takes considerable pains to make the terms and conditions of each issue widely known. The difference between the 'worst' outcome and the 'expected' outcome is zero. A decision to invest in such bonds involves so little risk and uncertainty that it is often described as a 'risk-free' investment; there is little scope for entrepreneurship here.

Risk is multidimensional. There is no single opposite to 'low risk', but practically every investment in anything other than government-backed bonds involves less certainty about the amount and timing of the investment and the size and phasing of the returns. More research will usually reduce the uncertainty in any given case, but this research takes time and costs money. The time taken by extensive pre-commitment research actually increases the risk that some other entrepreneur will pre-empt the market, while the money spent on it increases the investment and reduces the rate of return to the investor. The time and cost of this research is the cost of reducing the investment risk to some defined level.

Entrepreneurs are frequently described as risk-takers, but they don't talk about themselves that way and in any case risks are insurable. Entrepreneurship is much more than risk assessment and actuarial calculation: entrepreneurs might buy insurance against known risks, they may even start an insurance company but entrepreneurship is not simply another form of insurance. Psychologists describe entrepreneurs as risk-tolerant. They might not like uncertainty, but they aren't paralysed by it. Entrepreneurs are usually very good at assessing and balancing risks in their proper context; doing nothing involves all sorts of risks in a world where other entrepreneurs may be active. The random walk model shows how a succession of well-defined risks can lead to a truly uncertain outcome: an entrepreneur chooses the best option whenever she is called upon to make a decision, evaluates the outcome and makes a new best choice once the effects of earlier decisions are known. Entrepreneurs are explorers of the realms of possibility, avoiding dead ends and endless circles, staying out of bottomless pits and emerging having obtained a worthwhile objective, not necessarily the one they originally went looking for.

The entrepreneur's advantage

A number of factors combine to create a successful entrepreneur and people who are capable of successful entrepreneurship in one industry and culture might be less successful in another. All entrepreneurs must have the ability to make decisions with uncertain outcomes, based on the best available current information. Equally, entrepreneurs must be able to reverse decisions as soon as circumstances make such a reversal necessary and abandon policies as soon as they are found to be inappropriate. One role demands a robust self-confidence, the other fundamental humility. Entrepreneurs don't have to be specialists in the industry in which they are operating or leading experts in the underlying science and technology, but they need to know enough about both to take advice from genuine experts and recognise and reject the urgings of fake ones. When Christopher Columbus set sail to 'discover' the West Indies, the public view was that such a journey was impossible and the risks were infinite. Columbus had researched the issue by reading ancient Greek authors and he knew that the world was round. By applying logic, roughly the argument that one patch of ocean was much like another, he formed the private view that the risks of the voyage were finite and manageable. The project's success made Columbus famous and extremely rich, although not, in the end, particularly happy. Columbus could not have succeeded if he had not been a fine sailor, but many other fine sailors made no bold discoveries. Columbus had the self-confidence to assert the feasibility of his voyage amid an almost universal belief that it was impossible. In his subsequent career as a colonial administrator, this same self-confidence led to him disregarding the opposition of his peers and subordinates in matters of more immediate interest to them and so to his subsequent removal from office.

Sir John Monash was Australia's greatest soldier, and the only general on either side to emerge from the Western Front of the First World War with a reputation for success unstained by one for butchery. Before the war he founded the Monier Concrete Company and after it he was the foundation chairman of the State Electricity Commission of Victoria. Monash combined the abilities to analyse, plan and evaluate to an extraordinary degree, while retaining a remarkable emotional detachment. If a civil or military project was going to fail, he knew it and, within the limits of his authority, stopped it, no matter whose idea it originally was. If the plan was going to succeed, he knew that too and would not be deflected by other people's doubts, whether the doubters were the staff of the commander in chief (he ordered his signallers not to pass on messages) or the Victorian cabinet (he called the cabinet to a meeting, told them what they were about to do and left without waiting for questions).

Part of the entrepreneur's advantage, as shown by Columbus and Monash, is the ability to form an opinion based upon the facts, disregarding unfounded prejudices and popular superstitions along the way. Part is the ability to function under pressure. These two attributes are seldom sufficient. An entrepreneur must be able to lead and contribute.

An entrepreneur's contribution will usually be based on some particular competence that sets her apart from her likely competitors. Columbus was an expert sailor, while Monash was a professional engineer and had been an officer in the volunteer artillery for many years before the war. A business entrepreneur must have a strong grasp of some key aspects of a project, whether marketing, sales, development or production, or in general terms, some skill or capability that enables the entrepreneur to be personally essential to the project's success.

Leadership can be both over- and understated. Leadership divorced from any useful skill becomes a mockery and its achievements nugatory. Leadership may involve flamboyance, but integrity, competence and the ability to communicate effectively are the defining qualities of leadership. Monash became profoundly admired and respected, but he was anything but charismatic. He did not lead his troops over the parapet, he sent them and they went willingly because of their absolute – and repeatedly justified – faith in his generalship.

Learning entrepreneurship

Can entrepreneurship be taught and learned? The answer is yes and no. There are unlimited ways in which people express themselves and becoming an entrepreneur is just one of these. People whose talents and ambitions do not include building teams of people to achieve an economic or social objective can be taught to pass exams in entrepreneurship but this won't turn them into entrepreneurs.

The world is full of opportunities, but only those people who recognise an opportunity and create an enterprise to realise it are entrepreneurs. Many entrepreneurs fail at their first attempt; some of these are discouraged, while others learn some lessons from their experience and try again. Sometimes a new enterprise fails for reasons that could not have been foreseen, but far too often the failure can be traced to pure ignorance: the entrepreneur or product champion, in their enthusiasm, ignored some elementary rule of management, finance, accounting or marketing.

Some projects get into trouble because of a failure to integrate the skills available: such projects go through an unnecessarily long gestation and a difficult birth while various critical issues are raised, only partially resolved and raised again. If the effect of these incessant reviews is to keep changing direction, the ultimate result may be to abort the project completely. Entrepreneurial education can spread a general recognition of the significance of innovation and entrepreneurship through the community. At the same time it can give people with entrepreneurial ambitions the skills they need to seize opportunities and avoid the most common causes of failure.

This book focuses specifically on three critical aspects of entrepreneurship:

- *Opportunity screening:* how do you make sure that the project to which you are about to commit yourself has a reasonable chance of success?
- *Revenue forecasting:* how do you set phased revenue targets? What sales and marketing budget will be required to meet these targets?
- *Entrepreneurial business planning:* how do you document your project proposal so as to make it intelligible to those who will review it and attractive to those whom you wish to join it (as partners, financiers, key employees, key suppliers, launch customers and others)?

These are by no means the only skills needed by an entrepreneur. An entrepreneur, or a trusted member of an entrepreneurial team, will need skills in:

- *Ethics:* How do you preserve your self-respect, and the respect of your community, without fudging the hard decisions? We discuss ethics in Chapter 2, because of the essential role of ethics in creating teams and building value-creating relationships.
- *Accounting:* What has to be done to keep track of the money passing through a new enterprise? How do you use your accounting data to help you to manage the new business?
- *The law:* What must a business do, and what must it not do, to obey the law? What is the right structure for the new enterprise? How can the venture's intellectual property be protected? What do directors do? We provide a brief overview of the relevant laws in Chapter 7.
- *Finance:* How do you measure the value created by a business? How do you build a financial operating plan? How do you structure an offer to potential investors? How do you find potential investors? Once you have them, how do you keep their confidence? Finance plays a significant role in every stage of venture creation.
- *Team creation:* How do you recruit and motivate the people you will need to launch the venture with you? How do you decide what sort of team you are going to need? Chapter 5 explains the salient facts about designing new venture organisations.
- *Marketing:* How do you bring your product to the attention of potential customers?

Entrepreneurs who learn these skills before they launch their new venture are not certain to succeed, but they will be able to identify, and avoid, the most common causes of failure. Entrepreneurs who start the business first and try to learn these skills on the job need a great deal of luck if their venture is to stay afloat. People who never learn them never become successful entrepreneurs.

A well-structured entrepreneurial education programme provides an opportunity for potential entrepreneurs to develop and test their skills at planning and leadership in a relatively safe environment. Such programmes often involve teamwork and a substantial element of team assessment, and while the students' projects may lead to live enterprises, they don't have to. Where possible such programmes should include exposure to practising professionals in finance, marketing and other critical areas, particularly in the plan evaluation process. This can give students a foretaste of the type of questions they will face and the directness of the criticism they may be subjected to, when they set out to practise their entrepreneurial skills on a truly live project.

'Lifestyle' entrepreneurs, people who intend to start or take over a small business, cannot neglect any of these issues. One person, planning to start a new retail business, will take a day or a week to stand outside a possible site and count the number of people, and likely customers, who go past. That person is practising marketing. Another person might lease a site in a shopping centre from an agent because the rent is especially low: that person is not practising marketing. The second person's site may turn out to be one of a row of otherwise empty shops in an isolated corner; the business's failure is a marketing one, even if the word was never used.

The economics of entrepreneurship

Orthodox ignorance

The entrepreneur is an important figure in the work of the classical economists such as Adam Smith, but as the discipline became more mathematical and less pragmatic from the last quarter of the nineteenth century onwards the entrepreneur became squeezed out. The major tool in the orthodox economists toolkit is general equilibrium theory, which considers the 'state of the world' long after the last innovation has taken place and no further changes can be expected.

Baumol (1968) describes one role invented for the entrepreneur. Marx suggested that the natural development of a capitalist system involved ever-increasing concentration, as successful firms grew and those that failed to grow were taken over or forced into bankruptcy, until a handful of firms dominated those industries that did not collapse into total monopoly. Marx, following Adam Smith, had noted that as firms got larger they got more efficient, through a better use of the labour force, each member of it becoming more specialised. Even the overheads of supervision increase more slowly than the number of lowest level workers, again favouring the largest firms. In order to preserve competition in theory if not in practice, the economically orthodox postulated that every firm required a unique entrepreneur whose influence became ineffective if the firm exceeded a certain size, forcing costs up as output exceeded some finite level. Graphically, the entrepreneur becomes a heavy object dropped on the falling average cost curve to put a downward kink into it and flick the tail upward.

From the 1980s the entrepreneur crept back into orthodox theory in the form of principal–agent theory. According to this theory, the shareholders in a company collectively constitute the entrepreneur and they hire a manager to carry out their wishes. This construct has absolutely no basis in practice, for all its theoretical elegance. Shareholders don't even have a legal right to direct the managers of a company, as if a volatile group of investors whose membership changes daily could even be said to have a common opinion on a company's direction. In practice investors subscribe to a company or buy shares in it because they believe it has good management. In countering the assertion that shareholders own a company and the managers are therefore required to obey their wishes, Kay and Silberston wrote (1995: 88):

> As a legal matter, an English company does not appear to be owned by its shareholders, despite frequent statements to the contrary by corporate managers – a striking illustration of the substitution of rhetorical for real accountability. 'The company is at law a different person altogether from its subscribers.' (Lord Macnaghten in *Salomon* v. *Salomon & Co.* 1897, AC 22 HL) 'Shareholders are not, in the eye of the law, part owners of the undertaking. The undertaking is something different from the totality of the shareholdings.' (Evershed, LJ in *Short* v. *Treasury Commissioners*, 1948, AC 534 HL)

The continued reference to shareholders as 'owners' in the press and some academic writing does suggest that some economists are prepared to recommend illegal behaviour if it conforms to economic theory. As far as entrepreneurs are concerned, it is not certain which view of them is the more humiliating: do they merely exist to bend a downward sloping line into a U-shaped one or are they the agents of the investment firms that dribble other people's money to them from the safe haven of limited liability? If orthodox economic theory cannot contribute to our understanding of entrepreneurship and innovation as they occur in the real world, we must move to the fringes of the discipline.

When orthodox economists are challenged to explain economic growth, they cite three factors: the natural increase in the labour force; there is the accumulation of capital; and technological change (sometimes referred to as 'total factor productivity' or TFP growth). Robert Solow (1956) estimated the relative importance of the three factors and observed that the increase of labour and the accumulation of capital could only account for 20 per cent of the growth of the US economy over a 50-year period. Using the normal assumption that knowledge is instantaneously transmitted so there can be no economic incentive to produce it, the missing 80 per cent, sometimes called the 'Solow residual', is described as 'exogenous' or coming from outside the economy. Having written entrepreneurs out of the economy, there was no way to write innovation back in, leading a sceptical commentator (possibly Joan Robinson) to describe the orthodox view of technological change as 'falling like manna from heaven'.

Schumpeter and creative destruction

Joseph Schumpeter is a complex figure in the development of economics. As professor of economics at Harvard he presided over a large, diverse and creative department and corresponded with the leading figures of the discipline across the world. Schumpeter was not an unorthodox economist except in his interests: rather than studying the long run equilibrium he focused on entrepreneurship and economic growth. Schumpeter thought that economists who studied a hypothetical equilibrium were missing an essential point:

> The essential point to grasp is that in dealing with capitalism we are dealing with an evolutionary process. It may seem strange that anyone can fail to see so obvious a fact which moreover was long ago emphasised by Karl Marx. Yet that fragmentary analysis which yields the bulk of our propositions about the functioning of modern capitalism persistently neglects it. Let us restate the point and see how it bears upon our problem.

> Capitalism, then, is by nature a form or method of economic change and not only never is but never can be stationary. And this evolutionary character of the capitalist process is not merely due to the fact that economic life goes on in a social and natural environment which changes and by its change alters the data of economic action; this fact is important and these changes (wars, revolutions and so on) often condition industrial change, but they are not its prime movers. Nor is this evolutionary character due to a quasi-automatic increase in population and capital or to the vagaries of monetary systems of which exactly the same thing holds true. The fundamental impulse that sets and keeps the capitalist engine in motion comes from the new consumers' goods, the new methods of production or transportation, the new markets, the new forms of industrial organisation that capitalist enterprise creates. ([1942] 1967: 82)

Having little sympathy for equilibrium, Schumpeter had less, if that were possible, for those economists who interpreted competition solely in terms of price:

Every piece of business strategy acquires its true significance only against the background of that process and within the situation created by it. It must be seen in its role in the perennial gale of creative destruction; it cannot be understood irrespective of it or, in fact, on the hypothesis that there is a perennial lull.

But economists who, *ex visu* of a point of time, look for example at the behaviour of an oligopolist industry – an industry which consists of a few big firms – and observe the well-known moves and countermoves within it that seem to aim at nothing but high prices and restrictions of output are making precisely that hypothesis. They accept the data of the momentary situation as if there were no past or future to it and think that they have understood what there is to understand if they interpret the behaviour of those firms by means of the principle of maximising profits with reference to those data. The usual theorist's paper and the usual government commission's report practically never try to see that behaviour, on the one hand, as a result of a piece of past history and, on the other hand, as an attempt to deal with a situation that is sure to change presently – as an attempt by those firms to keep on their feet, on ground that is slipping away from under them. In other words, the problem that is usually being visualised is how capitalism administers existing structures, whereas the relevant problem is how it creates and destroys them. As long as this is not recognised, the investigator does a meaningless job. As soon as it is recognised, his outlook on capitalist practice and its social results changes considerably.

The first thing to go is the traditional conception of the modus operandi of competition. Economists are at long last emerging from the stage in which price competition was all they saw. As soon as quality competition and sales effort are admitted into the sacred precincts of theory, the price variable is ousted from its dominant position. However, it is still competition within a rigid pattern of invariant conditions, methods of production and forms of industrial organisation in particular, that practically monopolises attention. But in capitalist reality as distinct from the textbook picture, it is not that kind of competition which counts but the competition from the new commodity, the new source of supply, the new type of organisation (the largest-scale unit of control for instance) – competition which commands a decisive cost or quality advantage and which strikes not at the margins of the profits and the outputs of the existing firms but at their foundations and their very lives. This kind of competition is as much more effective than the other as a bombardment is in comparison with forcing a door, and so much more important that it becomes a matter of comparative indifference whether competition in the ordinary sense functions more or less promptly; the powerful lever that in the long run expands output and brings down prices is in any case made of other stuff. ([1942] 1967: 83–4)

Schumpeter's hope that economists were emerging from an exclusive focus on price competition was based on the widespread acceptance of the work of Robinson and Chamberlin on imperfect competition, but his hope has proved illusory. The tradition of Robinson (1969) and Chamberlin (1933/1960) is preserved in the study of industrial organization (IO) economics, but this is seen by the generality of economists as a specialist branch of the economics profession dealing with those rare special cases where the assumption of perfect competition cannot be sustained. The major focus of IO economics is not how capitalism works but how firms can be forced to act as if they were in a state of textbook competition. The lack of clout possessed by IO economists was well illustrated in 1996, when the newly elected Liberal (that is, conservative) government in Australia closed the Bureau of Industry Economics (in which IO economists were employed) and transferred its functions to the Productivity Commission, where general equilibrium theory is worshipped with exemplary devotion.

Schumpeter's last major work was *Capitalism, Socialism and Democracy* ([1942] 1967), in which he predicted that socialism would supersede capitalism. This is often read as a sign of the weakness of his judgement, although readers of the book will find that by 'socialism' he meant the welfare state rather than the practices of the Soviet Union. While there are plenty of noisy advocates of a return to the red-blooded capitalism of the nineteenth century, it is by no means clear that they are going to succeed in destroying the welfare state, which is still quite definitely with us 50 years after Schumpeter's death.

Schumpeter's major academic book, as we now see it, was his *Theory of Economic Development* which first appeared (in German) in 1908 but which he kept working on until an English edition appeared in 1934. (Schumpeter himself may have placed more weight on his work on the theory of economic cycles, which from today's perspective looks like an interesting but ultimately unproductive endeavour. Modern developments in chaos and complexity theory have destroyed Schumpeter's hopes of developing a set of predictive tools, and cast doubt on his reliance on arguments based on cycle theory for producing precepts of economic policy.) Entrepreneurially led economic growth followed, according to Schumpeter, along the following path:

1. An entrepreneur fastens upon a potential innovation, a new product, a higher quality product, a new method of production or a new way of organising production.
2. The entrepreneur raises capital from a bank or banks: Schumpeter was writing about what we now refer to as merchant banks, but even if the capital comes from investors, they will raise it by drawing down their bank deposits or borrowing against security; all new money eventually can be traced back to a bank.
3. The entrepreneur uses part of this capital to obtain the use of premises and equipment, hire labour and purchase materials. It is a critically important part of Schumpeter's argument that the labour, in particular, is hired away from its previous employer by the offer of higher wages or benefits; the entrepreneur does *not* rely on access to previously unemployed resources.
4. The entrepreneur now markets the newly produced products, some of which may be bought by the entrepreneur's own workers but most of which will be bought by other firms' workers. Part of the profits from these sales will reward the bankers or investors, part will be reinvested and part will reward the entrepreneur personally.
5. To simplify a complex argument, the existence of a firm paying higher wages than were previously customary will force up the general wage level as older firms attempt to retain their workforces. The most marginal firms will be unable to afford higher wages and will fail. At the same time, the money spent on the entrepreneur's products may be diverted from that previously spent on other,

inferior products and the firms making these must innovate in their turn or contract to meet the reduced demand.

6. Consumers outside this loop will now have access to superior or cheaper products and workers generally will enjoy higher real wages, so the economy will have developed in a positive way.

7. The creativity of the entrepreneur will be less warmly welcomed by those firms rendered unviable by the rise in general wage levels or those whose markets have shrunk: the creative activity of the entrepreneur will have led to the destruction of the marginal firms and those relying on inferior products, but measured by the level of real wages, society as whole will have advanced.

In Schumpeter's pithy summary, the creativity of the entrepreneur leads to the destruction of the less entrepreneurial and less efficient firms: society and the economy advance by a process of 'creative destruction'. We have no doubt that creative destruction, led by entrepreneurs and product champions (or intrapreneurs), is the primary force for economic and social development.

Evolutionary models

Edith Penrose is credited with identifying embedded knowledge as a key factor in the success of competitive enterprises and set this out in *The Theory of the Growth of the Firm* ([1959] 1995). Whereas the orthodox neoclassical assumptions are that labour, capital and resources are in short supply while knowledge is free and instantly disseminated, Penrose took the view that knowledge was hard to create and hard to learn, while labour, capital and materials were generally available. She also identified the firm itself as a source of embedded knowledge; while different individuals might have a grasp of particular aspects of technology, production or the market, their combination underpinned the firm's performance – no one individual had a complete grasp of the entire operations of a successful firm once it had grown to a significant size.

Penrose's focus is on the firm, while Schumpeter is more interested in the broader implications of entrepreneurship for industries and whole economies, but there is no fundamental inconsistency. Schumpeter can be read as identifying the embedded knowledge of the firm with the private knowledge of the entrepreneur, but an alternate reading is possible, and in any case Schumpeter was dead well before Penrose's work appeared. It is clear that Schumpeter saw the unique capabilities of particular firms as far more important than the efficiency with which firms used resources in explaining both competition and economic development. Associating these unique capabilities with embedded knowledge should raise no problems.

The neo-Schumpeterians and the evolutionary economics schools preserve Schumpeter's tradition although they are relegated to the fringes of the economics profession, and Schumpeter's tradition is respected at some distance beyond the fringe by the advocates of bionomics. (Those interested in bionomics can search the web or read Rothschild (1992), the book that launched the concept.) The concept of the embedded capabilities of each corporation as a source of economic growth, which is closely related to Schumpeter's approach, was moved to the centre of management thinking by the article 'The core competence of the corporation' by Prahalad and Hamel, which appeared in the *Harvard Business Review* in 1990. Hamel and

Prahalad were following Penrose and the business historian Alfred Chandler, and in a significant departure from the 'purest' interpretation of Schumpeter, they pointed out that an entrepreneur had to build a team and an enterprise, not merely assemble a fleet of robots to carry out her directions.

It is hard to imagine any dispassionate observer rejecting Schumpeter's assertion that economic growth has been driven by 'the new consumers' goods, the new methods of production or transportation, the new markets, the new forms of industrial organisation that capitalist enterprise creates'. There were, and to some extent still are, gaps in the Schumpeterian narrative. Although the orthodox economic position is falsified by our daily experience, it has considerable intellectual appeal: why doesn't society settle down into an unchanging equilibrium state? Isn't there a logical limit to the process of improvement? Are there not 'diminishing returns' to innovation?

The analogy with evolution is a strong one: if evolution leads to the 'survival of the fittest', why doesn't it stop when all the weak have been eliminated and only the fit survive? We know it doesn't stop, but explaining why it doesn't requires considerable theoretical subtlety.

The foundation text of modern evolutionary economics is generally considered to be Richard Nelson and Sidney Winter's *An Evolutionary Theory of Economic Change*, first published in 1982, although the enigmatic Norwegian-American economist Thorstein Veblen raised the issue in 1898 and it was a commonplace of Schumpeter's work. In some contexts, 'neo-Schumpeterian' and 'evolutionary economics' are practically interchangeable terms. The critical difference between an evolutionary and a neoclassical approach to analysing a market economy is that the neoclassical view assumes progress towards an equilibrium state accompanied by increasing economic efficiency, whereas an evolutionary view has no end state and no particular trend in economic efficiency (as distinct from productivity). A firm may have an advantage over its competitors in either view of the world, but the orthodox neoclassical theory suggests that such advantages are temporary; the result of a slight blip in the normally perfect and instantaneous transmission of knowledge, and other firms will catch the initial leader. In the evolutionary view a firm with an advantage may build on this advantage to gain market share and the increased market share will lead to an improved cash flow relative to its competitors, which enables it to extend its lead further. To take a golfing analogy: match play golf follows the neoclassical model, with the players starting square at every hole; while multihole golf is more evolutionary, with players carrying any advantage from one hole, or round, into the next.

The descriptive advantages of the evolutionary models are not enough to shake the orthodox economist's devotion to the concept of equilibrium, and one form of the orthodox critique of evolutionary models is that these are purely descriptive, and while most evolutionary biologists see the gene as the unit of evolution, there are a number of candidates for this role in evolutionary economics. As Geroski points out (1999), the unit of evolution may be variously described as the firm, the business unit, a routine or a core competence; he argues that this failure of members of the evolutionary economics school to even agree on what they are talking about means that their discipline is immature at best.

Stuart Kauffman took the decisive step in producing a formal description of evolution and explains this in *The Origins of Order* (1993). He takes as his mathematical substructure work on the physics of spin glasses and identifies the crucial property driving evolution as frustration: however things are arranged, some elements are out of their ground state – 'You can't please everyone'. More colloquially, not only is there no equilibrium in which both foxes and rabbits are happy, there isn't even a perfect fox: the fox must be fast to hunt rabbits in the open, but robust to hunt rabbits in the undergrowth, to say nothing of holding his place in fox society; but increased speed and increased robustness are simply not compatible. A healthy fox is an excellent compromise, but a compromise nevertheless.

Kauffman succeeded in explaining not only why foxes are such efficient predators, but how wolves and foxes could emerge from a common ancestor. By treating evolution as an iterative process on a complex landscape, he was able to demonstrate the process of speciation, the process of adaptation, and the relative stability of species in a way that was both theoretically consistent and reflected the known behaviour of the real world. Kauffman went further, demonstrating with his random grammar models that state space contained frozen regions, in which change was impossible, liquid or chaotic, regions in which change was continuous and order impossible and a region 'at the edge of chaos' where new order could emerge. As with the complex landscapes, the statistics and patterns that emerged from Kauffman's work on random grammars reflect reality.

Kauffman answers Geroski's question: the unit of economic evolution is 'all of the above'. Economic state space defines public knowledge, individual capabilities, embedded knowledge and the boundaries of firms and markets. It is the combination that evolves. The evolution might involve a succession of slight improvements to a particular operation: this is Kauffman's adaptive walk, known in business practice by the Japanese term *kaizen*, the 'way of improvement'. Economic evolution also embraces multiple simultaneous changes, bringing about a 'new combination' in Schumpeter's phrase, or an 'evolutionary leap' as described by Kauffman. One of Kauffman's critical insights is that, even in biology, a focus on the gene can be misleading. Every living creature is the result of the interaction of a number of genes with both the environment and the previous development of the organism; this explains how a mere 30,000 or so genes are sufficient to guide the development of a human being. Talking of the 'fitness' of any single gene is misleading; it is only fit when accompanied by a given set of complementary genes in the individual's genetic inheritance, and then only because of the current state of the biosphere. A firm is superior when its combination of individual skills and embedded knowledge allows it to serve a given group of markets better than its rivals; but because a person is an outstanding contributor in a firm making motorcar tyres does not mean that that person would be an automatic choice for a leading role in a ballet company. This does not mean that ballet dancers are superior to production workers or vice versa, just that their contribution is meaningless outside its context.

Kauffman's model extends and clarifies Schumpeter's. One important aspect of Kauffman's insight affects our view of creative destruction: the evolution of the wolf did not cause the extinction of the fox, although it may have altered the boundaries of its niche and triggered a few further adaptations. Likewise the invention of the aeroplane did not lead to the extinction of the shipping line or the railway, although it forced both to adapt their roles to altered circumstances.

Romer and spillovers

The American economist Paul Romer has made a number of attempts (1986, 1993, 1994) to explain economic growth without abandoning neoclassical theory. The attempt is necessary because neoclassical theory, with its focus on equilibrium, cannot explain technological change – why, if knowledge is instantly and costlessly disseminated, should any firm invest in discovering it? And if one relaxes the assumption that knowledge is costlessly and instantly disseminated, why don't firms that have discovered new knowledge simply use it internally to increase their profits, as Adam Smith thought they would:

> A dyer who has found the means of producing a particular colour with materials which cost only half the price of those commonly made use of may, with good management, enjoy the advantage of his discovery as long as he lives, and even leave it as a legacy to his posterity. (Smith [1776] 1835: 25)

Romer argued that, in the normal case, firms could only appropriate part of the value of their new knowledge, but this part was sufficient to provide an incentive to invest in R&D in the first place, while the part that they could not appropriate 'spilled over' into other firms and into the community, raising the general level of knowledge. He then proposed replacing the standard production function $Y=f(K,L)$ with $Y=A(K,L)f(K,L)$ where A represents knowledge or technology or something, Y represents output, K capital and L labour; f is the 'standard' production function. Romer (1994) described his contribution to the development of endogenous growth theory. He defends it as a model that reproduces, to some extent, horizontal and longitudinal data sets covering productivity, but does not claim any great realism for it.

His conclusion that the development of new knowledge is important for economic growth would seem to be unexceptional, but the rate at which the governments around the world are piling fees onto university students while slashing funding for academic research suggests that the body of work which he represents is not taken seriously by those who determine public policy.

CHECKPOINT

Entrepreneurs are ordinary people; few if any of them leap tall buildings in one or even several bounds. They are distinguished from the rest of us by their determination to create an enterprise devoted to delivering some product or service, or achieving some form of social change. Some of them become rich in the process, but for many of them this is a secondary objective, if it is an objective at all.

Entrepreneurship plays a key role in the development of modern societies and economies; to the extent that rising real wages and an improved quality and diversity of the goods and services available to consumers constitute progress, entrepreneurs drive progress.

Given the degree to which economic theory shapes public policy and constrains public discussion of economic and social issues, the lack of attention paid to entrepreneurship by the generality of economists, and the misapprehensions of most of them when they do consider it, is unfortunate. It means that entrepreneurs won't be well understood by governments, but at least in a modern capitalist society governments won't actively hinder them either.

Exercises

This book covers both the 'why' and the 'how 'of entrepreneurship but if you are reading it as a student your practical interest might be at least as strong as your intellectual curiosity. The exercises in this and subsequent chapters will mainly cover issues that we see as important to people planning or considering an entrepreneurial venture.

1 Why are you interested in the subject of entrepreneurship? If you are considering launching a new venture, or participating in such a launch, write down a few notes describing your objectives (you don't have to show them to anyone).

2 In the light of your answer to 1, why should other people want to join your venture? Write down a few notes setting out the reasons you expect your prospective colleagues may have for joining you.

3 What particular advantage will you bring to an entrepreneurial venture? What critical skills do you think that you lack and will have to find in your venture colleagues? Make some notes and store them safely: we suggest that you revisit them at the end of this book.

4 Explain, in half a page or so, the difference between the orthodox economist's explanation for economic growth and Schumpeter's.

5 Is an instance of *kaizen*, the Japanese system of improving manufacturing processes by frequent, minor improvements, an innovation? Would the introduction of *kaizen* to a country where manufacturing had previously been organised on Taylorist principles be an innovation? Explain your answer.

6 Adam Smith thought that a dyer could exploit the benefits of an innovation for his lifetime and that of his children and grandchildren. Explain why this might not be true.

Notes

1 Soichiro Honda was the cofounder of Honda Motor; Akio Morita founded Sony; Josiah Wedgwood, in the course of establishing the pottery firm that bears his name today, innovated both marketing and the factory system of manufacture; Matthew Boulton was James Watt's partner in the firm Boulton and Watt; Boulton was the entrepreneur who complemented the inventive James Watt in the innovation of steam power.

2 One of the most comprehensive analyses of business cycles was provided by Joseph Schumpeter – an economist whose work on defining the process of entrepreneurship we will encounter in subsequent pages. See Schumpeter (1939).

3 Braudel (1981) chronicles the rise of modern capitalism readably and comprehensively.

4 Foster (1987) provides a very readable demonstration of the nature and importance of innovation and technological cycles. Freeman and Soete (1997) describe the major features of each of the great cycles of innovation from the Industrial Revolution onwards.

5 Heilbroner (1986) provides an enjoyable introduction to the history of economic ideas through the lives of their creators.

6 Keynes' 1936 book is generally regarded as his major work, and the one in which he set out his theory of depression and recovery, but he was a prolific writer and much of his earlier as well as his later work is still regarded as valuable, at least by those who believe that the future is unknown and unknowable.

7 The economics of large firms is a branch of economics known as industrial organisation (IO) economics. Most work in IO economics, in the view of the present authors, relies on an unduly static view of the economy and understates the importance of entrepreneurship and innovation. IO economists have not (as at 2003) provided an agreed, much less a convincing, account of large, multiproduct firms.

8 Arthur and Arrow give a short account of these recent developments in economics in Arthur (1994: ix–xx).

9 The Model T Ford stayed in production until 1926 but, in hindsight, this was too long.

10 J. M. Keynes.

2 Entrepreneurs in society

This chapter

■ Businesses and markets are part of a broader society, one in which the relations between people have more dimensions than contracts for the supply of goods and services, and where most people have more ambitions than the simple accumulation of financial assets. In developed countries other than the USA, there is general acceptance that there is a degree of mutual responsibility and obligation that links businesses, people and society. Firms that recognise and respond to these obligations are more likely to be successful in the market and more likely to attract and retain top-class employees than firms that do not accept obligations beyond immediate profit maximisation.

■ In this chapter we will explain the concept of ethical entrepreneurship and set out a series of principles for ethical conduct in an entrepreneurial economy.

Entrepreneurs

Human society is made up of a large number of unique individuals. One of the many ways in which each person differs from those around them is in their ambitions, hopes and dreams. Some people wish to become outstanding athletes, dancers, scientists, politicians, writers or musicians. These ambitions need not be engraved in stone; as people go through life, their circumstances and ambitions change. Some people, at some stages in their life, feel a powerful urge to build an organisation that will do something, or produce something, that has not been done before. When they put these urges into practice, they become entrepreneurs.[1] If their intentions are ethical, we refer to them as 'ethical entrepreneurs', or simply 'entrepreneurs' in this book. Other authors (for example Baumol 1990) use the term more broadly.

Who are they?

The word 'entrepreneur' was first applied to Frenchmen who 'entered and took charge' of royal contracts. Typically, the king would grant some nobleman the right to build a road or a bridge and collect the tolls, in return for a suitable donation to the royal treasury or some other favour. The nobleman would appoint an entrepreneur, who would arrange finance, supervise construction and manage the completed facility. The entrepreneur guaranteed the nobleman a fixed annual payment and kept anything that was left over. Noblemen generally wished to earn a steady income without getting their hands dirty. They could do this by engaging an entrepreneur. The entrepreneur accepted the uncertain outcome in return for the chance of earning a profit. Since these early

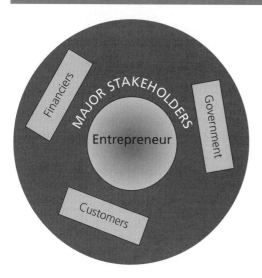

Figure 2.1   **The entrepreneur – always in the middle**

entrepreneurs tended to be smart and closely involved with the project, and the noblemen who nominally owned the projects were usually neither, the profits were often very substantial.

The fundamental principle of entrepreneurship has not changed: entrepreneurs earn their reward by managing projects and accepting and managing the associated uncertainty. This does not make an entrepreneur a gambler: far from it. The best entrepreneurs are not risk-takers, although part of their task is to manage risks. Uncertainty, not simple statistical risk, rules the world; no venture is certain to succeed. Entrepreneurs choose to 'enter and take charge' of projects where they have some special advantage which means that the dangers the uncertain world presents to the project are less, as long as the entrepreneur is managing it, than they would be if the government, or the financier or customer, attempted to manage the project directly.

Figure 2.1 shows the entrepreneur 'in between' the major stakeholders in an enterprise. There is the government, in our enlightened days representing the community rather than the king. The government sets the limits on what is acceptable, while still requiring a more or less substantial donation to the treasury in return for the needed approvals and permits. There are the financiers, because without money an entrepreneur can run no more than a cottage industry. Last, but not least, are the customers for the new enterprise, because without customers there can be no profit.[2]

Entrepreneurship

1 It is initiated by an act of human volition.
2 It occurs at the level of the individual firm.
3 It involves a change of state.
4 It involves a discontinuity.
5 It is a holistic process.
6 It is a dynamic process.
7 It is unique.
8 It involves numerous antecedent variables.

9 Its outcomes are extremely sensitive to the initial conditions of these variables.

Taken together, these characteristics create a set of parameters and criteria that will have to be met by any 'ideal' model of entrepreneurship.

Bygrave and Hofer (1991: 17)

This brings us to the kernel of ethical entrepreneurship:

- the entrepreneur *takes charge of* some project that will deliver valuable benefits and brings it to completion
- the entrepreneur *manages uncertainty*,[3] overcoming the many unforeseen dangers that face a venture and preserving the other stakeholders' investments

■ the entrepreneur has some *advantage* which means that a project in the entrepreneur's charge will succeed in the face of challenges that would destroy a less well-managed and planned venture.

Wealth and greed

Some entrepreneurs have become extremely wealthy and no doubt more will become so in the future. Some people, entrepreneurs and others, have demonstrated extraordinary greed. Active entrepreneurship is not compatible with uncontrolled greed or any other form of uncontrolled passion, but someone who has created, or inherited, a major wealth-generating enterprise will have a disposable income considerably greater than is needed to sustain an extremely comfortable lifestyle. People who are driven from the start by greed seldom become ethical entrepreneurs or entrepreneurs at all under our definition; fraud, theft and deception are far quicker routes to wealth, while outright banditry and extortion provide a quicker route still in those countries in which they are tolerated.

In most countries there are many people on the edge of society or altogether outside it and the redistribution of wealth from those who are conspicuously dissipating it to those who have none at all is often just. Practically every civilised society confiscates the proceeds of crime: why, might it be asked, should entrepreneurially gained wealth be treated differently? There are two linked reasons: one is that the ethical entrepreneur creates new wealth, most of which passes to the new enterprise's workers, suppliers and customers, and a relatively small fraction stays with the entrepreneur and the entrepreneur's wealth is not gained by unjustly depriving others; the second is that prospective entrepreneurs might be discouraged by the prospect of confiscation and public disgrace, and so society would, over all, be worse off.

The former Soviet Union provides a dreadful example of what can happen to a society in which entrepreneurship is outlawed; ethical entrepreneurs are useful members of society. The conditions in which ethical entrepreneurship could develop and make such a contribution are, however, very new when the whole of human history is considered.

Zero sum and positive sum

Polluters who don't pay

There is no stronger advocate of free-market capitalism than myself. As a small businessman who is founder and operator of a bottled water company, I believe in and understand the free market a lot better than Sean Hannity ever will. But in a true free-market economy, you can't make yourself rich without making your neighbors rich and without enriching your community. What polluters do is make themselves rich by making everyone else poor. They raise standards of living for themselves by lowering quality of life for everyone else. And they do that by escaping the discipline of the free market. Show me a polluter and I'll show you a subsidy, I'll show you a fat cat who's using political clout to escape the discipline of the free market and forcing the public to pay his costs of production.

David Talbot (2003). This article first appeared in Salon.com, at http://www.Salon.com. *An online version remains in the Salon archives. Reprinted with permission.*

The win–win enterprise

Successful business entrepreneurs are usually richer at the end of the process than they were at the beginning and it may be wondered where the money came from. The simplest answer is that entrepreneurial firms create wealth by introducing innovations.

The entrepreneur offers a new service, or delivers a new good, that costs less to provide than people are prepared to pay; in turn, the value that the average buyer receives exceeds the price they are required to pay. In particular, the value the buyers get, after adjusting for the price they pay, is greater than the net value they used to receive for their money before the innovation became available. The entrepreneur is better off, as the owner of valuable shares in a successful enterprise. The entrepreneur's employees are better off, since they are getting a more attractive package of benefits than they were before they took a job with the entrepreneur. The entrepreneur's customers are better off, receiving more value for money than before.

Clearly, now that some money is being spent on the entrepreneur's products, there will be a smaller fraction of the total expenditure in the economy going on everything else. As the effects of the innovation work through the whole economy, the money supply increases sufficiently to ensure that the average producer is no worse off than they were before: everybody wins; there are no losers.

When an innovation directly drives some previous product from the market, some workers may lose their jobs and some shareholders may see the value of their shares fall. They may not be consoled by the thought that everyone, on average, has been made better off when they have so obviously been hurt. There are two possible answers. One is that casualties are inevitable if society is to progress and the social safety net is there to keep them from destitution. The other is 'Go and do likewise'.[4] Innovations may displace older products but they seldom compete with other innovations. Firms that develop an innovative culture have little to fear from other innovators.

The money manipulator

Most of the time prices will even out across a market; a beer brewed in one city will cost about the same in every local outlet that sells it, and the price in more distant markets will be roughly the home price adjusted for freight costs. The average price of a firm's shares over a sufficient period will reflect the risk-adjusted discounted value of the firm's future cash flows quite accurately. Most of the time, in most markets, there are no super profits to be made by buying and selling the same thing.

There are, however, times when the market gets things wrong, and goods, or more often shares, are on offer at a price much lower or higher than they are in some other place or will be in some short time. Buying when or where something is cheap and selling where or when it is much dearer, or reversing the process by short-selling before a price fall, can produce large gains for the successful speculator. Speculation is often described as gambling and often it is, but sometimes it is a response to superior information. In 1815, for example, Nathan Rothschild learned the result of the Battle of Waterloo several hours before the official despatch arrived and made another large fortune by buying up government bonds cheaply. Today's market traders have the 24-hour news channel CNN showing at all times.

Speculators have been known to get information by more devious means than watching television. Staff of companies and governments have been bribed to pass over advance information about facts that will change bond or share prices. Press releases with lucky 'errors' in them can distort a market. Companies may be managed so as to report unsustainable profit increases leading to a sharp rise in their share price, or a 'concert party' may coordinate the buying and selling of a large parcel of shares and take advantage of the price differentials this causes.

However it is obtained, a speculative profit is the clearest possible example of a win–lose combination. The people who bought before the price fell, or sold before the rise, lose exactly as much as the speculator gains. The speculator makes money without adding value. This makes speculators unpopular among the losers, who make up the majority. In what was basically a public relations-driven attempt to improve the image of speculation and prevent governments trying to control it, some of the worst speculators of the 1980s called themselves 'entrepreneurs'. This was a travesty, and in the 1990s the swindlers and speculators of the 1980s were usually referred to as 'paper entrepreneurs' when the word was used to describe them at all.

Big wheels and little wheels[5]

All entrepreneurs are not equal

Innovative projects come in all shapes and sizes. Landing a man on the moon was a project, but so is rejuvenating a small mixed retail business. No one is compelled to be an entrepreneur, but it is very difficult to run a business, or even play a significant role in a commercial or community organisation, without making entrepreneurial decisions from time to time. While the success of any project is going to be defined by its stakeholders, the success of any one person's entrepreneurial career is very likely to be defined in terms of that person's objectives.

People's objectives change as they pass through their lives, but broadly speaking a person who achieves what they set out to do is a success. An entrepreneur should not consider their life a failure if they retire without ever founding a multibillion-dollar enterprise.

Creating a growth venture

Some businesses seem to grow without any apparent limit from their founding or the entry of an outstanding individual. In 1904 Henry Ford was a young man building motorcars as much for fun as for sale. In 1923 Alfred Sloan wondered whether General Motors was worth more as property than as a manufacturer. In 1945 the Toyoda family owned a medium-sized textile machinery factory and a small work-shop assembling military trucks, neither of which was actually operating in the aftermath of Japan's defeat. In 1958 Ken Thomas and Peter Abeles decided to merge their trucking businesses under the name TNT. In 1968 Andy Groves and his friends Robert Noyce and Gordon Moore founded Intel to make 1024-bit DRAM chips. In 1980 Bill Gates' Microsoft was one of hundreds of small businesses writing software for the hobbyists and pioneers who were trying to make microprocessors do something useful or at least interesting.

Often there is a baton change during the development of a company, when the founding entrepreneur passes control, not always willingly, to a new management team. Bill Boeing founded the Boeing Aircraft Company, but it got into difficulties, and the Boeing name is the sum of the Boeing family's interest in the present company. In many cases the entrepreneur who led a company from its foundation or refoundation to greatness did not create the opportunity that became their company's strength. If Henry Ford had been less pig-headed, churning out Model T Fords long after GM had demonstrated that the market wanted variety and colours other than black, Alfred Sloan's task would have been much harder. Bill Gates actually told IBM to go and buy a product called QDOS instead of giving him the order for PC-DOS; IBM gave Gates the order anyway, and so it was Gates who bought QDOS, polished it into PC-DOS and began the process of turning Microsoft into the world's largest software company.

What all these successful entrepreneurs have in common is that they recognised their opportunity when it came and pursued it single-mindedly. Another common factor is that they did not do it on their own: successful entrepreneurs build, lead and inspire teams of people to create their new enterprises. There is nothing routine about the creation of a new growth enterprise and little chance to repeat learned behaviour. The new enterprise is seldom in a position to pay the high wages and salaries or make the promises and grant the perquisites that would be needed to recruit proven top performers. The new enterprise can only succeed by drawing extraordinary performances out of ordinary people.

The enterprise creator

Bill Boeing had to be prised apart from the enterprise he had founded, but there are also people who deliberately build enterprises and sell them as soon as they have grown to the point where management begins to replace leadership. These people are less 'lifestyle entrepreneurs' than people who choose an entrepreneurial lifestyle.

Managing an established enterprise has challenges and opportunities, but these are different to those facing the creator of a new one. There are some people who find the challenges of starting a new enterprise attractive and such people often find the task of managing an existing one boring. The archetypical entrepreneur in American textbooks founds a new business, builds it for seven years and then sells it to a larger firm for a net personal gain of at least a million dollars. Having created and sold one enterprise, these entrepreneurs frequently start another, often investing their entire capital: having made a million dollars once, they believe they can do it again.

Other successful entrepreneurs may sell their enterprise or hand it to managers while they involve themselves in other activities. Some entrepreneurs who exit their enterprise in this way then use the time to pursue greater wealth still; but a significant number of successful entrepreneurs spend their time and wealth on increasing public well-being by political, charitable or artistic activities, working as a sponsor or volunteer. Such activities are particularly important in the USA, where it is hard to imagine the political, cultural or charitable systems surviving without such support; but entrepreneurs who move from accumulating to distributing their wealth occur in most societies.

The lifestyle entrepreneur

Many people find that working for a boss is irksome, even when their managers have outstanding human resource management skills and their employer is a leader in empowerment and a provider of outstanding benefits. When the boss believes that fear and insecurity are essential tools of the active manager, the delights of working for someone else diminish further. When previously loyal and hardworking employees are told they are no longer required, they frequently ask themselves whether the rewards of working for someone else are worth the pain. People in this position may set themselves a target: in such and such a time they will be the proprietor or major shareholder in a business that will provide an adequate income without making extravagant demands on their time or, at least, pay the bills while they are doing things they want to do.

American books often call firms created by entrepreneurs with such closely defined ambitions as 'mom and pop' operations; they may also be called 'jobs without a boss' and starting or buying such a business may be called 'buying a job'. However the resulting businesses are described, creating such an operation involves most of the problems, although usually on a smaller scale, that face the creator of a new growth venture. Judging by the statistics on survival rates these firms are not significantly less likely to fail than new firms with less well-defined ambitions, but because the scale of the problems is smaller, they may receive less attention. While the risk of a cash crisis or a technological debacle are less, the risks that stable small and medium-sized firms face from major changes in the market or the economy are probably greater.

Many large companies have introduced lean production and single sourcing, following the lead set by Toyota. When firms such as Ford or GM cut their supplier roster to a fifth of its original size, thousands of small and medium-sized businesses are pushed to, or over, the brink of disaster. Major retailers extend their market reach by building 'category-killer' stores such as Toys R Us and B&Q, and as such businesses grow, they draw custom away from hundreds of small and medium-sized retailers, many of whom will be forced into drastic retrenchments or out of business altogether.

Stable and lifestyle firms face risks that need managing because they service changing markets in turbulent economies. They will always face challenges that force the owners and managers of these firms to make decisions. Whenever the owners and managers of small and medium-sized businesses assess risks and make decisions, they are entrepreneurs and the lessons of this book are relevant to them.

Product champions: the 'intrapreneur'

New, high-growth companies eventually become established, stable ones. One day they reach the limit of growth in their main market. Once a company has reached half or thereabouts of its potential market, its growth phase, at least with that product line, is over. From this point leadership becomes less important and management more so. Independent decision-making is frowned upon; staff are expected to obey the rules and submit their proposals for change to a committee. The committee may reject or ignore them if they are not prepared in the proper format. Worthwhile ideas can easily become buried in such an atmosphere. In extreme cases such a firm may fall into the hands of a chief executive who sees new product development and marketing as an unnecessary expense; those who propose such a development may experience a career hiccup.

Some major corporations have made strenuous efforts to avoid such fossilisation. The American corporations 3M and Hewlett-Packard and the Japanese firm Sony have implemented procedures intended to encourage innovation and avoid relying on the cash flow generated by older products. While the average age of all the products on developed country markets, and all the processes used to make or deliver them, is between six and twelve years, innovative firms strive to keep the average age of their product lines to much less than that. Hewlett-Packard explicitly charges its business unit managers with keeping their product lines young: the average Hewlett-Packard product is less than three years old in the market.

Over recent years many firms have aggressively 'delayered' their management structure, cutting out middle and supervisory managers and relying on teamwork and cooperation to keep their enterprise functioning. A bureaucracy sets in place many barriers to change, but it also provides a mechanism for implementing changes once a decision is formally taken. Firms that have removed their bureaucracy have removed the barriers but they have also removed the mechanism. A sandy desert has replaced the brick wall and it may be no easier to cross. The individual teams within a flattened organisation may have an extremely flexible and effective approach to their defined tasks, but they often become fiercely protective of them. Their interests and their commitment may be to the team goals and not to those of the overall organisation.

Some people who work for large companies cease having business-related ideas. They may become keen gardeners, golfers, pillars of their local community or the devoted secretary of a sporting club. At work, however, they arrive punctually, greet their colleagues, managers and subordinates courteously, discharge their duties punctiliously and switch their brains back on as they get into their car or catch their train to go home. Other people take their ideas and leave, intending to start their own businesses. A few people are, however, trapped.

People who work for large corporations are sometimes struck by ideas that cannot work anywhere else. It may be an idea for reorganising the flow of work or an extension to the current product line, or it may need access to key people in the corporation plus lots of money. In the first two cases the project is meaningless outside the original corporation, while in the third case it is only major corporations that can mobilise major amounts of money. In all three cases the idea will lapse unless it is taken up by a product champion, an intrapreneur, who will secure corporate agreement to the project.

In a traditional bureaucracy this may involve the painstaking submission of forms and reports, every one of which carefully observes the bureaucratic rules. Alternatively, the product champion may find a way to short-circuit the process, lobbying the key decision-makers of the firm, building a tower of godfathers to the top, until the innovative project becomes part of the firm's official objectives. This may seem to be an extremely wasteful process, particularly to the many product developers who believe that the superiority of their invention is so self-evident that only fools or rogues could fail to acknowledge it. It is still the only proven route to get private sector projects with capital requirements in the hundreds of millions of dollars or more off the ground.

In a flat organisation the champion must be able to create a meta-team, a team of teams, that will accept the challenge of creating a new product and the risk that one or more of the original teams will find their own product lines superseded. Ultra-flat organisations are relatively new and there are few documented cases of such an organisation coming together around a major initiative. More frequently, the innovations such organisations produce are limited to the capability of one or a small number of teams.

Successful product champions cannot rely solely on their sales skills or the cunning with which they subvert a bureaucracy. The projects they propose must make technical and financial sense, for at least two reasons. One is that bureaucrats and other defenders of the status quo will seize on any technical or financial weaknesses to damn the project. The other is that the product champion is tied to the project and the corporation: there is no particular joy in being the inspiration for a monumental failure.

Many of the innovations that shaped the second half of the twentieth century came from corporations that committed everything they had, and a little bit more, into a single project. Boeing did it twice, once by innovating the commercial jet airliner,[6] and subsequently by innovating the wide-bodied passenger jet. IBM created the modern information technology industry with the System/360, announced in 1964 and delivered in volume from 1966 on. In 1964 an IBM spokesman was asked whether the System/360 was important to IBM: he answered, 'You bet your company it is!'

Changing society: the public benefit enterprise

Terrible social evils often only appear so in hindsight, at least to the majority of citizens. Before 1777, the common opinion of educated men from the beginning of recorded time had favoured slavery: in that year Dr Samuel Johnson published his considered opinion on a suit to return an escaped slave from Scotland to his master, and the court, accepting Johnson's argument, set the former slave free and effectively abolished slavery in Britain. It took two more years before the right that Johnson had won for a black man was extended to coal miners in Scotland. In 1806 the young Lord Palmerston stood for the parliamentary seat of Cambridge (and lost) on a pro-slave trade platform.

By 1833 the same Lord Palmerston was enthusiastically directing the Royal Navy to enforce an international ban on the slave trade. Palmerston's biographer (Ridley 1972) noted that the man was a perfect weather vane; never leading public opinion, but never far behind it. Palmerston's conversion shows that it took just 56 years from opposition to slavery being the preserve of a tiny minority of eccentrics to it becoming mainstream opinion.

History records that Bishop Sam Wilberforce created and inspired the anti-slavery movement in Britain, showing all the energy and leadership associated with successful entrepreneurship. Half a century after Wilberforce's triumph General William Booth inspired and led the Salvation Army, another huge entrepreneurial endeavour undertaken without the expectation or achievement of any personal financial rewards.

The leaders of social change must employ many of the planning, organisational and leadership skills of entrepreneurship. As Booth said to critics who complained that Salvation Army bands were playing popular tunes, 'Why should the devil have all the best music?'

Should entrepreneurs act ethically?

At least one reviewer of an earlier edition of this book was critical of the prominence given to ethical and moral issues. In that reviewer's eyes, ethics was a matter of public relations: firms should not get caught doing anything unethical, at least if this was likely to affect the willingness of its customers to deal with it, but beyond that firms should let nothing stand between them and a lawful profit. We find this attitude morally repellent, but our reasons for putting ethics up front go beyond our own preferences.

Ruppel and Harrington (2000) provide a recent example of a study concluding that 'moral management may be good management'; that employees are more committed, and effective, when they believe that their firm's managers observe high ethical and moral standards. This provides another example of what Kay (1996, 1998) calls the 'principle of obliquity'; the paradox that the best way to gain or improve profits seldom involves the single-minded pursuit of them. Paine (1994, 1996) offers more evidence and argument in favour of operating a business from a primarily moral perspective, paying due attention to the firm's obligations to all its stakeholders. Such a perspective recognises the firm's obligation to pay its investors a fair return, but does not allow the single objective of profit maximisation to displace any responsibility of the firm to its employees, customers and host communities.

Axelrod (1984) demonstrated that totally egotistical agents would find it in their interests to act cooperatively in circumstances where they expect an ongoing relationship with other agents. There is, of course, a clear difference between doing something because it is 'right' and doing the same thing because it is profitable, but at least Axelrod demonstrated that there is no automatic conflict between moral and profitable behaviour. Axelrod's argument unravels if we assume a certain or an actuarially predictable future, as many economists do. (When two selfish agents realise that the current interaction is their last, the inhibition against purely selfish behaviour vanishes; at the second to last interaction, knowing that they will be stabbed in the back the next time, each will strive to get her retaliation in first, and so on back to the first interaction.) In a genuinely uncertain environment, agents cannot be sure that any interaction will be their last and selfishly motivated but superficially ethical behaviour will persist even between totally egotistical rational agents. It is important to appreciate that Axelrod was not arguing that apparently moral behaviour is simply disguised egotism, but rather that there is no essential conflict between moral behaviour and broadly defined self-interest.

Managers of established, profitable businesses are frequently tempted by short-term profit-making opportunities, especially when they have been employed on a fixed-term contract or have few expectations of job security. They can make a short-term decision knowing that others will have to manage the long-term consequences. Managers of new ventures, entrepreneurs, do not have this luxury; the short term is all hard work and investment while profits, if any, lie in the future. Only by persuading all stakeholders that the firm has long-term, and therefore ethical, objectives is it possible to secure the investment of commitment as well as money that gives the venture a chance of success.

A decision to adopt a moral code does not provide much guidance on which moral code to adopt, how to cope with complex rather than simplistic dilemmas. Business morality embraces more than refraining from stealing thy neighbour's ox or lusting after thy neighbour's handmaiden. We look to philosophers, in our case Jane Jacobs, for help.

Are commercial morals different?

Some people believe that morals are prescribed by divine authority while others believe that they have evolved with the development of human society. There is little difference in practice: an evolved morality would include rules that promoted a prosperous and harmonious society (because those societies that adopted less suitable rules would have declined and vanished), while a benevolent deity would have dictated rules that produced a prosperous and harmonious society.

Jacobs (1993) observed that humans don't observe a single, universal morality, but that there are two quite distinct sets of moral precepts in common use in developed societies. She refers to them as the 'guardian' and the 'commercial' syndromes.[7]

Guarding the territory

Humans must eat to live but we also need shelter, access to water and materials from which to make essential tools. People in modern developed nations expect a lot more than these basics, of course, except after a disaster, when such basic life-preserving facilities will usually be acceptable enough. The simplest human societies live much closer to the basic subsistence level than most readers of this book. Like practically all animal species, the most basic human societies support themselves within a well-defined territory, hunting here and gathering there. People who rely on a territory face two major hazards: they may be invaded and lose access to the most productive areas; and they may overexploit their territory, killing all the game or burning all the timber.

The rules that emerged from hunter-gatherer societies are familiar to modern humans and many people would claim that they are the only true morality. Since the survival of the tribe depends on the preservation of the tribe's territory, guarding the territory is the first duty of every able-bodied member. Jacobs suggests that our earliest sets of moral rules applied to the specifically male guardians of the tribal territory. Many human females are faintly amused by the antics of men in uniform, and while they may not like the consequences of conquest much, women adapt to it much more rapidly and successfully than men. Accounts of the end of the Second World War in Europe concur in relating how German women took the lead in first protecting their families, including their husbands and adult sons, from the occupying forces and then in securing food and accommodation for them. General Eisenhower's stern anti-fraternisation orders had to be abandoned in a matter of days; the charm offensive launched by German womanhood at the GIs was more than a match for the general. Jacobs' 'guardian' rules come with more than a hint of testosterone. Her guardian rules are:

- *Shun trading* and be suspicious of strangers: trade requires you to give something away which might be more valuable than that which you receive in return. Trading encourages judgement of the relative value of the various options on offer, an approach that may not be consistent with defending an outpost to the death.
- *Exert prowess* both by being a skilled hunter and a brave warrior; be skilled and active, and be seen to be skilled and active, in feeding the tribe and defending and extending its borders.
- *Be obedient and disciplined* because success in the hunt and in battle depends on obedience and self-control.
- *Adhere to tradition* because our forefathers knew more than we do and their rules must be observed if we are not to put our territory at risk.
- *Respect hierarchy* both in deferring to your superiors and enforcing the obedience of your subordinates.

- *Be loyal* and obey orders without question.
- *Take vengeance* and punish any infraction of the rules with exemplary severity.
- *Deceive for the sake of the task:* trick strangers and trap prey before they do the same to you.
- *Make rich use of leisure* because hunting and warfare are only sporadic activities and idleness leads to trouble.
- *Be ostentatious* to impress and terrify your enemies and assert your own status in the tribe.
- *Dispense largesse,* not only charity to the deserving, but rich gifts to guests and dependents: wealth is for display, not for hoarding.
- *Be exclusive* and only be intimate with equal status individuals from the same tribe, because any other behaviour will subvert the hierarchy upon which the security of the tribe depends.
- *Show fortitude* and bear discomfort and pain without complaining.
- *Be fatalistic* because thinking too much about outcomes is subversive in military and hunting discipline.
- *Treasure honour,* defined as rigid adherence to the standards of guardian behaviour, irrespective of the consequences.

Jacobs gives plenty of examples of well-documented historical societies where these guardian standards formed the basis of the moral code. Rules such as these formed the lifeblood of the English aristocracy well into the twentieth century. Lord Palmerston, British foreign secretary between 1830 and 1851 and prime minister from 1855 to 1865, dispensed largesse and practised ostentation so effectively that he was frequently short of cash, an embarrassment he resolved by not paying the tradespeople who supplied his various mansions. When his butcher, desperate for payment, forced his way into Palmerston's presence, the noble lord put on a pair of gloves, wrote out a cheque and, while the butcher was still trying to make a graceful exit, flung the pen and the gloves out of the window (Ridley 1972).

Different guardian qualities were illustrated by the exchange between the Duke of Wellington and Lord Uxbridge at the Battle of Waterloo, immediately after a cannon ball had narrowly missed the duke and shattered Uxbridge's knee: 'By gad sir, I have lost my leg.' 'By gad sir, so you have.' Uxbridge was then carried to the operating table, where he discussed dancing while the surgeon removed his leg (in the days before anaesthetics) and the duke continued directing the battle from roughly the same place with the cannon balls still whizzing past and removing various members of his staff from time to time.

Jacobs traces the guardian syndrome back to Plato (*c.* 427–347 BC). Plato was strongly influenced by the practice of the Spartans. All the citizens of Sparta were brought up to be soldiers or soldiers' mothers, while the Spartans maintained an underclass of Helots to do all the productive work. The guardian moral syndrome can be found at work in ancient Rome: the destruction of the Roman Republic by the strife between Caesar, Pompey and Crassus was the result of an insane rivalry to be supreme in public honour, totally separated from any considerations of personal or family advantage, and ending in the violent deaths of all three men and, in due course, the utter destruction of their families. It is not simply a western phenomenon: it was fully developed in India before the British conquest in 1763 and the British ruling caste in India adopted guardian behaviour to the point of parody. The same set of values can be found in feudal Japan (before the Meiji restoration of 1868), with echoes persisting today.

In Britain one consequence, at least partly intentional, of Mrs Thatcher's government in the 1980s was a permanent reduction in the level of deference attached to titles and honours, but a substantial degree of deference remains. The USA is not a deferential society in the English sense, but the cultural background encourages successful people to be at least somewhat contemptuous of those of lesser attainments – the 'losers'. Excessive deference stops ideas being passed up a hierarchy, while an excessive pride in personal achievement may stop those higher in the hierarchy from listening. The many entrepreneurial successes in both countries show that these issues are far from insuperable, but from time to time they do appear to inhibit innovation in the larger corporations in those countries. Many US writers, in particular, deny that significant entrepreneurship is possible in a corporate environment, a position often held with far greater vehemence than any available facts substantiate. Medium-sized and large organisations have proved profoundly innovative in Japan and Germany, nations where cultural mechanisms have evolved to bypass hierarchical barriers to the flow of innovative ideas in either direction.

Trading up

The starting point of Jacobs' analysis of the two moral syndromes is an example of trust in the financial system: anyone can walk into a bank, practically anywhere in the world, hand money to a perfect stranger and expect with near-total confidence that the sum, less the agreed (and generally modest) charges, will be accurately and promptly remitted to an account in a completely different bank in a completely different part of the world. Jacobs calls this an example of the 'commercial syndrome' at work. In the most primitive of societies trade enables mutual benefits to be realised. If one tribe's territory is rich in game, while another's is rich in edible plants, each tribe will be malnourished – unless they can agree to swap surplus meat for surplus vegetables. Even this simple transaction cannot proceed without breaking three or four of the guardian moral precepts.

Jacobs suggests that trade was originally 'women's business': since women were not expected to be hunters or warriors, they were not required to adhere so rigidly to the guardian code. In modern west Africa the 'market mammas' dominate commerce while their menfolk perform various antics that serve to disguise their unemployment when they are not demonstrating their prowess by joining coups against their government or provoking riots with the men of other tribes. The Global Entrepreneurship Monitor (GEM) study showed that, in Australia and several other developed countries, women were disproportionately represented among entrepreneurs; a study of 'business angels' (Hindle and Wenban 1999) revealed that women with a choice between becoming informal partners of an entrepreneur and becoming entrepreneurs themselves almost invariably chose the latter option. Jacobs lists a set of moral principles that she refers to as the 'commercial syndrome'; these are described below:

■ *Shun force*, commerce is impossible under threat, and when people meet to bargain they implicitly agree to come to a voluntary agreement or none at all. As a corollary of shunning force, merchants attempt to *come to voluntary agreements*, since otherwise their attendance at a market becomes a waste of time and trouble.

- *Be honest;* effective merchants are always looking past the current transaction to the future, and deceit in one transaction will create distrust in the negotiations for further ones.
- *Collaborate easily with strangers and aliens* because these are the people with whom the most mutually advantageous bargains may be struck. Jacobs points out that the ancient Roman laws governing markets were known as the 'law of foreigners'.
- *Compete* to expand your business; do not use force or deceit to damage your competitors even when the opportunity arises.
- *Respect contracts* even when circumstances change and it might be advantageous to break one: the boot may one day be on the other foot.
- *Use initiative and enterprise;* whatever the traditional way of doing something, or a traditional place or manner of trading, may have been, it is worth looking for a better one.
- *Be open to inventiveness and novelty* wherever or whoever it comes from.
- *Be efficient* and sparing of effort and resources.
- *Promote comfort and convenience* at the expense of ostentation and self-indulgence.
- *Dissent for the sake of the task;* don't blindly obey orders.
- *Invest for productive purposes;* the purpose of wealth is to create more wealth, not fritter it away.
- *Be industrious* and don't waste time in unproductive activities.
- *Be thrifty;* when there is no good reason to spend time or resources, don't spend them.
- *Be optimistic;* difficulties can be overcome and adversity can be deflected, or at least moderated, by foresight and perseverance.

It doesn't take much thought to see some glaring contradictions between the guardian and commercial codes of behaviour. When Lord Palmerston ignored his butcher's bill he was asserting their relative places in the social hierarchy. A few hundred years earlier in England, and persisting into the nineteenth century in Russia and the southern states of the US, the butcher would have been a serf or slave obliged to prepare meat for the nobleman's table in return for permission to live on the estate. The English butcher, adhering firmly to his more modern commercial morality, defied Palmerston's social and political eminence and insisted on him fulfilling his half of their contract.

A man travelling to a far country called his own servants and delivered unto them his goods.

And unto one he gave five talents, to another two, and to another one; to every man according to his ability; and straightway took his journey.

Then he that had received the five talents went and traded with the same, and made another five talents.

And likewise he that had received two, he also gained another two.

But he that had received one went and digged in the earth, and hid his lord's money.

After a long time the lord of those servants cometh and reckoneth with them.

And so he that had received five talents came and brought another five talents, saying, Lord, thou deliverest unto me five talents: behold, I have gained beside them five talents more.

His lord said unto him, Well done, good and faithful

▶

servant: thou hast been faithful over a few things, I will make thee ruler over many things: enter thou into the joy of thy lord.

He that had received two talents came and said, Lord, thou deliverest to me two talents: behold, I have gained two other talents beside them.

His lord said unto him, Well done, good and faithful servant: thou hast been faithful over a few things, I will make thee ruler over many things: enter thou into the joy of thy lord.

Then he that had received the one talent came and said, Lord, I knew thee that thou art an hard man, reaping where thou hast not sówn, and gathering where thou hast not strawed:

And I was afraid, and went and hid thy talent in the earth: lo, thou hast thine.

His lord answered and said unto him, Wicked and slothful servant, thou knewest that I reap where I sowed not, and gather where I have not strawed:

Thou oughtest to have put my money to the exchangers, and at my coming I should have received mine own with usury.

Take, therefore the talent from him and give it unto him which hath ten talents.

...

And cast ye the unprofitable servant into outer darkness: there shall be weeping and gnashing of teeth.

Matthew 25: 14–28, 30

The medieval Catholic Church represented the guardian morality in stone and marble, while the Protestant Reformation celebrated commercial virtues. The philosopher Weber went so far as to ascribe capitalism to the 'Protestant work ethic', but modified his opinion when it was pointed out that the great trading cities such as Amsterdam, Geneva, Florence, Venice and London had been commercial long before the Protestant Reformation, and the cities of northern Italy remained commercial, and Catholic, after it. The Catholic Church itself adapted to the reality and value of commerce in a long process beginning with the Council of Trent (1545–63) and culminating in the Second Vatican Council, called by Pope John XXIII over the years 1962–65.

Ethical entrepreneurs

Here, and in the rest of this book, the word 'entrepreneur' will be reserved for the man or woman who creates an enterprise, either as a new organisation or as an initiative from within an existing organisation.[8] Some journalists have used the word to describe anyone who buys and sells, no matter how disgracefully and no matter how much damage is caused to society in general or to the people and enterprises that fall into their hands. Many corporate swindlers of the 1980s and 90s were called 'entrepreneurs' by their sycophants and their acts of plunder and ostentation were praised by many politicians and business journalists as if they had earned the wealth that they dissipated.

Ethical entrepreneurs create wealth in the form of valuable enterprises, but the value of these enterprises is based in the trust of their customers and the dedication of their staff. Commercial ethics involving the sacrifice of temporary advantage and the exercise of restraint are essential to the running of a commercial society. There have been tests of people's reaction to opportunities to exercise restraint and share in the results with others who did likewise, as opposed to taking advantage of a short-term opportunity. Roughly seven out of every ten people challenged will choose restraint and cooperation, while the remaining three will grab at an immediate opportunity and let the future take care of itself.[9] The balance between the value creators and the value takers is quite fine and has developed over many millennia.

Societies in which everyone acts like a Spartan warrior cannot develop and grow because every shoot is eaten before it ripens. Societies in which everyone is trusting and commercial can prosper hugely, as did the cities of northern Italy during the Renaissance until they clashed with a society of warriors. Societies in which a balance is struck between the value creators and the value shifters may represent the best possible compromise. London was the undisputed commercial capital of the world for 228 years, commencing with the exquisitely commercial Glorious Revolution of 1688 and only starting to decline during the insane slaughter of the First World War. London's supremacy commenced when the City and its friends invited William of Orange, the successful warrior leader of the eminently commercial Dutch, to become their king. Its end commenced when Britain's imperialist policies (then a word to be used with pride, not a form of political abuse) clashed with the imperial dreams of the German empire and provoked a fratricidal war. Modern warfare requires a 'military–industrial complex', a deadly combination of guardians in command and a commercial supply organisation. The escalating military capability delivered by modern industry makes a very bad marriage with the stubborn refusal to compromise inculcated into military commanders.

Ethics for entrepreneurs

In most contemporary societies people are permitted to follow their own commercial interests within fairly widely drawn legal guidelines. Even societies where freedom of expression is severely curtailed encourage business. As we have already shown, the pursuit of self-interest may, but does not have to, advance society's broader goals. We choose to restrict our definition of 'entrepreneurs' to people whose activities contribute to society's overall interests and exclude people whose businesses only thrive by reducing the welfare of others.

Entrepreneurship is a matter of choice; becoming an entrepreneur involves a conscious decision to create more value than you can capture personally – no matter how well you do, the world at large will be even better off. Entrepreneurial behaviour, in this light, is moral behaviour, and the rules of conduct are ethical rules that set out a preferred form of behaviour for individuals who will, from time to time, have an opportunity to gain personally by behaving otherwise. There is no proof available that following these rules will produce the best personal financial outcome for every person under all circumstances, but equally there is no convincing evidence that a life devoted to selfish exploitation is either long or happy.

Honesty

The requirement to act honestly is not an injunction to make a complete disclosure of everything to everyone. To quote Robert Townsend (1970: 136), commercial honesty means that if you are asked a question, you answer it if you can, but 'if you don't know, say so, and if you know but won't tell, say so'. The commitment to be honest means making an active effort to avoid deceit, whether by outright lie, implicit falsehood or concealed fact. The duty of honesty extends to customers, suppliers, employees and competitors.

The command to be honest sounds easy, but it can lead to painful dilemmas in real life. If a new product is going to be late, fall short of its specification or even fall short of a customer's exaggerated expectations, it is all too easy to avoid revealing the painful truth until facts pre-empt discussion. If a subordinate, or worse still, a superior, carries out a task in a substandard way, it is all too easy to mutter a few words about 'good effort' and let one lapse grow into an addiction. In either case a short, painful conversation early will pre-empt a major row later.

The command to honesty is not a call for impolite directness: the customer, or the underperforming colleague, may be a problem but they are also, potentially at least, part of the solution. If the product can never be delivered or, if delivered, will never perform as expected, the problem is as serious as it is with an irredeemably incompetent colleague. When, as is more usual, the problem is not absolute and a satisfactory compromise is possible, the customer, or the colleague, has a positive interest in finding that solution. Every commercial culture will have developed ways in which problems can be raised and conflicts resolved without permanently damaging an otherwise mutually satisfactory relationship.

You are walking in a lonely area when you find an old man dying from injuries caused by a fall. He is still conscious and gives you a scrap of paper:

'It's fifty units on the winning treble at Ascot', he says, 'please give this ticket to my old mate Bert Smith of Erehwon East', and lapses into unconsciousness.

You put the paper in your pocket and go for help, but when you return the man is dead. A little while later you remember the bit of paper, which really is a betting ticket, and check the newspaper. The ticket is worth over £45,000.

How hard do you look for Bert? Before you get very far you see a short note in *The Erehwon Messenger* to the effect that one Bert Smith, late of Erehwon East, has died in a Salvation Army home for the indigent. What do you do next?

People who trade in the global economy still retain their personal expectations of appropriate behaviour and their cultural traditions must be respected if a mutually beneficial relationship is to develop. In some societies even formal contracts are often subordinated to the informal give and take that marks effective personal relationships. In 1995 the Chinese government decided that the laws applying a 25 per cent tariff to wool imports should be enforced, and so the Chinese importers simply deducted 20 per cent from their remittances to their suppliers, even for shipments that had been bought under their explicit instructions. The contracts to purchase, in their view, incorporated an implicit caveat against changed circumstances.

Secure voluntary agreement

Few individuals go through life without ever being in a position to compel someone to do something. In commerce and enterprise management, the temptation to use these moments of power can be strong, and occasionally irresistible, but every such occasion must be recognised as an aberration.

Contrast:

'I'm the boss and you will do it my way or be sacked',

with:

'Please do it my way for now, because I know it will work, and we will talk over your idea tonight.'

Or contrast:

'Our price for this job is $25,000 – take it or leave it',

with:

'For a job this difficult, and so urgent, I would normally ask $30,000 but if we go through the spec together we may find a way of getting it down to $25,000 or so.'

By aristocratic or guardian standards any attempt to secure voluntary agreement when it could have been compelled is an act of condescension at best and a display of weakness leading to a loss of status and authority at worst. History is littered with tales of generals who led, or sent, their troops to disaster rather than take the advice of a junior officer or NCO.

Truly ethical entrepreneurs take the requirement to 'secure voluntary agreement' seriously, to the point of ensuring that the other party's consent is truly voluntary, and not based upon limited or deceptive information. Firms selling to children or marketing habit-forming drugs need to examine their sales and marketing practices carefully if they are to maintain their self-respect and the respect of society. The type of statement that would be unexceptional in a corporate boardroom might be out of place in a television commercial scheduled during a children's programme.

People suffering from syndrome confusion sometimes think that becoming the owner of a business, or even a promotion to a position of authority inside one, gives them not just an opportunity but an obligation to order their subordinates about.[10] They may get an opportunity to indulge their power fantasies, but they are unlikely to build a successful, growing enterprise. There is sometimes a place for peremptory behaviour, such as a crisis when people's lives will be at risk unless someone takes charge and gives orders. People who provoke such crises in order to justify authoritarian conduct should not be encouraged.

Trust strangers and foreigners

Modern economies run on knowledge as much as on valuable goods, and your unique knowledge is more likely to be valuable to people who do not know you than to those who do. Trade within the circle of family and friends, 'taking in each other's washing', may add some value but never very much. The broader the marketing endeavour, the more likely that high value bargains will be struck.

The command to 'trust strangers' is not a call to be recklessly indifferent to the risk of fraud and deceit. By all means ask for the customary deposit and secure enough personal and address information to enable a credit check to be run. Having been prudent, approach the stranger as someone with whom it may be possible to create a valuable commercial relationship, not as a mark to be taken down or an intruder to be resented. If a reasonable discussion reveals no grounds for either a commercial or a personal relationship, the stranger has become an acquaintance to whom politeness, but no more, is required. The stranger, after all, may have acquaintances with whom more useful bargains can be struck.

The BBC series *Fawlty Towers* reached a huge and devoted audience in many countries. It could not have been seen as funny by so many people unless they had been exposed, possibly in less extreme form, to the types of customer abuse depicted by John Cleese. Some of the laughter must have come from people who were uncomfortable with strangers themselves.

Don't attack or subvert competitors

Ethical competition is about satisfying customers, not destroying rivals. Those of your competitors who are better at satisfying customers than you set a standard that you must rise to, and those who are not as good must catch up with you or do less well. Some firms will be unable to keep up and will go out of business, others may be forced to retreat from the main market and focus their efforts on niches. If that happens, it should be the result of their bad management or unlucky decisions and not your successful scheming.

From time to time firms get the opportunity to subvert a competitor by direct attack, such as spreading rumours about their solvency or their product or by dumping look-alike products at below cost into their chief market. Other opportunities for subversion may come about with chances to control a common supplier or an important distribution channel. However it is done, effort directed to subverting a competitor represents an investment intended to be recovered from a firm's customers, through higher prices and reduced service, once the competitive threat is removed.

By and large, attempts to subvert a competitor by manipulating distribution channels or suppliers are illegal in most countries and any company that makes such attempts may face both criminal and civil penalties. Unfortunately there is no general ban on unfair competition, as when a large company launches a cheap copy of an innovator's successful product or steals an innovative service or retail concept. Intellectual property law leaves some large loopholes for copying products and services. Ethical entrepreneurs may not steal their competitors' concepts, but they should not assume that their competitors will display the same forbearance.

Refraining from subverting competitors is not an injunction to help them actively by giving them essential information without fair compensation. In Chapter 7 we provide a short overview of intellectual property law: there is nothing unethical about using the law of the land to defend an enterprise's intellectual assets against those who would rather steal than create.

Respect the intention of contracts

Only fools fail to respect properly drawn up, legally binding contracts. The full majesty of the law can be landed on the head of any such defaulters in most countries. Formal contracts have their place, but it is simply not practical to conduct most business and employment on the basis of written contracts. While the law can be invoked to enforce implicit contracts under some circumstances, recourse to law is expensive and the result both uncertain and unlikely to fully compensate the injured party. Ultimately, the performance of the type of implicit contract that dominates commercial relationships depends on the good faith of the various parties.

A related form of immoral behaviour under the sanction of the law involves reneging on implicit commitments given to junior partners or skilled employees. Partners and employees who put in work 'above and beyond the call of duty' in the early life of a new enterprise have been frozen out or fired when they requested a share of the rewards for success. Suppliers who supported a growing business with extended credit and extensive technical support find themselves discarded as soon as their advice is no longer vital and the business has less need of credit. This form of behaviour is a type of creeping systemic corruption, because it means that the trust needed to build a winning team in the early days of a new enterprise will be harder and harder to secure. The skilled worker may demand overtime, in advance, before working evenings and weekends. The junior partner may start secret negotiations with a rival, hoping to sell out before being sold out. Suppliers may demand cash in advance where previously they offered credit. In the end, there are no winners.

Respect initiative and tolerate dissent

Entrepreneurs, particularly when their enterprise is new, are painfully aware of the urgency of getting their new products to market and expanding their distribution, and the dangers of wasting time and effort on distractions. It is extremely tempting to summon up traditional 'guardian' attitudes: 'get on with your work, don't argue with me, you're employed to do a job, not talk about it.'

Executive training

Most large companies have their mythologies: this story comes from two at least.

A regional executive of a multinational firm saw a marketing opportunity and he booked advertising time, ordered stock and launched a vigorous promotion to exploit it. Alas, the opportunity was a mirage and by the time the campaign was wound up the firm had lost at least a million dollars.

The group chief executive was on the telephone within hours:

'Don't tell me, sir: I'm clearing my desk right now, my resignation is in the mail.'

'You can't leave now, not when we've just spent a million dollars teaching you to qualify opportunities!'

This temptation must be resisted, because the people who are doing the job are often the first to discover problems with it. Their statement of the problem may be imprecise and their proposals for resolving it implausible: a crushing remark or a few minutes of public mockery will suffice to shut them up, then and forever. The truly great entrepreneur realises that subordinates who practise initiative or express dissent have discovered a problem in the approach they were told to implement. The problem may only exist in their imagination, but it is then real enough: if members of the team think there is something wrong, they will not be able to stop the rest of the team, and the firm's potential customers, from catching a hint of their disquiet. Working through the problem, even if the answer was to go ahead exactly as planned, greatly increases the chances of success. More importantly, some of the concerns that will be raised will be the result of real problems and some of the initiatives that subordinates take will be in response to real opportunities.

By listening to all concerns and extending the maximum possible tolerance to initiative, the entrepreneur gains the widest and earliest information about the problems and opportunities that lie ahead.

Look for the better way

People brought up in the guardian tradition believe a practice that has remained unchanged for many years, or centuries, should be preserved on that account alone. Entrepreneurs, on the other hand, feel that the longer something has been unchanged, the more likely it is to offer an opportunity for a successful series of innovations.

St Jerome (c. 345–419) was concerned that the Bible was only available in Greek, the language of the aristocracy, and Hebrew. He set out to translate it into the common (or vulgar) tongue, in those days, Latin. His translation was adopted by the Catholic Church and is known as the Vulgate. Over ten centuries later the scholar William Tyndale (c. 1494–1536) observed that Latin was no longer widely spoken, particularly in England, so he prepared a translation into the common language of his time and place, English. The orthodox were so outraged at this breach of tradition that they had Tyndale burned at the stake for heresy. One must hope that Tyndale and Jerome had a quiet chuckle in a better place about these matters.

Value comfort and convenience

Heroes of myth and legend prepared themselves for future ordeals by extraordinary feats of self-denial and privation, completed their quest in spite of fearful dangers and terrible hardships and as soon as the celebration feast was over they set out again. English public schools maintained this tradition well into the twentieth century: a British officer, liberated after four years in a Japanese POW camp, explained: 'it was nothing really, not after being a boarder at an English prep school'.

Many established companies treat comfort and convenience as a reward for holders of exalted positions, while the lower orders are expected to rough it and like it. Such firms may have a travel policy under which the chief executive and a few of his intimates travel first class, the rest of the senior managers travel business class and the serfs ride in steerage. The more entrepreneurial companies have a common travel policy: if anyone rides in the back, everyone does.

Most people, given a choice, will avoid discomfort and choose the most convenient of various options. Expecting them to suffer pain and endure inconvenience for a marginal cost saving will simply restrict the market for a new product. Successful products in today's affluent societies are those whose benefits are delivered with comfort and convenience, and an entrepreneur who sets out to supply such products should be able to appreciate the results.

Spend time and money carefully

Successful entrepreneurs will have a lot of money around, even in the relatively early stage of marketing their new products. If they want to go on enjoying it, they will have to spend a great deal of it on the needs of the business until it reaches early maturity, and then they will have to start spending money preparing their firm's next generation of products. After the early days of their first successful enterprise, there will, however, be money that is not needed for sustaining the firm and intervals of time during which the entrepreneur's personal attendance at the business will not be needed.

This time and money can be directed to increasing the entrepreneur's, and the entrepreneur's family's, quality of life, but since the firm may make a renewed call on the entrepreneur's time or money or both, the personal expenditure must be controlled as carefully as the business investment. First-generation entrepreneurs should aspire to comfortable houses, not mansions; modern appliances, not live-in

---

An investigating accountant from an investment bank visited a new enterprise in a provincial town and, after careful inspection of their accounts and plans, agreed to a substantial loan against very doubtful security. The accountant finished this task on a Friday afternoon and, having friends in the area, spent the weekend in the country.

On his way back to the capital city, he passed the new enterprise, just in time to see the owner taking possession of a new, large, black BMW.

The loan was cancelled by midday.

servants beyond the need for childcare; charitable donations, not foundations. Marble-faced offices may be suitable for lawyers and accountants but not for the new and growing enterprise. Heroes of romantic fiction may fling their purses to a beggar or stake the family fortune on the turn of a card: the true entrepreneur gives the beggar a well-judged gift and gambles, if at all, with no more money than would be spent on an alternative entertainment.

As soon as entrepreneurs can no longer endure modest affluence, they must sell their business to a person or firm that will go on developing it and splurge the proceeds in any and every direction that takes their fancy. As long as they remain in charge of an active firm, their obligations to their staff, partners, customers and suppliers demand that their investments are ruled by prudence, not by ambition or ostentation.

Never threaten and waste no time on revenge

Threats are a waste of breath unless the threatener intends to carry them out, and punishing someone is a waste of time and effort that could better be spent gaining new customers or recruiting new associates. Revenge is a distraction from the main tasks of building a business. Every entrepreneur, every human, will feel let down by some person at some time, often with good cause. In many cases the most appropriate response is to withdraw cooperation from that person until he has demonstrated that he can be relied upon again. Sometimes the entrepreneur should practise a little self-examination: did he secure an agreement with the offender in the first place by subtle threat and implicit intimidation? If so, the breakdown in their relationship is the entrepreneur's fault as much as the other party's. On many occasions one party or the other reverting to hunter-gatherer morality will cause the breakdown: 'It was there, so I picked it up.' 'You would have cheated me if I hadn't got in first.' 'No one trusts [insert appropriate minority group here] like you.'

If a criminal offence has been committed, the police should be informed and then left to do their duty by their own lights. If the offence is merely a breach of morality or more general commercial etiquette, depriving the offender of any further benefits from mutual trade is an adequate punishment. Even then, an entrepreneur should be prepared to resume a commercial relationship with a defaulter who takes the first step to reconciliation. There is no need for the entrepreneur's firm to go without the future benefits that a renewed relationship may offer.

Be optimistic   The moral antonym of optimism is not pessimism but fatalism. Soldiers sit under an artillery barrage believing that they won't die unless the shell with their number on it is fired and that they will die when it is. Until very recently many crew members on English fishing boats in the North Sea didn't learn to swim, because 'if the sea wants you she'll take you' or even if you cheat her by swimming 'she'll take someone else' and the swimmer will have that death on his conscience (Gill 1994).

The entrepreneur, to paraphrase an ecological slogan, should be optimistic globally but pessimistic about details. The entrepreneur's global optimism asserts that the enterprise can succeed, and if this one fails, then valuable lessons will be learned in time for the next attempt. Every detail must be examined with a pessimist's eye: entrepreneurs should by all means hope for good luck, but they shouldn't rely on it more than absolutely necessary. Whenever risks can be reduced by judgement and planning, they must be. At the end of the day the entrepreneur expects to succeed, approaches problems believing that they can be overcome and, if everything falls in ruins, picks through the rubble gathering materials for the next attempt. The entrepreneur travels bravely, and arrives.

CHECKPOINT

Entrepreneurs act in, and are part of, society. They conceive of innovations and create enterprises to bring the idea into reality. An entrepreneurial enterprise may be a new firm, a new division of an existing firm, a project team inside an established firm or even an unincorporated public interest organisation. The entrepreneur must adopt, and encourage the members of his team to adopt, appropriate patterns of behaviour because these are right in themselves and will increase the chances of the team's efforts leading to a successful conclusion. The type of behaviour appropriate to an entrepreneur and an entrepreneurial enterprise is different from, but by no means inferior to, that expected from an officer of the Brigade of Guards or the regiments in that brigade.

A successful entrepreneur may gain personal wealth and the innovations introduced by the entrepreneur's enterprise may cause some hardship to the stakeholders in firms affected by the entrepreneurial enterprise's success. If the innovation has been genuine and the entrepreneur's activities ethical, this damage will be more than offset by the general social benefits of innovation, including access to superior or cheaper products and a rise in the general wage level.

Exercises

1 If you are reading this book as a text for a course of study, you will probably be expected to submit a business plan as part of your final assessment. You should now be making notes about the sort of innovation that you might be interested in pursuing, at least as your business plan topic. If the assignment is to be completed by students working in teams, you should have a reasonable idea of who you expect to be working with.

2 Do you want to become an entrepreneur in order to get rich? If so, how will you persuade anyone else to help you (as distinct from workers acting purely according to your instructions)? If not, what objective do you have in mind? Take a few minutes to write your thoughts down.

3 How do you think Lord Palmerston's contemporaries would have reacted to his treatment of the butcher? Do you see anything wrong with it? Note down your thoughts.

4 Assume that you have started your own business and every penny is needed to keep it going. You look at your cleaning contract and find that it has been

mistyped and what was clearly intended to be a monthly payment amount has been entered as an annual payment. Do you pay what is intended or what you have contracted for? Some cleaning operations are small family businesses; others are divisions of major multinational corporations. Does the size of your cleaning contractor make any difference to your actions? Explain what you would do and why.

5 Your business is well established and you have raised capital by bringing in outside shareholders. The largest of these new shareholders asks you to give his nephew a job; you know, or soon learn, that this young man is reputed to be untrustworthy, incompetent and lazy. Do you give him a job? If you learn that he is not really untrustworthy or lazy, just incompetent, does this change your mind? Explain what you would do and why.

6 Spend a little time with a business magazine or the business section of a broadsheet newspaper (in hard copy or on the web) and find a firm whose share price is rising and is attracting favourable comments from journalists and their sources. Do you consider that the success of this firm is due to the entrepreneurial acts of its managers or some other reason? Write down a few notes, giving your opinion of the reasons for the firm's current success.

7 From the same business magazines or newspapers, identify a firm whose share price is falling and whose managers are being criticised. Do you see their problems as arising from failed attempts to innovate, failing to attempt to innovate or some other reason? Write down a few notes, giving your opinion of the reasons for the firm's current problems. Try to avoid being facile: the firm will be criticised because it has too little money or is making too little money, but these are symptoms of its problems, not causes.

Notes

1   At least, we use the term 'entrepreneur' when the intention and effect of the enterprise is a socially positive one. Baumol (1990) uses the term to cover enterprise creators with less benign objectives as well. A treatment of the many ways that entrepreneurship can be, and is, theoretically perceived and explained is contained in Jennings (1994).

2   Defining entrepreneurship is no simple matter because it is a phenomenon embracing multiple perspectives and activities. In presenting their views on ethical entrepreneurship, the authors have worked in accordance with the definitions embodied in two works: Bygrave and Hofer (1991: 13–22) and Stevenson et al. (1999). Bygrave and Hofer state three definitions and a nine-point scorecard which can be used to estimate the degree to which processes are 'entrepreneurial': an *entrepreneurial event* involves the creation of a new organisation to pursue an opportunity; the *entrepreneurial process* involves all the functions, activities and actions associated with the perceiving of opportunities and the creation of organisations to pursue them; an *entrepreneur* is someone who perceives an opportunity and creates an organisation to pursue it. Stevenson et al. write of entrepreneurship as a behavioural approach to management but define it with a greater emphasis on resource control: 'From our perspective, entrepreneurship is an approach to management that we define as follows: the pursuit of opportunity without regard to resources currently controlled.'

3   Risk is a statistical concept, but is always characterised by a stationary mean (or expected) value and a well-defined standard deviation. The risk, to a casino, that any given number will come up on a roulette wheel is 1 in 37 (or 1 in 38 for a wheel with a double zero) and so a casino can promise odds of 36 to 1 and be assured of a substantial profit. Uncertainty applies when the mean is not stationary and/or the standard deviation is not well defined; under uncertainty there is no a priori way of guaranteeing a positive outcome. Standard insurance policies generally refuse to cover losses from uncertain events such as acts of God, war or civil disturbance, but that does not stop them happening.

4   The first Duke of Wellington's response to a complaint from a number of generals whom he had passed over for colonel of the 33rd Regiment of Foot in favour of a less senior but more efficient officer (see Longford 1972).

5   Sir Laurence Hartnett (1973) *Big Wheels and Little Wheels* is an informal autobiography of a fascinating man who was a successful corporate entrepreneur in General Motors during the Alfred Sloan era, working successively in England, Scandinavia and Australia. After leaving GM to start an ultimately unsuccessful enterprise to manufacture a competitor to General Motors' Holden, he went on to the successful creation of the first enterprise importing Japanese cars to Australia. During the Second World War he served in the Australian Munitions Directorate and among other things created an optical glass and optical munitions industry from scratch, which by the end of the war was supplying the US Navy's Pacific fleet with periscopes.

6   As British readers may know, Boeing did not invent the commercial jetliner: the de Havilland Comet was indubitably first. Unfortunately, the Comet, for technical reasons (its tendency to explode in mid-air), was not a commercial success. It showed that the product was practical and the market existed, but that was all.

7   Jacobs borrows the word 'syndrome' from medicine, where it describes a group of manifestations that, when seen together, indicate that a particular condition is present. It does not automatically imply the presence of a disease.

8   Thinking about entrepreneurship as 'the creation of new organisations to pursue opportunities' is the focus of much of the work of American academic, William B. Gartner. See, for instance, Gartner (1985), Gartner et al. (1992), Gartner (1993).

9   Practising and teaching microeconomists show a remarkably different psychological profile to other professionals, reversing the normal balance between cooperation and predation.

10 'The working class/Can kiss my a–e/I've got the foreman's job at last' (to be sung to the tune of 'The Red Flag' aka 'Tannenbaum').

3 Entrepreneurs and cycles

This chapter

■ While the future is unpredictable and uncertain, this does not mean that there is no point in trying to learn from history. There we can learn that certain classes of events have followed each other several times; we also learn that certain sets of circumstances are propitious for some acts and unfavourable to others. Kondratieff, Schumpeter and others have built quite elaborate theories around the idea of cycles of events and, with the benefit of hindsight, these cycles can be fitted into the historical record surprisingly well. As predictive tools they have not performed so well, a matter that modern chaos and complexity theories have done a lot to explain.

■ In this chapter we attempt a less ambitious approach: we describe some historic sequences and demonstrate that certain forms of entrepreneurial action are appropriate under some circumstances and inappropriate at other times. We will provide guidance to an entrepreneur establishing the current state of the various significant cycles in order to determine how propitious the times are for her proposed venture.

About cycles

Humans are all too aware of the cycle of birth, growth, maturity, decline and death. It is tempting to use this sequence as an archetype of much that we observe in society. Like all analogies, it is easy to get carried away. Some facts should always be kept in mind when the term 'life cycle' is applied to anything more dynamic than an insect or plant species.

First, a cycle goes around and eventually returns to the place it started from. Neither the sequence of human life nor social and technical development ever gets back to exactly the same place: 'no man can step in the same river twice'. Human and economic development is not cyclical; it is chaotic. This does not mean that near-cyclical repetition will not occur, just that every sequence of apparently similar events will eventually get broken, often after the repetition has been consistent for so long that most people have come to believe that it will continue for ever. Even biological evolution seems to show this pattern; species that appear to have stayed unchanged through tens of millions of years evolve rapidly over a period of a few hundred thousand years and then settle down again in a new form until the next burst of change.

Second, there is no single cycle or sequence that can adequately describe either history or contemporary society completely. Humans are organised into nations, tribes, clans, families, companies and other forms of association: each of these has its own pattern of development and interactions, many of them unanticipated, with all the rest. Humans are only part of the biosphere and rely on it for air, water and food while fearing the emergence of diseases and famines. The biosphere itself is affected by the state of the atmosphere and the earth's crust, both of which are affected by human activity.

Finally, humans are not perfectly 'rational' in the sense of doing the objectively reasonable thing under all circumstances. This is partly because the objectively reasonable thing to do can only be determined in hindsight in most interesting situations; but also because humans have hormones as well as brains. They are living organisms, subject to emotions that can, on occasion, quite overwhelm reason. Humans are not instinctual like insects either, doomed by their genes to repeat a certain pattern of behaviour until they die, whether it works or not. Most of the higher animals can learn from experience, a few can learn from watching others and humans can learn by hearing or reading about other people's experiences as well. The result of learning is often a change in behaviour. When the change spreads through a community and affects the way people behave, the sort of things they buy, the way things are made, sold or delivered, markets, technologies and products move through their so-called life cycles.

This chapter describes the patterns of technological and market development and change that have been observed in the past. We know that the future will be different, but we don't know just how different. Every entrepreneur sets out to reshape the future so as to include her enterprise as a successful part of it, but many entrepreneurs make the mistake of thinking that the changes they are planning are the only ones that are going to take place. For those aspects of the future that are totally unknown, the assumption that the future will be like the present is false, but may still be the best possible guess. Some aspects of the future are relatively predictable and in these cases the cautious entrepreneur will assume that the indicated changes will actually occur.

Nobody can tell what the most fashionable colours will be in four years' time, but all the children who will start school within the next four years are already born. An entrepreneur whose business is likely to be critically dependent on the use of fashionable colours should put off making any irreversible decisions for as long as possible, but an entrepreneur whose business is related to the number of children in a nation's schools can find out the most probable numbers, by year of schooling, for nearly 20 years ahead with relatively little effort and a high degree of confidence.

Some definitions

Unfortunately, it is not possible to provide perfect and exclusive definitions of products, markets and technology, much less of their life cycles. When someone buys a product, they simultaneously grow a market and help to spread the adoption of some technology. Products, markets and technology can only make sense as concepts if it is remembered that every definition is only partial. Practically every product on the market today is the output of a complex production and delivery system, with each of these production systems linked to many others. People who ignore these underlying linkages and try to deal with a single aspect of an economy, an industry or even a business in isolation are generally incapable of explaining or predicting the actual result of any action in the real, interlinked world.

Technology

Technology, broadly speaking, represents a set of techniques and capabilities that can be used to create a consumer product, or an industrial precursor to a consumer product, rather than a consumer product itself. Many consumer products involve a range of technologies in their implementation and still more in their preparation and delivery.

A household DVD player, for example, relies on advanced materials technology to produce its semiconductor laser, detector and other electronic components. The purity of the materials used and the precision with which they are turned into a DVD player today were both unimaginable 60 years ago and available only in sophisticated research laboratories as recently as 20 years ago. Another range of technologies are needed to produce its variable speed drive and some sophisticated software is required to recreate an analogue audio signal and stable picture from the digital recording. The housing involves more sophisticated materials technology; even the corrugated cardboard box the player was delivered in is the end product of some complex ways of rearranging trees.

Many different technologies are embodied in the DVD player; many more were used to produce it. Further technology was used to deliver it and some of its components may have been air-freighted: heavier-than-air flight was first demonstrated in 1903; jet engines were not put into service until 1944; and the triple-shaft 'jumbo' engine that makes long-haul air-freight economic was not introduced until 1974. Practically every good produced on earth spends some time in a diesel-powered truck: the truck, its electrical system and its pneumatic tyres are all twentieth-century technologies.

The marketing of the DVD player involved still more technology: the owner may have read about it in a newspaper (printed on a high-speed, multicolour, web-offset press, first available in the 1980s), seen it on television (1938) or talked about it on the telephone (dating back over a century). It may have been bought in a shop, but more likely a speciality supermarket (first seen in the US in the 1930s) and taken home in a mass-produced motorcar (1908). The store was stocked under the control of a sophisticated computer (first demonstrated in 1950, delivered in industrial quantities for commercial use from 1961 and not mass-produced until 1981).

Technology is ubiquitous, even when the product that is bought and consumed looks absolutely natural. If some nineteenth-century Rip van Winkle was woken today, he might be at least as surprised at the sight of ordinary Europeans eating fresh fruit and vegetables in the depths of winter as at any of the gadgets on display in the shops. Although the fruit and vegetables themselves have not changed much, the technology used to grow, order and deliver them has changed radically over the past 100 years.

Products

A product is some thing or some effect deliberately produced by one person or firm with the intention of exchanging it for some different thing or effect. Usually the term means a good or a service that its producer intends to sell for money or the equivalent. Life is quite possible without 'products' in this sense: feudal lords lived off their estates and, in theory at least, saw merchants as either the providers of decadent luxuries or parasites who added to the price of what they sold without adding value to the product itself. When the European powers first colonised tropical countries, they found people living quite well by hunting, fishing and gathering with little desire for European products and less for becoming wage-labourers.

The wiser modern managers and marketing executives start their definition of a product with the prospective buyer. The consideration to be offered in exchange is assumed to be money. Medieval merchants added nothing physical to the products they sold, but they performed many services on behalf of their customers: among other things they selected suitable products from the range on offer in distant markets, undertook the journey, often a long and hazardous one, from the source to the destination market, provided essential advice on the use of novel products and financed their stock. Today's consumers and industrial buyers need these services as well, so looking at a product as if it is nothing more than some physical object is a mistake. Every product is a package of goods and services; the goods are optional but the services are not.

From the earliest recorded time many products have consisted entirely of services: physicians, surgeons, advocates and teachers offered their services for a fee in classical Greece, five centuries before Christ. Military officers from classical times onwards would contract to a city or a tyrant to raise and command soldiers in any number from a company to an army on a fee and incentive basis. This army would then fight who, when and where their customer directed – until their commander received a better offer from someone else.

Fee-for-service warfare in Renaissance Italy

Fee-for-service warriors in the Italian Renaissance were called *condottieri*. These men often dispensed with fighting altogether: the commanding officers would meet, discuss the size, morale and disposition of their respective forces and from this decide who would win a battle. Having decided, no battle was needed: the 'defeated' army would abandon its customer and go and look for another one, while the 'victor' would conduct an auction in which its original employer and the city whose army it had just defeated could buy victory.

Trying to distinguish between 'products' and 'services' tempts people to forget that all products include a substantial service element. Buyers spend their money to resolve a problem and will select the option that they believe best matches their needs (including the need to have some money left over to spend on other things). Often the same effect may be achieved with a good or a service: a man needing a shave can visit a barber or buy a razor. The same man may make different choices at different times.

Using a customer-focused definition of product means that a significant change in the delivery or sales method represents the introduction of a new product. Biscuits sold by weight from a tin by a traditional grocer are a different product from identical biscuits sold prepackaged in a supermarket, just as they are different from speciality biscuits sold in a patisserie.

Brands

Once a consumer has decided to buy the resolution of some need or desire (as distinct from doing it themselves or going without), they are 'in the market'. In most cases their problem, unless defined extremely tightly, will have several solutions, all of which are reasonably likely to succeed. Once the choice has narrowed to a small selection, a prudent consumer will recall that purchased solutions can be disappointing or even hazardous. Packaged food may look appetising in the picture on the box, but once the contents are on a plate the box itself might taste better or be more nutritious. The holiday hotel at the beach resort that looked so delightful in a brochure may turn out to be designed and run along the lines of a prisoner-of-war camp, while a few square metres of polluted sand may be visible from a corner of the roof, if a sufficiently powerful telescope is used during a break in the rain.

A Japanese consumer seeking a culinary delight may order a dish of fugu, or blowfish. If the meal is not prepared meticulously, it may well be the last one that that particular consumer eats.[1]

Consumers and industrial buyers often want to minimise the risk of disappointment or hazard when they are about to use an unfamiliar product for the first time. One way they do so is to look for a well-known, reputable brand. The brand may be marked on the product (as the origin of the word implies) or it may be the name of the supplier. If the product worked as expected and the anticipated benefits were realised two things follow: first, the buyer may prefer that brand the next time a related need requires satisfaction; and second, the buyer may tell others about the satisfaction obtained, enhancing the reputation of the brand and making other people more likely to rely on it.

A foreigner was visiting London for the first time, and felt the need for a change from English pub food. He was passing a steak house at the time, and so he went in. In the event the steak was small, tough and overcooked, the salad limp and skimpy and the service slow and surly.	Two years later the same person was visiting London again and the same urge arose. He saw a steak house that seemed vaguely familiar, and it wasn't until a slow and surly waiter delivered a small, overcooked steak accompanied by a limp lettuce leaf that he remembered why.

As always, brands must be evaluated from the point of view of the customer, not the supplier. Sometimes a customer chooses a familiar brand because she recalls a favourable association between that brand and that product. On other occasions a customer enters a familiar and trusted store, or engages a familiar contractor, and relies on the store's or contractor's choice of product supplier. The two forms of brand association are often complementary, in that a highly reputed store may make a point of stocking highly regarded brands.

Marks & Spencer, the British clothing and fresh food chain, built an international reputation for the quality of its products; so much so that products marked with its house brand 'St Michael' were often sold at premium prices in countries where Marks & Spencer does not operate. There were no supplier brands available at all in Marks & Spencer's British stores; the only supplier identification was that of Marks & Spencer itself. Even product categories dominated by strong consumer brands, such as chocolate and alcoholic drinks, were packed and labelled to Marks & Spencer's requirements before being put on sale.

It's all over the shop

Catherine Bennett

Christmas is coming to Oxford Street. The austerity decorations are up, the tube stations are plugged solid with people and the gutters, soon to flow with festive vomit, are already serving as a pedestrians' overtaking lane. Anyone desperate enough to join the throng might be interested to know that in the midst of this retailing hell there is a haven of space and silence: the Oxford Street branch of Marks & Spencer.

In the recent past there would have been crowds jostling through the swing doors, women grappling among the hangers, much sighing and tutting in the queues. On Tuesday expanses of this vast shop were deserted, great vistas of tops and troos opened up, empty of both shoppers and shop assistants. No one was looking at the slippers. No one showed interest in the 'looks like sheepskin' coats that looked more like fuzzy felt. No one was checking out the reading glasses, nor the teddies, nor the financial services. No one was inspecting the evening clothes. Despite their display near the front doors, no one was going anywhere near the doleful rows of nighties, nor the Bart Simpson advent calendars, nor the thick-pile lavatory seat covers.

In Cafe Revive, a coffee and cake shop in the basement, recently done out with snazzy new chairs and wood-look flooring, there were 10 brooding shoppers, including me. None of us appeared to have bought any clothes. The place felt uncanny and, if the death throes of a once-thriving business can ever merit the word, it felt sad. Even sadder, I would argue, than the death of Inspector Morse, that other icon of middle-class, middle-brow Britishness. After all, around 70,000 people work for M&S.

As financial commentators have often remarked during the company's recent lurch from prosperity to prostration, the shop is unusual in being a warmly regarded institution as well as a business. If, like me, you come from Leeds, it means even more: along with Alan Bennett, Billy Bremner and Valerie Eliot, M&S is one of the few notable names that city has ever produced. Harrogate had a spa. Sheffield had knives and forks. Ilkley had a moor. We basked in the reflected glory of Marks.

It was founded in 1884 as a market stall, grew into Marks & Spencer Penny Bazaar, then into the mighty chain that – in the days when Leeds's proudest boast was 'Motorway City of the 70s' – sometimes seemed a bit too posh, what with its overpriced knits and crumpets, for its own home town.

How M&S so quickly reversed from profitability to its current pitiful state is still a matter for conjecture. City writers have talked a lot about management failure, autocracy and overexpansion. Some believe that the competition from places such as Next and BHS, compounded by the success of the discount store Matalan, just became too keen.

Last week a truculent shareholder, Annette Johnston, publicised her own diagnosis in several newspapers. Touring the shops, she had recently failed to find 'washable tweed-look trousers' for her husband, 'cord trousers with elasticated waist' for herself, brushed cotton checked blouses and a tweed jacket. In short, Johnston wanted Morse-wear. 'If you are over 40 there is just nothing in the shop', she complained. 'You might as well just jump off a cliff as far as they are concerned.'

In the scuffed and stained Oxford Street store, there was, as alleged, a distinct shortage of ladies' tweed jackets. On the other hand, so much of the store seemed dedicated to the needs of this supposedly neglected generation that it is unlikely there are still enough traditional, cardie-loving grans left to buy it. But who else would want the beige 'secret support' ski pants (with underfoot strap), the sludgy mid-length anoraks, the yoked nightie marked 'cosy', the funny little fleece hats with contrasting trim? More youthful styles exist, but these are so well concealed among the racks of camouflage for senior citizens that you might spend half an hour in the shop without finding them.

As you trudge the shop floor, much of the mystery surrounding Marks's misfortune evaporates. It isn't selling enough clothes because so many of its clothes are now tacky, rather than dull or dowdy, without being cheap. The children's clothes have been colonised by Disney, the lingerie by Agent Provocateur. Even when a decent conventional M&S idea such as a plain jumper has emerged, it has been executed in vile knitting-shop colours: doll-flesh pink, leaf green, greeny-yellow, Tweenie blue, tomato red. A child's party dress with a handstitched bodice, costing £30, is made out of velvet so synthetic that it appears almost electrically charged.

True to its recent 'I'm normal' campaign, featuring a mighty-bottomed model scampering up a hill, most of the clothes come in a comprehensive range of sizes, often with the size 22s, waistbands stretched taut on their hangers, arranged defiantly to the fore. Some stands are decorated with photographs of the quince-

▶

shaped one: a beacon to the broad-beamed, although not, one suspects, an inducement. In fact the ostentatiously brave plumpness campaign seems unlikely to have beguiled the disaffected. On the contrary. More sensitive young shoppers may prefer not to be seen with a carrier bag that might as well be a placard reading I'm Outsize, Me. The rest of us already knew about their generous range of body squashers and concealers.

Last week, with the news that sales were still in decline, the company sounded contrite. 'We are still working to improve our clothing offer, particularly in womenswear and menswear.' It seems unlikely to improve its 'offer' though, unless it decides which particular kinds of women or men it is aiming at. Young or old? Extravagant or frugal? Staid or showy? Morse or The Bill? The current female target appears to be a fantastic hybrid, part-Gran, part-slapper: an impecunious, size 22 slack-and-slipper-wearing Simpsons fan in her 60s who exists on a diet of prepared Caesar salad and jam roly poly and is currently saving up for a baby blue pashmina and a pair of Salon Rose Embroidered Mesh High Leg Briefs (£12, sizes eight to 22). If such beasts exist, they were not, I'm afraid, shopping in the Oxford Street branch last Tuesday.

Then again, nor was anyone else. That's because the over-50s think it's for the 14-year-olds, and the 14-year-olds think it's for the over-50s. Last month sales of clothes and footwear fell by a further 17%. Much more of this self-inflicted identity crisis and M&S will go the way of Inspector Morse. RIP.

Guardian *Thursday 16 November, 2000*

The history of Marks & Spencer in the late 1990s and early in the twenty-first century demonstrates that brand strength may not be enough if people cease to want what the brand stands for (see box). Not long after this article was written, new top managers were appointed to Marks & Spencer, and the company's market share was stabilised and its financial status rectified after some shop closures and a new approach to sourcing that de-emphasised 'British made'.

The British grocery chain Sainsbury's also has a premium reputation and is a strong user of house brands, although not to the same extent as Marks & Spencer. Over 60 per cent of the product lines carried in a typical Sainsbury's supermarket will be house-branded. The major Australian grocery chains tend to follow American rather than British practice, and about 30 per cent of their lines will be house brands, usually matching each house-branded line with one or two supplier-branded ones. American studies suggest that a choice between three product lines is sufficient to maintain a store's reputation among consumers, while stores that carry house brands only, or only one outside brand, may, in the US, acquire a downmarket image and must charge below-average prices to maintain their volumes.

There have been a number of American retail chains that developed an international reputation in the period since the end of the nineteenth century but at the present time none of them appears to have created and maintained the brand strength of Sainsbury's or Marks & Spencer. One factor in this may be the Robinson–Patman Act, an American law, now seldom invoked, that was intended to prevent supermarket chains making full use of their buying power. Wal-Mart has grown to an unprecedented level of dominance in US retailing since Sam Walton opened the first Wal-Mart store in 1962, but by an aggressive low price strategy based initially on shrewd store location decisions and now supported by a close focus on operating efficiency and the effective use of the group's buying power.

Markets

The most obvious sign that a market has emerged is when people start paying an independent supplier to satisfy a need that had previously been neglected or satisfied within the firm or the household. Equally, a market can contract when people draw an activity back into the household or firm, having previously bought services, or when some new market develops that eliminates the original need altogether.

Until the 1950s in most developed countries, most households used a wash boiler and mangle for their household laundry. The work was heavy, unpleasant and moderately hazardous, and so many families, even those of very limited means, were prepared to pay for a washerwoman to visit and either do the washing or take the dirty laundry and return it washed and dried. With the widespread availability of washing machines and the introduction of widow's pensions, the cost of engaging a washerwoman went up and the inconvenience of doing the household laundry within the household fell: the market for domestic washing services contracted drastically, while the demand for washing machines rose.

The underlying need, for clean clothing and household linen, was more or less universal in the developed world by the 1960s. It had risen steadily since the early nineteenth century, when cleanliness began to become a middle-class virtue from having been a sinful luxury indulged in by a few foppish aristocrats. (The cotton spinning innovations of the Industrial Revolution played a key role: cotton became cheap enough for artisanal and lower middle-class families to afford a change of underclothing. Clothes-washing would have seemed eccentric, at least, to people who would have had to remain naked until their laundry was finished.) Before 1800 there was no market for either washing machines or laundry services; the aristocracy and upper middle classes had servants who did their washing while everyone else stayed dirty.

It could be claimed that, since 1800, there has been one growing market in 'the means to achieve socially acceptable levels of personal and domestic hygiene', or that there have been two markets, one for contracted washing services and one for household washing machines, or even that there has been a succession of markets as each generation of washing machines replaced the previous one.

This semantic minefield simply illustrates that markets are best defined by reference to the customers who use them. On this basis the novelty of a market should be assessed in terms of the changes (if any) in the pattern of user behaviour involved. An industrial laundry whose salespeople collect and return washing involves little if any behavioural change, as far as the customer is concerned, from giving the wash to a local washerwoman; such a laundry might be said to be competing against the washerwomen in the laundry services market. By contrast, buying a washing machine and using it personally involves a significant behavioural change, so the introduction of domestic washing machines could be described as creating a new market. A newer model of washing machine incorporating a spin-dryer to replace the wringer did not require a behavioural change and could be seen as a new product entering an established market.

By starting from the buyers' habits the entrepreneur can learn some useful clues about their likely response to a new product, whether it is a novel good, a new service or even a new sales or distribution method applied to a familiar product. Habits tend to change slowly and the sales of any new product which requires its buyers to make such a change will start slowly, no matter what the apparent advantages of the invention. By contrast, a new product that carries out, or helps its user to carry out, a familiar task in a faster, cheaper or better way may face few barriers to adoption. Business travellers showed no reluctance to be flown in Boeing 747 'jumbo' aircraft when they were first introduced, since the main change from narrow-bodied jets was (in those happy days) that there were lots of empty seats in economy. The capacity of the aircraft had doubled but the number of passengers had not.

It took ten or so years from the introduction of wide-bodied international jet aircraft for the market in long-distance tourism to develop to the point that all the seats were regularly sold and the airlines could start working on ways to squeeze more in. Taking an international instead of a local holiday represented a major change in behaviour, so the habit of taking such holidays spread relatively slowly through the population of potential users.

Industry life cycles

Many industries have shown a consistent pattern of development as the technologies that they relied on matured:

- When an industry is very new individual firms tend to be vertically integrated, not only performing practically all the tasks involved in transforming raw materials to finished goods, but even making their own machinery. At one stage Henry Ford not only owned iron ore mines, he even owned a cattle ranch so as to have guaranteed supplies of leather for his cars' seats.
- The success of the earliest firms leads to the entry of many competitors, most of whom will also be vertically integrated to some extent. The growing market for the final product also involves increased demand for intermediate products, offering a chance for industry-wide scale economies. One of the earliest opportunities to be exploited often involves the formation or spinning out of specialist firms to produce the industry's machinery.
- The industry's structure undergoes a 90° rotation, as firms merge or drop out at the final product end and the survivors disaggregate, transferring much of their common production to specialist firms.
- The disaggregation process continues, with firms outsourcing services such as transport, cleaning and plant maintenance to specialists. Even apparently core activities such as design and procurement may be contracted out (Langlois and Robertson 1994).

Figure 3. 1 illustrates this process graphically.

The trend to disaggregation is one of the drivers of the developed world's move towards a 'service' economy. When breweries owned their own delivery trucks and employed their drivers, the costs of delivery were counted as part of the brewing industry. Now that the breweries have contracted out their transport to specialists, the delivery operations are counted with the service fraction of the economy.

Vertical integration is superficially attractive to an entrepreneur, as it was to Henry Ford. The more vertically integrated a firm is, the more control the firm's management has over every part of the production and distribution chain. The downside is

Industry innovator has
no choice but vertical
integration

New entrants copy innovator and
vertically integrate

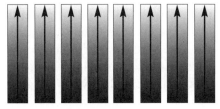

Mergers and failures reduce
horizontal competition

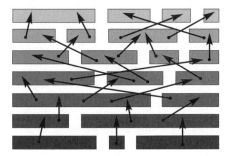

Mature industry marked by horizontal
concentration, vertical disaggregation

Figure 3.1 **Evolution of industry structure**

the commitment of time and capital to activities that have nothing to do with the entrepreneurial firm's particular advantages. There is, of course, a risk that an entrepreneur who outsources some critical component or service to a specialist firm may find that the specialist captures too much of the total value added. This risk can be exaggerated: the specialist usually needs the innovator's business too. If an entrepreneur encounters a specialist supplier whose margins are wholly out of line with its contribution, the entrepreneur might consider suspending work on the original innovation and going into direct competition with the excessively greedy supplier. Trying to compete with the established intermediate supplier and launch an innovation at the same time may be an unduly risky option.

Entrepreneurs should be very wary of being drawn into activities where they have no distinct advantages. Many parts of the production and delivery process will be needed by their business but will have nothing to do with their innovation. The more of these that they can contract out, the greater the leverage that their own particular advantages will provide. The need to concentrate on those parts of their business where unique value is created is driving many large firms to move towards 'lean production' where every activity that does not contribute to the firm's unique operating advantages is a candidate for buying in or outsourcing. This is, in turn, creating numerous new markets which provide opportunities for new and growing firms.

When a firm spins off a technologically proficient unit that has historically contributed to the firm's competitive advantages, the firm has clearly lost control of something valuable. This will be offset in two ways: first, the selling company will be paid, in cash, shares and other valuable considerations for the unit; and second, the newly independent unit will incorporate market, product and technological innovations inspired by the original owners' competitors in the products that the original owner can now buy. Firms that share a common supplier can use their supplier relationship to build a mutually beneficial communications channel through which technological and market intelligence can be exchanged.

The tendency to vertical disaggregation and horizontal aggregation is not a particularly recent one, going back at least to the medieval wool-processing industry. It is clearly shown by the history of the nineteenth-century railway industries. The very earliest railway companies did their own surveying, designed and built their own structures, laid their own permanent way and designed and built engines, as well as carrying people and goods. By the end of the nineteenth century specialist firms were carrying out most of the civil and engineering works and the railway companies generally restricted themselves to track maintenance and train operation. The 1994 restructuring of the British rail system separated the maintenance of the track and operation of the signalling systems from the running of trains, carrying disaggregation even further.

The development of the US and British cotton industries offers another example. The medieval textile industry in England was almost totally disaggregated. Different specialists scoured, carded, spun, wove and dyed the fabric. This pattern was maintained as the industry moved from cottages to factories during the Industrial Revolution of the eighteenth and nineteenth centuries and as the cotton-processing industries around Manchester grew to rival the wool-processing industries in Yorkshire. The US textile industry was established in New England in the early nineteenth century in direct opposition to the British industry and in the teeth of considerable hostility from it.[2] Early American textile factories were almost totally vertically integrated, with mill owners making their own machinery and processing raw cotton into fabric. By the beginning of the twentieth century the US industry had disaggregated almost as completely as the English one.

There is a long and consistent pattern of industries moving from vertically integrated monopolies to vertically disaggregated differentiated oligopolies[3] selling unique but mutually substitutable products. This strongly suggests that the move adds to the aggregate value of the industries concerned and so is likely to continue into the future.

Market life cycles

The adoption process

Every technology, market, product and brand has a starting point in historic time: once no one used it and at some later time it was used by at least one person. Every successful technology, market, product and brand was, at some time, used by many people and there must have been a time when some intermediate number used it. The thought precedes the deed and the idea of using a new product must have preceded the decision to use it in most buyers' minds.

At the individual level there is a need to learn at least some elementary facts about a novel technology, market, product or brand before making a decision to become a user. Prospective users of the Sony Walkman needed to learn that it was light, portable and could entertain them as they moved around. They did not have to learn the principles of transistor operation or understand how Sony had designed and built the tape drive system. Buyers could learn the facts they needed by trying the product in a shop, talking with their friends or reading a Sony advertisement.

The hard decisions

Until around 1970 the dominant steel-making technology was the Siemens-Marten 'open hearth' furnace, a huge brick frying pan in which a charge of pig iron and scrap steel was slowly cooked until it reached the right composition.

The basic oxygen converter was developed in Austria in the 1950s, and began to be adopted by the world's steel industry from 1960. The basic oxygen converter was smaller, faster and less labour-intensive than the open hearth. The major US steel companies delayed adopting the new technology because of the profit impact of writing off their open hearth furnaces.

Japanese, Korean and Brazilian steel makers were not so dilatory, and in just ten years the US steel industry plunged from market dominance to a minor player in the global steel market.

Sometimes the knowledge needed is much greater. Steel, in every sense, provides the foundation for modern industrialised societies. It is produced in huge quantities in huge plants; even a 'mini-mill' dwarfs most factories. A decision to change technology represents a massive investment commitment and may involve a huge write-down of the value of previous investments, forcing the steel-making company to declare a reduced profit or even a loss. Decisions with these implications are not going to be undertaken in a hurry.

Middle-class families face at least three sets of decisions that are proportionately, if not absolutely, comparable to a choice between major industrial technologies. They buy houses to live in, they buy motorcars and many of them arrange private education for their children. All these decisions involve a major upfront investment, the full results of which may not be known for many years. Often a decision in these areas will be preceded by months or even years of anxious discussion and eager information-gathering.

Entrepreneurs promoting a new technology, or trying to create a new market by proposing the outsourcing of some internal process, are often frustrated and upset by the apparent stupidity of the people they are trying to sell the idea to: something that seems blindingly obvious to them is met with suspicion and even hostility from the people it is intended to benefit. Many decisions are irreversible, or only reversed at great cost, and even a small chance of disaster will make most people hesitate as long as the alternative is not equally unpleasant. Rather than fret about the stupidity of those who do not rush to embrace their new concept, entrepreneurs should imagine themselves choosing a school for their only child: if the match between child and school proves to be a bad one, they cannot wipe the slate clean, reset the child's age and start her at an alternative establishment. Of course, for some people their child's schooling presents no problems at all: 'I went to St Y's, and that is where my son is going.' Quite.

The diffusion of innovation

Most entrepreneurs will not realise their ambitions by securing one customer, they need lots of them. When the focus 'zooms out' from the individual to the group, the correct approach is to use statistics rather than case studies or the sales manual. Fortunately the progressive adoption of a new concept by a population is relatively easy to handle statistically.

There are two processes at work behind the progressive adoption of an idea:

1. There may be a deliberate attempt, or series of attempts, made to convince people that the new idea is valid and should be adopted. If the idea is a religious one, the process is described as 'proselytising' and the people who carry it out are called missionaries; if it is political, it will be called 'education' by its proponents and 'sedition' by its enemies; if it is a new scientific concept, it will be announced by a letter to *Nature* followed up by a series of learned articles; while if it is concerned with the sales of a new product it should be called 'promotion'.

2. Prospective users will progressively learn by observation, direct or reported, of the successful experiences of others who have adopted the new concept. This may lead them to accept the validity of the idea themselves. This form of adoption can be split into two subgroups:

(a) decisions which are regarded as complex and important to the person making them may be preceded by a process of conscious or partly conscious research, seeking the opinions of others and taking opportunities to observe the actions and learn about the experiences of prior adopters

(b) the adoption by a trusted surrogate may be sufficient when the level of trust placed in the surrogate outweighs the risks inherent in a decision – a Ford buyer trading up to the latest model without visiting any other manufacturer's dealers, or someone buying a new frozen desert from a Sainsbury's or Tesco store, is acting in this way.

Method 2(b) usually follows a successful application of method 1 or method 2(a): the first visit to a Tesco store, or purchase of a Ford car, may have been a response to a promotion by the supplier or the result of a search by the user – the trust needed to make the supplier a surrogate will have been built up over repeated visits to stores in the Tesco chain or the continued satisfactory use of the previously owned Ford car.

The known statistics about method 2(a) show a remarkable consistency between products and across cultures.[4] For every two people who have adopted an idea and found it satisfactory, one more is likely to adopt the idea as a result of their influence in any given year. There are two provisos: one is that only a limited number of people will adopt two mutually exclusive ideas; and the other is that, as the adoption of an idea spreads, much of the influence of prior adopters will have the effect of reinforcing each others' beliefs rather than persuading members of the uncommitted group to adopt the idea. While a new idea begins to spread with a growth rate of up to 50 per cent per year, this tails off sooner or later.

The interaction between adopters and the previously uncommitted members of a population generates the characteristic 'logistic' curve shown in Figure 3.2.[5] The exact shape of the curve depends critically on the number of adopters in the population at the time of the first introduction of the new idea, and on the fraction of the adopters who are sufficiently satisfied to influence others. Growth patterns similar to that generated by this curve have been found in the history of early Christianity, the

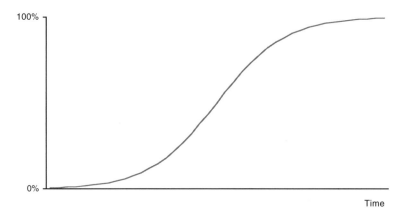

Figure 3.2   **Simple logistic curve**

sales of powered lawn mowers in California, the number of citations of learned articles; in fact, practically everywhere the spread of new ideas has been measured.[6]

A simple diffusion model fails to explain how the first few adopters enter the population. It cannot, without assuming unrealistically high levels of satisfaction and/or influence, explain the actual pattern of diffusion observed in many markets or the relatively short time such markets take to develop. These deficiencies are made up, for commercial markets at least, by assuming that a certain amount of adoption is induced by deliberate promotion: type 1 processes from the list above.

While the rate of idea diffusion resulting from interpersonal interaction is known fairly accurately, attempts to find some single number, or even range of numbers, to describe the effect of deliberate promotion have failed to determine it to within six orders of magnitude. This suggests that human response to the unsolicited offer of a new product is not a constant; at the very least, the degree of response seems to vary with the degree of effort put into promoting it. This idea will be developed in the section on market life cycles below.

Technological cycles

The idea of 'technological cycles' comes from economics and in particular the work of Schumpeter, Kondratieff and others, who identified what they believed were 'long cycles' in economic development.[7] Such cycles started with the introduction of a new technology, resulting in a spurt in economic growth. Growth then continued for many years as the new technology was applied in more and more areas, but it finally petered out as the technology approached its physical and commercial limits. Technology cycles may be more relevant to students of the macroeconomy than to entrepreneurs, but understanding the nature of technological development may assist many entrepreneurs to recognise that there are more and less propitious times to launch a new technology.[8]

The development of military technology has been thoroughly documented[9] and the process can provide many analogies to the application of technology to commercial purposes. Some highlights of the development of military technology in Europe include:

- the Spartan hoplite, a heavy-armed infantryman trained to fight in line, could defeat peasant levies even when outnumbered five or more to one
- the Macedonian phalanx, a battle formation of hoplites advancing behind a wall of overlapping shields, could defeat sword-carrying, heavy-armed infantry
- the Roman legion,[10] a combination of heavy-armed and light-armed infantry trained to manoeuvre and fight in ranks and columns and supported by light cavalry, could defeat a phalanx
- the invention of the stirrup and girth enabled the Gothic tribes to create armies of heavy cavalry whose long spears and even better manoeuvrability could defeat a legion
- the invention of armour-piercing projectile weapons, the longbow and the arquebus, enabled infantry supported by pikemen to defeat heavy cavalry
- and so on to today's cruise missiles and stealth aircraft.

One of history's most profound lessons is that major military innovations seldom if ever came from the nations that had raised themselves to dominance by an earlier military innovation. The Romans introduced the legion four centuries before Christ, and for the next 700 years progressively refined the weapons, the command structure and the training of the legions as they expanded their empire. Only after the Goths captured Rome did the Roman army take the development of heavy cavalry seriously. The Goths' heavy cavalry enabled them to hold Rome and found the Holy Roman Empire. Our word 'knight' comes from the Gothic word for an armoured cavalryman. Knights ruled the battlefield – and the countryside – for 1000 years until the Welsh longbowmen at Agincourt demonstrated that the horse-powered heavy cavalry era was over.

There are good examples of something similar happening with national technical capabilities. Britain led the Industrial Revolution, and the two technologies that the British became pre-eminent in were the application of steam power and the smelting, casting and machining of iron. British steam engines powered most of the railways of the world until the world's railways switched to diesel in the 1960s. British researchers and innovators worked in other fields as well. Faraday laid the groundwork for the practical application of electricity and Perkin founded the world's first synthetic chemical manufacturer; but Germany, rather than Britain, became the home of the world's leading electrical (Siemens) and chemical (I G Farben) firms. British managers and investors were too comfortable with the technology they knew to put sufficient effort into alternatives. Even the apparent British dominance of railway technology was lost to the Japanese and French as high-speed trains were developed: the British became locked into the view that the speed limit for steam-hauled trains was a limitation of the system rather than the engine.

This lesson is often repeated in the history of individual firms, at least in English-speaking countries: product-based companies that have been built on one innovation are seldom successful in the successor markets. IBM did not invent the computer, but it did take it from being a laboratory toy to an essential tool of commerce. IBM's archetypical product was the mainframe, a powerful computer that needed a special environment and a team of specialist operators, analysts and programmers to make it useful. The mainframe was a sort of central power station, where all the computing work of a major organisation would be carried out. At one stage IBM held 80 per cent of the mainframe computer market and only respect for the US anti-trust laws stopped it taking over the rest. IBM's success over the years 1955–85 is unparalleled: for 30 consecutive years IBM increased its sales and its profits by more than 15 per cent per year, every year. This very success led to the near failure of IBM in the years after 1985, as neither the staff nor the management could see that PCs and PC networks presented a threat to IBM's mainframe business or its business model. IBM had been so accustomed to success that it could no longer recognise threats. Only a radical reorganisation under a new chief executive appointed from outside the company enabled IBM to recover.

The minicomputer, less powerful but much more environmentally tolerant than the mainframe and cheap enough to be used for one task rather than having to be managed as a central utility, was innovated by Digital Equipment Corporation.

Digital in turn saw its market shrink as its customers abandoned the minicomputer for the interactive workstation, innovated by Sun Microsystems and Digital Equipment itself was eventually taken over by the PC firm Compaq. Compaq failed to thrive after the merger and was taken over by Hewlett-Packard, while Sun found its business model becoming increasingly irrelevant by 2003; its revenue fell and it recorded a trading loss for the first time in many years. IBM launched the PC, taking it away from hobbyists and putting it onto the corporate desk, but failed to secure control over either the hardware architecture, embodied in the microprocessor, or the software environment. The dominant innovators in the history of the PC market to the time of writing are Intel and Microsoft; the rest of the players, IBM included, are essentially their distributors.

An example of overcoming technical limits: the development of the computer

The computer industry did not spring from nothing. Calculating machines go back to the eighteenth century, and Babbage designed and started building his 'analytical engine' in the first half of the nineteenth century. Tabulating machinery was in widespread use for commercial calculating applications before the Second World War. 'Colossus', the British code-breaking machine built and commissioned at Bletchley Park during the Second World War, incorporated most of the essential features of a modern computer.

The computer could not become the basis of an industry while two major technological barriers remained. Computers need components to implement logic and they need to be able to store and modify data. As Babbage discovered, mechanical logic could be used to build an adding machine, but it was not technically possible to put enough of it together to make a working computer. More components meant that each component had to be smaller and therefore more fragile, but more components meant more friction and therefore more force needed to drive the machine. The lines 'more force' and 'more fragile' crossed before a working machine could be built with nineteenth-century materials and lubricants. In the 1990s the British Museum, using modern materials and metalworking machinery, constructed a working 'analytical engine' to Babbage's design.

Hollerith invented the tabulating machine and built it out of mechanical components only, but the cost, complexity and fragility was such that the machines Hollerith built stayed where he built them – in the US Bureau of Census. Hollerith's machines stored data on punched cards and modified it by punching new ones. The electromagnetic relay could be used to implement logical functions and electrical brushes could detect holes in punched cards, which seemed to solve the problem that had stopped Babbage and restricted Hollerith, and electromechanical tabulators entered the commercial market and were used for account keeping and other purposes. The first machines used at Bletchley Park, the 'bombes', got their name because of the audible ticking that came from their electromechanical components.

Electromechanical technology could be used to carry out quite complicated tasks, whether in Bletchley Park's bombes, IBM's tabulators or automatic telephone exchanges, but it was 'hard-wired logic': the components were joined with soldered wire, and if the logic had to change then the wire had to be cut and rejoined in a different way. As the British genius Alan Turing pointed out, a true computer had to be able to change its own logic and this was impractical, to say the least, with soldered connections.[11] IBM tabulating equipment cut down on the soldering problem by bringing some of the connections onto a plugboard where the functions could be controlled by inserting little wire links. The people, invariably female, who plugged up these boards were referred to as 'programmers'. While changing plugs on a board was quicker than soldering, it fell far short of the flexibility a true computer needed, and in any case most of the logic connections in a tabulator were still soldered and could not be modified on the plugboard.

Colossus, ENIAC, Mark 1, MANIAC and the other early computers used electronics to give them the flexibility they needed to implement programmable logic, but the only active electronic components available to the people building these machines were thermionic 'valves'. A thermionic valve consisted of a cathode, which had to be at red heat for the device to function, an optional number of grids and screens, which could be used to control the current flow, and

▶

an anode that had to be maintained at a high enough voltage to attract electrons from the cathode. All these components had to be enclosed in an airtight, evacuated container; the most compact thermionic valves were about the size of an acorn, while the standard size was similar to a man's thumb.

Force and friction had defeated Babbage: heat and statistics fought the early developers of computers. Each logic element or 'latch' needed active elements (one or two valves) as well as several other components, which meant two cathodes, two heaters and a power demand of four to six watts. The most basic computer needed 10,000 thermionic valves which gave out 40–60 kilowatts of heat: enough to keep several suburban homes comfortably warm in the middle of winter. Getting rid of all this heat was one problem and the effect of it on the components was another. The internal heat ensured that thermionic valves drifted off their specification or failed altogether fairly quickly. The expected life before failure of each thermionic valve was about 1000 hours, but the time before one of the 10,000 failed was a matter of a few hours only. The first computers were slow, hot and very unreliable.

Computers became generally practical once William Shockley of Bell Laboratories had invented the transistor, a solid state electronic device that did not need a heater and which had an indefinite service life. Even before the development of the integrated circuit it had become possible to build reasonably reliable – and cool-running – computers. IBM's 1401, introduced in 1961 and wholly transistorised, became the first commercially successful computer range.

One of the lessons of this and many other examples of industrial history is the sheer magnitude of the time lags: it took over 100 years from the time the concept of a computing machine was formulated to the development of a commercially successful product. Turing published a formal proof of the logical feasibility of computing machines in 1938, 23 years before computers reached commercial success. Mark I and MANIAC were both demonstrated in the laboratory by 1951, ten years before computers achieved commercial success. The key enabling technology, the transistor, was demonstrated in the laboratory 14 years before the IBM 1401 system was launched.

The growth phase of the mainframe computer market did not really start until 1966 and its growth phase did not end until 1984. If any of the key inventions had been patented, only Shockley's transistor could have earned any royalties from licensing, and then the amount would have been minuscule by comparison with the ultimate size of the computer and communications industries.

History teaches us that technical inventions and scientific discoveries are neither a necessary nor a sufficient condition for the development of a new enterprise. One of the most successful enterprises of the twentieth century was IBM, yet not only was IBM not the inventor of the computer, but from 1956 on IBM was legally obliged to license any and all of its patents at no charge to any US corporation that wished to make use of them. Entrepreneurs in control of a secret or patented invention would be silly to give their rights away, but they should not imagine that the invention on its own will bring success to their enterprise.

The ecological model

While the term 'cycle' may not, as we suggested above, be an appropriate way to describe the history of any particular technology, there is certainly a fairly well-established general pattern:

1. *inventors and researchers*, in or out of laboratories, discover physical phenomena or logical relationships that are intriguing to specialists, but which have only a limited, if any, immediate practical application
2. an *entrepreneur* links several of these ideas to create a product which addresses a sufficiently wide market at a sufficiently profitable price to become commercially successful
3. *success* in the first market leads to increased volumes, falling costs and prices, and

the use of the innovation in other applications, extending the original market and creating new ones

4. *other entrepreneurs* see that the functional elements of the new product, combined with apparently unrelated inventions (not necessarily their own), can be used to create a newer product again, further extending the original market and/or creating more of them

5. *still further entrepreneurs* see that certain components of the original or one or more of the derived products can be replaced with an enhanced version or produced by a superior process, improving the final product's performance and/or reducing its cost

6. eventually various *physical limits* will be reached and no further progress can be made with products based on the original core technology.

The elaboration of the original innovation does not trace a straight line from a primitive device to a modern one. One quite good analogy is that of the growing bush: the original innovation resembles the trunk, while each subsequent innovation represents a new branch. At each stage the branches get smaller, while there are many more of them. Finally an innovation, like a bush, reaches the limits to its growth. The outer boundary is fixed by physical limits, the zone of superiority of other products or the end of market demand, while inside the bush the spaces that remain are too small to allow leaves to develop. Renewed growth may be triggered by cross-fertilisation with a new technology; or growth may turn into decline when the technology may cease to develop, and products relying on newer technologies invade its market space.

Until the fifth step in the list above is reached the new technology is unquestionably driving economic growth. As each new market segment is opened up, or as superior products displace older ones, both consumers and producers gain. At the fifth step some of the innovative drive turns on the technology itself, cutting its cost rather than widening its application. These internal improvements will lead to lower prices and, in the early stages, actual market growth as the rise in the number of users overcomes the lower average prices they are paying. Eventually the point is reached where further price cuts do not widen the market sufficiently for revenue to grow and the technology ceases to contribute to economic growth; rather, it starts to subtract from it.

The first great technological thrust of the modern era came from the steam railway: the era is generally dated from the opening of either the Liverpool & Manchester Railway or the Baltimore & Ohio Railroad in 1830.[12] Human civilisation had previously been limited to thin strips around natural harbours and along the banks of navigable rivers; the railway turned this one-dimensional pattern into a two-dimensional one. The effective completion of the US railway system in the 1890s coincided with a great, worldwide economic crisis. The slackening pace of railway building may not have caused the crisis but it removed an underlying force for growth.

The second great technological thrust came with the development of the mass-market motorcar, generally dated from the introduction of the Model T Ford in 1908. The motorcar industry had not developed sufficiently to hold off the Great Depression of 1930–33, but it did underpin the long boom following the Second World War. In the 1970s the US car market slowed down markedly, as did the economy of many western nations.

By the end of the twentieth century no single technology or industry had appeared to take over economic leadership from the motorcar. The computing and communications industries, although huge, did not seem to have the scope for further growth that would award either of them the title of 'most significant industry'. The term 'information superhighway' was introduced in 1993 to promote the development of computer networks offering near-universal access. Its proponents clearly hoped that the information superhighway would boost the development of information service industries as successfully as the US interstate highway programme of the 1950s and 60s had boosted the development of the motor industry, and provide a new engine of long-term economic growth. After the 'tech wreck' in early 2001, the bankruptcy of many Internet companies and the clear signs of saturation in the PC market, such hopes looked unrealistic at best.

It is possible that no single industry will replace the motorcar as the primary engine of economic growth, that nothing will dominate the economies of the twenty-first century the way the railway dominated the nineteenth and the motorcar the twentieth. There are certainly people who will argue that the industrial era ended with the twentieth century. Whether this means that economic growth is also ending, or that future growth will be driven by forces that are different in impact and organisation, as well as technology, from those of the past, is for the future to discover.

Markets and users

Markets

A market comes into existence when an identifiable group of people begin to satisfy a need by purchase when they had previously left that need unsatisfied or dealt with it within the household or the firm. Using the definitions set out above, a market may also emerge when a new way of satisfying a previously purchased need becomes available: 'new' in this case means that the users will be required to do new things to acquire and use the new product, and says nothing about the technology it embodies.

Clearly there must be someone who is prepared to supply the new good or service, or deliver an established good or service in a new way before a new market can appear. A new product is first offered by an entrepreneur or an innovative firm, hoping to create or expand a business by satisfying the future demand for the new product. Once the market is established, demand is self-sustaining as satisfied current users make repeat purchases and influence other potential users to try the product. At the point where the entrepreneur or the innovative firm is first ready to supply the new product, however, it has no current users, satisfied or not: the demand is wholly potential. Before the new product can have a lot of users it must have a few of them, and it is worth considering the relationship between the entrepreneur and the first few users.

Users

A potential user of a new product is in the same position as an experimental subject: the entrepreneur, like the experimenter, promises the subject that nothing but good can come of trying out the new product. The potential user, like the experimental subject, will see that the entrepreneur, or the experimenter, is bound to get some good out of the trial, but the user benefits are by no means so certain. Experimental subjects are often paid for their time, with cash or other benefits, and indemnified against risk. Early users of new products expect no less.

Ways in which early users obtain benefits that offset the risks they are being subjected to include the following:

- Extensive personal attention from a salesperson backed up by a team of support staff during the period of installation and early use. This is common practice in the marketing of major industrial products. The early user does not merely get the benefits of risk control: suppliers of new products to key users will carry out many of the commissioning and early operating tasks that later users will have to perform for themselves.
- Extensive advertising of a new product may offer potential early users the assurance that the supplier is even more exposed to the success of the product than they are, giving an implied promise of performance.
- Celebrity endorsement of a new product may encourage new users to give it a trial, particularly when the persuasiveness of the advertising is sufficient to convey the impression that the celebrity is already a user,[13] and therefore further buyers are less subject to first-user risks.
- Samples of a new product may be given away, or sold on an extended free trial basis, relieving the early buyers of any financial exposure in the event of the product failing to perform.
- Early users may be offered inducements greatly exceeding their apparent exposure. Party plan and similar sales schemes promise early users a commission on those future sales they will arrange.

Harmless cigarettes

A world-famous operatic tenor of the 1930s allowed his photograph to be used in a cigarette advertisement over the words '[A particular brand of] cigarettes don't affect my singing voice.'

A personal friend of the tenor remonstrated that the tenor was a lifelong non-smoker.

'Right,' said the tenor, 'that's why they don't affect my voice.'

All these approaches require the supplier to offer a substantial, and expensive, inducement to the early buyers of a new product. A new customer will spend a certain amount with a supplier in the course of the first year of their relationship, while the supplier will spend money on promotion and selling. As a general rule, the promotion and selling costs needed to secure a typical new, unreferred customer for an expensive consumer durable or an industrial product will approximate the gross margin on one year's business from such a customer. For packaged consumer goods as much as five times the product cost may need to be spent to gain one new user. This is not really a matter of one-on-one accounting, with so many dollars spent on each new customer. Rather, it represents the likely return, measured in customers, to an investment spread across a large population. This is most obvious with media advertising; for many products a TV or newspaper advertisement will be seen by large numbers of people lacking the means or the desire, or both, to buy the advertised product. The great majority of the people with a need which the new product addresses and the means to pay for it will not buy as a result of seeing one advertisement either. The value generated by sales to a small fraction of the exposed population must be sufficient to compensate for the cost of advertising to all of it.

Since every customer introduced to a new product involves a large accounting loss, and often a cash loss as well, the prospects for a supplier with a new product look dim. Dim they are if the 'three Rs' of product marketing cannot be brought into service. These are recommendation, repurchase and replacement.

Recommendation

Recommendation is the dominant engine of market growth for durable goods and high value, infrequently purchased services. The recommendation can be tacit, as when early motorists aroused public interest merely by driving their cars around, but it is often volunteered or sought. It would probably be possible to construct a chain of common directors linking every listed company in any major commercial city, for example, such that a few telephone calls would be sufficient for a company director to get a personal recommendation about practically anything or anyone.

'Internalised recommendation', perhaps better described as familiarity, may be important in some markets, if early users increase their own usage faster than competition and experience drive costs and prices down. Over a somewhat longer timescale a combination of rising community affluence and falling real supply costs can also lead to significant market growth, as products that were initially luxuries bought on special occasions become routine purchases. Such factors probably underlie the global growth in sparkling wine consumption among other products whose consumption implies a minimum level of affluence.

Some ideas are spread with very little paid-for promotion. The concept of mass overseas travel was effectively diffused through Australia by returning travellers' slide nights. The comedian Barry Humphries satirised the Australian slide night hilariously, but at the same time spread the concept of overseas tourist travel even further. Home video became popular in much the same way. Any concept where early users gain an increased benefit by bringing others into the market is likely to diffuse very rapidly: building tradespeople were the first occupational group to become major users of mobile telephones in Australia. One of the major applications was coordinating trades at a site; clearly, if the plasterer wanted to know if the plumber had finished the pipework it was easier to telephone than visit, but this was only possible if both were on the mobile network. There wasn't much for the early mobile telephone salespeople to do apart from collect the money, because the early users did the real selling work.

Some marketers have successfully used the Internet to simulate a network effect. The film *The Blair Witch Project* was successfully launched on little more than Internet 'buzz'; its successor flopped when the same buzz told cinema goers to go elsewhere for their entertainment. Recommendation may create a customer, but repurchase and replacement purchases by that customer generate the cash flow that sustains a business.

Repurchase or replenishment

Repurchase beyond the familiarisation period generates cash for the suppliers of frequently purchased products, cash which can either be harvested or invested in gaining new customers. Often the repurchase decision is triggered by the purchase of a durable product: the Gillette Company sells a package containing a handle and some blades at or below cost, counting on future sales of razor blades to generate profits. Some prescription drugs need to be taken for the rest of the patient's life: the profits on these future sales provide a return on the investment in persuading doctors to prescribe the drug as well as on the cost of developing and proving it. Repurchasing is the dominant source of cash flow for packaged consumer goods, making consumer goods marketing profitable if churn rates can be held down, even when recommendation rates are low and the promotional costs per customer gained are relatively high.

Consider a supermarket product that will retail for €5.00 with a wholesale price of €3.50 and a fully allocated production cost of €2.45. Users will use everything in the packet during a month and, if satisfied, will need to buy a new packet to continue enjoying the experience. The supplier may engage merchandisers to give free samples to users at a cost (supply plus fees) of €3.00; perhaps only one in four people who get a sample decide to buy the product, so the supplier has paid €12.00 to earn €1.05. This does not look good; but suppose the typical user stays with the product for two years. Our €12.00 outlay has been paid back in 13 months, and the marginal rate of return on our investment in gaining a customer and keeping her for two years has been 121 per cent per annum.

Replacement
Replacement sales offer a useful chance of future cash flow to the marketers of durable goods, since durable goods purchasers tend to return to their original supplier when they need an upgraded product. The tendency to return erodes over time, but when users are particularly satisfied with their current product their loyalty erodes quite slowly. During the 1980s Japanese motor manufacturers, especially Honda and Toyota, had a better reputation in America for reliability and holding their value than American manufacturers did. This led to a steady growth in Toyota's and Honda's market share as their customers traded in their vehicles for new ones (most of them made in 'transplants' in the USA and Canada) and owners of American-branded vehicles also traded them in for Toyotas and Hondas. During the late 1980s the Honda Accord was the best-selling car in the US, although the Ford Taurus overtook it in the early 1990s.

The exact figures are not easy to obtain, but assume that the average American new-car owner trades it in after three years, and that Toyota's customer retention rate was 90 per cent against General Motors' 70 per cent during the 1980s. General Motors spends about 1.8 per cent of its gross revenue on advertising and at least as much again on other forms of selling and promotion, so for each car sold at an average price of US$18,800 GM spends about $680 on sales and promotion. Treating the new vehicle market as basically a replacement one, if 70 per cent of buyers had intended to buy a GM vehicle anyway it cost GM $2270 to win back or replace each disgruntled user. Scaling Toyota to GM's size and profile, Toyota would have only needed to spend $227 per vehicle sold (still $2270 per disgruntled user, but now there are a lot fewer of them) to maintain its market share. When you consider that

GM's average net profit per vehicle sold was $204 in 2002 (and near zero in the late 1980s) these numbers become quite significant.

Market development

A new market often starts slowly, as one or a small number of innovative suppliers attempt to generate customer interest within the constraints of a tiny or non-existent advertising and general marketing budget. The onset of rapid growth may coincide with the entry of a major company, as when IBM entered the PC market in 1981, or when one of the early entrants gets access to an adequate source of capital, as when Sun Microsystems formed an alliance with AT&T. The additional capital allows the early products to be refined to marketable standards and a properly organised sales and marketing effort to be initiated; this will build a pool of early users whose influence and repurchasing will cause rapid growth in industry revenues.

Eventually, which usually means within seven or so years of the professional stage of marketing commencing, more than half of the potential customers will have joined the market and revenue growth will slow quite sharply, eventually stabilising as the flow of new users becomes limited to those people whose changing economic or demographic circumstances bring them into the market. Looking back to the standard diffusion curve (Figure 3.2), the onset of maturity can be seen as the point of inflection, the centre of the 'S'. Until this point sales have been accelerating, after it, they are still growing but decelerating.

Markets show birth, growth and maturity, and lovers of analogy would look for periods called decline and a time of death as well. These may be rare: since markets grow when people decide to satisfy a need by purchase, their decline and death would require that people should cease to have certain needs, cease to purchase their solution or that some alternative market should arise that completely eliminates the original one by satisfying the needs in a significantly different way.

There are many examples of markets stabilising at some level, possibly below their peak, and then declining relatively slowly, if at all. The market for men's hairdressing services declined sharply with the growth in the market for safety razors as the product – a clean-shaven appearance – was drawn back into the household. The men's hairdressing market suffered a second shock when the 'short back and sides' appearance ceased to be mandatory for all working men and schoolboys. A residual market remains.

Marketing implications

Obviously an entrepreneur will want to see her company leading the development of a new market or expanding rapidly into an established one. The diffusion process offers the key: advertising and other forms of promotion can persuade potential users to try a product, but unless the user experience is both satisfactory and superior to any alternatives of which the trial user is aware, the trial won't create a customer. Only customers generate profits by repurchasing the product and recommending it to other potential users. Good marketing can't save a bad product, it may even hasten its demise.

If a product does achieve a high rate of trial success, the entrepreneur will wish to see the diffusion process accelerated by encouraging satisfied customers to recommend the product to potential users. Industrial product companies may achieve this by forming user associations, membership of which can reinforce the users' general satisfaction with their supplier (particularly after the annual user conference, when the supplier sponsors the cocktail party) and predispose them to acting as positive referees for the supplier's products. Suppliers of clothing and footwear may enlist their users as recommenders by labelling their products prominently, as with Nike's 'swoosh' or Adidas's three stripes. Retail stores may pack purchases in bags prominently branded with the store's name and logo.

Toyota entered the Australian motorcar market in the early 1960s, a time when memories of Japanese atrocities against Australian civilians and POWs during the Second World War were still strong and raw. They had one decisive product advantage over both the locally built cars and European imports of that period: Toyotas were far more reliable than their competitors.

Advertising would have had some trouble conveying this information, both because of residual distrust of the Japanese and because Japanese products had a partly deserved reputation for being poor quality imitations of Western ones.

Toyota solved the problem by putting a decal strip across the bottom of the rear window of each new car, reading 'Talk to me about my Toyota.' Within a matter of months the reliability of Toyota cars became common knowledge among Australian car owners and drivers and Toyota's market share began to climb.

In Chapter 4 we will discuss ways to estimate the cost of persuading potential users to try a product and the economic implications of an inadequate number of successful trials or an excessive rate of customer desertion.

Product life cycles

Markets may have an open-ended life cycle, but products, taken as precisely defined packages of goods and services offered to customers, do not.[14] Products are introduced, modified and eventually withdrawn following executive decisions made by specific suppliers. Some suppliers are obstinate, some are timid and some are unlucky; this means that the exact length of time between a product's launch and withdrawal, its price trajectory and its sales volumes can be estimated but cannot be determined precisely in advance.

It is possible to suggest an idealised product life cycle, the sequence that would have been followed if every decision had been perfect. Real product histories cannot be any better than this and they may be significantly worse. In general terms products follow the following sequence:

- There is an *introduction* – or *launch* – phase, during which the product will be new to the majority of people who notice it. Some of them will give it a trial; those who give it a trial, being human, will have differing reactions, ranging from great satisfaction to utter disgust; and if too large a fraction of the early trials generate a lukewarm or worse response, there will be few repurchases and recommendations, and sales will fall sharply. The supplier may withdraw the product or the distributors refuse to carry it. Either way, the life cycle ends at this point.
- Products enter a *growth* phase when a significant fraction of the early users of a product are sufficiently satisfied by it to repurchase it and/or recommend it. Sales will begin to rise, encouraging the supplier to increase production and the distributors to give it greater prominence; the success of the product will generate more recommendations, more repurchasing and more sales, giving the supplier rapidly

rising revenue and accounting profits, although cash flow is often still negative or marginal as profits are ploughed into growth.

- The rapid growth phase, and the high earned margins, will attract other suppliers who will offer directly comparable products in competition with the innovator. A combination of optimistic growth forecasts and overconfidence among entrants, together with the inevitable slowing of growth as the market knee (the inflection point of the sales curve) is passed, means that supply will run well ahead of demand and at least some of the entrants will try to move their inventory or fill their capacity by discounting. This phase is known as a period of *competitive turbulence*.

- Many of the suppliers will withdraw once they find that the promised high margins are a mirage and their earlier market share forecasts are revealed as being hopelessly optimistic. The remaining suppliers will compete on features and service rather than price and concentrate more on keeping their own customer base happy rather than poaching other suppliers' customers. Such co-respective behaviour, to borrow a term from Schumpeter, is typical of the *mature* phase of the product life cycle. Firms that survive into the mature phase of the product life cycle generally enjoy strongly positive cash flows and relatively stable profits.

- Eventually other innovators will introduce superior products, or products which remove the need for the original product altogether, and the *decline* phase commences and the revenue earned by the original product is no longer sufficient to provide an adequate return on the capital tied up in producing it. The product will be progressively withdrawn.

One of the most common management mistakes is to delay the last step, keeping a product in the market for too long. At the point where the margins earned by a product can no longer justify the capital resources needed to support it, they are still positive, and some managers may argue that a product should be kept available as long as it is earning any money at all. Such managers need their aim redirected: businesses do not succeed simply by making a profit, but by adding the greatest possible value to a given stock of capital. Maintaining an ageing product line may appear to maximise current profits but it depresses future ones. The value of a company reflects both its current and its prospective future profits.

Intel gets cunning

The first microprocessors made by Intel for the PC market were known as the 8088 (in the original PC), the 8086 (in the PC/XT) and the 80286 (in the PC/AT and the first generation of clones). Each of these stayed in the market, more or less unchanged, for four or five years with a certain amount of overlap.

By the time the 80286 had been in the market for a year or so, the value and growth rate of the PC market attracted other chip suppliers, whose products were near-perfect substitutes for the Intel one, and prices began to fall precipitously.

When it launched the 80386, Intel followed it with a few variants with different speeds and power consumption, and regained control of the market. The 80486 launch was followed by a variant of some sort every two or three months, ensuring that Intel always had some high margin chips in the market. Intel's revenue, profits and share price all boomed. Intel maintained the pattern with the Pentium followed by the Pentium II, III and IV, each of which was released in a series of variants with successively higher clock speeds at correspondingly higher prices.

Another mistake that many managers make, particularly those in high technology industries, is to exaggerate the degree of change needed to make a product sufficiently new to restart the product life cycle at the first step. With some packaged consumer products, little more is needed than new packaging, new advertising and some new varieties, but even with quite sophisticated products, a product can be new to the market without being new from the ground up. New products must be sufficiently novel to bring about an increase in perceived value that will, in turn, justify a profitable price. Often a series of relatively minor product changes will achieve this: 'All-singing, all-dancing new' products are the necessary exception, at least outside the theatre, not the general rule.

Whose is the product?

Many marketing text books refer to the 'four Ps' (the four factors making up the 'marketing mix': *product*, *promotion*, *place* and *price*) in their discussion of the factors affecting the success of a new product. Clearly, when all other things are equal, consumers will prefer the product that is available in the most convenient place. When products are clearly differentiated, people will seek the better product even at some inconvenience. For any single product, one factor will tend to dominate the other.

Most packaged consumer products are offered in supermarkets of one sort or another and consumers make the decision to go to a particular supermarket and then select the products they need from the range available. The choice of supermarket determines the selection from which the choice of product will be made. The fraction of the consumer population inside one supermarket will tend to divide their choices of product within a category to reflect the amount of shelf space each product occupies.

Things are never quite what they seem – two distinct processes underlie the decision to display a product in a supermarket and the allocation of shelf space between those products selected:

- Supermarkets want to be attractive to customers, which means that they must stock popular brands. In addition, they know that customers who visit a supermarket to buy an advertised branded product will usually buy most of their other requirements as well on that trip, and may increase their tendency to patronise supermarkets in that chain.
- The managers of a supermarket will tend to increase the space allocated to a rapidly moving product, while that of slower moving products will be contracted. Since the rate of sales is affected by the amount of space allocated, success builds on success.

Suppliers of branded consumer goods advertise, in the first instance, to justify and maintain their place in retail outlets and, second, to ensure that the space they are allocated pays its way and is maintained and extended. Rather more than half of the sales of packaged consumer goods come from people who enter the store intending to buy from a category (like toilet soap) and only decide on a brand (like Lux or Pears) once they have seen the selection on display. Only a minority of supermarket sales are to people who decide to buy a specific product before they enter the store. If a successful consumer product advertising campaign draws people into supermarkets looking for the advertised product, the attracted customers will buy many other products as well. This generates a certain amount of tension between branded goods suppliers and the major retailers, since the retailers are clearly beneficiaries of the packaged goods suppliers' advertising; even more so when people whose interest in a category is aroused by the branded goods supplier's advertising buy the retailer's own brand product instead.

In the US there are firms which specialise in producing imitations of new branded goods, copying the package design, the colours and even the typefaces on the label, and selling these copies as own brands to supermarket chains. In some countries, but not in the US, an original package design can be protected by registration. In most countries the common law on 'passing off' has failed, on occasion, to protect branded goods suppliers from what they saw as unfair copying of their products.

The high returns generated by the successful introduction of a packaged consumer good make such innovations look attractive to new as well as established firms. By no means all this margin sticks to the supplier, however, and the smaller and newer the supplier, the more of the margin gets soaked up by the supermarket chains. The large retail chains insist on keen wholesale prices, but this does not upset branded goods suppliers as much as the retailers' demands for 'cooperative' advertising and promotion. Many branded goods suppliers find that the costs of cooperative advertising and promotion can reach 10 per cent of the wholesale price, sometimes even more. While it is described as 'cooperative', not much cooperation is sought from the suppliers: the retailers simply designate a line as a 'special' for a period, mark down its price and subtract the markdown from their remittance to the supplier; or they may mention the supplier's lines in an advertisement and, again, deduct an appropriate share of the advertisement's cost from their next remittance.

There is a clear lesson to anyone whose products are to be sold through major retailers: either such suppliers must be so fantastically efficient that they can earn decent profits while selling at wholesale prices too low for any competitors to undercut them, or they must have such strong brands and such distinctive products that the retailers' house brands cannot get a free ride on the supplier's advertising. Packaged goods suppliers are often offered quite tempting deals for supplying retailers with their products in house-branded packaging. On a narrow accounting view, these deals are bound to look attractive, taking up spare capacity with guaranteed orders and no co-promotion or other levies. When the broader picture is considered, things are not so simple and some leading packaged goods suppliers, such as Nestlé, refuse to manufacture for house brands on any terms.

Large companies, either supplying or planning to supply packaged goods to major retailers, must plan on vigorous and continuing new product programmes in order to keep their products distinctive, and must be prepared to support each new product introduction with a major advertising and promotional campaign in order to boost sales while the margins are still reasonable and before imitators and house brands are positioned to take a free ride on the original supplier's advertising.

Small companies and entrepreneurs should look very carefully at their distribution plans before relying on major retailers to sell their products. Many small businesses have found that party plan or other forms of direct marketing can be used to build their business without the commitment of capital to manufacturing and promotion that the large retailers demand. Once a product has proved itself through direct marketing channels, it will be much easier to attract investors who will fund further market development, if the original entrepreneurs' wishes run that way. Some small businesses that grew large through direct marketing, like Avon, have chosen to stick with the methods they know. Others, including many healthcare brands, started with direct selling and moved their products into supermarkets once their market success was established.

Cycles and the entrepreneur

An entrepreneur must consider the state of the technology, market and product life cycles when preparing to launch a new product. In extreme cases a careful review of these issues will lead to a proposal being abandoned, but in nearly every case they can be used to refine the product introduction plan.

Product or process?

We mentioned this distinction in Chapter 1 and will return to it in Chapter 5, but very broadly speaking a product is a good or service produced in order to be sold, and a process is used in the production of products. When dealing with business-to-business sales the seller may be providing a product while the buyer is acquiring a process, or a physical product to support one. The distinction is sharpest with commercial software: the selling firm is clearly producing a product but the purchaser gets a pure process. Services can fit this pattern: a company offering training is selling a product but the purchaser hopes that its employees, once trained, will support the firm's value-creating processes more effectively.

The distinction is important because firms only become concerned about process improvement when the first phase of rapid market growth is over. Well-run firms in a period of rapid market development don't want to 'lock in' what may prove to be an inappropriate technology and they don't want to be distracted from the critical tasks of finding new customers and delivering their products to them. Once market growth has slowed, cost and quality become more important and process innovations, whether purchased or developed internally, become more interesting.

Technology

Technology must be taken into account in at least two dimensions: the technology *in* the new product and the technology used to *make* and/or *deliver* the new product. There is a third direction, one that is not easily taken into account: the possibility of someone else introducing a new technology that will radically reshape the market for the entrepreneur's product. The Internet has opened up the possibility of applying technology to the marketing of products as well; even after the first rush to e-everything has subsided, it is still not clear whether Internet-based marketing represents a revolutionary innovation or simply an improved form of catalogue selling.

The world is full of inventors, but relatively few inventors turn into successful entrepreneurs or are adopted by one. Very few inventions reach the market and even fewer become the foundation of a successful enterprise. Many inventions that do reach the market enjoy a brief flash of market interest before dropping into the museums and history books. When the impossible and the fraudulent are weeded out, two of the common reasons why an innovation does not succeed in entering and holding a significant market are mismatch with the market cycle and wrong state of technology cycle.

The ideal point to launch a technological innovation is at the stage when the existing technologies are at or approaching their physical limits, while demand for the products enabled by these existing technologies is rising strongly. The jet engine was first developed as a power plant for fighter aircraft at a time when the demands of the Second World War were encouraging the rapid development of piston engine technology, and it wasn't until the very last months of the war that jet aircraft were put into service. With the onset of the Cold War, however, it became apparent that the speed of sound represented an absolute performance limit for propeller-driven aircraft, and the jet engine (and its close relative, the gas turbine) became the dominant technology for powering military aircraft. It took approximately 40 years from the first laboratory demonstrations of jet engines to the maturity of the technology with the triple-shaft turbofan engines as used on modern wide-bodied passenger aircraft. The companies (General Electric, Pratt & Whitney and Rolls-Royce) that were prepared to invest at a sufficient rate to grow their capabilities in line with the growth of the technology prospered, although not without some anxious moments.

The penalty for attacking at the wrong point in the technological cycle can be seen in the relative failure of a series of attempts made by Sun Microsystems from 1990 to 1995 to get their Solaris software technology out of the technical niche which it (very profitably) occupied and into the general PC market. Purists might have had some reservations about Solaris, but the comparable technology on PCs, MS-DOS, was dramatically inferior.

The MS-DOS world was not, however, standing still. User software suppliers, such as WordPerfect Corporation, Lotus Developments and others, worked tirelessly to improve the products they sold to MS-DOS customers, overcoming the limitations of the technology. Microsoft Corporation relaunched their Windows software, a step that improved the usability of MS-DOS dramatically, and finally overhauled Solaris with Windows 95, launched in 1995. Those MS-DOS users approached by Solaris salespersons did not, in general, simply compare that product with Solaris, but estimated the time and effort required to convert their work to Solaris and compared it to the state that the MS-DOS world might have reached by the time their conversion was finished. The general conclusion seemed to be that MS-DOS users would get all the benefits of Solaris, in the same time and for much less effort, if they waited for Microsoft to get around to providing them. Sun Microsystems launched at the wrong point in the technology cycle, long before the technology they were attempting to displace had reached any serious barriers to its own development.

Microsoft showed itself aware of the challenge and the intrinsic limitations of the MS-DOS technology underlying Windows 95–98, by investing in Windows NT, a new product technologically even though most of the older application interfaces were preserved. Over a period of six or seven years Microsoft stabilised and enhanced it until, rebadged as Windows XP, Microsoft could offer it as a general replacement for Windows 95–98–Me. The timing is significant: Microsoft was actively working on a replacement for Windows 95 even before it launched that product.

Sun, having failed to overtake Microsoft's lead in software, saw its core business under attack at the start of the twenty-first century. Sun had been formed to exploit a gap in the market for interactive technical applications: in 1981 the normal way for an engineer or scientist to perform technical computing involved a dumb terminal linked to a mainframe or powerful minicomputer; Sun's founders realised that it was becoming technically possible to substitute a smart terminal, or workstation, and deliver a comparable performance to a dumb terminal linked to a larger system at a comparable total cost of ownership. For the next 10–12 years the workstation market proved very profitable for Sun, but in the mid 1990s Intel introduced its Pentium range of microprocessors and ordinary PCs were able to offer performance comparable to Sun's workstations at a substantially lower price. Sun had realised during the 1980s that users did not wish to sit at isolated workstations and developed a series of fast minicomputers to provide common services to groups of workstations; Sun called these 'servers' to distinguish them from 'traditional' minicomputers. As growth in the workstation market slowed and reversed, Sun picked up the slack with servers, and as the Internet boom started Sun servers were the hosts of choice for serious websites. Intel did not stand still, however, and by 2001 its Pentium IV and Itanium microprocessors achieved performance levels that permitted the construction of servers with a performance comparable to Sun's servers but at half the price or less. Sun, this time, had nothing in the wings and in 2002 reported losses and declining revenues, and some analysts predicted that it would soon be taken over. If this happened, Sun would have survived just over 20 years, having surfed two technology waves but missed the third.

The market

A product can only succeed in the market if sufficient people want, or can be persuaded to want, to buy it. The ideal point to launch a radically new product is at the beginning of the market life cycle, when there are a large number of potential users, none of whom have developed any form of loyalty to any other supplier. There is a risk involved in basing a strategy around being first into a new market, and that is the possibility that the market does not, in fact, exist; that whatever people said to market researchers or when shown samples, the net benefits of the new product were not sufficient to justify an adequate, or any, price. Some large companies make a point of being 'fast followers' for this reason; they wait until a pioneer has shown that the new market is real before launching their own product.

Companies that do pioneer a market must expect the entry of major competitors if their product is successful, and they should assume that the entering competitors will invest generously in promotion, selling and product development in order to overcome the first mover's advantages. The English company EMI invented the first CAT scanner (computerised axial tomography: a technique using computers and new-generation sensors to build up a cross-sectional picture of the body rather than the simple shadow seen in a conventional X-ray) and launched it in 1972. Early technologies for non-invasive medical imaging had reached a series of physical limits, while demographic, economic and other technological factors had precipitated an explosive growth in demand for medical services. The demand for scanners was enormous, yet the scanner proved a financial disaster for EMI. EMI began building production capacity and ordering components to meet the huge demand their sales staff reported, but the first of their competitors had a superior machine on the market just 15 months after the first EMI scanner was delivered; EMI's order backlog evaporated and their technological triumph turned into an inventory nightmare. EMI's strategy did not allow for the entry of competitors.

The fast follower's window may be open for up to four years, depending on the type of market, the technology involved, the speed with which the first mover has updated the original product and the effort the first mover has put into promotion. If the first mover and other early entrants have produced excellent products that are strongly recommended by their users, the fast follower's window shuts long before the onset of market maturity. Maturity is generally seen to set in when 50 per cent of the potential users have become actual ones and from this point until the market reaches a post-mature stage new firm entry is very difficult. Because each satisfied current user casts a 'future shadow' of potential users who will follow that user's recommendations, effective maturity may occur as much as two years before apparent maturity.

IBM and Digital Equipment Corporation both chose to adopt a 'fast follower' strategy in the market for engineering workstations that Sun Microsystems and others pioneered in the early 1980s. By the time they were ready to enter, mid 1988, Sun Microsystems had an impregnable position, and while both IBM and Digital Equipment enjoyed modest success, neither went close to challenging Sun Microsystems' dominance. This relative failure in the workstation market led to an equally disappointing performance in the market for office server systems, where Hewlett-Packard converted an early entry into market dominance; while Hewlett-Packard was a slightly smaller company than Digital Equipment in 1985, by 1995 Hewlett-Packard was twice Digital Equipment's size; shortly afterwards, Digital Equipment was taken over by Compaq and in early 2002 Hewlett-Packard took over Compaq: the 1975 minnow had become the alpha shark in 17 years.

Sun Microsystems and Hewlett-Packard had been in the workstation and office server markets respectively, earning a strong reputation, for nearly six years when IBM and Digital Equipment tried to enter it. This reputation, far more than any technical details about their products, ensured that Hewlett-Packard and Sun Microsystems would continue to prosper in the teeth of the attempts by IBM and Digital Equipment to seduce their customers.

For some time after a market has reached maturity, entry remains difficult. The firms who entered during the early growth phase of the market will have secured a huge 'share of mind' among both the actual and potential user population, and their mutual competition will have ensured that they have left very few technological or market niches unexplored. The prize that the established firms are fighting for, the secure market share and strong cash flows enjoyed by participants in a mature market, is sufficiently attractive to make sure that interlopers will be seen off.

Many markets enter a post-mature phase, as the established suppliers find that there are few rewards left for technical innovation or marketing effort, and turn inwards, looking to cut their own costs rather than increase their sales. During this post-mature period there is often a substantial concentration of ownership followed by rationalisation of product ranges and distribution channels. Such rationalisation can lead to growing numbers of dissatisfied customers, people who are in the market but are actively dissatisfied with all the suppliers they have been able to try. This can create an opportunity for an entrant, or a rejuvenated competitor, to seize a substantial and valuable share of the market.

In 1987 Australia's retail grocery industry was dominated by three firms: Coles Supermarkets, Woolworth[15] (trading as Safeway in Victoria), and Franklins. Franklins was doing well with its 'no-frills' discount image, Coles Supermarkets was also doing well, more because of the excellent sites that the Coles Myer property arm had acquired than for any particular retailing excellence, while Woolworth was not doing well at all. A couple of years before, Woolworth had purchased Safeway's Australian operations from RJR-Nabisco in the aftermath of the 'Barbarians at the Gate' takeover.[16] Safeway's upmarket reputation had enabled it to earn better margins than Woolworth, but in a fit of misplaced corporate pride Woolworth's managers had renamed the Safeway stores in New South Wales as 'Woolworth'. The effect had been a major loss of market share in New South Wales, near-zero profits and a collapsing firm value.

Woolworth was taken over and Paul Simons recruited to the position of executive chairman. Simons observed that no Australian supermarket chain was doing a particularly good job of fresh food marketing. The margins on fresh produce are good and the customer appeal considerable, but all the Australian retailers had become used to handling packaged goods with a shelf life of weeks or months and tended to treat the produce section in much the same way. Simons relaunched Woolworth as 'the fresh food people'; he appears to have decided that the various issues were so urgent that he did not wait until the computer systems had been modified to cope with the demands of fresh food but trusted the staff to clear away any stock that was less than perfectly fresh. Neither of Woolworth's main competitors had a strong reputation for their fresh produce at the time that Woolworth relaunched itself: Franklins had problems with selling space and Coles was suffering from serious management problems which led to its stores paying premium prices for compost-grade produce.

At the time Simons was appointed at Woolworth its market share was 21 per cent and falling and its shares were worth little more than the paper that they were printed on. When Simons stood down as chief executive seven years later, Woolworth's market share had passed 29 per cent, the company had been successfully floated for A$1 billion and the new shareholders were sitting on a substantial capital gain. Woolworth's market share continued to grow, passing 36.1 per cent in 1999, while Franklins suffered from a falling market share and reduced margins, to the point that its owners wound the operation up in 2001. With Franklins gone, Woolworth's market share in the supermarket category jumped to 44.5 per cent by the end of 2002, and Woolworth became rather coy about it, preferring to refer to its share of the entire food, liquor and groceries sector, even that being a remarkable 26.5 per cent. Simons demonstrated that entrepreneurial success is still possible in a very mature market.[17]

CHECKPOINT

An entrepreneurial concept can only succeed in a window of opportunity, or more properly, when a series of windows coincide. The entrepreneur must be able to access an appropriate level of technology and the market must be capable of absorbing a sufficient quantity of product. These two factors are not entirely independent: the market's capacity to absorb a product will be affected by the price, which will in turn be affected by the state of the available technology.

There are many historical examples of ventures failing because the market was not ready for their product; there are many other examples of the market willingly accepting a new product only to reject it when the technological limitations became apparent. Even when the technology works and the market wants it, there may be social or physical barriers to its widespread adoption. Excellent technology may fail in the market if the older technology it must compete with has sufficient remaining development potential and a well-established position in the market.

Above all, *invention is not innovation*. Just because something can be made does not mean that people are prepared to pay for it.

Exercises

By now you should have formed your business planning team if the plan is a team assignment and, whether you are in a team or flying solo, you should have a few ideas for a subject for your plan. The first few questions relate to these topics and may help you to refine your choice of project.

1 Do any of your proposed innovations involve technology, other than incidentally? If so, is the technology developing so rapidly that you may lock yourself out of the mainstream or developing so slowly that a new technology may be poised to replace it? Qualify each of your proposed innovations according to the state of the technology it will use or with which it will compete.
2 Who are your potential users and why will they buy your proposed product? What are they doing now, before your product is made available to them? How sure are you that they won't go on doing it? Qualify each of your proposed innovations according to your confidence in a favourable user response.
3 Do any of your potential users satisfy their requirements in a market at present? If so, what state is the market in? Set out the implications for each of your proposed innovations.
4 Are your products intermediate goods or services, provided to other firms, or will they be consumed or used by final consumers? If they are to be offered to

other businesses, what is the state of development of your customer industry? Set out the implications for each of your proposed innovations.

There are lessons to be learned from other's experience, even if their actual field of activity is remote from anything you are currently considering. The following exercises are intended to help you in this direction.

5 Look through a few recent issues of a business magazine or the business section of a broadsheet newspaper and find a company that appears to be doing very well at the moment, with growing sales and profits. Try to establish, either from your research or your own experience, at what stage this company's products are in the relevant market, technology and industry life cycles and decide what impact these factors have had on its success.
6 Look through a few recent issues of a business magazine or the business section of a broadsheet newspaper and find a company that appears to be doing poorly at the moment, with static or falling sales and falling profits or even actual losses. Try to establish, either from your research or your own experience, at what stage this company's products are in the relevant market, technology and industry life cycles and decide to what extent these factors have caused its problems.

Notes

1 The liver of the fugu, or blowfish, is acutely toxic, such that if it is even scratched during the preparation of the dish the diner may be fatally poisoned.

2 Contemporary economists argued that the US was making a terrible mistake by establishing manufacturing industries: the 'law' of comparative advantage (invented by the English economist Ricardo) stated that manufacturing should be done in Britain while foreigners concentrated on raw material production. The British government took a strongly pro-south view during the American Civil War: the south grew cotton to supply English factories, while the north was home to a protected textile industry that competed with the British.

3 American economists tend to follow Chamberlin and refer to competition between a few large companies selling substitutable but differentiated products as 'monopolistic competition' and reserve the term 'oligopoly' for competition between a few large firms selling indistinguishable products, while British and European authors may describe this as 'oligopoly with product differentiation'.

4 For a comprehensive survey of market life cycle models and the evidence supporting their use, see Mahajan et al. (1990). For the results of a study showing the consistency of certain model parameters, see Sultan et al. (1990).

5 Most books concerned with mathematics in business applications find space for a description of the basic logistic or 'S' curve which has the general form $y' = \lambda x(1 - x)$.

6 Modis (1992) is an entertaining book devoted to the predictive power of 'S' curves.

7 See Schumpeter (1933, 1939).

8 The nature and importance of innovation and technological cycles – focused on the practical utility of 'S' curves – is described in Foster (1987).

9 See Ropp (1959); or Jones (1987); or any of the many other specialist books on this subject.

10 The phalanx and the legions clashed for the first time when the Macedonian King Pyrrhus invaded Italy in the third century BC. Pyrrhus won both his battles, but his losses were so great that he lost the war; thus the term 'Pyrrhic victory'.

11 For an excellent account of Turing and his achievements see Hodges (1983).

12 George Stevenson's Stockton and Darlington line of 1825 is generally discounted because only some of the haulage was by steam: passengers travelled in horse-drawn rail coaches. The B&O started revenue generating steam-hauled passenger traffic some months after the L&M, but the American system was developed independently and incorporated some unique inventions.

13 Under the law in most jurisdictions it is an offence to claim an endorsement that has not been actually provided. The trick with the tenor (see box) might well be caught under the laws banning misleading conduct if tried today.

14 An early positive view of the utility of the product life cycle as a useful marketing concept is found in Levitt (1965).

15 No relation to the US or British firms of that name.

16 Burroughs and Helyar (1990) wrote an entertaining account of the takeover of RJR-Nabisco by KKR.

17 The story of a A$24 billion turnover supermarket chain operating exclusively in Australia and New Zealand might seem of little general interest; but the fact that Simons achieved this turnaround with *no* downsizing and in 1992 abolished casual employment in his group, making all employees, whether full or part time, permanent staff with full employee benefits makes the story unusual in a wider context than just Australia.

4 Proving the business concept

This chapter

- The world of possibilities is unlimited, but the world of ideas is even larger. Some ideas are ready to be turned into a profitable, growing business immediately; some will have to wait until critical technological problems are overcome; but most will never be both practical and profitable. In this chapter we discuss the process of opportunity screening, a systematic way of discarding unfeasible ideas, and identifying unfeasible aspects of otherwise practical ideas, before an entrepreneur invests the time needed to produce a complete business plan and long before the entrepreneur or anyone associated with him commits money or other significant resources into an attempt on the impossible.

- As part of this screening process, you will need to make projections of revenue and marketing expenses for your venture: we describe some powerful tools for guiding such projections in this chapter. These, or similar, tools are incorporated into various revenue-forecasting packages, some free on the Internet, others available for purchase, and we have included sufficient technical detail in an appendix at the end of this chapter to enable competent programmers to develop their own forecasting tool.

- The body of this chapter includes tables and material based on advanced theory, but the theory itself is summarised in the appendix at the end of this chapter where it will prove useful to model builders and those who wish to expand on the issues raised without confusing those who are comfortable accepting the authors' mathematical bona fides without personally verifying them.

Screening for practicability

Figure 4.1 contains a stylised map of the enterprise creation process. The starting point of every new enterprise is a problem and an idea for solving it. We do not consider that either the identification of problems or the generation of ideas needs to be dealt with at length in this book, because while the availability of an idea is a precondition for entrepreneurship, it is not part of the entrepreneurship process. Many successful enterprises are based upon an association of an entrepreneur or entrepreneurial team and an 'ideas person'.

Every idea is the product of a human's imagination and some ideas are bound to stay there. Ideas must be tested for fatal flaws before they can be set out as a concept. Concepts are a combination of an idea for resolving a problem and a practical pro-

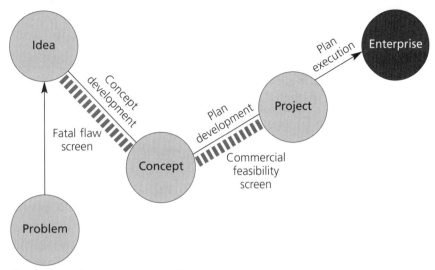

Figure 4.1 **The innovation track**

posal, in outline form at least, for delivering that solution. Many nascent concepts suffer from fatal flaws, as we discuss below.

A concept may address a real problem and be technically feasible, and yet it may be commercially unfeasible: the total cost of turning the concept into a marketed product and then supplying the product to customers may be too high in relation to the revenue the new product would generate. The development of a business plan, the major theme of this book, is fundamentally about turning a concept into a commercially feasible proposal. Developing a complete business plan takes time and effort and it is disappointing, to say the least, to get to the end of the process and discover that the concept cannot be turned into a commercial proposition.

In this chapter we describe the process of turning an idea into a concept and then applying a fairly simple set of commercial feasibility tests that will screen out commercially hopeless concepts before investing the effort required to develop a complete business plan. Effective, low-cost screening has another useful effect, in that the less effort invested in a flawed idea, the less psychological pain involved in abandoning it. While the logic is ludicrous, the argument that 'we have put so much effort into this plan already that we must carry on with it' has a great deal of practical and emotional force; it has been the trigger for some of history's greatest disasters.

Ideas

Good ideas are legion. Some people like to talk about their ideas, while others keep their own counsel, but it is hard to spend more than a few minutes awake without coming across some inconvenience or irritation. Many people, confronted by a nuisance, will grin (or not) and bear it; some will repeat the everlasting cry of the English lower middle classes: '"They" ought to do something about it.' Lots of people will wonder whether anything really could be done about it, and if they have the habit of letting their imagination work, many of them will come up with an idea.

Every innovation starts with an idea, but only a few ideas become innovations. There is no certain link between the idea and the innovator: Hero of Alexandria, in the first century AD, had the idea of steam power and made a few gadgets, like self-opening doors and moving altars, but no industry arose and Hero's ideas were largely forgotten. They were revived by Newcomen, who built steam-driven pumps for mines, the first in 1712. A few copies of Newcomen's engine were made, but demand was slight, and several of the few engines that were built were used infrequently, if at all. In 1769 the engineer James Watt secured the first of his many patents for improvements to the steam engine. In 1776 James Watt and his partner Matthew Boulton put steam engines incorporating Watt's improvements into serial production (and Jefferson wrote the United States Declaration of Independence); the power and the American revolutions started in the same year.

Watt and his partner Boulton became extremely rich, as Watt and his colleagues added a series of innovations to the basic idea, improving the flexibility, efficiency and applicability of Boulton and Watt engines. Watt did not invent steam power, but he and Boulton were the entrepreneurs who turned steam power from an idea to a commercial reality. Watt is justly credited with responsibility for the innovation 'steam power'. If a contemporary entrepreneur had considered commercialising either Hero's or Newcomen's work, they would have discovered that, given the markets, technology and business environment of the day, it would have been impossible. A proposal to commercialise steam power at any date significantly earlier than 1776 would have encountered one or more 'fatal flaws'.

Fatal flaws

Fatal flaws are facts about an opportunity that make it impossible for a new enterprise based upon it to succeed. They should not be confused with fatal stumbles, operating or management errors that destroy a product or a business but which, in the glare of 20:20 hindsight, could have been avoided. The following list of potential fatal flaws is not exhaustive and we accept no responsibility for ventures that find a new way to attempt the impossible. Nonetheless, if this list was routinely consulted before people put their time and money into a new venture, a lot of heartache and disappointment might be avoided:

- *Scientific feasibility:* Does the product depend on the suspension of any of the laws of nature, such as the special or general theories of relativity, the second law of thermodynamics or the laws of conservation of energy and momentum?
- *Economic feasibility:* Does the product involve an economic absurdity, such as a selling price lower than the minimum cost of its components, or a service provider's income insufficient to support life?
- *Technical feasibility:* Can the product be made, or if a service, delivered, using currently available, or at least feasible, technology?
- *Marketing feasibility:* Does anyone want it? Has the product any features that would persuade someone to choose it ahead of currently available products?
- *Fundamental legality:* Is it legal?

The laws of nature

The laws of nature serve humanity well; if they were only slightly different, we would not be here. This may be some compensation for the repeated disappointments nature's laws inflict on inventors and the occasional gullible investor. Elaborate urban myths have circulated in Australia and other countries about the water-powered motorcar and the supposed conspiracy of the oil companies to suppress it. The oil companies, in this matter at least, are innocent. Water represents the most stable, and therefore the lowest energy, combination of hydrogen and oxygen. It cannot be used as a source of energy, and the inventors who demonstrate water-powered motorcars to the popular press and populist politicians every few years may possibly be fools, but it is more likely that they are rogues. All real-world processes are dissipative; they require a source of energy to keep them going. Perpetual motion machines do not exist and cannot be produced, which does not stop people trying to invent them and persuading investors to back them.

The silent and irrevocable operation of the laws of nature should not be confused with the squawking of assorted pessimists and congenital knockers. The difficult and the unusual should not be confused with the impossible. There are large published collections of quotations from people who should have known better saying that something was impossible or would never happen. Investors and entrepreneurs who do not understand the second law, or the work of Newton, Einstein, Maxwell, Heisenberg and others, should consult a physicist or engineer before putting money into an amazing invention. When briefing their consultant they should make sure that the report distinguishes 'improbable' from 'impossible'. In the latter case they should get out at once; in the former, they may consider investing a little more money in a full technical report – if the inventor will let a consulting engineer anywhere near his product.

Some inventors are profoundly reluctant to allow their concept or prototypes to be examined in detail by experts. As a broad generalisation, an entrepreneur or investor who backs a product so secret that a reputable consulting engineer cannot be trusted to examine it and prepare a confidential report is putting their money at high risk.

Economic absurdity

The standard form of economic absurdity is a system for winning at gambling (not to be confused with a proposal to operate a casino or a totalisator, or with schemes involving rigged bets or unequal contests). One of the most common gambling schemes is known as the 'martingale'. Many of these schemes appear quite logical and some fairly subtle argument is needed to show why they must eventually fail. There is a famous statistical proof known as 'gambler's ruin', which demonstrates that a gambler with a finite purse playing a fair game against a strong house must, eventually, be ruined. 'Ruin is certain, but the time it takes is indefinite.'

The martingale

There are various forms of martingale, but the principle is always the same. At roulette the martingale player puts a unit bet on one colour (say black). If it wins (and the croupier returns the original stake and the same again as winnings), the gambler pockets the winnings and repeats the original bet. Otherwise the gambler doubles the stake and repeats the process. When black turns up again (as it statistically must) the gambler will make a profit of one unit. The fatal flaw in the martingale is the existence of house limits on the one hand and the finite resources of the gambler on the other. If the wheel is a fair one, it is certain that there will eventually be a losing streak so long that the gambler will no longer be able to afford a doubled bet, or the house will refuse to accept it.

The system is called a martingale after the piece of harness that can be used to stop an unruly horse turning its head; once a gambler starts on a martingale he cannot stop or turn aside until he is ruined.

Other forms of absurdity can be shown to be the logical equivalent of proposals for selling hundred-dollar bills at a discount. One of the hero-entrepreneurs in Ayn Rand's novel *Atlas Shrugged* (1985) invents a new alloy of iron and copper with all sorts of marvellous properties, including being cheaper than steel. Since copper is vastly more expensive than iron, this imaginary product is economically absurd. J. R. R. Tolkein imagined an equally impressive material, mithril, in his *Lord of the Rings* (1966), but he had the economic good sense to make mithril rare and expensive.

Some entrepreneurs have been known to make dramatic mistakes in their estimate of the likely competitive response to their initiative. Among the many flaws that eventually grounded Compass Airlines Mk I[1] was a confusion of average and variable costs: because the *average* cost per passenger experienced by the established airlines on the Melbourne–Sydney corridor was A$180, the management of Compass assumed that it could set a fare of A$160 and capture all the traffic. The *variable* cost per passenger was, however, less than A$25 and the established airlines were better off flying passengers at A$160 (and as the price war developed, for fares as low as A$79 and even A$69 for one week) than flying an empty seat. Both the established airlines and Compass lost money during the price war; Compass, as the newest and smallest airline, ran out of money first.

Product feasibility

A product can be scientifically and economically feasible without being practical given the current state of technology. Newcomen's engine was dreadfully inefficient, not only because it lacked an external condenser, but also because the fit between the piston and the cylinder was so poor. In the early 1700s there were no precision metal working machines available capable of boring large cylinders or turning large pistons, and so Newcomen's cylinder was a ring of rough castings bolted together and the piston a rough wooden framework built up with leather and cloth stuffing. Boulton and Watt were able to buy large-scale lathes and boring machines; with the better fit and the external condenser, a Boulton and Watt engine did ten times more work per tonne of coal than a Newcomen engine had been capable of.

More recently, the Danish architect Joern Utzon's original design for the Sydney Opera House was based on ellipsoidal shells, reflecting the shape of the sails on the yachts in Sydney harbour.[2] The design of such shells cannot be completed using readily soluble equations, and if one of the computers available in 1960 had been set to the task it might still be running without having found a feasible design. Utzon and the consulting engineer Ove Arup redesigned the roof with spherical segments, which could, with difficulty, be designed using the mathematical and computing tools available, and construction of the Opera House proceeded.

If an innovation involves manufacturing something, and if unusual shapes or materials, or extremes of performance are required, then the project should proceed cautiously until there is some confidence that the product can actually be produced and have the appropriate performance. If the product is to be used in mission-critical or life-critical applications, then it must be possible to manufacture it at a guaranteed quality level. Often, as with Utzon's Sydney Opera House, the concept will stay but the prototype will need significant modification before it can be put into production.

Lack of manufacturability can become a fatal flaw when there is some aspect of the plan that eliminates the time needed to work through potential manufacturing problems. Rolls-Royce set out to design and build the RB211 triple-shaft, high-bypass engine on the timescales demanded by the Lockheed L1011 'Tristar' project. Its original concept involved carbon fibre composite blades on the first stage fan; when these could not be made to work to the demanding specification set for them (a number ten chicken arriving at 120 km/h while the fan was spinning at its rated speed), the cost of rushing alternatives into production made Rolls-Royce bankrupt in 1972.

Innovations involving service products can fail for similar reasons: if the prototype works because of the unique talent of one or a small group of individuals, it must be possible to train ordinary people to deliver the service at a similar standard in order to grow the enterprise. One of the keys to the continuing success of the McDonald's organisation is its refusal to offer any products that it cannot reproduce using semi-skilled staff, and another is the ingenuity with which it has standardised some difficult tasks. Making good French fries consistently is quite difficult, in general, but McDonald's, by standardising the size of each chip and the breed of potato it was made from and controlling the heat of the cooking oil by thermostat and the cooking time by a timer, have made chip-making a routine task.

Is it legal?

Visitors to Ireland report an extensive demand for the services of fertility control clinics, and those who do not study the sociopolitical background may wonder why until very recently there weren't any. Visitors to Thailand may be surprised to see that there are no T-shirts on sale bearing caricatures of the king. No one in Singapore publishes a popular newspaper or magazine disrespectful of Senior Minister Lee. Many citizens of the US get extremely irate at any misuse of the 'Stars and Stripes'. Some Americans are surprised at the bureaucratic hurdles in the way of anyone wishing to sell or buy handguns in other countries. There are many products that are freely available in some countries and strictly banned in others.

There are also many products whose sale is only conditionally legal. In most developed countries pharmaceutical preparations may only be sold once regulatory approval has been obtained. Many types of business may only be conducted in premises that have been approved, either specifically or in general terms, by one or more levels of government. Entry into certain trades and professions may be regulated. Very strict standards, backed up by severe penalties, apply in many countries to facilities where food is prepared or stored. Appliances that may be connected to the water, gas or electricity supplies, or the telecommunications network, must meet strictly enforced standards.

The existence of rules and regulations often creates the illusion that a business opportunity is available by breaking them and, in countries where exemptions from the laws are traded in an informal market, the opportunities may be very real and very profitable. If a country embarks on a programme of deregulation, permitting a more general right of entry to various forms of economic activity, then rather too many entrants may try to seize the opportunity: the US deregulated its airline system in 1978 and there was a rush into the market, which peaked with 28 competing carriers. As of mid 2003 there were five major and a few large regional carriers left, while two of the major carriers were operating under Chapter 11 bankruptcy protection.

If laws and regulations block an opportunity, the entrepreneur can plan to secure an exemption or lobby to have the regulations amended. In the absence of an exemption or deregulation, such a proposal is fatally flawed.

Specialists and experts often fall into the trap of doing something because they can and assuming that other people will want the result. Other specialists and experts don't want it, because they would prefer to do it themselves, while prospective users can't see the point at all. The Newton hand-held computer launched by Apple in 1994 seems to have been close to this category: Apple had made some technical advances in handwriting recognition and rushed a product into the market to allow customers to admire their cleverness. The Newton achieved a certain distinction as the first electronic device to be ridiculed in an internationally syndicated comic strip, but not as one of the world's great marketing success stories. The later success of Palm demonstrates that there is a market for hand-held computers, but the Newton clearly failed to meet that market's expectations.

Marketing legends tell the tale of a pet food company in England, whose technicians discovered a new way to process dog food. The product seemed to be a certain winner and the company invested in substantial advertising and negotiated extensive distribution. The first few days' sales were fantastic: the product 'walked off the shelves'. The company stepped up production and waited for the repeat orders, but none ever came. Dogs loathed the stuff!

Planning spreadsheets

The development and elaboration of the concept of 'management by objectives' represented one of the twentieth century's major landmarks, relieving entrepreneurs and chief executives of the God-like responsibility for ordering every aspect of an operation and allowing them to delegate without threatening their organisation's integrity. There is still the problem of developing the objectives. For the continuing operations of an established organisation this is relatively simple: the chief executive, with or without the help of a planning unit, examines the firm's historic performance data and sets objectives based upon some projection of it. Monitoring is then a matter of comparing actuals with the projections and taking action to control any variations from the phased targets. Those chief executives who earn their salaries do so by resolving the conflicts that arise when various objectives become incompatible: when manufacturing can't meet the increased volume projections, reduce variable costs and avoid any capital expenditure; when the sales manager cannot meet the revenue forecast without allowing salespersons to overspend their petrol allowance; or when the service manager can't increase customer satisfaction and halve the number of service personnel in the same period.

Entrepreneurial businesses must be managed, often much more carefully than established ones, since there is so little room for error. There are, however, no historical records from which objectives can be derived. A planning spreadsheet may be used to generate, among other things, 'pro forma' sales and cost projections which can serve two major purposes:

■ they can provide a pseudo-historic base upon which objectives can be set and the performance of the organisation in its early months monitored

■ they can provide a tool which can be used to test the financial feasibility of a proposal and refine the marketing and organisation plans of a feasible one, without going to the trouble of developing a full set of operating financial projections.

Financial modellers have used spreadsheets for centuries; but until the 1980s these were usually paper and pencil efforts. Marketing models can be developed systematically and automated by using a spreadsheet and we describe one way of doing so in this chapter. Putting a marketing model onto a spreadsheet is still relatively unusual, but the methods described here are based on over 25 years of published research on marketing, economics and sociology.[3]

Fear, facts and fantasies

Models were once made of balsa wood and a few still are, but the models that entrepreneurs use to help them to plan and run their businesses are made out of numbers and stored and calculated on a computer. Stored program computers are relatively new, dating from about 1950, and personal computers cheap enough for most people to own and powerful enough for most people to find useful have only been available since 1985 or thereabouts. Most managerial workers in the developed world now regularly use a computer at work, but relatively few develop their own basic or application software or even build their own Excel® models, and for this group the computer remains something of a mystery.

In one very real sense, computers do not 'do' anything on their own: a computer is a machine which obeys a detailed program, such that if the same computer is given the same data and made to execute the same program, it will produce the same result. Programs often have 'bugs' in them, meaning that, for at least some data values, the result may be different from the one that the people who programmed the computer intended. This is not a 'computer error'; it is a person error. If the data given to a computer is not a good reflection of the real world, the results may be equally unrealistic: one of the earliest computer acronyms was GIGO, meaning 'Garbage in, garbage out'. Bad computer output generated from bad input is not a computer error either; it too is a person error.

There is a sense in which computers do more than simply carry out their instructions; the sheer calculating speed of a modern computer means that calculations which would take a human a lifetime or longer to complete are finished in a matter of minutes on a computer. Such results can't be checked by hand, and so they can be said to be 'computer-generated'. Computer-generated results can be in error even if the program used has no bugs. This can be because of subtle (or not so subtle) errors in the data, or the program used is not a perfect model of the real world, or the problem does not have a calculable solution. People who use computers in business need to develop an intuitive sense of what is reasonable so as to avoid relying on computer models incorporating egregious errors. Work in chaos theory has demonstrated that even good models based on accurate data cannot be used to make accurate long-term predictions.

Computers are tools, just as hammers are. A hammer can drive in nails or crush a thumb. A computer can be a useful tool or a way of accelerating disaster. We don't blame the hammer for a broken thumb and we should not blame a computer for a rotten outcome to a venture. We would laugh at a carpenter who tried to drive in nails with his bare hands for fear of hitting his thumb with a hammer. An entrepreneur who refuses to use a computer for fear of making a mistake with it is just as foolish.

Perfection

The world that people live in is messy, full of unexpected events, some pleasant but many downright nasty. The ancient Greek philosopher Plato suggested that people felt this way about the world because they did not understand it. Plato used the analogy of people sitting in a cave, with their backs to the entrance, watching the shadows made by people and events happening on the outside.[4] Humans, Plato suggested, are trapped in their illusions; the messiness of the world that we perceive and the apparent randomness of the events that batter us is an artefact of the limitations of our senses. The real world, the world outside the cave, is perfect, obeying immutable laws and moving in a perfectly predictable way. If we want to understand the real reality, said Plato, we should disregard the flawed evidence of our senses and look for the underlying truth in mathematics and logic.

Theoretical physicists and neoliberal economists still follow Plato's advice. Orthodox economists talk in formulas and equations; they refer to perfect markets and general equilibrium. When anyone confronts them with evidence from the real world they dismiss it as 'anecdotal'. Theoretical physicists concern themselves with the first billionth of a second after the 'big bang'. Nobody is going to go back and take a look, so the problem of contrary evidence does not arise. Theoretical physicists are 'often in error but never in doubt'; the same is true of too many economists.

The words 'perfect' and 'ideal', when used by theoretical physicists and orthodox economists, mean 'explained by our equations'. The opposite to 'perfect', in this sense, is not 'imperfect' but 'real'. The opposite of 'rational' is not 'irrational', but 'practical'. An entrepreneur does not require or expect perfection or certainty. He is not afraid of 'perhaps': 'perhaps it won't work out this way, but I'm here to maximise the chances that it will.' This is how entrepreneurial market and financial models are intended to be used: they help the entrepreneur to eliminate the impossible and the very unlikely, improve the route to his objective but they don't replace the real world or try to deny its richness, complexity and endless capacity for surprise.

Chaos and complexity

The Platonists based their stand on mathematics, so much so that the entrance to Plato's Academy in ancient Athens had the sign 'No entry without geometry' engraved over the entrance. From the 1890s on, a series of discoveries in mathematics have shattered this foundation. These can be summarised under the headings 'chaos' and 'complexity'.[5]

Work on chaos or, more properly, 'deterministic chaos' goes back to the French mathematician Poincaré. He was the first to observe that, even when 'perfect' equations are available, it can be impossible to produce an accurate prediction. Technically, as soon as the equations that describe a multielement system, no matter how perfectly, have non-linear terms, the implicit error may grow without limit. All predictions about the future state of such a system are strictly less accurate than the data about the present state and the possible error grows exponentially with time.

There is nothing special about 'non-linear' behaviour. A perfectly straight horizontal beam made of perfectly uniform material and balanced on perfectly frictionless hinges is mathematically linear, but the same beam stuck in the ground to make a column is not. Even the stars in the heavens are affected by chaos. Astronomers know the position of the moon to a precision of about one second in a thousand years, and so a prediction of an eclipse in a thousand years from now would be good to the nearest second. A prediction for ten thousand years into the future, ten times as long, would not be good to the nearest 10 seconds, but could be out by as many as 1000 seconds. A prediction for a million years into the future would be no better than a random guess.

Related work on complexity theory has shown that the medium- and long-term behaviour of complex systems comprising multiple interacting components cannot be predicted by studying, no matter how perfectly, the pairwise interactions of the components. The equations governing such a system do not have 'perfect' analytical solutions, and the best numerical solution processes are 'NP-complete', meaning that the time needed to compute a solution grows exponentially (or worse) faster than the number of components in the system. We don't need to search the heavens for an example: one shopper in one supermarket could spend the lifetime of the universe (or longer) trying out all the ways to fill a simple shopping list.

Commercial lottery games, where subscribers pick a few numbers from a list and win when all or most of their numbers are drawn, demonstrate how even a small number of choices can lead to a huge number of outcomes. Only one choice of numbers will win the first division prize in any draw; finding the optimum, the best possible, state for a real system is about as hard as picking the winning lottery numbers.

Reality   The real world is built on compromises, most of them quite satisfactory. A table of eclipses that is good for ten thousand years satisfies most practical requirements. Most people who enter supermarkets emerge eventually with their immediate needs satisfied. Architects and engineers are quite good at specifying columns that don't buckle. Even when we do not have exact information about the future, it is often possible to make a very accurate guess of the limits to the range of possibilities: the next Epsom Derby will almost certainly be won by a horse.

An entrepreneur planning a venture can make guesses about the future and, as long as the guesses are based upon a reasonable base of research and experience, they can be used in a business plan. The planning process should recognise two sources of variance:

1. the initial guesses will have an explicit or implicit margin of error – these errors compound with time, so the longer the forecast, the less reliable the numbers at the end of it
2. the plan, like every human endeavour, is subject to systemic upheaval or catastrophe; factors that no one was taking any account of may interact in ways that no one would have imagined, leading to an outcome that nobody forecast.

The entire point of the plan is to anticipate the first type of errors and either counter them or build on them as the plan evolves. If early sales are slower than planned, actions can be taken that will bring them back on track. If they are better than anticipated, the plan will help the entrepreneur to avoid a cash flow crisis as the new venture takes advantage of the favourable turn of events.

The word 'catastrophe' has a mathematical and colloquial meaning. To a mathematician, a catastrophe is a sudden, discontinuous change in a system. A cool change in a hot summer, when storms break up a hot spell and the temperature drops ten or more degrees in an hour, is a catastrophe in the mathematical sense. Colloquially, a catastrophe is a disaster but, in retrospect, most systemic shocks have been turned into disasters by human action. All too often, the human action has consisted of following a plan even after its major premises are shown to be wrong.

Many years ago there was a near disaster at a major international airport, when an aircraft that had just landed turned across the main runway in error just as another aircraft was cleared to take off. The subsequent investigation showed that the aeroplane taking off, whose crew could see the obstruction clearly, could have aborted their takeoff and stopped hundreds of metres before a collision. Alternatively they could have applied emergency thrust and taken off more rapidly than planned, in which case they would have cleared the obstruction by fifty or more metres.

Instead, they performed a completely routine takeoff, striking the roof of the aeroplane in their path with their main landing gear, severely damaging the aircraft on the ground but causing no casualties, and were able to land safely on their bent but otherwise operable landing gear. Two highly trained, perfectly fit pilots confronted with a totally unexpected event completely lost their powers of judgement.

A myopic entrepreneur may not be able to see the difference between a variation from the plan arising from the inevitable imprecision of forecasting and the effects of a catastrophe. A small-scale entrepreneur might open an ice cream stall and find that sales on the opening day are 50 per cent down on budget. The marketing textbooks explain that sales can be boosted by more promotion and so the entrepreneur might erect a bigger and more colourful sign. This might be an unnecessary expense if the weather had been unseasonably cool on the opening day: the weather fluctuates and ice cream sales with it. One day may be too short a time in which to decide that a trend has been established. On the other hand, if the Environment Protection Authority has just erected a huge sign banning swimming and setting out a list of vile pollutants contaminating the nearby beach, every day the entrepreneur stays on that site is one more step on the road from catastrophe to disaster.

Creating a marketing model

Writing computer programs, including complex spreadsheets, and, more importantly, validating them requires aptitude and training and, since a number of forecasting models exist, there is no need for budding entrepreneurs to reinvent that particular wheel. The input to such models is a list of parameters while the output is a phased revenue and direct cost projection. Just as power steering won't keep a car out of an accident if the driver chooses to steer into one, a computer model, no matter how well written, won't produce useful results if it is fed useless data.

In the following section we build the concepts described in Chapter 3 and show how they can be quantified. Before a product has been launched, the parameters are no better than informed guesses, but after the launch they can be refined as sales data comes in and the model can then be used as an active aid to the ongoing tasks of product management.

Product price and cost

Parameters that you must estimate

Marketing a new product (whether a good or service) involves asking people to pay for it. This introduces at least two constraints:

- The perceived value to the buyer must exceed the price, which in turn must exceed the cost
- The targeted buyers must be able to afford the product.

You are not going to get very far with your planning if you have not developed a reasonable idea of your proposed price and associated direct costs; the price then has two roles to play, in that your revenue is the product of the price and the number of sales, while your market is limited to those people who can afford your product. If your planning horizon is more than a matter of months, you will also need to estimate likely trends in prices and costs. Prices, unless supported by added features and improved performance levels, generally trend downwards, while hourly labour costs trend up. Material, equipment and production costs trend down, while the costs of providing a service with human servers tend to rise. You need to estimate these effects in your planning and you will need to track the trends after your venture is launched to verify or adjust your estimates.

Customer behaviour

There are three general classes of purchasing event in the life of the relationship between a supplier and a customer:

1. The customer makes a first purchase to initiate the relationship; this may be indistinguishable from subsequent purchases, as when a customer buys a particular packaged consumer good for the first time, or it may be quantitatively different, as when a customer buys a new car from a particular maker for the first time or a new member joins a golf or other club and pays a joining premium
2. There may be ongoing transactions, such as regular servicing of a motorcar, green fees or buggy hire at a golf club or simply routine repurchasing of a consumer good or service
3. There may be subsequent 'lumpy' transactions, such as the replacement of a motorcar after a period of use or the payment of annual renewal fees at a club or on an insurance policy.

Often a venture that would be marginal if it could only rely on one source of income from a customer relationship becomes profitable if more than one can be brought into play. One of the most famous examples is King Gillette's launch of the safety razor, where Gillette offered the handles at an actual cash loss, relying on the extremely profitable sales of blades for the prosperity of his business (Drucker 1985: 245–7).

Defining the market

Failure is always distressing, but failure in the pursuit of an impossible objective can be worse: you don't just feel disappointed, you feel stupid as well. The most fundamental error anyone can make is to launch a product into a market that is simply too small to generate enough revenue to cover the venture's basic operating costs. Modelling starts by quantifying the market the new venture intends to satisfy and this estimate of the size of the target market will become a key model parameter. The market for this purpose consists of the people or firms who could gain net benefits from the use of the new product, have the means and will be offered the opportunity to buy it. Note that this defines three intersecting sets: obviously people and firms that could not gain a net benefit from using a product are unlikely to become users of it; but people and firms who can't afford it won't become users; and neither will people and firms with no access to the product. Products with a superficially wide appeal may prove to have a much narrower market after this subsetting is carried out.

Markets aren't static: firms or people who have been in the market and been at least potential users of a product will leave it eventually and other people or firms may join it. People and firms entering a market have no established supplier allegiance and represent an opportunity for each supplier to gain customers without first detaching them from a different supplier; while when a firm or a person leaves a market, their customer relationships are disrupted and their previous supplier loses both the direct benefit of revenue generated by sales to them and the indirect benefit of their recommendations. These effects can be significant even in markets in which the buying population changes relatively slowly; but they can become dominant factors in markets with a rapid turnover of buyers, such as markets serving persons in a narrow age range. It is always useful to estimate market entry and exit rates; in some cases it may be critical.

If a plan covers an entry into more than one market or addresses clearly differentiated market segments, the data for each segment should be estimated and the estimate recorded. When actually generating a revenue forecast, segments can be aggregated or each such segment can be forecast separately, but common sense should limit the complexity of this part of the forecasting process. Once a business commences operations, segment tracking can become very important indeed and a failure to recognise segment boundaries at the planning stage can prove costly.

Market response parameters

It is one thing to estimate how many potential customers the world holds for a new product; it is another, and even more critical, task to estimate how many of these people or firms will become actual, revenue-generating customers and, once they have become customers, how long they will maintain that state. Market researchers including Bass, Midgley and others have provided tools that can be used to estimate new product adoption rates and Figure 4.2 summarises their conclusions, at least for a single supplier to a new and relatively large market. (See the technical appendix to this chapter for a discussion on the extension of the model to other situations.)

In this model potential customers become actual ones after a two-stage process: initially they are trial users and only if the trial is satisfactory do they become cus-

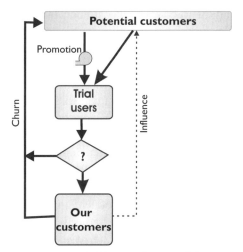

Figure 4.2 **Hybrid adoption model**

tomers. Potential users become trial users because of 'external' or 'internal' influence (Mahajan et al. 1990); external influence is created by a supplier's promotional efforts, while established users recommending the product and being visibly satisfied users of it exert internal influence. Internal influence creates the positive feedback that makes the successful marketing of durable goods possible.

Marketing effort may be wasted if a product fails to satisfy its trial users and, churn, when previously satisfied customers leave the market or revert to being potential customers only, can become financially fatal if it rises too far. How far is too far depends on the product, the market and the product's marginal profitability, but studies by Reichheld (1996, 2001) and others suggest that quite small changes in churn rates can have dramatic impacts on the bottom line, with a 5 per cent change in the churn rate changing net profit by 25–100 per cent.)

New entrepreneurial businesses are less concerned with profitability than survival and this will be determined by the interaction of two effects: how much it will cost to persuade a potential user to become a trial user and what the probability is of a single trial converting a trial user into a customer. Repeated measurements have confirmed that the prompt returns to promotion are negative, that is, the earned margin from the extra sales induced by an advertising or other promotional campaign is less than the cost of the campaign. This is most obvious when the promotion takes the form of giving away samples: not only does the supplier have to pay the cost of producing the samples, but also the cost of distributing them. Positive returns are only earned from promotion when enough of the new customers induced to try the product are sufficiently satisfied to keep purchasing it or recommend it to their friends and acquaintances – hopefully, both.

The survival and profitable growth of a business depends on the churn rate for all businesses and the effectiveness of internal influence on those selling infrequently purchased products. Simple observation of users may lead to underestimating churn rates: a purchaser of a durable product, such as a motorcar or refrigerator, may become dissatisfied and resolve not to buy a replacement from the same supplier, while refusing to recommend the supplier to others; but this change in status will not become apparent until the time comes to replace the original purchase. Buyers of some types of goods and services may even continue purchasing a product after they have ceased to consider themselves a customer of its supplier, choosing it as long as it is the cheapest or most convenient – and no longer. When low-cost airlines appeared in the US and European markets, they rapidly attracted a substantial number of apparently satisfied users of the full-service airlines: these users' previous 'loyal' behaviour had reflected a lack of alternatives rather than a conscious commitment to their previous supplier.

The four critical parameters are: the cost of securing a trial; the probability of a trial creating a customer; the churn rate; and the rate at which customers influence potential customers to become trial users. The actual value of these parameters will be different for different markets and often different for different suppliers to the same market. Some guidelines for initial estimates are:

- The cost of securing a trial for a new product in a new market can easily exceed the direct cost of one unit of the product concerned; it may approach the end user price and is unlikely to be less than the gross margin.
- The probability of a trial leading to the trial user becoming a customer ranges upwards from zero. Obviously if it is zero the product will fail and the venture may fail with it; packaged consumer goods companies generally regard a trial to customer rate of less than 20 per cent as being symptomatic of product failure, while 40 per cent is considered very acceptable. Major purchases, whether by firms or individuals, tend to have a high trial to customer conversion rate, at least in part because the buyer does not wish to admit to making a major error of judgement.
- Churn rates vary from trivial to 100 per cent per year and more. As shown in Chapter 3, an apparently small difference in churn rates can have a major effect on profitability. Frederick Reichheld, a former director of Bain & Co, built a successful consulting career by showing his clients how to reduce customer churn and demonstrating how much such a reduction would be worth to them in profit. He has shared his accumulated wisdom with the rest of us through a number of articles and books, including Reichheld (1996).

The late Soichiro Honda was listening to an internal presentation when one of his engineers referred to 'satisfying our customers'. Honda exploded: 'We don't just *satisfy* our customers. We amaze and delight them!'

- Observed rates of internal influence, or less formally, word of mouth promotion, vary from slightly negative to almost 300 per cent per year (see box 'Telstra MobileNet®'). Rates over 50 per cent per year are inevitably associated with powerful network effects, when users can gain significant benefits from recruiting new users. When such incentives are absent, internal influence will only occur if adoption is visible to others, either because of the nature of the product, as with a new model of motorcar, or because users wish, for personal or professional reasons, to describe their experiences with the new product. A meta-study of diffusion estimates found that the mean level of internal influence for consumer durable products was 28 per cent per year (Sultan et al. 1990).

The main point of a forecasting model is to link marketing expenditure to revenue forecasts, or alternatively, to take a set of revenue forecasts and estimate the marketing expenditure necessary to achieve them. If there is a single major cause of the failure of new ventures, it is to underestimate the cost of marketing by a factor of two or more. Even if a product is destined to become a major success, marketing costs will send the initial cash flow negative.

Telstra MobileNet®

When Telstra first introduced mobile telephones to Australia their promotion emphasised the 'yuppie toy' aspect of mobile telephony, but this was not where the major early sales came from.

Australia has a unique system of home building, where the builder typically employs no one and acts as the owner's agent in engaging a succession of independent subcontractors to do the actual work. Each builder would typically have a number of projects running at the same time and the coordination was often faulty; the plasterer might arrive before the electrician and the plumber had finished their initial work and have to go away again, or the electrician might return to fit the switches and outlets only to find that the plastering was incomplete.

Building subcontractors ('subbies' in the vernacular) saw the possibilities of mobile phones very quickly: rather than driving to a site they could ring the tradesperson whose work theirs depended on and find out if the site was ready for them. Obviously this didn't work until the person they were calling had a mobile phone as well, and so those subbies with mobile phones had a strong incentive to persuade those who did not to acquire one.

This internal influence-driven adoption of mobile phones by subbies in the Australian home building industry led to overall sales growing at 12 per cent per month, equivalent to 290 per cent per year.

An example   A corporate entrepreneur intends to launch a new product into a supermarket category where research has shown that there is little customer loyalty and most purchases are based on price. The new product will cost a little more than established product lines but will be of a far higher quality, and so the entrepreneur confidently expects that at least 30 per cent of trials will lead to the trial user becoming a customer, and that customers will make one purchase a month with a churn rate of no more than 20 per cent per year. There are at least a million potential users in the launch segments.

The entrepreneur also knows that he must achieve sales at a rate of at least £3 million per year by the end of six months if he is to maintain his supermarket slotting. The recommended retail price of his product is £3.60 and his wholesale price will be £2.40 while his direct supply cost will be £1.40. The £3 million per year is, of course, £250,000 per month, which means he needs just under 70,000 customers, of whom about 1200 will drop out in any month and need to be replaced by new recruits. Assuming that the cost of securing a trial equals the retail price and the trial success rate is 30 per cent, each customer recruited will cost his venture £12.

It is easy to see that he will need to maintain a standing marketing budget of at least £14,400 per month and on top of this he must spend £840,000 on marketing over the first six months to build up his customer base to the minimum level acceptable to his supermarket outlets. He doesn't want to commit to an excessive expenditure upfront in case his marketing research has misled him and the product won't achieve the minimum level of acceptance it needs; but he doesn't want to 'snatch defeat from the jaws of victory' by falling just short of his target. He decides to budget £220,000 per month for four months, at the end of which time he will know whether the product is worth backing or not. His financial/marketing plan includes Table 4. 1 or something similar.

He projects an introduction cost of about £530,000, on top of previous development and marketing research costs, to produce an income stream of about £60,000 per month or £720,000 per year. At a corporate hurdle rate of 25 per cent per year, this will be valued at £2,880,000 so he is confident that the initial investment is justi-

Table 4.1 **A sample marketing projection**

Month	1	2	3	4	5	6
Marketing spend (£)	220,000	220,000	220,000	220,000	14,400	14,400
Trials	61,111	61,111	61,111	61,111	4,000	4,000
New customers	18,333	18,333	18,333	18,333	1,200	1,200
Lost customers		(306)	(606)	(901)	(1,192)	(1,192)
Total customers	18,333	36,360	54,087	71,519	71,527	71,535
Unit sales	61,111	79,138	96,865	114,297	74,327	74,335
Value of sales (£)	220,000	284,897	348,714	411,469	267,577	267,606
Contribution from sales (£)	61,111	79,138	96,865	114,297	74,327	74,335
Contribution after marketing (£)	(158,889)	(140,862)	(123,135)	(105,703)	59,927	59,935

fied. Of course, his initial market research suggested that there were a million potential users, so his planned market penetration is only 7 per cent or so; there is still plenty of upside. Success on this level would be sufficient to justify the capital expenditure needed to expand production, increase penetration and diversify into new markets.

An entrepreneur launching a new venture and hoping to access venture capital would need a more elaborate model, because simply exceeding a 25 per cent hurdle rate is not enough to get venture capitalists excited. Using the same product parameters but projecting the period of high marketing investment for a full year, promising to keep other overheads down to £20,000 per month and limiting prelaunch expenditure to £750,000, leads to a projected internal rate of return of 70 per cent, which might attract venture capital; but generally a worksheet as simple as Table 4.1 will not be enough in a business plan offered to venture capitalists and a more elaborate underlying model may be needed. Even corporate entrepreneurs may find opportunities quite as attractive as this one hard to identify and a more elaborate model may be needed to build a convincing business case for a valuable but more marginal proposition.

Seasonality

Some products are sold more easily at certain times of the year. If a model uses annual periods in which to forecast, this doesn't matter, but if a model is used to forecast months or quarters, a seasonal adjustment should be applied. Seasonality comes in at least two guises: there are seasonal events and conditions, such as Christmas or winter, and there is the fact that different months have different numbers of working and non-working days. As long as the model is being used for venture planning, the pattern of the weeks is not critically important, but if it is retained as a management tool after the venture is launched, a good understanding of seasonal factors is essential.

Small populations and prediction errors

When the expected number of sales per period is small and the marketing budget constrained, there may be less than one sale per period expected in the early life of a venture. A simple, or even a sophisticated, model may predict that, for example, there will have been sufficient money spent on sales and marketing to bring in the first customer by month seven of the plan. This may be an excellent, unbiased prediction but it is far from a certainty, and a venture that expected its first sale in month seven should be able to survive even if that elusive first sale does not turn up until month nine or ten. After twelve months without any sales, a modest level of panic might be appropriate, but even then a statistician would be reluctant to say that the initial projection had been wrong.

Predictions are subject to error, no matter how soundly they are based, and the probable error will usually be no more than the square root of the number of units expected. If the plan, or even a forecast based on a series of successful periods of selling, predicts 10,000 sales in a period, the probable error range is ±100, or about 1 per cent. Quite small variances from the forecast, assuming that it has been seasonally adjusted correctly, are a matter of concern. By contrast, if the number of sales per period is expected to be 1, the error range is ±1, and an actual sales achievement of 0, 1, or 2 units should not cause any great surprise. If the sales per period are expected to be about 1, then only about 37 per cent of periods would be expected to see exactly one sale; about the same number of periods would see no sales at all, and in around a quarter of the periods more than one sale would be expected.

Given an expectation of one sale per period, every eight months or so you should expect consecutive periods with no sales at all. Panic in such situations is understandable, if statistically unjustifiable. It is possible to make a computer model simulate vile tricks such as this, which is useful for simulation purposes when very large amounts of money are at stake. It is, however, somewhat dangerous to include random or pseudo-random numbers in a forecast that is going to be used to build financial projections.

Promotional quality

The most direct way of securing a trial is a sampling programme or the equivalent. When introducing a new packaged consumer good the supplier may engage a merchandising firm to distribute free samples of the product to shoppers in the target segments; a new service business may distribute leaflets through its catchment area offering a free or heavily discounted service to those who present the leaflet before a certain date; prospective buyers of a new car may be offered a test drive. Alternative forms of promotion, such as media advertising or event sponsorship, will be justified either on the basis that they will reach potential users inaccessible to a sampling programme or they will incur a lower cost per trial.

The continued use of sampling programmes is a proof, of sorts, that media promotion and event sponsorship are not guaranteed to be a more economical way of securing a trial than sampling programmes and, for planning purposes, it is wise to assume that the cost per trial will be that of a sampling programme, irrespective of the actual promotional strategy adopted.

The possibility remains that a promotional campaign will be less effective than a sampling programme, either because of defects in the media planning or the promotional material itself. In spite of the confidence projected by advertising agencies and media planning consultancies, campaign failures still occur. What we discuss in this chapter is a way of setting marketing budgets that should be sufficient for a competent marketing team to be able to generate the expected number of trials. The development of an effective marketing plan, and the appointment of people competent to administer it, is largely out of the scope of this book, but that does not mean that the development and execution of an effective marketing plan is anything but central to the success of most new ventures.

Encouraging internal influence

On the face of it, internal influence is pure gold to an entrepreneur, with satisfied users persuading potential ones to try the product without drawing a penny from the marketing budget. As we mentioned in Chapter 3, a little discreet encouragement can make such persuasion more effective at a relatively modest cost. Capital goods suppliers may encourage the development of user associations; consumer product companies may place a discreet (or even blatant) product identifier on their goods such that merely wearing or carrying them makes the user a walking endorsement.

Wal-Mart, the behemoth of American retailing, brands its discount warehouses 'Sam's clubs' to give its users a sense of being part of a community rather than mere consumers patronising a large and impersonal corporation.

For an established company launching a major innovation, user association meetings can be an excellent place to guarantee an enthusiastic initial reception; but for a new venture with no customers an investment in a user association or other means of encouraging internal influence might be considered premature. A new venture should still plan to develop a user association, or some other means of building user linkages, as soon as there are enough customers to make such linkages reassuring.

These activities are properly part of the marketing plan rather than the venture business plan, but a reference to them in the master document may encourage those developing the marketing plan to make provision for them in due course.

The financial planning model

Estimating budgets

Most business planning packages allow you to enter detailed information about your staff establishment and asset register, but of course this assumes that you have completed your organization and process design. It will often be necessary to project a basic set of pro forma accounts before these tasks have been completed. Your estimate of revenue and the direct costs of earning it leads to a forecast of the gross margin (sometimes referred to as the gross profit); and if you followed the methodology described above or used a soundly based forecasting package, you even have a forecast of the cost of promotion, a charge against the gross margin. Before anyone can claim to have earned a profit, they must pay the 'fixed' or 'other' costs of operating, meet the depreciation charges on the assets they use and pay interest on any money borrowed to support the business. Often the final step in screening an apparent opportunity is to produce a provisional profit and loss (P&L) forecast, using algorithms to estimate the various charges against the gross margin.

'Fixed' or 'other' costs

Even large and successful companies often find that three headings are enough to estimate the fixed costs of operating a business. These are sales and marketing, research and development, and general administration. In the perfect world imagined by mainstream economists, there would be no fixed costs: all of them represent an 'imperfection' in the real world, which it suits economists to ignore (at least, until they start to run a real business).

Sales and marketing activities are only needed because consumers do not have perfect information about all the products that might be useful for them; research and development costs are only incurred because producers lack perfect information on what consumers want and how best to produce it; and general administration is only needed because the contracts under which both production workers and other staff are employed are 'incomplete' and from time to time workers and staff may need guidance or correction. Because these costs would not be incurred in an economically perfect world, there is a tendency to call them 'overheads' and to regard any reduction in expense under these headings as a Good Thing. This attitude, while it has gained considerable influence since 1979, can in many cases be deeply mistaken, as later chapters of this book, and other works on management and entrepreneurship, make clear.

The Roman model (see box) had a 'span of control' of a little over eight. 'Ultra-flat' and team-based organisations may give the impression of having a larger span of control than Julius Caesar specified; but this is often a matter of developing an informal structure where the first and even the second line managers are recognised by the team as leaders but not rewarded by either status or wage increments. There may be a slight saving in front line management wages but any gain from this may be lost in the time taken for the informal structure to emerge and resolving the problems when the emerging informal leader is working to an idiosyncratic agenda.

Tables 4.2 and 4.3 show the number of front line employees and the number of managers required to manage them for various values of the span of control parameter. Table 4.3 shows the number of managers needed when the total staff is at the

Table 4.2   **Number of front line employees**

Management levels	Span of control			
	5	7	10	15
1	5	7	10	15
2	20	42	90	210
3	95	287	890	3,135
4	470	2,002	8,890	47,010
5	2,345	14,007	88,890	705,135
6	11,720	98,042	888,890	10,577,010

Table 4.3   **Maximum number of managers**

Management levels	Span of control			
	5	7	10	15
1	1	1	1	1
2	6	8	11	16
3	31	57	111	241
4	156	400	1,111	3,616
5	781	2,801	11,111	54,241
6	3,906	19,608	111,111	813,616

limit for the span and level parameters. For example, if the span of control is going to be seven, then there will have to be one manager until the front line staff numbers pass seven; three managers for a front line staff count of eight to fourteen, four managers for a front line staff count of fifteen to twenty one and so on. The mathematics behind the tables can be found in the appendix at the end of this chapter.

Administration is not the only problem: firms cannot simply allocate a budget to promotional activities; they must appoint suitable staff to administer it. Most of the actual promotion will be subcontracted to advertising agencies, event managers and the like, but someone has to choose the subcontractors, give them their instructions and correct them when they deviate from the agreed programme. In a complete business plan there may well be a full description of a sales and marketing organisation, but at the preliminary planning level some metric such as '€x per front line marketing manager' will provide a basis for discussion, at least. Plans, even provisional ones, which assume that multimillion euro marketing budgets can manage themselves will not carry a lot of conviction.

The Roman legion

The Roman legion, as it evolved from 150 BC until 400 AD, was one of the first purpose-designed organisations with an indefinite life. Each legion had an identity quite separate from its commander or any of its soldiers, an identity that was, in some cases, maintained for hundreds of years. Becoming a legionary was a career decision, with soldiers signing up for twenty years; but in return they were promised training, promotion opportunities, a pension (or land grant) on their retirement and generous performance bonuses for those who survived a successful battle. In most countries, before and after the Roman period, armies were created from peasant levies, drafted for a campaigning season and dismissed, or abandoned, at the end of it.

Roman legionaries were formed into maniples ('handfuls') under the command of a decurion; ten maniples made up a century (following Caesar, of about 80 legionaries) under the command of a centurion; six centuries made up a cohort, and the commander of the senior century doubled as the commander of the cohort; and ten cohorts made up a legion, with the commander of the senior cohort doubling as the senior continuing commander. Legions also were given a commanding officer, or legate, chosen from the Roman nobility; but with rare exceptions legates accepted the suggestions of their senior centurion on operational matters more often than they gave him orders.

Ignoring the legate and his staff, a legion at full strength had 4800 men and an operational command structure of 660 decurions and centurions. Robert Graves, in his historical novels, adapted British army terminology, with decurions described as corporals, centurions as sergeants and the senior centurions as battalion or regimental sergeant majors, equating the legion to a British regiment, the cohort to a battalion and the century to a company. Within the limitations of historical fiction, this is quite a good contemporary analogy.

Since no entrepreneurial venture is likely to be more focused or disciplined than a Roman legion, any attempt to operate with much less than one manager to each eight workers is likely to lead to less than optimal performance.

The third heading is R&D: companies that want to stay afloat in rapidly evolving markets must generally have planning for a product's successor well advanced before the product is even launched. New ventures that don't want to be 'one trick ponies' need to at least match their industry in the fraction of their revenue spent on R&D; for example, Microsoft spends approximately one-sixth of its revenue on R&D, making that the lower limit for companies hoping to share Microsoft's markets. Firms in other industries should find out the R&D intensity of their likely competitors and be prepared to match or exceed it. Published statistics should be interpreted with care, since the published R&D figures may exclude some product development costs if they are not carried out by laboratory scientists; work on packaging and formulation may be neglected in the statistics in spite of its marketing significance.

The quick P&L   Estimating the fixed costs, either as described above or for corporate ventures, by using rules provided by the controller's office and adding these to the estimates of revenue and direct costs described earlier, allows the construction of a 'quick P&L' forecast, at least down to the EBDIT[6] line. Such a forecast makes no account of leasing or depreciation charges, beyond an office rental element that may or may not be included in the estimate of the cost of executive employment (which, once included, turns the EBDIT into an EBIT) or interest and taxation expenses; but it still conveys a lot of useful information about the project.

Proposals for internal corporate ventures are generally accompanied by a quick P&L such as that shown in Table 4.4 or an even simpler forecast; although capital and financing charges will still be considered as part of the project evaluation, these will be calculated by the controller's department using rules that are, as far as outsiders go, tablets of stone, not to be queried or challenged.

Non-promotional marketing expense

While developing the revenue forecast we showed how to estimate a promotional budget. We included in this budget money that would persuade potential customers to become trial ones; this will include money spent on advertising, promotion and sales incentives. It did not include the salaries and other costs of product managers, a marketing manager, a sales manager and payment to salespersons while they fill out their expense claims, complete call reports and spend their time in other unproductive ways. Not every new venture will need separate product, marketing and sales managers and salespersons at the venture's inception, but practically every venture will need some effort along these lines, and if it grows at a satisfactory pace, all these positions will need filling and budgeting for.

The plan should include a reasonable estimate of the annual cost including payroll overheads of employing executives in these various roles: there should be an additional budget to cover accommodation and technical services and, in the case of salespersons, company-maintained vehicles and a generous entertainment allowance. It will always be tempting for a new, cash-strapped venture to try to minimise these expenses, but if penny-pinching leads to the job being done badly, the costs will far outweigh the savings. This is especially true for the sales positions: although some incompetent salespersons manage to earn high incomes, no competent salesperson will be attracted by low ones.

A new business can separate the sales sheep from the goats by offering a basic retainer and a bonus scheme with a substantial boost for high performance. For a position with on target earnings of £70,000, the salesperson might be offered a retainer of £35,000 plus a maintained prestige car, with a bonus of £35,000 for achieving 100 per cent of target plus £700 for each percentage point past 100 per cent. If a 'gun' salesperson achieves 300 per cent of target, they will earn £210,000, probably the highest salary the venture will pay in its early years by a substantial margin. Anyone who finds this a problem is no entrepreneur.

Table 4.4   **Example of a quick P&L statement**

ExampleCo project budget (£)

Year ending	30/6/04	30/6/05	30/6/06	30/6/07	30/6/08
Sales					
Initial or trial purchase	1,315,750	1,137,535	1,374,814	1,456,730	2,018,373
Regular supplies	187,670	484,239	794,086	1,130,588	1,522,666
Replacement	1,100	14,013	49,018	101,046	162,134
Sales total	1,504,520	1,635,787	2,217,918	2,688,364	3,703,173
Direct costs					
Materials	123,623	143,665	203,389	257,661	364,517
Services/subcontractors	42,018	37,801	48,264	54,684	78,857
Labour	328,850	393,191	561,904	718,300	1,014,695
Production management	60,000	80,000	80,000	80,000	80,000
Direct costs total	554,491	654,657	893,557	1,110,645	1,538,069
Gross margin	950,029	981,130	1,324,361	1,577,719	2,165,104
Other costs					
Sales and marketing	810,000	680,000	780,000	780,000	1,080,000
Research & development	75,000	75,000	75,000	75,000	92,579
Administration	275,301	256,789	285,896	309,418	360,159
Other costs total	1,160,301	1,011,789	1,140,896	1,164,418	1,532,738
EBDIT	(210,272)	(30,659)	183,465	413,301	632,366

Production/delivery expense

When estimating the direct costs of operating a business, whether manufacturing or service, the entrepreneur or his specialist advisers will 'walk through' the process of manufacture or delivery to estimate a standard cost in materials and labour hours. It is then a relatively automatic task to work back from the revenue projections to the direct costs and the size of the front line workforce. These are not, however, the only costs of operating a manufacturing or service delivery operation.

The venture will need an executive in overall charge; since most manufacturing operations have a service element, they may need both a manufacturing and a service manager. The budget must allow for the annual cost of these executives including overheads: this should be the loaded salary of a typical production executive and/or service supervisor, including related costs such as statutory overheads (including payroll tax, superannuation and worker's compensation insurance), fringe benefits (company car and so on) and direct overheads (secretarial services, computer and network, office rental and so on).

As a manufacturing business grows it may require a production planner and a logistics manager, and as the direct labour force grows there may be a need for foremen and forewomen. A growing service business will need a process analyst to refine and script the service delivery process and plan enhancements, and where services will be delivered from several locations there will have to be arrangements for supervision, not necessarily continuous, at each delivery point. A credible budget must allow for these salaries as well as the associated statutory and other costs.

R&D budget   As mentioned above, a venture that does not maintain an R&D programme in line with those of others in its market is doomed to eventual eclipse. At the planning stage it is important to set out a realistic R&D budget, even if, in practice, it might be neglected for the first few years of the venture's existence. It will be easier to allocate funds to an R&D programme once they become available if this was forecast in the original plan, while venture investors might regard an attempt to start an R&D programme without such prior signalling of the entrepreneur's intentions as an illicit diversion of funds that should be returned to them.

General administration expense

A new venture will need a CEO and an internal venture will need a project manager; in either case they will need a salary, an appropriate package of benefits, budgetary allocations for the related statutory overheads and accommodation and secretarial and technical support. Entrepreneurs are often tempted to underpay themselves and call the gap 'sweat equity'; venture investors are reluctant to see too much 'sweat equity' in the mix, at least partly because they may have to replace the entrepreneur as CEO and the replacement will certainly not join a troubled venture for less than a fully competitive salary and package.

Any new venture with external shareholders will need someone to ensure that the accounts are properly maintained and the venture's cash position secured by timely issues of equity and raising of loans. A significant internal project in a corporation will also need someone to prepare progress and budget reports and authorise expenses. Whether their title is CFO or project secretary, they will need a salary package, budgetary allocations for the related statutory overheads and accommodation and secretarial and technical support. A plan that fails to include such a person may cause prospective venture investors to suspect that their money would not be treated with the proper respect.

In addition to such prominent positions, there will have to be a sufficient allocation for costs not specified elsewhere, including billing and collection, the personnel/HR function, legal services and legally required accounting services, rents and servicing costs for common areas in the head office and other such items.

Uncertainty

A working market model should produce three critical numbers for the financial projection: the marketing expense, the unit sales and the size of the user population. The financial model will in due course turn this into a set of forecasts covering profit and loss, asset values and cash flow. The main reason for a planner to produce these financial forecasts is to get the answer: yes or no. The most basic question the financial model sets out to address is: Do the prospective returns from this investment justify the associated risks?

There are two slightly different ways in which this question may be put into financial terms:

■ Does the risk-weighted net present value of the projected returns from this investment exceed the cost of it?
■ Does the prospective internal rate of return exceed the hurdle rate appropriate for this class of investment?

Each method has its advantages and, taken to the limit, the two methods converge in any case. The theory of investment under uncertain conditions is fairly new and the leading workers are Avinash Dixit and Robert Pindyck, whose papers and books on this subject have been appearing since 1989.[7] Their argument has been relegated to the mathematical appendix to this chapter, but in brief they demonstrate that it is possible to calculate an appropriate hurdle rate for a venture, given knowledge of the return expected from an alternative, riskless investment and the uncertainty associated with the specific venture. Their measurement of uncertainty can be summarised as being the standard deviation of the expected outcome per unit of time or, more colloquially, a variation from targets which will not be exceeded with a probability of five out of six (see Table 4.5 for typical hurdle rate values).

To take an example more or less directly from Dixit and Pindyck's (1994) book, a company considering opening up a new copper mine at a cost of $10 million could put the money instead into high quality securities paying 8 per cent per year. The historic uncertainty of the copper price is 25 per cent per year. If, at the current copper price, the mine could make a profit of $1 million per year into the indefinite future, this looks better than the bonds, but they show that, in practice, the miner would be unwise to invest until the prospective profits were at least $1.47 million per year. The 14.7 per cent return is the *hurdle rate* which investments of this class should be expected to exceed. In a Monte Carlo simulation of the effect of probable changes in the copper price, five out of six outcomes would be better than $800,000 per year, an 8 per cent return, if the mine was not opened until the expected return equalled or exceeded 14.7 per cent.

Table 4.5 **Hurdle rates**

Riskless, or lowest acceptable, rate	Project risk				
	20%	40%	60%	80%	100%
5%	9.3%	16.5%	27.1%	41.4%	59.6%
10%	15.6%	23.8%	35.2%	50.0%	68.5%
15%	21.6%	30.7%	42.7%	58.1%	77.1%
20%	27.4%	37.3%	50.0%	65.9%	85.3%
25%	33.1%	43.7%	57.0%	73.5%	93.3%

A second Dixit and Pindyck result allows a planner to adjust the risk-adjusted hurdle rate when the profit stream is expected to run dry after some number of periods. If the ore body in the mine above had an expected life of ten years, the expectation of failure is one failure per ten years or 10 per cent per year and this should be added to the hurdle rate: in this case, the mine should not proceed until the prospective profits were $2.47 million. Again, uncertainty demands a higher return: if the mine was known to have reserves that would last *exactly* ten years, the appropriate risk-adjusted rate of return would be rather lower and the profit stream would be acceptable at $1.71 million per year. The effect of discounting over time means that the risk of the mine running out early has greater weight than the possibility of the profit stream continuing past the expected life of the mine.

Example 1

An entrepreneur is considering a new retail concept in fashion clothing. The minimum acceptable return is 10 per cent. No profit is expected in the first year, a profit of $500,000 per year is then expected until competitors imitate the format and thereafter a profit of $200,000 per year until the concept is buried by a superior one. The entrepreneur estimates that competitors will enter at the end of year three and a superior concept will appear at the end of year ten.

Table 4.6 **Reducing mulitple sources of uncertainty to a single number**

Source of variation	1:6 worst case (std deviation)	Variance (square of of std deviation)
Economy may go into recession	–5%	0.25%
Fashion trade liable to significant swings	–25%	6.25%
Range of outcomes for marketing campaign	–10%	1.00%
	Total variance	7.5%
	Estimated risk	27.3%

The risk is the square root of the variance, and is estimated, as shown in Table 4.6, to be about 27 per cent per year.

The expected profits can be divided into two phases:

a from year two for about two years: $300,000
b from year two for about nine years: $200,000.

From Table 4.5 it appears that a reasonable hurdle rate for this venture is 20 per cent. Since phase *a* is expected to last two years, the adjusted discount rate becomes 70 per cent and the value, as at the start of year two, is about $430,000. Phase *b* is expected to last nine years, the adjusted discount rate is therefore 31 per cent and the value at the start of year two is about $640,000. At the start of year two the venture will be worth about $1,070,000. Discounting it back one year produces a project value of about $890,000.

The maximum day one amount that a rational investor would subscribe for 100 per cent of the equity in the business is $890,000, even though the business is expected to return $2.4 million over the ten years it is expected to operate. A term certain annuity for ten years at 10 per cent would pay a little over half this amount.

Example 2

An entrepreneur has developed a concept for a novel consumer durable and has borne all the costs of getting it ready for the market. He has completed a business plan showing that the product will break even by the end of the second year on the market, while profits will rise to a steady £2 million per year from year four until his patent expires after 12 years, after which competition will reduce the profit stream to £1 million per year. He asks an intelligent private investor for £1 million to finance initial production and advertising.

The private investor would rather keep his money under the pillow than earn less than 10 per cent, which is the rate that he regards as 'riskless'. He recalls that new ventures such as this have a 1:6 expectation of total failure and the uncertainty of the prediction is therefore 100 per cent. The appropriate hurdle rate from Table 4.6 is about 69 per cent and the present value of the promised profit stream is only £690,000. The investor shows the entrepreneur to the door.

On the Robert the Bruce principle, the entrepreneur raises a small sum of money from his friends and relatives, postpones his nationwide rollout and markets his product through a regional network marketing group, where sales exceed expectations. After two years he returns to the investor, shows him the results of this market trial and once more asks for £1 million for a national retail rollout. The investor believes that the one-in-six worst-case result for a venture with two years of trading history is a 60 per cent shortfall against expectations and an appropriate hurdle rate from Table 4.5 is 35 per cent. On this basis the profit stream is worth about £2.35 million. After some haggling, the investor offers the £1 million in return for 45 per cent of the equity in the business.

Asset classes

Different assets are affected by uncertainty in different ways. Completely liquid assets, cash and deposits of up to 90 days maturity in major banks, are conventionally treated as riskless. Less liquid assets are subject to greater uncertainty and their use must be rewarded with a higher rate of return. Risk-weighting as calculated using the Dixit–Pindyck equations is only appropriate for that part of each investment that will be lost if a business fails. Marketing and product development expenses create intangible assets that are only valuable as part of a continuing business and therefore money under these headings is wholly at risk. Buildings and land, on the other hand, will usually have a continuing value, although a sale by the receivers may not get back all the money spent on them. Plant and machinery will also have some value in bankruptcy, but if it is industry-specific, not very much: if a business failed because of low demand and prices for its product, no rational investor will want to pay very much money for plant and equipment which is only useful for someone wanting to enter that industry in spite of the low demand and inadequate prices.[8]

To be super-logical, an entrepreneurial business plan should analyse all the expense items in asset classes: those that are lost with the business, those that will have only a low value on disposal and those that may have a substantial value on disposal, and use a separate risk-weighting calculation and discount rate for each. In practice, firms and investors use a single discount rate to evaluate the cash flow from a proposed project, implicitly placing a very low salvage value on any assets. From the view of an investor in a new enterprise, this is quite reasonable: very few firms are wound up at the point where all creditors can still be paid from liquid assets and so the hard assets will be sold to satisfy the creditors. It is possible that a firm that was so well managed that it could anticipate failure in this way would not actually fail.

New entrepreneurial businesses are wise to lease as many of their assets as possible, even though this means sharing the eventual profits with lease financiers. By leasing these assets the business minimises its upfront cash requirements and improves the risk-weighted return for the investors: the returns can be higher even though the profits are lower.

Corporations are not usually in the position of investors in a new venture, in that the assets can, in general, be put to use elsewhere in the corporation even if the venture itself is terminated. Those that are not required can be disposed of in an orderly manner, and even the marketing and product development expense may not prove to have been totally wasted. The Apple Lisa was, by any measure, a failure as a product, but its software technology was reused for the Apple Macintosh and the marketing and sales effort devoted to it built public awareness of Apple as an exciting company, an effect that may have had a positive effect on early Apple Macintosh sales.

Even assets like cars and computers, which receivers struggle to give away when winding up a bankrupt firm, retain most of their value inside a corporation. The economist George Akerlof (1970) described the difficulties experienced by receivers as a 'lemons problem': once the firm has ceased to trade there is no one who knows which of the cars or computers were properly looked after and which weren't, and they are sold at prices which assume that they are all no better than the worst of them.

Corporations which do not intend to put up artificial barriers to innovation should be careful not to lump in the purchase of reuseable assets with the sunk marketing, development and tooling costs when evaluating proposals, since this would involve an exaggerated risk-weighting. Either the corporation should set up a notional leasing arrangement for the reusable assets or it should use a separate asset class for them.

Example 3   A financial services company decides to offer a new service after a successful pilot. The major cash outlays and the relevant salvage value will be as shown in Table 4.7.

Table 4.7 **Sunk and recoverable investment**

Outlay	Cash	Salvage
Working capital including launch promotion	$2.5 million	nil
Computer programming	$3.0 million	nil
Computing equipment	$1.5 million	$800,000
Premises	$2.0 million	$1.5 million
Total	$9.0 million	$2.3 million

Their planners estimate that there will be a zero net profit in year one, $1 million in year two, $3 million in year three and $5 million in year four and subsequent years. The estimated variance is 40 per cent, based upon 20 per cent observed variation in demand for similar services over the economic cycle and 20 per cent specific project risk based upon analysis of the pilot project results; that is, the uncertainty is about 63 per cent. They can earn 5 per cent on their high-grade bond portfolio. The appropriate hurdle rate from Table 4.6 is about 30 per cent.

The present value of the $9 million cash investment into the project is $8.2 million, which seems to be inadequate, but the at-risk expenditure is $6.7 million, and on that basis the project should proceed: its risk-weighted present value *exceeds* the required at-risk investment.

Estimating uncertainty

The variance of an estimate is the measure of our ignorance about the future. The square root of the variance, or standard deviation, can be thought of as defining a comfort zone: the outcome of an 'experiment' will, most of the time, be no further away from the expected value than one standard deviation. Roughly, four times out of six the result will be no more than one standard deviation away from the expected value, once in every six tries it will be less than the expectation minus the standard deviation, and one in every six tries it will be greater than the expectation plus the standard deviation. For example, if we observed 16 consecutive spins of a roulette wheel, we would expect black to appear 8 times and red to appear 8 times; but since the standard deviation in this case is about two, we should not be surprised to see as many as 10 reds or 10 blacks appear. The longer that we observed the wheel, the tighter, relatively, we should expect the balance to be. In 64 consecutive spins, we could have no reasonable doubts about the wheel if the number of reds was between 28 and 36, we should view fewer than 24 reds or blacks with surprise and fewer than 20 with suspicion.

Investment in a new venture is a matter of uncertainty, not simply risk and, strictly speaking, variance is a meaningless concept when applied to an uncertain outcome. We are able to rely on concepts such as variance by assuming, along with Dixit (1992), that the type of uncertainty that can be modelled by a geometric random walk is reasonably typical of business ventures. The variance used in the Dixit–Pindyck formulae is not the uncertainty associated with the final outcome, but the uncertainty associated with a single year (or period, when the discount interval is other than a year).

A business that puts a product on the market makes certain assumptions about the size of the potential market, the fraction of the potential users who will give the product a trial after a certain amount of advertising and at a particular price, and the fraction of those who give the product a trial who will become regular users and/or recommenders of it. Each period the product is on the market can be considered a statistical test of these assumptions. The standard deviation of these test results declines with the square root of the number of trials: if the number of sales in the first period was ten and the standard deviation was 80 per cent, this means that the plan should not be treated as faulty if it had projected anywhere from 2 to 18 sales in the first period. After four periods the standard deviation is down to 40 per cent, and if the cumulative sales forecast was within plus or minus 40 per cent of the actual, the plan should not be considered discredited.

If:

n is the total number of sales reported over a number of consecutive periods and

M is the total number of potential sales in the market then (4.1) produces the standard deviation of n where n is the best estimator of the 'true' or 'share of mind' sales the supplier gained.

$$\sigma_n = \frac{\sqrt{(n+1)\left(1-\dfrac{n}{M}\right)}}{n} \tag{4.1}$$

For example, the product manager of a firm selling a new, infrequently purchased product estimated the total market size at 10,000 users and in its first six months the product achieves 100 sales; σ_n equals 10.0 per cent and as long as the plan predicted something between 90 and 110 sales at this stage, there is no reason to doubt the validity of the original plan forecasts. If, as happens all too often during the launch of a new product, the actual result is well outside the implicit range predicted by the forecast sales and their standard deviation, the marketing model should be adjusted until it produces a result that fits the data: there should be no attempt made to fit the world to the model.

At the planning stage, there are no real sales at all from which to estimate σ. The planner must rely on his experience, supplemented by such advice as they can get and such research and interviewing that they can carry out. In principle, a quite small sample of the population can produce useful results; in practice, it is very hard to estimate the repurchasing and recommendation behaviour of potential users from interviews and experiments. Advertising response can be estimated and is, routinely, by major advertisers and their agencies, but good advertising, of itself, does not guarantee the success of a new product.

It is possible to estimate σ_0 (the standard deviation at time zero) with great precision, if with rather less realism, by setting each of the key parameters in the market model to their one-in-six worst case, observing the shortfall in the predicted sales revenue, expressing each shortfall as a percentage and finally taking the square root of the sum of the squares of the percentage shortfalls. A simpler, and generally satisfactory estimate of σ_0 is 100 per cent (or for true pessimists, 150 per cent). In real life, each month's sales returns provide information that reduces σ and, as long as the sales themselves are meeting expectations, justifies a continued investment in product marketing.

The plan should anticipate real life and, in particular, allow for review points at which the plan can be revised or abandoned if reality is not coming up to expectations. The critical marketing parameters (see above for a fuller description) are going to be one or more of:

- the advertising response rate
- the trial to user conversion rate
- the churn rate
- the repurchase frequency
- the effective recommendation
- the exit rate.

The uncertainty about the planner's estimate for each of these parameters will be reduced with actual marketing experience, but not all the 'real' parameters emerge together. The advertising response rate can be determined almost as soon as the first buying cycle is complete. The rate at which the other parameters emerge depends on the expected repurchase frequency. For a frequently repurchased product, the conversion rate and the repurchase frequency will become apparent within a couple of months of the product's introduction, and the churn rate, if it is going to be significant, will emerge within six months. For an infrequently repurchased, durable-type product, the most critical market parameter is the effective recommendation rate, which is hard to estimate without two years of sales history or a marketing research budget that permits relatively intensive customer tracking.

Quick checks on viability

Proposals for independent ventures will need more complete pro forma accounts and the collection of data for these and their ultimate preparation is described in Chapter 10. The quick P&L may still be used to give a basic check on the venture's viability, and if the report is negative, the effort of completing an organisation and process design, preparing a complete set of pro forma accounts and writing a full business plan may be applied to some more hopeful purpose.

■ If the per period EBDIT is not positive by the end of the second trading year, and the cumulative EBDIT is not positive by the end of the fourth year, it may be impossible to attract finance for a new venture on any terms. Most financiers would be looking for quicker returns than this.

■ The EBDIT, as its name implies, must be adequate to cover all the financing and taxation costs of the business and provide a return to investors, and net losses will generally be unacceptable by the end of the third trading year if not earlier. The third year EBDIT therefore can be used, by dividing it by an appropriate rate of return, to estimate the total amount of capital the venture can support. The rate of return needed, including depreciation/amortisation, is unlikely to be less than 20 per cent and so each $1 million of year three EBDIT cannot support more than $5 million of assets and can generally only support less.

These requirements may be relaxed somewhat in a corporate environment, although public companies in the English-speaking world have to be very careful not to frighten the share market analysts and institutional investors by committing to long-term strategies. In the early 1980s the Pilkington Group was subjected to a share market raid with the sole, and well-publicised, motive of forcing the Pilkington management to spend less on R&D, declare higher current profits and pay larger dividends or other forms or shareholder reward. The group was able to fight off the raid and maintain most of its R&D programme, but the lesson was not lost on the management of other British firms with large R&D budgets. More recently, the Boeing Commercial Aircraft Company appears to have deliberately surrendered leadership in the large passenger aircraft market to Airbus Industrie because Boeing's managers did not believe that the share market would tolerate an investment programme costly and sustained enough to produce a competitive successor to the 747 range.

The AAGM

A second, simple way to estimate the viability of a proposal starts from the annual available gross margin (AAGM). The planner will have an estimate of the total number of customers (actual and potential) in the market, the average annual expenditure of each actual customer and the average gross margin earned per year per actual customer. The AAGM is the gross margin that would be earned in the impossible but delightful situation where every potential customer became an actual one. It can be used to estimate the maximum amount of capital a prudent investor would commit to a given project when the product is new and the market untested. Table 4.8 sets out the relevant ratios.

Table 4. 8 **First stage financial screening**

Product security	Launch day value (fraction of AAGM)
The product is an unbreakable, unavoidable and indefinite monopoly	14%
Competitive entry will not occur for at least four years from the full launch (that is, after market testing completed)	7%
Otherwise	4%

Example: A modest proposal declined

An entrepreneur considers preparing a superior study guide for students taking the Scottish Higher Still examinations. He determines that his potential market consists of 40,000 students per year. The students are used to paying £15 or so for a textbook; he finds that the variable costs of book production are about £12 including the reseller margin. He computes the AAGM: 40,000 x (£15 − £12) = £120,000. He notes that the market is an easy one to enter and so the last line from Table 4.8 is appropriate: the launch day present value is £120,000 x 4% = £4800. He decides not to resign from his job to write and publish the book.

Launch strategy

The launch of a new product takes place under circumstances of considerable uncertainty and the appropriate planning discount rate is high; this in turn limits the amount a prudent planner will commit to the launch of a new product. After the product has been on the market for a reasonable length of time, the uncertainty will be greatly reduced and the appropriate discount rate will be much lower. If the market has responded more or less as expected, this suggests that the planner's estimate of the key market parameters was close to their actual values and a much more vigorous promotional effort may be appropriate.

For a sound product, with a reasonable rate of trial to conversion, a low churn rate and a reasonable level of recommendations, marketing operations become cash positive very rapidly and are profitable almost from the launch. Even when a high discount rate is applied, the optimal strategy when marketing costs alone are considered may involve very heavy launch expenditure, sometimes even pre-empting the 'major' launch. The best strategy for any particular product will depend on the non-marketing, scale-related fixed costs.

When scale-related fixed costs, such as leasing equipment and premises and recruiting and training production, delivery and service staff are substantial, the best strategy may involve a low-key pilot launch followed by a major one once the market response parameters have been determined to a reasonable level of accuracy and the market has shown its readiness to accept the new product. The time needed to gain confidence in the market response parameters can be as little as three months for a frequently repurchased consumer product to as much as two years for a durable one. Every innovation is unique by definition and so we cannot set down any immutable rules, but a plan that involved a test market expenditure of less than a tenth of a per cent of the AAGM (see above), to be followed, if the test was successful, by a major launch spending 5 per cent or more of the AAGM would not seem unreasonable to us.

When scale-related fixed costs are very low, the plan tends to become a pure marketing one and the best strategy may involve a single launch with a budget of 5 or more per cent of the total available gross margin. For instance, magazine publishers can subcontract their printing and distribution, so once they have covered their scale-independent editorial and composing costs they have few other fixed commitments: the single launch strategy is appropriate in their circumstances.

Amstrad became a major PC supplier in the UK and Australia over the years 1986–92; its product supply strategy was to subcontract manufacturing, transport and distribution, eliminating scale-related fixed costs. Amstrad launched each new package with an advertising blitz and promptly abandoned any that disappointed. Amstrad's PC business was eventually eclipsed by pressure from two directions: rival marketing companies and retail concepts eroded its market share, and its suppliers, firms such as Acer and Samsung, began to develop their own distribution channels and promote their own brands and became less ready to concede large margins to a pure marketer.

Firms that, for one reason or another, can't or won't pursue the Amstrad route and intend to develop more than a marketing shell may find themselves in a stalemate: once the market acceptability of their product is proved, it appears likely to be extremely profitable, but the cost of the capital equipment needed to make test market quantities of their product is such that they can't justify a market trial to prove market acceptability.

CHECKPOINT

At this point in the planning process, the planner should have a good estimate of:

■ the most probable sales and revenue per period
■ a reasonable estimate of the gross margin and the directly related marketing expense per period
■ a good estimate of the fixed and variable costs that will be incurred in supplying the goods and delivering the services that make up the sales and revenue forecast and hence
■ a soundly based estimate of the per period earnings before depreciation, interest and tax (EBDIT) for a number of years into the future.

The EBDIT can be turned into an estimate of the maximum capital commitment that the venture could support, using an appropriately risk-weighted discount rate, and if this is not greater than the minimum value of the assets (including working capital, which must necessarily exceed the proposed budget for the launch promotion) needed to start the business, there is no point in making the attempt. This value will be sensitive to several of the model assumptions and often an apparently unviable project can be shown to be viable by modifying its plan: a common error is to underprovide for promotion and therefore place an artificial limit on the venture's growth rate; if the product is going to be a success, then marketing expenditure is returned, in the form of increased gross margins, quite rapidly. Other model parameters are not under the control of the entrepreneur in the real world, even though they can be altered in the model in seconds. If the original estimates for factors such as the cost of securing a trial, the internal influence and the trial success rate were soundly based, changing them may make the plan look better but such games will certainly not improve the outcome of the eventual project.

The best of planners will overlook more possible problems than opportunities; 'cooking' the parameters to make a doubtful project look viable increases the risk of ultimate failure by relaxing the search for a truly viable way of bringing the product to market. There should be no shame attached to the planner who, after a conscientious effort to develop a viable plan, aborts a project. Very great blame should fall on a planner who bends the data to make an unviable project look attractive and encourages people to commit time and money to a probable failure.

Exercises

1 Review the process by which a potential customer becomes an actual one; apply this to the project on which you are basing your current business plan or, if you are not working on a business plan, to a number of products used in your household.

2 Re-establish the basic feasibility (scientific, economic, technical, marketing, legality) for a number of possible products your proposed venture could launch.

3 Prepare a revenue forecast and marketing budget for the most promising of your ideas as screened in answer to question 2. Start by estimating the key marketing parameters; write them down. For each parameter, work out how you would test your assumption before launching your venture and verify or adjust it after the venture is launched.

4 Securing trial is relatively simple, if expensive; but for a venture to succeed it must convert a substantial fraction of its trial users into customers and keep them in that state. Write down the expected ratio of trials to customer creations for some of your more

promising ideas and your expected rate of customer churn. How do you justify these assumptions? How do your assumptions compare with the actual performance of comparable products sold in similar markets?

5 Identify a branded product that you or your household used to purchase regularly but now no longer purchase. Estimate your value as a customer to the supplier of this product. Set out the reasons why you are no longer a customer: were they under the supplier's control? If so, how could the supplier have kept your custom? Does this experience have any relevance to any venture you may be considering, as a student exercise or for any other purpose?

6 If you have not already done so, transcribe or recalculate the forecast prepared in answer to question 3 to a spreadsheet and develop a quick P&L forecast from it.

7 Your spreadsheet will obviously cover a finite number of years, but if the EBDIT is positive at the end of your last forecast period, the business will have a marketable value of the order of five times the EBDIT. Estimate the present value of the EBDIT row at the prevailing business loan interest rate using the NPV spreadsheet function. (The leading banks regularly publish their lending rates in the financial pages of the broadsheet newspapers and on their Internet sites.)

8 Estimate the uncertainty associated with your venture and, using this figure and the current business loan interest rate, use Table 4.5 to estimate an appropriate hurdle rate; use this value to re-estimate the present value of the EBDIT row on your quick P&L forecast. Does this change your view of the viability of the venture?

Mathematical appendix

The information in this appendix involves relatively advanced mathematics. It will be useful to those who wish to write their own forecasting models or study the operation of forecasting models; but readers who have no such interests, and are prepared to use an existing revenue-forecasting model or methodology for their revenue projections, should skip to the next chapter.

Diffusion models

It is possible to prepare models that have considerable explanatory power over the whole period from the time of a new product's introduction to its share of a relatively mature competitive market. Midgley (1977) was one of the earlier workers in this field; for a more recent work in this area see Cooper and Nakanishi ([1988] 1999). The models described below are best seen as simplified versions of the complicated and well-validated models used by advanced researchers. They achieve what we regard as an adequate balance between formal accuracy and user simplicity, but they should not be considered as the 'last word' in this area or anything approaching it. It is always important to remember that understanding the theory does not necessarily mean being able to put it into practice successfully. The officers of the *Titanic* understood Archimedes' laws perfectly well, but this did not enable them to save their ship after it struck an iceberg.

Mahajan et al. (1990) provided a definitive account of the development of diffusion models, at least from an American perspective. The basic socio-contagion model goes back to the eighteenth century with the development of the logistic or epidemic equation:

$$\frac{dx}{dt} = x(1 - x); \ 0 > x > 1.$$

Integrating the logistic equation produces the characteristic S curve generally associated with the product life cycle. The basic logistic curve is not very useful for revenue forecasting because its zero point is a minus infinity at which time

$$\frac{dx}{dt} = 0:$$

something additional is needed to start an actual product life cycle. Frank Bass

(1969) filled in the gap by proposing a modified logistic curve with an additional parameter (4.2):

$$dm = \left[p(M - m) + qm\left(1 - \frac{m}{M} \right) \right] dt \qquad (4.2)$$

In (4.2) M is the size of the potential market, m is the number of adopters at time t and p and q are the coefficients of innovation and imitation respectively, Mahajan et al. (1990) argue that these coefficients are more properly described as the coefficients of internal and external influence respectively and we prefer this usage.

$$\text{At } t = 0, \frac{dm}{dt} = pM$$

this model has no starting problems. While the Bass model is a substantial advance on the simple logistic curve, it has its limitations: it is a model of adoption, not sales; it models the entire market, not any individual participant; and there are logical and practical objections to treating p as a constant through the product life cycle.

Midgley (1977) made an effort to resolve these issues: a somewhat simplified version of his model is depicted in Figure 4.3. Using the subscript 1 for 'us' and 2 for 'them' and dropping out some unlikely pathways leads to (4.3). In this version of the model p and q retain the use assigned by Bass; but two new parameters appear, c and s. c is the rate of churn, the rate at which customers revert to being potential customers, and s is the trial success rate. Since not all trials create a customer, but each trial represents a sale, the number of trials is estimated by x. We do not know whether (4.3) can be integrated analytically; but solving it numerically is not difficult.

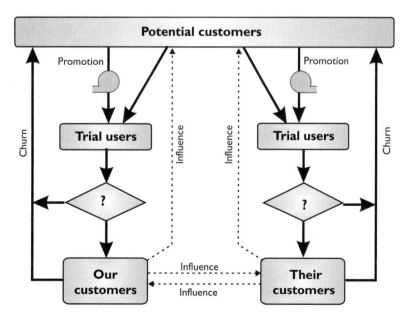

Figure 4.3   **Midgley's model (simplified)**

$$dm_1 = \left\{ p_1 s_1 (M - m_1 - m_2) + q_1 s_1 m_1 \left(1 - \frac{m_1 + m_2}{M}\right) - c_1 m_1 \right\} dt$$

$$dm_2 = \left\{ p_2 s_2 (M - m_1 - m_2) + q_2 s_2 m_2 \left(1 - \frac{m_1 + m_2}{M}\right) - c_2 m_2 \right\} dt$$

$$dx_1 = \left\{ p_1 (M - m_1 - m_2) + q_1 m_1 \left(1 - \frac{m_1 + m_2}{M}\right) \right\} dt$$

$$dx_2 = \left\{ p_2 (M - m_1 - m_2) + q_2 m_2 \left(1 - \frac{m_1 + m_2}{M}\right) \right\} dt$$

$$(4.3)$$

Figure 4.3 and (4.3), with nine parameters that need to be estimated, have more theoretical than practical appeal to entrepreneurs contemplating the introduction of a new product. Major consumer products companies, who have the resources needed to measure and track the relevant parameters, could use models of this level of sophistication in their product planning and while tracking the launch of new products.

Figure 4.2 is reproduced from Legge (2002) and shows a simplified version of Midgley's 1977 model (or a more sophisticated version of Bass's 1969 one). It differs from Bass's in explicitly linking trial and adoption to promotional effort, and by introducing churn and trial failure and from Midgley's model by omitting competitors and the distinction between pre-aware and aware potential users. Leaving out competitors is a reasonable simplification for a new product where early sales, by the modelled venture or any others, will only reach a fraction of the potential users. With a careful definition of the market so as to exclude 'rusted on' users of competing product, this model can still produce relatively useful results in an established market. Legge (2002) argues that Bass's model is oversimplified and that Midgley's, while formally complete, has too many parameters to be a generally useful predictive tool. The equations (4.4) reflect Figure 4.2 and while they apply strictly to an entire market (which could be supplied by a single early mover), they can be useful for new entrants to a new and largely unexploited market or entrants to a market where there is significant churn and modest or no internal influence.

Initial purchase is treated in this model as a response to one of two stimuli: there are the externally influenced adopters, responding to advertising, promotion and sales effort, and there are those who join as the result of influence from earlier adopters. Those who try the product may be insufficiently satisfied to become regular users and revert to being potential customers; similarly, existing customers may become dissatisfied or leave the market and they, too, return to the pool of potential customers.

$$dm = \left\{ ps(M - m) + qsm \left(1 - \frac{m}{m}\right) - cm \right\} dt$$

$$dx = \left\{ p(M - m) + qm \left(1 - \frac{m}{M}\right) \right\} dt$$

$$p = 1 = \exp\left(-\frac{MEXP}{M \times CST}\right)$$

$$(4.4)$$

Equation (4.4) can be integrated analytically if somewhat messily – p should be treated as a constant for each integration interval and recalculated for different intervals. *MEXP* is the rate at which sales and promotional effort is being expended in support of the product and *CST* is the cost of securing trial, as discussed in the main body of the text.

Management headcount

If the span of control is constant across a model organisation, the number of management layers required is the logarithm whose base equals the span of control rounded up to the next integer. Obviously only a fraction of the possible front line headcounts can be managed with every position at every level filled and responsible for exactly 'span of control' subordinates, and this is the number used to generate Table 4.2 and Table 4.3. Logarithms to the bases *e* and ten are found on most calculators and spreadsheet packages (usually called 'ln' and 'log' or 'log 10' respectively); to compute the logarithm to a base other than *e* or ten, simply divide the log to the base *e* or ten of the number of interest by the log to the base *e* or ten of the base required. For example,

$$\log_7 100 = \frac{\log_{10} 100}{\log_{10} 7} \approx 2.36$$ computes the logarithm to the base 7 of a hundred.

The Dixit–Pindyck equations

The level of demand in any given market tends to follow a 'random walk' such that each period's demand can be analysed into three components: a base level, a trend (up, down or flat) and a random component, again up or down. If demand takes a large fall (purely by chance) it may take some time before it ever comes back to its previous level or trend; similarly, if it takes a large jump up, it may remain above its average or trend level for some time. At any given time no one knows whether the next move in demand will be up or down:

- If an investment is made just before demand drops, it is relatively unlikely that the project will achieve the level of returns that had been planned for on the assumption of constant, or at least definite, future returns. If the investment had been a borderline case, and demand did drop, the investor will be disappointed, at least, with the eventual returns failing to meet his minimum expectations.
- If there were ways to buy insurance against the risk of markets turning down (as there are, in the form of traded options, commodity futures, currency hedges, and derivatives plain and fancy in financial markets), a prudent investor would have paid an insurance premium to guard against loss, and the cost of the investment should be considered as the sum of the cash required by the project and the cost of the insurance premium (or the price of an appropriate portfolio of derivatives, futures and options). Since this is larger than the cost of the investment alone, the true expected returns are lower than the apparent ones.
- A prudent investor will therefore only invest in projects where the expected return is sufficiently high to justify both the cost of the investment and an appropriate insurance premium.

Dixit (1992) showed how these assumptions may be incorporated into a model that can be described as a differential equation, the relevant solutions of which are equations (4.5) and (4.6), the hurdle rates which a rational investor would use to value an uncertain opportunity. Dixit and Pindyck (1994) extend the valuation methodology to more complex scenarios; while theoretically very interesting and potentially useful for managing large-scale corporate investments in a limited number of industries, few entrepreneurs would find the effort of mastering this advanced textbook and applying its conclusions to their plans a cost-effective use of their time.

Concepts and variables

ρ (rho) is the *riskless* rate of return per period, the return to an investor in gilt-edged government guaranteed stock: obviously, no one would wish to put their money into anything that earned less than this.

ρ' (rho prime) is the *risk-adjusted* rate of return per period, the lowest return acceptable to a rational investor with access to riskless investments returning ρ when offered an opportunity whose (perpetual) profit stream has a variance of σ^2 in a market with a long-term growth expectation of μ.

μ (mu) is the trend growth rate per period, either of the general economy or some other indicator that will result in an effortless increase in the profit stream.

σ^2 (sigma squared) is the normalised variance of the detrended expected profit stream per period. (Note: the variance is the square of the standard deviation.)

β (beta) is a Dixit and Pindyck parameter that must on no account be confused with beta in the capital asset pricing model.

Equations (4.5) and (4.6) show how ρ' can be derived from the other parameters:

$$\beta = \frac{\sigma^2 - 2\mu + \sqrt{\left(\sigma^2 - 2\mu\right)^2 + 8\rho\sigma^2}}{2\sigma^2} \tag{4.5}$$

$$\rho' = \left(\rho - \mu\right)\frac{\beta}{\beta - 1} + \mu \tag{4.6}$$

ρ' is the minimum acceptable rate for a perpetual but variable income stream; if:

λ (lambda) is the expected length of time the income stream will flow

ρ'' (rho double prime) is a discount rate that can then be used as if the revenue stream was actually perpetual.

Equation (4.7) allows the discount rate ρ' to be adjusted when the revenue stream has an expected (not a certain) time before the profit flow will cease, and the expectations are in a Poisson distribution:

$$\rho'' = \rho' + \frac{1}{\lambda} \tag{4.7}$$

Notes

1   Compass Airlines Ltd started operations in Australia in late 1991, following deregulation of the domestic airline market, and failed after approximately a year. A couple of years later Southern Cross Airlines Ltd bought the name 'Compass' from the receivers and operated a discount airline from August 1992 to March 1993 before it, too, failed and was liquidated. The Branson organization launched a discount carrier in Australia

under the name 'Virgin Blue' in August 2000; this carrier is still operating at the time of writing, but its entry led to the demise of the established full-service airline Ansett Australia which appointed an administrator in September 2001 and ceased operations in March 2002.

2   Strictly speaking, sails form a catenoidal shape, but Utzon did not seek this level of precision; his winning entry in the Opera House design competition used freehand sketches of the proposed roof shells.

3   Some of the books and papers consulted in developing the marketing models used here are: Bass (1969); Midgley (1977); Dodson and Muller (1978); Foxall (1988); Dockner and Jorgenson (1988); Mahajan et al. (1990); and Bass et al. (1994).

4   The most cited English translation of Plato's *Republic* is Cornford (1966).

5   See, for example, Waldrop (1992) or Coveney and Highfield (1995). Both these works provide a reasonable, accessible overview of recent developments in the field. Rosser (1991) provides a reasonable economist's overview of this area.

6   EBDIT = earnings before depreciation, interest and taxation.

7   The definitive text at this stage in the development of the theory of investment under uncertainty is Dixit and Pindyck (1994).

8   Some very successful entrepreneurs have got their start by exploiting the dynamics of bankruptcy: the receivers are under pressure to sell as quickly as possible, so may accept offers that amount to little more than scrap value for modern equipment in good condition. Operating with such a low asset cost base, such entrepreneurs may be able to operate profitably at times when their competitors, who paid full value for their productive assets, are struggling to meet their finance costs and report significant losses after depreciation.

5

Creating the business model

- The previous chapter covered the issues determining the fundamental viability of a concept, this chapter is therefore relevant to concepts which are both technically feasible and where there appears to be a market of sufficient size to justify a significant investment.

- 'Might' is not 'will'; many good concepts have been destroyed by poor execution. In this chapter we will discuss how to design an enterprise capable of turning a feasible innovative concept into a successful innovation.

Practical planning

A business plan is a model of a world the entrepreneur hopes to make real and, in particular, a world including the entrepreneur's new enterprise. The fully developed plan will have an organisational design as described below, a set of pro forma accounts as described in Chapter 10 and a number of other sections as described in Chapter 11. These describe the complete plan, but there are a number of important decisions to be made before the final plan can be drafted.

Before you can complete the organisational design you will have to resolve the following issues:

- the new enterprise will need a strategy, a word picture of where the enterprise and the entrepreneurs want to be in the future (or for a venture launched within a corporation, a persuasive explanation of how the proposed enterprise will support the established corporate strategy)

- the new enterprise will need an organisation, a number of people sharing the tasks in some systematic way

- the new enterprise will need some assets in order to commence operations and, as the business develops, it will create and acquire more of them

- the new enterprise will create value by some process, the core activity of the new business.

This chapter deals with the design of the value-adding process and the creation of valuable products which we defined and then valued in Chapter 4 and will protect in Chapter 7.

Fundamentals of strategy

Behaviour and opportunity

Strategy is built on two foundations: where you are now and where you want to get. Obviously a strategy without an objective is meaningless – 'if you don't know where you're going, any road will take you there' – but a strategy that ignores its starting point is equally invalid.

One useful way to characterise strategies has emerged from studies of evolution and evolutionary economics and is characterised by Andersen (1999) as the distinction between r-strategy and K-strategy. Andersen starts with the equation of the simple iterated logistic curve, where x grows from marginally greater than zero towards K, with an initial growth rate of r.[1] When x is small, the growth rate[2] will be approximately r, but as the number of iterations rises and x increases, growth will slow until, when x approaches K, growth will approach zero. When this formula is plotted as a graph (as in Figure 3.2) it will show a characteristic S-shape with x rising from (almost) zero to (almost) K; if the growth rate is plotted, it will decline from r towards zero.

Evolutionary success is defined as reproductive success: when successive generations of a species are more numerous or at least not less numerous than their predecessor, they are described as being evolutionarily fit, while species whose numbers decline from generation to generation are less fit. When a new ecological niche emerges or a radically new species enters one, there will be no species ideally suited to exploit it, but there will be a lot of resources available; these conditions favour species that grow their range rapidly. After a sufficient lapse of time, which in evolution may be a million years or so, the new niche will have become saturated and the fittest species will be those that make the best use of the available resources. Rabbits, above all introduced species, did well in Australia because there were few predators or entrenched rabbit diseases and their ability to produce large litters several times a year led to an extraordinary explosion in their numbers.

There is a clear analogy with firms intending to exploit an innovation: if the market is new, potentially large and poorly serviced, the most successful firms will be those that grow most rapidly; in Andersen's term, those that pursue an r-strategy. Price and features are relatively unimportant in such a market. Since most potential buyers have nothing at all at present, any functional, safe product will satisfy them. Once such a market approaches saturation there will be few naive users and one firm's growth will come at the expense of others. Features and price will both become important and the successful firms will be those that make the best use of their resources by pursuing, in Andersen's terms, a K-strategy.

Sustaining a competitive advantage

A firm, by setting out a strategy, establishes some objectives with dates at various times in the future, but no firm can survive for long without some form of competitive advantage. The essence of an entrepreneurial plan is the creation, protection and development of the firm's sustainable competitive advantages.[3]

The fact that a competitive advantage is sustainable is no guarantee that it will, in fact, be sustained. Secrets leak out, patents expire and newer innovations let rivals break into previously secure markets. Firms that achieve superior performance will find their techniques and procedures imitated. At the same time, firms may suffer from competitive disadvantages that, if allowed to flourish, will offset the benefits of their advantages. New firms, in particular, suffer from a number of inevitable disadvantages: they are small, have no credit history and no market recognition; entrepreneurship would not be challenging if there were no problems to overcome.

Entrepreneurs planning new businesses around innovations have two clear advantages over all their established rivals: the entrepreneurs have their innovation and the rivals do not; and the entrepreneurs can design an organisation to maximise the competitive advantage their innovation offers, while their rivals are more or less saddled with their current organisation. The decisions an entrepreneur makes at this time about the firm's structure and its place in the final value chain cast long shadows; they are strategic, and while strategic freedom offers opportunities it also involves hazards.

Planning, as we will make clear in Chapter 6, focuses on one opportunity; it implements a strategy but it does not establish one. The strategic context, however, constrains the plan: obviously, the strategic approach chosen must be compatible with the current opportunity, but pursuit of the current opportunity should not be allowed to close off too many future possibilities.

Core competencies

The economist Edith Penrose first drew attention to the concept of a firm as a collection of competencies ([1959] 1995) and, in fairly sharp distinction from the majority of her profession, saw modest levels of organisational slack as a virtue that allowed time to pursue innovation. She saw, as many people don't, that a 'perfect' organisation with every person and asset 100 per cent occupied in productive activities is profoundly dysfunctional; such an organisation has no way of responding to environmental changes, whether threats or opportunities. She saw firms as organisations that can 'do things' but also as capable of learning to do 'new' things and improving the way that they performed established activities. While other economists tolerated her and management theorists and teachers profoundly respected her, her ideas became very widely disseminated by Prahalad and Hamel's article in the *Harvard Business Review* (1990).

Economists often have trouble with the idea of corporate competencies. Knowledge and skill clearly reside in individuals, while data, procedures and equipment can be replicated – what more can there be? In fact, relationships between individuals also carry knowledge, in that a team, accustomed to working together, can solve problems and complete activities that none of the members could have solved or completed on their own. Moreover, such a team comfortably outperforms a group of equally qualified strangers working together for the first time. As the football coach's cliché has it: 'A champion team will always beat a team of champions.' Economists may have trouble with this set of concepts because of the importance their education places on competition between individuals, with cooperation seen as competition's antithesis. As Adam Smith put it, 'People of the same trade seldom meet together, even for merriment and diversion, but the conversation ends in a conspiracy against the public, or in some contrivance to raise prices' ([1776] 1835: 54). The idea that cooperation could be socially valuable or commercially important is shocking to the well-educated economist.

Fair shares?

Americans are brought up with a view of leadership that recognises the added value that effective teamwork contributes to an organisation, but attributes an unreasonable proportion of this added value to the leader. To many Americans it is quite acceptable to pay the chief executive of a successful enterprise hundreds of times more than the pay of the average worker in that enterprise. This view may, however, be mistaken: gross income disparities do not improve team performances and may detract from them.

Defenders of large income disparities often point to the high incomes of some sporting stars; but huge disparities between the pay of members of the same sporting team are unusual. In the Australian football league there is a roughly ten to one limit on the difference in match payments between the highest paid star and the lowest paid rookie and when the Australian team won the Cricket World Cup in 2003

the prize money was divided equally between members of the touring party, with those players who were not selected for any match receiving the same as the most glamorous stars. English football league payments are less transparent than Australian ones, but examining the Manchester United plc annual report for 2001–02 reveals an average of 495 employees, of whom 66 were players, and a total wages bill of £70 million. If the non-players earned the English average wage of approximately £23,000, this would remove about £10 million from the pool, making the average player payment about £900,000. According to www.manchester.com (4 April 2003), the highest paid player got £2.6 million, just under three times the average. (Of course the top players of the time such as Keane and Beckham earned more from sponsorships than from their playing salaries, but even counting this income leaves the ratio between the best paid and the average player at less than twelve to one.)

Cooperation is, however, central to the development and maintenance of core competencies and so the prospective division of the rewards for success is a critical factor in the design of entrepreneurial organisations. The concept of 'fairness', while largely absent from economics, is very important to ordinary people. If an entrepreneur wishes to secure the cooperation of her employees to ensure the success of the enterprise, she must necessarily offer more than the minimum legal wage for their participation. Even a substantial increment or promised bonus will not bring commitment unless the offer is seen as 'fair'.[4] No reasonable employee or junior partner in an entrepreneurial venture expects the same level of rewards as the entrepreneur, but neither do they expect their contribution to be trivialised. This may not matter if the employee concerned is clearly outside the value chain: the commitment of the catering staff at a football club is a great deal less critical than that of the players; but in enterprises less stylised than the management of a professional sports team there can be significant hidden costs incurred in treating a subset of the employees as mere biological robots obeying their instructions, from whom nothing is expected beyond obedience and to whom nothing is owed beyond the legal minimum wage.

As a practical matter, an entrepreneur attempting to create an enterprise that can survive the onset of competition and the eventual obsolescence of its initial product lines needs to pay as much attention to the development of core competencies as to the protection of more formal forms of intellectual property. The competency- or resource-based view of an enterprise sees profits, and profitable growth opportunities, arising from excellence in task performance; Freeman and Soete, summarising the investigations of the science policy research unit of the University of Sussex (1997: 197–226), conclude that the one essential competence without which no enterprise can excel is the ability to understand the enterprise's current and potential customers. Competence at using or creating technology is ineffective unless allied to a deep understanding of user needs. This in turn leads to a need for an inclusive organisation: often the people who actually meet real users and learn about their problems are a long way from the centre of the organisation, and unless strong communication flows are encouraged in every direction, this information may never reach the people who could act on it.

News from the periphery

For some reason the [NEC Corporation's Kumamoto semiconductor] plant turned out a good many more defective chips than any other NEC facility. The factory manager and employees met daily to try to fix the problem. They took corrective action and tried novel solutions without success: they could not reduce the rejection rate below a certain point. Everyone was puzzled why only Kumamoto could not meet company-wide norms.

One day the heroine of this story was walking to work and stopped at the railroad crossing in front of the factory while a very long freight train passed. She felt the ground vibrating as the heavy cars rumbled by and suddenly it occurred to her that this shaking might be the culprit. Later, on the job, she felt no vibration. Nevertheless, thinking that perhaps the precision machinery might be affected, she told the foreman. Shortly after [the factory was protected by a vibration barrier and] the defect rate dropped sharply. The woman was only eighteen years old, but she took pride in her job and in NEC …

Ishihara (1991: 40)

A narrow economic view of an enterprise might see time spent coaching and effort spent on internal communications as a wasteful diversion from the proper pursuit of profit and, if only today's profits are concerned, this view is quite correct. Once longer term effects are considered and it is recognised that coaching and communication build an organisation's ability to sustain shocks and exploit opportunities, the fallacy of the narrow view becomes obvious. An economist might argue that long-serving employees earn more than new ones and so a cull of the older workers will improve the firm's financial performance by reducing wage costs. This has two longer term effects: the older workers take with them part of the structure of the corporate competencies, putting the whole fabric at risk; and those who escape the cull learn that their employer places a zero value on their loyalty and offer little loyalty or commitment in return. Building an enterprise takes time and restraint, and a willingness to accept that today's organisational slack is a key contributor to tomorrow's core competence.

A firm that understands its core competencies is better able to identify opportunities where its competencies will give it an advantage and avoid diversions into areas where others may outperform it. Hamel and Prahalad (1994) discuss the development and deployment of core competencies at some length. One example they use is Canon, whose initial expertise in optics and precision mechanics enabled it to broaden its camera range; the development of electronic metering and autofocus capabilities saw it develop competencies in the application of microelectronics which allowed it to move into video cameras, gaining expertise in electronic imaging; these new competencies saw Canon build market leadership positions in mid-scale photocopiers, laser printer engines and microelectronic production equipment among other things. Any field in which precision optics and mechanics, microelectronics and imaging are brought together is one in which Canon can play and win.

Failure to understand core competencies can lead to less happy consequences. ICL was formed as a British 'national champion' in 1968, determined to wrest leadership of the computer industry from the US in general and IBM in particular. At that time computers were large, slow and very expensive and software was given away to those who purchased the hardware. IBM, as industry dominator, had no commercial interest in improving the efficiency of its software, since more efficient software earned it no revenue and might even offer customers an alternative to upgrading their hardware. The British companies that were to be merged into ICL had lacked IBM's economies of scale and were unable to match IBM's prices for machines of equivalent instruction-level performance, and so were forced to bridge the gap by writing more efficient and capable software. The result was that ICL, at its birth, was endowed with a huge competitive advantage in software design and development, some patriotic fervour and little else. At a time when even simultaneous printing and program execution was impossible for most IBM customers, ICL offered a multiuser interactive system (George 3) and an outstanding base for real-time transaction processing (J/Driver), both with a combined hardware and software cost/performance advantage over the best equivalent IBM systems of a factor of two or more. Over the next 20 years ICL's development teams built on this advantage until its VME system, with a functional level that Microsoft's XP could not deliver for another 12 years and a level of intrinsic security that Microsoft conspicuously failed to deliver even then, could outperform IBM's price/performance on interactive and transaction processing tasks by a factor of three or more. On top of this, ICL's QB suite, first delivered in 1985, could slash the cost of developing transaction processing systems accessing extensive databases by a factor of ten.

From its foundation until the remnants were absorbed into Fujitsu 33 years later, ICL's strategy was dominated by what it wanted to be rather than what it was. From 1968 to 1981 it struggled to build its own hardware until, under pressure of near bankruptcy, it negotiated a technology collaboration agreement with Fujitsu. Between 1981 and 1983 ICL worked on its one true competence, combining its software expertise with Fujitsu's technology to produce the Series 39, but when the integration of ICL's software with Fujitsu's technology took a little longer than had been hoped for, ICL switched strategies again. From 1984 to 1995 ICL struggled to become a marketing organisation, adding products from a wide range of other also-rans to its catalogue and losing money on every sale of them while only the profits from the sales of Series 39 and its Fujitsu-powered successors kept the company solvent. From 1995 to its final extinction ICL tried to succeed as a services company and failed again. ICL's failures are clear enough in hindsight, but the lesson is a general one.

Core competencies are activities that a firm can do well, not just those it wishes it could do well.

Strategic intent and competitive advantage

To summarise the last few pages, the critical strategic choices an entrepreneur must make include identifying the core competencies that the enterprise will start with and those that it will create; and choosing between *r*-strategic behaviour, focusing on sales growth, and *K*-strategic behaviour, focusing on quality and efficiency. Only when these choices have been made can there be a reasonable chance of completing a relevant organisation design.

A competency is an internal property of an enterprise; a competitive advantage is its external manifestation. Such advantages can take a variety of forms; some examples are set out in Table 5.1.

Table 5.1 **The relationship between competencies and competitive advantages**

Competitive advantage	Related competencies
Exclusive control over some scarce resource, such as a rich mineral deposit	■ Finding and securing extraction rights to resources including negotiation with prospectors and governments ■ Efficient extraction and transport to market of resources ■ Effective marketing of output
Effective patent protection or other legal monopoly over the production of some widely demanded product or over the use of a process that significantly improves the manufacture of such a product	■ Research into products and related processes leading to the grant of patents, the creation of trade secrets etc ■ Defence of intellectual property against infringers ■ Use of the protected product or process to create products that can be marketed profitably
First mover advantage	■ Identification and rapid exploitation of emerging opportunities ■ Ability to understand user expectations and track changes in them ■ Ability to devise and rapidly implement effective responses to competitors' initiatives
A reputation for consistently superior service delivery and/or product performance	■ Ability to manufacture products or deliver services to standards consistently higher than achieved by its competitors without incurring disproportionate costs ■ Ability to correct mistakes rapidly, effectively and unobtrusively ■ Ability to understand and anticipate user expectations and track changes in them

Life's unlimited variety

All firms are different

No two firms are identical, if for no other reason than the legal requirement to have different names for different firms. New entrepreneurial ventures go further than this; they should be essentially different from any existing firm because, if they were too close a copy of an existing firm, they would be permanently second to market, doomed to low growth and eventual failure. Sometimes there is one clear difference between the new firm and existing ones, while every other aspect is as close as possible to an established model. Franchising succeeds when each new franchise preserves the successful features of existing ones while opening up a new local market segment. At the other extreme, radical innovations may involve processes, organisational structures and distribution methods never previously used.

A new venture starts with an opportunity. In Chapter 4 we discussed how to screen and value opportunities. If the resulting product is easily and cheaply copied, the opportunity may be of little value unless it can be, to some degree, exclusive. In Chapter 7 we will give a brief overview of intellectual property law and its use in delaying the entry of imitators. In this chapter we will assume that the opportunity exists, is valuable and can be protected to a sufficient extent. This chapter will discuss the type of organisation implied by the nature of the opportunity and set out, in necessarily general terms, the success factors specific to that class of organisation.

One shot strategies

An entrepreneur may have a closely defined set of objectives, focused on a single opportunity. This may be because the enterprise has a clearly defined objective and no purpose once this has been achieved, such as organising the Olympic Games; or it may be that the entrepreneur has a clearly defined objective, that of selling the business in a relatively short time and severing her connection with it.

A plan for a singular event will involve winding up the enterprise and selling whatever assets it has at some point in the future. Entrepreneurs running such enterprises may find it difficult to motivate staff, especially during the closing down phase, so only enterprises where the great bulk of the intellectual and management contribution will be coming from the entrepreneur and the entrepreneur's partners are suited to this approach. Bob Reiss, whose successful creation of a board game is described in Stevenson et al. (1999: 63–77), is a canonical example of an entrepreneur whose venture had a single, well-defined objective and could be wound up when that objective had been reached.

The clean break between the entrepreneur and the enterprise follows another stylised model of entrepreneurship. In this model the entrepreneurs who create a business sell it as a going concern, either by a stock market flotation or to a larger business, after no more than seven years. At this time the growth phase of the product life cycle, at least in the original market, is over and with it the relevance of an r-strategic approach to venture management. The new owners should realise some further value growth by imposing cost disciplines or through synergies with their existing operation, but they must change the enterprise's approach to a K-strategic one.

Entrepreneurs planning such a break should keep the business as a tightly saleable entity, with none of the loose ends or commitments that a growth strategy requires, so as to make the business's sale as expeditious and remunerative as possible.

Growth business strategies

The managers of a growth business cannot choose between r-strategic and K-strategic behaviour for the organisation as a whole, since there will some products in or entering the 'cash cow' phase of their product life cycle, for which a K-strategic focus is essential, while the business's growth is propelled by its new products which must be managed in an r-strategic way.

The founding entrepreneur, if she chooses or the investors allow her to remain chief executive after the initial growth phase ends, cannot remain a full-time entrepreneur once her enterprise has several product lines in different stages of their product life cycle, possibly in different markets as well. The single-minded pursuit of a clear objective serves an entrepreneur well, but will cause great problems if the chief executive of a multiproduct, multimarket company adopts the same approach. In such a company individual ventures rely on the leadership and planning skills of their product champions but the chief executive's primary role is to allocate resources between the competing demands of the various initiatives. Takeo Fujisawa and Soichiro Honda were the entrepreneurs who founded the Honda Motor

Company; but when Honda burst onto the US market, Kihachiro Kawashima led the initiative (Sakiya 1987).

An entrepreneur who intends to create a lasting business must build an organisation that can manage multiple concurrent product strategies. Most importantly, the business must be designed on the premise that work will begin on replacing its products, including the launch product lines, before their growth peaks; when lead times are significant, work may have to start on replacement products before the product they will replace is even launched. Similarly, even while the firm is pursuing an r-strategy, as it drives its launch product into the market it must be building its competencies in K-strategic product management as the product line moves from its growth to its cash cow phase.

Multiproduct, multimarket firms were not generally popular with the finance markets from the mid 1990s until 2001, which was partly a matter of ideology as analysts repeated what they were taught as economics undergraduates, but was mostly a reflection of the speculative nature of the 'bull' market that ran over that period. During a 'hot' bull market buyers are more interested in growth than earnings quality and a diversified company cannot have every division growing at the same rate. Some of the most recent dramatic examples of growth enterprises have come in Southeast and East Asia, where many major companies are still under their founder's, or their founders' first generation descendants', control and the dynastic ambition to build an empire has overcome the temptation to cripple their companies' growth so as to maximise the share price. News Corporation and Virgin Group provide two examples of major growth enterprises that have bucked the trend and in both cases their managers are largely immune from share market fashion. News Corporation has a share structure that entrenches its control by the Murdoch family, while Virgin Group Ltd is a private company controlled by Sir Richard Branson. The many diverse enterprises in the Murdoch empire at least share a media focus, while the Virgin Group seems to be involved in everything that has seized its founder's fancy; its website listed 34 discrete enterprises and 9 alliances in early 2003 and there has been no indication from Branson that this marks the limit of his ambition.

Branson's personal style grates with some people but clearly not with everyone and, as the website honestly claims, his group has achieved real success. Branson's flamboyance distracts attention from his genuine patience and self-control: at any time since the early 1980s he could have floated Virgin Group and collected hundreds of millions of pounds (at least) and let professional managers teach his staff to think about shareholders rather than their customers or each other. He didn't and even his various stunts have served to build his brand's awareness, while apparently giving him considerable enjoyment.

One clear lesson from the success of Virgin Group, News Corporation, Sony and many other new growth businesses is that accessing venture capital and selling unrestricted shares to the public may mean trading off the venture's long-term prospects for the entrepreneur's short-term personal wealth. Those who do wish to build a major, lasting enterprise may not be able to imitate Branson but they can surely learn from him.

'Success has a thousand fathers; failure is an orphan' runs the proverb; in strategy

The Virgin story

Virgin – the third most recognised brand in Britain – is now becoming the first global brand name of the 21st century. We are involved in planes, trains, finance, soft drinks, music, mobile phones, holidays, cars, wines, publishing, bridal wear – the lot! What ties all these businesses together are the values of our brand and the attitude of our people. We have created over 200 companies worldwide, employing over 25,000 people. Our total revenues around the world in 1999 exceeded £3 billion (US$5 billion).

We believe in making a difference. In our customers' eyes, Virgin stands for value for money, quality, innovation, fun and a sense of competitive challenge. We deliver a quality service by empowering our employees and we facilitate and monitor customer feedback to continually improve the customer's experience through innovation.

Virgin began in the 1970s with a student magazine and small mail order record company. Our growth since then has not only been impressively fast, it has also been based on developing good ideas through excellent management principles, rather than on acquisition.

We look for opportunities where we can offer something better, fresher and more valuable, and we seize them. We often move into areas where the customer has traditionally received a poor deal, and where the competition is complacent. And with our growing e-commerce activities, we also look to deliver 'old' products and services in new ways. We are pro-active and quick to act, often leaving bigger and more cumbersome organisations in our wake.

When we start a new venture, we base it on hard research and analysis. Typically, we review the industry and put ourselves in the customer's shoes to see what could make it better. We ask fundamental questions: is this an opportunity for restructuring a market and creating competitive advantage? What are the competitors doing? Is the customer confused or badly served? Is this an opportunity for building the Virgin brand? Can we add value? Will it interact with our other businesses? Is there an appropriate trade-off between risk and reward?

We are also able to draw on talented people from throughout the group. New ventures are often steered by people seconded from other parts of Virgin, who bring with them the trademark management style, skills and experience. We frequently create partnerships with others to combine skills, knowledge, market presence and so on. Contrary to what some people may think, our constantly expanding and eclectic empire is neither random nor reckless. Each successive venture demonstrates our skill in picking the right market and the right opportunity.

Once a Virgin company is up and running, several factors contribute to making it a success. The power of the Virgin name; Richard Branson's personal reputation; our unrivalled network of friends, contacts and partners; the Virgin management style; the way talent is empowered to flourish within the group. To some traditionalists, these may not seem hardheaded enough. To them, the fact that Virgin has minimal management layers, no bureaucracy, a tiny board and no massive global HQ is an anathema.

Our companies are part of a family rather than a hierarchy. They are empowered to run their own affairs, yet other companies help one another, and solutions to problems come from all kinds of sources. In a sense we are a community, with shared ideas, values, interests and goals. The proof of our success is real and tangible.

www.virgin.com 2003

---

development the road to failure is easy to see but the paths to success are hard to find and easy to stray from. Simply avoiding mistakes may be the best route to promotion in a bureaucracy, but it is no guarantee of success in an entrepreneurial venture.

The limits of military analogy

A lot of popular writing about strategy uses military examples and, since wars and battles are often intensively researched, it is possible to make some very interesting observations and draw plausible analogies with business. We do so in this book. There are, however, some major differences between military activity and business. War is a 'negative-sum game'. Winners and losers are both generally worse off at the end of a war than at the beginning; although one side may suffer more than the other, everyone loses. Some businesses are conducted on zero-sum principles, but many are managed to build value and do not waste time or resources on irrelevancies like damaging potential rivals. The study of the history of wars and battles can be extremely useful in explaining and testing problem-solving principles, but an appeal to the glamour, heroism, courage and triumphs offered by warfare is misplaced.

There is a second crucial difference between war and business: private soldiers have historically been conscripts, forced by law and custom to fight and submit to military discipline. Even soldiers in volunteer armies surrender many of their civil rights for the period of their enlistment: refusing to obey a lawful order is a military crime and officers are generally empowered to compel battlefield obedience on pain of death. Businesses cannot compel obedience by any threat more violent than dismissal and, in many cases, the special talents or unique knowledge of the refractory staff make even that threat a hollow one. 'I can call up spirits from the vasty deep', said Glendower. 'Aye, so can I or so can any man,' responded Hotspur, 'but will they come when you do call them?'

Many historians rate the Russian Marshal Georgi Zhukov the outstanding general of the Second World War. He is recalled for his strategic brilliance, but also for his way of phrasing orders.

'Capture the objective by 10 o'clock or be shot at midday', he advised one officer.

Marshal Rokossovsky, his subordinate and admirer, wrote that Zhukov sometimes 'displayed unjustified sharpness'.

Zhukov's account of his 'unjustified sharpness' towards Rokossovsky on 30 November 1941, when he was caught between defeating the advancing Germans and catering to the dictator Stalin's advanced paranoia can be found in his memoirs.   *Zhukov 1969: 86–7*

The greatest military leaders were as remarkable for their ability to secure the willing cooperation of their allies and their subordinates as they were for their military insights. That is a lesson that every entrepreneur should take to heart.

Personal and strategic objectives

Someone who decides to build a growing business must recognise that they will, themselves, be intimately bound up with the business for many years; an entrepreneur's personal and business strategies are closely linked. There is no point in entrepreneurs condemning themselves to a lifetime of torment, so they should devise strategies that will reward them when they are successful, not the reverse.

In general terms people perform better when they enjoy the work and entrepreneurs are no different. Most good opportunities involve the deployment of multiple skills in a variety of tasks, all of which contribute to the development of a competitive advantage. It is hard to imagine a new enterprise being totally self-contained while remaining part of a modern economy and society, and, in practice, the boundaries of the enterprise, the point at which outsourcing starts, are readily changed.

The core parts of an enterprise are those that are, by definition, not eligible for contracting out. If the strategy defines the core so as to include those activities the founding entrepreneurs are happiest doing, there is little reason to challenge this choice and the entrepreneurs will at least know that the success of their enterprise will not mean the failure of their personal ambitions.

Growth strategies

Why grow?

Before assuming that every business must grow, it is worth looking at the reasons why growth is an imperative for many, but not all, enterprises. The most direct way to approach the subject might be from the economic fact of rising productivity, both from the development of new technology and the inexorable operation of the learning curve. In a market economy part of the benefit of rising productivity will be captured as rising real wages and part of it as falling real production costs. Competitive forces, while by no means as prompt or efficient as the authors of economics textbooks assume, will ensure that no firm can isolate itself from either effect: its real wages will rise and its real output prices will fall and, unless it makes technology investments at least the average rate for the economy, its margins will be squeezed; but if it does maintain its level of technology investment, its cash flow will be squeezed. The effect will be particularly pronounced when the technological developments relevant to a firm's industry increase their users' capacity.

The technological improvement may, for example, take the form of operating speed. A new machine may be able to produce twice the output of the models it succeeds, while costing only 50 per cent more. This is highly satisfactory for firms whose markets can absorb the output of the faster machine, but places smaller firms in an impossible situation. As long as the technology continues to improve, every static firm will be caught eventually and squeezed into a merger or forced into bankruptcy. A growing firm is more likely to be the predator than the prey in a takeover, and if it does get taken over, its shareholders are likely to be richly rewarded and its staff cosseted by the acquirer.

Technology may not be the primary issue: globalisation and reduced transport and communication costs mean that retailers can source their stock from anywhere in the world; but smaller ones may be unable to maintain a global buyer network and be forced to watch as their larger rivals offer a better range of goods at lower prices. There are economies of scale in advertising: a television advertisement costs the same amount whoever is paying for it, or sometimes the larger advertiser has access to volume discounts that increases its advantage. More importantly, an enterprise capable of serving customers throughout a viewing area knows that everyone who sees its advertisement has ready access to its services, while its smaller rivals know that, should they use television advertising, many of the viewers will reject their offer for its inconvenience; or the required travel will make many viewers too costly to service, no matter how attractive the offer might otherwise be.

Even in some fields of professional service, such as accounting and law, large firms appear to have major advantages, even though their product, being delivered by a single provider, is largely unaffected by technology or operating scale. In such cases the large firm's advantages in marketing and operating flexibility may be decisive: they certainly aren't cheaper than their suburban sole practitioner rivals.

Higher, wider or thicker

In Chapter 3 we discussed the progressive transformation of industries from vertically to horizontally aggregated. It may help to consider the delivery of a consumer product, whether a good or a service, as the final step in a series of transformations and combinations. Some of the operations and components will be unique to a single product, particularly when an industry is new, while others will be part of the history of many products. McDonald's provides a fairly elementary series of products and its business is built on the reliability and consistency with which it delivers them. Part of most children's McDonald's experience is a serving of French fries; but in most countries McDonald's don't grow the potatoes, clean or slice them, freeze them or deliver them; neither do they make the fryers, thermostats or timers that their staff use.

When McDonald's opened a Moscow store in the last months of the communist regime, few of the goods and services it uses in America or Britain were available. One of its first activities was to find farmers willing to grow appropriate breeds of potato, explain to them how the job should be done and arrange transport, cutting and freezing services. As the Russian move to a market economy continues, McDonald's is progressively shedding these peripheral activities to concentrate on its core business.

The core strategy of every business should include activities that protect its key sources of competitive advantages, but such precautionary actions do not produce growth. A firm's current competitive advantages, its core competencies, can be leveraged into growth in one of three ways: deeper, with the firm undertaking more of the transforming activities itself; wider, as when the firm finds new markets for its products; or higher, when the firm introduces higher quality products to draw more revenue from its established markets.

Vertical integration

Backwards integration is essentially self-limiting: if McDonald's were to move to extensive backwards integration, it would become a much larger and more complex company, but it would have no more revenue. McDonald's has, in fact, been becoming even thinner vertically over its history, outsourcing much of the final operations of its business through franchising. Even the core element of the original McDonald's product, the hamburger patty, is produced by separately owned partner companies in most countries.

Forwards integration represents an attempt to seize a thicker slice of the value chain. It often looks attractive as part of a growth strategy: each step forwards will offer a substantial growth in revenue and value added. It is so attractive that it may be wondered why it is so rare. Many Australian dairy farmers sell their produce through a cooperative. At least one of these, Murray–Goulburn, has developed a major business exporting milk-based manufactured products, to the great profit of its farmer members. Dairying is an exception: no substantial wool-processing industry ever developed in Australia, even to remove burrs and grease from the fleeces before export.

Australia is a major exporter of coking coal and iron ore which mills in other countries will use for iron and steel-making, transporting 1.6 tonnes of unwanted material for each tonne of desirable iron, yet until the Kwinana HIsmelt plant comes on line there have been practically no iron or steel exports from Australia. Attempts at forward integration are certain to face a number of hurdles:

■ a company that decides to integrate forward may find itself competing with its customers who may in turn take pre-emptive action such as switching their own purchasing
■ whether the traditional customers of a company planning downstream integration retaliate or not, the new downstream operations represent a new venture into an established market; such operations are usually cash negative for one or more years, and the firm may find this drain on its liquidity hard to support

■ the management and operating techniques appropriate to the new operations may be quite different to those familiar to the managers of the existing company and the resulting cultural clashes may make synergy impossible.

HIsmelt

CRA Ltd, Rio Tinto's Australian subsidiary, began the development of the HIsmelt direct smelting iron-making process in collaboration with Klöckner Werke of Germany in 1975, and from 1989 with Kobe Steel. When Kobe Steel dropped out in 1995, Rio Tinto continued the project on its own, completing the successful operation of a demonstration-scale pilot plant in 1999. A commercial scale plant is expected to go on line at Kwinana, Western Australia, in late 2004.

   The principle method of iron making is the blast furnace, a technology invented by the ancient Sumerians, or possibly the ancient Nigerians, during the second millennium BC; although the scale of operations has grown immensely, the basic chemistry and principles of operation are all but unchanged. Blast furnaces generally require sinter plants and batteries of coke ovens, both of which are environmentally hazardous and a cleaner, more efficient technology has long been overdue.

   From Rio Tinto's point of view, one overwhelming disadvantage of blast furnaces is that they could not remove phosphorous from iron ore if it was present, and phosphorous contaminated iron was useless for steel making. Rio Tinto had mining rights over six billion tonnes of iron ore in the Brockman region of northwest Australia which was contaminated with phosphorous to a level that made it commercially valueless.

   Unlike blast furnaces, a HIsmelt plant does not need an associated sinter plant or battery of coke ovens, and even substantial levels of phosphorous in the ore can be removed before they contaminate the pig iron output.

Rio Tinto's move into direct smelting was possible because at least some of these hurdles could be circumvented. Rio Tinto's expectations for the product of the HIsmelt direct smelting process are based in part on the fact that it will not be competing directly with its iron ore customers. Integrated steel mills consume iron ore, while direct smelted iron will be consumed by mini-mills. Rio Tinto's established competitors for direct smelted iron are scrap merchants, and Rio Tinto's product will be a suitable feed for mini-mills producing higher quality steel products, while much of the available scrap steel is only suitable for producing relatively low-grade reinforcing bar and light structural members. HIsmelt may also be licensed to integrated steel manufacturers to replace their blast furnaces and coke ovens, a move which may upset the contractors who may have hoped to rebuild the older plant, but one that may enhance rather than damage Rio Tinto's relationship with its iron ore customers.

Rio Tinto has shown no desire at all to get involved with the marketing of iron or steel; practically all its efforts to market HIsmelt have focused on finding an established steel maker as a partner, and while Rio Tinto may supply the technology and the raw materials, the partner will have the task of disposing of the finished product. In 2002 Rio Tinto announced the decision to build a commercial-scale HIsmelt plant at Kwinana, Western Australia, with Nucor, Mitsubishi and Shougang as its steel-making partners.

Horizontal extension

Vertical integration involves developing new assets to increase a firm's slice of its industry's value added while supplying the same final users with essentially the same product. Horizontal extension policies attempt to use the existing assets more intensively. These assets include the technology and core competencies of the firm, but they also include the favourable view of the firm taken by its satisfied users, its goodwill and brand equity.

One common form of horizontal extension is by increasing the geographic range over which the product is offered; from local to regional, regional to national, national to world trade. At each stage the knowledge gained from serving the existing customer base can be used to improve the product and marketing strategies in order to secure a foothold in the next group of markets rapidly and economically. There are a number of ways in which such market broadening may be carried out. Franchising and licensing are commonly used for service products and fast moving packaged consumer goods. Industrial goods and services can be offered through agencies, licensees, partnerships, branches or subsidiaries. The markets can be served by exports, local manufacture or an appropriate combination of the two.

Horizontal extension can be by brand leveraging. This involves offering a wider product range, with the intention of increasing the revenue per customer or per geographic market segment. The chief asset used to support this form of horizontal growth is the goodwill of the established customer base, which predisposes the people in it to consider the supplier as a suitable source for their additional requirements of related products and prompts them to influence other potential users to give the supplier's products a trial. Since the cost of developing a customer base is often the largest of the investments needed by a successful innovation, development of the customer base itself should always be considered carefully as a first option. McDonald's now offer chicken salads and even (in some markets) McVeggie Burgers as a result of successful efforts to broaden its customer base to include those who do not wish to eat beef. Attempts at horizontal extension do not always succeed; McDonald's in the US has been trying for years to build up its evening patronage without any dramatic signs of success.

At least two factors must be present before a firm can successfully leverage its brands:

1. the chosen extension must relate, in the customers' perceptions, to those aspects of the supplier's product that attracted them in the first instance
2. the chosen extension must represent an extension of the supplier's established business strengths.

The other major basis for horizontal growth is by *capability leveraging*. While brand leveraging builds on a firm's superior reputation in the market, capability leveraging starts from inside the firm. Firms planning this form of growth look for opportunities to use the established organisational knowledge and facilities to create new products directed to new or extended markets. Honda Motor started with tiny auxiliary engines for bicycles and its products can now be found practically anywhere petrol engines are in service, from lawn mowers and portable electric generators to Formula One racing cars.

Growth through 'quality'

Quality can imply freedom from defects; but it can also be a measure of value, with higher quality products attracting a higher price. Scotch whisky can have varying proportions of malt to grain spirit and varying ageing periods. A three-year-old grain whisky would be the cheapest legally offered product, while aged malts from famous distilleries may command fabulous prices. Economists describe the malt as a higher quality product than the cheap grain whisky.

Improving the quality of whisky is largely a matter of patience but sometimes a more active strategic move is involved. The De Bortoli family have operated a vineyard in the Murrumbidgee irrigation district of New South Wales since 1928, where the warm climate and guaranteed water supply allowed them to become a significant producer of 'cheap and cheerful' wines, often sold as bag in a box 'casks', retailing at A\$10 and bringing the vineyard no more than A\$4 for four litres after tax. During the 1980s the family decided to move into higher quality lines and established a vineyard in the cooler Yarra Valley region of Victoria and planted slower maturing, lower yielding grape varieties there. De Bortoli wines from the Yarra Valley have won prestigious Australian and international prizes, and the wines sell for A\$15 or more for a 0.75 litre bottle, returning A\$6 after tax to the family, an eightfold increase in the return per litre sold. It is unlikely that the family could have gained the same return from buying more land in the Murrumbidgee irrigation area to produce more of the same cheap, wine. The cash generated by the move into the Yarra Valley allowed De Bortoli to open a London office in 1996 and allow British consumers the privilege of enjoying their fine wines. Their strategy worked because of the order in which the moves were made; it was only when they had moved into higher quality production that they had the cash, and the product, that could make a geographic expansion succeed.

Toyota introduced the Lexus range in a successful move into the luxury end of the car market and the revenue and profit from Lexus supported Toyota's growth in spite of a slowdown in some of its established markets.

To some extent 'quality creep' is an essential feature of a developing capitalist economy. In the 1970s Ford UK sold a model called the Escort Popular as their entry-level vehicle, a two-door sedan with plastic seats, no chrome and no more than the statutory minimum level of features. The nearest 2003 equivalent from the Ford product range would be a Fiesta Finesse, which comes with adjustable fabric-covered seats as part of a list of features, some of which had not been invented when the Escort Popular was on the market. Rising affluence in Britain has dried up the market for cars like the Escort Popular; even if Ford had kept it or a similar car in production, its potential buyers could have bought better equipped second-hand cars for less than Ford could have afforded to sell them an Escort Popular.

Built-to-a-budget cars such as the Escort Popular are still manufactured in developing countries for sale to their domestic emergent middle classes (never for export) but in the developed world rising affluence and falling real manufacturing costs have made such cars obsolete. The Australian Falcon marque has been on the market continuously since September 1960, essentially a four-door 'family' saloon car with ample power to tow a boat or caravan, internal space for five adults and a boot that can carry a family's luggage for a long holiday. In the 2002 incarnation as the BA model it is one of the largest, safest and most comfortable cars available in the world at its price point of A\$34,500 (€19,400 or £13,300, including tax). When the Australian Ford Falcon first appeared as the XK model adapted from the successful US version in 1960, the price was A\$2274, equivalent to A\$22,600 in 2002 money, so superficially the price has risen by over 50 per cent. A review of the quality improvements suggests that the price rise has been more than worth it. While ageing enthusiasts may recall the XK Falcon with misty eyes, its features included an engine that tended to fall out of the car if it hit an Australian outback bump at speed, a live rear axle that was always ready to take over the steering, air conditioning that consisted of a front quarter-pane that could be turned to blow air onto the driver's body, brakes that worked quite well as long as they were dry, plastic upholstery over a driver's bench seat with a fore-and-aft adjustment only and safety provided by optional seat belts. Modern drivers might happily pay $11,000 to be let out of such a car if they found themselves inside it; needless to say, a modern Falcon has shed all these defects and acquired a long list of rather more attractive features.

The design of the firm

Success factors

A number of issues should be resolved before the structure of a new venture is finally determined:

- What is the competitive advantage the firm will have at venture launch and what will be the main advantage three and ten years later?
- How will these competitive advantages be protected from competitive imitation and emulation and, as they are eroded, how will new advantages be developed to replace them?
- How will the value implicit in this competitive advantage be captured, immediately following the launch and three years later?
- What are the critical success factors for the venture, immediately following the launch and three years later?

When a new venture succeeds it makes profits, typically much larger profits, relative to its capital base, than established firms are accustomed to. Before the venture succeeded, these high returns were needed to justify the implicit risks, but once the venture has succeeded, the risks vanish in the full 'glare of perfect hindsight' and other firms will want a share of the new market. In most cases the entry of direct competitors can be delayed but not halted by measures such as patents. Major firms tend to watch each other and generally plan on the assumption that a new product will not be alone in the market for more than 15 months. Unless there are special reasons to the contrary, it should be assumed that any worthwhile innovation will be matched on the market within three years.

Imitation is, of course, the most sincere form of flattery, and entrants to a new market generally want to share in it, not destroy it. If the original product was sound and its launch well managed, competitors who don't enter within two years will not challenge the entrepreneur's leading position, and competitors who don't enter within four years will not, without a genuine innovation of their own, make a successful entry at all. Those determined competitors who followed the innovator into the market rapidly would have launched their own development projects. If they were 15 months behind the innovator, they will require no more than another 15 months to bring their own innovation to market. In a keenly contested market, products superior to the original one are to be expected within 30 months of the first product's launch.

Entrepreneurs planning to create growth enterprises should start work on their product's successor, or a major enhancement of their product, at or before the time of the original product's launch. At the same time they should avoid giving their prospective competitors any more help than necessary. Few things can be as helpful to a competitor as the arrival on their doorstep of disgruntled ex-partners or former senior employees of their main rival. When an innovation has been sponsored from within a major corporation, few events are so disconcerting as the appearance of a group of former colleagues launching a directly competitive entrepreneurial venture.[5]

Having a competitive advantage and capturing value from it are not the same thing. Of Porter's (1980) five competitive forces, the threats from entrants and substitutes are latent at the time a new venture is launched. The threats from suppliers and buyers are, however, magnified. The new firm may need credit, it will certainly need a reliable source of supplies (whether of components, consumables or services doesn't matter at this level of abstraction). Unless the venture is dealing directly with final consumers, it will need orders from major customers or listings with distributors, wholesalers or retailers; all of these are in a position to strike a tough bargain with a new firm offering them an untried product.

People factors

Success factors are relatively abstract concepts, which become practical when they are used to guide the planner in designing an effective organisation. The practical value of success factors continues once the venture is running, because they help the people in the organisation to get their priorities right. For the entrepreneur and her senior associates, one critical success factor will be the morale and commitment of the new venture's staff.

If the product must be sold through established distribution channels, the firm will need a sales manager with experience in the relevant area or the profits will vanish into a series of wholesale price rebates. If particular components, services or supplies will be needed, and there is only one or a very few suitable suppliers, then the new venture must consider recruiting an experienced purchasing executive, or special charges will eat up whatever profit the wholesale rebates leave. As an alternative, a firm in this position could try to form alliances with the critical suppliers, offering them exclusivity or even equity in the venture to secure their fullest cooperation.

McDonald's is only one of many retail service concepts created by successful entrepreneurs. Establishing a retail venture is relatively easy, although earning a fair return on the effort put into running it is harder; growing a retail venture usually means more outlets. Every new outlet is, by definition, physically separate from the rest and so will have many of the management problems of an independent enterprise, including recruiting, training and motivating and supervising staff. At the same time, all the staff and managers at all these locations are expected to pursue company aims and strategies, even when these are not those that the people in the various locations would naturally support. Large, dispersed enterprises face formidable problems of supervision and control as they strive to keep each of their operating units focused on the corporate objectives and restrain their tendency to subvert each other. Excessively forceful or obtrusive control will demotivate staff and suppress initiative and innovation, while a more relaxed form of control may lead to the loss of corporate coherence.

One common form of retail expansion is by franchising. The franchiser preserves its capital and the additional direct cost of each new outlet is relatively small. Problems of recruitment and motivation are delegated to the franchisee and the franchise agreement, reinforced by an appropriate incentive structure, restrains destructive competition among outlets. McDonald's typify the crucial skills needed for successful franchising: the type of systems analysis that enables the complete task to be broken into easily learned and repeated steps, and the training and supervision system that ensures that franchisees earn a fair return on their investment while preserving the integrity and reputation of the brand.

Organisation designs for success

Critical success factors should not be confused with the causes of sudden death. If a relatively young person dies of a heart attack, the immediate cause of death is usually obvious in the form of a clot in or obstruction of the coronary arteries. Health professionals do not go around telling people to avoid clots and keep their coronary arteries clear: they tell them to adjust their lifestyle long before the symptoms of heart disease appear. Firms all fail the same way: they are wound up when they can no longer pay their bills or when such a situation is imminent. Telling a business on the point of failure that 'it mustn't run out of cash' is like telling a man in the middle of an acute heart attack that he mustn't obstruct the flow of blood through his coronary arteries.

Those little hints ...

A coal-mining company with spare capacity received a fax from a Polish steelworks asking for a quotation to supply a large annual volume of low-sulphur coking coal. They ignored it, as they ignored another four messages over the next six months; finally the Polish mill placed an order with a mine in a different country at a price considerably higher than the original miner was used to receiving.

The critical success factors are those indicators that can tell a firm that things are going wrong long before the receivers are called in. For a growth business, capturing the small hints that, when acted on, lead to new markets and new products are also critical success factors. The critical success factors differ dramatically from one firm to another even when they are in similar industries. They also change as a firm develops and its products move through their life cycles.

The critical success factors for some firms are mainly financial; all firms must watch their cash flow and available financing capacity. Firms that have overdrafts, fixed interest debt or venture finance agreements will find that these all have conditions that must be observed. Measures like average debtor days can show important trends, including an early warning of sales staff padding the order book to boost their bonuses. When a firm's performance depends on the fast turnover of low-margin products, purchasing prices and terms are critical. Firms where a small change in a financial statistic can have a rapid effect on its viability need to ensure that they have staff with the right skills, and the right access to the entrepreneur, to spot a deviation and recommend an effective corrective action.

The viability of firms serving consumer markets directly is critically dependent upon the level of customer satisfaction. For frequently repurchased products the rate of conversion of trial to regular use, the churn rate and the level of positive recommendation reflect the satisfaction conveyed. In the case of infrequently purchased products, the strength of the positive recommendations made by users to prospects will reflect the level of satisfaction users enjoy. Firms must be able to collect, analyse and take action on measures of customer satisfaction. Bad publicity following a product failure or a major customer relations error can be fatal: failure to respond promptly and effectively to one customer complaint can be the stone that starts an avalanche of them. All firms serving the consumer market must have an effective complaint response mechanism in place; if there are health or safety implications in the product there should be a PR emergency plan prepared as well.

Firms serving business markets inevitably have fewer customers relative to their turnover than firms serving consumers and they are also likely to find that a few customers account for the majority of their sales, revenue and profit. This presents a double challenge: the firm must be able to prevent the loss of any of its major customers; at the same time it must be able to either control the service cost or build the revenue it gains from its smaller ones. Keeping the large customers allows the firm to survive; improving the handling of smaller ones allows it to grow. In contrast to consumer products, components and services sold to businesses generally earn quite large margins; short term at least, financial data will be less useful as an indicator of the firm's progress than indexes such as the number of customers and the average revenue per customer.

Firms that provide professional services have traditionally been invited to do so on a fee-per-service basis, in which case an accounting and billing system that captures a record of every service performed is essential. There is a trend for fee-per-service to be replaced by price-per-job, as, for example, when corporations put their audit requirements to tender or when health insurance funds start paying on a casemix basis. Success under such circumstances depends on tight project control rather than on good accounting and, in many cases, good task analysis skills will also prove vital. Such changes in the contractual relationships expected in a market may put established firms, and their suppliers, at a significant disadvantage, offering a corresponding opportunity to an entrepreneurial entrant.

The process model

Firms earn revenue by performing services and delivering goods that customers want keenly enough to pay for. If the firm is to earn a profit, the price must exceed the firm's costs, while at the same time being less than the cost to the customer of doing without, doing it themselves or getting an equivalent benefit from an alternative supplier (including, but only over the relatively short term, the trouble and expense of finding an alternative supplier).

Every firm buys some inputs, performs some transformation processes and produces some valuable products. The process and organisation design must be built around the factors that enable a firm to gain and keep customers while still making a satisfactory profit. Each of a firm's operations can be replicated by a firm's rivals and its customers: the firm survives because it creates more value for its customers than its rivals or the customers themselves could provide for the same cost. Remember that customers face search costs and an uncertain satisfaction level if they change suppliers, and so a supplier with a good reputation and a record of consistently high quality performance does not necessarily have to match its lowest price rival.

The value can be relatively high because the firm performs an ordinary task extraordinarily well, or the firm's product is truly unique and customers who have the relevant need will not believe that there are any comparable products available. When the Channel Tunnel installed VESDA fire detection systems, it was because it was believed that the performance of VESDA systems was essential to protect the £5 billion asset and the 2000 people or more who can be in the tunnel at any one time. By contrast, successful grocery chains sell the same types of food and groceries as competing retailers at similar prices: they attract and keep their customers by the selection of products that they offer, the layout of their stores, the courtesy of their staff, the freshness of their products and all the other factors that distinguish a good retailer from an ordinary one.

Table 5.2 **Examples of competitive advantage**

Competitive advantage	Product	Process
Unique features	Pharmaceutical companies with desirable drugs protected by strong patents have both a strong demand for their products and a relative freedom from competitors; in general, any firm whose products are both desirable and hard to imitate effectively may be in this quadrant. The long-term competitive advantage such firms enjoy is their ability to create and recreate such products.	'Top' professionals in any field, often but not only surgical and legal, whose reputation is so strong that they will be the first choice for anyone who can afford them are in this quadrant, as is any service organisation which is generally believed to be the 'best' at performing its designated tasks.
Value for money	Most firms try to deliver reliable, well-made, competitively priced products that consistently meet or exceed their users' expectations. A few, most notably Toyota, have proved able to do this consistently over a long period, in Toyota's case, over 30 years.	Outsourcing contractors generally claim to be able to perform various business processes more efficiently and/or at a lower cost than any available alternative, and sometimes this is true. The low-cost air carriers, such as Ryanair, Virgin Express, Virgin Blue and the original innovator South West Airlines, succeed by offering a keenly priced product that is otherwise only marginally differentiated from their rivals' offerings.

The entrepreneur must answer questions about the firm's competitive advantage before starting the process design:

■ Is the competitive advantage based upon the product or the process? Will the firm attract and keep customers because of what it provides them or how it delivers it?

■ Is the competitive advantage based in unique features or unique value for money? Can competitors remain in the market in the short and medium term by cutting their prices or must they replace their current product range?

Table 5.2 shows four major classes of competitive advantage. In the two 'value-for-money' quadrants there is no 'magic bullet' to drive competitors away; rather, the total product offered is sufficiently good to bring customers back when they need to replenish their stocks of a consumable product or replace a durable one, while building a reputation that attracts new customers and improves the effectiveness of the firm's advertising and promotion. Success in these quadrants is often a matter of being lucky with one's competitors: Toyota enjoyed great success in the American market in the 1980s while Ford and Chrysler were struggling with financial problems and General Motors was dissipating its vast resources on a series of management fantasies. South West Airlines built a network of point-to-point services while its larger rivals cut back on direct services to concentrate on a hub-and-spoke strategy. Wal-Mart's rise in the US and News Corporation's global growth might not have been possible had the families of the chief executive not also been major shareholders. They could invest their cash flow in growth while their competitors were distracted by the demands of the share market.

Entrepreneurs with good concepts may look at Table 5.2 and feel that it is a little too easy: their competitive advantage will fit into all four quadrants. The point of planning is to decide which of the quadrants must not be surrendered to competitors while the business survives and, therefore, which of the quadrants their organisation will be built around. In three of the quadrants industry standards will be good enough, but in one, at least in the eyes and hearts of the firm's customers and targeted prospects, the firm must be unique. The industry standards may be extremely stringent: airlines whose planes crash and hotels whose guests get poisoned don't stay in business long, but these are not matters on which competitive advantages are built.

Documenting the model

When a new enterprise will enjoy high gross margins, as in packaged software development and marketing, direct costs are not important and so a detailed development of the process model can be deferred. In other cases direct costs can become critical: if an enterprise has a gross margin as high as 60 per cent and expects a net profit of 10 per cent of sales, a 25 per cent error in the estimate of direct costs can, on its own, wipe out the entire prospective profit. Such errors are easily made, especially by people with limited production planning experience, and for a major innovation it may well be that no one has any directly relevant experience.

The only way to get it right is to walk the entire process: in manufacturing, from goods inwards to despatch and invoicing; for service industries, from first contact to final farewell and invoicing or cash collection. To be thorough, the process designer should walk the process in both directions, recording what each step is, what sort of human skills are required, what equipment will be needed and what energy and other supplies may be consumed in the process. For a manufacturing proposal, the planner should read *The Goal* (Goldratt and Cox 1993) if she hasn't already done so and then repeat the process.

When aggregating the numbers, the planner must remember that no one can work more than 100 per cent of the time or be in two places at once or even do two different things at the same time. For any process that involves a single service point, loading that point to over 70 per cent of its capacity is a recipe for unpredictable service times. If any point in a process is loaded to 100 per cent of its capacity, the likely consequences include service times, and therefore work in progress levels, that grow without limit. Assuming that a worker, paid for eight hours, can actually work flat out for 480 minutes is likely to be falsified by experience; equally, planners who neglect weekends, public holidays and annual and other leave from their calculations are likely to find that reality doesn't make that mistake.

Mistakes will be made, as they are even on Toyota's fabled production lines. Mistakes at Toyota are invisible because the worker that makes the mistake generally detects and corrects it; but matching Toyota's investment in training and worker-friendly personnel policies isn't cheap. Overall, when estimating the effort required by a process, a planner without expertise in the industry involved should make her best estimate of the labour hours a task should take – and double it.

The firm's assets

Every firm is involved in a minimum of two quite separate groups of activities: the firm must maintain and develop its asset base and carry out some value-adding processes that attract customers and generate sales revenue. The assets and the cash flow from operations can be separately valued; a firm only creates value when the value of the cash flow is greater than the value of the assets.

A firm's assets can be grouped into four categories:

1. *Physical assets*, such as buildings, land, plant and equipment
2. *Intangible assets*, such as intellectual property and customer goodwill
3. The firm's *human capital* made up of the firm-specific skills of its principals and employees and the various team competencies they have developed
4. The firm's *financial assets*, such as cash, bank deposits and the debtors ledger, net of financial obligations such as creditors and loans.

It is important to note that, strategically, something is an asset as long as the firm can use it in its operations; the question of legal ownership is quite separate. Most firms need premises to operate from and so the business plan must show these, but new firms usually need to be careful with their money and so they often choose to rent or lease their premises and major items of equipment. A decision between renting and buying is essentially a financial one, but one way or another the firm will pay.

Physical assets

The entrepreneur must develop a list of all the physical assets that the new firm will need to control in order to operate. For each item there will be a cost of acquiring it and a separate cost of maintaining it; there will also be an implicit throughput limit. When a firm's growth leads to equipment or premises becoming redundant, there will be a salvage value or disposal cost. Some items of equipment and the premises needed to house them may not be needed until the business has grown to a certain size, with the relevant operations being carried out on a service basis beforehand.

Preparing a good estimate of the fixed assets required is worth the effort, both for the confidence it will give the plan evaluators and the fact that these assets are potential security for debt or lease finance. There is no need to be obsessive, listing individual office chairs, but if there is no line at all for office furniture or the amount provided is not commensurate with the number of professional staff that will be employed, the plan will be considerably less credible than it could have been.

Particular care is needed to define the scale dependencies of each asset, showing at what revenue level the asset will need to be augmented, what the augmentation will cost and how the augmented asset will perform. Sometimes the relationship between revenue and asset is obvious, as when a growing supermarket comes to need more checkout lanes, but sometimes it is not obvious at all, at least to an outsider, as when a manual batch manufacturing process might get replaced by an assembly line operation or parts of an assembly line are replaced by robots.

Off-balance sheet assets

The total value of the assets a firm owns, even if they are mortgaged or otherwise encumbered, is shown on the balance sheet. An asset is important to a firm because of the flow of productive services that it can be used to generate and, in many cases, ownership is not a precondition for use. One common form of having an asset available for use without owning it is the 'operating lease', discussed in more detail in Chapter 12. The firm rents the asset and, at the end of the agreed leasing period, the firm may walk away from it with no further obligations.

Sometimes the set of operations involving the asset may be subcontracted to a specialist firm; this has become very common in manufacturing industry, with individual components being transported between six or more specialist subcontractors before they are assembled into the finished product, an instance of the general process of vertical disaggregation described in Chapter 3.

New enterprises have a lot to gain from alliances as an alternative to subcontracting arrangements as a means of gaining access to specialised equipment and particular skills. An ally may extend favourable terms in return for promised future benefits, so over the long term an alliance may be more costly than a subcontracting agreement but in the short term there may be less of a drain on the new firm's cash, and only when a firm has survived in the short term will the longer term become relevant.

Intangible assets

Intangible assets can readily be divided into goodwill and brand equity on the one hand, representing the value to the firm of its reputation among current and potential customers; and intellectual property, the value of its unique corporate knowledge, on the other. In practice these are two effects of the one cause: the firm's corporate knowledge leads to the delivery of unique products that gain an appropriate reputation.

These assets are referred to as 'intangible' because, with limited exceptions, they are of no value to the firm's creditors in the event of bankruptcy. Plant and equipment can be seized by the bailiffs or receivers and auctioned, but by that stage the firm's goodwill and brand equity will not be worth much even if they could be crated up and offered for sale. Intangible does not mean unimportant or immortal, however.

Intellectual property is only valuable as long as it is unique, and yet product innovations will be imitated in as little as 15 months, while process and management innovations can only remain confidential for a few years. A firm can only maintain the value of its intellectual property by ongoing research. This does not necessarily mean a formal R&D or market research department. It could be as simple as a regular tour of the appropriate trade shows and a press clipping service, but, simple or elaborate, the business plan and proposed organisational model must show how the firm's intellectual property will be maintained and developed.

Goodwill and brand equity need looking after if they are to maintain their value. Too many firms don't return telephone calls, leave people hanging on a line and put coupons marked 'return this for more information' in their advertisements and trade show brochures and don't send anything to the people who do return them. In an established company this sort of behaviour leads to a slow erosion of customer confidence, but in a new one a few serious errors in dealing with customers and prospects can spell doom. An entrepreneur looking for a market with quick growth possibilities could do worse than look for one dominated by a firm that combines an essential product with a poor reputation. People will flock to an alternative even if there are few tangible differences between the incumbent's and the entrant's products. Being polite can be an innovation in some circumstances.

Human capital

There is no business without people. A firm can only grow and be profitable if it secures a good reputation among its actual and potential users. Two of the critical factors in establishing and maintaining a reputation are the quality and consistency of the product and the quality of the customer contacts with the firm's staff. With a new business, the *esprit de corps* is likely to be sufficient to ensure that customers are properly attended to, that bad products aren't shipped and that service standards stay high.

Once a business expands to the point that new staff need to be employed, there will be employees with less commitment and less understanding of what the firm is about. Many firms have found that the telephonist/receptionist can be the most important single member of staff when customer satisfaction is measured, but in these communication-intense times, any member of staff may find themselves answering the telephone to a customer or prospect. Devices like orientation programmes and company handbooks may seem dreadfully pretentious to a business with half a dozen people, but they may be an essential insurance policy: the person who gets a crass response from the storeman or who won't leave a contact number because the telephonist said 'we don't do that' might be the one who was going to give that critical order.

Training programmes serve the direct purpose of transferring and enhancing skills, but they also serve a secondary role in bonding employees to the organisation and each other. Well-managed firms spend a lot more on training than less well-managed ones, not just because their managers want to be nice to their staff, but also because reducing staff turnover rates can have a dramatic effect on the profitability of a business. Staff with four years' experience (the average for Japanese manufacturing firms in the early 1990s) can be 30 per cent more productive than staff with 18 month's experience (the average for US manufacturing firms during the same period). Working faster plays a role but so does working smarter: experienced workers make fewer mistakes, meaning that less rework is needed, and they don't stop to ask advice as often.

Several techniques can be used to build a cohesive team. Personality tests can be used to obtain an overall profile of employees. This can then be used to try to match different employees to appropriate lines of work and build teams of individual employees with complementary skill sets. Other successful team-building exercises include activities like orienteering, in which employees practice cooperation outside the work environment, in a social context that is often less personally threatening than the workplace. People often relax enough to enable an atmosphere of trust and friendship to develop, which can have significant benefits when employees return to their normal duties.

Some sensitivity is needed in the design of team-building activities when female staff are involved, particularly if the females make up a relatively small fraction of the group. Men whose only previous experience with teams has been their college rugby club may find that some modification to their own behaviour and expectations is required. Male sporting teams often have bonding rituals involving consuming large quantities of beer and spirits, singing obscene songs and securing the services of workers in the sex industry for visual and more intimate entertainment. Relatively few modern females take delight in getting paralytically drunk or singing 'The Good Ship Venus'; almost none wish to be mistaken for sex workers. Firms and organisations which do not take these considerations seriously risk prosecution and public contempt; at the very least, misconceived bonding exercises will have a seriously negative effect on the morale and commitment of the female members of staff.

There is a marketing reason for taking some care of the ordinary staff of the business, which is that these are the people who get to learn about customer and process problems first. One of the reasons for the success of Japanese manufacturing industries since the mid 1970s is their success at involving all the staff in product and process development. Some Japanese firms have staff suggestion programmes that yield a workable suggestion per employee per year: these Japanese employees know what their company is trying to do and want to be part of doing it.

Counter staff, process workers and delivery personnel are part of the human capital of a firm: they can, with good management, become part of the product and market development process as well.

The asset model

The process only exists to capture value from the firm's assets: Figure 5.1 presents this graphically. The financial assets are on top, because they are part of the rules of the game: the firm is legally obliged to maintain certain financial standards and an entrepreneur may be committing an offence if a firm continues to trade with negative net assets. The intellectual property of the firm is placed, in Figure 5.1, second only to the firm's financial assets. Entrepreneurship and innovation are fundamentally about ideas, not things. The firm's reputation, or goodwill, is treated here as part of the intellectual property portfolio, because marketing (securing trial) and product development (ensuring that trial is satisfactory) must be treated as a com-

Figure 5.1   **The process and asset model**

bined activity. Readers familiar with Harvard's Professor Porter (1985) will know that he puts marketing and sales together as part of the process line. We disagree: sales are part of the delivery process, realising the value embodied in currently available products and existing customer relationships. Marketing is about building future value, new customers and new products.

We put the firm's human capital below its intellectual assets because people form the link between the idea and the real process. It is a two-way flow: people, often the same people, contribute to the intellectual property of the organisation as well as carrying out the various tasks implicit in the process. Entrepreneurial firms are often exciting and satisfying places to work, but excitement and satisfaction should be the result of the proper implementation of an entrepreneurial value creation process, not the chief object of it. Buildings, plant and equipment are properly placed at the lowest level of the asset hierarchy. These are transient incidents in the life of an entrepreneurial firm.

CHECKPOINT

In Chapter 4 we explained how to use a marketing and financial model to establish the viability of a proposed enterprise. The integrity of the financial model depends on the integrity of its assumptions, most particularly the assumptions about the recurrent and equipment costs that will be required at each level of revenue as the firm and its markets grow. The most critical are those that occur soonest: the minimum viable organisation and asset base that can create and deliver its product at and immediately after the product launch.

The design of the organisation and the process will interact with the financial model and constrain it: in real life, there may be several iterations of the organisation and process design needed to find a viable one and some more to look for the best possible launch structure. Firms launching new products must walk a narrow path between not making their project viable because of too much excess baggage, staff, inventory, equipment, and launching and failing because the organisation is simply too anaemic to deliver its promises.

A more subtle error comes from launching with an ultra-thin organisation structure and asset base, then failing to build sufficient muscle as the market grows and the demands on the firm's staff multiply. Such firms appear to make a successful launch, but fail, or at best stall, one or two years after the launch because they fail to support their customers and this cuts off the cycle of recommendation and repurchasing upon which all long-term success depends.

To avoid this, the organisation, process and asset planning should reflect two market states: at the time of the launch, uncertainty is high and capital precious; after two years for a durable product, rather less for a consumable one, the market response is in. If the market response is negative, the project is over, but if the market response is favourable, uncertainty is far lower and capital, while still to be used with care, is more readily available. Having an 'exploitation' structure complete, if only on paper, avoids the waste of precious time when a decision to move from market trial to major launch is made.

Entrepreneurial business planning is not an 'efficient' process, as we explain in Chapter 6. For all practical purposes each successful proposal emerges from the debris of many failed ones. There is no dishonour in declaring at any stage that the concept cannot be successfully elaborated along the lines currently being pursued. The concept may or may not survive, but the doomed route must not.

Look at the strategic, organisational, process and asset decisions that you have recorded: Do they make sense? Can the people they need be recruited and, if they can, will they work in this structure? If they don't, can't or won't, *stop now*, rework the organisation or the process or the asset base, or even go back and redevelop the concept, but don't go on to complete a plan for certain failure.

Exercises

1 Explain why new entrepreneurial ventures generally adopt an *r*-strategic approach to their organisation, while innovative initiatives launched from within established businesses are more often regarded as *K*-strategic.

2 Find an example, from your experience or from reading some business magazines and the business section of one or more broadsheet newspapers, of a cost reducing initiative undertaken by a public company over the past year and decide, from the information available to you, whether the initiative is genuinely *K*-strategic or is intended to produce a short-term boost to reported profits without regard to the long-term consequences.

3 In discussing the relationship between the chief marketing executive and the chief financial officer, the chief executive of a company said: 'It is marketing's job to work out how much money they need to meet our revenue targets, and finance's to find the money.' Does this comment suggest an *r*-strategic or a *K*-strategic focus? Explain your answer.

4 By now you should have selected an innovation for your business plan. Is this innovation best suited to an *r*-strategic or a *K*-strategic approach? Explain your answer.

5 Again, considering your chosen innovation, what primary competitive advantage will it have when it is launched? What core competencies will underpin this competitive advantage? What new core competencies will you develop as your venture progresses?

6 Considering your proposed venture, how will it create the necessary competencies, or if it is being launched from within an established enterprise in which the required competencies already exist, how will it gain access to them?

7 Again, considering your proposed venture, do you see it as a one-shot venture, with the entrepreneurial team disbanding on achieving a particular milestone (if so, what milestone?) or a continuing growth business?

8 Whether or not you are proposing the creation of a continuing growth venture, if your venture was in fact to be maintained with growth in view, what do you see as the likely directions that growth will take? What competencies will the venture possess that will give growth in these directions a competitive advantage?

Notes

1   $x_i = x_{i-1} r \left(\dfrac{K - x_{i-1}}{K} \right)$

2   $\dfrac{x_i}{x_{i-1}} - 1$

3   Porter (1980, 1985) is a widely used source of ideas on corporate strategy. Equally stimulating views may be found in Kay (1993), Prahalad and Hamel (1990) and Hamel and Prahalad (1994). The subject attracts a considerable literature: the search term 'corporate strategy' returned 1088 articles from the ABI-Inform database.

4   Daniel Kahneman, the psychologist who shared the 2002 Nobel Memorial Prize for Economics, and his colleagues conducted many experiments. In one they paired off their subjects, and one member of each pair was given $20 and told to make an offer to share it with the other. The second member of the pair could accept the offer, in which case the money would be divided according to the first member's proposal, or reject it, in which case the experimental coordinator would confiscate the $20, leaving both participants with nothing. Economic theory suggests that the offer need only be trivial, a few cents at most, since the player who

received the offer should 'rationally' choose a few cents over nothing. Kahneman showed that second players who were offered less than $5 nearly always refused the offer; they preferred nothing to letting their playing opponent get away with an unfair division of the prize.

5   Staff who leave their employer and immediately join a competitor may be accused of unlawfully disclosing trade secrets and may be pursued through the courts; except in the most egregious cases, the law in this area is uncertain and the original employer must consider the possible bad publicity and damage to its corporate image if it goes to law, offsetting this against the damage to its business if it ignores the defections. Large corporations tend to avoid lawsuits, or make relatively generous settlement offers, but when defectors from one entrepreneurial business turn up in a rival, personal issues may lead to a lawsuit that cooler heads might well have avoided. The circumstances of the staff's departure may be critical: if they were dismissed or treated in a way that made their departure inevitable, the courts might rule that their right to earn a living trumped their obligations to their previous employer. If they left well-paid, secure jobs to join or start a rival their case may be weaker.

6 Entrepreneurs and planning

This chapter

- In this chapter we describe the essential nature and attributes of an entrepreneurial business plan. Rather than giving you a prewritten plan and suggesting that you fill in a few blanks and add some numbers, we are asking you to consider what makes a plan different from a novel or a coroner's report and what makes an entrepreneurial business plan different from an 'ordinary' business plan.

- This chapter commences by explaining what an entrepreneurial business plan is and how it differs from other types of plan. Starting from these definitions, we explain what an entrepreneurial business plan must contain and what tools must be provided to support it. We set out these requirements in the most general way so as to minimise the constraints on an entrepreneur's creativity while maintaining a focus on the development of an effective plan. We set out principles, not straitjackets. The sensitive, competent entrepreneur or entrepreneurial team will be able to use them as a tailor uses his tools of the trade to stitch a custom-made suit. They are not prefabricated solutions pretending to fit every situation. We show how these principles can be used to aid the writing and rating of a good plan and show that there is well-researched empirical support for them. We follow this with a brief section containing a plan design that shows one way that the entrepreneurial business planning principles might be implemented. We conclude the chapter by outlining the EBPAR methodology for evaluating business plans.

Plans and entrepreneurial plans

The kind of plan an entrepreneur needs differs in many ways from all other types of plan. The word 'plan' can mean both a schematic description of something, usually a structure, and a proposed course of action. Sometimes, as in the plans for a new building, the word means both. Practically all large businesses, many medium-sized and a few small ones use business plans. Mostly these are plans based on an extrapolation of recent history: the plan period is assumed to be like the previous period with a relatively small amount of change. Business plans can be extremely elaborate and involve large sums of money; bringing an updated model of a popular car into production can take three or more years and involve spending a billion or more pounds. The marketing assumption behind such a plan will, however, be that the new model will sell at roughly the same rate as the current one is selling. The plan may include some allowance for growth but it will be in line with a long-term trend.

An entrepreneurial business plan, on the other hand, often starts from a market with no sales history at all. When there is an existing market, an entrepreneurial plan envisages major changes in it. When Takeo Fujisawa and Soichiro Honda came together in 1949 to make 58 cc engines as auxiliary power for bicycles, the market was practically unlimited; their problems were largely on the supply side.[1] The decision to make their own frames for the Honda Dream was entrepreneurial after a fashion, but it sprang from frustration with the frame supplier more than a conscious decision to pursue a market opportunity. Honda etched his name in history with the decision in 1959 to open the US market to his bikes. Honda's motorcycles were lightweight, highly engineered and targeted in Japan at young professional couples. American motorbikes were large, low-tech and oily, and most Americans associated motorbikes with Hell's Angels, riot and mayhem.

Kihachiro Kawashima, Honda's executive vice president, and Grey Advertising came up with an advertising campaign based on the slogan 'You meet the nicest people on a Honda' and, as the 'swinging sixties' started, 'The nicest things happen on a Honda'. They started a revolution that totally restructured the worldwide motorcycle industry. In due course Honda and other Japanese motorcycle manufacturers launched heavyweight machines and captured a major share of the large machine market as well. The British motorcycle industry was wiped out; the American industry nearly followed it until new managers and owners at Harley-Davidson rose to the Japanese challenge.

Haig's strategy, Monash's plan

One of the lessons of military history is that a good plan can overcome a bad strategy. Lord Haig, the British commander-in-chief on the Western Front during the First World War, had a strategy of going to Berlin by the shortest possible route. A succession of army commanders adopted this strategy as a plan: large numbers of men would be assembled, given rifles with bayonets attached and told to walk through the German lines killing any of the enemy who did not promptly surrender. Officers who had the temerity to complain about obstacles like barbed wire, machine guns and semi-liquid mud ten feet deep were told that they were 'defeatist' and 'lacked fighting spirit'.

A series of events led to Lt General Sir John Monash being appointed to command the Australian Army Corps. The Corps was one of the few intact fighting units left to the British in August 1918. Monash did not criticise Haig's strategy, but insisted on his 'entrepreneurial' right to plan his own offensive, to the point of threatening to cancel the battle of 8 August if the high command interfered. On 8 August, as in every

other battle, the strategy was Haig's of going straight to Berlin, but the plan was Monash's and the offensive reached and then stopped at the line Monash had drawn.

The impact on the Germans was profound: in the evening of 8 August Ludendorf wrote, in the official German war diary, that the war was lost. Normally attackers expected to lose more than the defenders: Monash's Australians swung the balance ten to one in their own favour. Most First World War offensives ended at a ragged high water mark, leaving scattered and exhausted men vulnerable to a counterattack. Monash's offensive ended in a perfectly straight line, and the German counterattack withered under the fire of 5000 pre-ranged guns before an Australian soldier suffered ruffled hair. It wasn't pretty and it certainly wasn't glamorous, but it was effective.

All Monash's plans had a number of things in common:

■ he insisted on a clear and unambiguous definition of the immediate objective

▶

- he insisted that individual initiative should be encouraged within the boundaries of the plan
- he insisted that the plan should be understood by those carrying it out
- he insisted that, if circumstances changed to the point that the chief assumptions upon which the plan was based could not be treated as reliable, the plan should be suspended and redeveloped for a later implementation and not attempted with

inadequate resources or under conditions of remediable uncertainty

- but above all Monash insisted that the plan should be practical – when Monash planned, failure was exceedingly unlikely.

Monash's rules are still valid for a business developing an entrepreneurial business plan.

Honda and Fujisawa made another major entrepreneurial decision when they took Honda into motorcars. Japan's Ministry for Trade and Industry opposed this move on roughly the same grounds that would have led to such a proposal being killed inside most western companies: the investment required was huge and immediate while the returns were distant and uncertain. Unanticipated events played a part in Honda's ultimate success: when environmental concerns in the US led to strict motor vehicle emission laws being passed, Honda Motor's experience with super-efficient, low capacity motorcycle engines enabled it to meet the first stage US limits without catalytic converters and without sacrificing fuel efficiency. The rise in fuel prices following the first 'oil shock' of 1972 turned fuel efficiency from an academic to an extremely practical matter and Honda received a second major boost. The Honda Motor Company, more or less on its own, redefined the world's view of motorcar engine technology.

An ordinary, non-entrepreneurial plan will succeed unless some extraordinary events disrupt it. Until 1972 the American motorcar industry had been used to building inefficient and highly polluting cars; when they were forced to make them less polluting they took the path of least resistance and made them even less efficient. Their ordinary plans assumed that their customers would go on buying them anyway. A successful innovation brought to market by an entrepreneur is the sort of extraordinary event that sends businesses relying on ordinary plans off a cliff. The American motor industry might have gone on selling its dinosaurs indefinitely if their customers had not been able to see Hondas, not merely using a quarter of the fuel, but leaving them behind at the traffic lights as well.

Key questions

This chapter is about three words: *entrepreneurial business planning*. Entrepreneurial business planning is the midwife of new ventures. Without entrepreneurial business planning, and the business plan that results from it, a new venture is likely to be stillborn, unable to attract the physical and financial resources it needs to get it started and sustain it until it reaches profitability, positive cash flow and self-sufficiency.

One point needs to be made right now. Every so often it becomes popular to decry the importance of entrepreneurial business planning. Articles appear – even in learned journals – with provocative titles advising would-be entrepreneurs to tear up their business plans because investors do not use them or believe in them. No doubt very popular books will be sold devoted to this thesis. Be aware that what is really being said is something like this. If you are silly enough to try to write a plan in a mechanical way, according to a formula – from this or any other textbook or software package or any other source – it will be a bad plan. The fundamental principles of good entrepreneurial business planning – as we will show in this chapter – are sound and have a basis in empirical research. However, the attempt to 'shortcut' the application of those principles by mindless conformity to a formulaic regime is akin to trying to fit a tall man into an 'off-the-peg' suit two sizes too small for him. The suit won't fit the man. The plan won't suit the business. That is the valid point made by the 'tear up your business plan literature'.

The invalid point is that purveyors of this literature often try to pretend that all plans are bad or unnecessary. A moment's reflection will cure you of ever subscribing to this fallacy. Simply imagine a new venturer too lazy or incompetent to be able to communicate and justify his new venture vision and a way of making it happen. Who would invest in his venture? No sensible person could because they would have no structured or even clear basis for an investment decision. So, make sure that periodically popular rhetoric about tearing up your business plan never confuses you. By all means, tear up the notion that a formulaic, perfunctory approach will work. But accept the necessity of the difficult task; the vital need to articulate a vision if you wish to make it happen. That is what an entrepreneurial business plan is for. Of course a plan may be presented in many different ways. The traditional formal document is just one way (although still a very efficient one). The medium for presenting your entrepreneurial business plan might be quite creatively chosen. It could be on video or DVD, or in a series of cogent slides accompanied by a superb verbal presentation. The point is simply this: whatever the degree of formal 'writing' that embodies it, development and articulation of an entrepreneurial business plan is an essential component of the entrepreneurial process.

A second argument from the 'throw away your plans' school comes from a confusion of business planning with choreography. A dancer only has to drop the principal ballerina once to reduce a ballet performance to a shambles; a single member of the chorus line can achieve the same effect in a musical by failing to keep in time. A sound business plan must incorporate the assumption that any particular expectation may be disappointed and any action may have an unexpected result; but the resources assembled, the control systems in place and the training and familiarisation provided for the people in the enterprise will ensure that every difficulty can be overcome and every unexpected opportunity exploited.

> They [the French marshals] planned their campaigns just as you might make a splendid piece of harness. It looks very well; and answers very well; until it gets broken; and then you are done for. Now I made my campaigns of ropes. If anything went wrong, I tied a knot; and went on.   *Duke of Wellington (Longford 1969: 534)*

So, how do we prepare a useful, adaptive plan? Three key questions must be answered before we can say with any confidence that we can offer valuable guidance to an entrepreneur engaged in planning a new venture.

In everyday speech, 'planning' is a word capable of a great many meanings and is often used very loosely. So, our first question is one of definition. What do we say distinguishes planning as undertaken by entrepreneurs from all the other activities than can legitimately be called 'planning'?

The second question concerns entrepreneurship as a distinct field of human endeavour. We must relate business planning to the more general concept of entrepreneurship before we can answer the question: When should a given business planning process be called 'entrepreneurial'?

A third question remains. What distinguishes a good entrepreneurial business plan from an ordinary one?

Only when we can give useful answers to all three questions are we able to set out a definitive set of prescriptions which, when applied to a specific opportunity, will guide an entrepreneur to the production of a high quality entrepreneurial business plan.

We first discuss the concept of 'planning'. Henry Mintzberg (1994) set out a comprehensive model of planning, plans and planners and we adopt and adapt his perspectives and definitions to come to our definition of what planning is and – most importantly – is not.

We then explore the definition of 'entrepreneurship' itself and important related concepts. Bygrave and Hofer (1991) have given us a checklist of nine parameters which they suggest can help us to determine whether any given process should properly be called 'entrepreneurial'. By applying these parameters and drawing on some other well-accepted definitions of entrepreneurship we will define an entrepreneurial business plan (EBP).

What is planning?

Mintzberg's model of planning, plans and planners

We have adopted the definition and perspectives on planning set out by Henry Mintzberg (1994) in his book. The major part of Mintzberg's book is concerned to refute all assertions to the effect that some person, group or company has developed a systematic process for developing strategic plans for modern corporations. A strategic plan represents the highest level of a corporate planning process and sets out the markets and industries that the corporation should invest in and the amount to be spent in each, often including the choice between expansion by acquisition or development. It is possible to use complex systems theory to show that the existence of any universal strategic planning paradigm is extremely unlikely, but Mintzberg chooses to proceed by showing the internal inconsistencies in each of the most widely praised strategic planning methodologies and recounting the awful disasters they caused to the corporations that adopted them. Note once again that this is not a rejection of planning itself but of the misconception that planning can be turned into an automated, formulaic approach to solving problems without proper sensitivity to particular circumstances.

Mintzberg acknowledges that once a strategy is in place, it is not merely possible but essential to develop a series of mutually consistent sub-plans that express that strategy. A complete set of plans:

- describes the actions needed to give effect to the predefined corporate strategy
- describes the expected outcome to some level of detail
- shows the resource commitment, primarily but not exclusively financial, that will be needed to put these plans into effect.

Nobody, simply by studying architecture textbooks, can decide whether a corporation should put the building of a new head office into its current year strategy (and by implication pay a smaller dividend to shareholders or defer investment elsewhere), but if a corporation has decided to build a new head office, it would be reckless in the extreme to start building it before a complete set of architectural plans have been prepared and reviewed. The essential defining statement of the Mintzberg perspective is: 'Organisations engage in formal planning, not to create strategies but to programme the strategies they already have, that is, to elaborate and operationalise their consequences formally.'

Mintzberg and Waters had made the same point in slightly different words some years earlier:

> Companies plan when they have intended strategies, not in order to get them. In other words, one plans not a strategy but the consequences of it ... Planning gives order to vision, and puts form on it for the sake of formalized structure and environmental expectation. One can say that planning operationalizes strategy. (1982: 498)

Figure 6.1 is a schematic representation of Mintzberg's model of the elements and relationships linking planning, plans and planners.[2] The diagram provides an illustration of the key elements of Mintzberg's planning–plans–planners process model and the integrated flow of activities that connects them. For planning and plans, the 'stone tablets' of strategy are taken as given. Planning as a process and plans as process outcomes can only commence subsequent to a strategy having been formulated or 'found'. The roles of 'planning', 'plans' and 'planners' must then be carefully distinguished.

Planning turns a strategy into a programme, converting a given set of strategic directives into a set of plans that can in due course be carried out. In Mintzberg's model planning proceeds in three ordered steps:

1. the strategy is codified, turning it from a set of aspirations to a set of objectives with magnitudes and dates
2. the codified strategy is then elaborated, taking each of the objectives and analysing it to determine the necessary antecedent actions
3. the elaborated strategy is then recorded in a hierarchy of functional area plans (such as: a marketing plan; a production plan; a human resources plan and so on) which can, once approved, become the authority to carry out the actions determined in 2 above.

The completed, integrated plan, Mintzberg suggests, has three distinct roles and so can be used in three distinct ways:

1. it is a communications medium: those charged with carrying out particular

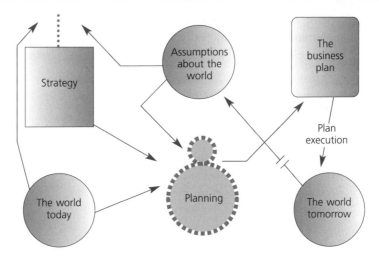

Source: Adapted from Mintzberg 1994: 392

Figure 6.1 **Mintzberg's model**

actions can refer to the plan and expect those charged with carrying out complementary actions to be consulting the same plan

2. it is a control device: senior management, having approved a plan, expect their subordinates to adhere to it and report progress against the targets documented in the plan

3. a plan can be used as a simulation device, testing the effect of different assumptions and modified strategies, with a view to arriving at an improved plan or, where necessary, abandoning an unrewarding strategy entirely.

Planners have, in Mintzberg's model, three roles that go beyond their programming and simulation duties:

1. they find the strategy, decoding the corporate mission statement and other Delphic utterances from senior management as a necessary precedent to formulating quantified objectives

2. they analyse the found strategy as a necessary precedent to programming it

3. they may act as catalysts in the strategy formation process, offering senior management a palette of options and data with which a realistic strategy may be formed.

We discussed core competencies in Chapter 5 and pointed out that proposals which were not based on core competencies seldom succeeded. In organisations where the mission statement and other official definitions of the corporate strategy represent pious hope rather than competent reality, planners are well advised to give priority to the known corporate competencies in framing their plan, ignoring or paying lip service only to the 'official' mission and strategy.

The planner may or may not have been involved in strategy formation, but that is irrelevant to planning and the production of plans. Simulations (feeding alternate data into a plan's information evaluation instruments) may or may not be useful in amending strategy, but the essential feature of Mintzberg's model is his insistence that planning is conceptually distinct from, and subsequent to, strategy formulation.

A brief elaboration of the roles Mintzberg assigns to planners, plans and planning follows.

Planning has one role – achieved in three steps

Mintzberg writes:

> Planning helps to translate intended strategies into realised ones, by taking the first step that can lead to effective implementation. We present this not as our first role for planning but as the only one. All other roles we shall discuss pertain to plans and planners but not to planning ... Planning as programming is clearly decision making, or more exactly a set of coordinated decision processes evoked by the dictates of strategy. And it clearly involves future thinking, and often controlling the future as well – specifically the enactment of desired end-points. (1994: 333–4)

Achievement of this single role – developing the programme – involves three steps.

First, Mintzberg (following Hafsi and Thomas 1985: 32–7) stresses the key codifying attributes of planning: to make all implicit assumptions explicit; to consider all major hurdles; to 'take everything relevant into account' and uncover and eliminate all inconsistencies. He writes 'Planning thus brings order to strategy, putting it into a form suitable for articulation to others' (Mintzberg 1994: 337).

Second, elaboration of strategy is the decomposition of the codified strategy into a three-part hierarchy: sub-strategies; ad hoc programmes; and specific action plans. The result (quoting Katz 1970: 356) is 'a timed sequence of conditional moves in resource deployment'.

The final step – converting the elaborated strategy – involves proceeding from arrangement (of strategic hierarchies) to performance (establishing budgets and control mechanisms).

Plans have three roles

The first two roles for plans are as communications media and control devices. Mintzberg writes:

> Plans, as communications media, inform people of intended strategy and its consequences. But as control devices they go further, specifying what behaviours are expected of particular units and individuals in order to realise strategy, and then being available to feed back into the strategy-making process comparisons of these expectations with actual performance. (1994: 361)

The third role of a plan is as a simulation device. Mintzberg goes on:

> Plans, especially in the operational form of budgets, can be used to consider the impact of possible changes on the organisation's current operations, including the testing of new strategies ... In other words, plans can feed back into the strategy-making process and so find a third role for themselves in the organisation, namely as simulations (although this would seem to be less common than the roles of communication and control). (1994: 377)

One can almost see the evolution of Mintzberg's thought development in these two passages, separated though they are by 16 pages. The key linking concept is 'feed back'. All control systems feature feedback. So, it is not inconceivable to regard certain simulations as part of the feedback (and hence control) process. However, a great many simulations transcend feedback and feature 'feed new', that is, the input of new data based on an alternative strategy. His final position is to distinguish simulation as a third major role for plans.

The several roles of planners

Finally, Mintzberg (1994: 361) argues, uncontroversially, that planners can have several roles, depending on the circumstances confronting the business. At one time a planner may be primarily fulfilling the role of analyst; at another time the planner may be acting as a catalyst of change. The discussions of a selection of some of the unlimited number of roles which planners might play are interesting but the empirical, logical and modelling components of Mintzberg's work are complete without them.

What is entrepreneurial business planning?

Setting some limits: the boundaries of entrepreneurship

Although it is a very ancient economic phenomenon, the study of entrepreneurship is not a 'mature science'. The American Academy of Social Sciences formally admitted entrepreneurship as a distinct discipline as recently as 1989. In many of its major sub-fields this has not been long enough for scholars to articulate and secure general acceptance for paradigms that scholars and practitioners might use as a foundation for practice and further research.

A starting point in the determination as to whether a given proposal or process is 'entrepreneurial' is to test it against the following three definitions (Bygrave and Hofer 1991):

1. an entrepreneur is someone who perceives an opportunity and creates an organisation to pursue it
2. an entrepreneurial event involves the creation of a new organisation or new project within an existing organisation to pursue an opportunity
3. the *entrepreneurial process* involves all the functions, activities and actions associated with the perceiving of opportunities and the creation of organisations to pursue them.

These tests do not provide a complete definition, since they omit the subject of resources. At least one extra test must be applied (Stevenson et al. 1999: 5):

■ an entrepreneurial approach to problem-solving involves the pursuit of an opportunity when this will involve the use of resources not currently controlled by the entrepreneur.

We are sympathetic to, if not entirely convinced by, Stevenson et al.'s attempt to contrast an entrepreneurial or 'promoter' approach to management with the traditional or 'trustee' approach across six dimensions: strategic orientation; commitment to opportunity; commitment of resources; control of resources; management structure; and compensation/reward structure. One of the most serious difficulties we have with this dichotomy is the implicit denigration of the corporate entrepreneur by excluding *K*-entrepreneurship (Andersen 1999; Chapter 5) from the definition. Process innovation is firmly included in Schumpeter's definition (1934) and this activity is overwhelmingly carried out inside corporations. Introducing the reward structure as a discriminating criterion is likely to exclude social entrepreneurs as well as corporate entrepreneurs by definition, a step we are reluctant to endorse.

From the resource perspective, the essence of entrepreneurial behaviour is the introduction of an innovation by employing resources that the entrepreneur does not control at the start of the endeavour to create a new set of resources, possibly but not necessarily including the competencies embedded in a new, viable enterprise.

In the market sector of an economy the current holders of the necessary resources cannot be compelled to offer them to the entrepreneur; they must be convinced by the attractions of the offer and the possibilities of the new enterprise. These stakeholders include, at the start of an enterprise, key staff and critical component and service suppliers. As the enterprise develops, customers and distributors will also become stakeholders. Nearly every entrepreneurial project cannot start until it has secured finance beyond the personal capacity of the entrepreneur. All those stakeholders who are expected to make a substantial commitment of their time and resources to the new enterprise may reasonably ask to see a plan that lets them make their own judgement about the enterprise before joining it or offering it useful support. Professional financiers, whether offering equity or debt, may refuse to consider any opportunity not described in a well-prepared business plan. The project authorisation process in many corporations now demands a fully articulated business plan in support of every significant capital expenditure proposal; the world is littered with the debris of failed projects that would never have been launched if they had been subjected to a rigorous entrepreneurial business planning process before they were commenced. The preparation of such a plan is of central importance to the entrepreneurial process.

One good definition of a business plan is:

> A business plan is a document that articulates the critical aspects, basic assumptions, and financial projections regarding a business venture. It is also the basic document used to interest and attract support – financial and otherwise – for a new business concept. (Stevenson et al. 1999: 43)

The following two points distinguish entrepreneurial business planning from all other forms of planning:

1. its *subject matter* – it will be a programmed strategy to create a growing enterprise, either by launching a new venture or reinvigorating an existing organisation whose returns (essentially the sum of the current return and growth rates) are no longer adequate to justify its resources
2. the *audiences* for whom the plan is intended – the audience can be considered as made up of two groups of people: external prospective investors and/or lenders;

and stakeholders whose personal and corporate commitments are essential to the achievement of the performance projected in the plan.

An entrepreneurial venture includes four key ingredients (Timmons 1990: 30):

1. a talented lead entrepreneur with a balanced and compatible team
2. a technically sound and marketable idea for a product or service
3. a thorough venture analysis leading to a complete business plan
4. a clear statement of the cash required, phased over the period until the venture becomes cash flow positive, and an indication of the minimum equity component.

The emphasis on financing in the definition is a theme that will recur in later chapters of this book. All reader-users of entrepreneurial business plans have one crucial thing in common: they use the information the plan contains to help them to make decisions about committing themselves and the resources they control to the venture. The target audience for an entrepreneurial business plan consists of 'resource providers'. In economic theory, if not always in practice, all resources in a market economy can be represented by dollar values and evaluated using discounted cash flow techniques. In theory, the whole audience for an entrepreneurial business plan can be treated as investors.

In practice, while there are some people who can be excited by a 'beautiful set of numbers', there are many who cannot. There are people who, on hearing the term 'good figures', do not think about balance sheets and cash flow statements.

All entrepreneurial business plans must deal with certain key issues in essentially the same way, although individual examples may be different depending on who (as an individual or a member of a well-defined group) controls the key resources a new enterprise needs. Everyone who is asked to go beyond the normal conventions of trade to support a new enterprise is making an investment in it, sacrificing the current use of some asset in the expectation of an adequate future return. Labourers paid hourly wages, and business service providers paid on their monthly invoice, are not investors. Experts who are asked to sacrifice the security of a public service or corporate career (such as it now is) and the opportunity of selling their skills elsewhere are investors. Suppliers who are asked for long credit terms are investors, as are those bankers who advance money on terms more generous than a secured overdraft callable on 30 days' notice.

The entrepreneur should consider anyone who takes any sort of risk to support the new venture as an investor. People who subscribe equity capital are, although vitally important, still just one class of investor.

Summary: two core definitions

Entrepreneurship is a process of opportunity realisation through a creative approach to resource control. The entrepreneurial business plan is the entrepreneur's major device for defining and gaining control of the resources a new venture needs. Now that we have established the nature of the entrepreneurial process and described the investor audience, we are in a position to provide formal definitions of entrepreneurial business planning and the entrepreneurial business plan. The definitions make use of the categories of the entrepreneurial process defined by Bygrave and Hofer, the emphases supplied by Stevenson, the boundaries defined by Timmons and the concepts of planning employed by Mintzberg:

- Entrepreneurial business planning is the process of convincing the owners and controllers of certain resources of the feasibility and desirability of participating in a new venture. The process takes a predefined strategy and determines the set of resources that will be needed to implement it and how they must be deployed. It leads to a forecast of the economic outcome to be expected, a determination of the sensitivity of this forecast to the value of various antecedent factors and an assurance that the proposed plan represents at least a locally optimum outcome.
- An entrepreneurial business plan is a formal document that sets out the expected results of the entrepreneurial business planning process, including, inter alia, the assumptions that the planner relied on and the confidence that can reasonably be placed in each of them, the resources that will be used and how they will be combined, the key managers and their qualifications and experience, detailed financial forecasts covering revenue, expenditure, investment and returns and, in general, all the facts and arguments needed to obtain, with the consent of their current owners and controllers, the resources needed to carry through an entrepreneurial venture.

From guidelines to implementation

Communications

The plan is a means of communicating with investors (in the economic sense); people who are being asked to sacrifice the opportunity to use certain resources in other, undefined ways in order to dedicate them to this particular project. While in general, all members of the target audience are investors, in particular they will have different motives for examining the plan:

- equity investors will wish to see that the risk-weighted return on their investment is better than any of the alternatives they are currently considering or consider themselves likely to be offered in the near future
- debt financiers will wish to see that their loan is backed by good security and the business will generate cash flows sufficient to cover the agreed interest and principal repayments
- owners of private (proprietary) companies will wish to see that their key personal objectives are not placed at undue risk – these may be non-financial objectives; one accountant discovered that a promise of 'golf every Wednesday afternoon and all day Saturday' meant far more to the small business owners that he dealt with than concepts such as return on investment
- managers of public companies will wish to see that the new venture will support, rather than cannibalise, their existing sources of revenue and shareholder value
- the finance directors of public companies will seek assurance that the costs of the venture are fully declared and the commitments being sought are all that will be sought
- licensors of patents and other providers of intellectual property will seek to max-

imise their revenue consistent with preserving their reputation and the security of their property

■ key employees will want to see that their skills are being complemented by the venture and that the rewards they are promised are both adequate to the risks they are being asked to take and likely to eventuate.

Entrepreneurs may find it necessary to prepare variants of the plan, or at least of the executive summary, tailored to each of these audiences. In each of these versions, while the core data, research results and arguments are retained, the presentation will be adjusted to the interest and capabilities of the particular audience. It is not ethical to prepare different plans incorporating different data for different audiences and, quite apart from the possibility of criminal proceedings for fraud, an entrepreneur should allow for the probability that the recipients of different versions will compare notes.

The writer of the plan is setting out certain promises and declarations on behalf of an entrepreneur or an entrepreneurial team. Ideally, the writer will be the lead entrepreneur, and in many cases he will be, but excellence at entrepreneurship is not always associated with excellence in written expression. When a specialist writer is engaged, it must be on the basis that the writer will set out the entrepreneur's plan, not merely prepare a document to bemuse the local bank manager.

By far the most important of the messages conveyed by a plan is that the entrepreneurial team are capable of carrying out their promises, have the right combination of skills and experience to complete the tasks they set themselves and recruit employees and partners to complete the rest. The second most important message is that the team are committed to the project, that they are not trying to pass the risk to an investor or lender and keep the profits or, worse still, the subscribed capital for themselves.

The technical excellence of the project is important but many potential investors may understand the technical aspects less and deem them less critical than marketing and management issues. Relative outsiders will know less about the industry and the markets the venture will address than the entrepreneur and the entrepreneurial team. By describing the project in the business plan, the entrepreneur and the entrepreneurial team should set out to convey confidence in their judgement and ability rather than make a technologist or marketer out of a bank manager. A serious potential investor will, nevertheless, have the technical sections of the plan reviewed by an expert in the appropriate field: errors or omissions are likely to be detected.

Plan boundaries

The fundamental assumption of every entrepreneurial business planner is that there is a significant obstacle to overcome, and something valuable to be gained by overcoming it. If there is no obstacle, there is no call for entrepreneurial skills; if there is nothing valuable to be gained, there is no point in deploying them.

First, entrepreneurship is a deliberate act, not purely driven by a change in circumstances, and one that is closely associated with a single economic entity. Second, the result of a successful entrepreneurial process will be a change that extends beyond the original entity's boundaries and one where the 'before' and 'after' circumstances are clearly different. Third, each entrepreneurial process is unique; it attempts something that has not been done before and, even if it fails, it establishes a new knowledge base from which further attempts will begin. Fourth, the entrepreneurial process starts from a state of significant uncertainty, in that small flaws in the assumptions, or apparently minor incidents, can have major effects on the direction and outcome of the process.

The major exclusion we make from our definition of the entrepreneurial process is the strategic choice of industry and market and decisions such as the minimum and maximum scale of any single initiative. These are strategic decisions and establish a prior framework upon which an entrepreneurial process can be built. This distinction is not very important to an entrepreneur creating a new, freestanding enterprise, but it can be critical to the chances of an internal venture launched within a major corporation.

A proposal that a firm should seek certification to the appropriate world quality standard in the ISO 9000 series is not entrepreneurial; success will not be a unique event except on the most pedantic definition, and in any case will not result in a significant change to the external economic environment. By contrast, a proposal to establish a firm that will assist, through consultancy and training services, many other firms to achieve ISO 9000 series certification may be entrepreneurial because it opens a new market or introduces new techniques and, if the firm succeeds, it will change the external environment by increasing the number of firms with ISO 9000 series certification and the flow on effects from that.

An article in a newspaper in the mid 1970s disclosed that the Sydney harbour bridge (built in the 1930s by Dorman and Long, the British steelmaker) had been designed to withstand a wind of 110 miles per hour. A minor panic ensued in Sydney: 'What', wrote the editorials, 'would happen if a 115 mile per hour wind blew in Sydney?'

The last survivor of the bridge design team neatly punctured the hysteria with a letter pointing out that, if a wind of 100 miles per hour should blow in Sydney, the harbour bridge would be the only structure left standing.

A proposal to buy a twentieth truck for a mine in order to meet rising demand is not entrepreneurial, because it is an incremental decision without any implied discontinuity; but a proposal to replace all the delivery trucks at a mine site with a conveyor system running to the wharf or rail loader may well be entrepreneurial, since it will involve a radical change in the economics of the mine operation, with consequences that may go well beyond the original firm. A firm that rebuilds a warehouse after a fire is not being entrepreneurial, since it is merely responding to external events, but a firm that builds a new warehouse in order to establish a new warehousing and distribution business may, if its technology, organisation or marketing is sufficiently innovative, be carrying through a genuine entrepreneurial process.

Simulation

Rational investors proceed on the 'bad news' principle; their first concern is not to lose what they have and only then do they look to what they might gain (Bernanke 1983). During the development of a business plan the authors will attempt to provide generally reassuring information; but a good plan can also be a simulation tool with which to explore the impact of adverse and favourable events. All investors know, or ought to know, that failure cannot be excluded altogether; but simulation lets them find out how close to the edge they are being asked to travel. A well-developed business plan becomes a simulation tool with which to explore this 'possibility space'.[3] The only limits to the simulation process are the laws of humanity and nature.

An entrepreneurial planning process explores the effect of what can happen, not just what might happen. Statistics show us that, when a large number of variables are present, it is practically certain that one or more of them will take 'unlikely' values. Murphy's Law – whatever can go wrong, will go wrong – is soundly based in theory and experience.[4] The simulation model is constructed to answer the type of 'what if' questions that potential stakeholders may ask. An inability to answer them, or to provide a qualitative answer, must reflect badly on the entrepreneur.

The practice of working with numbers can obscure the essential asymmetry of many outcomes. If an engineer orders too much concrete and steel for a new bridge, it will end up costing more than it had to; but if he orders too little the structure will fail, at great cost in money and possibly lives as well. When in doubt, a civil engineer adds strength. Likewise in a new enterprise: a cautiously phased entry into a new market, or a contingency on the product development plan, may lead to lower profits; but the consequences of seeking to maximise the expected profits from an enterprise is that risks are also maximised, and the consequence of failure is not lower profits, but bankruptcy, the loss of the equity capital invested in the firm and often the loss of the founding entrepreneurs' personal assets as well.

In general, entrepreneurs set out to create enterprises with an indefinite life, and events that are unlikely in any single period become almost certain when enough consecutive periods are considered. An entrepreneur planning the introduction of a new oilseed harvesting system into Britain and Europe would need to keep a sharp eye on the WTO negotiations and the various disputes over agricultural policy between the EU and the USA. While few observers believe that a drastic reduction in the common agricultural policy (CAP) support for the oilseed and other agricultural industries is imminent, it has been conceded in principle and may even happen one day. Another entrepreneur might see the heatwave of 2003 as an indication that he should establish a domestic air-conditioning business in southern England; but a couple of mild or more traditional summers could see the end of such a venture.

Summary: attributes of an effective plan

An entrepreneurial business plan must include information on a certain number of matters of interest to potential investors and other stakeholders; we could consider this list of essential components as defining an entrepreneurial business plan, to the point that a document omitting some or all of these components and attributes is simply not such a plan. Formal conformity is not the same thing as excellence and there are certain 'success rules' that we recommend planners to follow.

We need to distinguish between the rules of conformity and 'success rules'. This is fundamentally a distinction between the mandatory and the optional. A law is a rule recognised by a community as binding. The rules of conformity circumscribe. They are closely related to boundaries because non-conformity puts one outside the community. On the other hand, success rules, as the name implies, are indicative rather than prescriptive. Not being successful does not place one outside the community. Success rules are principles intended to increase the probability of solving the types of problem that fall within the purview of a particular paradigm. The rules of conformity (together with boundaries) define what that purview is.

An illustration may be useful. The boundaries of a tennis court are clearly marked. One of the many laws of tennis is that the server gets only two chances to land the ball in the designated landing area. One of the success rules of tennis is to 'get a high percentage of first serves in play'. Someone who cannot achieve a high percentage of first serves (or fails to implement any other success rule) does not cease to be a tennis player. However, anyone who breaks the rule that states that 'two serves are all you are allowed on any given point' or any other law, or continues to play after a shot lands outside the appropriate boundaries, has left the community of tennis players and is playing some other game.

The essential attributes and the success rules are discussed below, grouped under the three functional headings.

Boundaries and conformity rules

**Communi-
cations**

An entrepreneurial business plan is a document addressed to the controllers of various resources generally including but not limited to financial resources. It explains to them why it is in their various interests to commit these resources to the planned venture. The author(s) of the document are members of, or are writing on behalf of, an entrepreneurial team that wishes to proceed with the planned venture and needs the nominated resources to do so. The document must place the plan in a strategic context and set out its objectives.

The plan document must include an explanation of why the proposed venture is likely to succeed and identify the risks facing it. For each identified risk there must be a proposal to respond to it, while the reasons for the venture's expected success must be placed in the context of the obstacles the venture may reasonably be expected to face.

Success rules

Each class of investor approached must be shown that the prospective rewards for participating in the proposed venture are at least as attractive as those that an alternative deployment of the resources under their control can offer, while not exposing the resources, or their controllers, to risks whose probability or magnitude lie outside their prudential boundaries.

Prospective investors must be convinced that the entrepreneurial team is trustworthy and competent to complete the tasks that starting and operating the venture will involve, that the resources requested will be sufficient without being excessive and that the rewards proposed to be earned by the team will represent a just division of the fruits of success.

Members of the target audience must understand the plan and the role they and the resources they control are expected to play in pursuing it. They must be empowered by being given the information they need to make a decision whether to participate, without feeling pressured by a biased or emotional presentation of the circumstances under which the venture would be undertaken or the consequences of their declining to participate. The more radical the proposal, the more dispassionate the presentation of it should be: people who are being asked to endorse a brave decision should not be given the option of withdrawing their support later because they were rushed into it. The plan document must be of a sufficient length to contain the information that prospective investors need, it must be structured so as to ensure that this information is readily accessible and comprehensible and it must be free from padding, verbiage and irrelevant material.

Finally, the plan must be read as an invitation to a dialogue, not as a take-it-or-leave-it proposition: the investors must feel invited to join the entrepreneurial team, not simply surrender control of their resources to it.

Control

Boundaries and conformity rules

The plan must be for an innovation, a significant, irreversible change in the social and/or economic fabric of society. The change must be well defined and the planning document must describe a number of milestones, the achievement of which will, during the execution of the plan, demonstrate that the venture is making satisfactory progress towards the achievement of its objectives.

These milestones must include pro forma financial statements for each year until the achievement of the major plan objectives and a cash flow projection on a finer timescale from the initiation of the venture to the projected date at which it is expected to generate enough cash to be self-supporting without any further call on equity investors.

Essential activities involving substantial resources or taking a significant amount of time on the main path should be documented in sub-plans, with their cash flow and resources budgets documented in the main document along with their specific purpose and objectives.

Success rules

The financial statements in the plan document should be generated by a computer model capable of exploring the effect of various contingencies; where appropriate the revenue forecasts should be generated by a linked computer-based marketing model, with parameters that can also be used to explore contingencies; and when the plan envisages a project with more than a trivial number of linked and interdependent activities, there should be a computer-based project plan justifying the planning timescales and allowing various contingencies to be explored.

The pro forma financial statements must be structured so as to facilitate the development of a value-adding financing deal and the basis of such a deal should be outlined. All investors must be shown a clear proposal to realise their gains and recover their investment in line with the expectations appropriate to that class of investor.

Simulation

Boundaries and conformity rules

There should be no boundaries to the possibilities of simulation provided by the plan, in the sense of there being contingencies for which the implications cannot be explained. The plan document, and the associated computer-based tools, must be able to answer all the questions that the target audience might reasonably be expected to raise, showing both the financial and the other impact of changes in the basic assumptions and the occurrence of various contingencies.

Success rules The simulation tools must have been used during the development of the plan to ensure that it represents at least a local optimum, in that no single parameter change can significantly improve the expected outcome.

The plan, and the simulation tools, should be intelligible to and usable by an appropriately skilled person who has had nothing to do with their development. The tools should not, when supplied with any reasonable combination of parameters, fail or produce a ridiculous or plausible but deeply erroneous forecast.

The plan, and any accompanying tools, must be based on a mutually consistent set of assumptions.

What other researchers say

Planning generally produces better results than does trial-and-error learning (Ansoff 1991). A proliferation of academic and practitioner literature stresses the importance of planning, promoting models of the planning process and offering normative advice on how to design and implement effectively strategic and operational plans. Fundamentally, the objective of planning in business is to minimise the impact of uncertain future events on the pursuit of a goal.

The nature of planning is distinctly different for new ventures than for existing ones. A critical review of the business planning literature (Pearce et al. 1987) and a meta-analysis (Schwenk and Shrader 1993) reveals that firm size and stage of development are critical factors in understanding business planning. Hindle (1997) and McGrath and MacMillan (1995) suggest that planning for new ventures is entirely different from planning for firms in later stages of development. These scholars argue that new ventures begin with a high ratio of assumption to knowledge and inevitably experience deviations from original targets that require fundamental redirection. Thus, new ventures must practise more 'discovery-driven planning'. Applying business practices valid for a mature business can cause failure for new ventures (Block and MacMillan 1982, 1985, 1993; Kanter 1989; Sykes 1995). Greiner (1972) concluded that what works for a mature business will cause failure for an early stage business.

Hindle and Mainprize (2003) provided distillation of 22 pieces of literature related to business planning. It supported the contention that an entrepreneurial business plan has two fundamental purposes (see Table 6.1):

1. *Communication:* entrepreneurial business plans must be a tool that clearly communicates the future and its uncertainty.
2. *Credibility:* entrepreneurial business plans must portray credibility by providing for revision and iteration.

The literature synthesis revealed ten fundamental entrepreneurial business planning principles, comporting strongly with the twelve laws and the six success rules of Hindle's (1997) enhanced entrepreneurial business planning paradigm.

Table 6.1   **Results of selected literature relating to business planning: summary of theoretical rigour, overall goals and presence of fundamental EBP principles**

Selected literature relating to business planning	Theoretical rigour (high, medium, low)	Overall goal(s) of a business plan	10 fundamental principles of an entrepreneurial business plan									
			Expectations	Milestones	Opportunity	Context	Business model	Team	Elaboration	Scenario integration	Financial link	The deal
Amis and Stevenson (2001)	H	Communication document to secure capital										x
Muzyka (2000)	M	Mapping and defining opportunity			x							
Hindle (1997)	H	Communication, control and simulation of the new venture	x	x	x	x	x	x	x	x	x	x
Bers, Lynn and Spurling (1997)	H	Presenting multiple future scenarios								x		
Sahlman (1997)	M	Communication of the opportunity and team			x	x	x	x		x	x	
McGrath and MacMillan (1995)	M	Communication of the venture assumptions and learning (discovery) plan		x								
Sykes (1995)	M	Minimising risk by communicating critical assumptions								x		
Weltman (1995/1996)	M	Forecasting the financial future								x	x	
Timmons (1994)	H	Communication document to secure capital			x	x	x					
Block and MacMillan (1993)	M	Communication document to secure resources		x								
Schwartz (1991)	M	Communication of the venture's future								x		
Sandy (1990)	L	A 'conversation' of business objectives into performance objectives	x		x	x						
Wyckham and Wedley (1990)	M	Communicates the feasibility analysis process								x	x	x
Rich and Gumpert (1985)	M	Accurately and attractively communicate the proposed project	x		x		x	x			x	x
Block and MacMillan (1985)	M	Communication of quantitative milestones		x			x		x			
Fry and Stoner (1985)	H	Communication of the vision to internal and/or external audiences	x		x		x			x		
Hills (1985)	H	Communication of the market analysis and opportunity			x	x				x		
Timmons (1980)	M	Communication document to secure capital			x			x			x	
Webster and Ellis (1976)	H	Communication of the characteristics of the company, competition and financial projections						x			x	x
Mancuso (1974)	L	Communication of the risk and reward structure of a new venture	x		x		x	x			x	x
Deweerd (1967)	M	Communicate multiple future scenarios								x		
Schumpeter (1934)	M	New venture must be founded on a new combination			x							

Source: Hindle and Mainprize 2003

Table 6.2 Entrepreneurial business plan assessment regime (EBPAR)

Dependent variables	Independent variables	Assessment questions		Rating criteria
Communication	Expectations	Does this EBP meet an investor's reasonable expectations for efficient provision of sufficient information upon which to make the screening decision? The reviewer will expect that: ■ key success factors and risks can be clearly identified and are understood ■ the venture has a large projected market with good potential market penetration ■ a strategy for commercialisation, profitability and market dominance is present ■ a strong proprietary and competitive position can be established and protected	Low	Only 1 or 2 of the expectation items are present in the EBP
			Med	3 of the expectation items are present in the EBP
			High	All 4 of the expectation items are present in the EBP
	Milestones	Are milestones in the EBP clearly communicated primarily as: ■ quantitative values? ■ financial targets?	Low	Either there are no milestones or they are without any quantitative values or financial targets
			Med	Some of the milestones use quantitative values or financial targets
			High	All milestones use quantitative values or financial targets
	Opportunity	Does this EBP provide a comprehensive description of the venture opportunity by describing: ■ the innovation at the heart of the venture? ■ the magnitude of the opportunity (market size) and source of this estimate? ■ market growth trends and the source(s) of these estimates? ■ venture's value from the market (% of market share or proposed market share value in dollars)?	Low	Only 1 or 2 of the opportunity items are described in the EBP
			Med	3 of the expectation items are described in the EBP
			High	All 4 of the opportunity items are described in the EBP
	Context	Does this EBP demonstrate awareness of the context by describing the: ■ industry structure? ■ competition (including indirect competitors)? ■ the changes that the venture team expect in the industry over time? ■ factors that will inevitably change but cannot be controlled by the team?	Low	Only 1 or 2 of the content items are described in the EBP
			Med	3 of the context items are described in the EBP
			High	All 4 of the context items are described in the EBP
	Business model	Does this EBP outline the business model by explaining: ■ who pays (paying customer)? ■ how much (average transaction value)? ■ how often (repetition)?	Low	Only 1 of the business model items is explained in the EBP
			Med	2 of the business model items are explained in the EBP
			High	All 3 of the business model items are explained in the EBP
Credibility	Team	Does this EBP describe the entrepreneurial team addressing: ■ what they know (qualifications and experience)? ■ who they know? ■ how well they are known?	Low	Only 1 of the aspects of the entrepreneurial team is addressed in the EBP
			Med	2 aspects of the entrepreneurial team are addressed in the EBP
			High	All 3 of the aspects of the entrepreneurial team are addressed in the EBP
	Elaboration	Does this EBP elaborate the overall strategy into sub-plans by: ■ linking the milestones to sub-plans? ■ using a timeline or a simple PERT diagram to show how tasks, milestones and sub-plans interconnect?	Low	Either there are no sub-plans or they are without any linkage to milestones
			Med	Some of the milestones linked to sub-plans
			High	All milestones are linked to sub-plans and a timeline shows their interconnectedness
	Scenario integration	Does this EBP employ simulation techniques to obtain a variety of logically developed future scenarios, establishing a: ■ most likely case? ■ best case? ■ worst case?	Low	Only 1 scenario is presented
			Med	2 scenarios are presented
			High	3 scenarios are presented
	Financial link	Does this EBP link the selected strategy discussed in the body of the plan to the financials by addressing: ■ how much money the company needs over what period? ■ the level of sales to break even? ■ when established, how much profit the company is likely to make? ■ when cash flow turns positive? ■ the main assumptions that the forecasts are based on?	Low	1 or 2 of the aspects of the financial link are addressed in the EBP
			Med	3 of the aspects of the financial link are addressed in the EBP
			High	4 or 5 of the aspects of the financial link are addressed in the EBP
	The deal	Does this EBP articulate a value-added deal structure by describing: ■ the funds required; the amount of cash investment required for growth; and the use of the proceeds? ■ the offer; for equity financing the offer is almost always stated as a % of the equity in the venture? ■ the return; is commonly stated as an annual return on investment? ■ the exit strategy; the most likely mechanism in which in the investor can expect to receive the initial investment back plus the return? ■ the exit horizon; the approximate length of time the investment will be illiquid?	Low	1 or 2 of the aspects of the deal are addressed in the EBP
			Med	3 of the aspects of the deal are addressed in the EBP
			High	4 or 5 of the aspects of the deal are addressed in the EBP

Source: Hindle and Mainprize 2003

Hindle and Mainprize (2003) found five principles relating to the first goal (Communication of an uncertain future). They summarised these as:

1. expectations
2. milestones
3. opportunity
4. context
5. business model.

The second essential goal of an entrepreneurial business plan is credibility and is achieved by providing for revision and iteration under the principal headings of:

1. team
2. elaboration
3. scenario integration
4. financial link
5. the deal.

EBPAR – establishing plan quality

Mainprize and Hindle (2003) then codified the principles described above into an 'entrepreneurial business planning assessment regime' (EBPAR). Table 6.2 summarises the way in which applications of ratings of each of the ten principles may be applied to a new plan as you write it or an existing plan as you rate it.

A visual summary can be created from the results of EBPAR to further extend its utility. The visual summary uses communication and credibility as dependent variables on a graph when applied respectively to x and y axis (see Figure 6.2).

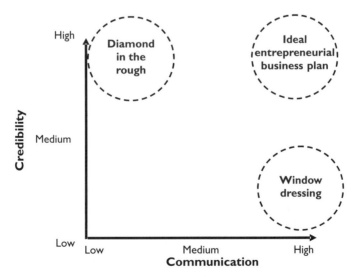

Figure 6.2 **Selected positioning profiles of EBPs using EBPAR visual summary**

Using EBPAR

Hindle and Mainprize (2003) began their search for an entrepreneurial business plan assessment regime with three questions.

1. What is the theoretical basis for writing entrepreneurial business plans?
2. What are the fundamental principles synthesised from the literature?
3. How can these principles be operationalised? The discovered regime – EBPAR – provides some answers. The new question becomes how can the assessment regime be best used?

Initially, its principal utility will be as a taxonomic device. Entrepreneurial business plans can now be practically classified and arranged in meaningful clusters. Two brief examples of hypothetical entrepreneurial business plans will illustrate. EBP1 describes a venture that proposes to manufacture a new type of sailing boat. The vision for the sailing boat, the market opportunity and the revenue model for the new venture are articulated with excellence throughout the plan. However, the plan fails to demonstrate credibility by not discussing possible scenarios and contingency strategies. This entrepreneurial business plan would rate high on communication and low on credibility using EBPAR. It would be positioned as 'window dressing': it reads well but lacks credible flexibility (see Figure 6.2). EBP2 describes a 10-minute oil change service. Present in the plan are a variety of capacity scenarios, detailed timelines, financials and management team responsibilities. However, the vision for the service and its execution are poorly articulated. This entrepreneurial business plan would rate high on credibility and low on communication. It would be positioned as 'a diamond in the rough', the well-thought-out credible flexibility of the venture is eclipsed by poor expression (see Figure 6.2). An entrepreneurial business plan positioned as a 'diamond in the rough' goes undiscovered by potential investors and often remains in the ground unmined.

Assessment of both entrepreneurial business plans would result in different positioning profiles but the insight would be equally valuable. The result of assessing entrepreneurial business plans by using EBPAR can be used as guidelines for improving them. The intended goal is to improve the fundamentals that are identified as weak by the EBPAR. Improving individual fundamentals moves an entrepreneurial business plan toward the position of 'ideal entrepreneurial business plan' (see Figure 6.2). More generally, entrepreneurs benefit from EBPAR during the writing process by illustrating the principles that should guide the preparation of a compelling and convincing entrepreneurial business plan. Venture capital firms have a regime for rating the quality of entrepreneurial business plans and thus potentially improving their investment decisions. Instructors on entrepreneurship programs have a tool to aid their assessment of plans prepared as student assignments.

With the development of EBPAR, Hindle and Mainprize have provided a tool whereby the quality of entrepreneurial business plans can be assessed systematically based on theoretical principles. Improving the communication and credibility aspects of an entrepreneurial business plan could have the potential to improve the likelihood that the plan passes any investor's deal screening process. Determining a visual profile of a particular entrepreneurial business plan provides insight for the entrepreneur and investor alike. An entrepreneur is able to improve the articulation of his plan. For an investor, the EBPAR is a refined lens providing new insight to improve deal screening. The focus of future research should progress towards greater standardisation for the writing and rating of entrepreneurial business plans. Standardisation – the formal framework of a systematic approach to process improvement – is not an end in itself but it could become a means of achieving more consistency and greater transparency in the highly volatile area of deciding whether or not to invest in a new venture. Of course, the most important component influencing that decision will always be the entrepreneurial business plan.

Testing EBP principles in the real world

Entrepreneurial business plans are written by many but mastered by few. Equally, the frameworks to help guide the creation of entrepreneurial business plans are espoused by many and researched by few. Hindle and Mainprize have attempted empirically to study the principles important for the assessment of entrepreneurial business plans that can be used as guidelines for their improvement. In another study, Mainprize and Hindle (2003) used a statistical technique called 'logistic regression' to identify which of the ten EBPAR factors did most to increase the likelihood that an entrepreneurial business plan would 'pass' the investment screening stage in a venture capital evaluation. The aim was to find support (or otherwise) for the proposition that a business plan embodying the ten EBPAR principles would have an enhanced likelihood of passing the investment screening stage of a venture capital deal screening process. The unit of analysis, the investment screening decision, stemmed from decisions made about entrepreneurial business plans. The sample of business plans was taken from a collection of plans raised to obtain venture capital funding in the USA. The study's sampling frame utilised data gathered from over five years of academic–practitioner collaborative efforts with a major North American venture capital conference provider, the Wayne Brown Institute (WBI) (see www.venturecapital.org). Mainprize and Hindle examined 129 entrepreneurial ventures seeking venture capital funding.

The results of logistic regression indicated that the quality of the entrepreneurial business plan as an input correctly predicted a positive investment screening decision at a level of 89.9 per cent. Four of the ten EBPAR variables turned out to be particularly important. They provided a statistically significant indication of propensity to increase the likelihood that the venture would receive positive investment evaluation in the deal screening process. They were:

1. Clearly describing the *entrepreneurial team* made it 2.29 times more likely that a plan would receive a positive investment decision (p = 0.001)
2. A well-articulated *opportunity* made it 1.95 times more likely that a plan would receive a positive investment decision (p = 0.018)
3. Employing simulation techniques to obtain multiple future *scenarios* made it 1.67 times more likely that a plan would receive a positive investment decision (p = 0.038)
4. A clear description of the *business model* made it 1.53 times more likely that a plan would receive a positive investment decision (p = 0.046).

The remaining six EBPAR variables remain important, in that a plan that fails to reach a minimum standard on each of them may be rejected without further analysis. Students are used to an evaluation process that is ultimately additive: if they earned 5/5 for their description of the entrepreneurial team but 2/5 for their description of the opportunity, they would expect to be given 7/10 (a credit or distinction) for the two sections combined. A real-world assessment by an investor is better modelled as a multiplicative process and the combination of 5/5 and 2/5 may be 10/25, that is, 4/10 (a fail). A student exercise that rated 50 per cent on a conventional evaluation might be viewed as anything from zero to 35 per cent by an investor (who, on the other hand, would not expect 100 per cent and might well take such a plan as a good basis for further development).

The dangerous bit: an example entrepreneurial business plan layout

We started this chapter by saying that it was more important to understand the general principles of entrepreneurial business planning than slavishly copy a prefabricated regime prescribed by a textbook. We presented those principles in the form of a description of the entrepreneurial business planning paradigm and showed both how other writers had treated the entrepreneurial business planning problem and how principles distilled from our entrepreneurial business planning paradigm had borne the scrutiny of empirical research. Now we take the dangerous step of suggesting a prefabricated regime of our own. Are we hypocrites? We hope not.

What is offered in this concluding section is an illustration. It shows just *one* way (not the one and only way) that the general principles of good entrepreneurial business planning might be incorporated in a document that *might* be a good format for implementing the principles in a well-designed, readable, comprehensive document. We stress once again that this particular presentation format is indicative, not prescriptive. We encourage you to vary the format as vigorously and creatively as the particular circumstances of your new venture may demand. With all these caveats in mind, here we go.

A good plan does more than communicate with its target audience, it opens up a dialogue with them. The dialogue can be wordless on the other side: it is conceivable, but unlikely, that a professional investor will read a plan and then silently reach for a cheque book. A good business plan must empower the plan reader. This is necessary because the typical reader starts from a position of technical inferiority, knowing substantially less about the industry, the markets and the product than the entrepreneur. By the time readers reach the end of a plan, they should feel that they understand the key facts about the industry and the project. They do not aspire to an equality of knowledge with the entrepreneurial team but to a level of understanding that makes them feel competent to assess the risks and benefits of participation.

Plan design and writing and presentation skills can be critical: the plan readers do not wish to feel patronised, condescended to or lectured at. Equally, different readers will have hugely different tolerance levels for detail. For instance, in the part of a plan describing a new product, a professional engineer or industrial chemist will look for a level of detail that would have a bank manager or venture capitalist reeling in confusion. The best way of satisfying such a disparate audience requires a soundly structured approach to the plan's development and presentation. This is not to say

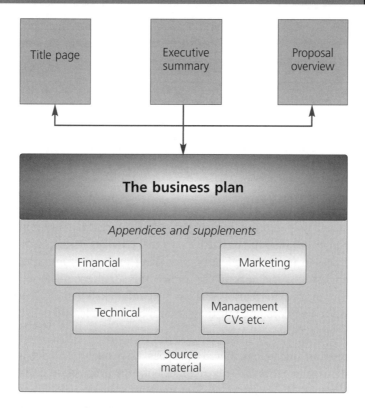

Figure 6.3   **The elements of a business plan**

that there is a single structure that every plan can fit: the entrepreneur must develop a structure that is appropriate to both the project and the audience.

Figure 6.3 shows some of the elements of such a business plan:

- a title page, with sufficient clarity and design to ensure that everyone who picks up the plan will at least read the title and that the target readers will actually look inside the plan
- an executive summary of one or two pages, which makes it clear from the first line who should be reading the plan, what they are being asked to contribute and what they can expect to get out of it
- an overview of the proposed enterprise, written, audio-visual, or multimedia; not a home shopping programme hard sell, but dispassionate and informative
- the business plan itself (described in more detail in Chapter 11 of this book), containing the minimum amount of material that every target reader needs to be presented with
- a series of appendices or supplements containing information that some, but not all, the target readers will wish to review.

We provide more detailed guidance in Chapter 11, but we hope that by the time you have got that far you will have gathered all the material your plan will need, understand why it is important and how to present it, and that you will understand that our overview is more of a checklist than a plan design, something to help you make sure that nothing important has been left out.

Executive summary

This plan has been prepared under the direction of the general manager of the steel division for presentation to the finance committee of the board. It seeks authority to invest US$110 million in a joint venture to build and operate a mini-mill in California. The expected return on this investment will be between 22 and 27 per cent, which comfortably exceeds the current corporate hurdle rate ...

It may be advisable to prepare more than one executive summary when the expected readership is diverse: the risk of a target reader failing to read the body of the plan because the executive summary makes it seem irrelevant is high, while the cost in time and effort of preparing multiple summaries is relatively low. In general terms the appendices and/or the supplements should not be bound with the main plan, for fear of making the combined document hard to carry and terrifying to contemplate, but they should be available and delivered promptly if they are requested.

Flexibility and credibility

Almost anyone who is offered a proposal on a 'take-it-or-leave-it' basis feels an immediate urge to 'leave it'. This includes both the proposition and the plan itself; even if the proposal looks attractive and the plan seems convincing, the prospective stakeholders will wish to feel that they are active participants. One reason is that they do not wish to see their own knowledge and experience slighted; another is that their questions test the entrepreneur's ability to cope with the unexpected during the evolution of the plan.

Questions can be probing and uncomfortable: 'Have you thought of ...'; 'What if you don't get ...'; but enthusiasm can be even harder for the unprepared to cope with: 'Gee, that's great, but you're rollout is so slow that you'll lose half the market. Let me put up double [treble, ten times...] what you asked for and we'll really give the competition a run for its money.' Good answers raise the credibility of the plan, but often good suggestions raise the value of it even further.

Think of the audience

Many people, preparing their first business plans, fail to give much or any weight to the interests of their readers. Broadly, every reader will have two key interests: one, 'due diligence' strictly speaking applies to the officers of a corporate investor or stakeholder and the way they take proper account of their own companies' interests; the other, the return or harvest, enables them to compare the proposed investment with the alternatives that may be available to them.

The plan must address both these interests. The 'due diligence' requirement is satisfied by making the plan complete and intelligible: whatever the actual outcome of a given stakeholder's participation, they should be fully informed, or as fully informed as is reasonably possible, at the time they enter. The plan should not include any false statements, neither should it omit any relevant true ones. The proposed return must be set out clearly and in general terms the deal offered to any prospective participant should represent a proposal laid on the table for discussion. Most professional investors will feel professionally obliged to restructure any deal they are offered, so the entrepreneur should concentrate on showing them the size of the needed investment and the practicality of making a return on it.

It is not sufficient to show that a new enterprise will be profitable: it must either, come harvest time, be generating large amounts of cash such that the venture's investors can receive a capital return, or it must be a saleable enterprise such that the venture's investors can sell their interest, either to a larger company or by way of a public float.

Conclusion: making a plan successful

A plan is successful when it secures the commitment of the owners and controllers of the resources that the plan requires to the project described in the plan. The fact that a plan is successful doesn't guarantee that the implementation of the plan will be a success, but if the plan fails to gain the resources for which it argues the implementation must also fail, either because the project will be aborted or because the project will start without vital requirements. When Compass Airlines started operations in Australia in 1991, the business plan as described in the prospectus showed that it would need $110 million in equity capital to succeed. The public offering only raised $65 million, but instead of either handing back the money or preparing a new plan, Compass Airlines followed the original plan, went broke and the investors lost all their money.

CHECKPOINT Not only are there an infinite number of possible innovations, the number of ways in which one concept can be commercialised is also infinite. Although there must be a 'best possible' plan associated with any concept, there is no known way of finding it. The best we can do is develop a 'locally optimum' project, developed by taking a feasible proposal and 'tuning' each of its significant parameters. The 'first guess' proposal for implementing a new concept is, for all practical purposes, capable of significant improvement with relatively little effort. The base case scenario described in an entrepreneurial business plan must have been refined to the point that there are no easy ways to improve it, which means that it should not be a 'first guess' but a thoroughly refined proposal.

The entrepreneurial team's experience should provide prospective participants with an assurance that the starting assumptions were well chosen, but no amount of experience leads to a perfect first attempt. Every project proposal involves some controllable and some uncontrollable variables. Two sets of simulations are needed, and they need to be kept clearly separate during the planning process: one tests the effect of changes in the uncontrollable variables on the plan outcome, systematically analysing the intrinsic risk of the proposal; the other tests the effect of changes in the controllable variables, systematically searching for an optimal plan.

Factors such as the timing of the entry of the first major competitor are uncontrollable variables; some plans may only offer attractive returns if competitive entry can be deferred for some minimum period. The planners should determine, using sensitivity analysis, what this minimum period is and explain why they believe that competitors will not, in fact, enter before this critical period is over. Factors such as the distribution channels, pricing and marketing expenditure are controllable variables, and the planners should use simulation to find the best values for these variables.

We described model building in Chapter 4, and we consider that computer-based models are an essential tool for all but the most trivial planning exercises. Having a good model does not guarantee that the sensitivity analyses will be carried out completely, and the computer certainly can't do the job on its own, but it does increase the planner's, and the readers', confidence in the quality of the entire plan.

In summary, the entrepreneurial business plan is an active model of the proposed venture. It is used to produce a 'base case scenario', which is the entrepreneur's view of the most likely outcome if all the resources noted as required in the plan are obtained and deployed according to the plan. The same model can and normally will be used to explore a variety of different scenarios, both different environmental constraints and different resource sets. The world is constantly changing: it will certainly be different on the day the plan is completed from its state when the plan was commenced and will change further between the completion of the plan and the start of its implementation. The mark of an excellent entrepreneurial business plan is that it can be brought up to date rapidly: there should never be an excuse for launching a venture based on a plan incorporating assumptions that are known to be false.

Exercises

1 What are the three functions of a business plan?

2 What is wrong with using a business planning package to prepare a plan for your proposed venture?

3 Why do entrepreneurs need plans? Shouldn't they just respond to circumstances as they arise?

4 The executive summary appears at the front of a plan. Does this mean that you should write it first?

5 Investors are likely to take a close look at the marketing sections of a business plan. What are they looking for?

6 An economists' proverb runs, 'there are no $100 bills lying on the pavement', by which they mean that no valuable opportunity will be neglected. This is clearly wrong, but why?

7 Potential investors are interested in the quality of the business model. What is meant by this term and how is a high quality business model distinguished from a low quality one?

8 Investors prefer projects led by experienced entrepreneurs: if you have no previous entrepreneurial experience, does this mean that you cannot launch an entrepreneurial venture? If it doesn't, how can you get around the experience problem?

9 If your student assignment is a business plan and your instructor marks it at 80 per cent, would you expect a venture capitalist to support it without further amendment? If not, why not?

10 If your student assignment is a business plan and your instructor gives you maximum marks for your sections on the entrepreneurial team, the opportunity, your scenario development and your business model, but lower marks for other sections, is your plan ready for submission to an investor? If not, why not?

Notes

1   For an approachable account of the rise of the Honda Motor Company see Sakiya (1987).

2   The inspiration for this figure originally appeared in Mintzberg (1994: 392, Figure 6.7).

3   Well-based systems theory can be used to demonstrate that no finite process can be guaranteed to produce a globally optimum outcome to any non-trivial problem: technique, including entrepreneurial business planning, is limited to refining a given concept, not to creating an ideal one.

4   Consider also O'Toole's corollary: 'If nothing can go wrong, it will.'

7

The legal environment

This chapter

- The law is extensive and dynamic and in common law countries changes every time a superior court issues a judgement. It is far too complex for a chapter such as this to give any more than a long distance overview. When an entrepreneur meets the law, it is essential that she engages a lawyer and, in many cases, obtains specialist legal support as well. Lawyers are expensive, but the problems a business can get into if it attempts to resolve legal matters without involving a lawyer can be more expensive still.

- This chapter will describe a number of areas of business activity where incorrect or ill-advised behaviour could lead to substantial business and personal losses. Ignorance is seldom an acceptable excuse. The chapter is not a legal text and most lawyers will find the treatment of the law simplistic. The readers should, however, learn when and where to be careful.

- Readers who want to learn more about the relevant law could consult a text such as Judge (1999) for British business law, or Pentony et al. (1999) for Australian commercial law, or a reputable textbook in other countries, but owning and even reading one of these books will not turn you into a lawyer; it may, if you have a vivid imagination, put you off an entrepreneurial career entirely. Law books necessarily focus on contraventions and the associated consequences; but most entrepreneurs, most of the time, are not in breach of the law and so are safe from these consequences.

Evolution of the law

Modern law represents the blend of two ways of looking at the world. There is the traditional view of society as a complex network of duties and obligations and there is the law of the market, where caveat emptor (buyer beware) once ruled, subject only to fair weight and honest coinage. Both traditions go back to classical Rome and beyond. The Roman law of the markets became medieval merchant law and is the basis for modern contract law, while traditional law evolved into the modern equity jurisdiction maintained in England by the Chancery Division of the High Court of Justice.

Contract law is conceptually very simple, if complex in practice. An enforceable contract involves two promises or a promise and an act: either one party offers to supply some goods to the other or perform some services for the other or both in return for a 'valuable consideration' and the other party accepts that offer; or one party promises to do something if the other party performs some act or refrains from performing some act and the other party performs or refrains from performing that act. Purported contracts are void if one party used fraud or force to persuade the other party into them, if the performance of the contract involves an unlawful act or acts or if the contract fails various other tests. The law recognises that contracts may be frustrated, in that a change of circumstances makes the performance impossible, and has rules for resolving the outstanding issues; but a contract cannot be repudiated just because one party regrets having entered into it.

Traditional law looks at a person's acts and decides whether they are 'right' or 'wrong' and if there is a dispute attempts to resolve it 'justly'. A contract may be overturned in a traditional jurisdiction if enforcing performance would be unfair or unjust.

Two trends can be observed: one is the growth of contract law to cover steadily wider areas of human activity, such that when a contract clashes with a traditional obligation, the contract prevails. Even matters of marriage and the raising of children, once a bastion of traditional law, have been invaded by contract law in many jurisdictions, with the recognition of prenuptial agreements and the enforcement of surrogacy contracts. At the same time issues of right and justice have encroached on contract law, abolishing caveat emptor when businesses deal with consumers, setting enforceable minimum standards for employment contracts and establishing wide-ranging limitations on the agreements businesses are permitted to make with each other, to list a few of many such encroachments.

A further trend has been the creation of artificial forms of property. Patents, copyrights, trademarks and the like constitute 'intellectual property', which can be traded and carry certain enforceable rights. Other rights may be created by law and then traded: these include fishing quotas, resource exploitation leases and riparian rights among others.

Entrepreneurs

There is relatively little in the law intended specifically to help or hinder entrepreneurs, and patent law, which was specifically intended to encourage entrepreneurship well before the word had entered English usage, has costs and limitations that limit its applicability to a small fraction of new ventures. Copyright was instituted initially as part of the royal censorship system and evolved into a way of freeing authors, composers and artists from the tyranny of patronage; it has proved useful to many entrepreneurs, notably in the IT industry, while failure to understand or use it properly has proved costly to many others.

Contract law clearly antedates modern entrepreneurship but is a necessary condition for it to succeed. While the evolution of contract law gives a modern entrepreneur far greater freedom of action than that enjoyed by a medieval merchant or artisan, there are still many points on which statute law limits an entrepreneur's freedom. For small and new ventures contracts embodying an attitude of common decency towards employees and honesty towards customers are unlikely to get an entrepreneur into serious trouble; but as a business gets larger and its customer base expands and diversifies, good nature and honest intentions may not be enough.

The law has entered a third area unknown in medieval times, the protection of the environment. Every business that produces any waste in the course of its oper-

TO THE RIGHT HONOURABLE THE EARL OF CHESTERFIELD

My Lord,

I have been lately informed, by the proprietor of the World, that two papers, in which my Dictionary is recommended to the public, were written by your Lordship. To be so distinguished is an honour, which, being very little accustomed to favours from the great, I know not well how to receive, or in what terms to acknowledge.

When, upon some slight encouragement, I first visited your Lordship, I was overpowered, like the rest of mankind, by the enchantment of your address, and could not forbear to wish that I might boast myself 'le vainqueur du vainqueur de la terre'; that I might obtain that regard for which I saw the world contending; but I found my attendance so little encouraged that neither pride nor modesty would suffer me to continue it. When I had once addressed your Lordship in public I had exhausted all the art of pleasing which a retired and uncourtly scholar can possess. I had done all that I could, and no man is well pleased to have his all neglected, be it ever so little.

Seven years, my Lord, have now passed since I waited in your outward rooms, or was repulsed from your door; during which time I have been pushing on my work through difficulties, of which it is useless to complain, and have brought it at last to the verge of publication, without one act of assistance, one word of encouragement, or one smile of favour. Such treatment I did not expect, for I never had a Patron before.

'The shepherd in Virgil grew at last acquainted with Love, and found him a native of the rocks.'

Is not a Patron, my Lord, one who looks with unconcern on one struggling for life in the water, and when he has reached ground, encumbers him with help? The notice which you have been pleased to take of my labours, had it been early, had been kind; but it has been delayed until I am indifferent, and cannot enjoy it; till I am solitary, and cannot impart it; till I am known, and do not want it. I hope it is no very cynical asperity not to confess obligations where no benefit has been received, or to be unwilling that the public should consider me as owing that to a Patron, which Providence has enabled me to do for myself.

Having carried on my work thus far with so little obligation to any favourer of learning, I shall not be disappointed though I should conclude it, if less be possible, with less; for I have been awakened from that dream of hope, in which I once boasted myself with so much exaltation, my Lord,

Your Lordship's most humble, most obedient servant,

S. J.

                                          Boswell ([1791] 1896): pp 212–3

ations must comply with the relevant environmental laws or face heavy penalties for breaching them. Tipping unwanted chemicals into the sewer or heavy metal scraps into the municipal dump, even in small quantities, can be a very expensive mistake.

There is one area of the law that was specifically developed with entrepreneurs in mind, company law. A traditional merchant's 'word was his bond' and was backed by all that merchant's resources: there was no distinction between the man and the business. If two or more people conducted an enterprise, they were partners and as such jointly and severally liable for the debts of the business. If an enterprise failed, the result could be ruin for the entrepreneur, her partners and their families. During the nineteenth century legal changes and judicial decisions made it relatively easy for an entrepreneur and her partners to establish a 'limited liability' company, which could trade as if it was a person, but if it was wound up the shareholders ('members of the company') were only liable to the company's creditors to the extent of their share subscriptions, and if all their shares were fully paid for, not liable at all. This meant that the failure of a business did not mean automatic ruin for the entrepreneur and, even more importantly, it meant that entrepreneurs could raise capital by issuing shares to members of the public and the subscribers' liability was strictly limited.

Patents and quasi-patents[1]

Patents are granted for inventions and are basically industrial in application.

The definition of an invention in the Statute of Monopolies passed in the reign of James I included 'any manner of new manufacture' and this is still the usual definition. This actually has three or four elements:

Requirements
for a patent

- *Manufacture:* This can be a product itself, the method of making a product or any other part of the manufacturing process.
- *Newness:* This is critical. An invention must not be disclosed before a patent application is filed. Too often, in their initial enthusiasm, inventors publish their invention and then find that they cannot get a valid patent. Prior publication by anyone else, anywhere in the world, of a description of an invention invalidates a patent.
- *Invention:* An invention cannot be validly patented if it is 'obvious' in the light of what has been known and used before and to the use that can be made of the prior art base by a person 'skilled in the art'. This is a most difficult matter when patents are contested and the courts consider each case on its merits.
- *Utility* (or usefulness): This refers to the patent itself, not the product or process it protects: to be valid, a patent must describe the invention clearly and completely enough for a suitably equipped reader to replicate it.

How do you
get a patent?

Patents are granted by the national Patent Office of each country, or by the European Patent Office for patents covering all the countries of the European Union. In general an inventor must submit a claim with the appropriate fee, pay further fees to have the patent validated by a patent examiner and, assuming that the patent is accepted, a fee for its initial issue and further fees to renew it, if that is desired, until the maximum permitted time has expired. The initial fees are substantial, at approximately €2000 per country per patent on top of patent attorney costs, while the renewal fees are also substantial.

An inventor does not have to make a separate application in every country. The International Convention for the Protection of Industrial Property permits applicants to maintain the priority of their home application, provided applications in other offices are filed within 12 months of the home application. The Patent Cooperation Treaty (PCT) enables a single filing to give notional protection in most countries of the world (with the exception of some Asian countries, notably Taiwan, and some South American countries) for a further period of 18 months before it is necessary to file in individual countries (or 'enter the national phase', in the language of the Treaty). The PCT can be used in association with the International Convention, which means a PCT application can be lodged up to 12 months after the first home application.

The PCT allows an inventor to avoid the cost of overseas patent applications until a firm decision has been made to exploit the invention commercially in foreign as well as domestic markets, but if an entrepreneur or inventor desires global or multi-country protection, they will eventually have to pay the fees applicable to each relevant patent office.

While the law in most countries permits anyone to visit a patent office, submit an application and pay the fees, the patent that may follow, if any, is unlikely to be enforceable unless an experienced patent attorney prepared the claim. Minor defects in drafting or slight omissions in the specification can be turned into loopholes big enough to drive a London bus through when discovered by a specialist lawyer acting on behalf of an infringer.

When more than one inventor claims to have made a particular invention, the law in most countries other than the USA dictates that the patent must be awarded to the 'first to file', and one of the first steps every national patent office will take when a new application is submitted is to record the date and time the application is received. Because of a peculiarity of the US patent law, where there are two inventors of the 'same' invention, the patent office can decide who was the first inventor and the first inventor can be granted that patent even though her application was the later filed one. Non-American inventors are at a disadvantage as the earliest date they can claim, if they are working outside America, is the date of their earliest application.

Are patents worth the time and expense?

If there is any doubt, we suggest that an entrepreneur should lodge a patent application. It is conceivable that more money has been made from applications that cannot be granted or patents that would be held by the courts to be invalid than from valid patents. An applicant can license an application that never goes to grant and can keep the application alive for a number of years, possibly equal to the commercial life of the invention.

Further, the existence of a patent application can act as a deterrent to possible copiers or infringers. There are three types of these:

1. Some people will take positive steps to make sure that they do not infringe on anyone's patent. If they see a patent application number, they will immediately abandon plans to produce a potentially infringing product.
2. Others are cautious about potential legal costs and penalties if they are caught infringing. They will take some time to decide whether or not to risk infringing a patent. This time can be most valuable to an applicant who markets the new product vigorously.
3. The third are the cowboys who will copy and be damned. There is little you can do about these, but they are by far the smallest group in the developed countries. (Politicians and law enforcement agencies in lesser developed and developing countries often regard patents and other intellectual property as tools of neocolonial oppression, 'more honoured in the breach'.) The US has, in recent years, been a strident advocate of intellectual property rights in international forums, but through the nineteenth century and well into the twentieth, the US treated free access to foreigners' intellectual property as the birthright of every American.

What happens if someone infringes a patent?

Because a patent monopoly is closely defined, proving infringement, except in the most blatant of cases, can be a highly technical matter and the patent holder should seek advice from a patent attorney or specialist solicitor before taking any action. Assuming that the specialists agree that there is an infringement, the first step will usually be to write a letter, demanding that the infringing activities cease and threatening action without further notice if it does not.

Such a letter of demand serves three purposes. It may lead to settlement of the dispute but, if not, it ensures a positive date for damages or an account of profits. If it is necessary to start litigation, then this can be done without further notice. Courts do not like litigation to be commenced without the infringer being given an opportunity to cease infringement.

Taking a claim to court is going to be an expensive business; you may have to spend €3000 before the first word is said in court and €50,000 or possibly much more before you get a judgment. If the infringement is in another country, your expenses will be increased by travel and accommodation costs and the need to duplicate specialist and legal resources. Litigation should be avoided if at all possible.

Minor patents

Some countries, including Australia and Germany, offer a simplified patent with a shorter maximum lifespan and an easier and lower cost application process. Intellectual property specialists regard these devices with some suspicion. Many of them consider that the reduction in the cost of securing a minor patent is trivial compared with the reduction in protection offered.

Other people's patents

Quite apart from the value of having one's own patents, patents can be of great value to entrepreneurs. Why reinvent the wheel? A search of the patent records will reveal substantial information about what has been done before. Quite apart from informing the entrepreneur what she can't do, because there is a subsisting patent or application, the complete specification of a patent or patent application must include 'the best method known to the applicant of performing the invention'. This means, first, if one can find a good invention that has not been commercialised, and in respect of which the patent or patent application has lapsed, one is well on the way to getting a product without the work needed to start from scratch. Second, it means that entrepreneurs can find out what their competitors are doing and this can lead to 'spring boarding', rapid development of superior products and processes to the benefit of the public and the entrepreneur.

Registered design

In law, a design refers to the appearance of an article and can relate to one or more of the shape, pattern, configuration or ornamentation of the article. It does not protect the principles of manufacture or operation of an artefact: if these are to be protected at all, they must be protected by patents. A design does not extend to two-dimensional impressions; these are covered by copyright. Note that the term 'design patent' is used in the USA for that which is referred to as a 'registered design' elsewhere.

A design is registered by lodging representations of the design, normally drawings or photographs, at the appropriate offices. The actual forms are usually simple, although in the US a specification similar to a patent specification (although simpler) must be filed. In the US, the protection granted is a design patent, which may give some functional protection in certain cases.

A design is infringed if the design or a fraudulent or obvious imitation is applied in the country of registration to an article; by importation of an article which, if made in the country of registration, would be an infringement; or if articles under the above categories are sold or offered for sale or hired or offered for hire.

If you believe that a registered design has been infringed, you should consult a patent attorney or a solicitor, who will probably recommend writing to the infringer and demanding that infringement cease. The demand will also often request several further actions, such as the destruction of infringing articles and the payment of damages and costs. If an infringer can prove that she took all reasonable steps to avoid infringing, there can be no damages in respect of the period before the letter was sent.

If writing to the infringer does not produce the desired result, it is open for the proprietor to take the matter to court. Unless the infringement is point-for-point exact, the decision may be a matter of opinion and success in court is not guaranteed. As with patents, the costs of taking an infringer to court are high and you should satisfy yourself that the potential rewards justify the risks and expense before proceeding.

Specialist protection

Circuit layout protection

Specific circuit layout laws to protect the owners' copyright in the layout of integrated circuits have been implemented in most jurisdictions that support the Trade Related Aspects of Intellectual Property (TRIPs) Agreement of the General Agreement on Tariffs and Trade (GATT) treaty which established the World Trade Organization (WTO).

Basically, like copyright, generally, it is not necessary that the copyright be registered but there is a necessity to obtain a written assignment if the author is not the owner or is not employed by the owner. The protection of TRIPs is that it gives the owner the right to copy the layout, the right to produce integrated circuits in accordance with the layout and the right to exploit the layout. These rights are infringed by copying the layout, whether directly or in a material form (that is, by the manufacture of integrated circuits in accordance with the layout). There is protection against innocent infringement: if the infringer did not know and could not have been expected to know there was infringement, no liability accrues.

In order to prove infringement for an integrated circuit, it would normally be necessary to section and polish the chip and then take micro-photographs of the etched circuit. A chip or circuit designer might feel that demonstrating that a competing chip or circuit board performed to exactly the same specification and used an identical pattern of terminations ('plug compatibility') was sufficient to prove infringement, however, a number of plug compatible chips have survived challenges by proving that they were different in design.

Plant breeders' rights

It is possible in most jurisdictions that support the TRIPs Agreement to obtain protection for new varieties of plants but it is also possible in some cases to obtain normal patent protection. A new plant may be deemed to be a manner of new manufacture and to get protection it is necessary for the plant to meet the other requirements of invention: it must be new and it must be inventive, or non-obvious. Because the newness requirement for protection of plant varieties is generally less stringent than for a patent, there may be occasions where protection can be sought under the provisions for plant breeders' rights where they could not be sought under the patent laws.

The specific requirements for securing plant variety protection are: that the variety was originated by a person (that is, natural variation cannot be claimed); it must be homogeneous and stable; it must be distinguished from other varieties by one or more important characteristics; it must not be a species or genus which is excluded from protection; it must not have been offered for sale in another country for more than a statutory period (which may vary between plant types), prior to filing for protection.

The period of protection is generally 25 years for trees and vines and 20 years for other varieties. It is not an offence to grow the variety, provided this is for private and non-commercial use, nor is it an offence to grow the variety for experimental purposes. If protected plants or seeds are properly purchased by farmers, it is not an infringement for them to save and use seed derived from them for their own purposes.

Copyright

Copyright is created automatically by creating an original literary or artistic work, including a new technical manual or computer program. When publishing such a work it is advisable to ensure that its copyright is respected by including the following line close to the title:

© Copyright [Name of person(s) or firm(s) who own copyright] [year of first publication][, year of a revised publication]...

Copyright protects the results of creative endeavour, meaning the sequence of words or notes or the form of a literary work, musical composition or work of art. The ideas expressed in the work are specifically excluded from protection, so someone who independently produces a new work expressing the same ideas but in substantially different words, note sequences or form is free to publish it.

Copyright is not a monopoly protection; it is purely a protection against copying. Thus, unless the work has been available to the alleged copyist, there can be no breach of copyright. For example, two persons with cameras can stand side by side and take effectively identical pictures and each will have copyright in her own picture. If a third person copies one of these pictures, she infringes the copyright in the picture concerned but not the other and so, for infringement to be proved, it is necessary to show which picture was copied.

When assigning copyright great care is needed: such assignments must be done in writing. A contract to produce material which is the subject of copyright is not, in itself, sufficient to transfer the copyright to the purchaser, it will simply give an implied licence to use the material. To protect against subsequent disputes it is essential that, where an entrepreneur makes an agreement with an unrelated party to develop copyright material, such as a user manual or a computer program, there should be, as part of the agreement, an obligation on the contractor to execute an assignment when asked to do so.

The purchase of a copyrighted work does not transfer copyright. If you buy a painting, this does not give you the right to use it on Christmas cards; such use is an infringement of copyright. There can also be an infringement if a video or film is made in an area where copyright works are displayed, if the works are placed on film more than incidentally. A clip for television which shows copyright material could infringe copyright.

Trademarks and registered trademarks

A trademark is any sign used to distinguish the goods and services of a trader from those of other traders. Simply by adopting a particular word or device (or even a sound or a scent, as described below) as a symbol to distinguish goods or services, it becomes a trademark. Of course, it may not be a very 'good' trademark and may not be able to be protected.

In the common law countries, including the UK, Australia, the US, Canada, South Africa and New Zealand, as well as in most countries whose legal systems are based on the British tradition, the first user of the trademark has unassailable rights although a concurrent user may also develop rights. In the civil code countries, generally Continental Europe and Japan, rights go to the first applicant for registration although the first user will normally be entitled to continue to use the mark.

Historically, a trademark was a word, a number of words or a device, or a combination of word(s) and a device; but nowadays the definition can relate to anything which can be set down in writing, including the more historical forms of trademarks, such things as sounds and scents.

A good trademark should be distinctive and preferably inherently distinctive at the time of adoption but, on use, even inherently non-distinctive marks can develop a secondary meaning and become distinctive. Most people would have little difficulty in associating Bollinger with champagne or IBM with computers. Acceptance by the market-place is most important to marks.

A trademark must distinguish the goods or services of the application and so a word which is completely descriptive of a class of goods or services has not been able to be registered as a trademark, no matter how distinctive it has become. For example the Oxford University Press was not permitted to register 'Oxford' in respect of publications, although it could show about 400 years' use. If a word used as a trademark passes into common use by other traders, that mark may be removed from the register. The Univac Corporation first applied the word 'computer' to a programmable calculating machine and registered it as a trademark, but they were unable to prevent the term 'computer' passing into general use and so they retain no particular rights over the use of the term. However, 'Biro' and 'Thermos' remain on the register in Europe; although they are used generically by the public, they are not so used by other traders.

It is desirable for a user of a trademark to assert that the word is a trademark whenever it is used. The 'TM' symbol, as in 'to use Splodge™, first prepare...' can be used to assert the rights of the proprietor in the word 'Splodge' and counters the contextual implication that it is a general term for products used in the manner described.

Registration

Additional protection for a trademark may be secured by registering it with the appropriate statutory authorities. This may be particularly important for a new trademark, where there is no trading history to establish the owner's rights to it.

A major advantage of the registration of a trademark lies in the protection of the mark. Registration gives rise to a monopoly right to the use of the mark and prohibits the use of deceptively similar marks in respect of the goods for which the mark is registered. If the same or a deceptively similar mark is used on goods which are of the same description as the goods for which the mark is registered, provided that there is a likelihood of deception or confusion, then there is infringement. In some jurisdictions, if a mark is a well-known mark, there can be infringement by the use of the same or a deceptively similar mark on unrelated goods, if there is likelihood that the infringing mark would be taken to be connected to the registered mark.

These provisions substantially broaden the protection given by registration. They have been adopted by countries harmonising their laws with those of other countries as agreed in the TRIPs Agreement. The actual registration process and the related fees may change from one jurisdiction to another.

While the '®' symbol may not be specifically recognised in all jurisdictions, it may be desirable to use it in association with the mark after registration to assist in maintaining the rights in the trademark. Marks cannot be hoarded; they can lapse if they are not used.

Protecting and defending trademarks

Owners of valuable trademarks should be active in discouraging their use as generic terms, particularly in relation to their application to similar products by other traders. Descriptive use by others is not in itself damaging; but it is important to guard against the use of a trademark as a noun: the IBM Corporation was not seriously troubled by the frequent (and unflattering) references to 'IBM machines' in Joseph Heller's *Catch 22*, but if Heller's book had referred to 'IBMs', his publisher could have expected a visit from IBM Corporation's lawyers. The sole proprietor of the Big Blue laundromat in suburban New York was astounded by the arrival of three partners in one of America's largest legal firms, accusing him of damaging IBM's reputation and demanding that he adopt a different name. One edition of the Merriam-Webster International Dictionary decided not to identify trademarks and was withdrawn after very substantial complaints by trademark owners.

If you suspect that one of your trademarks has been infringed, you should consult a patent attorney or solicitor. They will probably recommend an initial demand on the infringer requesting that the use of the mark cease. The demand may also include a request for other remedies. If this does not produce a satisfactory result, then infringement actions can be commenced.

Common law protection of intellectual property

Passing off

The common law offence of 'passing off' arose from merchant law as a form of consumer protection; merchants were not allowed to make false claims about the provenance of goods offered since this might deceive buyers into paying too much. 'I promise you that this is an original Michelangelo, offered to you for the astounding price of two gold florins.' Merchants who defied these rules could be deemed to have brought their guild into disrepute, and could be sanctioned by fines or even exclusion from the trade. As now adopted into the common and EU[2] law, there is a general prohibition on deceiving buyers by giving them misleading or false information, either about the product, 'This pill will make you irresistible to ...' or endorsements of it, 'Approved by the Royal College of ...'. The simplest defence against passing off charges is honesty: entrepreneurs who make no false or misleading claims about their products and do not cite false testimonials or permit their product to be confused with those supplied by others are unlikely to get into trouble.

In some jurisdictions lawyers have been able to use the passing off provision on behalf of the supplier whose name has been misused, claiming that they would suffer in reputation if buyers believed that they had, in fact, produced the inferior product that was being sold as if it was theirs. Case law varies from country to country; in the USA the standard for passing off is very high and packaging or labelling that a British or Australian court might consider deceptively similar to a plaintiff's product might be held, in the USA, to be legitimately competitive. There are specialist firms in the USA that produce knock-off packaging to order, including those minimal changes which will create a defence against a passing off claim in the US courts.

If an entrepreneur can register a design or a trademark it is wise to do so, rather than rely on a common law claim. Most of the EU countries do not follow common law, and even in Britain an infringer might argue that an entrepreneur's failure to use the available statutory protection suggests that there was little value in the designs, trademarks or trade dress that was copied.

Trade secrets

Firms often have confidential information that, if it was taken and wrongly given to some other party, perhaps by a disaffected staff member leaving the firm's employ, could cause great damage to the company. Generally, if the company treats this information as confidential, the courts will regard it as being so. Information about a firm which is readily available through publication in a catalogue or an annual or other report cannot be confidential.

If there is a breach of confidentiality, it is possible to obtain an injunction to prevent further breaches, but this may be like unscrambling an egg and the only practical action is to seek recompense for the damage that has occurred.

Inventors or entrepreneurs may wish to disclose their invention or a concept, perhaps to a manufacturer, a prospective investor or a potential lead customer. If, prior to the disclosure, the material is stated to be confidential and the person receiving the material accepts this as a fact, then a relationship of confidentiality has been established between the two parties. This does not have to be more than a verbal agreement but for the purposes of proof, it is desirable to have some form of written statement in which the person to whom the material is disclosed agrees to respect confidentiality. If the material is not confidential, that is, it is already available to the person to whom it is disclosed, it does not matter what documents are signed, this does not give the material any status which it did not have before.

Some companies, particularly American ones, to whom material is to be disclosed, have their own form of confidentiality agreement which must be signed by the discloser before the company is prepared to consider material given to it. These agreements are to protect the company against being informed of something of which they are already aware, but which has not been published. For example, the company may have been carrying out research in an area to which a disclosure made to it relates and may have already made a development that is the same or very similar to the material disclosed to it. The company, of course, wants to ensure that the value of its own knowledge is not affected by the disclosure. A disclosing company achieves protection by limiting what is accepted as being confidential to what the discloser can obtain a valid US patent for.

One substantial advantage of seeking confidentiality is to bring the situation to the attention of the person disclosing information. Most breaches in this area are inadvertent rather than deliberate and if people are told that certain information is confidential, they are generally likely to respect its confidentiality.

Note that most countries and the EU have implemented 'whistle-blower' protection laws, making it impossible to prevent disclosure of unlawful behaviour by claiming that the discloser has a duty of confidentiality by reason of the way in which she learned of the offence. Obviously there is a grey area where the behaviour disclosed is arguably legal although unethical and immoral; an enterprise that pursues a whistle-blower for disclosing such activities may be seen by the public, and possibly its customers, as compounding the original offence against acceptable standards of behaviour.

Products

In practically all developed countries firms, whether incorporated or not, that offer goods and services to the public must meet certain minimum standards of conduct. The following list is not exhaustive:

■ suppliers owe a qualified duty of care to those who may use their products or be affected by the use of their products
■ suppliers offer certain statutory warranties when they sell goods and services.

The duty of care

The concept of a 'duty of care' is an ancient one, but was originally limited to a supplier's obligation to direct customers and could be qualified by the supplier's understanding of the purchaser's competence. A naive buyer was protected but a sophisticated one was not. This worked well enough when most commercial dealings were direct, but tends to leave aggrieved users without a remedy in a modern economy with its multistage manufacturing and distribution processes.

Statute law and case law have progressively extended the duty of care to the point that a supplier, filling an order from a manufacturer exactly as specified, might still be found negligent if the component was unsuitable for its intended purpose and harm to persons occurred as a result. The courts may look beyond such issues as whether the product was being used as directed, or even used legally, and ask whether the supplier could have reasonably anticipated harm coming to third parties. If a motorcar accident was caused by brake failure, itself caused by the fracture of an underengineered component, and bystanders were hurt, the bystanders might have a case against the brake manufacturer even if the car had been speeding and under the control of an unlicensed driver before the accident.

US case law has gone further than that of most other countries in extending the duty of care to remoter and remoter parties, and firms planning to export goods to the US, or offer services to US citizens, should endeavour to ensure that their product will not cause unexpected harm in any circumstances in which it may reasonably be expected to be used. A manufacturer of hammers would probably not be liable to the estate of someone murdered with one of their products, but might well be liable to someone blinded by a chip flying from the head, even if the placard under which the hammer had been sold had phrases like 'Use eye protection' and 'Not for use with hardened nails' in bold print.

US law does not, in general, recognise territorial boundaries where US citizens or businesses are involved. Since it is generally impossible to ensure that a manufactured product is never sold in the US, or that a service is never provided to a US citizen, prudent entrepreneurs will operate as if the US standard of care applies universally.

Statutory liability

Statute law supplements the common law in many jurisdictions. Article 6 of the EU Directive on product safety (85/374/EEC) states in part:

> A product is defective when it does not provide the safety which a person is entitled to expect, taking all circumstances into account, including:
> (a) the presentation of the product
> (b) the use to which it could reasonably be expected that the product would be put
> (c) time when the product was put into circulation.

All relevant circumstances may need to be considered, including: the manner and purpose for which the goods in question had been marketed; their packaging; the use of any marks in relation to them; any instructions for, or warnings with respect of, their use or misuse; what might reasonably be expected to be done with them; and the time when they were supplied by the manufacturer.

The law may protect suppliers who improve the safety of their products from the inference that previous versions of them were unsafe, and provides a state-of-the-art defence if the manufacturer can prove that the defect could not have been discovered, given the state of scientific and technical knowledge at the time of manufacture. Manufacturers who can prove that the goods complied with a mandatory standard; or that they only became defective because they were incorporated into finished goods; or that they became defective after shipping are usually protected.

Statutory conditions and warranties

Article 2 of Directive 1999/44/EC of the European Parliament and the Council of 25 May 1999 states:

Conformity with the contract

1. The seller must deliver goods to the consumer which are in conformity with the contract of sale.
2. Consumer goods are presumed to be in conformity with the contract if they:
   (a) comply with the description given by the seller and possess the qualities of the goods which the seller has held out to the consumer as a sample or model;
   (b) are fit for any particular purpose for which the consumer requires them and which he made known to the seller at the time of conclusion of the contract and which the seller has accepted;

(c) are fit for the purposes for which goods of the same type are normally used;

(d) show the quality and performance which are normal in goods of the same type and which the consumer can reasonably expect, given the nature of the goods and taking into account any public statements on the specific characteristics of the goods made about them by the seller, the producer or his representative, particularly in advertising or on labelling.

(e) There shall be deemed not to be a lack of conformity for the purposes of this Article if, at the time the contract was concluded, the consumer was aware, or could not reasonably be unaware of, the lack of conformity, or if the lack of conformity has its origin in materials supplied by the consumer.

3. The seller shall not be bound by public statements, as referred to in paragraph 2(d) if he:

(a) shows that he was not, and could not reasonably have been, aware of the statement in question,

(b) shows that by the time of conclusion of the contract the statement had been corrected, or

(c) shows that the decision to buy the consumer goods could not have been influenced by the statement.

4. Any lack of conformity resulting from incorrect installation of the consumer goods shall be deemed to be equivalent to lack of conformity of the goods if installation forms part of the contract of sale of the goods and the goods were installed by the seller or under his responsibility. This shall apply equally if the product, intended to be installed by the consumer, is installed by the consumer and the incorrect installation is due to a shortcoming in the installation instructions.

Subsequent articles of the Directive set out further consumer rights. In most countries the law sets out a similar default set of conditions that apply to all sales of merchandise.

What does change from country to country, and in the USA from state to state, is the ease or difficulty of evading these conditions. In the EU the conditions cannot be overridden by contract conditions for goods sold to consumers for their own or their household's use: for such consumer-type goods the statutory conditions override any terms in the contract of sale that would tend to weaken them. In other jurisdictions some or all of the conditions can be voided by a contract, but even there simply printing a waiver on the back of the receipt may not suffice to protect the seller.

Ethical entrepreneurs should not seek to evade these quite reasonable conditions.

Fitness for purpose

The common law, supplemented in the EU and some other countries by statute law (see 2(a) and 2(b) above), states that whenever a purchaser, whether a consumer or not, expressly or implicitly makes known the use to which a proposed good is to be put, the supplier may be legally obliged to make good any loss incurred by the purchaser if the goods were not, when supplied, capable of satisfactory use in the manner expected. In some jurisdictions (but probably not in the EU) a supplier can defend a claim, including claims from final consumers, under this heading by proving that the purchaser did not rely, and could not have been reasonably expected to rely, on the supplier's recommendations.

This legal rule makes it smart for a buyer to be dumb, not to say 'I want that...', but rather 'What do I need for...'. Firms are often drawn into trouble under this heading by overeager salespersons, or the entrepreneur in a selling role: when a potential customer is on the point of agreeing to buy a product and asks for some reassurance that it will not merely work as specified, but do the job that the buyer wants, it takes some discipline, backed up by training, to avoid giving a warranty of fitness for purpose.

In cases where a fitness for purpose warranty is unavoidable, as with a design-and-construct contract, a prudent firm will insist on seeing a full specification of the user's requirements included as part of the contract.

Correspondence to description

The common law, supplemented in many jurisdictions by statute law (see 2(a) above), forbids suppliers from supplying goods that do not conform to a description used in advertising or marked on the goods or their packaging.

In practically all jurisdictions buyers are legally entitled to refuse to accept or pay for shipments of goods that do not conform to their advertised or marked description and to sue for the recovery of any damages caused by such goods. In some jurisdictions it is a criminal offence to deliberately supply consumers with goods or services that fail to conform to their description.

Merchantable quality

Merchantable quality is a traditional legal term that generally protects purchasers from unpleasant surprises caused by hidden defects or faulty workmanship; in the UK it has been replaced by the concept of 'satisfactory quality'. Consumers in the EU are guaranteed goods of merchantable or satisfactory quality by clause 2(d) of the Directive cited above. It does not imply perfection (unless the normal standard for that class of product is zero-defect). Goods explicitly sold for repair, as damaged or for scrap are not generally required to meet this quality standard.

Express warranty Buyers generally have a right to the performance of any claims made by a supplier or the supplier's representative that induce them to make a purchase. Commercial purchasers will usually be offered a contract limiting the warranties to a limited number of documents and excluding other representations or material. Under normal circumstances, the courts would be expected to uphold such a contract between businesses.

In some jurisdictions, contracts and terms of sale purporting to exclude the right to performance on an express warranty are void if consumers normally buy the relevant goods or services for their own or their household's use. As with 'fitness for purpose', express warranties are usually offered by salespersons trying to close a difficult sale, and entrepreneurs and managers should ensure that they provide sales training and set out sales procedures that help staff resist the temptation to make such promises.

Promotional practice

Merchant law forbad, and following it the common law forbids, 'misleading and deceptive conduct'. In many jurisdictions this vague and general term has been clarified by statute as well as case law and some classes of misleading or deceptive conduct are singled out and specifically prohibited. The courts in most jurisdictions have refined the definitions by their decisions, and an entrepreneur who sets out to skirt the edge of the law may be able to do so if she can secure the help of an equally unethical lawyer. As at 2003, the EU had begun a process of developing a uniform standard for trading practices, but until a directive is passed, national laws will apply.

In England the relevant laws are administered by the Department of Trade and Industry, and outlined on their web site http://www.dti.gov.uk/ccp/topics1/adprice.htm.

Endorsements and comparisons

It is generally an offence to claim an endorsement or approval that a product does not, in fact, have or to say that some person or firm is a user if they are not. In many jurisdictions it is an offence to make a false claim about a product, whether or not any one is actually deceived and whether or not any person or company suffers harm by believing the claim. It may also be an offence to assert, falsely, that the use of a particular product or class of products is mandatory or essential when it in fact is not. An exception is often made for commercial hyperbole, or 'puffery', covering claims that are so outrageous that no reasonable person would take them seriously.

In general terms, a company may compare its products to those of its competitors, but it is prohibited from making false statements about its competitors' products on matters of objective fact such as the normal trading price or measurable aspects of performance. Firms have got into trouble by quoting their competitor's list prices in markets where the normal trading practice involved substantial discounts, for example. Equally, firms should avoid claiming or implying that their product is the same as that of one of their competitors. Such assertions do not have to be explicit to be caught by the law; in many jurisdictions a firm that uses packaging that is deceptively similar to that of one of its competitors may be committing an offence and may also be the target of legal action by the affected competitor.

Spurious claims

In many jurisdictions firms may not advertise a product at an especially attractive price and then claim to have 'sold out' the special offer with a view to switch-selling consumers onto a higher priced product. Neither may they use terms like 'limited quantity' when supplies of a product are, for practical purposes, not limited. The word 'new' must be used with care and firms have been successfully prosecuted for using the word 'new' to describe reconditioned goods sold with an as-new warranty; other firms have been prosecuted for selling unused goods as 'new' when they were not from current production.

Games and contests

Promotions offering prizes in return for coupons may be treated like illegal lotteries in some jurisdictions. The law on illegal lotteries is complex and changes from place to place. Putting a card into a package and promising that 'those who return a completed card will be entered into a draw for a prize' may constitute a crime in some places or require a special permit in others. Many entrepreneurs and small business operators flout these laws almost routinely and, as long as no one complains, they will continue to do so. The gaming police generally have bigger fish to fry. Breaking the law gives, however, a hostage to fortune and the prudent entrepreneur will consult a lawyer before starting a promotional game.

Even when a contest is conducted perfectly legally, the offer may create an enforceable contract between the seller and its buyers, and a carelessly run game may prove very expensive. In the UK the Hoover Company promised all buyers of certain of its products in a given period a free air trip to New York; so many took advantage of the offer that the company was forced into bankruptcy. In Australia a company selling instant lottery tickets defined one of the winning conditions for a major prize ambiguously and was forced to pay out on more tickets than it had planned to.

Trading stamps and coupons

It was once a common practice to attach or print a coupon to the packaging of some commonly purchased good and promise buyers a gift if they collected a sufficient number of them. In the UK, New South Wales and elsewhere certain companies ran merchant schemes, where buyers would receive stamps in proportion to their purchases, which could then be redeemed from a catalogue. These practices are now subject to regulation or even bans in some jurisdictions and the prudent entrepreneur will avoid them or consult a lawyer before doing something similar.

In the USA frequently, and in other countries somewhat less frequently, manufacturers may add a coupon to the packaging of certain goods promising some value on presentation, such as a discount on the next purchase or even cash back on presentation. Such coupons create a contractual obligation and they may create a contingent liability which should be recognised in a company's accounts. For this reason it is important that the wording on the coupons and that used in any associated promotions is unambiguous and includes an end date.

Electronic versions of these schemes are now relatively common, with holders of a loyalty card or a co-branded credit card entitled to various benefits in return for their patronage of the suppliers associated with the loyalty card or their use of the credit card. These schemes create enforceable contractual obligations and associated contingent liabilities; they may also attract the attention of the consumer protection authorities if the benefits are described deceptively. 'Frequent flyer' schemes that offer 'free' flights in return for points cannot unreasonably restrict access to such flights: Qantas, for example, made an undertaking to the Australian competition authority to reserve some seats for frequent flyers on every scheduled service.

Gifts and free samples

Gifts as such, like a free brush with each large can of paint or a glass with a bottle of drink, are unlikely to run foul of the law. Things may be more tricky when the buyer does not know the value or nature of the gift until after the purchase is concluded, as with prizes for finding certain symbols on the inside of the packet; if the prizes are valuable enough the promotion may constitute a lottery requiring an appropriate permit. Free samples are also generally safe, although there may be regulations limiting such offers in particular cases and places. If the product could cause damage in the wrong hands, like razor blades that might fall into the hands of young children if left in letterboxes, the firm responsible for the promotion could find itself in considerable trouble.

Summary

Entrepreneurs should be honest about their own products. They should not make any claims about third parties, whether competitors, customers, or standards and testing authorities, unless these claims can be backed up by sound, documentary evidence.

Companies

Company law is vast and complex, and the following overview sets out the general principles that the law in most jurisdictions implements. Entrepreneurs should consult their lawyers and accountants before setting up a company and for guidance into how to manage it; they should *not* assume that practices that are acceptable in one country would be acceptable in another.

A company is a legal person, separate from its directors and shareholders. It is capable of entering into contracts and incurring debts, but the actions of a company are, in fact, the actions of people. There are several classes of people who may be identified with any company:

- there are shareholders, essentially passive investors, who receive a portion of the profits in the form of dividends when such are paid and in the event of liquidation, who are entitled to any of the company's assets not already pledged to someone else
- there are directors, who are elected by the shareholders but whose primary duty is to act in good faith in the company's interest – they are ultimately responsible for the company
- there are senior executives, who are appointed by the directors (and in some cases may be directors) and enjoy the delegated authority of the directors between board meetings
- there are other employees, who (at least in theory) do what the senior executives tell them to do.

Ethical entrepreneurs will usually operate through companies, both because of the possibility of receiving more appropriate treatment by the tax authorities and the possible need to be able to raise capital by the sale of shares, if not immediately, then in the reasonably near future. Taxation law is complex and frequently changed and an entrepreneur should consult an accountant and/or a lawyer, both to advise on the most appropriate company structure and for assistance in drawing up and registering the necessary documents.

The company form will allow the entrepreneurs to keep their private affairs separate from those of the business, and their investors will be protected from risks beyond the possible loss of their investment. Ethical entrepreneurs will not treat the company as a device for diverting investors' money to their own pockets or swindling the firm's creditors or employees. Unethical entrepreneurs who do abuse the corporate form may be prosecuted and on conviction have their gains confiscated, although the risk of such prosecution varies with the jurisdiction. There are enough examples, in most jurisdictions, of such swindlers escaping conviction and avoiding total confiscation of their gains to encourage further attempts.

Companies may be 'private' or 'proprietary' with no market in their shares or 'public' when, at least in principle, the shares may be traded and the statutory reporting requirements are accordingly much stricter. Companies often indicate their status by a suffix to their name. Private companies must use 'Ltd' in the UK, 'SARL' in France, 'GmbH' in Germany, 'Pty Ltd' in Australia and are encouraged to use 'LLC' in the USA. Public companies may use the suffix 'Inc' in the USA, 'plc' in the UK, 'SA' in France, 'AG' in Germany or 'Ltd' in Australia. A more up-coming corporate form in France is the Société par actions simplifiée (SAS), which can also be a one-person company – the Société par actions simplifiée unipersonelle (SASU).

There is a special form of company called a 'company limited by guarantee', which is useful for those social entrepreneurs who are not motivated by personal profit. (Such enterprises are often referred to as 'not for profit', a term that seriously irritated at least one entrepreneur of the authors' acquaintance, She was determined to make a satisfactory profit, because without it her enterprise could not survive or grow; but she wished to apply the profits to the social purpose of the business, not to paying dividends to shareholders or bonuses to directors. She did not mind being associated with a 'pro bono' enterprise.) The shareholders in a company limited by guarantee do not subscribe money, but they do guarantee to contribute, up to a certain maximum, to the company if it is liquidated and there are outstanding amounts owing to creditors. Companies limited by guarantee are forbidden to pay dividends and, if they are wound up, any remaining assets must be applied to the company's purpose. When the company's purpose satisfies the relevant statutory and regulatory conditions, it will be permitted to dispense with the 'Ltd' or equivalent suffix.

Directors

The directors of a company are elected by the shareholders but they are responsible to the company: if shareholders wish to limit the directors' freedom of action, they can pass a resolution amending the company's articles at the company's general meeting, but they can't, or at least shouldn't, treat the directors as their employees or their delegates. In the UK case law establishes that directors are obliged to act in the interests of the company and not those of any shareholder, and the new Companies Act (introduced as a bill in mid 2003) may give more specific guidance.

Australian law includes a list of obligations for directors of small and medium-sized enterprises, but large company directors are left to the common law and the corporate regulators. The conditions, which are explicitly binding on the directors of small and medium-sized Australian enterprises, but with minor interpretative changes probably apply to all company directors in most jurisdictions, are:

- to act in good faith
- to act in the best interests of the company
- to avoid conflict between the company's interests and the director's interests
- to act honestly
- to exercise care and diligence
- to prevent the company trading while it is unable to pay its debts
- if the company is being wound up – to report to the liquidator on the affairs of the company
- if the company is being wound up – to help the liquidator (by, for example, giving the liquidator any records of the company that the director has).

Company directors who fail to perform their duties may be guilty of a criminal offence with a penalty of a fine or even jail. They may also be personally liable to the company and others for any loss or damage that the directors' actions or omissions cause. They can also be prohibited from serving as a director of their current or any other company. A director's obligations may continue even after the company has been dissolved.

There is extensive law dealing with the relationship between the directors and the public, as potential investors, customers and creditors of a company. Company directors who allow a company to continue to trade when it is unable to pay its debts as they fall due may be sued personally to make up any losses suffered by creditors. Uninformed ignorance is no longer an excuse in most jurisdictions: directors who could, by reasonable inquiry, have discovered that their company was insolvent can still be liable for its debts even if they made no such inquiries and remained blissfully unaware of the firm's problems.

A company, as a legal person, can commit crimes and be punished for them if tried and found guilty. If a penalty is applied, a company can be fined but not put in gaol; if it is a crime for which the penalty may include gaol, the directors may, under certain circumstances, be prosecuted. Companies and their directors can usually avoid punishment by showing that the crime was committed by a junior employee acting against the policies of the company and the instructions the employee was given, unless the crime was one for which 'strict' or 'absolute' liability applies, in which case the company can be found guilty, even if the employee who actually caused the offence was acting against her instructions and did so without the knowledge of the directors. Offences against environmental and competition laws may involve strict liability and, as the backs of a million hotel doors testify, so may carelessness with a guest's property in an inn.

In many jurisdictions including the UK, a person may have the legal responsibilities of a director if she acted like one and is treated by the other directors as if she were one, even if never formally elected to the board. Senior executives and, in some cases, senior consultants may be included under this rule. The rule guards against villains hiding behind 'men of straw' as directors, protecting their own plunder from creditors and leaving the creditors to persecute a group of paupers. The rule may also catch an overenthusiastic employee who winds up suffering the civil and criminal penalties for corporate misbehaviour without having ever enjoyed the perquisites or income of an executive director.

Other employees

Most company employees are neither directors nor senior executives and will generally be assumed to be following their company's policy in their actions. Except where statute law has intervened, companies inherit the common law rights of 'masters' and employees owe the duties of servants. These duties include the diligent discharge of any assigned duties and the careful protection of their employer's property and commercial interests. Employees cannot use the instructions they are given or the policies within which they are required to operate as a defence against criminal charges, but they are generally indemnified by the company for the civil consequences of actions they take in the pursuit of the instructions they have been given and in accordance with the firm's policies as explained to them.

In small firms generally, and in most entrepreneurial ones irrespective of size, the relationship between ordinary employees and senior executives does not follow the master and servant model. Employees have wide responsibilities and a corresponding amount of discretion. Under the *kanban* system innovated by Toyota and now used by most of the world's car makers, ordinary production employees are responsible for ordering parts worth millions of dollars annually.

Efficient and entrepreneurial companies want their employees to operate under the most general instructions and do not expect them to be perpetually referring to a policy manual. As long as both sides act in good faith, empowered employees using their devolved authority are unlikely to get themselves or the company into serious trouble, but entrepreneurs (and progressive managers) need to be clear in defining how far the empowerment extends. If junior employees are in an environment where a mistake could lead to an offence being committed, they should be given appropriate training. Most managers are well aware of this where safety issues are concerned; training in matters of contract, environmental and competition law may also be important.

Investors

The law in most jurisdictions attempts to protect investors in two ways: they are protected from invitations to subscribe capital to a firm where the invitations contain misleading information or exaggerated forecasts of the prospective returns; and when trading in shares in public companies, investors are protected, to some extent, from losing money by buying or selling shares where the other party has privileged access to information that might have changed the investor's view of a fair price.

Prospectuses

In Australia and the USA companies that raise capital from members of the public may be legally obliged to prepare a 'prospectus', a document that contains 'all' the material information an intelligent investor would need to make an informed judgement. In the UK a prospectus is required when a company raises money from the public for the first time (an initial public offering – IPO). A prospectus will generally include financial information going back for several years as well as directors' forecasts (if such forecasts can reasonably be made) for the future of the firm and their statement of the purpose for which the capital is being raised. In principle (and in the US, in common practice) the directors and advisers to a company can be sued by aggrieved investors if the firm fails to perform as forecast in the prospectus; in the US (but not yet elsewhere) the writs may fly if the share price of a new company falls below the issue price, even if no defect can be demonstrated in the prospectus.

In many countries the law is deliberately vague about the contents of a prospectus, but the fear of the civil and criminal consequences of publishing a misleading prospectus leads firms to draw up elaborate documents and have them certified by senior partners in leading accounting and law firms. The cost of such a prospectus can run into hundreds of thousands or even millions of euros.

In most jurisdictions, no prospectus is required in certain closely defined circumstances. These may include offers where the minimum subscription is so large that it can be assumed that only fully informed professional investors would consider it, offers made to persons sharing some common interest or characteristic or offers that only go to a limited number of people. It would be reckless in the extreme for an entrepreneur to attempt to raise money from anyone except members of her immediate family without consulting a lawyer, both to advise whether an offer in the proposed form is legal and, if it is, whether the entrepreneur fully understands the implications of publishing it in its present form.

In the UK a listed company raising further funds by the sale of shares to the public is required to prepare a statement of 'listing particulars' which, apart from the change of name, is subject to most of the requirements that would apply to a prospectus.

Continuous disclosure

The stock exchange rules of many countries require that all circumstances that may affect the share price of a firm should be notified to the stock exchange as soon as the directors of the firm learn about them. This rule is intended to make insider trading impossible by ensuring that the general public is as well informed as any director, adviser or employee of the company, as well as preventing a false market developing in the shares.

The USA is undoubtedly the global leader in the provision of information, although the scandals at the start of the twenty-first century revealed that some chief executives at least felt no obligation to ensure that the information provided was correct. North American firms routinely disclose far more operating information than firms in most other countries do and willingly answer analysts' questions about their product and marketing initiatives in considerable detail. Major US corporations regularly report their progress with major new products, but generally only once they are nearly ready for launching or actually on the market.

Employment

Employment law is vast and complex and differs from country to country and in federations like the USA and Australia, from state to state. This section provides a bare overview of the principles governing employment law.

A growing enterprise will need to expand the number of people doing the work, and while some of this extra effort may be provided by new partners or contractors, some of it, and in general, most of it, will be supplied by employees. Employees may be described as 'staff' employed at an annual salary, or 'workers', or some equivalent term, and paid an hourly wage rate, but they are, as far as the law is concerned, employees and the relationship between employer and employee is governed by a number of laws and regulations.

The law recognises that genuinely independent contractors may perform some services, but because of the number of attempts made to evade either taxation or employment law by reclassifying employees as contractors, the law in the EU is intricate and complex. The general principle is that anyone who performs tasks as directed for a single enterprise is an employee, whatever their position is called.

Taxation and statutory payments

Employers are directly liable for some taxes and may be required to collect personal income tax and other levies from their employees and possibly from their contractors. PAYE income tax collections have brought many firms to grief: the money is part of an employee's gross pay and must be forwarded promptly to the tax collector. Employers who apply any of the tax or social security contributions they collect to any purposes of their firm, and consequently fail to forward it to the tax authorities on time, are not simply being slow at paying a bill: they are defaulting on their statutory obligations and may be subject to criminal prosecution.

Employers may be required to make other payments in respect, or on behalf, of their employees such as the Central Provident Fund in Singapore or the Superannuation Guarantee Levy in Australia. Ignorance of the relevant law is never an acceptable excuse for not making these payments and failure may lead to substantial penalties being demanded as well as prompt settlement of the outstanding taxation or other statutory obligations.

Conditions of employment

Employees may come under a relevant law or regulatory body, in which minimum standards of employment are set out, covering matters such as hours of work, overtime and shift rates, annual, long service and special leave as well as the actual rates of pay for employees carrying out the duties described in the documentation.

Other people may be employed under personal or collective employment contracts; such contracts are also subject, in most countries, to statutory minimum conditions. Employment law is complex and large firms generally employ specialists to draw up and maintain employment contracts or conduct negotiations with unions. Small firms should engage an appropriately qualified consultant to draw up contracts unless they can follow a template prepared by the regulator.

Dismissal

In most countries employees may be dismissed 'for cause' if they breach their conditions of employment; in some cases the breach must be flagrant or repeated after a formal warning if the dismissal is to be legal.

Different countries have different rules covering 'without cause' dismissals; in Australia, for example, employment may be terminated because the duties of the position have been superseded by a reorganisation or the introduction of new technology: this is termed 'redundancy'; or because the employer's trading performance has declined and the employee can no longer be profitably employed: this is termed 'retrenchment'. Australian employees who are retrenched or made redundant are usually entitled to a payment based upon their period of service, but they are not usually entitled to dispute their termination.

The EU Charter, Chapter 4, Article 30, bans the 'unjustified dismissal' of employees but qualifies this by reference to 'national customs and practices'. The clause is repeated in the draft EU constitution. National laws and practices vary widely: Britain provides no general protection against unfair dismissal apart from a minimum notice period of a week for employees with less than two years' service and two weeks for the rest (although the courts have found that an implied contract guaranteeing a longer notice period exists and can be enforced in various circumstances); Austria prescribes notice periods as long as five months for long-serving employees; Germany provides for compensation amounting to as much as 18 months' pay. Most European countries are closer to the Austrian or German practices than the British ones.

Statutory conditions, or a union contract, typically cover hourly paid 'blue-collar' workers, while salaried staff members are usually employed on individual contracts. In most countries individual contracts cannot be used to undercut statutory minimum conditions.

Health and safety

Until quite recently, certain occupations were regarded as naturally hazardous and dangerous to health and, if a worker suffered death, injury or illness, this was considered that worker's bad luck, but the risk 'came with the territory'. Employers could only be sued or prosecuted if their deliberate acts had caused an accident. Lion taming, for example, was considered hazardous and a lion tamer who got mauled by a deaf lion would have to write it down to experience; only if the employer had provoked the accident by, for example, stuffing cotton wool into the lion's ears or poking it with a sharp stick before its entry could the lion tamer sue.

More prosaically, workers were often routinely exposed to noisy or hazardous machinery or dangerous chemicals, and if they became deaf or contracted cancer or liver disease, this was unfortunate, but no blame attached to the employer. If an unguarded guillotine removed a few fingers, the worker received a settlement from the workers' compensation insurer as set out in the Table of Maims from the relevant Act, but that was all.

The law in most countries still recognises the possibility of accidents and the concept that certain activities are naturally hazardous, but there is generally a strong obligation placed upon employers to make the workplace safe, both in respect of accidents and the employees' long-term health. Hazardous chemicals must be contained in enclosed vessels and employees whose tasks require them to be exposed must be equipped with respirators and protective clothing. Guillotines and presses must be intrinsically safe and rotating machinery must be enclosed.

Employers are generally obliged to provide a healthy, safe workplace. This requires them to take all the steps necessary to eliminate all the hazards of which they are, or could reasonably become, aware. There are some very limited exceptions for tasks which cannot be completed without a degree of hazard, such as fire fighting (or lion taming), but even in these cases the employer is obliged to take all practical steps, in terms of both training and the provision of protective equipment, to limit the hazard while permitting the task to be completed.

In many countries employers may also be obliged to insure themselves against claims from injured workers and the insurers may use bonuses and penalties to distinguish between safe and unsafe workplaces.

Equal opportunity and harassment

Employers in the EU as in most developed countries are obliged, when recruiting, assigning duties, providing training, offering promotion, selecting staff for retrenchment or redundancy and, in general terms, in all the ways in which they conduct their business to refrain from discriminating between employees on various statutory grounds. The EU seeks to prohibit discrimination on the basis of racial and ethnic origin, religion and belief, disability, age and sexual orientation. In Australia the list covers race or national origin, sex, age, union membership, political or religious beliefs. In England similar prohibitions apply, although equal opportunity and racial equality policies are separately administered.

Employees who are discriminated against may seek redress and they may be assisted by specialist agencies; the punishment on conviction may go well beyond any monetary award, as many highly qualified (and therefore potentially mobile) workers will avoid employers who are notorious for their unfair treatment of their staff.

In the EU sexual harassment is prohibited, including activities ranging from occasional touching or lewd suggestions to the explicit or implicit offer of promotion or job security in return for sexual favours. Other forms of harassment involving mockery or maltreatment are prohibited on similar grounds to the prohibition against discrimination, whether the employer is actively involved or not. Harassment occurs when the working atmosphere is one in which a 'reasonable person' would feel threatened or uncomfortable. Employers in most developed countries are obliged actively to prevent one group of their employees acting in threatening, harassing or intimidating ways towards other employees. Discrimination and harassment on the grounds of age will become unlawful across the EU from 2006.

As with unlawful discrimination, the penalties for perpetrating or tolerating sexual, racial or other harassment go beyond any civil or criminal penalties that may be applied: firms that become notorious for harassment may have great difficulty in attracting top quality staff to work for them and the economic cost of being restricted to hiring second tier staff may dwarf the legal penalties.

Competition law

A great deal of economic theory is concerned with the desirability of 'perfect' competition, to the point that most introductory economics texts present a mathematically false 'proof' purporting to show that perfect competition minimises prices and maximises consumption. Even this claim depends on the assumption that the typical firm's output is limited by the rising cost of extra production, not by the extent of demand for its products. Since practically every manufacturing and service firm ever studied experiences falling unit costs when it is able to sell an increase in its output, the relevance of perfect competition theory to the real world can hardly be said to be proven. Schumpeter dealt a strong blow to the assertion of the perfection of perfect competition:

> Many theorists take the opposite view which is best conveyed by example. Let us assume that there is a certain number of retailers in a neighbourhood who try to improve their relative position by service and 'atmosphere' but avoid price competition and stick as to methods to the local tradition – a picture of stagnating routine. As others drift into the trade that quasi-equilibrium is indeed upset, but in a manner that does not benefit their customers. The economic space around each of the shops having been narrowed, their owners will no longer be able to make a living and they will try to mend their case by raising prices in tacit agreement. This will further reduce their sales and so, by successive pyramiding, a situation will evolve in which increasing potential supply will be attended by increasing instead of decreasing prices and by decreasing instead of increasing sales.

> Such cases do occur, and it is right and proper to work them out. But as the practical instances usually given show, they are fringe-end cases to be found mainly in the sectors furthest removed from all that is most characteristic of capitalist activity. Moreover, they are transient by nature. In the case of retail trade the competition that matters arises not from additional shops of the same type, but from the department store, the chain store, the mail-order house and the supermarket which are bound to destroy those pyramids sooner or later.

Now a theoretical construction which neglects this essential element of the case neglects all that is most typically capitalist about it; even if correct in logic as well as in fact, it is like *Hamlet* without the Danish prince. ([1942] 1967: 85)

Economists remain deeply wedded to the desirability of perfect competition in spite of the many theoretical and practical problems with the concept, and so eloquent is their advocacy that governments throughout the world have created extensive bureaucracies to police industry and force it to behave as much like the textbook models as possible. The economist Harberger (1956) used the tools of economic analysis to measure the cost of departures from perfect competition to the American economy, and concluded that it was no more than 'one steak dinner per family per year', and far less than the cost of maintaining the pro-competition bureaucracy. His paper was published in a leading journal and then ignored.

The EU Competition Directorate (http://europa.eu.int/comm/competition/index_en.html) is a powerful and aggressive organisation that investigates corporate practices throughout, and in some cases beyond, the EU and prosecutes offenders vigorously.

Market power

One of the things that makes perfect competition so attractive in theory is the assumption that every firm is so small that it cannot influence the general price or output level by its own acts (or this would be the case if the laws of mathematics were as flexible as economists assume). Large firms, on the other hand, may have considerable power, not only to set their own prices, but to reward and punish other firms. An established firm might, perhaps, tell its suppliers that if they supplied a smaller but aggressive rival they might be deleted from the larger firm's list of authorised suppliers. The pressure need not be overt: the (relatively) small supplier or distributor might choose to act in a way that it believes will cause least grief to the dominant partner in its relationship and so refuse to assist potential rivals entirely on its own initiative.

Having market power is not an offence in Europe or Australia, as long as it was acquired lawfully, but abusing it to do damage to a potential rival or even to affect its conduct may be a criminal offence. In the USA even a lawfully acquired position of market power can be challenged in the courts and a large firm may be broken up into smaller ones by court order. This happened to Standard Oil in 1911 and AT&T (the Bell telephone system) in 1984. An order to break up Microsoft was rescinded on appeal in 2001.

In Europe, Australia and the USA, the competition authorities may challenge mergers and acquisitions if they would create a new source of market power or increase the power of an already dominant firm. The remedy might be to forbid the merger, acquisition or alliance, but often it is allowed to proceed after giving various enforceable undertakings intended to prevent the unduly baleful use of the new power.

Entrepreneurs starting new firms might feel that this aspect of competition law is unlikely to affect them, but if their chosen method of harvesting their investment is a trade sale, and their business had developed a unique technology or franchise, the anti-trust authorities may choose to intervene on the grounds that a sale to their preferred purchaser would increase the purchaser's market power unacceptably. As mentioned in Chapter 8, entrepreneurial firms have been forced into liquidation by the refusal of the competition regulator to allow them to accept a takeover from a large competitor.

Collusive pricing

In a competitive market in theory, and to a somewhat lesser extent in practice, prices are below the level that firms, if free from competitive worries, would charge. If a group of nominal competitors should come together and make an agreement to follow a common price list or operate in mutually exclusive territories, it is possible that the result will be a higher level of prices than before they formed their agreement. Such collusion between competitors has been illegal under common law for centuries and statute law in most developed countries has now widened the definition and strengthened the penalties for such price fixing.

The addition of statute law has weakened the standards of proof required for a conviction and increased the number of ways in which price fixing might be inferred. In some (hopefully not all) jurisdictions small and entrepreneurial companies are more likely to be targeted under these provisions than their behaviour truly warrants; the regulator knows that small and new firms will not have the resources to sustain an effective legal defence in court and that they may lack the sophisticated legal advice needed for those who wish to collude but don't want to be caught at it.

Exclusive dealing

When large firms deal with small ones, especially when small suppliers deal with large retailers, it might be regarded as a misuse of market power if the large firm threatened the small one with adverse consequences if it also supplied the large firm's rivals. It might be possible, however, that a small firm might offer, without any pressure at all, to deal exclusively with a single retailer in return for favourable display or credit arrangements. In an industry where large firms left the last step in the distribution chain to dealers, as with the motorcar industry, a dealer might offer to sell a single manufacturer's products exclusively in return for promotional support and favourable credit arrangements.

Competition laws in many countries may permit the regulatory authorities to review and possibly forbid such arrangements on the grounds that they tend to restrict consumer choice. In Europe, and particularly Britain, car buyers have been affected by substantial price differentials between countries, with the gap between British and Belgian prices particularly notorious. The car manufacturers maintained these differentials by appointing a limited number of dealers and imposed conditions on them such as to reduce competition between different dealers selling any given manufacturer's range, While these arrangements were legitimised by an exemption from European competition law, the EU Competition Directorate has taken steps over the past few years to restrict the scope of the exemption and introduce more competition among dealers. The exemption was redefined to limit its scope in 1995, and a new, narrower exemption took effect in mid 2003.

Audi, for example, had purged its dealer list; the EU Competition Directorate discussed the matter with Audi, who decided to reinstate the purged dealers. In a speech delivered in February 2003, Commissioner Monti told the car industry of further investigations and, if necessary, further reviews of the exemption to ensure that the contracts between car manufacturers and dealers were purged of anti-competitive effects.

'Third line forcing' is the practice of including in a contract between two parties a condition that requires one of them to deal with a nominally unrelated third party for some related product or service. As an example, before the practice was banned, Australian banks and building societies would require home buyers to insure their new property with a designated insurance company as a condition of their mortgage. Typically the premiums charged to such customers were two or more times higher than the premiums charged to untied clients and this was reflected in the high commissions paid by the insurers to the banks and building societies concerned.

Not all third line forcing contracts are illegal; the competition authorities will attempt to balance the possible damage to competition against any offsetting consumer benefit. McDonald's franchise agreements in most countries specify the supplier of the fries and the meat patties; this is acceptable because the competition authorities recognise that the arrangement guarantees McDonald's customers a consistent product and the benefits of this outweigh the disappointment felt by those firms not on McDonald's list of suppliers. If McDonald's was the only operator of fast-food restaurants in a country, these agreements might cause greater concern.

A boycott may be a variation on third line forcing ('you may deal with anyone except "X"') or it may be a broadly organised attempt to damage a particular business, as when a group of firms make an agreement not to deal with a nominated firm. Boycotts may be undertaken as a form of bargaining ('none of us will deal with you until you change your prices/terms/behaviour') or it can be intended to drive a firm out of the market altogether. Under common law such boycotts might be considered unlawful conspiracies and in most developed countries there are statutory prohibitions enforced by the competition authorities as well.

Resale price maintenance is the practice of requiring trade purchasers to adhere to a set price list or observe a minimum price rule when they sell on certain goods and services. The laws against this practice vary from place to place and in the USA from state to state. Resale price maintenance is generally illegal under EU and British law, and exemptions from this part of the law have been progressively withdrawn. In Britain the pricing of books was maintained under the Net Book Agreement until the agreement itself collapsed in 1996, for example, and now publishers' prices on books sold in England, as in most of the world, are advisory only.

A firm might be tempted to insert a price maintenance clause in order to ensure a high level of sales support or a premium sales environment for its higher quality product lines by guaranteeing high reseller margins. While the level of service provided to end users is regarded as a legitimate subject for a contract between a supplier and its dealers or distributors, the price they charge will generally not be. For this reason dealer and distributor agreements for products where the service levels and sales professionalism are important should set out minimum standards for these and avoid any mention of prices or margins.

Environmental law

Humans have, from time immemorial, treated the environment as an infinite sink for household and industrial wastes and the environment has struck back from time to time. Poor disposal of household rubbish encouraged rats who brought the plague with them; poor disposal of human excrement created the conditions in which cholera and typhoid could flourish; chimneys belched soot and noxious gasses, devastating the countryside and destroying human lungs; and for far too long this was tolerated on the grounds that 'where there's muck there's brass' as Yorkshire tradition has it.

By the end of the nineteenth century most major cities had been sewered and supplied with clean drinking water and cholera and typhoid retreated from the first world's cities to the third world's slums. Britain in particular struggled with the smoke problem through the nineteenth and the first half of the twentieth centuries until in December 1952 the great London smog locked up the city for five days and killed 4000 people. The Clean Air Act of 1956 followed and the sulphurous smogs that were once a regular feature of London life are now only seen in period films.

Clean air was followed by clean water: the Thames Water Company noted in a millennium press release that 113 species of fish could be found in the Thames at London, a substantial advance on the zero found in a 1960 study. Across the developed world rivers are returning to health and air quality is rising.

One legal weapon that the environmental authorities have used is blunt but effective: many offences against the environment are 'strict liability'. This means that if your firm causes pollution of the air, water or surrounding land, you can only avoid penalties by proving that no reasonable steps that you could have taken would have prevented the unlawful discharge. If an employee caused the discharge by a deliberate act or failure to act, even if the employee was acting against his instructions, your firm may still be found guilty.

Environmental pollution is broadly defined and there are almost no general exemptions. If an enterprise generates any waste at all beyond natural human excretions, it is almost certain to require a permit to discharge it or be obliged to engage a licensed contractor to dispose of it. If the waste products are directly harmful to health, the civil penalties for illegal discharges may be dwarfed by the damages claims. Whatever complacency there had been in Europe was dissipated with the Seveso accident in 1976 in Italy.

Seveso

A dense vapour cloud containing tetrachlorodibenzoparadioxin (TCDD) commonly known as dioxin was released from a reactor to the atmosphere following a plant failure at Seveso in 1976. Although no immediate fatalities were reported, kilogram quantities of the substance lethal to man even in microgram doses were widely dispersed which resulted in an immediate contamination of some ten square miles of land and vegetation. More than 600 people had to be evacuated from their homes and as many as 2000 were treated for dioxin poisoning ...

http://europa.eu.int/comm/environment/seveso/

In a tribute to the impact of the Seveso incident, the EU Directives on chemical pollution are referred to as 'Seveso Directives'; the Seveso II Directive, of 1996, now defines the minimum legal requirements for firms handling dangerous chemicals. (National standards in EU countries may be more severe, but not less so.)[3]

The direct penalties for environmental crime are steep; but the costs of remediation and the effects of the bad publicity can dwarf these costs. Even small infractions are severely punished, not just because a minor breach may be the 'thin end of the wedge' for the infringer, but when all the firms or households in a major city repeat a minor breach, the accumulation of minor problems can become a major one.

Some firms in pollution-prone industries have been tempted, following the suggestion of Lawrence Summers when chief economist of the World Bank, to relocate their plants to third world countries where environmental laws may be less onerous or less strictly enforced. Their respite tends to be temporary: Greenpeace and similar organisations are proficient at naming and shaming firms who treat the life and health of people in the third world as a matter of minor importance and what such firms gain in reduced effluent treatment costs they lose, perhaps many times over, in bad publicity.

CHECKPOINT

The law both supports entrepreneurship and places constraints on what entrepreneurs are allowed to do.

The law is extensive, and in the common law countries goes well beyond that set out in statutes. Much of the law is common sense or common ethics and intelligent, ethical entrepreneurs should have little trouble with it. In many areas the law is far from intuitive and entrepreneurs need professional advice if they are not to come into costly conflict with it.

This chapter, and similar overviews, cannot describe the law in any depth and certainly do not equip an entrepreneur to make her own legal decisions. All it can do is erect some signposts, marking areas of business activity where the wise entrepreneur or manager will take advice before proceeding further.

Exercises

1 You have a great idea for improving the organisation of your business. Can you patent it? Would it be wise to do so, if you could? How else can you protect your idea from your competitors?

2 You discover that a remote tribe in Mongolia use juice from a plant not previously known to science to cure skin diseases. Can you patent the use of juice from this plant? If chemists in your laboratory extract the active ingredient and work out a way to synthesise it, what, if anything, can you now patent?

3 You place a contract with a technical writing firm to prepare a user manual for your new software. How can you stop them using slabs of your manual when they get a contract from your competitor?

4 You discover a way to make a Japanese motorbike sound like a Harley-Davidson. When you sell your gadget the local Harley-Davidson distributor sends

you a letter accusing you of infringing the Harley-Davidson trademark (being the characteristic exhaust sound) and demanding that you desist from selling your gadget. Do you have anything to worry about?

5 You run a cake shop; one day a VIP sends his chauffeur into your shop to buy one of your cakes. Are you allowed to put up a sign saying 'My shop is recommended by 'X' (the VIP)?'

6 You import a gadget for driving screws and market it. Unfortunately your supplier has not heat-treated the bit correctly and it breaks after a few uses. When customers complain you direct them to a notice on the packet that disclaimed any responsibility for the performance of the product, and suggest that they get in touch with the manufacturer in China. Does this discharge your responsibilities?

7 You start a new business with the support of a

number of 'business angels' (private investors) who buy shares in your company. One of them suggests, very firmly, that you should transfer your legal work to his brother's firm, even though this firm has a poor reputation and is unfamiliar with your industry. What are your legal obligations in this matter?

8 A wheelchair-bound person applies for a job in your office for which she is well qualified. Can you refuse to employ her on the grounds that you have no disabled toilet?

9 You open a restaurant in your village specialising in French cuisine; the existing restaurant offers Italian cuisine. You meet the other restaurateur in your local golf club, and he suggests that he might broaden his menu to include some popular French dishes. If you suggest that this might be a very bad idea, are you breaking any laws?

10 Your restaurant uses about 100 litres of oil a week for cooking. You have been paying €40 per month to a disposal contractor; a new contractor appears and offers to do the job for €20. You give him your business. A few months later you hear a rumour, easily confirmed, that your new contractor is simply pouring the waste oil into a ditch from where it leaks into the local river. Are you committing an offence?

Notes

1   This and the following two sections were originally contributed by Mr Alfred Tatlock, lawyer and patent attorney, and edited into its present form by the authors.

2   Strictly speaking, in matters of law one should refer to the 'European Community' (EC) rather than the 'European Union' (EU), and observe that EC 'law' is actually a treaty obligation on member states to pass laws that implement its Directives, but both distinctions are becoming blurred in practice.

3   http://europa.eu.int/comm/environment/seveso/#1.

8 The role of governments

This chapter

In this chapter we will explain the nature of pressures on governments and the reasons why a good government may well respond favourably to some of these pressures. We then describe the range of options open to a government in a market economy, classifying policies both along an active/passive dichotomy and according to the degree of impact such policies may have and the (often parallel) strength of the opposition that they may arouse. We expect readers to take three main things from their study of this chapter:

■ some understanding and appreciation of the orthodox economic position on the arguments for, and against, government intervention in a market economy

■ some insight into why the study of complex, evolving systems leads to a different set of recommendations on some issues

■ a systematic way of classifying and understanding government policy as it affects firms operating in a market economy, so as to recognise the intentions of particular policies, guide entrepreneurs seeking to take advantage of them and assist those who make public policy to do so successfully.

Pressure on governments

However a government is organised, a democracy, autocracy, monarchy, republic or hybrid of any or all of these, it will find that there are interests it must satisfy if it is to achieve its objectives, as well as interests it wishes to satisfy for reasons of friendship, political affiliation, philosophical direction, return of favours received or some other reason. In countries with elected governments a failure to reconcile the 'must' and the 'want' will lead, eventually, to electoral defeat; if changing the government through an election is impossible, other means will be tried and history suggests that they will eventually succeed.

This chapter follows a plan suggested by Jerry Courvisanos of the University of Ballarat whose help, both with the plan and subsequent advice, is gratefully acknowledged.

In autocracies and dictatorships, at least some of the interests pressed upon the government will be purely personal, as men jostle and women intrigue for favour; but once some democratic institutions are accepted, governments and their petitioners feel obliged to appeal to the broader public interest, no matter how narrowly their proposals are really targeted.

Interests in a modern society are pursued by interest groups of one type or another, sometimes organisations formed for a different purpose and sometimes by specially formed organisations. Sometimes a group will advocate a change of policy, such as increased (or less) environmental regulation or more or less regulation of working conditions; or a group may pursue a single issue, such as clemency for a particular prisoner, the designation of a particular building as a national monument or a particular area as a national park.

A common, and often successful, political tactic adopted by those opposed to a particular interest group is to accuse its spokespersons of pursuing private (or 'vested') interests while, often hypocritically, asserting that their recommendations favour the public good. Trade union leaders may be accused of giving themselves a comfortable, or better, lifestyle on their members' fees while only pretending to defend workers' rights. Industry groups that lobby for national development policies may be accused of trying to create protected monopolies in order to exploit the public.

History has many accounts of special interest groups perverting government policies in pursuit of selfish ends and ministers and others abusing government authority to 'feather their own nests'. Sometimes the issues are far from clear-cut. When 'Engine Charlie' (Charles E. Wilson, then president of General Motors) was nominated by President Eisenhower to become his secretary of defense in 1953, a senator at Wilson's confirmation hearing asked him whether his loyalty to General Motors might conflict with his duties as defense secretary. 'I cannot believe that what was good for the country could be bad for General Motors,' he responded, and then to his lifelong regret continued, 'or vice versa'.

Wilson's regret was political, because of the furore that his remark caused, not because his original statement, in its entirety, was anything but sincere. As president of General Motors he never thought there could be a conflict, probably because his ethical blinkers were so firmly fixed that the possibilities never occurred to him. GM was a major manufacturer of battle tanks for the US armed forces during and for some years after the Second World War, and using inferior materials could have been financially good for GM if not for the crews of the tanks. Wilson could not even imagine himself or any other GM executive making such a decision; it lay outside their moral universe.

There have, of course, been men (and a few women) whose morality tolerated any act that progressed their immediate self-interest, irrespective of its effects on others. History suggests that such an approach to government fails even in its ostensible aim, since the hostility of those offended or disadvantaged by the selfish acts of their rulers leads more or less directly to their overthrow. Nero may have felt that the Romans should regret the loss of an emperor as artistic as himself, but the Romans swallowed the damage to their artistic sensibilities and overthrew him anyway.

Learned ethics, social norms and other factors make it easy for people to believe that the satisfaction of their special requirements is consistent with the good of the country as a whole; but the fact that they believe it does not make it wrong. The existence of externalities (see below) means that governments can, sometimes, make

'You'll be treated with honours if you secrecy mark, sir
For my master is noble, and I am his clerk, sir'

A reference to Mary Anne Clarke, a young lady who so charmed the Duke of York in the early 1800s that he dictated his correspondence to her and allowed her to apply his seal to it. Since this was the 'grand old Duke of York' who was commander in chief of the British Army, much of the correspondence concerned appointments and promotions in the army, but since the Duke was a great landowner, many appointments in the Church were also under his influence. Young Ms Clarke enhanced her allowance from his grace by composing letters on behalf of any aspiring officer or clergyman who showed the right kind of appreciation.

When the scandal finally erupted in 1808 a committee of the House of Commons summonsed Mary Anne and her charm and wit, compounded by the Honourable Members' reluctance to accuse the king's second son of corruption, enabled her to evade all punishment.

decisions that favour specific interests but that also progress the general interest. Proving that a specific interest has been favoured does not prove that the general interest has suffered. The art of good government requires making decisions that lead to 'everybody (or nearly everybody) wins' outcomes; successful bad governments are those that can conceal the partial favours they perform for their friends and campaign donors under a veil of public interest.

Historical background

When Colbert, the French chief minister to Louis XIV, asked a bourgeois merchant[1] for advice on making France prosperous, the answer was 'Laissez-nous faire' – 'let us do it'. In one sense this was a call for economic freedom, and that is how, with the benefit of hindsight and the burial of Marxism, most people now regard it. Literally, however, Colbert was being asked to implement a transfer of power from the aristocracy to the bourgeoisie, from an economy organised in the interests of the landowning class to one more responsive to the demands of the town-based merchants and manufacturers. Neither Colbert nor any other French government implemented any radical deregulation of the French economy; but Colbert and his successors recognised that entrepreneurs had a legitimate place in it.

Something resembling laissez-faire developed in Britain, between approximately 1780 until the 1920s in political theory, and between 1832 and 1871 in practice. The period 1780 – 1914 was one of near-miraculous economic transition in England and southern Scotland, as bare fields in the Midlands, the English northwest and the Firth of Clyde were transformed into mighty manufacturing cities whose products dominated the markets of the world. A politically pivotal moment was 1846, when the Tory government under Sir Robert Peel repealed the Corn Laws and allowed unrestricted imports of wheat and other food grains to the UK.

The repeal of the Corn Laws was justified on two main grounds: the global economic crisis of the late 1840s was restricting British exports, causing unemployment and part-time working in the manufacturing cities and the distress (and revolutionary ardour) of the working classes would be reduced by lowering food prices; one reason for the reduction in British exports was that Britain's potential customers overseas were running out of gold with which to purchase British manufactured products; by making Britain a market for their agricultural products this imbalance of trade would be corrected and British exports could resume their growth.

While these arguments found great favour in England, at least until the First World War, they had less appeal to Britain's main economic rivals, Germany and the USA. Free trade and laissez-faire seemed, to manufacturers and politicians in these countries, as a way to keep them as economic backwaters, exporting rural commodities in exchange for manufactured goods. Britain would have the profitable manufacturing industries and the economic growth associated with them, while the USA and Germany would remain dominated by smallholding agriculture.

In Germany the economist Frederich List and others argued that the British dominance of manufacturing was not the result of free trade or laissez-faire, but simply a result of first mover advantages. In response, the German states implemented the Zollverein, a free-trade area embracing the German-speaking states with a common tariff on imports. This was supplemented by subsidies and even administrative orders fostering key industries. The first major reward for the Germans came

▶

at the expense of the French, when, in 1870, 500 Krupp steel cannon blew the French forces away at Sedan. While the first three industries of the Industrial Revolution, pottery, cotton and iron, were based in Britain, the next three, steel, chemicals and electricity, were dominated by Germany.

In the USA abstract theory had little say in the matter of tariff protection: the North had industrialised to win the Civil War, and the newly rich industrialists had no intention of rejoining the agricultural poor once the fighting stopped. High tariffs made sure that cheap British imports were going to make no headway in the American market.

The US experience became important in another way. Because of the peculiarities of the international capital markets and the lack of laws, customs or regulations to control the US ones in the nineteenth century, shady entrepreneurs found it very attractive to build new railroads (but not to operate them). Typically, the US entrepreneurs would draw up a prospectus for a new railroad; raise money for it on the London market, and let exorbitant construction contracts to their cronies. These contracts would send the original company broke

and the bankruptcy administrators would sell its assets to another firm. The end result was desperate overbuilding with, for example, three double-track lines running between New York and Chicago competing for traffic that any one of them could have easily carried on its own.

This was great for freight shippers operating between New York and Chicago, who could bid the rates down to a derisory level, but the backlash was felt in those areas of the US served by only a single railroad. The railroad companies were desperate to cover their losses on the trunk routes, and did so by charging extortionate rates to farmers and small manufacturers in middle America. These aggrieved men (no votes for women then) let their representatives know of their feelings, and the US Congress passed the Sherman Antitrust Act, the first of its kind in the world, to prohibit monopolisation. Congress also established the Interstate Commerce Commission with the power to regulate railroad rates.

America thereby led the world both in the creation of anti-trust law and the government management of markets.

Mainstream economic opinion

The subject of political economy deals with the interaction between governments and businesses and is accordingly the subject of many books in which many points of view are expressed. Since 1975 or so, the dominant school of political economy has taken the 'neoliberal' approach. The most vigorous neoliberals argue that all advocacy groups are fronts for vested interests and all government policies should be judged purely in terms of their conformance to economic theory – as set out by neoliberals. Neoliberal theory generally asserts that 'leaving it to the market' will produce better social outcomes than any form of 'intervention'. The more common neoliberal view is that, in general, less government is better government; but they recognise some circumstances in which markets may fail and governments may play a constructive role.

Market failure, in the most general sense, occurs whenever the preconditions for perfect competition are not met, that is, everywhere and always. In many circumstances, however, competition works sufficiently well to make it unlikely that the net cost of imposing additional regulations will be justified by the possible benefits. Most orthodox economists recognise situations where the cost of a market failure substantially exceeds the costs of action to rectify it. Market failures, in the orthodox view, may be caused by externalities, sunk costs, the emergence of monopoly power or conflicting social and economic objectives.

Externalities

Externalities are said to occur whenever the benefits or costs of an activity affect more than the direct participants. Policy measures may be called for when the social costs of such externalities become intolerable. Discussion of externalities often focuses on the negative ones, such as pollution, but once it is accepted that entrepreneurship and innovation are essential factors in economic growth, externalities that tend to suppress or encourage innovation may need to be considered.

Three specific examples of such externalities are discussed below.

Disproportionate consumer benefit

Most products are offered at a single price to all comers, even when the value to some greatly exceeds the value to others. The aggregate benefit gained by those who pay much less than the product is worth to them is referred to as the 'consumer surplus' and represents a fraction of the value generated by an innovation that is inaccessible to the innovator. Since the innovator must, in general, share the full reward for innovation with the public at large, many socially worthwhile innovations may be neglected unless a social incentive is added to the prospective profit.

Public health measures are an obvious case in point: each individual's intrinsic optimism makes them assume that the risk they face is slight and therefore the price they will be prepared to pay for prophylaxis is low. Health insurance and social security may transfer many of the costs of an incident to the public at large in any case, making individuals even less willing to pay for prophylaxis and the development of prophylactic treatments even less attractive to entrepreneurs and innovative companies. Agricultural improvement is another area where the externalities are widely accepted by economists: improved production techniques may offer huge social benefits from cheaper, better quality food. To the farmer such innovations may just mean larger crops and lower prices with little net benefit.

For these reasons few economists oppose substantial public support for innovations in health and agriculture. In the USA, for example, the National Institutes of Health are well supported; in 2003 the federal government allocated them over US$23 billion. Their discoveries are offered to the private sector for exploitation at a nominal or zero charge. The US Department of Agriculture is also well supported: its 2003 research budget was just over $1 billion with another $2 billion for cooperative research and extension services. The expenditure on extension services is in effect a marketing subsidy in support of manufacturers of agricultural technology, no doubt justified by the need to raise agricultural productivity by using the most modern equipment.

Free rider issues

An essential feature of the market system is that products are offered to all comers, including an innovator's rivals. These rivals may reverse engineer an innovation and put their own version onto the market, capturing part of the profit the original entrepreneur had been counting on. Innovations that offer considerable social value but only modest returns to their entrepreneur may be neglected unless this 'free rider' problem can be overcome.

Most governments enforce certain intellectual property rights, giving innovators a measure of protection against free riders; many also offer grants and other subsidies to research and development, reducing the innovator's outlays and therefore reducing the adverse consequences of reverse engineering and early competitive entry. Publicly funded research results are also offered to innovators free or on generous terms: in the UK and Australia, for example, a substantial fraction of each university's public funding is based on the number of papers its researchers publish.

Since publication precludes patenting, such information is effectively free to those who can make profitable use of it.

Some economists, whose admiration for competition exceeds the average even for economists, argue that intellectual property protection is always anti-competitive and society would be better off if all forms of intellectual property protection were abolished and replaced by prizes and pensions for worthy innovators. This was the system that largely applied until late in the eighteenth century; most people who examine the social history of the 1700s and contrast it with society today are unconvinced.

Economic and social development

Much economic theory deals with price as the critical issue and many economists argue that the principal or sole aim of public policy with respect to business should be to maximise output and minimise price. When, for any reason, a business has some pricing discretion, there are few examples of win–lose contests as stark as that which divides producers from consumers. If the price is raised, consumers will suffer, while if it is lowered, the producer gains the pain. The introduction of new 'qualities' of products confuses the issue: are consumers suffering from blood poisoning made better off by reducing the cost of the attendance of witchdoctors, or by providing penicillin, even if the producer makes a profit?

Work generally associated with the US economist Paul M. Romer suggests that matters are even more complex. Innovations, these economists suggest, generate total returns that substantially exceed the rewards to the innovator, with the community at large capturing at least part of this 'spillover' benefit in the form of general economic growth. When the Bobcat replaces the wheelbarrow, the productivity of the operator is obviously improved, but the Bobcat manufacturer and the machine operator are unable to keep the benefit entirely to themselves: some is shared with the workers at the Bobcat factory and some with the people whose building works progress faster and more economically, so the benefits spread through the community. If an innovator wants a personal reward, he must provide rewards to the broader community as well and for this reason even the most self-interested innovator contributes to general economic growth.

There have, of course, been spectacular examples of broad social returns to innovation. Mechanical refrigeration was invented by the US inventor John Gorrie and first patented in 1851, but when it was used to cool air in living or working environments, the result was fog and condensation rather than increased comfort, because cooling air raises its humidity. Willis Haviland Carrier invented a practical dehumidifier in 1902 and with others founded the Carrier Engineering Corporation in 1915. Carrier is now a division of United Technologies Corp., with divisional revenues in 2000 of US$8.4 billion and operating profits in that year of $795 million. If Carrier's family have retained even a small fraction of the company they must be wealthy today; this might be considered an adequate reward for Carrier's innovative efforts.

The financial benefits captured by Carrier himself and the company he founded are, however, trivial compared to the benefits they did not capture. Tropical and semi-tropical cities such as Singapore, Hong Kong, Brisbane and Miami would be backwaters today without air conditioning. The modern textile and printing industries could not operate in their present locations, or as efficiently anywhere, without air conditioning. The US Congress could not operate for four months of every year until it was air-conditioned in the 1920s.

Romer (1984), supported in this instance by the systems theorists (see below), argues that innovations such as Carrier's are merely the most visible members of a general trend; practically all innovations facilitate other innovations leading to positive social returns at the point where the prospective entrepreneurial returns are no longer sufficient to justify the effort. The implication that innovation generally should be supported has proved alarming to many economists, including Romer himself, but it has never been convincingly refuted.

Sunk costs One of the preconditions for perfect competition is free entry to and exit from industries and markets, not merely in the sense that no regulations control or limit entry, but that no one who decides to exit an industry or market need suffer a capital loss. As a strict condition this is obviously impossible, but there are markets and industries where it is almost true. In cities where taxi licences are limited, for example, anyone who meets the fairly simple regulatory requirements can buy a plate and start driving: if they don't like the job, they can give it up and sell the plate to someone else, possibly even at a profit.

Of course, even such apparently safe investments can go sour, as when the economic reformers in New Zealand in the 1980s simply abolished taxi licensing restrictions. Drivers and operators who had spent hundreds of thousands of dollars buying licences found that their money had gone, while additional entrants squeezed the already tight margins in the industry. The economists on whose advice the New Zealand government inflicted this catastrophe on a few thousand small business people were unabashed: licences restricted competition, competition was an unqualified public good and anyone who bought a competition-restricting licence only to see its value evaporate deserved, in their loudly stated opinion, all that they got.

More generally, entry to an industry and a market involves sunk costs, in product development, acquiring industry-specific knowledge and advertising the new firm's attributes to its potential customers. Once the US budget airline Valu-Jet became known as 'swims with alligators', its owners had no choice but to relaunch it under a new name; their substantial promotional investment in the name 'Valu-Jet' was totally lost.

For the initial innovator all the investments in product development and initial marketing are at risk should the innovation fail in the market: there is little value in the intellectual property that covers the secrets of making an unsaleable product or the brand equity of a firm no longer in business. Even setting this aside, where the sunk costs of entry are large, an industry may experience the integer problem, where a market is served by less than the 'optimum' number of firms because prospective entrants see that their likely market share cannot generate sufficient profit to justify the investment required to secure it. In the extreme case, the prospective sunk costs of entry are so high that no entry will take place, and the first mover advantage becomes the basis for a monopoly.

Many economists are quite happy to propose government intervention in such cases, usually to aid entrants at the expense of incumbents. Australia's National Competition Policy, for example, permits a company's assets to be 'declared', after which potential competitors may secure access to them at an arbitrated price. The Foxtel consortium, for example, built a cable network passing about 40 per cent of Australia's homes. The courts ruled that the National Competition Policy obliged Foxtel to distribute channel C7, produced by a media rival to one of the Foxtel partners, on the Foxtel cable.

Monopoly power

It is easy to imagine that a monopolist, the only supplier of some product or service, can set any price that its managers like, while when there are a number of suppliers, consumers can shop around and competition for their business will lead to lower prices. In practice, and even in theory when realistic assumptions are used, this is only a short-term effect. While competition may not limit the prices a monopolist can charge, the unwillingness or inability of consumers to pay high prices means that a monopolist's self-interest will keep prices from rising indefinitely; while in most markets competitors will use brands, advertising and customer relationship management systems to become monopolists over their own market share, bringing prices close to the level a single monopolist would have charged.

A monopoly innovates – then doesn't

Thomas J. Watson Sr became the manager of CTR (later to become IBM) in 1911, and one of his first acts was to raise money for an R&D programme into superior tabulating equipment. While Watson is remembered as an inspired salesman, he never neglected R&D and IBM rapidly became the global leader in calculating technology.

Under Thomas J. Watson Jr, IBM moved from electromechanical tabulators to electronic computers, and having achieved dominance of business computing with the 1401, IBM 'bet the company' on the System/360 in 1964. IBM became America's most admired, and most valuable, company, holding over 70 per cent of the corporate computing market in its own right with another 10 per cent held by 'IBM-compatible' manufacturers.

In 1977, some time after Thomas J. Watson Jr stepped down as chief executive, IBM faced another critical decision; whether to make the next architectural leap with 'FS' (future system) or go on squeezing money out of its dominant market position with the obsolescent 360 architecture. The new managers balked at the challenge and for seven years their decision appeared to have been correct, as IBM continued to grow; but in 1984 IBM 'hit the wall'. Growth stalled, and shortly after, profits dived.

IBM had to be rescued by a new management team under Lou Gerstner, and survives as a large and profitable company but no longer an unchallengeable industry leader.

Watson and Petre 1990; press reports

Sometimes, the consolidation of a market from many competitors to a few oligopolists or even a monopolist may deliver considerable consumer benefits. As Schumpeter pointed out many years ago, when corner shops were replaced by supermarkets consumers benefited from substantially lower prices: typically the retail price of goods in a supermarket was comparable to, or lower than, the wholesale price charged to the many small firms that it displaced. At the district level, monopolies replaced competition but consumers were unquestionably better off.

Monopolies may be harmless but they may also be malign, not so much in the sense of gouging customers as in neglecting innovation: the real problem is not what a monopoly is doing 'today' but rather what it won't attempt to do 'tomorrow'. Rational, wise and far-sighted managers of a monopoly will recognise that a vigorous programme of innovation is the best way to maximise their company's value;

but less far-sighted managers may see innovation as a real current expense, with uncertain future benefits and an unwelcome drain on profits, and decide to neglect it. Eventually a rival or rivals will find the energy and support needed to pick up these neglected innovations but, at least in hindsight, there will have been a significant social cost incurred because of the delay.

An exaggerated concern about monopoly power has proved very rewarding for the many economists in the extensive bureaucracies formed to fight it, such as the Federal Trade Commission in the US, the Competition Directorate of the European Union, and the Australian Consumer and Competition Commission (ACCC).

The prosecution in the Microsoft case in the USA did not attempt to demonstrate consumer harm because of excessive prices: one key point of contention, Microsoft's Internet Explorer, was given away for nothing. The prosecution argued that Microsoft, having competed its way, ostensibly legally, to dominance in the market for PC operating systems, was illegally using its advantages to deter entry and damage competitors in other fields of computing. Consumer harm, such as it was, occurred because unknown innovators were deterred from offering products that might have been superior to Internet Explorer because, at a zero price, they were unlikely to make much of a profit.

Putting competition ahead of consumers

The fear of monopolies is such that if a company, because of its internal efficiencies and the large scale of its operations, can offer lower prices than any competitor it may be committing the criminal offence of attempted monopolisation by doing so. In order to give consumers the benefits of low prices arising from competition, prices may have to be held up. Consider this paragraph from the EU Competition Directorate's press release celebrating its judgement against Michelin in June 2001. Commenting on the case, Competition Commissioner Mario Monti said:

Dominant companies must be careful not to engage in practices that exclude other players from the market. Rebates and bonuses are normal commercial practices but, as confirmed by the European court, some types are illegal when they are granted by a company in a dominant position and have an exclusionary effect.

As critics, including some less committed economists, have noted, competition law may have the effect of preserving less efficient competitors rather than furthering the interests of consumers; it also requires assumptions that may be very hard to prove: do Michelin's competitors have a low market share because of Michelin's anti-competitive behaviour, or are they simply less efficient at addressing buyer needs in Michelin's core markets? One of the assumptions required by perfect competition theory is that of 'perfect knowledge', that, by assumption, except where Michelin holds specific patents, every other company, or at least, every other tyre company, could make tyres that matched Michelin's specification at Michelin's cost level. This may be a theoretically useful assumption, but it is hard to see how it could be proved; such evidence as is available suggests that the assumption is not supported by the facts.

One instance of high farce in the Microsoft case occurred when the prosecutors were working on a proposal to set up four competing operating systems companies, each starting with a complete copy of Microsoft's source code, but then free to go their own way in a state of near-perfect competition. The members of the lobby group supporting the prosecution recoiled in horror when they were asked to become some of the four competitors: it became clear that the main problem was not monopoly, but that Microsoft had one and they did not.

Microsoft's Windows became a monopoly because network effects dominate the market for such products: the more people who used Windows, the more attractive it became to writers of useful application software; and the more application software was available the more attractive Windows became to computer buyers. As Arthur (1989) suggested, when strong network effects are present, a technically inferior product may rise to dominance, by luck as much as by good management.

The argument against monopoly on the basis of excessive consumer pricing is not supported by either logic or econometric studies. The economist Harberger demonstrated in 1954 that the total cost of monopoly in the US economy was no more than 'the price of one steak dinner per family per year' and far less than the cost of maintaining the anti-monopoly bureaucracy. The more subtle argument used in the Microsoft case, that a monopolist may suppress or deter beneficial innovations that would provide consumers with a superior alternative, is less easy to disprove. While urban mythology is well populated with tales of large companies suppressing innovations, most of the stories turn out to be totally unfounded when properly examined.

New ventures are not under much threat from the anti-monopoly sections of the law; it took even Bill Gates 16 years to grow from a hobbyist to an alleged monopolist. In the US, more than in most other countries, the anti-monopoly law offers some opportunities for entrepreneurs, since large companies may prefer settling to being sued in a country where in general each side pays its own costs. If some action of the larger firm has damaged the entrepreneur's interests, the anti-monopoly law places the burden of proof on the monopolist to prove that the larger firm's actions were neither deliberately hostile nor recklessly indifferent to the welfare of its competitor.

The public interest

The economy is a subsystem of human society and so it is possible that socially or politically determined priorities may override strictly economic ones. This may lead to governments subsidising entrepreneurs or protecting them from competition by tariffs, quotas and preferential purchasing policies, even when it could be argued that the same results could have been achieved at a lower cost by allowing market forces to complete the task.

The most common arguments are those from national defence: if the cheapest supplier of munitions and military equipment is also a potential enemy or a nation with whom trade may be disrupted at a time of conflict, then politicians may argue successfully that their countries should establish their own defence industries. Sometimes these may take the form of state-owned arsenals, but often local firms and entrepreneurs will be given preference in ordering and offered subsidies and incentives in order to establish a national defence manufacturing capability.

Orthodox economists greet more general arguments for government support of industrial development with suspicion verging on outright hostility. Either by assumption or an appeal to the 'law' of comparative advantages, they may argue that the costs of any government intervention to support entrepreneurs necessarily exceeds the benefits; even if industrial development policies appear to have been wildly successful, as in Singapore, South Korea and Taiwan, there are plenty of economists available to argue that pure laissez-faire would have produced even better outcomes.

The complex systems approach

People clearly differ in their ability to 'grasp the broad picture'; someone who fails to do so may be told that 'they can't see the wood for the trees'. We accept that someone can be a good landscape gardener without knowing much about plant physiology, or a good psychologist without being an expert on the biochemistry of neurotransmission. Such similes and examples bridge a major philosophical debate: can understanding the parts of a system lead to a proper scientific understanding of the properties of the whole? Complex systems theorists believe that a system of many interacting components may have properties that cannot be discovered purely be examining the parts in detail, if for no other reason than the information-processing task grows combinatorially with the number of components (there can be two interactions between two components, six interactions between three components, 1,814,400 interactions between ten components and so on).

The dominant contemporary economic school today relies on general equilibrium theory to analyse economic problems. A theoretical state of general equilibrium will be one from which change cannot occur from within the system itself; it must be imposed by external forces. When general equilibrium theorists study change, they do so by the method of comparative statics: solve their equations for the state before the shock that induced the change, solve them again, for the situation that would be expected once the effects of the change had worked through the system, and compare the two solutions to find the differences. These differences are the effects that economists using this method consider to be caused by the initial change.

There are a number of critiques challenging the relevance of the study of a system of statics when the subject is as dynamic as a modern entrepreneurial economy, not all of them recent. Schumpeter's comments on this issue, in which he pointed out the intrinsic evolutionary nature of capitalism, were quoted in Chapter 2.

More recently, Kauffman's investigations of complex evolutionary systems (1993, 1995) have introduced an even more fundamental criticism: in the words of the old Irish joke, sometimes 'you can't get there from here'. Although a static analysis (or some other approach) may show that an alternative state may be more desirable than the present one, there may be no feasible path between the two. In Kauffman's terminology, no 'adaptive walks' link the two states; if the change is to be achieved at all, it requires an 'evolutionary leap'. Adaptive walks are a process of individual, disconnected decisions, while evolutionary leaps imply a number of simultaneous changes, potentially, in human societies at least, coordinated ones. A less humorous but more precise response from the Irishman whose advice the motorist sought could have been 'first, turn your car into a helicopter.'

A simple complex system

Newton's law of gravitation deals with the attraction between two bodies, but because the sun is much more massive than any of the planets, Newton was able to calculate the planetary orbits by treating each planet in turn as if it was then only one, and then calculating how the larger planets would perturb the orbits of the rest.

In the late 1800s the mathematician Poincaré attempted to calculate the orbit of a small planet around two equal-sized large suns, the 'three body

▶

problem' the solution of which had eluded Newton. Poincaré discovered that the orbits could only be determined by assuming an impossibly precise measurement of the initial position and velocity of the planet: the tiniest of differences would send the planet into a completely different orbit. Still worse, for practically all starting conditions the planet did not 'orbit' in the conventional sense at all, tracing out an endless path that never repeated itself.

A system of three bodies acting under gravitational attraction is too complex for its behaviour to be predicted.

Suppose, for example, a US manufacturer decided, in order to improve its access to global markets, to use metric rather than American nuts and bolts. It could simply change the bolts in its stockroom. This would provoke a crisis since the bolts would no longer fit the holes and new drill bits would be ordered. Another crisis would occur when the nuts didn't fit the bolts, another when the spanners didn't fit the nuts and more still when angry customers found that their maintenance drawings did not describe the products correctly. Long before this, in all probability, the firm would have failed or a more interventionist management team appointed and the one step at a time approach replaced by a 'big bang' as every change was coordinated and planned.

No economist, to our knowledge, advises firms to rely on simple adaptation in order to solve their problems, but a group of economists known as the Austrian School does take this position with regard to social problems. This group, supported from the sidelines by a group inspired by the book *Bionomics* by Michael Rothschild (1992), argues that 'imposed' order created by government policy will necessarily be worse than 'emergent' order arising from a laissez-faire market. The French biologist Jacques Monod anticipated this argument in *Chance and Necessity* (1971), in which he pointed out that we have no logical reason to believe that evolution is benevolent: Hitler and Stalin were evolutionary outcomes as much as were Mahatma Ghandi and Martin Luther King Jr.

The Austrians and their allies have opened a second front with the theories of public choice and regulatory capture, which assert that even if, in theory, a socially coordinated change would be beneficial, in practice politicians and public servants would corrupt the initiative to their own benefit; while if regulation appeared to improve the social outcome when contrasted to a laissez-faire market, in short order the regulators would identify with the industry they were regulating and jointly conspire to rip off the public.

It is important to recognise that the 'Austrian' arguments are not based on experiments or even comparative historical studies: they analyse an actual outcome and contrast it with a superior one that, they assert, would have been arrived at under laissez-faire conditions. Ultimately, as Monod pointed out, the argument is about God: Is there a God? Is He omnipotent and benevolent? Does He choose to intervene in markets to ensure that laissez-faire outcomes are superior to socially imposed ones? Unless the answers to these questions are 'yes', complex systems theory suggests that it may be possible (never certain, and sometimes not even probable) that any given set of social problems may respond better to a socially managed solution than to a laissez-faire one. After all, even the most devoted Austrian theorist expects the state to interfere with the activities of criminals whose actions might infringe their property or other rights.

Systems theorists who countenance government action in an economy do so on a number of grounds: the public infrastructure may be inadequate to support an optimal number of entrepreneurs and maintain an optimal rate of innovation; firms and entrepreneurs may lack the capacity to adopt new technological paradigms; technologically obsolete or inferior processes may have become locked in by historic processes; and public and social institutions may be inadequate or inappropriate to the task of encouraging innovation.

Clusters and differentials

One of the deepest differences between orthodox economists and complex system theorists is summarised in the distinction between the phrases 'comparative advantage' and 'competitive advantage'. The former comes from the classical economist David Ricardo's theory of free trade, which asserts that, under free trade and in the absence of interfering governments, every industry will be located so as to make the best possible use of the available resources. The latter term is practically the trademark of the Harvard economist Michael Porter (1980, 1985, 1990), but substantial contributions to the underlying theory and the collection of relevant evidence were made by the historian Braudel and the complex systems theorist Arthur.

The theory of competitive advantage asserts that the location of firms in an industry may be affected by the earlier location decisions of other firms, such that a firm entering an industry is more likely to do so in proximity to established firms in that industry than at other locations. Arthur and Porter describe such industries as forming 'clusters' around a focal point; the most globally famous example is Silicon Valley in California, where high-tech firms cluster around each other and Stanford University. 'Silicon Fen' around Cambridge and the concentration of the English software industry along the M4 corridor west of Heathrow are clusters of this type.

The theory of comparative advantage makes exactly the opposite prediction: if there are already several firms from a given industry in a single location, the best land will already be occupied and the best staff recruited. Competition between firms will already be pushing land prices, service costs and wages up. Firms seeking to establish low-cost operations should, suggests the theory of comparative advantage, go as far as possible away from such blighted neighbourhoods. The physical evidence, set out in great detail by Porter (1990), suggests that the attraction of clusters may overcome considerable cost disadvantages.

The high cost of operating a business in a major cluster is, of course, the flip side of the high wages that may be earned there and nations and regions aspire, with reason, to be the location of such clusters. While competition between workers might be expected to keep wages down, the competition between different employers in a cluster for workers will tend to push them up.

The economist James Galbraith has produced (1998) a convincing explanation for wage and salary differentials, drawing in part on complex systems theory and the use of sophisticated statistical analyses. He showed that the workforce could be divided into three categories: the K-sector (K being economists' shorthand for capital, but it could also signify knowledge) whose products are required by the producers of consumer goods and services; the C-sector, where the K-sector's products are put to work to produce consumer goods and services; and the S-sector, whose products are either pure services or the manufacture of goods with little capital or knowledge content.

Galbraith found that the K-sector, typified by firms like Boeing, Siemens and Microsoft, pay higher than average wages, irrespective of the job: even Microsoft's janitors are better paid than janitors in less glamorous industries. The high value added in K-sector firms and the high cost of mistakes ensure that employers in these industries want committed, long-service workers and are prepared to pay enough to make their workers' jobs worth keeping and worth doing well.

Wages in the S-sector, typified by the fast-food and hospitality industries, hover around the minimum wage except at times of general prosperity when competition between employers exerts a slight upwards pressure. The net value added per worker in these industries is low, as are training and recruitment costs, and the consequences of occasional mistakes are trivial (compare the consequences of mucking up a hamburger order with crossing critical wires on an aeroplane's safety systems).[2]

C-sector wages span the difference: workers with substantial personal responsibility, such as miners, forestry and construction workers, earn similar wages to K-sector workers, as do workers in major manufacturing industries such as motorcars and defence equipment. In the latter two industries the need for inter-worker cooperation and the high value of the equipment they use make their commitment and diligence important to their employers. As the value of the production equipment and the value of a single unit of output drops, so do the wages until, with the clothing and footwear industries, wages and conditions merge with those in the 'pure' service sectors.

For those who accept the arguments of Porter and Arthur and the evidence assembled by Braudel and Galbraith, governments may have a significant role to play in enhancing the welfare of their communities. Best of all is to create a centre of attraction for K-sector industries; it may have been accidental in the case of Silicon Valley, but it was anything but in Bangalore or Ireland. Next best is capital-intensive manufacturing industry, the basis of the Japanese and Korean 'miracles' of post-war development. Doing nothing may earn the praise of neoliberal economists, but as Shakespeare's King Lear said, 'Nothing will come of nothing'.

Public infrastructure

Innovations occur in time and space, and for every innovation there are preconditions without which it could not have been undertaken. Some of these preconditions will have been satisfied by prior, privately undertaken innovations; but in most cases public infrastructure will have also played a role in making an innovation possible. The development of Federal Express is one of the best-known, or most studied, cases used in entrepreneurship teaching; and yet Federal Express would be, literally, inconceivable without America's publicly provided airfields and highways.

Today's entrepreneurs, at least in the developed world, assume that when they flick a switch the lights will come on and when they pick up a telephone they will be connected to the person to whom they wish to speak. While privatisation and deregulation have been the rule since the 1980s, most of the communications and electricity supply infrastructure in the developed world was either publicly provided or built by regulated private monopolies. Where such infrastructure is lacking, whole fields of innovation are foreclosed.

Systems theorists consider that innovation and economic development will not proceed unless the physical infrastructure is provided, and those who wait for market forces to build their airfields, roads, electricity supply systems and communications infrastructure will wait a long time. More subtly, purely profit-driven providers of such infrastructure will underinvest and overcharge when compared with public providers; unreliable and expensive services are simply more profitable to their suppliers than reliable, inexpensive ones. Elected officials, on the other hand, realise that their constituents are more concerned about performance than profit.

Physical infrastructure is only part of the story: entrepreneurs need employees and customers who are sufficiently literate and numerate to make and use their products. For some innovations, bare literacy may be enough, but for others PhDs are a barely adequate qualification. Educated and trained individuals are seldom enough on their own; there must be information sources, such as libraries and databases.

Systems theorists have little difficulty in demonstrating that, except under the most unreal assumptions, such infrastructure will be poorly supplied under laissez-faire conditions. (Typically, proofs of the efficiency of laissez-faire in infrastructure provision include the assumption of perfect foresight, a concept not merely ridiculous in itself, but self-contradictory: why should perfectly foresighted entrepreneurs invest in research, since their perfect foresight must surely reveal the conclusions before they start?)

Transition problems

Innovations are a form of creative destruction, some more drastic on the destructive side than others. In the systems theory view, every innovation sets the scene for further ones, and to minimise social disruption and maximise the speed with which the potential benefits are realised, it is socially and economically desirable that people and firms associated with the old order of things should play an analogous role in the new one.

As motorcars replaced horses and carts, blacksmiths and coachbuilders adapted relatively easily to the new economy, but as electronic calculating devices replaced mechanical ones, the people who had been trained to make, maintain and operate electromechanical equipment had nowhere to go. Every technological transition creates winners and losers, and if society simply abandons the losers or waits for market forces to re-educate them, the economy will suffer from a restricted supply of appropriately skilled workers and a deficiency in total demand.

Systems theorists recognise the need for social institutions to support retraining and redeployment. Intriguingly, a number of neoliberal economists, faced with irrefutable evidence that the policies they promote have caused significant hardship and distress, also now argue for 'restructuring assistance'. When the Australian dairy industry was deregulated in accordance with neoliberal principles, over a billion dollars was provided in restructuring assistance to dairy farmers whose businesses had been rendered unviable.

In some instances transition can be managed at the firm level, minimising the destruction. A firm may have a good reputation and well-established markets, yet its capital base may be too slight and its margins too thin for it to be able to afford a new generation of production equipment or systems. Even when the suppliers of the new equipment offer generous terms and delayed payment, a firm may be leading such a hand-to-mouth existence that it cannot afford to release workers for training or suspend production while the new equipment is installed. In a globalised industry when some firms have made the generational transition early, the laggards may slip further and further behind. Appropriate assistance, possibly in the form of training and deferred taxation as much as outright cash grants, may enable such firms to make the generational change and carry a substantial number of their workers with them.

The distinction is probably that humane (or pragmatic) neoliberals see restructuring assistance as an exception to their general laissez-faire principles and a way to diffuse the political opposition to the reforms they favour. Systems theorists would argue that the need for restructuring assistance is continuous insomuch as innovations are also continuous: the normal operation of an economy involves driving obsolescent products from the market, making learned skills obsolete and putting those firms at the back of the technology wave under severe stress. Because of this social institutions to support retraining, restructuring and redeployment should be an essential part of a high productivity economy.

Dead ends

Path dependency can lead to more than an arguably inferior technology becoming the 'dominant design'. Path dependent development can lead to entire industries being stuck in a technological backwater, unprofitable as they are and unable to draw in sufficient private capital to support restructuring. Whole communities can become trapped in a kind of time warp: employers whose assets cannot be sold for more than scrap value; workers whose skills are so specific that the only alternative is unemployment or work as unskilled labourers. The economist Keynes meticulously documented the British cotton-spinning industry's 40-year decline from 1890: its final death in the midst of the Great Depression was almost a relief to its victims. The Appalachian coal-mining industry went through a similar period in the middle of the twentieth century. The oil shocks of the 1970s threatened to force the Japanese aluminium industry into a similar hopeless state, as the price of electricity generated from oil rose in line with the rising oil prices.

Systems theorists recognise the possibility that a series of carefully judged choices could lead an industry and its victims into such a situation and only governments have the resources and the power to force an effective restructuring: the Japanese government's controlled elimination of Japan's domestic aluminium-refining industry and the development of alternative sources of supply in low energy cost locations such as America's Pacific northwest and Australia is a textbook example of a successful intervention of this kind.

Many neoliberal economists prefer to argue that industries, communities and people in such situations have brought the situation on themselves and to assist them is to 'reward failure'.

Institutional problems

(Institutions, in the economic sense, cover systems of government administration as well as organisations.) Entrepreneurs need more than a technological and a social context, they operate in an institutional one as well. They must be able to collect debts and defend their physical and intellectual property at the very least. They need reasonable opportunities to promote and sell their products; which includes measures to give customers reasonable confidence in buying them.

Society has broader objectives than the convenience of entrepreneurs and some laws and customs restrain them. Entrepreneurs can use the law to collect their debts but others can enforce their claims against an entrepreneur. Some products, or product attributes, may be banned or subject to restrictions; workers and customers may have specific rights; buildings may be subject to zoning regulations and construction standards; companies may need to be registered and submit statutory reports; in these and other ways entrepreneurs' interactions with their employees, their customers and society at large will be affected by society's institutions.

Institutions, laws and regulations sometimes outlive their usefulness and may, in the course of time, cost society more in deterred entrepreneurship and abandoned attempts at innovation than can be justified by any benefits they offer.

The possibility that institutions might need reform and regulations may have outlived their usefulness is common ground between systems theorists and neoliberal economists. The major point of difference is that neoliberal economists tend to see all institutions and regulations as the product of vested interests and therefore obstacles to progress, at best a poor substitute for easily enforced property rights, while systems theorists recognise that institutions have both positive and negative aspects.

Government in a market economy

Markets have existed since the earliest recorded time, so the practice of exchange is no novelty; but market economies have only existed in theory for 400 years or so and even today there are no practical examples of 'pure' market economies in the world: in every developed and developing country there are governments playing an active economic role.

For a market economy to bear any resemblance to the economic textbooks, every economic actor is engaged in a win–lose game with every other one. Workers are expected to compete with each other by offering to work longer hours for lower wages until deaths from starvation, exhaustion and workplace accidents create a labour shortage. Manufacturers and farmers are expected to produce flat out whatever the state of demand, even when prices fall below the cost of production and they face personal ruin: if their competitors are ruined first, they are considered successful.

This presents the government of a market economy with two problems: making people compete when it is clearly in their best interest not to; and, when people do compete, making sure that they do so in an 'economic' way as distinct from using force or fraud. Workers, if allowed to choose freely, may join or form trade unions (opinion polls in the USA, where less than a sixth of workers are members of unions, suggest that over half of them wish they were in one), farmers may join marketing cooperatives and manufacturers form trade associations. In each case they are clearly better off individually if they are allowed to join unions, cooperatives or trade associations; but in received economic wisdom, if not in fact, 'society' can be better off by making all its members act against their own immediate interests and compete when cooperation would suit them better.

Cooperation has been part of human behaviour since well before there was such a thing as human society: a cooperating group of primeval men could kill and feast on a mammoth that could have killed them individually without breaking stride. Competition, of a sort, has also been around for a long time. If clan group A thought that clan group B had the better hunting grounds, a successful ambush followed by a massacre would allow group A to enjoy the benefits.

In post-Soviet Russia this form of competition became quite significant for several years as successful businessmen were allowed to borrow unpaid soldiers from the army and use them to collect debts or eliminate creditors. In societies where capitalism has become firmly established, including today's Russia, such activities are frowned upon. Spreading rumours about a competitor can be nearly as damaging, while giving short weight or lying about ingredients is another long-established way of securing a competitive advantage without risking a price war.

A government in a 'pure' market economy might restrict itself to forbidding cooperation and limiting the ways in which competition may be practised, but most developed and developing countries now have governments that feel obliged to respond, to some extent, to the wishes of their populations; and in spite of 400 years of earnest economic argument, the great majority of people expect more from their governments than supervision of the market – the 'level playing field' of popular economic writing.

Types of government intervention

It can be useful to think of potential government actions in a number of dimensions. Policies may be passive, respecting laissez-faire but trying to give it the best chance of delivering its presumed benefits, or active, when governments recognise that a laissez-faire market cannot solve a particular problem or group of problems. In each group policies may be negative, aimed at preventing harm, or positive, aimed at improving outcomes. Finally, policies in each category can be considered as lying on a scale of intensity, starting with laws, regulations and actions that attract near-universal support and moving to policies and practices which may arouse serious contention, both from laissez-faire advocates and people, firms and organisations that believe the favours provided to another group are the equivalent of discrimination against them.

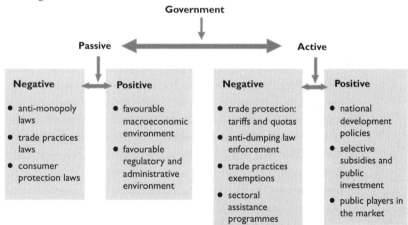

Figure 8.1 **Ways governments intervene in markets**

Passive policies

By and large, the policies on the passive side of the balance will attract widespread approval in principle, although the practice can be the subject of more debate. We split such policies into two groups: those that prohibit certain activities and those that require certain others.

Passive/negative The proclamation and enforcement of laws against the use of force or fraud to change the outcome of market transactions is now uncontentious. Even burglars and armed robbers accept their general validity, only challenging them on the grounds that they were not, on the occasion in question, the malefactors. This could be considered historically and geographically naive; the rights of merchants, farmers and artisans to defend their property against noblemen and royal favourites were only established by bloody revolutions in 1642, 1688, 1776 and 1789 in the UK, the USA, and Europe. There are still too many countries where arbitrary seizure, while nominally illegal, is both frequent and unpunished.

At the next level we could consider laws that regulate the way firms compete in the market. This is not entirely uncontentious; although the US Congress passed the Sherman anti-trust Act in 1890 it was not enforced at all until 1911 when Standard Oil was 'trust busted' and its enforcement has been only sporadic ever since. Australia's first anti-trust law was not passed until 1975; English competition laws were passed in 1976. A number of economists are prepared to argue that the pure outcomes promised by laissez-faire are jeopardised by the Sherman Act, its successors and imitators.

By and large, few economists and even fewer governments believe that laissez-faire can survive without protection and so firms in most countries are prohibited from combining to set prices, control quantities or limit competition by agreeing to divide the market into exclusive areas. Individual workers in most countries are allowed to join trade unions, which may then bargain collectively with their employers, but unions are often subject to heavy legal restrictions. The legal position of trade unions in common law countries, such as the USA, the UK and Australia, is that they are prima facie unlawful conspiracies which are allowed certain ways to avoid criminal prosecution or suits for civil damages. Many economists see the legal toleration of trade unions as a blemish and seek to have the legal protection of trade union activities abolished.

The laws favouring competition are typically broad and seek to close off indirect limitations on competition, even prohibiting or limiting contractual arrangements with an ostensibly innocent purpose. The international farm machinery company Massey Ferguson, for example, has a policy of appointing dealers who are required to carry Massey Ferguson lines only, in return for favourable credit arrangements and promotional support. In Australia these contracts were set aside on the grounds that other companies might not have the volumes that justified the appointment of exclusive dealers, so if these smaller manufacturers were excluded from Massey Ferguson dealerships they might be excluded from the market entirely, thereby limiting competition. This interference in the market may have been one of the factors, but a minor one, leading to Massey Ferguson's takeover by Agco Inc. in 1994.

A further group of laws and regulations seek to protect workers and consumers from coming to harm at the hands of profit-seeking firms. Various countries balance prevention and cure in different ways, but inevitably there will be some mix of prescriptive regulation ordaining some acts and prohibiting others and less prescriptive statements of principle, such as requiring employers to provide a safe workplace and supply products that will not harm their users.

The twist that makes both the theory and practice of this area interesting is the problem of punishing companies. A company can't be put in jail and a fine is effectively a penalty on its shareholders, who, in the case of a publicly held listed corporation, have nothing at all to do with its management. If the fine is large enough to threaten the viability of the company, then employees may also be punished by losing their jobs and possibly other entitlements, even those who had nothing to do with the offence.

Punishing companies

Since directors are responsible for the acts of a company, when companies commit offences or cause harm it might seem reasonable to punish the directors as if they had personally committed the offence or caused the damage. The English courts, at least, have ruled that this would be unjust on the grounds that the directors may not be aware of the consequences of their decisions.

When the vehicular ferry *Herald of Free Enterprise* capsized and sank while leaving Zeebrugge harbour the bosun whose job it was to close the vehicle doors was asleep after working for 36 hours without a rest break; and the third officer whose job it was to supervise him was also required to supervise the release of the mooring rope at the other end of the vessel.

The vessel had taken on a much heavier cargo for the home voyage than the outward one, and was 915 mm (three feet) deeper in the water than it should have been, but sailed before the ballast pumps had made much impression on the excess displacement. Cost cutting ordered by the directors had led to the retrenchment of the fourth officer and the relief bosun, and the directors' demands for operating efficiencies had inspired the order to sail before trimming the ballast correctly. The combination made some sort of accident inevitable, but the courts acquitted the directors of manslaughter on the grounds that they could not be held responsible for this particular accident. Attempts to prosecute the third officer and the bosun for their part in the tragedy aroused public outrage and were abandoned, so at the end of the day a company's reckless indifference to human life could kill 192 people and yet no-one was guilty.

Boyd 1996

The Law Commission in 1996 proposed to create an offence in England of 'corporate manslaughter' with the possibility of jail sentences for the directors of companies found guilty of the offence, and a bill to give effect to this recommendation was introduced to the British Parliament in 2003.

Passive/positive   Government macroeconomic policies can have a major effect on the prospects for entrepreneurial success and the fraction of the population who act entrepreneurially. The two effects are not closely linked and international evidence suggests that the two measures do not always move in parallel. Government policies can be considered under two headings: monetary policy and the fiscal/regulatory regime.

Monetary policy

As both Schumpeter and Keynes pointed out, and every entrepreneur learns again with every mail delivery, access to money is the sine qua non of entrepreneurial success. Real interest rates must be kept low in countries that wish to encourage entrepreneurs and inflation must be kept stable (not necessarily lower than 10 per cent per year or so, on the evidence). Keynes argued that the real interest paid on government debt should be progressively reduced to zero: 'no risk, no reward'.

Since the late 1970s dogma has trumped reason and governments throughout the world have been urged to make their currencies freely convertible, so that citizens and foreigners may buy and sell their national currency without any restriction.

When governments who had maintained low interest rate policies made their currencies convertible, they accepted the risk that their currency would be sold to buy bonds in countries where real interest rates were higher, leading to a falling exchange rate, rising domestic inflation and irresistible pressure on their monetary authorities to raise interest rates.

The Southeast Asian countries accepted further advice from the International Monetary Fund (IMF) to fix their currencies against the US dollar, making speculation on interest rate differentials a 'one way bet'. In 1997 Thailand, Malaysia, Indonesia and South Korea were plunged into crisis as speculators (mainly local, although international hedge funds were in on the act) sold their currencies. Malaysia avoided the crisis by reimposing exchange controls in the teeth of the most dire warnings from neoliberal economists; South Korea minimised its impact when the government socialised the currency speculators' losses by taking over their debts at extortionate interest rates; but Thailand and Indonesia lacked the political will to defy the IMF or the national economic strength to buy off the Wall Street predators and remained mired in crisis for several years.

Countries have three choices: they can be the USA, who as the issuer of the global trading currency can set its own interest rates; they can maintain convertibility and so have higher real interest rates than the USA but bask in the admiration of neoliberal economists; or they can institute exchange controls and regain control over their domestic interest rates. The Washington Consensus, administered by the IMF and the World Bank, prescribes convertibility, thereby making all entrepreneurs equal in their access to money and American entrepreneurs significantly more equal than the rest.

Fiscal policy

Fiscal (taxation) policy can be used fairly readily to bias economic activity in a direction desired by a government. US policies are widely seen as 'entrepreneur friendly', the three key areas being the favourable treatment of limited partnerships, the low rate of capital gains tax and the manner in which employee share options are taxed.

Limited partnerships, as implemented in the US, allow venture capital investors to share in the early losses of new ventures, deferring their own tax liability, without becoming full partners in a venture and potentially liable for its debts. The investors do, of course, stand to lose their investment if the venture fails entirely, so the limited partnership structure does not entirely eliminate risk. When a venture succeeds and can be sold profitably by trade sale or an initial public offering (IPO; see Chapter 12), the investors must pay capital gains tax on their proceeds, but with luck and good management (which is how venture capital funds earn their fees) they will never be exposed to any income tax obligations in respect of their investment. The capital gains tax concessions become an incentive for other investors to support new ventures as equity investors and participate in IPOs.

New ventures often need to lure technical and other specialists from their existing employment, expecting them to give up their relative security, perks and high incomes. The new ventures seldom have the free cash to offer golden handshakes and high salaries and are tempted to offer their new recruits equity. In the US, this often takes the form of share options, while in more fiscally conservative countries such as Australia and the UK, the traditionally preferred incentive has been partly paid shares.

In the US, the employee is only liable for tax on such options when he exercises them (turns them into shares), while a tax loophole, still open in 2003, allows the employer to claim the difference between the exercise price and the market price as a deduction from taxable income. The Australian or European tax on partly paid shares would be based on their value at issue, usually one penny in the pound, and so is also minor; but partly paid shares may be called by a venture's creditors in the event of its bankruptcy and may also have some voting power. In Australia and most European countries share option grants are seen as too close to tax evasion, and so options in unlisted companies are taxed at the date of grant as fully taxed income on their notional exercise value, not on the date of exercise as concessionally taxed capital gains, making them unattractive as salary substitutes when offered by new companies.

Thomas J Watson Sr used share options in partial substitution for salary to carry IBM through the Great Depression, and later remarked, somewhat sadly, that practically every employee so paid had sold his shares as soon as the price rose to the point that the options were 'in the money', while if they had held them only a few years until IBM become a stock market darling in the 1950s they could have become millionaires many times over. Bill Gates and Paul Allan used options as compensation in the early days of Microsoft, making over a thousand of their employees millionaires as the company's share price boomed.

During the height of the dot com boom (1995 to April 2001), some lucky employees made gains that dwarfed anything that employee investors in IBM or Microsoft had enjoyed, as share prices in companies like Cisco, Amazon and Yahoo! rocketed to fifty times their issue price in a matter of months. Those who held out for even greater gains had to settle for a lot less, while the many employees of 'dot bombs' wound up with little or nothing.

The arguments for favourable tax treatment of employee share option schemes are rather less persuasive in the aftermath of the popping of the dot com bubble than they were at its height.

Regulatory policy and administrative practice
There are few topics on which the political debate is louder and less accurately focused than the subject of regulation. The costs of regulation are frequently claimed to hamstring business and deter entrepreneurs; but too few commentators point out that regulations, in general, *benefit* entrepreneurs by providing a 'safe haven' against civil and criminal claims. Once an entrepreneur has secured regulatory approval for his operations, he is safe from those who may claim, in the future, that he has damaged their interests and must pay compensation. Their claim, if it proceeds at all, must be against those who granted the approval, not those who operate under its protection.

There are, of course, wide differences in national practice concerning regulation, with the English-speaking countries generally being, or at least claiming to be, less regulated than the Continental Europeans and those who follow their tradition. The Anglophone tradition is based on common law and the assumption that the primary responsibility for alleviating damage should lie with the courts, acting at the instigation of those who were harmed. The tradition started well before the emergence of independent judges and fearless juries:[3] originally the courts were quite literally the manor, baronial or royal courts and the litigants appealed to the squire, baron or king as appropriate. Appellants openly argued that their previous or prospective service to the squire, baron or king should sway the decision in their favour; moral concepts such as 'justice' took second place. Reforms, from the time of King John and Magna Carta, have only established that cases will be dealt with 'according to law'. Justice may or may not be the result.

From the entrepreneur's perspective, going to court, as plaintiff or defendant, is expensive, time-consuming and uncertain. Black letter law or regulation, complete with a properly stamped certificate of compliance, offers certainty and convenience.

Some regulations are profoundly anti-entrepreneurial, such as those that limit entry to a given market or industry, but in these cases there is often a strong case to be made that the costs imposed by a regulated monopoly, whether public or private, may be outweighed by the social benefits such as imposed service obligations and performance standards. Deregulating and privatising regulated and publicly owned industries may create entrepreneurial opportunities, but experience across the world since 1979, when the deregulation movement got into its stride, have shown precious little consumer benefit in many cases and serious actual harm in several.

Other regulations, such as the German requirement for entrepreneurs to under-stand basic accounting before they start their business, might be dismissed as 'nanny state' – if someone wants to go broke in a rush, why stop them? – but even then there are social costs of business failure that go beyond the entrepreneur personally and an outright condemnation of the German system might be unjustified.

Workplace regulation is a matter of vigorous debate, with many economists arguing that every regulation necessarily increases the cost of employing someone and therefore regulations raise unemployment levels. An Australian federal court judgment in 2001 scandalised economists by stating that there was no practical evidence that the regulations being challenged affected employment at all, no matter how convincing the theory. Even more to the point, the American economists Card and Kreuger demonstrated in papers published in 1994 and 2000 and a definitive book published in 1997 that raising the minimum wage by a modest amount increased welfare and did not increase unemployment. There is simply no direct link between workplace regulation and unemployment.

The administration of regulations is, however, a matter that most definitely impacts on employment levels and entrepreneurial activity. Where regulations are set out openly, the fees for compliance and other certificates are published and moderate and the administration of the regulations open and just, entrepreneurs can flourish. Even when mild corruption enters the system and bureaucrats require an incentive from applicants to do their duty, entrepreneurship will not be seriously inhibited. In countries where approvals, once given, can be revoked by a rival paying a larger bribe, entrepreneurship, in the sense used in this book, becomes impossible.

Active/negative   This group of policies includes border protection, in its various guises, to stop foreign-based industries damaging domestic ones and competition policy, intended to prevent individual firms from weakening its magical effects.

Protection

Protective, as distinct from revenue, tariffs have a long history. The German political economist, Friederich List, in his book published in the USA in 1856 as *National System of Political Economy*, proposed their use during the nineteenth century to enable Germany to catch up with Britain, and the *Zollverein*, a common market of German states, preceded Bismarck's unification of Germany by many years. List was aware of two facts that most modern economists choose to ignore: one is the cumulative effect of experience (the more you do something, the better you get at it); and the other is the need for a fixed investment in capacity before a manufacturing (or sophisticated service) firm can begin production. This meant, in the first half of the nineteenth century, that British manufacturing industry had lower average costs than German industries, ensuring their global competitive success; but worse, British firms could manufacture for the German market (or the market in any other country with the temerity to develop a manufacturing industry) using plant that was fully paid for by other production and sell it at its variable cost. German firms were locked out of global markets by British competitive advantages born of experience and liable to be strangled at birth in their own market by ultra cheap 'dumped' imports.

Governments that follow List and protect their domestic industries from the threat posed by imports may act generally with tariffs and quotas or specifically with anti-dumping actions and market access agreements. Such policies clearly conflict with the principle of free trade, and while neither the empirical nor the theoretical arguments in favour of completely free trade are particularly compelling, its advocates make up in stridency what they lack in evidence. In practice practically every government protects parts of its domestic industry. The USA is a vigorous advocate of free trade in global negotiations, yet its automobile industry is protected by 'voluntary' restraint agreements with Japan, its textile industry is protected under the multifibre agreement, its shipbuilding industry is protected by the Jones Act, its steel industry is protected by the vigorous use of anti-dumping tariffs and there are more examples for those who want to look for them.

In Australia, from federation in 1901 until the early 1980s, protection was accepted policy and any entrepreneur who wished to start a new industry in Australia could have a tariff applied to competing imported products more or less as of right. Unfortunately for manufacturing entrepreneurs, this policy was abandoned in the mid 1980s and tariff protection is not, in general, available to new industries in Australia. Many developing countries still use tariffs to protect their new industries, but they are under pressure from the WTO to reduce or eliminate them.

Competition law enforcement
In the EU, most US states and Australian suppliers are not allowed to determine the prices at which their dealers, distributors and retailers should trade, for fear that this might limit competition between them. When companies are judged to have 'market power', actions, which would be legal and conventional under other circumstances, may be deemed criminal if they might have the effect of limiting competition or even having a 'chilling' effect on competition. A chilling effect is deemed to occur when a company's actions make entry to a market look unattractive to outsiders, even if it cannot be shown that any outsiders were, in fact, chilled.

The most public face of competition policy is the administration of the law governing corporate mergers. Clearly a law forbidding collusive price fixing would have little effect if the potential colluders could simply agree to pool their interests in a friendly merger. Mergers and acquisitions are, however, extremely lucrative events for merchant bankers and other corporate advisers and their voices are generally heard quite clearly by governments: most proposed mergers are allowed to proceed. When merger proposals are rejected, as when the EU Competition Directorate blocked the takeover of Honeywell by GE in 2001 or the Australian government blocked the takeover of the gas producer Woodside Petroleum by Shell later that year, considerable controversy generally follows.

Entrepreneurs may brush with merger laws if they decide to sell their venture in a trade sale as the best form of harvest (see Chapter 12). Companies such as GE, Microsoft and Cisco supplement their in-house research with a substantial acquisition and licensing budget, used to acquire promising developments from their smaller rivals. Such transactions might be considered as restricting competition if the smaller firm's technology or other assets conferred a substantial competitive advantage on the purchaser, so could face scrutiny and possible blockage by the competition authorities. Sun Microsystems argued, during the anti-trust proceedings against Microsoft, that one suitable penalty would be to ban all acquisitions by Microsoft for five years.

Broadcom, later Australis Media, was one of the first firms to offer subscription television by satellite in Australia, but encountered cash flow problems in 1997 and accepted a takeover offer from the News Corporation/Telstra joint venture Foxtel that would have cleared its debts and allowed its shareholders some return on their equity. The ACCC called in the takeover proposal for review, forcing Foxtel to withdraw their offer and Australis Media failed, rendering its shares worthless and inflicting heavy losses on its bondholders. (Foxtel then bought half of Australis Media's rent book from the receiver for a nominal sum, but since Australis was already dead this transaction could not be said to reduce competition.)

Sectoral policies

While industry policies (see below) are generally concerned with the fostering of new industries, sectoral policies (which can involve protection) are generally intended to preserve established industries or at least manage their orderly adjustment to changed circumstances.

By far the largest of these schemes are the agricultural support schemes maintained by the EU and the USA. Since the EU and the USA are both international advocates of trade liberalisation, these enormous schemes are something of an embarrassment. The EU justifies the Common Agriculture Policy on social and environmental grounds, although its administration does not always seem to be in line with these protestations. The USA argues that its farmers must be supported to offset the unfair competition from the EU, although a study of the operation of the various schemes suggests that domestic political considerations are at least as important to the scheme's authors as international trade.

Britain, before it entered the EU (and Australia), tended to use marketing boards rather than subsidies to support agriculture. The marketing boards were basically grower organisations doubly exempt from competition laws, in that they had a monopoly over the sale of a designated commodity and were able to assign production quotas to individual members, establishing and enforcing market sharing agreements. The boards were an extension of the earlier cooperative movement within which groups of primary producers had established jointly owned production plants.

The Milk Marketing Boards in Britain

Milk Marketing Boards were established in England, Scotland and Wales in 1933 to relieve the distress caused by the Depression. As well as establishing quotas for individual farms, the boards operated a price averaging scheme, using part of the high price earned by fresh milk sales to raise the returns to farmers selling milk for manufacturing into cheese, butter, ice cream and other milk-based products. Consumers benefited by receiving a consistent supply of fairly priced milk while farmers earned higher and more consistent returns.

According to John Empson:

> The Milk Marketing Board was – by any measure – the greatest commercial enterprise ever launched by British farmers. Indeed, in terms of its main activity – the collection and sale of milk from farms – it was the largest such organisation in the world.

The boards tried to maximise the sales of fresh milk, and encouraged the sale of milk door to door by local dairy companies; to keep these companies viable milk was sold in returnable glass bottles. Supermarkets disliked handling glass, and disliked the need to handle returns even more, so they offered little competition to the door-to-door sales channel.

When Britain acceded to the European Community, the Milk Marketing Boards were grandfathered in spite of their apparent conflict with EC competition policy, but the farmers' devotion to them preserved them until 1992. In their later years a triple alliance of pro-competition economists, the EU's Competition Directorate, and the supermarket operators lobbied against the boards, and in 1992 the British government initiated their dissolution by executive order, a process that was completed during 1994. The successful Dairy Crest operation was divested from the successor cooperative, so while Continental dairy cooperatives kept their marketing arms the British milk producers lost theirs; the effect showed up clearly in the sales figures.

Over the ten years from 1992 door-to-door sales of fresh milk declined by about 68 per cent while supermarket sales rose by 147 per cent. Total milk sales declined by 11 per cent. The support that the boards had previously given to farmers was replaced by the various schemes in the EU's Common Agricultural Policy.

www.defra.gov.uk/foodrin/milk/faqs; Empson 1996

Since 1995 the various Australian marketing boards have lost most of their coercive powers and have been dissolved or turned into conventional shareholder-owned marketing companies. While these new policies have been applauded by neoliberal economists and championed by lobby groups and multinational agribusiness corporations, they have been bitterly resented in rural Australia.

Active/positive   Governments in general go beyond banning activities in the interests of competition and social welfare and actively promote those that they favour. These measures can be ranked according to the degree of opposition they attract from orthodox economists, from 'market-friendly' initiatives such as competitive research grants through national and regional industry policies involving subsidies and tailored infrastructure provision, exceeded by direct investment by the state in specific firms and capped by the formation of state-owned enterprises, either to compete in an existing industry or establish a new one.

Liberalisation and privatisation

Governments who accept the neoliberal arguments for the superiority of competitive markets over all other forms of organisation, and those whose policies are under the control of the World Bank and IMF, have adopted active policies intended to create or simulate markets in areas of the economy previously dominated by government enterprises or regulated private firms. The US airline industry was deregulated in 1978 and other countries have generally followed. In 1983 the AT&T telecommunications monopoly in North America was deconstructed under a court order, in 1986 British Telecom was privatised and most other countries have since moved in this direction. Public utilities in many countries have been deregulated, privatised or corporatised, most particularly the electricity supply industry. In few if any cases have the results been unequivocally good for consumers, although merchant bankers and consulting firms have done spectacularly well from their involvement in the process.

In Australia competition has been deemed to be so important that property rights, often considered the foundation of capitalism, can be set aside where they prevent competitive entry. Owners of copyright in recorded music are not allowed to specify the source of recordings sold in Australia, making 'grey' or parallel imports legal, and the ACCC has lobbied for all copyrights, patents and licences to be restricted in this manner. Owners of privatised railway lines have been ordered to allow competitors to use their tracks at rates that the owners claim are below their own fully allocated costs.

Cogeneration

One of the persistent criticisms of publicly owned and private but regulated electricity supply systems is their reluctance to pay for cogenerated power. On the face of it this seems absurd: cogeneration is a way of turning one of nature's dirty tricks inside out. In a normal power station, at least half and as much as three-quarters of the energy supplied is discharged to the environment; but when an industry needs process steam (for example for drying paper in a paper-making plant) it is possible to generate electricity at almost no additional operating cost by operating the boiler at a slightly higher temperature and pressure and passing the steam through a small turbogenerator before it reaches the plant – where, of course, all the heat is needed. Paper plants, especially, need lots of heat and only modest amounts of electric power and can easily generate much more electric power than their plant needs.

Rather than welcoming this cheap power, public and regulated utilities may refuse to pay for it, or even demand reverse power trips on the supply circuit breakers, refusing to even accept it for nothing.

The utilities are not being entirely perverse: because they are publicly owned, or operating under public interest regulation, they are obliged to install enough capacity to meet the peak demand in their area and since cogenerating plant is operated to suit its owners' convenience, it cannot be relied upon at peak times. If the utilities were to offer the plant owners more than the variable operating cost of their own lowest cost generator, accepting cogenerated power would actually increase their overall costs and therefore the price to the public. When a utility has access to hydropower, its lowest variable cost plants are the hydro plants and their variable cost is zero – and that is the most they offer to pay for cogenerated power.

Liberalisation policies create entrepreneurial opportunities and the proponents of such policies often claim that this is one of their major benefits. The spectacular rise of Enron Inc. as electricity and gas deregulation took hold in the US west and south-west from the mid 1990s, and its even more spectacular fall in 2001, in the aftermath of the Californian electricity crisis of that year, suggest that entrepreneurial activity, on its own, is not necessarily a force for public good.

R&D grants and concessions

Most basic research and a great deal of pre-market development is carried out in universities and institutes affiliated to them, but in order to increase competition an increasing number of grantors accept applications from other bodies.

Entrepreneurs can therefore apply for such grants directly; but more commonly, they will form an alliance with a university or a not-for-profit research institute with the academic institution making the grant applications. Australia's Cooperative Research Centre programme institutionalises this type of arrangement, and most other developed countries support similar systems, either formally or informally. World Bank and other international funding may be available to entrepreneurs in developing countries.

Expenditure on R&D is often tax-privileged in one way or another; for example, in Australia firms may deduct 125 per cent of their eligible research costs from their pre-tax income, effectively claiming a 7.5 per cent subsidy. Until 1996 Australian firms were permitted a 150 per cent deduction and the proportion of business expenditure devoted to R&D climbed steadily; after the cut to 125 per cent, this proportion started to decline, suggesting that a 7.5 per cent subsidy is insufficient to encourage firms to expand their R&D activities. Malaysia and Singapore have similar schemes with a 200 per cent deduction rate.

Britain introduced a 150 per cent tax credit system for small and medium-sized enterprises in 2000 and planned to introduce a complementary scheme for large companies in 2003. The USA has had a 'temporary' R&D tax credit scheme in place since 1981.[4]

Small business support

One unintended consequence of the growing influence of neoliberal economists has been an increased concern for the welfare of small businesses, often supported by exaggerated claims of their role in innovation and as a creator of employment. In practice, only a bare majority of small businesses employ anyone at all and perhaps one in two hundred demonstrate the entrepreneurial flair that leads to rapid growth.

Policies to encourage small businesses are nevertheless seen as harmless by the most doctrinaire economists and laudable by most of the rest. Many national and regional governments will have specific small business initiatives, offering advice, perhaps assistance with regulatory paperwork and sometimes subsidised business planning support. These services may be offered from offices or shopfronts and, in some cases, through incubators, buildings or estates where entrepreneurs are invited to rent space and offered easy access to various forms of assistance as well as extensive networking opportunities.

Industry policies

To an economist in the neoliberal or Austrian tradition, or American politicians defending the interests of industries clustered in their electorates, industry policy is anathema. The general argument runs, if a particular industry is favoured, this must be at the expense of other industries and, by implication, consumers. Galbraith (1998), as discussed above, showed that workers, at least, would be favoured by successful industry policies that replaced S-sector employment by K-sector or upper C-sector jobs.

The classic example of an industry policy is the role of Japan's Ministry of Trade and Industry (MITI) in the years following the Second World War. Japanese wages were low in the aftermath of defeat and the subsequent economic collapse, and the near-universal advice of economists was that Japan's recovery should be based on its comparative advantage in the supply of labour. Instead, MITI, with the support of the Ministry of Finance, focused on the development of capital-intensive industries and achieving global leadership in the related production technologies. The success of these policies was such that their result is generally referred to as the 'Japanese miracle'. Korea and Taiwan imitated Japan and they too enjoyed 'miracles' (Wade 1990).

When governments structure industry policies, they generally do so in a budgetary context, which gives them an incentive to distinguish between a system of cash grants and other extraordinary expenditures and concessions, without an immediate cash impact on the budget. The logic can be somewhat tortured; but in general a government would prefer to grant a firm access to public land than spend cash buying an equivalent area from private hands, even where the potential market value of the public land concerned is worth as much, or more than, the cash required to acquire the private land. Similarly a subsidy to a new firm's wages would appear as a cash outlay in the budget, while a payroll or income tax waiver need not be so recorded.

The use of concessions from the standard taxation regime is commonly described as a 'taxation expenditure', and the UK Inland Revenue estimated that these amounted to £138 billion in 2002, a figure that may be compared to the total amount raised by Inland Revenue and Customs and Excise taxes of £207 billion. Even after removing personal income tax allowances and the capital gains tax concession for owner-occupied housing, the tax expenditure total came to £83 billion, over 40 per cent of the total revenue collected.[5] Of this some £3.4 billion could be considered support for entrepreneurship and small businesses. The Australian Treasury calculated that in 2001 the Commonwealth spent A$32 billion in this way, or more than one-sixth of the Commonwealth's actual budgeted expenditure.

Industry policies can be broad or narrow in focus and general or specific in their application. Governments that choose to be specific in the industries they decide to support, and narrow in the award of that support, are acting entrepreneurially (or perhaps, meta-entrepreneurially) and clearly enjoy the greatest upside; but equally, if the industry they favour fails to develop in the way they hope, or the firms they support fail to secure a viable place in it, their decisions may be criticised in hindsight, at least in countries where such criticism can be uttered safely.

There is a general criticism of industry support schemes and one that is more pointed in the case of narrowly focused schemes: the incentives may be used to corrupt the decision-makers rather than progress the aims of the underlying industry policy. When the favoured firms succeed in generating high quality employment, the political opponents of the government or the scheme may argue that other firms would have done even better if they had not been corruptly excluded; and if the favoured firms fail, accusations of corruption will be coupled with allegations of incompetence.

Even when there is no reason to suspect corruption, firms in politically attractive industries are quite capable of playing off different jurisdictions against each other to get the best deal, such that the support offered may well exceed that strictly necessary to attract the industry. When GM announced in 2000 that it proposed to build a new engine factory in Australia, a vigorous if silent bidding war developed between the states of Victoria and South Australia for the privilege of being the host. Rumour suggested that Victoria won the contest with a package of benefits worth about A$50 million, about a tenth of the capital cost of the facility. Given that GM had

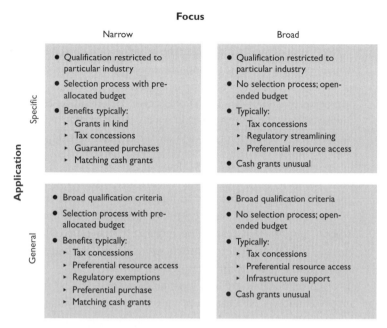

Figure 8.2 **Industry policies**

already announced its intention to build the plant in Australia, it might be argued that the incentive was pure profit to the company – but it could also be argued that GM's expectation of such an incentive was factored into their decision to build in Australia in the first place.

Hindsight is always perfect, of course, but theoretical opponents of industry schemes use a Morton's Fork approach:[6] if the scheme appears successful, they assert that it is only because the new industry would have appeared and developed without the scheme, possible even faster; while if it fails, their general condemnation of such schemes appears vindicated. History can never be wound back and restarted to test such assertions, but when those without obvious ideological barrows to push have studied the post-war history of East and Southeast Asia, the activist industry policies pursued by Singapore, South Korea, Japan and Taiwan are given much of the credit for the outcomes.

While the US federal government regularly appears in trade forums to state its adamant opposition to industry policies in any form, the US states go their own way. When BMW decided to locate a plant in the US in the early 1990s, South Carolina decided that a major auto industry was just what the state's economy needed. The state acquired the land for the factory at Spartansburg, demolishing a number of newly built houses to clear the site, and built access roads; when BMW queried (with reason) the educational standards of the local labour force, the state built a technical high school and training facility that 'guaranteed BMW five qualified applicants for every position'.

Broad, general policies carry the least risk of either corruption or encouraging uncommercial investment, but carry the twin risks that they will provide subsidies and benefits to at least some firms that would have proceeded anyway and the cost cannot be determined in advance so that a successful policy may destabilise the relevant government's fiscal position.

Neoliberal orthodoxy suggests the broadest and most general policy of all: the effective elimination of tax on companies, or at least large ones, to maximise the rewards for investors. In 2001, for example, the Bush administration in the US refused to adopt a treaty prepared by the OECD to control the operation of tax havens, It was widely suggested that the administration was concerned that the treaty might have exposed multinational corporations to the same tax liabilities that purely domestic ones faced.

Direct government participation

From antiquity until the mid 1980s, it was considered normal for governments to finance, own and operate key industries. Various grounds were cited: in some cases the government itself was the major customer and there seemed little reason to expect the private sector to be more responsive or efficient than a government-operated business. Where 'natural monopolies' like water and electricity supply are concerned, a private industry will underinvest unless promised adequate profits through regulation and a government-owned business may provide a more reliable supply at a lower cost than a private or deregulated business simply by accepting a lower profit rate; or an investment may be made on social grounds by a government where the returns are too low to attract commercial investment.

Famous historical examples include the Venice Arsenal, where the weapons were forged and the fleets built that made Venice the Queen of the Mediterranean; the English Royal Dockyards, where the ships of the Royal Navy were built and maintained from the navy's foundation by Henry VIII until the dockyards were closed or privatised under the Thatcher government. The German railways were built by the state for a number of reasons, among them a critique of the inadequate loading gauge[7] on the private British system and the risk that the private sector would not run railways to the places that the military wanted them; the German railways also proved far safer for passengers than the British ones, with about a fifth the number of deaths and injuries per million passenger miles. Even in the USA the private sector has not been entrusted with manufacturing nuclear weapons or weapons-grade uranium or plutonium.

The CEGB in Britain, and public power utilities such as the TVA in America and the SECV in Australia, enabled a large-scale, highly efficient electric supply system to be created after the private sector had signally failed to attempt anything of the kind.

CHECKPOINT

Whether, and how, governments should support industry is a matter of considerable debate and has been for many years; while the fully planned economy of the USSR is now regarded, at best, as a failed experiment, arguments for the total separation of state and business are unconvincing in theory and widely ignored in practice.

Entrepreneurs seeking government assistance clearly need to offer something in return. If an entrepreneur already has access to substantial resources, government assistance in the form of grants, loans and tax breaks may ease the cost of an R&D programme. Such assistance is usually available to all firms that meet the stated conditions, although the conditions and value of the assistance may vary from country to country and from time to time.

Entrepreneurs seeking help with commencing or continuing commercial operations may be able to get useful government assistance:

- if their innovation has significant military potential, they may be able to access a defence support scheme
- if their business plan suggests rapid employment growth in the relatively near future and they are prepared to locate in an area of high unemployment, they may be offered various concessions and incentives
- if their business is centred on an innovation using sophisticated technology and they are prepared to locate in a country or region suffering from Silicon Valley envy, they may also be able to negotiate a programme of concessions and incentives...

but unless their business plan is viable (not necessarily sufficiently profitable to justify the proposed investment) without government assistance, no well-run government agency will assist it except in the most perfunctory way. Government assistance programmes cannot be analysed without considering the photo opportunities they provide, as elected officials seek to share the glamour that surrounds successful entrepreneurs. They are not about giving the kiss of life to the near dead: the risk of failure, and the bad publicity and worse that follows, sees to that.

Readers who wish to find out exactly which programmes may offer support for a given enterprise or industry will find the Internet a valuable resource. All the regional development programmes available in England are indexed from the Department of Trade and Industry site www.dti.gov.uk/regions/rdapage.htm; British industries with a defence aspect may examine the options for export support at www.deso.mod.uk/. Australian readers (or readers generally interested in Australia) can visit the site www.business.gov.au where, at least in principle, all the programmes available to Australian business are described. The central and state or regional governments in most developed and many developing countries maintain similar websites.

Exercises

1 Patents, copyrights and other forms of intellectual property protection restrict competition and create monopolies. Explain whether society would be better off if these legal privileges were abolished.

2 What are externalities? Do these justify the use of public or regulated private monopolies to provide water and sewage services to modern cities? Do they justify subsidies to urban public transport systems?

3 Some governments offer restructuring assistance to businesses damaged and workers rendered unemployed by foreign competition following trade liberalisation. Is this the rational act of a government concerned to maximise economic development or merely wasting taxpayer's money on a populist gesture?

4 Consider the 'corporate manslaughter' law recommended by the Law Commission: is it fair to punish the directors of companies for acts which they neither intended nor ordered?

5 Competition produces winners and losers and if the losers are eliminated, there will eventually only be a single monopolist left; after all, by the end of the football season only one of the hundreds of football clubs in England holds the Coca-Cola FA Cup. If you have completed a microeconomics subject, explain why competition does not degenerate into monopoly; if you haven't, look up an introductory economics text for the explanation. In either case, explain how the textbook argument relates to your experience.

By now your research for your business plan should be well advanced.

6 Locate the appropriate authorities for the region in

which your venture will be operating, examine the various support schemes they operate and decide which, if any, of them are applicable to your proposed venture. Prepare an outline application for support under the most promising of the schemes.

7 National, regional and local authorities may have discretionary budgets, which can be used to promote employment and economic activity within their jurisdiction. Prepare a letter addressed to the appropriate officer in one of these authorities requesting assistance (which might be a grant, expedited regulatory approval or access to some local resource) and explaining why your venture is an appropriate recipient of such assistance. Imagine yourself in the chair of

the recipient and see whether you could have made your proposal more convincing.

8 As your national government prepares its annual budget, it will receive numerous suggestions from individuals, lobby groups and associations of various bodies for alterations to the taxation system or particular expenditures. These may be indexed on a website (for example www.hm-treasury.gov.uk/Consultations_and_Legislation); most of them will be reported in the broadsheet press and can be found in their online archives. Find such a proposal and write a letter to the editor of your favourite newspaper supporting or opposing it (you don't have to send the letter).

Notes

1   That is, a town-dwelling merchant owing allegiance to the king and his town, but not to any aristocratic landlord. 'Bourgeois' is sometimes used as a term of abuse, but here it is intended to be understood in its factual sense.

2   In 1989 a British Midlands Boeing 737 crashed at East Midlands Airport in England after one engine failed and the crew shut down the other one. Initial reports suggested that a Boeing worker had crossed the fire alarms, but close investigation cleared Boeing of this error and blamed cumulative pilot errors – including a failure to read Boeing's bulletins on controlling a 737-400 on one engine and, during the crisis, not actually looking at the instrument panel for the engine vibration warning.

3   Originally juries were panels of unwilling commoners dragooned into accepting the blood guilt that might otherwise have damned the judge or exposed him to reprisals.

4   Bloom et al. (2002) consider the significance of R&D incentives and conclude that they generally have a significant effect. Their paper includes an appendix describing the incentive schemes in a number of countries.

5   Including personal income tax allowances suggests more than a little ideological input to the compilation of the estimate; neoliberal economists and ultra-high income earners see flattening the income tax scale by abolishing such allowances as highly desirable by (although it would be considered economically reckless by Keynesians). The treatment of owner-occupied housing is quite complex in theory: on a perfectly 'level playing field' householders should pay income tax on their imputed rent while claiming deductions for their interest and other expenses. The sheer complexity of such a scheme for householders and the taxation authorities alike has prevented, and probably will continue to prevent, its adoption.

6   Wikipedia explains Morton's Fork as follows: 'The expression originates from a policy of tax collection devised by John Morton, Lord Chancellor 1487, under the rule of King Henry VII. His approach was that if the subject lived in luxury and had clearly spent a lot of money on himself, he obviously had sufficient income to spare for the king. Alternatively, if the subject lived frugally, and showed no sign of being wealthy, he must have had substantial savings and could therefore afford to give it to the king. These arguments were the two prongs of the fork and regardless of whether the subject was rich or poor, he didn't have a favourable choice.' http://en2.wikpedia.org/wiki/Morton's_Fork

7   Not the track gauge (George Stephenson's 4' 8½" track gauge became the Continent's 1.435 m track gauge) but the maximum size of a rail vehicle that could run the length of the track without striking any structures such as tunnels, bridges, platforms or stanchions. The Stephensons adopted a fairly limiting loading gauge such that there are a number of tunnels in Britain that cannot accommodate a standard shipping container on a standard flatbed wagon; by contrast, the US loading gauge permits containers to be carried stacked two-high on most routes. The German loading gauge was also very generous, big enough to allow a Krupp cannon to be transported to any part of the network. At the start of the First World War as the Germans advanced through Belgium they discovered that Robert Stephenson had designed the Belgian railways and the German army's Krupp cannons had to be disassembled for transport across Belgium. The delay was used by the French to marshal their forces in time to stop the German advance at the Battle of the Marne.

9 Entrepreneurship in corporations

This chapter

- A substantial fraction of the total innovative activity in a developed economy takes place inside large corporations. Much of it is incremental, involving relatively minor improvements to existing product lines and processes but, because of the sheer size of major corporations, the absolute scale of such innovations can be quite dramatic and the planning and approval process correspondingly serious.

- Occasionally, very occasionally, a major corporation undertakes an innovation that calls on its complete resources, a project of 'you bet your company' importance. Some person, or a small group of people, lies behind such innovations, establishing their feasibility and persuading their company's management to support them.

- By and large, the difference between corporate and start-up entrepreneurship are matters of degree rather than alternatives: both need a sound business plan, can only proceed with the support of a team brought together to support the proposal and need the approval of the controllers of various critical resources, usually including money; but for corporate venturing, the authority of the corporation is at least as important. The scale of a corporate venture is one important difference, as is the number of people whose careers are at risk in the event of failure.

- In this chapter we will describe some of the essential characteristics of large companies and set out some principles and related techniques for securing their commitment to an innovative expenditure on a relatively significant scale.

Large companies

Great trading corporations dominate the climax state of a capitalist economy, comparable to the great trees that dominate a mature forest. Like the great trees, they were once seeds and then saplings and, like the great trees, they will fall one day. Some will last longer than others and, when their time is up, some will crash while others will rot in place. Some will seem to be on the point of collapse and yet gain a new lease of life; others will be cut down while still strong and turned into sawn timber or even firewood.

There are huge differences between corporations: their industries, ambitions, public images and the respect with which their stock is treated in the market all differ. The one thing they all have in common is their sheer size: their financial resources, expenditure level and the number of people who work for and deal with each of them.

Entrepreneurs creating a new enterprise face all sorts of conflicting problems, but not recognising their colleagues is seldom one of them. One person is enough to start a new enterprise; four or five founding partners may be something of an upper limit. As the enterprise grows, employees and subcontractors will be needed but there will be no organisation charts, no staff development programmes, possibly not even a telephone list.

The passage from a small to a medium-sized organisation is often traumatic, both for the enterprise and its staff. People start having specific duties and responsibilities on which they concentrate, resenting interference from others and not interfering themselves. This can lead to dramatic disasters when some critical task, like updating the insurance policies, is omitted altogether; but equally it can lead to a gradual hardening of the arteries, with the amount of effort devoted to internal communication rising and the proportion of the firm's efforts devoted to its markets and other external factors declining as a proportion of the total effort expended.

If these early problems do not stop the new enterprise, it will eventually become a large business. One mark of becoming large is that the firm starts having middle managers, people whose jobs carry neither responsibility for making critical decisions nor the responsibility for carrying them out. Even medium-sized firms need some staff people, a pay officer, a personnel person, someone to chase debtors and fend off creditors. Large firms have staff departments headed by senior executives, directors of information technology and human resources. Employees get job descriptions and personal training plans.

Why do firms get large?

Some people wonder why firms get large. The subject provides economists with many opportunities to produce learned papers and present them at conferences. The most probable answers focus on the efficiency gains produced by specialisation. A full-time debtors' clerk will be far more effective at controlling the amount of working capital the debtors' ledger represents than someone for whom overdue accounts are an irritant and a distraction. A firm with 500 employees growing at 10 per cent per year and with a moderate staff turnover rate must recruit three or four new employees every week. Placing advertisements, interviewing and selecting these new employees is a full-time job and the bureaucracy of job descriptions and organisation charts is essential if anyone except the chief executive is to carry it out.

Whatever people are doing, they get better at it the more often they do it. In numbers, someone who has been concentrating on one task for four years will be at least 60 per cent more productive[1] than someone who has had to deal with three other equally complex and time-consuming tasks over the same period. The employees inside a large firm are usually far more effective at their particular tasks than small firm employees or sole traders, because they get the chance to perfect their approach and they enjoy a degree of freedom from distractions. People efficiency is only part of the story. Many expensive modern machines are only available in relatively high-capacity versions and a large firm is better able to keep such expensive equipment busy than a small one.

Service firms may need supplies; all firms need supporting services. Large firms are able to secure better bargains with suppliers and supporting service providers, not just by bullying but by spreading the marketing and sales costs their suppliers must defray over larger and more consistent orders.

The efficiency advantages enjoyed by large firms are, to a significant extent, cumulative. If an industry is at some point in time dominated by small, competing firms and chance or some apparently irrelevant factor favours some of them, the lucky ones will become a little larger than the rest. This will make them more efficient and able to keep their prices down while paying more for marketing effort, reinforcing their initial advantage. In a matter of a few years, the more successful firms can become several times larger than their competitors.

Dynamic performance

The dynamic reason for the success of large firms is that they are capable of applying large resources to pursue an opportunity. Some assets cannot be purchased in small pieces: a single new motorcar assembly plant will cost at least £200 million, which is only a fraction of the total cost of getting a new model car into production. Sums that an ordinary person would find terrifyingly large can be spent by large firms without undue angst: a corporation as large as Microsoft could spend $50 million on a new version of one of its lines of software, scrap it and start again without causing a flutter in its share price.

Schumpeter ([1942] 1967) suggested, and recent research has confirmed, that large firms are the major source of innovation in a developed economy, simply because they can afford to be. Bringing a new passenger aeroplane or a new model of a motorcar to market can involve the investment of several billion euros. Pharmaceutical companies regularly tie up hundreds of millions of dollars in the development and testing of a new product. Financial institutions spend tens of millions of pounds developing and implementing new service packages. A new holiday resort can cost tens or even hundreds of millions of pounds. Much of this money is borrowed, of course, but, in general, financiers prefer to lend to people who have a track record. An established leisure company will find it relatively easy to raise finance for a bland development, while an individual with a genuinely innovative idea but no record in the industry will find it hard to get interviews with bankers, much less get money from them.

Why aren't all firms large?

Schumpeter ([1942] 1967), having correctly identified large firms as the major source of innovation, went on to predict the virtual extinction of small ones. It hasn't happened in the 50 years since Schumpeter's death and does not look like happening at all. The basic reason is that efficiency comes at a price: the loss of adaptability. Large firms are efficient at producing and marketing a limited range of products and surprisingly bad at most other things. The Boeing Commercial Aircraft Company is deservedly famous for its passenger aeroplanes, but its forays into ground transport systems generated problems at least as rapidly as profits.

Much as there is a rich and flourishing undergrowth under the canopy of a climax forest, these implicit limitations on large firms give living room to smaller ones. Switching analogies, ants and elephants coexist, although those ants that find themselves directly under an elephant's foot may not do so well. Rarely, but often enough to be significant, the patch of ground ignored by the corporate elephants turns out to be extraordinarily productive and an ant grows to elephant proportions.

Most ants stay ants and most small firms stay small. There are a number of necessary functions in a market economy where larger firms, at least after a certain stage of growth, have no particular advantages over smaller ones. Taxi cab and messenger services can gain very little from being highly centralised, since the main activity involves reacting to essentially random customer demands. Large firms were needed to organise the railways, and later the airlines, because there was a large number of people who were prepared to pay for carriage between a limited number of main points. The more diffuse markets served by taxis and messengers offer few advantages to large firms and so few large firms are present.

Industries where the job is intricately intermingled with the holder's lifestyle tend to remain fragmented. Farming and long-haul trucking are industries with a continuing high proportion of small enterprises, because, in part, the benefits of the lifestyle compensate the operators for the uneconomically low financial returns they get for their time, trouble and capital.

Large and small firms coexist in the hospitality industries, because these markets can be segmented fairly easily into customers who want fast service with a consistent product at a predetermined price and customers who want a new, pleasurable or exciting experience. The same person may be, at different times, a customer in either segment, grabbing a McDonald's takeaway when the kids are hungry and the larder empty and going to a gourmet restaurant when the kids are safely parked with a minder or old enough to go off on their own. A business traveller stuck in a hotel overnight between meetings has one set of expectations; the same person travelling on a family or romantic holiday has others. The chains will always dominate the business travel market because predictability is an essential part of their offering, but specialists will always find niches in the leisure markets.

Discussing growth involves analogies, and while the trees in a forest can be used quite effectively as an analogy, there are two critical ways in which such analogies fail to capture important aspects of a modern market economy. One is that trees have little ability to take purposeful control over their own destiny; even if we should describe the top executives of a major corporation as being 'wood from the neck up', we would not expect to be taken literally. The second major weakness in the forest analogy is that it tempts us to think of the ground as constant, but in the commercial world firms live off the market and are part of it. The very success of one group of businesses creates the conditions that, sometimes, allow new large businesses to emerge. The ground upon which businesses rests is continually changing.

Dynamo or dinosaur?

Large corporations have a long history, but their emergence as major economic actors came in the mid-nineteenth century with the railways, which were organisations too large, too capital-intensive and too geographically dispersed to be run by an owner-entrepreneur. At the end of the nineteenth century large corporations emerged, initially in the US and Germany, in a number of major industries including chemicals, electrical equipment manufacture, electricity generation, steel-making and petroleum recovery, refining and distribution. By the middle of the twentieth century, the professionally managed corporation dominated the economies of the developed countries and, as Schumpeter noted, the emergence of the major corporation coincided with the greatest and fastest rise in living standards known to history.

▶

The emergence of gigantic corporations as major economic actors did not proceed without some criticism; from orthodox economists, whose theories stated that consumers would be better off if industries consisted of many small, competing firms; from many on the Left, who saw corporations, sometimes accurately but often not, as brutal exploiters and political manipulators; and from those who rejected the conformity that corporations imposed on their staff and the deliberate mediocrity of their products. While the post-war boom roared on, these voices could be, and largely were, ignored, but when inflation rose and economic growth faltered during the 1970s, the opponents of corporate dominance came to be heard more clearly.

Two trends emerged: a romantic idealisation of small business; and a demand for corporate managers to be more responsive to their shareholders. Managers of major corporations sought to 'increase shareholder value' by downsizing, outsourcing and divesting or closing underperforming business units; and many of the most creative employees, especially in the USA, ceased to believe in a corporate career and instead looked upon the corporation as a springboard from which they could launch their own enterprises.

Some downsizing and outsourcing provided opportunities for new small businesses, although most firms that accepted outsourced contracts were anything but small: when a major corporation outsources its IT operations to EDS or IBM, this does not represent a shift towards small business. Many downsized employees were invited back as contractors and incorporated themselves for tax and legal reasons. Such necessity-based entrepreneurship is also no evidence of a wish by employees to give up the comfort and regular incomes provided by a job in a major company.

The US consultant David Birch is responsible for a series of studies purporting to show that practically all job creation occurs in small and new enterprises; his analysis was, however, affected by a major conceptual error and his conclusions have not been independently verified. The generally accepted conclusion that new enterprises, *including new divisions of established ones*, account for most employment growth follows naturally from the dynamics of the technological, product and market life cycles (see Chapter 3) and in no way denies the continuing economic significance of major corporations. Outsourcing of various activities to specialist firms is not new but simply a continuation of the process of vertical disaggregation and horizontal aggregation that marks maturing industries.

The paternalistic corporation of the 1950s and 60s has gone, at least from the English-speaking countries; corporations in France, Germany and Japan still show some consideration for their employees. The corporation remains, as a major economic force, a major source of process innovation and, as a prospective purchaser, a major source of the rewards available to successful innovators.

The core competence of the corporation

We introduced the idea of core competencies in Chapter 5 as something that new enterprises must strive to create. Preserving and exploiting core competencies lies at the heart of corporate strategy; as we suggested in Chapter 5, the most successful firms are those that can separate their true core competencies from competencies they wished they had.

Corporations, however they are placed, seldom do well when they undertake initiatives in areas in which they are not competent. This reads like a truism but, in reality, many firms do not know what their core competencies really are. A dazzling salesman founded IBM and its major core competencies lay in the skill, education and discipline of its sales force. This powerful sales team gave IBM a unique ability to present complex concepts to the managers of large corporations in a readily appreciated way. The Watsons, father and son, understood this perfectly but, by the early 1980s, IBM's top managers came to believe that IBM had unique competencies in hardware design and manufacture and the production of complex software. They even believed that IBM's 360 architecture constituted an advantage. The personal computer and open systems revolutions of the later 1980s and early 1990s took IBM by surprise: it failed to realise that the computer industry was no longer under its control and it failed to find ways to leverage its one true competence into the future.

In the 30 years from 1954, IBM grew at a compound average rate of 20 per cent per year;[2] in the following ten years the rate was more like 1 per cent.

It is hard, perhaps impossible, to identify the core competencies of a large corporation from the outside by looking at its product range and examining its accounts, certainly unless the exercise is carried out over a decade or longer. The keys are found in its people, the things they talk about informally and the subjects that dominate discussion on the various informal networks that develop in every large organisation. Corporate mission statements, apart from those dictated by a committed and active founder, are seldom a good place to look for indicators of the core competence.

Occasionally top management succeeds in creating a new core competence. British Airways, on the eve of its privatisation in 1987, was not very popular with its passengers but kept them, in part, through political deals that limited competition on many routes. The arrangements British Airways made with the travel departments of its major corporate customers kept more and the dogged patriotism of many British travellers accounted for most of the rest. 'Belated Arrival' was one of the nicest plays on the letters 'BA' used by its frustrated customers. Lord King and Sir Colin Marshall, the chairman and chief executive, announced that British Airways was 'the world's favourite airline' (with a subtext focusing on high value business travellers) and shamed, shocked and trained the staff into turning the slogan into reality.

Corporate predation

Some opportunities are exploited by new, fast growth businesses, even in relatively mature industries. During the early 1990s regional banks in Australia showed marked growth, winning significant shares of the retail market. The opportunity was created by the policies of the major banks, who raised charges and reduced their service levels in order to repair the holes in their balance sheets left by their reckless corporate lending in the 1980s. When large companies discover that they have lost valuable market share points through inattention, they seek ways of regaining them. In the case of the successful Australian regional banks, the majors simply bought their upstart rivals.

One way an established corporation can set about regaining market share is for it to update its products and renew its marketing strategies, attracting new customers and reinforcing the loyalty of old ones. The other is simply to buy the companies that have invaded its markets. The first approach strengthens the large corporation in the longer term, while the second directly affects its short-term position but leaves the long-term weaknesses untouched. Companies that are managed so as to keep their share price high are only interested in the short term, so the merger and acquisitions route will seem very attractive. The following factors favour mergers over organic development:

- New product development expenditure and marketing activities are usually treated as a current expense, so when a large firm increases its spending in these areas, its current-period profit will fall, often taking the share price with it. By contrast, money spent on takeovers is recorded in the accounts as a capital transaction, so does not affect the current period's reported profit.

- Shares in smaller companies often trade at lower prices, relative to their assets, growth prospects and profits, than shares in larger ones. The major share-buying institutions tend to stick to larger companies: in Britain, firms in the FTSE 100 index (the 'Footsie'); in the United States, the Fortune 500; in Australia, the 50 Leaders. This makes it relatively easy for a large company to make a takeover bid that offers the smaller company's shareholders a substantial profit.
- There are sometimes quite genuine synergies available and efficiency gains to be realised from a merger. The larger firm's staff and service functions may be able to absorb the demands from the smaller one at little extra cost, while the energy and entrepreneurship that made the smaller company an attractive takeover target may be applied to improving the performance of its new parent.

Many individual entrepreneurs have found that a sale to a large corporation provides a relatively straightforward and remunerative form of exit. The pressures on corporate managers, as described above, ensure that willing sellers of successful growth businesses seldom have much trouble finding eager buyers.

Large company entrepreneurship[3]

Many large companies pursue 'organic' development instead of, or in addition to, their mergers and acquisitions. This may be because their industry is so concentrated that there are no small companies left to be taken over or the ownership structure is such that the company is managed for objectives more enduring than tomorrow's share price quotation.

The term 'organic' is often a poor one, because it suggests that a company can grow by doing 'more of the same'. Large firms are unlikely to find true organic growth rewarding unless they have gone through a period of neglect and underinvestment. Simply building more factories, opening more outlets or appointing more salespeople in the firm's existing markets will, for firms that have previously been well managed, increase their expenses faster than their income. Large firms can recover from an investment drought by simply raising the scale of their activities, but beyond that point they can only achieve profitable growth through innovation.

Innovation, as we have seen in earlier chapters, is not always or even often a matter of 'gee-whizz' technology. A successful entry into a new market is an innovation, as is the successful introduction of major new internal processes and the acquisition and forming of partnerships with firms that offer true synergy. Many attempts at corporate innovation are relatively safe, in the sense that a failure will be embarrassing but not fatal.

A few corporate innovations have involved the 'you bet your company' fervour, and uncertainty, of IBM's System/360 project. Boeing teetered on the edge of insolvency when its launch of the first series of 707 passenger jet aircraft was disrupted by a recession in the US airline industry, and the development cost of the RB211 triple-shaft jumbo jet engine caused the bankruptcy of Rolls-Royce. Most corporate innovation, however, involves less dramatic initiatives: serious enough for the people involved in them but not carrying a short-term risk to the survival of the organisation.

**What is
different
about
corporate
entre-
preneurship?**

The first and most obvious difference between start-up and corporate entrepreneurship is the scale. In money terms, most start-ups are launched with a few thousand pounds of capital, raised from family and friends, by mortgaging the family home or even by maxing out a few credit cards. If a start-up enterprise grows to the point that it seeks venture capital (VC), and only a small proportion do, the first tranche sought is likely to be between two and ten million pounds. By contrast, major corporations would not regard ten million pounds as 'serious' money, although they may be happy to feed it to the hairy inhabitants of their skunk works or laboratory; the investment in corporate ventures is likely to be measured in tens or hundreds of millions or, occasionally, billions of pounds.

A further significant difference is the acceptable timescale. Start-ups need to start reducing their credit card balance in a matter of months, and if they gain the support of venture capitalists, it will be on the assumption that the venture investors can harvest their investment in three to five years. Contrast this with Rio Tinto's HIsmelt direct iron smelting process, which should go into revenue-generating service in 2004, some 40 years and one hundred and twenty million pounds since the project started. The Boeing 747 jumbo took five years development and certifica-

---

The General Electric Company

The (British) General Electric Company (GEC) had roots going back to 1886, when Gustav Binswanger (later Byng), a German immigrant to England, and his partner Hugo Hirst (later Lord Hirst) founded an electrical appliance wholesale business. The business soon moved into manufacturing, servicing the rapidly growing telephone and electric appliance markets, and went public in 1900. The business continued to prosper, and over the years acquired other pioneering companies in the electrical engineering field, including Associated Electrical Industries (AEI), Metropolitan Vickers, British Thompson-Houston and English Electric.

Under the chairmanship of Lord Weinstock (1963–96), GEC continued to lead the consolidation of the British and then the European engineering-based industries, with a substantial share of the telecommunications, defence, transport, power generation and control, appliances and other businesses. Lord Weinstock proved a shrewd negotiator, reluctant to be rushed into any deal (or to approve poorly conceived internal ventures for that matter) and at the time of his retirement GEC had £2.7 billion net cash.

Not everyone approved of Lord Weinstock's caution; analysts and others in the City of London were appalled at the thought of this 'cash mountain' and when Lord Simpson replaced Lord Weinstock the share price began to rise. Lord Simpson cheerfully spent the £2.7 billion in the kitty on acquisitions in Britain, Europe and the USA, sold the defence business for £7 billion and spent that,

borrowed more billions and spent them too. Boring engineering businesses were also sold and, to make the point crystal clear, the group was renamed Marconi and became a major player in the Internet and telecommunications revolution. The share price rose from about £3.50 in 1996 to £11 at the end of 1999, valuing the group at over £30 billion. When Lord Simpson retired in July 2000 he collected a £10 million bonus as a reward for his outstanding performance.

In 2001, however, investors and analysts started looking at objective measures, like cash and profitability, and against these tests Marconi was found wanting. The share price dropped 96 per cent, taking the market capitalisation from a peak of £35 billion to £1.5 billion by the end of that year, and fell further as falling revenues led to rapidly rising debt. In December 2002 the company was restructured, with the creditors taking 99.5 per cent of the equity; shares that had been worth £11 two years earlier were valued at 1.5p, while the whole company was valued at £50 million.

The damage was by no means limited to the shareholders. Employment had peaked at 50,000; by the end of 2002 it was down to 17,000, with a further reduction of 3000 heads expected. Two generations of senior executives lost their jobs and, while a few floated off into the sunset on a golden parachute, most didn't receive enough to clear their mortgages.

Corporate venturing is a game played for high stakes.

tion to convert the prototype built under a military development contract to the design and certification of a civil jetliner, and a further ten years before the development investment was recovered from the profit on sales.

One more issue is the number of careers that are linked to the success of a corporate venture. Many start-up enterprises are wound up without fulfilling their entrepreneur's ambitions and a substantial proportion of VC-backed ventures either fail outright or yield only modest rewards but these outcomes are, broadly, acceptable. Either way, the pain falls mainly on the entrepreneur, her immediate family and any friends that she attracted to her venture. By contrast, the failure of a major corporate venture will be seen as reflecting on the competence and diligence of the corporation's board and senior executives, while the project champion's role in the failure will be largely ignored, in public at least.

Who is the corporate entrepreneur?

Corporations want to grow, if for no other reason than the impressive effect of prospective growth on their share price. To grow they must implement innovations and to implement innovations they must encourage corporate entrepreneurs. How?

One way to increase the number of corporate entrepreneurs is to widen the source of them: every employee of a corporation has a brain in which ideas ferment. Thinking is not the exclusive prerogative of the chief executive and her team of executive sycophants. The tendency, particularly noticeable in the US, but also very apparent in Britain and Australia, for chief executive salaries to rise without apparent limit tends to discourage innovation from outside the chief executive suite: if the chief executive is being paid 400 times as much as the average employee, she may be widely expected to contribute 400 times as many ideas.

Chief executives, however, are seldom appointed directly from the front office or the factory floor, and while they talk a lot to other chief executives, they have little recent experience of dealing directly with their firm's customers. If they do try to get involved with the details of innovations, they may see the problems in terms of the technology, markets and products of the period when they themselves worked in the front line. Such nostalgia-driven contributions assist some projects but are a hindrance to more. Chief executive officers, and a corporation's other senior managers, should be discouraged from getting involved in new project minutiae partly because their interventions may be less than perfectly helpful.

Project managers play a vital role in many large companies, controlling costs, keeping effort focused and ensuring that their projects secure and retain the confidence of the parent corporation's senior management. Some project managers are footloose, leaving a firm as soon as one project ends to find an interesting project with someone else. Others are an organisation's 'Young Turks', demonstrating their fitness for eventual promotion to the highest levels. Either way they are model cavalry commanders: they are given their objective and will attain it or die in the attempt. Casualties among their own team, and a certain amount of collateral havoc in other parts of the organisation, are an inevitable result of their operations. Like real cavalry commanders, they are seldom noted for the depth of their introspection or the frequency with which they ponder the meaning or intent of their assignment. Project managers are seldom the initial innovators in a corporation.

A project manager

An Australian company ordered a large and complex item of industrial equipment from an English firm in the days when English trade unions were more militant and industrial firms more important than they are today. The supplier engaged a project manager to see to the completion of the equipment in the factory, its delivery to Australia, installation and commissioning.

The project manager chartered an aircraft to collect the equipment and booked his flight to Australia. These plans looked like being disrupted when a group of workers began picketing the factory gate, holding the Australian (and some other) shipments as bargaining chips for their negotiations.

The elegant ritual that passed for bargaining was rudely interrupted when the project manager turned up with a gang of construction workers armed with picks and hammers.

'What are you going to do?' asked the astounded factory manager.

'Just knock down that old shed,' the project manager replied, 'so as to clear a landing space for the Chinook helicopter I have hired to lift my shipment over the picket line.'

The factory manager and the leader of the pickets had a very quiet discussion. 'Leave the building alone,' the factory manager told the project manager, 'and bring your truck around at 5 am precisely. We have agreed to open the canteen to the pickets at 4:55 am for twenty minutes, because of the cold weather.'

The shipment got to Australia on time.

Hsieh and Barton (1995), two McKinsey consultants, writing about leadership rather than pure project management, use the term 'young lions' to describe those rising young executives who accept project management and other change-making duties, and 'old warriors' for senior executives with their last promotion behind them who can also be effective in project roles, both as executives and mentors. They also introduce the idea of the 'high priest', the senior (but not quite top level) executive at the apex of his career who is respected as a thinker and analyst by the top managers of a corporation, but is unlikely to be given much or any executive responsibility. Such high priests are often the most senior people on the informal networks that define the corporation's core competence.

Hsieh and Barton's idea can be developed into an image of the innovation pathway in a typical major corporation. An innovative idea occurs to someone whose job exposes them to problems, either internal to the firm or as experienced by its customers. This person, the 'initiator', or her appropriate middle manager, 'the sponsor', approaches one of the high priests (or 'mentors') for blessings and advice. They may try to skip the blessing stage and make a direct approach up the management hierarchy: if they are lucky, they will be diverted to the high priest; otherwise they will simply be snubbed. The high priest will discuss the proposal and either explain why the firm will not adopt it or describe the informal project approval processes in use in the company, and give the would-be innovators the names of some likely supporters. The originator and proposer will be told to prepare a business case for the formal approval process to grind through and lobby the potential supporters to secure informal approval.

The corporate innovator can only succeed when the new idea can be aligned with one or more core competencies. When it is, there are no limits on the extravagance of the ideas that can be entertained. The internal networks will massage the impossible into the merely incredible and the practical will be embellished with sufficient relevant extensions to make it interesting to the informal network. The network can generate a wave of enthusiasm which top managers can ride or let swamp them.

Innovations from the top do not succeed unless they enlist the informal network or create a new one. King and Marshall personally initiated very few of the many small innovations that made British Airways attractive to business passengers, but they successfully empowered those staff who did not want to be associated with a 'bloody awful' airline to get their ideas adopted. Well-run corporations are generous with praise and photos of successful idea initiators and early sponsors will fill the house magazine. Corporations are less likely to trust people who have demonstrated the ability to think for themselves with a project management job. Once an idea is adopted and a project approved, a project manager will be appointed, usually neither the originator nor the first supporter being considered for this job. The project manager may coopt one or both of them onto the project, but usually in an advisory rather than an executive role.

The entre-preneurial process in a corporation

The initiator

Innovations start with a person, someone who sees a need and a means of satisfying it. This can be a production problem, where some waste of time or materials can be eliminated: the Japanese use the word *kaizen* – the 'way of improvement' – to describe the way in which shop floor employees contribute to the continuous improvement process through suggestions that are individually small but cumulatively significant. It may be a structural problem in an organisation, with some part of the operation being stifled by inappropriate controls or reporting lines. It may be an external opportunity, to form an alliance with or acquire a complementary business. It may, of course, be a market opportunity, a chance to create increased customer value through introducing a new product or enhancing or extending the distribution of an old one.

An initiator must propose a solution as well as identifying a problem: people who merely highlight problems without offering solutions are whingers, not contributors to corporate innovation. The solution need not be definitive or even particularly cost-effective, but it must address the identified requirement without being impossibly complex, ridiculously expensive or dependent on a radical revision of the laws of nature.

Initiators seem to be found at the ends of the organisational tree even more frequently than their statistical predominance would indicate. Ordinary research workers generate more good ideas than laboratory directors; production workers (in Japan at least) offer more ideas than production supervisors; shop assistants learn about customer problems faster than store managers; the list goes on. Some good concepts are injected into the top of an organisation; either when a new chief executive arrives from outside or while the members of the original entrepreneurial team are still in charge. Even then the top-down innovation is doomed unless the ordinary workers in an organisation get involved in the myriad of lesser innovations that make the concept a success: the concept of the Boeing 747 jumbo jet came from the top, but the aeroplane only flies today because of a vast number of lesser innovations, solutions to the long list of technical and operational problems presented by the decision to build a passenger aeroplane four times larger than those then in service.

The champion and the mentor

Most suggestions for operational improvement will be resolved at the operating unit or divisional level, because the payback will be so quick that the unit or divisional budgetary targets will not be jeopardised. This leaves many ideas that are potentially valuable, but, either because of the initial cost or the time before the return is realised, they cannot be hidden in operating budgets. The simple fact that a problem exists and has a possible solution is no guarantee of action. The concept, unless it springs fully developed from the head of the chief executive, needs a 'champion' or 'intrapreneur'[4] who will get corporate resources allocated to it. This may be the initiator or someone with more experience or standing in the corporation. When initiators from the lower ranks of a corporation set out to champion their own ideas, they need a sponsor, someone with sufficient seniority and experience in the corporation to guide them in its ways.

The champion, with or without sponsor, will still need the services of a mentor, either the corporate 'high priest' or a certified acolyte, who will guide the reformulation of the proposal into a form that can be understood by others in the corporation and eventually gain their support. Only founding chief executives can act as their own high priests; when a new chief executive wants to make an existing corporation embrace a particular set of innovative changes, he must enlist the support of the informal network or his efforts will fail. A new chief executive can appoint a new technical or marketing director, but new high priests emerge from within.

The corporate prelude to a business plan: The business case

Preparation of a complete business plan for a major initiative inside a large corporation is itself a major task and will involve securing commitment from a large number of people. A new product will need to be sold, so the senior sales managers must endorse it; it may need to be manufactured, if so, the production staff must be involved; it will often affect the corporate information systems, so the managers of the IS/IT function will need to endorse it; and people and functions that the champion has never heard of will need to be propitiated. Except in the most unusual corporations, these people will not want to expose themselves more than necessary, so they will not offer their support until they have seen the project authorised by people senior to them in the firm. They may still oppose it, overtly or tacitly, in spite of its formal approval, but they will not support it until this formal top management approval has been secured.

The mechanism for securing the formal blessing of senior management on an innovation is the business case, a relatively short document and a precursor to the full business plan and the creation of a project.

The basis of a business case

Successful projects inside corporations start with a business case, a document or process that is intended to help senior management choose the most appropriate projects to be given access to the corporation's executive and financial resources. Each business case sets out the costs (generally underestimated) and the benefits (frequently overstated) of financing a particular proposal, but when all the available requests are assembled they will, except in the most conservative firms, greatly exceed the total resources available. Large corporations generally have a formal planning and commitment cycle that culminates in the selection of those projects that will receive funding in the following year. Often the cycle culminates in an intensive planning session involving the chief executive and the rest of the senior managers of the corporation: such sessions may last a week or more and may be held at an exotic location.

Very few of the proposals put up to an annual planning festival will be genuinely innovative. Some will be 'organic' proposals masquerading as innovations, seeking extravagant funding to apply cosmetic changes to something that is already being done. Many will be for organisational changes: contract out this part of the operation, bring this other one back in-house, make more staff fly economy, re-equip this plant, close that one. Many may be 'more of the same' requests for independent spending authority, made by various turbulent barons concerned only with the glory of their own fiefdom.

Obviously it makes no sense for a proposal to be forced past the lowest level at which it is possible to get it accepted and financed, and where corporate practice involves a substantial devolvement of new product and process development funds, the manager of the devolved funds is the first person whose support must be sought. Divisional managers, even in nominally devolved organisations, will often be more enthusiastic in their vocal support than their financial support for a new initiative, since very few of them are able to maintain a true discretionary fund and those funds that they have nominal control of will be largely committed to current projects. A good proposal will often be seen by a corporate baron as the basis of a case to increase the fiefdom's total resource allocation, forcing the unpleasant decisions into other operating units.

Whoever actually rules on a business case, it has to be written so as to bear scrutiny at the highest levels of management.

The corporate objective

Directors, who are elected by the shareholders, control corporations. Unless the directors provide the shareholders with a satisfactory return on their investment, the shareholders may elect an alternative management for a corporation or even wind it up. Shareholder returns come in the form of dividends and capital appreciation on their shares. By and large shareholders prefer higher earnings per share over lower, higher growth rates over lower, and more consistent earnings over more variable ones.

Innovation may be applied to all three areas and sometimes more than one of them. A process innovation may reduce costs; if part of the saving is applied to marketing and part to price reductions, the result may be an increased rate of growth, as new customers enter the market and others are attracted from the firm's rivals. The increase in market share of itself reduces the variability of a firm's returns.

Product innovations, ranging from facelifts to radical forcing of the boundaries, generate revenue growth and a consistent product innovation policy holds the promise of sustained revenue and profit growth. Line replacements need a more carefully worked out justification, since part of their justification comes from the assertion that the line that the proposal seeks to replace is entering a period of slow growth or actual decline. Such messages are not always welcome, particularly when one of the executives who has to approve the investment in the proposed innovation built her corporate career on the product that is to be superseded.

Value and the share price

The commercial value of something is what people will pay for it, not the result of any calculation made by the seller. The value of a listed company is measured by its market capitalisation: the product of the number of shares on issue and the current share price. The logic behind the financial arithmetic of present values and risk-weighted discount rates is that they reproduce the calculations a fully informed and perfectly rational investor would make before deciding to buy or sell shares. Nobody, of course, is perfectly rational and, in markets where some traders are acting 'irrationally', even a rational trader might buy or sell shares at a price different to their logically computed value.

Internal investments by a corporation are usually justified by a prospective increase in profits; but innovations that improve the 'quality' of a corporation's earnings may be justified in spite of actually reducing current profits. As Dixit and Pindyck demonstrated (see Chapter 4), variability reduces the apparent value of a cash flow. A firm with an earnings standard deviation per year of 20 per cent and a trend earnings growth rate of 4 per cent should, in a rational world, be prepared to sacrifice as much as 2 per cent of its earnings per share to reduce the standard deviation of its earnings to 10 per cent per year. In practice few boards or chief executives would support a proposal that actually reduced earnings; but presented with two proposals, one of which promised a 5 per cent earning increase and no reduction in volatility, while the other promised a 3 per cent increase in earnings and a substan-

---

Southcorp

Few things are as reliable as the working man's taste for a glass of beer at the end of a day, but since the number of working men changes slowly and their capacity for beer is finite, it is not a market with any great upside. Well-managed brewery companies do generate a lot of cash and their managers are often tempted to invest a part of it rather than paying it out in dividends. So it was with the South Australian Brewing Company, which by the start of the 1990s had a major stake in the Rheem domestic hot water heater business, as well as owning a white goods manufacturer and a packaging company. There are few defensive investments quite like Rheem: while part of its business is supplying new homes with hot water heaters, a great part of it is in replacing heaters that have failed, due to the entirely predictable corrosion of the cylinder, after an average of 15 years' service. Australians do not like cold showers and they do not hesitate to replace their water heater when it fails, whatever the state of the economy.

The South Australian Brewing Company owned a number of public houses, and its managers had noticed that many of their patrons chose wine over beer, some or all of the time, so the company built up a stake in a number of wine-making companies, including Penfold, the makers of the fabled Grange, among others. As a

solid earnings generator, the South Australian Brewing Company was hard to beat: a brewery throwing off lots of cash, a wine business poised to soak up any demand the brewery lost from shifting consumer tastes, and the water heater business generating another recession-proof profit stream. Packaging and white goods also generated steady, if slowly growing, profits.

The board and managers of the South Australian Brewing Company did not congratulate themselves on their sound strategy as the boom of the 1990s roared on; rather they lamented that their shares were considered stodgy and lacking in growth potential. The board decided to become a 'pure play' in wine. They renamed the company 'Southcorp' and sold the brewery, the packaging business, the white goods manufacturer and finally the Rheem hot water heater business. They applied the cash to buying Australia's largest privately owned wine producer, Rosemount.

The timing was awful: the stock market boom ended in 2001, and in the ensuing bear market investors looked for earnings quality rather than growth; and as downsizing and bonus pruning struck the finance centres of London and New York, the demand for premium wine stalled, so Southcorp could not even offer earnings growth. The share price crashed, costing investors billions of dollars (and the chief executive his job).

tial reduction in volatility, there are times and circumstances when the second offer would be seen as the more attractive one.

Share markets are not 'rational' in any meaningful sense of the word. They have two basic modes of operation. When the share market is in a defensive mode, buyers are fearful that the value of their investment may fall. Buyers in such a market look to earnings and earnings quality, so a firm with steady, reliable profits, even if it is only growing slowly, will be highly regarded. Firms exposed to several different markets may meet the requirement for earnings stability. The share market's alternative mode is speculative, in which today's earnings and their quality is a matter of indifference, and the market will favour firms with a stake in a 'hot' market and firms with a spread of investments will be deprecated as 'lacking focus'.

From the mid 1980s a group of economists whose belief in the perfection of market outcomes was more like worship than the result of rigorous research gained wide influence over governments and many major financial institutions. They declared that, since markets were perfect and infallible, the performance of a publicly listed corporation could be measured accurately by the share price, so anything executives did that caused the share price to rise 'increased shareholder value' and was a Good Thing while everything they did which did not cause the share price to rise was a Bad Thing. It turned out that managers could keep the share price of their firms rising by a succession of strategies. First, they downsized and re-engineered, cutting costs faster than revenue and producing a short-term profit boost, which produced a gratifying jump in the share price and justified a large bonus for the senior executives, including share option grants. Second, they bought and sold parts of the business while taking on extra debt, concealing the negative impact of the initial downsizing and re-engineering; the share price continued to rise, justifying further large grants of shares and options to the senior executives. Third, when the problems could no longer be concealed by merger and acquisition (M&A) activity, the worst of them produced false and misleading accounts; when this triggered yet another share price rise, the senior executives sold their extensive shareholdings before the truth was revealed.

Following the stock market crash of 2001 and the corporate accounting scandals revealed in 2002, it became clear that the pursuit of 'shareholder value' was bad management practice, even in firms that had not reached the accounting fraud stage. From 1995 to 2001 the pursuit of 'shareholder value' led to one of the greatest stock market bubbles in history. All bubbles burst eventually, giving rational and irrational investors alike the chance to learn yet again that markets can have discontinuities: the price can fall from high to low without stopping long enough in between for speculators to unload their shares and cover their futures positions.

Until the next phase of irrational exuberance in the international share markets, business propositions whose sole justification is their prospective impact on the share price may receive a cautious reception; although when the next boom is properly under way many company boards will throw such caution to the winds.

Presenting a business case

Most large firms will have developed a preferred format for a business case presentation, and some of them even have manuals to follow, but the essence of all successful business case presentations is the same:

- be brief: senior managers often suspect that anyone who uses a lot of words is trying to hide something unpleasant
- be clear about the demands of the proposal: how much money, over what timescale, and how much call there will be on other key resources, whether people or facilities
- show a clear corporate benefit directly related to the proposed investment: claims of indirect effects will arouse suspicion unless they are clearly separated from the direct ones and are not required to complete the business case
- don't build a proposal around the supposed failure of other products or the adverse results of prior management decisions: at best this will shift the focus of discussion from your proposal to the product or project that you are criticising, and at worst you will arouse a pack of sleeping dogs, determined to tear your proposal apart, and possibly you with it
- avoid any technical jargon other than terms generally current in the relevant industry and, unless a specific technological breakthrough is critical to the proposal's success, avoid any discussion of technology at all except in the most general terms
- keep any written material short and readable, with all complex issues and long justifications dealt with in appendices or supporting documentation
- if presenting in person, use charts and handouts with care, don't use any numbers that you cannot justify and stick to the point when answering questions
- treat financial numbers with proper respect:
  - don't use broad brush or obviously overrounded numbers (like two million)
  - don't use excessive numerical refinement either (like $2,003,156.22)
  - make sure that all numbers add up, that balance sheets balance, that tax and interest are allowed for correctly
  - use approved numbers whenever possible, such as interest charges, head office overheads, depreciation rates and capitalisation policies
  - don't surprise or challenge the controller or the finance director with a freelance policy critique.

Development costs, risks and limits

Top managers in most corporations have learned, from bitter experience, that most attempts at innovation fail to bring the promised, or any, rewards. It is important to show, at the outset, the limits of the risks to which they are being asked to expose the corporation. This requires a phased expenditure budget, drawn up to align with the firm's normal accounting periods and showing liabilities in the period in which they are incurred, even when they are used to buy assets which can be leased. Internal costs must be shown, no matter how arbitrary the process of determining them may appear to be.

The expenditure proposal should not be allowed to become unduly complex and, in any case, it will often be in a form dictated by corporate standards, but the following items should usually be broken out into separate lines:

- wages and salaries and payments to contract staff
- wage-related oncosts and provisions
- equipment purchases

- consumables
- rent of premises (not currently rented by corporation)
- rent of premises (currently rented or owned by corporation and due to be vacated or not currently occupied)
- other external payments
- other internal payments
- project closure costs (assuming it runs to completion)
- contingency allowance.

Inexperienced corporate innovators often forget the contingency allowance, even though (assuming the other budgetary figures are best estimates) the absence of a contingency budget means that the project has a 50 per cent chance of failing by exhausting its cash allocation. Items like 'consumables' and 'rent' may be hard to estimate, but the controller's department will usually provide standard ratios that can be used to generate these cost lines.

Implementation and marketing cost estimates

The implementation and marketing costs will not need to be as detailed as the development budget, since they will be the subjects of later reviews if the development project proceeds. They will also be comparatively predictable once the development project has progressed to the point where there is a clearly defined product, whether a service offering to be packaged and distributed or a manufactured item to be produced or contracted.

A fairly general approach to this part of the budget will be adequate for an initial proposal, as long as the various cost lines are not significantly out of line with the appropriate corporate experience. Since these costs will, in conjunction with the revenue forecast, determine the long-term profitability projections, they should be set, for planning purposes, on the high side. The following lines are probably essential:

- capital amounts for premises, plant and equipment
- unit material and variable costs including standard overheads (unlikely to be zero, even for a service)
- warranty and service costs, if appropriate
- gross distribution allowances, including standard margins, co-promotion allowances, sales and promotional incentives and the like
- launch budget, including the preparation of promotional material, sales training, initial advertising costs
- continuing marketing and administration budget.

In practice several of these items may be shared with existing product lines, but this is not likely to be seen as an acceptable reason for trimming the estimates at the planning stage. A new initiative should be viable on its own; it should not be a way of locking in previous decisions. In any case the impact on existing product lines will need to be dealt with under the revenue forecasts and considering them under the cost section as well smacks of double counting.

Revenue projections

Revenue may come from sales, licences, royalties and service charges: projections can be made for each of these. The existence of revenue projections implies that there is a sales and price forecast: this, at the top level of most corporations, will be taken as supporting evidence rather than as a primary part of the case.

A sales forecast is difficult enough; what is more difficult, and more important, is to project the impact of an innovation on the corporation's existing product lines. Even when the proposal is for a line extension, it is not always easy to separate out the likely sales with and without the innovation. When the innovation is an obvious bit of 'creative destruction', and the sales of the new product will clearly be at the expense of some established line, the proposers of the innovation can expect to be met with quite passionate hostility.

The innovators may feel, equally passionately, that the established line is living on borrowed time and that if it is not replaced by their innovation, it will be by a similar product launched by someone else. There are plenty of recorded cases where the upholders of the established lines have won, only to see some other company, often an upstart, reap the rewards.

Foreclosing the future

In 1977, IBM announced that they had abandoned their 'Future System' (FS) project because of the possible impact of the implied product changes on their current customers (a coded way of saying, because of opposition from the supporters of the current product line). It took six years before the impact of this decision was made apparent by the stagnation of IBM's sales revenue and a further seven before IBM's profits collapsed as well and the company was forced into a massive reorganisation involving large-scale redundancies. In 1977, IBM accounted, on its own, for well over half the total revenue of the computer industry, with sales of $18 billion; by 2002, IBM's hardware sales were worth approximately $37 billion, or $50 billion including software. In 1977 HP's computer operations brought in a few hundred million dollars of sales only. By 2002, HP's computer hardware sales (including printers) had grown to over $46 billion per year; this is only part of the revenue that IBM sacrificed in order to defend the status quo in 1977.

When the success of an innovation is certain to destroy a significant part of the existing revenue base, the business case must be built around the combined sales of the old and new product. IBM's experience carries a slightly different message in this regard: their pre-1977 product line had considerable strength left in it and a business case built upon its premature replacement would have been fatally flawed. IBM was wrong to cancel FS, but the supporters of FS were equally wrong to demand that FS should immediately displace IBM's then-current product line. Technicians are quite good at predicting the impact of an innovation, but poor at predicting the time over which that impact will be felt. Computers were sold and are sold because of what they can do, not because of the virtues or defects of their logical architecture. An inferior logical architecture, like any product attribute that fails to attain the best possible standards, will eventually impact users by imposing excessive costs or restricting their flexibility. It often, particularly in industrial and commercial applications, takes several years before such impacts are widely felt.

If the receivers are in the outer office, it may be hard to get a corporation's management to allocate large resources to strategic innovations; but if they are not, senior managers will generally resent attempts to panic them into action by overblown predictions of the imminent failure of the current product line or the major processes.

The net value statement

Some innovations are so dramatic that the only way to evaluate them properly is to construct a financial model of the corporation, with and without the proposal. An aircraft manufacturer contemplating a new airframe design, a motor manufacturer considering a new marque, a retailer considering building a series of stores based upon a new concept, these are all innovations whose impact cannot be isolated to part of the corporation. The new model of aeroplane or marque of motorcar will gain some new sales, but it will also divert sales from the existing models and marques; it will require new manufacturing facilities, but it will also enable better use to be made of existing facilities; it will require extra staff, but it will also represent a career path for existing staff. People proposing such innovations will need to read more books than this one.

For every innovation on a billion-dollar scale, there should be a hundred million-dollar ones, and these are often significant enough to demand serious examination, but too small to justify building a special corporate model to evaluate each of them. The hundred projects pursued may be chosen from a thousand proposed and, since at least some of them will interact, the evaluation, to be complete, should be carried out on every possible combination of them. Such a calculation would, however, last far longer than the universe, so corporate finance departments use one of three quick and easy ways of ranking proposals. A fourth, based on the work of Dixit and Pindyck (1994), is described in Chapter 4 but it is not yet widely used at present.

The three shorthand ways of ranking investment proposals are the payback time, the net present value and the hurdle rate of return.

The payback time is determined by calculating the rate at which the innovation will earn profits, or cut costs, and dividing this into the expense of developing and introducing it. The answer is some number of years or months: proposals where the payback period is less than some maximum time are given further consideration, while the rest are rejected immediately. Payback limits vary from eighteen months to three years depending on the firm and industry. The payback method is appropriate for cost-reducing innovations whose total value is not likely to affect the overall position of a firm dramatically. It is less appropriate for revenue-generating innovations, projects with long lead times or cost reductions significant enough to give a firm new strategic options.

The net present value method of capital budgeting takes a firm's 'weighted average cost of capital', treating the earnings per share as the 'cost' of equity, and calculating the present value of the net income stream generated by the innovation. This method usually leads to far too many projects being considered; as Dixit and Pindyck showed, borderline projects chosen using this methodology are likely to perform poorly in reality. The main advantage of the approach is that it allows a large number of proposals to be sorted into the order of their net value: the highest value one is then selected, its capital cost is deducted from the funds available and the next highest value proposal selected; the process continues until all the available funds are fully committed. When applied injudiciously this can, as with the Victorian Economic Development Corporation (liquidated in disgrace in 1990), lead to worthless projects being supported simply because the worthwhile proposals run out before the available investment funds do (see Ryan 1989).

Another disadvantage of selecting projects by the net present value method is that it does not necessarily lead to the best outcomes. By the early 1990s it was apparent that

American manufacturing companies taken as a group used equipment that was on average eight years old.[5] By contrast, Japanese manufacturing companies used equipment that was, on average, three to four years old. This may be due to the prevalence of net present value-based planning in the Anglophone countries and the intense customer focus in Japan, where new machinery may be installed because it will improve the final product, not because it appears to be a good investment. A comparison of the performance of Japanese and American manufacturers suggests that investing in order to increase customer satisfaction may be better for growth and profits than judging investments on purely financial criteria. If the costs of customer base churn are properly brought to account, the difference may vanish, but that requires more detailed modelling than most companies, even large ones, currently undertake.

Hurdle rates of return can be used instead of the weighted average cost of capital in the net present value method, or projects can be ranked on the basis of their internal rate of return and the internal rate of return of each tested against the corporate hurdle rate. Internal rates of return cannot be determined by a formula, but all useful spreadsheet packages will have a function available to calculate them. Firms using the hurdle rate method will rank projects on the basis of their risk level and then reject those where the internal rate of return fails to exceed the hurdle rate appropriate to the project class.

As discussed in Chapter 4, Dixit and Pindyck have provided a formula for calculating hurdle rates, but most of the firms using hurdle rates set them on the basis of experience. These heuristic hurdle rates vary from 4 or so per cent above the current before-tax return on government bonds to 20 per cent higher, with most of them in the middle third of this range. Lower-end hurdle rates, around 15 per cent, are appropriate for very long-lived projects with secure returns, such as buying newly privatised public utility distribution systems. Hurdle rates of 25 per cent or more will be used to evaluate projects involving a significant amount of development expense and time, and for those that can only succeed by forcing an entry into an established market.

The hurdle rates used by any corporation will be fairly widely known inside that corporation, which means that would-be corporate entrepreneurs may be tempted to 'cook the books', padding the sales figures and understating the probable expenses and the development time. This is a self-defeating strategy, partly because corporate finance officers are very good at spotting such attempts and substituting their own estimates, well-padded in the other direction. Faking business cases is also self-defeating in the sense that it is like volunteering to be a target for live ammunition testing: if the project is accepted, and the returns are no better than the unpadded original estimates, the corporate witch-hunters will not have to look very far to find someone to blame for the debacle.

The product description and marketing plan

A business case should be accompanied by an overview of the proposed innovation, but not a detailed description or a technical discussion of it. Top executives do not expect to be presented with hoaxes: they need some idea of what they are being asked to support, but their technical input, if any of them are qualified to provide it, should have been sought long before a formal business case was put together.

Glossy pictures and celebrity endorsements (by an appropriate celebrity) are properly included: this part of the business case is a sales document, and the top managers who are being asked to support the case need to feel that the innovation is something that they personally, as well as the corporation, should be happy to be associated with.

The marketing plan overview in the business case should be no longer than needed to prove that there is a marketing plan and that some faith can be put in the marketing expense lines in the financial statements. As with the product itself, top executive input to the marketing plan can be sought while the business case is being put together. Collecting this input should not be allowed to confuse the evaluation process. The product description and the marketing plan should state clearly the degree of market novelty, and therefore strategic exposure, involved. The firm's senior executives will require answers to the following questions:

- Is it a new product entering a new market?
- Is it a product proven elsewhere entering a new market?
- Is it a new product entering an established market currently dominated by this firm's competitors?
- Is it a new product entering an established market to replace other products supplied by this corporation?
- Is it a line extension?
- Does this proposal concern process or sourcing issues only, with no direct market impact intended?

The development plan

The definitive development plan will have been presented in the first part of the financial proposal, so it is important that the descriptive material supporting the development plan is consistent with the proposed expenditure budget. Technical details of the development proposal are not usually required, but the strategic questions that senior management will wish to see resolved before they authorise a proposal include:

- Is any key technology being bought in? From whom? What special conditions, such as royalties or distribution limitations, will apply?
- Will there be any partners involved in the development? How will they be rewarded? How will the intellectual property rights in the innovation be divided? Who will have ultimate management authority?
- What are the firm's competitors doing in this area? Do they hold any key patents or other intellectual property rights? Will the firm gain any such rights?
- What is the degree of technological novelty?
  - Does the proposal depend on scaling up laboratory results?
  - Does the proposal depend on scaling up results obtained from a pilot plant?
  - Does the proposal require adapting technology proven in other industries?
  - Does the proposal only use proven technology?

Relationships and agreements with outside people and corporations that extend beyond sales and purchases are corporate strategy issues and are therefore the exclusive prerogative of the top management of a company. When the corporation is listed on a stock exchange, such matters that can be deemed material should be disclosed to the stock exchange or listed in the corporation's annual reports. Any employee who sets up such relationships without top management endorsement is almost certain to be guilty of conduct warranting instant dismissal and possibly a suit for damages or a criminal prosecution as well.

Senior managers are the 'receivers' of the product champion's plan and, as in most sales situations, matters that are blindingly obvious to the sender can be dark and obscure to the receiver. There is no doubt that senior corporate managers kill many good ideas and load those that they do approve with cumbersome reporting requirements. Sometimes good ideas are stifled out of incompetence or jealousy, and sometimes for good reasons that are never clearly explained to the champion or the initiator. Every senior manager aborts many projects for each one that gets approved; a manager who stopped every proposal would do a lot less harm than a manager who approved them all.

Some degree of conflict between senior managers and product champions is inevitable but, as we described in Chapter 6, strategy is the prerogative of senior managers and lies outside the boundaries of an entrepreneurial business plan. In initiating and carrying through the many small and medium-sized innovations that keep a corporation profitable, the senior manager's role is indirect. When the subject concerns major investments, relations with other corporations or the endorsement of strategic technological directions, the senior managers' role is central and their prerogatives absolute.

CHECKPOINT

Working within a major corporation has advantages and disadvantages. The disadvantages centre on the bureaucracy, the formality and the turf wars endemic to any large organisation; but the crucial advantage for the entrepreneurially inclined is that major corporations offer access to resources on a scale and over a period that are inconceivable for a start-up enterprise or even a successful medium-sized business.

While the processes required to access these resources might be bureaucratic and tedious, the fundamentals of a successful case are fairly simple:

■ the proposal must be presented clearly and unambiguously, with all significant risks identified and measures in place to control each of them
■ the proposal must be aligned with the current corporate strategy and build on the corporation's established organisational and market strengths
■ the success of the proposal will lead to an increase in the profitability of the corporation as indicated by its return on assets, relative to other corporations in the same industry, and other corporations generally.

Exercises

1 Consider a major corporation you have worked for or dealt with as a customer and recall some aspect of its products or conduct that you felt was capable of significant improvement. Draft a memo or letter to the chief executive, setting out your idea for improvement and estimating the costs, timescale and benefits. Keep it on one page, or edit it down to that.

2 Consider a major corporation you have worked for or dealt with as a customer, or have learned about in some other way (it may be the same corporation you used in Question 1), and attempt to identify its core competencies. Consider how effective these are at establishing and maintaining the corporation's competitive advantages and profitability. Consider whether and how these competencies could be strengthened. Record your thoughts in note form.

3 Identify a company that is drawing praise in the business pages of your favourite broadsheet newspaper or in a recent business magazine. Decide whether the company is being praised for its long- or short-term strategies. If the latter, decide whether there are any adverse long-term consequences likely to flow from its current measures.

4 Look at the stock market report in the business pages of your favourite broadsheet newspaper and identify a company with an unusually high price/earnings (p/e) ratio. Visit the company's website, run an Internet search on it and collect enough information to decide whether the company has the long-term growth strategies in place that could justify its share price; if not, try to work out why the share price is high.

5 By this stage work on your business plan should be well advanced. Prepare a five-minute presentation describing and promoting your proposal to the senior executives of a major company seeking their approval to proceed (if your plan is for a corporate innovation) or asking them to make a venture investment in your enterprise (otherwise).

6 An Austrian steel-maker innovated the basic oxygen steel-making process in the late 1950s; since this was faster, more productive and produced a higher quality of steel than the Siemens-Marten open hearth process that it replaced, most of the world's steel industry adopted it quite rapidly. The US was an exception: since their open hearth furnaces represented a major balance sheet asset, closing them down would require a substantial asset write-off and a reduced declared profit. Was this a correct decision? Set out the arguments for and against it.

Notes

1   Productivity is not simply a matter of working faster, although that happens. A major factor in increased productivity is that experienced employees make fewer errors, necessitating less rework and less spoilt material.

2   These numbers are dollar values uncorrected for inflation; but since the invention of the computer the nominal prices the industry charges have trended downwards; measured by the number of its customers, or the computing power delivered, IBM's growth was even more startling.

3   Professor Dan Jennings of Baylor University is an acknowledged expert in the field of corporate entrepreneurship. For an excellent commentary and overview series of readings on the field see, in particular, Jennings (1994), Chapters 11 to 14.

4   See MacMillan (1983). Here, MacMillan distinguishes the intrapreneur (operating under some form of corporate accounting system and not having to face the same degree of personal financial risk) from the entrepreneur who 'stands alone'. The authors of this book believe that being a product champion in a hostile corporate environment can be both lonely and risky. We use the term 'intrapreneur' with the meaning of 'product or project champion for a new venture initiative within an established organisation'.

5   See for example Bylinsky (1989), Currie (1992), Main (1990), Mansfield (1988), Sheridan (1990) and Stevens and Martin (1989).

10 The entrepreneurial financial model

This chapter

- All business plans for new ventures and prospectuses for the public sale of shares require a set of 'pro forma' accounts; many, but not all, proposals for a corporate investment in innovation will also require such projections. While normal accounts describe the past performance of an enterprise, pro forma accounts describe the accounts as they would appear if various assumptions were to hold: in the context of this book, if the business plan as described throughout the text is implemented and the market response and other projections prove to be accurate.

- In this chapter we describe how to build a set of pro forma accounts that will be readily understood by investors and lenders when they form part of the business plan or prospectus; but a set of accounts built as described here can be used immediately a venture is launched as a financial operating plan. As each period is completed, the projections can be replaced by actual figures, variations from the plan identified promptly and appropriate actions initiated.

- The method outlined in this chapter is based largely on the consulting experience of the authors and has served them and their clients well for many years. Other approaches by other people may be as good: someone with a methodology with which they are comfortable and which produces satisfactory results does not have to change to this one to be called an entrepreneur. The most important thing is to have a well-ordered, logical and comprehensive system for creating the financial model and producing the pro forma financial statements. For people with extensive experience, the precise methods will become a personal matter. What can never disappear, however, is the need for a systematic approach. We suggest that the one contained in this text book is simple, forthright and comprehensive. It will serve you well until your own experience enables you to enhance it.

Overview[1]

The key word is 'vital'

When a potential investor or other likely stakeholder picks up a business plan and reads it, the final point of their examination, the 'bottom line', is almost always going to be the financial statements, where the future performance of the business is projected. A useful business plan must include an integrated suite of projected financial statements – known as 'pro forma' statements – which are generated by an entrepreneurial financial model. The central feature of a good model is its ability to live.

Before the widespread availability of personal computers, the financial projections were usually a static typed table of figures that could not be adjusted without completely retyping them. This was a serious constraint when an investor or part of the venture's management team wanted to explore some alternative possibilities. Everything had to be reforecast from scratch. Modern PC-based models, when properly constructed, have a living capacity to produce changed results almost immediately after the inputs are changed. A vital entrepreneurial financial model must be capable of predicting the financial consequences of an unlimited number of alternative assumptions and revisions of data.

A dead set of figures has no role to play in creating or managing an entrepreneurial venture. The entrepreneurial business plan and the financial section of it, in which the results from using the entrepreneurial financial model are summarised, is not a 'report' in the sense of being just a record of a particular point of view at a particular time. It is a dynamic tool of practical management and must have the capacity to answer all kinds of interrelated 'what if' and 'what now' questions from all manner of readers of the plan. For instance, what if the material costs used in the original business plan rose by 2 per cent? What affect would this have on profitability? What if we were able to double the level of sales? Could we finance the working capital to support the higher throughput? Would we need new capital investments to support higher output levels? If so, how should these investments be funded? Should we seek to sell some equity or borrow the funds? If we did borrow the funds, would the interest payments on them be so high that the new level of business reduced profits? And so it goes on. One question leads to another.

The generation of integrated pro forma statements

Every business plan must include what accountants call 'pro forma financial statements'. When the venture moves from plan to reality, real figures will progressively replace the projected ones and the plan will serve to show the entrepreneurial team the financial consequences of any deviations from the plan and allow them to plan their responses. At a minimum, three financial statements must be produced. They are:

- the statement of [expected] financial performance (formerly known as the income statement or the P&L)
- the statement of projected cash flows
- the statement of financial position (also referred to as the balance sheet).

The number of such statements that should be produced and the time period they cover will depend on the planning horizon of the particular venture and the degree of detail it is appropriate to convey. Suppose that the planning horizon is five years. It would be usual to project a statement of financial performance, a statement of cash flows and a statement of financial position for each month of the first twelve, to consolidate those monthly statements into an annual statement of financial performance, financial position and cash flow and then produce annual statements of each for the next four years. Altogether, $17 \times 3 = 51$ statements: a great deal of financial information.

The chapter is organised as follows:

- First, we introduce the basis of all financial projections: a beginning balance sheet.
- Then we will move through each of the major sections of a complete financial statement, the balance sheet, the cash flow statement and the statement of financial performance (which was known as the income statement or the P&L, before the recent global standardisation efforts). In each case we start with the result and show how it can be developed in a systematic way.
- Next, we will look at what is needed in a set of projected statements of financial performance. We will make some general points about projected statement building and produce two examples of completed statements of financial performance for a hypothetical company, ExampleCo.
- Then we will put and answer the questions: How do we get there? What are the key steps to the statement of financial performance projection? And while following the steps by which ExampleCo's statements of financial performance were produced, we will demonstrate a systematic route which readers can use to prepare their own statements of financial performance.
- Further sections of the chapter will explain the cash flow statement and a further two sections will explain balance sheets. In each case the first step will be to state what is required of the set of statements and the second step will be to show how to meet those requirements: an outline of the key steps which culminate in the production of the cash flow statement and balance sheet.
- Finally, we conclude the chapter by describing some of the many uses to which the financial model can be put once it has been built. An entrepreneur who can produce an integrated suite of pro forma financial statements is in a position to apply the power of simulation to manage variance and change once the business is running, as well as investigating the financial implications of a host of alternative strategies and scenarios while developing the plan.

What the chapter will not do

This chapter is not an introductory text setting out fundamental accounting principles or spreadsheet construction skills. We will assume that those who intend to create an entrepreneurial financial model already possess a basic knowledge of double entry book-keeping and the production, structure and uses of financial statements, as well as the capacity to use an electronic spreadsheet, such as Microsoft Excel, at a moderately sophisticated level. It is unreasonable to expect anyone to be able to produce an integrated pro forma suite of financial statements – the core of the financial model and the heart of an entrepreneurial business plan – if they do not have a basic understanding of spreadsheet construction and accountancy. These are fundamental business skills, whether one is dealing with new or established ventures.

Readers without a good grounding in the basic principles of accounting may find this chapter heavy going. It is impossible to prepare a successful business plan without a good set of pro forma accounts, so budding entrepreneurs can plough on or skip the chapter and ensure that they have a good, entrepreneurially oriented accountant on their team.[2]

Introducing everybody's business: ExampleCo

The first rule of business planning and plan evaluation is that every business is different. This is a truism, but it still creates problems for a writer setting out the general principles of financial model creation. As a compromise between simply stating general principles with no illustration and providing so many illustrations that they become overwhelming, we are going to use data and format designs of a stylised business – ExampleCo – for illustrative purposes. The exact values of the data contained in the subsidiary schedules and financial statements projected for ExampleCo obviously do not matter. What does matter is that the examples draw out the general principles of model design and statement creation which can then be applied in a wide variety of situations.

With this emphasis in mind, let's make the acquaintance of ExampleCo.

The importance of a value-adding perspective

ExampleCo is a deliberately stylised and artificial creation, chosen to illustrate the importance of a value-adding perspective when it comes to building the entrepreneurial financial model for any business. Very simply, value-adding is the process of taking something acquired from somebody else – which may be called raw materials, but in practice may be components, semi-finished or finished goods, or for a professional service company, nothing at all – performing some of the firm's own processing upon it and then selling the result for more than the combined cost of the inputs and the processing.

ExampleCo is involved in three major areas of income-producing activity. It manufactures a useful device; it sells the consumable supplies that users of the device will need if they wish to continue to enjoy the benefits of owning it; and it sells replacements devices to those users whose original purchase has worn out. (NB: in most jurisdictions ExampleCo might not enjoy the revenue stream from the consumable supplies uncontested as this might be considered unlawful tying. The model presented here allows the simulation of consumable as well as durable products, which is why we have done it this way.) The traditional approach used in most accounting textbooks is to split the process of setting out fundamental accounting principles by first describing how to prepare accounts for a service business (the simplest form of organisation and trading), then describing how to prepare accounts for a retail business (more complicated) and, finally, teaching how to prepare accounts for a manufacturing enterprise (the most complex). We believe that by thinking of all businesses as value-adders, it is possible to approach the task of projecting the financial future of any business in the same way. There is no need for a three-way split.

ExampleCo will illustrate the flexibility that flows from a value-added approach to financial statement modelling. It is important that, despite its artificiality, readers take ExampleCo seriously.

A beginning statement of financial position

Lots of design options – but simple is often best

We ask readers to take a careful look at Table 10.1. It is the balance sheet for ExampleCo Pty Ltd as at 1 February 2002. As with every other illustration in this chapter, the specific figure for any amount is relatively unimportant. What the reader should be looking for in this and all other ExampleCo statement illustrations are the important general points that apply to the creation and design of all entrepreneurial financial models.

There are many ways of setting out a balance sheet. One of the best is also the simplest. The basis of all company accounting is that shareholders' funds are equal to assets minus liabilities and that's the format that ExampleCo has chosen to use for its balance sheet prior to creating its financial projections.

Information design principles: equity

Equity – also known as shareholders' funds – comprises three items. One is the capital subscribed, otherwise known as the issued capital. This is the amount subscribed by the purchasers of all the outstanding shares. It is the equity that shareholders have actually put into the business. When the financial engineers get their hands on it, this number may be split into two lines: the amount paid for the shares at their par or nominal value and a share premium reserve, being the difference between the par value and the amount actually paid for the shares. There are several reasons for this distinction: one is that, in liquidation, if there are any remaining assets they are divided among the shareholders on the basis of the number of shares each holds. If an entrepreneur declared the par value of shares as £0.01, issued himself a million of them and then sold a further 990,000 shares to the public at £1.00, consisting of £0.01 par value and £0.99 premium, and promptly liquidated the company, he would get just over £502,000 for his £10,000 investment, while the subscribers would receive just under £0.50 for each of the shares for which they had just paid £1.00. Put as baldly as this, such schemes are illegal in most jurisdictions, but variations on them are alive and well. A second reason for the distinction between par value and the amount subscribed is that a low par value allows the entrepreneur and his associates to issue themselves a lot of shares without putting up much money. The alternative of issuing 'partly paid' shares to the entrepreneur (for example, £1.00 shares paid to £0.01) means that, should the venture fail owing money to its creditors, the creditors could 'call' the unpaid capital (that is, force the entrepreneur and his associates to pay up to £0.99 to the creditors for each share they held, to continue the previous example).

Reserves follow the subscribed capital accounts. When you see any account labelled 'reserve', or 'special reserve' as part of shareholders' funds, what you are looking at is the fact that some capital or some retained earnings have been allocated to special purposes. Reserves are often used for 'extraordinary' income, such as the revaluation of assets or gains on disposal of assets above their written down value. Retained earnings, the third element of shareholder's funds, are simply the bringing forward of periodic profit or losses onto the balance sheet. ExampleCo is a new company, so it has no carried forward profits or losses. Companies that get into difficulty after a period of trading may have substantial losses,

Table 10.1 **The beginning balance sheet**

ExampleCo (Australia) Ltd - Opening Statement of Financial Position	
	Opening
3 Balance date	**1-Feb-02**
Balance sheet	
Shareholders' funds	
31 Capital subscribed	2
32 Reserves	
Retained earnings	
Total equity	2
Assets	
Current assets	
Cash and s/t deposits	2
GST/VAT input payments rebateable	
Accounts receivable	
Interest due	
33 Materials inventory	
34 Other current assets	
Total current assets	2
Non-current assets	
35 Plant and equipment at cost	
36 Land and buildings at cost	
Accumulated depreciation	
Security deposits	
Other non-current assets	3,000
Total non-current assets	3,000
Total assets	3,002
Liabilities	
Current liabilities	
Accounts payable	
S/T loans	
GST/VAT payable	
Income tax payable	
Interest payable	
Dividends payable	
Other current liabilities	
Total current liabilities	
Long-term liabilities	
L/T loans	
Concessional loans	
Finance leases	
LSL provision	
Other long-term liabilities	3,000
Total long-term liabilities	3,000
Total liabilities	3,000
Net assets	2

and an entrepreneur who is confident in his ability to restore the company's fortunes may see the accumulated losses as a convenient tax shelter, since no company income tax will be due until all these losses have been recovered.

Information design principles: assets

Moving to the way the balance sheet design arranges ExampleCo's assets, we see that there are two main divisions: current assets and fixed assets. This is standard, basic accounting practice. The company's current assets are cash and short-term deposits, accounts receivable, materials inventory and a general account called 'other current assets'. We note that the company will begin trading with $2 in the bank and no accounts receivable. Its only other asset is the prepaid costs of incorporation which is offset by an obligation to repay (one day) the person who paid for this activity. The balance sheet lists four categories of fixed assets: plant at prime cost; non-plant at prime cost; land and buildings; and accumulated depreciation. The key general point is that, in listing and recording the company's fixed assets, one ought to distinguish plant, that is, the productive equipment used in the fundamental value-adding processes of the company, from non-plant, items such as office equipment, furniture, motor vehicles used by administrative staff and so on, that is to say equipment that is a fixed cost of doing business, the expenses of which, particularly depreciation, will be recorded below the gross margin line.

Information design principles: liabilities

ExampleCo's liabilities are divided into two major areas, current and long term. The company lists accounts payable, short-term loans, income tax and a general 'other' category. Its long-term liabilities are 'long-term loans' and 'other long-term liabilities'. In this case the initial balance sheet shows that the company has no liabilities.

So it balances? So what?

As a necessity, net assets are exactly equal to shareholders' funds. This balance is absolutely fundamental and springs from the core accounting equation. It gives the balance sheet its name. It gives the statement reader a lot of valuable information. It also serves as a check on the construction of the spreadsheet. If the balance sheet doesn't balance, there is an error in the accounts, and accounting errors are like snags in tights: they run if they are neglected. A £1 misbalance today can explode into an error involving the loss or misappropriation of thousands, or millions, of pounds, dollars or euros in just one or two accounting periods if it is neglected.

ExampleCo is about to project its financial affairs over the next five years. The pro forma financial statements it is about to produce will form an integrated network of financial information, extremely useful to managers and of vital importance to potential investors in the company. So it is with all businesses contemplating an entrepreneurial future.

The first set of projected statements: statements of financial performance

Some general points

There are so many ways of projecting income and the costs associated with earnings that to try to classify all possible approaches would be an impossible task. The classic technique for a well-established business is to use past history as a guide to future performance, with the 'percentage of sales' method. This technique, about which there is plenty of information in almost all basic accounting and financial textbooks, relies on the establishment of gross income forecasts, usually based on past history, as the fundamental building block. Almost all other figures in the statement of financial performance are then projected as a percentage of sales. Thus direct labour might be x per cent of sales, materials might be y per cent of sales and so on. The main strength of this system is its simplicity. The many weaknesses are obvious. Most importantly, for an entrepreneurial business planner contemplating new and different activities, there may be no history of past sales and associated costs on which to base either the forecasts in the first place or the percentage of sales for other statement of financial performance items.

Chapter 4 of this book provided readers with a far better base for the important forecasts associated with a statement of financial performance than simple percentage projections. A new venture succeeds or fails in the market; the models described in Chapter 4 reflect this and the market is the only reasonable place to start developing a financial income model. To be credible, revenue forecasts have to be market-based, well documented and supported by evidence that will stand the scrutiny of a careful, critical reader of the business plan. The same holds true for every other line item in the statement of financial performance and all the other schedules and statements that this chapter deals with. In this chapter we describe a system for the generation and presentation of figures useful to an entrepreneurial venture, not the derivation of those figures. Chapter 4 presents a thoroughly researched technique for generating sales forecasts, but there may be cases where that technique is not appropriate and in every case there are alternatives. In this chapter we assume that the sales forecasts are available and present some sound general principles for arranging and presenting those estimates in formats useful to the planner.

Let's take a look at Table 10.2, one possible layout of ExampleCo's finished set of projected statements of financial performance for the next five years, before stepping back to break down the process of producing the finished statement of financial performance into its several steps.

Table 10.2 presents the finished statement of financial performance projections for ExampleCo's first five years. Consider the general format and layout of the statement. First of all there is a section on revenue, then a section on the direct cost of income earned which takes a reader down to what is called the gross margin line. Next comes a statement of general expenses. Notice that they are non-interest expenses and that they are classified by functional area: marketing, administration, and research and development. When all these expenses are subtracted from the gross margin, we have a line known by its initials as EBDIT (earnings before depreciation, interest and tax). Depreciation is deducted from the EBDIT to arrive at the EBIT (earnings before interest and tax). Next comes a section dealing with interest effects: additions for the interest which the business is projected to earn on its cash and short-term security deposits followed by a subtraction for the payments of interest that the business is projecting. Interest is often analysed further, but rather than clutter this statement the analysis is shown in Table 10.15 below.

When the interest effects are netted and subtracted from EBIT, the statement has arrived at the business's taxable income. It remains to subtract income tax at the projected corporate tax rate, remembering that the business is not liable to pay any

Table 10.2 **Financial performance statement pro forma in value-adding format**

ExampleCo Ltd - Statement of financial performance

		Year one	Year two	Year three	Year four	Year five
	Year ending	30-Jun-02	30-Jun-03	30-Jun-04	30-Jun-05	30-Jun-06
	Revenue					
1	Sales revenue		1,272,748	3,756,647	6,348,304	10,564,715
4	Extraordinary income					
	Revenue total		1,272,748	3,756,647	6,348,304	10,564,715
	Direct costs					
5	Production payroll		418,857	1,169,398	2,088,838	3,629,943
7	Materials		107,777	331,518	586,775	1,012,348
8	Other		237,513	436,984	640,216	979,372
	Direct costs total		764,147	1,937,900	3,315,829	5,621,663
	Gross margin		508,601	1,818,747	3,032,475	4,943,052
	General expenses					
11	Administration and marketing expenses	182,684	1,474,401	1,664,496	1,942,956	2,460,492
13	R&D expense	46,815	138,308	274,184	337,871	437,470
14	Other general expenses	7,193	20,760	39,326	64,044	94,209
15	Bad debts		25,456	75,133	126,965	211,294
16	Extraordinary expense					
	Total	236,692	1,658,925	2,053,139	2,471,836	3,203,465
	EBDIT	(236,692)	(1,150,324)	(234,392)	560,639	1,739,587
17	**Depreciation**	10,417	47,224	47,224	58,336	45,836
	EBIT	(247,109)	(1,197,548)	(281,616)	502,303	1,693,751
	Interest					
18	Interest earned	5,922	36,927	39,377	42,770	38,307
19	Interest charged	(2,932)	(36,100)	(83,300)	(86,911)	(84,578)
	Total	2,990	827	(43,923)	(44,141)	(46,271)
	EBT	(244,119)	(1,196,721)	(325,539)	458,162	1,647,480
	Taxation					
24	GST/VAT rebateable	(20,731)	(149,706)	(193,592)	(281,542)	(418,429)
25	GST/VAT collected		114,548	338,098	571,347	950,824
26	Income tax					106,022
	Total tax due (rebateable)	(20,731)	(35,158)	144,506	289,805	638,417
	Extraordinary Items					
27	Income		200,000	300,000		
28	Asset revaluation (devaluation)					
	Total		200,000	300,000		
	Profit (loss)	(223,388)	(961,563)	(170,045)	168,357	1,009,063
29	Proposed dividend					
	Retained profit (loss)	(223,388)	(961,563)	(170,045)	168,357	1,009,063

income tax until it has used up all its tax credits, that is, until all negative retained earnings (accumulated losses) have been eliminated.

Notice in Table 10.2 that every significant line of the projected statements of financial performance carries a note, in this case presented as a number on the left-hand side. These notes should be placed at the end of the entire suite of financial statements. They will add further detail and explanation to each line item occurring in the statement of financial performance suite. Of course, in the context of an entrepreneurial business plan, the notes may well refer a reader back to sections of the plan rather than merely providing additional numerical information. For instance, a business plan will have a significant section on marketing. The relevant note may well point readers back in the direction of the marketing sections of the business plan, where fully costed schedules and estimates of various expense categories, and the reasons for them, were presented. The administration, research and development and, indeed, potentially for every other item in the projected set of statements of financial performance may refer to other sections of the business plan as well as, or instead of, a reference to the notes to the pro forma accounts.

In addition – as the examples in the following section of this chapter demonstrate – all the aggregate numbers which get to be line items in the final statement of financial performance projections are supported by detailed subsections of the planner's spreadsheet. These will become sub-statements and subsidiary schedules in the Notes section of the printed statements. The next section of this chapter will describe some of the major subsidiary schedules that go into making up aggregate figures and therefore completing the entire statement of financial performance projection suite.

Breakeven analyses

We have called the financial performance statement format used in Table 10.2 a 'value-adding' format, for a very good reason. The layout clearly distinguishes between the main functions of value-added: that is the direct or variable costs of income earned, as distinct from the fixed costs which the business would incur, whether it produced at the planned level, at some other level or produced nothing at all. It is also important to distinguish non-interest expenses from interest expenses because the strategy and cost of financing a venture is quite a distinct matter from the actual operation of the venture. When costs are set out in the way we see in Table 10.2, many calculations are immediately possible, the most important of which is an easy to conduct breakeven and margin analysis.

We explain in Chapter 12 why potential investors want to look very carefully at the breakeven analysis. Briefly, a breakeven analysis enables the investor or other plan reviewer to determine how robust the planned business will be to variances in the level of sales. A supermarket, for example, has low fixed costs and high variable ones and one lost customer would not throw the plan for a new supermarket into confusion. An advertising agency or architect's office, by contrast, has negligible variable costs and high fixed ones: it can be thrown from strong profit into heavy loss by losing just one account.

In ExampleCo's case, we can see that the direct or variable costs of income earned include materials, direct labour and direct overheads. Direct overheads will include the various costs of employment above salary, including superannuation contributions and workers compensation insurance. Variable cost lines, in the main or subsidiary schedules, will cover freight and associated costs, production rentals, repair and maintenance of machinery and in some cases even the depreciation of plant.

The usual accounting procedure puts all depreciation below the gross margin line, that is, the depreciation of plant would be listed in an account together with the depreciation of non-plant such as office equipment and so on. There is a growing trend, however, in financial circles – and it is particularly important for new ventures – to directly relate the usage of equipment to the income it generates. Otherwise, quite a false picture of the gross margin can sometimes develop. The extreme case is when very expensive machinery wears out rapidly in service and must then be replaced rather than simply repaired. Another trend worth watching is the location of labour costs. Labour is a direct cost of production when the workers are paid piece rates or are casual staff whose rosters can be changed at short notice. A firm that has built up a team of skilled and specialised workers will not wish to break it up because of a short-term dip in revenue and it can't increase it overnight to take up an opportunity, so the ordinary time wages, at least, may get moved below the line to sit alongside staff salaries. The mining house Rio Tinto has had, since the early 1990s, an active policy of replacing all wage employment by staff employment in its Australian operations, by implication, making all labour a fixed cost, below the gross margin line.

Two major problems can follow errors in calculating the gross margin. One is that the resilience of the business to unexpected revenue changes will be misunderstood. The other is that pricing and discounting policies will be unsoundly based.

Looking at general expenses, the key general point to note is functionality. Standard accounting procedures usually distinguish between so-called financial accounts (those used for external audiences of the venture such as the Tax Commissioner, shareholders and potential investors) and management accounts (those used to provide operational information to internal audiences). An entrepreneurial financial model and the projected statements it produces should seek to do both jobs with a minimum of duplication. It should be simultaneously useful to management and its external users. Laying out the statement of financial performance in the value-adding format achieves this objective.

The naming of the aggregate lines and the item grouping in the statement of financial performance is also done for functional reasons. Anyone reading the ExampleCo income projections can see immediately the relative proportions that the company spends on marketing with respect to administration. They can see that, in its first year, it is spending very modestly on research and development. An entirely different basis rules the design of a cash flow statement. The key issue there will be timing rather than function. 'When does the firm pay for things' becomes more important than 'what does the firm get paid for' in the cash flow statement.

Once the EBIT has been calculated, our anticipated interest effects can be incorporated and the statement will show a taxable income. Notice that in ExampleCo's case, it is showing losses until the third year of its operations, but no income tax is due until the fifth year, when accumulated profits have wiped out these losses. New ventures may buy an entrepreneur's or inventor's business before it has earned any trading income, also creating negative retained earnings. Until such time as the accrued earnings become positive, no income tax will be due and the projected accounts should reflect this. In ExampleCo's case, tax is not projected to be payable until the fifth year of operation. Income tax will then be projected at the prevailing rate applicable in the economy and the country in which the business operates. Once tax is deducted, we have a profit after tax.

The basic principle: uncluttered information provision

There are a couple of features of the presentation of a statement of financial performance (that apply equally well to what we will have to say about the other statements) that have nothing whatsoever to do with figures or the logic that goes into producing figures. They are simply matters of good design and logical thinking.

For instance, it is highly desirable when presenting any information to any reader of anything not to overcrowd a page, clutter it up and make it messy. A good policy for pro forma financial statements is to make sure that the accounts and relationships that appear on the statements do not extend over a single page, usually an A4 or American quarto-sized page, or where a page break is inevitable, to put it in a logical place. It is most disconcerting to the reader of financial information to get, for example, halfway to the EBIT line only to have to turn over the page to pick up the thread. It is much more desirable to see the whole impact of each statement on one page.

The marketing expenditure account, for example, as we explain later in this chapter, is made up of many items. They are all listed in a subsidiary schedule and linked to the statement of financial performance by reference from the notes, or included in the Notes section of the pro forma accounts. They don't all get crammed onto the yearly statements of financial performance. Using statement notes and references to relevant sections of the full business plan, a reader of the statements is able to look up relevant subsidiary schedules and see in detail just what it is that justifies the aggregate figure for marketing. Imagine how crowded things would get if every item in the marketing subsidiary schedule were put onto the main statement of financial performance and the same thing were done for administration and the other summary lines. Where would one stop? For instance, would we have the expenditure for office stationery appearing or should there be a separate line for paperclips? By putting functional aggregates at the final statement level, each reader can follow the notes to investigate areas of special concern without being buried in trivia along the way. It is quite possible to present a column for notes, a column listing the account names and up to six columns containing figures representing, say, the first six months in monthly reports or five columns representing the five years of the five-year projection on A4 or American quarto paper.

Personal design and layout preferences then come into play. We dislike the unnecessary replication of currency signs in front of every figure. Equally, we feel that it is undesirable, unless one is dealing in billions of pounds (and very few businesses do that), to summarise figures to the nearest thousand. Every pound counts. It is quite possible, as Table 10.2 shows, for an accurate presentation down to the nearest pound to be accommodated in a layout comprising five or six columns and involving figures that run into the millions. If they are neatly presented, well laid out and the entire statement is covered in no more than one page, this is a neat, clean and useful mode of presentation.

Design for a variety of information needs

We now move from general principles of good design in information presentation to describing the flexibility which good entrepreneurial financial planning should permit.

Table 10.2 showed the statement of financial performance projections of ExampleCo in what we call 'value-added' format, whose main advantage, we have observed, is the clear distinction between fixed and variable costs and between inter-

Table 10.3 **Financial performance statement in merchandising format**

	Year ending	Year one 30-Jun-02	Year two 30-Jun-03	Year three 30-Jun-04	Year four 30-Jun-05	Year five 30-Jun-06
	Revenue					
1	Sales revenue		1,272,748	3,756,647	6,348,304	10,564,715
4	Extraordinary income					
	Revenue total		1,272,748	3,756,647	6,348,304	10,564,715
	Cost of goods sold					
	Goods component					
7	Inventory value brought forward		6,405	51,692	90,169	158,449
	Purchases in current period	6,405	153,064	369,995	655,055	1,108,981
	Total available inventory	6,405	159,469	421,687	745,224	1,267,430
	Inventory value carried forward	6,405	51,692	90,169	158,449	255,082
	Total stock used		107,777	331,518	586,775	1,012,348
	Other direct selling costs					
5	Direct labour		290,210	904,424	1,616,967	2,799,397
	Purchased services		33,122	90,129	143,358	237,648
5	Production management		55,986	57,952	79,618	116,580
6	Overheads		72,661	207,022	392,253	713,966
	Utilities and rates		51,004	69,022	89,442	123,488
10	Freight etc.		63,637	187,833	317,416	528,236
8	Production rentals		89,750	90,000	90,000	90,000
	Total other direct selling costs		656,370	1,606,382	2,729,054	4,609,315
	Total C.O.G.S.		764,147	1,937,900	3,315,829	5,621,663
	Gross margin		508,601	1,818,747	3,032,475	4,943,052
	General expenses					
	Marketing expense		945,173	1,159,468	1,407,470	1,918,578
	Administration expenses	182,684	529,228	505,028	535,486	541,914
	R&D expense	46,815	138,308	274,184	337,871	437,470
	Other general expenses	7,193	20,760	39,326	64,044	94,209
	Depreciation	10,417	47,224	47,224	58,336	45,836
	Bad debts		25,456	75,133	126,965	211,294
	Extraordinary expense					
	Total general expense	247,109	1,706,149	2,100,363	2,530,172	3,249,301
	EBIT	(247,109)	(1,197,548)	(281,616)	502,303	1,693,751
	Interest effects					
	Interest due	2,932	36,100	83,300	86,911	84,578
	Less interest earned	(5,922)	(36,927)	(39,377)	(42,770)	(38,307)
	EBT	(244,119)	(1,196,721)	(325,539)	458,162	1,647,480
	Taxation					
	GST/VAT due		114,548	338,098	571,347	950,824
	Less GST/VAT rebateable	(20,731)	(149,706)	(193,592)	(281,542)	(418,429)
	Company income tax					106,022
	Extraordinary items					
	Income		200,000	300,000		
	Asset revaluation (devaluation)					
	Profit	(223,388)	(961,563)	(170,045)	168,357	1,009,063

est and operational payments. Of course, many other layouts for projecting statements of financial performance are possible. One such alternative information presentation format is the often used and well-recognised form of statement of financial performance, which we display here as Table 10.3.

Table 10.3 is what might be called a 'traditional retail' statement of financial performance layout, although it is derived from the same spreadsheet that produced Table 10.2. All the revenue items appear as they did in the 'value-added' format but from then down things are different. Instead of laying out the 'direct costs of income earned', the conceptual framework moves to 'cost of goods sold' and we notice that in this format the reader of the statement becomes aware of just what has happened with the inventory of products which the business is selling. Since resale of inventory is the heart of retailing, this focus has clear merits. This form of ExampleCo's statement of financial performance projections also makes it clear, though, that the materials or the physical goods that are sold are not the only component of cost of goods sold.

There will be direct labour. If the business were a retailer, such as a supermarket chain, 'direct labour' might include blue-collar employees in the warehouse and storerooms as well as checkout staff. There are overheads. There are freight and associated costs and there are other items which might be more pertinent to a retailer than a manufacturer. Once the cost of goods sold is subtracted from the revenues, we again have gross margin and the statement then continues in the order of the previous format. Good entrepreneurial financial modelling, built from the ground up and well reported in spreadsheet format, is capable of a great degree of variety and flexibility in presentation.

How do we get there?

Having seen two examples of what one might call the 'finished product', two completed, neatly presented versions of the same statement of financial performance, we now set out the steps needed to get there.

Subsidiary schedules and the power of modern spreadsheets

At the risk of being facile, the short answer to the question, how do we build up a complex set of pro forma financial statements? is, by easy stages. This involves creating many subsidiary schedules, one or more for each line item in the aggregate statement of financial performance. The three great virtues of modern spreadsheet packages are:

- their ability to link with and combine data from many sources
- their ability to handle high volumes of data with ease
- their ability to recalculate the statements at high speed so that the numerical answers to a host of 'what if' questions can be seen almost instantly.

These are the three key virtues that an entrepreneurial financial model needs to have. Using spreadsheets, it becomes a relatively simple matter to take the output of one set of calculations and use them as the input to another table. Let's see how this power was employed to create ExampleCo's aggregate statement of financial performance projections and, in so doing, observe some general principles useful to the financial modelling of any entrepreneurial venture.

Gross revenue   Table 10.4 is an example of a gross revenue projection schedule. ExampleCo's customers have three different ways in which they can contribute to its revenue. So, very simply, what the gross revenue subsidiary schedule does is to capture the projections for each of these market segments and aggregate them. The actual creation of a gross revenue schedule is a simple matter. The hard part comes in estimating the market's response to a new product or firm and that is a function of how good one's marketing research and modelling has been; for readers of this book, how well you have understood and applied Chapter 4.

Figure 10.1 shows a gross revenue projection graph. The golden rules for presenting financial information graphically are: keep it simple and keep it clear. One can use bar charts, column charts, pie charts, line charts or any of the other alternatives in two- or three-dimensional presentations which are readily available and simple to use with modern spreadsheet packages. The main thing to avoid is confusing the reader of the financial information by overcrowding or overcomplicating the chart. When in doubt, don't graph. Unless a graph clearly adds to the clarity of information presentation, you and – more importantly – your audience are better off without it.

Table 10.4 **Revenue schedule**

ExampleCo - Revenue projection

	Year one 30-Jun-02	Year two 30-Jun-03	Year three 30-Jun-04	Year four 30-Jun-05	Year five 30-Jun-06
Original sales (units)		4,125	10,963	16,606	26,320
Price (excluding VAT/GST)		250	245	240.1	235.3
Original sales subtotal		1,020,165	2,669,922	3,961,429	6,155,443
Services and supplies (units)		12,154	53,400	114,189	207,769
Price (excluding VAT/GST)		19.95	19.55	19.16	18.78
Service and supplies subtotal		249,327	1,036,939	2,174,390	3,877,710
Replacements (units)		16	236	1,016	2,586
Price (excluding VAT/GST)		220	215.6	211.29	207.06
Replacement sales subtotal		3,256	49,786	212,485	531,562
Sales total		1,272,748	3,756,647	6,348,304	10,564,715
Other revenue					
Total revenue		1,272,748	3,756,647	6,348,304	10,564,715

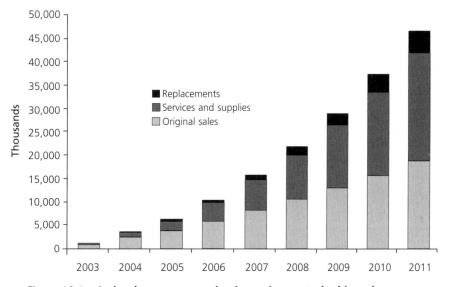

Figure 10.1   **A simple revenue projection using a stacked bar chart**

The direct (or variable) costs of income earned

Material inputs to production

Manufacturing businesses generally, and many service businesses, require material inputs, raw materials, components and finished products in order to create value for their customers. 'Materials' is a term that covers all these items and it can often be an area that causes confusion to the financial modeller. The key point to remember is that the financial treatment of materials has four distinct components:

1. There is *materials usage*, that is, a currency figure which records the volume of materials that go into production to earn the revenue of the period. Materials usage is the figure that needs to be entered in the period's statement of financial performance.
2. Then there are *materials purchases*. Purchases are the orders that the firm places with suppliers in a given period. Relatively few firms are able to purchase exactly the amount of materials they need when they need it;[3] purchases often support a safety stock. Usage is simply a function of the volume of activity. Materials purchases are very important but they don't actually feature in any statement unless one uses the 'retailing' or a similar form for the statement of financial performance.
3. The next line in the materials schedule is simply the *materials inventory*. This is the amount of materials stocks that we hold at the end of any given period and is a figure appearing on the balance sheet.
4. Finally, there are *inventory payments*. It is one thing to purchase materials but purchases are usually made on credit. When it comes time to actually pay for purchases by using cash, then we record this in a cash flow statement.

To summarise, materials usage forecasts will be used in the statement of financial performance projections, materials inventory forecasts will be on the projected balance sheets and materials payments forecasts will be in the projected cash flow statements. Materials purchases may never appear on any of these statements at all unless the cost of goods sold statement of financial performance format is used. The relationships between the 'four faces' of materials are illustrated in Table 10.5.

The schedule is straightforward. The first line lists the materials inventory at the beginning of the period, the next line is the estimate of materials purchases which will be made. Adding these two together gives the total inventory available. The next figure is the estimate for materials to be used. This is the figure that will appear in the statement of financial performance. We obtain the inventory at the end by simply subtracting usage from the total availability. Materials payments is a separate line altogether and is simply a function of company policy and the relative bargaining position of the firm and its suppliers. For example, if we were to pay all creditors on terms of 30 days, then the figure for materials payments in any month would be equivalent to the materials purchases figure for the previous month. Since

Table 10.5 **The four faces of materials**

	Year one 30-Jun-02	Year two 30-Jun-03	Year three 30-Jun-04	Year four 30-Jun-05	Year five 30-Jun-06
Inventory brought forward		6,405	51,692	90,169	158,449
Purchases in current period	6,405	153,064	369,995	655,055	1,108,981
Available inventory	6,405	159,469	421,687	745,224	1,267,430
Inventory usage		107,777	331,518	586,775	1,012,348
Inventory carried forward	6,405	51,692	90,169	158,449	255,082
Purchasing expense	6,405	153,064	369,995	655,055	1,108,981

these are annual statements, the estimates that have been used in the ExampleCo case are simply one-twelfth of the previous year's purchases plus eleven-twelfths of this year's purchases.

Labour, overheads, freight and so on

Table 10.6 shows the subsidiary schedules for direct labour, direct overheads and freight and associated costs for ExampleCo. Wages and the salaries of 'white-collar' production staff are listed, together with a schedule for all associated oncosts. These include payroll tax, staff training, superannuation, workers' compensation, long service leave provision and a general category for other oncosts. So, the labour subtotal in the final statement of financial performance is the total of the wages paid to staff plus all of these oncosts.

The schedule also provides the company's annual estimates for direct overheads and estimates for domestic and export freight costs associated with distributing its products.

Table 10.6 **Primary non-material costs projection**

	Year one 30-Jun-02	Year two 30-Jun-03	Year three 30-Jun-04	Year four 30-Jun-05	Year five 30-Jun-06
Employment costs					
Production salaries		55,986	57,952	79,618	116,580
Hourly paid wages		290,210	904,424	1,616,967	2,799,397
Salary and wages subtotal		346,196	962,376	1,696,585	2,915,977
Statutory superannuation		31,158	86,614	152,693	262,439
Additional superannuation		17,310	48,119	84,830	145,799
Workers' compensation		6,059	16,841	29,690	51,030
Payroll tax		8,623	36,983	75,681	143,601
Payroll tax rebate		(4,311)	(18,492)	(15,456)	
Training		9,494	24,928	43,608	74,647
LSL provision		4,328	12,029	21,207	36,450
Oncosts subtotal		72,661	207,022	392,253	713,966
Employment costs total		418,857	1,169,398	2,088,838	3,629,943
Freight and other costs					
Domestic freight		46,860	138,314	233,733	388,973
Export freight		10,414	30,736	51,941	86,439
Insurance		6,363	18,783	31,742	52,824
Utilities and rates		51,004	69,022	89,442	123,488
Freight and other costs total		114,641	256,855	406,858	651,724
Total non-material direct costs		533,498	1,426,253	2,495,696	4,281,667

Progress report: the statement of financial performance to the gross margin line

We now look at the results of combining the calculations of all subsidiary schedules so far. Figures appearing in the emerging statement of financial performance projections are aggregates of the greater detail that is contained in the subsidiary schedules we have just encountered. When combined, these figures take the business down to the 'gross margin line', that is, where the statements present an estimate of its earnings from operations – the fundamental picture of the company's value-adding activities.

You can now clearly see the importance of the notes attached to the statement of financial performance projections. For materials used a reader will go to the Notes and find a reproduction of the materials schedule as well as any necessary explanations. The reader can do this for most of the other line items in the statement. Each of the notes should include the relevant subsidiary schedule(s).

Table 10.7 **The statement of financial performance down to the gross margin line**

ExampleCo (Australia) Ltd - Statement of financial performance

		Year one	Year two	Year three	Year four	Year five
	Year ending	30-Jun-02	30-Jun-03	30-Jun-04	30-Jun-05	30-Jun-06
	Revenue					
1	Sales revenue		1,272,748	3,756,647	6,348,304	10,564,715
4	Extraordinary income					
	Revenue total		1,272,748	3,756,647	6,348,304	10,564,715
	Direct costs					
5	Production payroll		418,857	1,169,398	2,088,838	3,629,943
7	Materials		107,777	331,518	586,775	1,012,348
8	Other		237,513	436,984	640,216	979,372
	Direct costs total		764,147	1,937,900	3,315,829	5,621,663
	Gross margin		508,601	1,818,747	3,032,475	4,943,052

'Fixed' or 'other' costs

The one thing that all items used above the gross margin line had in common was that they varied with the volume of activity. This is why they are called direct costs or variable costs. They vary with the volume of activity and, while they are never strictly proportional to it, they are, by convention, regarded that way. From now on the remaining non-interest expenses with which we will be dealing are regarded as fixed costs. That is, they are costs that do not vary while output changes over its expected range in the course of an accounting period. They are a function of the business's basic capacity to produce. Subsidiaries of larger companies may be required to report their fixed costs using ratios determined by company policy; but even then, in the aggregate, fixed costs represent the business's capability, rather than its performance. Over the longer term, as economists like to point out, all costs are variable, but businesses, entrepreneurial or otherwise, will only be there in the long term if they successfully manage their way through each of the short-term periods in between.

A quite important point must be made here. In the ExampleCo case, all marketing expenses, administration and research and development expenses are listed as below the gross margin line; they are treated as though they are fixed costs. If there were some marketing costs, for argument's sake, which varied with volume, then those costs ought to be recorded above the gross margin line. A good example of this type of non-fixed marketing expense might be dealers' or salespeople's commissions directly tied to the volume of production and expected sales. If that were a significant line item and it was a variable cost, then it would be proper to record it above the gross margin line. For simplicity's sake, we have picked an example where all the company's marketing costs are treated as fixed in each accounting period, as are all their administration and R&D costs.

Assigning costs for accounting convenience can develop into an extremely bad habit. Many managers of firms, large and small, have slashed the marketing and product development budgets because they were 'overheads' and then received a painful lesson as they watched their firm's sales plummet. Bonuses, sales and promotional incentives and commissions are logically a variable cost, and it can be argued that promotional expense generally, since it is directly related to the volume of new name business, is also variable. It could be counter-argued that, since promotional expenditure is intended to win customers who will then provide an ongoing expenditure stream, promotion should appear as a capital expense. The accounts of a business are just a model: the best image of the real world that time, effort and the rules of accounting permit, but an image for all that. Facts are discovered in the real world, not by staring at spreadsheets. The world is changed by people going and working in it, not by putting different numbers into boxes.

We restate the importance of distinguishing salaries and non-salary components of functional cost areas. Any marketing costs, for instance, that are incurred in a given period – be it projected year one or projected month one or whenever – are going to have two components when the timing of payments is considered. Marketing salaries will be paid in the same period in which they are incurred, whereas the non-salary marketing expenses will ordinarily be bought on credit and if our terms of payment to suppliers are net 30 days, we will not pay for the non-salary marketing expenses until the next month.

Tables 10.8–10.12 contain ExampleCo's projected subsidiary schedules of fixed non-interest costs. They are virtually self-explanatory, illustrating as they do the two general principles which should dominate the modelling of fixed non-interest costs.

1. Observe the key distinctions between statements of financial performance and cash flow statements. For statements of financial performance, the key concept is 'functionality': to what distinct category does the expenditure belong – marketing, administration, R&D and so on? For the cash flow statement the key concept 'is timing of payments': when will this item be paid for?

2. Flowing from this key distinction in approach, it is vital to provide separate schedules of the salaries and non-salaries components of each category of expenditure before recombining them as a total figure.

Notice that for each of the three major functional fixed expenditure categories – marketing, adminis-

Table 10.8 **Projected salary expense**

ExampleCo - Non-production salary expense

	Year one 30-Jun-02	Year two 30-Jun-03	Year three 30-Jun-04	Year four 30-Jun-05	Year five 30-Jun-06
Staff salaries					
Administration	99,794	294,567	357,208	366,668	376,388
Marketing		160,050	221,280	227,140	233,160
R&D	18,028	88,534	152,784	156,836	160,988
Staff salaries subtotal	117,822	543,151	731,272	750,644	770,536
Oncosts					
Statutory superannuation	10,605	48,884	65,816	67,560	69,348
Additional superannuation	5,892	27,160	36,564	37,528	38,528
Workers' compensation	2,062	9,504	12,796	13,136	13,484
Payroll tax		10,019	27,873	33,259	37,838
Payroll tax rebate		(5,010)	(13,937)	(8,044)	
Training	4,713	21,728	29,252	30,024	30,824
LSL provision	1,472	6,787	9,140	9,384	9,632
Oncosts total	24,744	119,072	167,504	182,847	199,654
Non-prod. salary expense total	142,566	662,223	898,776	933,491	970,190

tration and R&D – the schedule contains a detailed list of all the items that go to make up the oncosts associated with the salary. One of the biggest mistakes made by prospective entrepreneurs when they use broad-brush financial modelling is to estimate the raw salary and wages figure for a particular activity and forget about the many, onerous oncosts that are associated with it.

Table 10.9 is a short but important subsidiary schedule: the payroll schedule. It produces the total figure for wages: direct labour (variable human resources costs) as shown in Table 10.6 and salaries (fixed human resources costs) as presented in Table 10.8. All entrepreneurs should plan their payroll schedules with great care because one week's failure to meet the payroll effectively means the demise of any business as a going concern.

Tables 10.10, 10.11 and 10.12 are the aggregate subsidiary schedules for marketing, administration and R&D respectively. They list the company's projections for all non-salaried components and then add the previously calculated salaried aggregates to come up with a total figure for the period. Look back at the statement of financial performance (Table 10.3) and observe that the figure listed for marketing is the total figure shown in Table 10.10. The administrative figure shown for any projected year in administrative expenses is the total figure shown in Table 10.11. The R&D figure for any given projected year is the total figure shown in Table 10.12. Shortly we will see that the separate salaries figures are aggregated in the cash flow statement.

Before we move on, one point needs to be made strongly. If you follow – and we strongly suggest that you do – the concept that functional area is the best way to list costs that occur below the gross margin line, the planner might have to split up the salaries of particular personnel into various components. For argument's sake, suppose that the CEO of a company had a £80,000 salary and spent 60 per cent of his time in marketing and 40 per cent in administration. From the point of view of recording the expenses in the statement of financial performance in a functional manner, £48,000 should be listed in the subsidiary schedule for

Table 10.9 **Payroll summary**

ExampleCo - Payroll summary					
	Year one 30-Jun-02	Year two 30-Jun-03	Year three 30-Jun-04	Year four 30-Jun-05	Year five 30-Jun-06
Wages		290,210	904,424	1,616,967	2,799,397
Salaries	142,566	718,209	956,728	1,013,109	1,086,770
Oncosts	24,744	191,733	374,526	575,100	913,620
Payroll total	167,310	1,200,152	2,235,678	3,205,176	4,799,787

Table 10.10 **Marketing expense projection**

ExampleCo - Marketing expense projection					
	Year one 30-Jun-02	Year two 30-Jun-03	Year three 30-Jun-04	Year four 30-Jun-05	Year five 30-Jun-06
Non-salary expenses					
Export market development		72,500	88,750	112,500	162,500
Trade shows		43,500	53,250	67,500	97,500
Marketing research services		58,000	71,000	90,000	130,000
Media advertising		398,750	488,125	618,750	893,750
Public relations		29,000	35,500	45,000	65,000
Internet, telephone and fax		72,500	88,750	112,500	162,500
Local travel		36,250	44,375	56,250	81,250
Other external services		25,000			
Other costs		14,500	17,750	22,500	32,500
Non-salary subtotal		750,000	887,500	1,125,000	1,625,000
Marketing salaries		160,050	221,280	227,140	233,160
Marketing salary overheads		35,123	50,688	55,330	60,418
Salary subtotal		195,173	271,968	282,470	293,578
Marketing expense total		945,173	1,159,468	1,407,470	1,918,578

Table 10.11 **Projected administration expense**

ExampleCo - Administration expense projection

	Year one 30-Jun-02	Year two 30-Jun-03	Year three 30-Jun-04	Year four 30-Jun-05	Year five 30-Jun-06
Non-salary expenses					
Heat, light & power	1,000	4,752	6,000	6,252	6,500
Stationery and office supplies	600	2,852	3,600	3,752	3,900
Internet, telephone and fax	1,200	5,700	7,200	7,500	7,800
Staff and visitor amenities	400	1,900	2,400	2,500	2,600
Cleaning and maintenance	600	2,852	3,600	3,752	3,900
Office rent	17,433	42,000	42,000	42,000	42,000
Other purchased services	40,500	109,250		12,500	
Rates and utilities	6,875	7,500	7,500	7,500	7,500
Non-salary subtotal	68,608	176,806	72,300	85,756	74,200
Administration salaries	99,794	294,567	357,208	366,668	376,388
Salary overheads	20,957	64,411	81,820	89,318	97,526
Salary subtotal	120,751	358,978	439,028	455,986	473,914
Administration expense total	189,359	535,784	511,328	541,742	548,114

Table 10.12 **Projected R&D expense**

ExampleCo - R&D expense projection

	Year one 30-Jun-02	Year two 30-Jun-03	Year three 30-Jun-04	Year four 30-Jun-05	Year five 30-Jun-06
Non-salary expenses					
Contract research	25,000	15,912	23,480	15,872	
Laboratory supplies		3,184	14,088	28,568	52,824
Travel and accommodation		4,772	23,480	39,676	73,368
Internet, telephone and fax		3,184	11,268	31,740	58,692
Cleaning and maintenance		3,184	14,088	26,980	49,888
Other purchased services					
Other costs					
Non-salary subtotal	25,000	30,236	86,404	142,836	234,772
R&D salaries	18,028	88,534	152,784	156,836	160,988
R&D salary overheads	3,787	19,538	34,996	38,199	41,710
Salary subtotal	21,815	108,072	187,780	195,035	202,698
R&D expense total	46,815	138,308	274,184	337,871	437,470

marketing salaries expense and £32,000 in the administration area. A bit of thought will soon enable a competent planner to allocate proportions of various people's salaries to their proper categories. Failure to do so simply means that your financial modelling is less potent than it could be because you lose the capacity to analyse cost areas in functional ways.

Fixed assets

Table 10.13 shows ExampleCo's pro forma asset register. The layout is straightforward. For each of the assets that ExampleCo will need for the foreseeable future, the table includes a brief description; an account identifier (to distinguish between facili-

Table 10.13 **Assets**

ExampleCo - Proposed asset register

Capital item description	A/c	Prime cost	Rental	Deprcn period	Acquire date	Disposal date	Finance method	Finance period	Finance interest	Finance residual
Office	N/P	125,000	2,500		1-Feb-02		Rent			
Computers	Plant	25,000	1,000		3-Feb-02		Op lease			
Factory	Plant	250,000	7,500		1-Jul-02	1-Feb-07	Op lease			
Bigger factory	Plant	750,000	15,000		1-Jan-07		Op lease			
Office fitout	N/P	100,000		4	2-Feb-02		Fin. lease	5	9%	20%
Manufacturing equipment	Plant	100,000		4.5	1-Jul-02	1-Jun-08	Cash			
Manufacturing equipment	Plant	50,000		4.5	1-Jul-04		Fin. lease	5	11%	
Manufacturing equipment	Plant	100,000		4.5	1-Jul-06		Fin. lease	5	11%	
Manufacturing equipment	Plant	250,000		4.5	1-Jul-07		Fin. lease	5	11%	
Manufacturing equipment	Plant	250,000		4.5	1-Jul-08		Fin. lease	5	11%	

ties, plant and equipment needed in production from facilities and equipment needed for other purposes); the prime cost of the item, the monthly rental (for items that will be rented); the depreciation period (for other items); the dates at which the item will first be needed and when it can be retired; how it is to be paid for (rent/operating lease, cash, or finance lease); and some leasing information where appropriate.

The treatment of an asset in the accounts depends on how it is paid for:

- if it is bought for cash, it is shown as a capital expense on the cash flow statement (below) and the cost will be progressively written off through depreciation (on the statement of financial performance)
- if it is acquired on an operating lease, or rented, the payments are pure expense, reflected in the statement of financial performance and the cash flow statement, but not affecting the balance sheet (hence 'off-balance sheet finance')
- if it is acquired on a finance lease, the prime cost is transformed into a lease obligation on the balance sheet and progressively written down by payments recorded on the cash flow statement, while the lease interest and the depreciation charges may be found on the statement of financial performance.

Depreciation

Table 10.14 is a depreciation schedule. Depreciation is a difficult topic for an operating business, with every capital item needing its own records maintained and being depreciated at its appropriate rate. The taxation authorities in each country set the minimum depreciation period for each class of asset and prescribe how the depreciation must be calculated.

There are two basic ways to record depreciation in the accounts: assets can be shown on the balance sheet at their prime cost and the depreciation accumulated, also on the balance sheet (the method illustrated here); or the depreciation of each asset can be deducted from its value at the end of each period and the written down value (WDV) shown on the balance sheet. Both approaches have their advantages and prob-

Table 10.14 **Depreciation**

ExampleCo - Depreciation

	Year one 30-Jun-02	Year two 30-Jun-03	Year three 30-Jun-04	Year four 30-Jun-05	Year five 30-Jun-06
Opening value of assets		100,000	200,000	200,000	250,000
Acquisitions	100,000	100,000		50,000	
Disposals at original cost					
Closing value of assets	100,000	200,000	200,000	250,000	250,000
Depreciation: opening balance		10,417	57,641	104,865	163,201
Additional depreciation	10,417	47,224	47,224	58,336	45,836
Write-back on disposal					
Depreciation closing balance	10,417	57,641	104,865	163,201	209,037

lems. If an asset is disposed of for a price different from its written down value, the difference must be shown on the statement of financial performance as an 'extraordinary' item or the accounts will no longer balance. Such non-cash extraordinary items must be carefully distinguished from cash ones, such as government grants or legal settlements, or it may become impossible to balance the accounts correctly.

In the accounts illustrated here, depreciation is shown as a single line in the general, or fixed cost, section of the statement of financial performance. As discussed above, some accountants prefer to record the depreciation of production plant under variable costs, above the gross margin line. As we describe in Chapter 12, potential investors calculate various ratios as a check on the realism of the plan and the management competence of the entrepreneurial team: the accounts must make these ratios easy to compute, or venture fund managers and other investors will save themselves the trouble by setting the plan aside and investigating a better presented one.

Interest effects

At a minimum, three projected average rates of interest need to be forecast and the forecasts shown: the interest the firm will earn on its own cash and short-term deposits; the average interest it will have to pay on all its short-term borrowings; and the average interest it will have to pay on all its long-term borrowings. The production of relevant subsidiary schedules based on these rates is then a simple matter.

Table 10.15 shows ExampleCo's schedule of projected borrowing intentions and the associated interest payments. Table 10.15 is typical of the schedules needed to calculate interest effects. We start with a beginning balance, list any extra borrowing, subtract any major payments and come up with a balance at the end for that particular loan category. It may be an overdraft, a fully drawn advance, or any one of a number of financial instruments. Every financial instrument that the company has, be it long or short term, ought to be planned in a similar way. There is then a line for the interest expenses and these are obviously calculated according to the contract struck with lenders. There is, of course, the additional matter of interest payments and, like wages and salaries, there is little or no room for late payment. Sometimes, interest expenses are accrued, in which case there will have to be a line providing for interest payable in the balance sheet. The more desirable situation and the more likely, because lenders want their interest payment promptly, is that inter-

Table 10.15 **Loans and other financial obligations**

ExampleCo - Loans and finance obligations

	Year one 30-Jun-02	Year two 30-Jun-03	Year three 30-Jun-04	Year four 30-Jun-05	Year five 30-Jun-06
Short-term loans					
Opening balance			200,000	200,000	200,000
Drawings		200,000			
Repayments					
Closing balance		200,000	200,000	200,000	200,000
S/T interest charges		9,334	14,000	14,000	14,000
Long-term loans					
Opening balance				500,000	500,000
Drawings			500,000		
Repayments					
Closing balance			500,000	500,000	500,000
L/T interest charges			37,500	37,500	37,500
Concessional loans					
Opening balance			500,000	500,000	500,000
Drawings		500,000			
Repayments					
Closing balance		500,000	500,000	500,000	500,000
Concessional loan interest charges		18,750	25,000	25,000	25,000
Finance leases					
Opening balance		95,903	82,831	68,543	94,883
Drawings	100,000			50,000	
Repayments	4,097	13,072	14,288	23,660	25,990
Closing balance	95,903	82,831	68,543	94,883	68,893
Finance lease interest charges	2,932	8,016	6,800	10,411	8,078
Total interest charges	2,932	36,100	83,300	86,911	84,578

est expenses, as they appear in the statement of financial performance, are identical to interest payments as they appear in the cash flow statement because they are paid in the same period.

Generally speaking, bank interest incurred for a period will be paid in that period by a transfer inside the bank's computer. Other loans may permit interest to be paid in the immediately following period.

Taxation

The creation of a subsidiary schedule for company income tax is relatively straightforward. Before a company has achieved positive retained earnings, it pays no income tax because it is in the situation that trading has not, in the aggregate, been profitable. Once it has positive accumulated earnings, a company's taxable income will attract tax at the appropriate corporate rate. Any tax incurred but not paid in a given period will be listed on the balance sheet as an accrued tax liability. Table 10.16 shows ExampleCo's projected taxation schedules for the coming five financial years.

Note that the tax due is calculated on the accrued net income, not the current year's profit; although as long as a firm, having paid off its accumulated start-up losses, stays profitable the tax will become a function of the current year's profits. Some firms show negative income tax on the statement of financial performance and accrue this as 'future tax benefits'. Most venture capitalists and other informed investors regard this as approaching sharp practice and distrust accounts in which such techniques have been used.

Table 10.16 also shows one method of dealing with value-added taxes, such as VAT or GST. The method illustrated in this chapter is similar to that implemented in popular accounting packages. All income and expenses are booked net of VAT or GST, and the tax collected and the tax paid are accumulated separately. Unlike income tax, a VAT or GST can be negative, as with ExampleCo's first year with expenses but no offsetting revenue, and this can prove a modest benefit to new enterprises.

Table 10.16 **Taxation**

ExampleCo - Taxation

	Year one 30-Jun-02	Year two 30-Jun-03	Year three 30-Jun-04	Year four 30-Jun-05	Year five 30-Jun-06
Company income tax					
Accrued income	(244,119)	(1,440,840)	(1,766,379)	(1,308,217)	339,263
Accrued taxation					106,022
Current period tax due					106,022
VAT/GST collected		114,548	338,098	571,347	950,824
VAT/GST paid	20,731	149,706	193,592	281,542	418,429
VAT/GST payable			144,506	289,805	532,395
VAT/GST rebateable	20,731	35,158			
Taxation due (rebateable)	(20,731)	(35,158)	144,506	289,805	638,417

Cash flow statements

Readers should spend some time examining Table 10.17. It is what one might call the long format for cash flow projections. The more you look at this statement, the harder it becomes to conceive that anything of great significance has been left out.

Cash inflows have been divided into:

- trading receipts
- capital receipts
- financing receipts.

Of course, the major trading receipt is the net cash flow from sales and this will depend on the collection time taken between sales made on credit and their conversion to cash. This is a key time lag in any business cycle. Capital receipts are going to be the sum total of all capital asset sales that were made. They are quite distinct from trading. For instance, if a business manufactures injection mouldings, the sale of its production of injection mouldings constitutes normal trading receipts. If the business had to replace some of the means of production by selling some of the old equipment prior to buying new, the proceeds of that sale are a capital receipt and not income in the normal sense of the word. However, it is a cash flow, and a positive one, and must be recorded as such.

Financing receipts are very comprehensively set out in Table 10.17. There are, of course, interest receipts, that is, the monies that flow to the firm from any balances on its holdings of cash and short-term securities (and indeed any holdings of long-term investments and securities). In addition, there is space in the design of the 'long' form of the cash flow statement to project additions to the short-term loans, additions to long-term loans, additions to other short-term liabilities, additions to other long-term liabilities, a section to record the cash received from the issue and sale of new shares and, finally, a place to record the cash flowing from any extraordinary income. Extraordinary income is income unlikely to be regularly received because it results from activities outside the business's normal mainstream activities. For example, if the business were a manufacturer but one of its officers had received some income by way of consulting for another manufacturing firm, but this was unlikely to be a regular source of income in future and had never occurred before, it would be best to call the income (and the ultimate resulting cash flow) 'extraordinary'.

Moving to the cash outflows section of Table 10.17, we notice that they exactly mirror the inflow section of the statement, being divided into three major areas:

- trading payments
- capital investment
- financing outlays.

Trading payments are listed in the order in which they occur in the statement of financial performance, with the exception that, in the cash flow statement, a distinction is made between aggregated salaries expenses and the non-salary components of marketing, administration and R&D. As has already been mentioned, the reason for this is that while subdivision into functional areas is the guiding concept for producing statements of financial performance, the key thing about cash flow statements is the timing of payments. And salaries will be paid in the period in which they incur whereas non-salary components will probably be purchases on credit and will be paid in a later period. The categories of capital investment are plant, non-plant, land and buildings and general 'catch-all' categories for other short-term purchases and other long-term asset purchases. Financing outlays involve major repayments on short- and long-term loans, short- and long-term interest payments and income tax. Add them up and one has a financing subtotal. The final line item is, of course, the payments involved for extraordinary expenses.

At this stage of the cash flow statement, we can add up the operating payments, subtract them from the total operating receipts and come up with an operating cash flow.

The next section of the statement involves non-operating disbursements. This can be thought of as reductions of equity which have nothing whatsoever to do with the day-to-day running of the business. They include dividends which may be paid from time to time to shareholders, any other equity reductions and any non-trading cash distributions that may be made.

When these items are subtracted from operating cash flow, we have a total cash outflow. We can now subtract to obtain a net cash flow for the entire 'ins' and 'outs' of the business for the period covered by the cash flow projection. When this net cash

Table 10.17 **Long form cash flow projection**

ExampleCo (Australia) Ltd - Statement of projected cash flows

	Year one	Year two	Year three	Year four	Year five
Year ending	30-Jun-02	30-Jun-03	30-Jun-04	30-Jun-05	30-Jun-06
Cash inflows					
Trading receipts					
Net cash flow from sales		616,639	3,199,954	5,400,259	9,208,002
Capital receipts					
Capital asset sales					
Financing receipts					
Interest received		35,610	27,859	46,745	35,817
Additions to S/T loans		200,000			
Additions to L/T loans			500,000		
Additions to concessional loans		500,000			
Addition to other S/T liabilities					
Addition to other L/T liabilities	100,000			50,000	
Addition to capital subscribed	1,000,000	750,000	750,000		
Extraordinary receipts					
Extraordinary income		200,000	300,000		
Total cash inflow	1,100,000	2,302,249	4,777,813	5,497,004	9,243,819
Cash outflows					
Trading payments					
Wages and salaries	117,822	889,347	1,693,648	2,447,229	3,686,513
Statutory superannuation	3,584	56,144	139,863	197,896	300,743
Additional superannuation		20,389	68,852	100,598	151,043
Workers' compensation	697	10,917	27,193	38,478	58,478
Payroll tax		3,550	28,343	61,053	161,260
Public liability insurance		9,546	28,175	47,612	79,235
Property insurance		4,068	3,714	3,651	8,932
Rentals	14,971	126,426	132,000	132,000	132,000
Rates and utilities	3,567	59,526	81,543	101,619	135,177
Insurances	4,921	142,162	356,758	636,844	1,078,690
Shipping		55,883	182,012	307,547	514,422
Other services	62,913	375,822	374,162	504,378	731,609
Training	3,983	29,257	53,333	72,108	103,418
Communications	1,059	76,020	105,753	147,602	224,435
Travel and accommodation		38,249	66,301	93,514	151,156
Other purchases	1,059	22,001	38,126	57,111	91,086
Media advertising		371,346	483,173	602,730	877,529
Trading subtotal	214,576	2,290,653	3,862,949	5,551,970	8,485,726
Capital investment					
Capital investment plant		100,000		45,833	4,167
Capital investment other equipment	100,000				
Capital investment land and buildings					
Other asset purchases					
Security deposits	7,500	22,500			
Capital investment subtotal	107,500	122,500		45,833	4,167

▶

flow is added to the beginning cash balance, we arrive at an end cash balance for the business – the figure which will go to the balance sheet. Of course, the ending cash balance for one period is the beginning cash balance for the next and the whole process begins again for the new period.

Table 10.17 **cont'd**

Year ending	Year one 30-Jun-02	Year two 30-Jun-03	Year three 30-Jun-04	Year four 30-Jun-05	Year five 30-Jun-06
Financing outlays					
Repayment, S/T loans					
Repayment. L/T loans					
Repayment, concessional loans					
Repayment, other liabilities	4,097	13,072	14,288	23,660	25,990
Interest, S/T loans		5,834	14,000	14,000	14,000
Interest, L/T loans			28,125	37,500	37,500
Interest, concessional loans		12,500	25,000	25,000	25,000
Interest, other liabilities	750	8,304	5,945	10,398	7,418
VAT/GST paid (rebated)	(16,548)	(59,472)	132,694	257,230	472,998
Company income tax					
Financing subtotal	(11,701)	(19,762)	220,052	367,788	582,906
Extraordinary expenses					
Operating payments total	310,375	2,393,391	4,083,001	5,965,591	9,072,799
Operating cash flow	789,625	(91,142)	694,812	(468,587)	171,020
Non-operating payments					
Dividend					
Other equity reductions					
Other non-trading distribution					
Non-operating total					
Total cash outflow	310,375	2,393,391	4,083,001	5,965,591	9,072,799
Net cash flow	789,625	(91,142)	694,812	(468,587)	171,020
Opening cash balance	2	789,627	698,485	1,393,297	924,710
Ending cash balance	789,627	698,485	1,393,297	924,710	1,095,730

Using the cash flow projection to explore financing options

The 'long' form of cash flow statement (Table 10.17) is very comprehensive. Virtually nothing has been left out that is needed for a detailed calculation of the company's cash situation. In this format, the cash flow statement is a useful device for projecting alternative financing scenarios. One of the biggest tasks facing an entrepreneur is the need to work out exactly how much financing and in what form his venture or responsibility centre will need during those stages when its growth outstrips its ability to be self-funding. Using the financial model proactively enables the entrepreneur to project a whole range of different financing scenarios and the cash flow statement is the ideal place from which to control these explorations. Look back at the statement. See how easy it would be, once a well-balanced spreadsheet is built, to experiment with different combinations of additions to short-term loans, additions to long-term loans and additions to capital subscribed. Better still, readers can build their own spreadsheet model and try it!

Various combinations can be simulated and all their effects can then be checked on the statement of financial performance to see which ones affect profitability in desirable or undesirable ways; they can be further checked on the balance sheet to see what equity consequences they have for the original shareholders of the venture. So, the cash flow statement is a useful device in many ways. Cash is the lifeblood of any venture. A detailed and regularly maintained cash flow model is the monitor telling the entrepreneur that the heart of the enterprise is healthy.

Meeting a variety of information needs

Of course, just as with the statement of financial performance, there are many other possible ways to arrange the presentation of a cash flow statement. Table 10.18 shows another possibility. In Table 10.18 the statement is divided into the key areas of trading, capital investment and financing – as in the previous design – but receipts and payments are netted by functional area to give first a trading cash flow, then a capital investment cash flow and then a financing cash flow. There is a section for netting extraordinary income and a section for netting non-operating disbursements. In this format of statement, which one might call the 'functional area' layout, it is easy to distinguish the positive and negative contributions to cash flow being made by each separate area of business activity.

Table 10.18 **Cash flow projection in 'functional area' format**

ExampleCo - Statement of projected cash flows

Year ending	Year one 30-Jun-02	Year two 30-Jun-03	Year three 30-Jun-04	Year four 30-Jun-05	Year five 30-Jun-06
Operations					
Receipts		616,639	3,199,954	5,400,259	9,208,002
Payments	(214,576)	(2,290,653)	(3,862,949)	(5,551,970)	(8,485,726)
Operating cash flow	(214,576)	(1,674,014)	(662,995)	(151,711)	722,276
Capital investment					
Asset disposals					
Asset acquisitions	(100,000)	(100,000)		(45,833)	(4,167)
Security deposits on rental items	(7,500)	(22,500)			
Investing cash flow	(107,500)	(122,500)		(45,833)	(4,167)
Financing and tax					
Financing and tax receipts	116,548	850,136	708,233	352,550	418,774
Financing and tax payments	(4,847)	(94,764)	(400,426)	(623,593)	(965,863)
Financing and tax total	111,701	755,372	307,807	(271,043)	(547,089)
Extraordinary items					
Extraordinary income		200,000	300,000		
Extraordinary expense					
Extraordinary cash flow		200,000	300,000		
Equity transactions					
Equity receipts	1,000,000	750,000	750,000		
Equity disbursements					
Equity cash flow total	1,000,000	750,000	750,000		
Net cash flow	789,625	(91,142)	694,812	(468,587)	171,020
Opening cash balance	2	789,627	698,485	1,393,297	924,710
Closing cash balance	789,627	698,485	1,393,297	924,710	1,095,730

The key steps to cash flow statement projection

Whatever layout you ultimately choose for presenting your business's cash flow projections, there are three key things to keep in mind:

1. ultimate output: it's one vital line in the balance sheet – the firm's cash position
2. the heart of the matter is timing: keep asking (and showing) when the firm gets money in and when it has to pay it out

3. never forget the essential simplicity of a cash flow statement's design: it is always cash in minus cash out equals cash held.

The ultimate output: one vital line in the balance sheet

Since cash flow is the lifeblood of any enterprise, it is possible for a business to go bankrupt while showing a profit: the nutrients (profits) have been ingested (net income earned) but they have not been digested and have not taken effect in the body of the business. If all sales were on credit but no purchasers ever actually paid for the goods a firm had sold them, that firm would have no cash and would be unable to pay its suppliers. They would stop supplying the firm, which would also be unable to pay its workers who would stop working for it. The business would go bankrupt while showing a profit. This is why the cash flow statement for the entrepreneurial financial model is at the heart of the enterprise.

But in one sense we ought never to forget that the cash flow statement, large though it is by subsidiary schedule standards, is simply that: a subsidiary schedule whose yield is one aggregate line item in the balance sheet, that is, the cash held by the business at the end of the period.

The heart of the matter: timing

Table 10.19 is a schedule of the timing of the expected cash flow from sales. We model in our spreadsheet a time module for receipts. How much is going to be received in 30 days? How much is going to be received in 60 days? How much of a month's sales do we expect to receive in 90 days? And so on. These figures can be related back to the statement of financial performance projections and we arrive at an aggregate figure for the collections expected in any period. The schedule shows, however, that we must allow for bad debts to reduce this figure. There are many ways of projecting bad debts and they will vary so much from business to business that no single recommendation for handling them will be generally applicable. Usually the estimate is calculated as a percentage of all sales that lead to bad debts. When bad debts are subtracted from the otherwise expected cash from sales, we come up with a projection for the net cash flow from sales and this is the figure that starts the cash flow statement.

People without small or medium-sized business experience often underestimate the difficulty of collecting money owed, even from debtors as creditworthy as governments or major multinational corporations. Table 10.19 is based on an average delay in payment of 90 days; keeping debtor days this low needs continuing hard work and won't happen without it.

Tables 10.17 and 10.18 presented the essential features of every cash flow statement in different formats, but these are not the only possible or even the only useful ones. In crude terms, any cash flow statement will have three major components: inflows, outflows and their difference.

Table 10.19 **Timing of cash receipts**

ExampleCo - Cash flow timing

	Year one 30-Jun-02	Year two 30-Jun-03	Year three 30-Jun-04	Year four 30-Jun-05	Year five 30-Jun-06
Sales as booked		1,272,748	3,756,647	6,348,304	10,564,715
Bad debt provision		(25,456)	(75,133)	(126,965)	(211,294)
Net receipts expected		1,247,292	3,681,514	6,221,339	10,353,421
Expected cash payment		616,639	3,199,954	5,400,259	9,208,002

The statements of financial position (balance sheets)

The basis of all our financial modelling began from a balance sheet immediately prior to the first projected period and we have already written, earlier in this chapter, about the design of that balance sheet and the presentation of the information in it. As we have been progressing through the production of income and cash flow statements, we have already built many of the subsidiary schedules that we need to produce figures for the balance sheet. For instance, retained earnings at the end of a period are simply going to be retained earnings at the beginning of the period (from the last period's balance sheet) plus the after-tax profit for this period (from the statement of financial performance). We already possess a materials' inventory figure: it is in the schedule we needed to calculate the materials purchases usages and payments (Table 10.5). The amounts of the written down value of plant and non-plant assets have already been calculated when we generated our schedules of depreciation (Tables 10.9 and 10.10). Cash, of course, is simply the net result of all the calculations on the cash flow statement.

There are really only two major subsidiary schedules left to generate and we will take a close look at them over the next few pages.

Design for variety of information presentation

Table 10.20 presents the projected balance sheets for the next five financial years for ExampleCo in 'narrative' format; the same information appears in Table 10.21 in an IASB-compliant format. The chart of accounts and the layout of those accounts is exactly the same as the beginning balance sheet on which the financial model is based.

Readers may experiment with different layouts for their balance sheets. One could, for example, set out the balance sheet in the form of a statement of all assets and then show how that balances with the total of all liabilities and shareholders' equity. Another possible design is to begin with working capital (a subtraction of current assets from current liabilities) and build up a treatment which adds net long-term assets to working capital and shows how this figure balances with shareholders equity. In short, one can balance almost anything with anything else and this gives an unlimited number of possible presentations for a balance sheet.

Key steps to balance sheet projections

Given the amount of subsidiary schedule building that has already been conducted in order to generate aggregate statements of financial performance and aggregate cash flow statements, there is very little that needs to be done in order to proceed to the production of a balance sheet. The two remaining vital subsidiary schedules that must be built are the schedule of accounts receivable (debtors) and the schedule of accounts payable (creditors).

Table 10.20, like Table 10.1, shows balance sheets in the traditional, or narrative, format where the shareholders' interests take pride of place. More recently the International Accounting Standards Board (IASB) and other authorities have revisited the subject of accounting presentation and formed the conclusion that the shareholders are not the primary audience for a balance sheet. Table 10.21 shows an

Table 10.20 **Projected balance sheets in narrative format**

ExampleCo (Australia) Ltd - Balance sheet

	Opening 1-Feb-02	Year one 30-Jun-02	Year two 30-Jun-03	Year three 30-Jun-04	Year four 30-Jun-05	Year five 30-Jun-06
Balance date						
Shareholders' funds						
Capital subscribed	2	1,000,002	1,750,002	2,500,002	2,500,002	2,500,002
Reserves						
Retained earnings		(223,388)	(1,184,951)	(1,354,996)	(1,186,639)	(177,576)
Total equity	2	776,614	565,051	1,145,006	1,313,363	2,322,426
Assets						
Current assets						
Cash and s/t deposits	2	789,627	698,485	1,393,297	924,710	1,095,730
GST/VAT input payments rebateable		4,183	39,363	52,581	78,318	113,790
Accounts receivable			630,653	1,112,213	1,933,293	3,078,712
Interest due		5,922	7,239	18,757	14,782	17,272
Materials inventory		6,405	51,692	90,169	158,449	255,082
Other current assets						
Total current assets	2	806,137	1,427,432	2,667,017	3,109,552	4,560,586
Non-current assets						
Plant and equipment at cost		100,000	200,000	200,000	250,000	250,000
Land and buildings at cost						
Accumulated depreciation		(10,417)	(57,641)	(104,865)	(163,201)	(209,037)
Security deposits		7,500	30,000	30,000	30,000	30,000
Other non-current assets	3,000	3,000	3,000	3,000	3,000	3,000
Total non-current assets	3,000	100,083	175,359	128,135	119,799	73,963
Total assets	3,002	906,220	1,602,791	2,795,152	3,229,351	4,634,549
Liabilities						
Current liabilities						
Accounts payable		27,049	168,184	238,449	389,035	563,527
S/T loans			200,000	200,000	200,000	200,000
GST/VAT payable			59,494	84,524	142,836	237,705
Income tax payable						106,022
Interest payable		2,182	11,644	21,874	21,887	22,547
Dividends payable						
Other current liabilities						
Total current liabilities		29,231	439,322	544,847	753,758	1,129,801
Long-term liabilities						
L/T loans				500,000	500,000	500,000
Concessional loans			500,000	500,000	500,000	500,000
Finance leases		95,903	82,831	68,543	94,883	68,893
LSL provision		1,472	12,587	33,756	64,347	110,429
Other long-term liabilities	3,000	3,000	3,000	3,000	3,000	3,000
Total long-term liabilities	3,000	100,375	598,418	1,105,299	1,162,230	1,182,322
Total liabilities	3,000	129,606	1,037,740	1,650,146	1,915,988	2,312,123
Net assets	2	776,614	565,051	1,145,006	1,313,363	2,322,426

IASB-compliant presentation, with a primary emphasis on the business, that is, the assets, and the creditors shown ahead of the shareholders.

The presentation in Table 10.21 reflects modern finance theory, including the Miller–Modigliani theorem and the legal point that shareholders are the 'residual claimants' only entitled to what is left after all the creditors have been satisfied.

Table 10.21 **Balance sheet in IASB-compliant format**

ExampleCo (Australia) Ltd - Projected statements of financial position

	Opening	Year one	Year two	Year three	Year four	Year five
Balance date	1-Feb-02	30-Jun-02	30-Jun-03	30-Jun-04	30-Jun-05	30-Jun-06
Assets						
Fixed assets						
Plant and equipment at cost		100,000	200,000	200,000	250,000	250,000
Land and buildings at cost						
Accumulated depreciation		(10,417)	(57,641)	(104,865)	(163,201)	(209,037)
Security deposits		7,500	30,000	30,000	30,000	30,000
Other non-current assets	3,000	3,000	3,000	3,000	3,000	3,000
Total fixed assets	3,000	100,083	175,359	128,135	119,799	73,963
Current assets						
Cash and s/t deposits	2	789,627	698,485	1,393,297	924,710	1,095,730
GST/VAT input payments rebateable		4,183	39,363	52,581	78,318	113,790
Accounts receivable			630,653	1,112,213	1,933,293	3,078,712
Interest due		5,922	7,239	18,757	14,782	17,272
Materials inventory		6,405	51,692	90,169	158,449	255,082
Other current assets						
Total current assets	2	806,137	1,427,432	2,667,017	3,109,552	4,560,586
Current liabilities						
Accounts payable		27,049	168,184	238,449	389,035	563,527
S/T loans			200,000	200,000	200,000	200,000
GST/VAT payable			59,494	84,524	142,836	237,705
Income tax payable						106,022
Interest payable		2,182	11,644	21,874	21,887	22,547
Other current liabilities						
Total current liabilities		29,231	439,322	544,847	753,758	1,129,801
Net current assets (liabilities)	2	776,906	988,110	2,122,170	2,355,794	3,430,785
Total assets less current liabilities	3,002	876,989	1,163,469	2,250,305	2,475,593	3,504,748
Financed by						
Long-term liabilities						
L/T loans				500,000	500,000	500,000
Concessional loans			500,000	500,000	500,000	500,000
Finance leases		95,903	82,831	68,543	94,883	68,893
LSL provision		1,472	12,587	33,756	64,347	110,429
Other long-term liabilities	3,000	3,000	3,000	3,000	3,000	3,000
Total long-term liabilities	3,000	100,375	598,418	1,105,299	1,162,230	1,182,322
Shareholders' funds						
Dividends payable						
Capital subscribed	2	1,000,002	1,750,002	2,500,002	2,500,002	2,500,002
Reserves						
Retained earnings		(223,388)	(1,184,951)	(1,354,996)	(1,186,639)	(177,576)
Total equity	2	776,614	565,051	1,145,006	1,313,363	2,322,426
Total equity and long-term liabilities	3,002	876,989	1,163,469	2,250,305	2,475,593	3,504,748

The schedule of accounts receivable (debtors)

Table 10.22 is an example of a satisfactory subsidiary schedule of accounts receivable. The schedule of accounts receivable is simple to construct. It starts with accounts receivable at the beginning of the period, a figure brought in from the previous period's balance sheet. Next, sales for the period (we assume here that all sales are made on credit terms) are added. The figure is, of course, the gross revenue figure from the statement of financial performance (Tables 10.2 and 10.3). From this gross estimate we must subtract bad debts calculated according to whatever formula seems appropriate to the business, which brings us, by subtraction, to a total of all the accounts receivable during the period. From this we subtract the net cash flow from sales because, as accounts receivable are paid, they are obviously removed from our list of accounts to be paid. The subtraction brings us to a figure for accounts receivable at the end. The fundamental layout of this subsidiary schedule (which of course can be made more complicated and have several more line items injected to add depth and information content to it) never varies from business to business.

Table 10.22 **Accounts receivable**

ExampleCo - Accounts receivable

	Year one	Year two	Year three	Year four	Year five
	30-Jun-02	30-Jun-03	30-Jun-04	30-Jun-05	30-Jun-06
A/c receivable opening balance			630,653	1,112,213	1,933,293
As booked					
Sales in period		1,272,748	3,756,647	6,348,304	10,564,715
less bad debts		(25,456)	(75,133)	(126,965)	(211,294)
Disposals, plant					
Disposals, non-plant					
Disposals, land and buildings					
Extraordinary income		200,000	300,000		
Total booked		1,447,292	3,981,514	6,221,339	10,353,421
As expected					
Expected cash flow from sales		616,639	3,199,954	5,400,259	9,208,002
Disposals, plant					
Disposals, non-plant					
Disposals, land and buildings					
Extraordinary income		200,000	300,000		
Total expected		816,639	3,499,954	5,400,259	9,208,002
A/c receivable closing balance		630,653	1,112,213	1,933,293	3,078,712

The schedule of accounts payable (creditors)

Just as we extend credit to people who buy from us, so do other suppliers extend credit to us and the balance sheet needs to show the schedule of the accounts that are payable to them at the end of any given period. There are many ways to build a schedule of accounts payable (creditors). One of the simplest and least likely to cause complications or error is demonstrated in Table 10.23.

This subsidiary schedule of accounts payable starts with a figure for accounts payable at the beginning of the period. Then, basically two things happen. All credit additions are totalled and added to the accounts payable at the beginning and all credit reductions are totalled and subtracted from that figure. The result is the accounts payable at the end of the period and that is the figure that we want for the balance sheet.

If you have been building your model according to the principles set out so far, all the figures that we want along the way already exist. The figures for credit additions are drawn from the statement of financial performance – direct overheads, non-salaries marketing and non-salaries administration. Our materials purchases are drawn from the appropriate subsidiary schedule (Table 10.5). Our credit reductions

Table 10.23 **Accounts payable**

ExampleCo - Accounts payable

	Year one 30-Jun-02	Year two 30-Jun-03	Year three 30-Jun-04	Year four 30-Jun-05	Year five 30-Jun-06
A/c payable opening balance		27,049	168,184	238,449	389,035
Credit additions					
Trade credit					
Statutory superannuation	10,605	80,042	152,430	220,253	331,787
Additional superannuation	5,892	44,470	84,683	122,358	184,327
Workers' compensation	2,062	15,563	29,637	42,826	64,514
Payroll tax		9,321	32,427	85,440	181,439
Public liability insurance		9,546	28,175	47,612	79,235
Property insurance	4,068	3,714	3,651	8,932	7,474
Rentals	17,433	131,750	132,000	132,000	132,000
Rates and utilities	4,125	63,256	82,522	103,194	137,488
Materials purchase	6,405	153,064	369,995	655,055	1,108,981
Shipping		63,637	187,833	317,416	528,236
Other services	66,100	392,320	379,797	517,462	746,436
Training	4,713	31,222	54,180	73,632	105,471
Communications	1,200	81,384	107,218	151,740	228,992
Travel and accommodation		41,022	67,855	95,926	154,618
Other purchases	1,200	23,380	39,038	58,564	93,124
Media advertising		398,750	488,125	618,750	893,750
Total trade credit	123,803	1,542,441	2,239,566	3,251,160	4,977,872
Capital equipment					
Plant acquisition		100,000		50,000	
Non-plant acquisition	100,000				
Land and buildings acquisition					
Total capital equipment	100,000	100,000		50,000	
Total credit additions	223,803	1,642,441	2,239,566	3,301,160	4,977,872
Credit reductions					
Trade credit					
Statutory superannuation	3,584	56,144	139,863	197,896	300,743
Additional superannuation		20,389	68,852	100,598	151,043
Workers' compensation	697	10,917	27,193	38,478	58,478
Payroll tax		3,550	28,343	61,053	161,260
Public liability insurance		9,546	28,175	47,612	79,235
Property insurance		4,068	3,714	3,651	8,932
Rentals	14,971	126,426	132,000	132,000	132,000
Rates and utilities	3,567	59,526	81,543	101,619	135,177
Materials purchase	4,921	142,162	356,758	636,844	1,078,690
Shipping		55,883	182,012	307,547	514,422
Other services	62,913	375,822	374,162	504,378	731,609
Training	3,983	29,257	53,333	72,108	103,418
Communications	1,059	76,020	105,753	147,602	224,435
Travel and accommodation		38,249	66,301	93,514	151,156
Other purchases	1,059	22,001	38,126	57,111	91,086
Media advertising		371,346	483,173	602,730	877,529
Total trade credit reductions	96,754	1,401,306	2,169,301	3,104,741	4,799,213
Capital equipment					
Plant acquisition		100,000		45,833	4,167
Non-plant acquisition	100,000				
Land and buildings acquisition					
Total capital equipment	100,000	100,000		45,833	4,167
Total credit reductions	196,754	1,501,306	2,169,301	3,150,574	4,803,380
Net additions (reductions)	27,049	141,135	70,265	150,586	174,492
A/c payable closing balance	27,049	168,184	238,449	389,035	563,527

are all figures that come from the cash flow statement (Table 10.17): materials payments; direct overhead payments; non-salary marketing payments; and non-salary administration payments. Plant acquisitions and non-plant acquisitions come from the relevant subsidiary schedules (Table 10.13). In this way, the accounts payable subsidiary schedule draws on all the work previously done in building the financial model and generates the last liability figure needed to produce the finished balance sheet projections shown as Table 10.20.

Other bridging issues

The shareholders' funds section of the balance sheet is calculated by referring to the relevant figures in the cash flow statements and the statements of financial performance. Retained earnings for this period will simply be the retained earnings of the previous period plus the profit, after tax, on this year's statement of financial performance. Reserves are a matter of policy and will simply represent an allocation of retained earnings (reserve goes up, retained earnings goes down, a simple subtraction). Capital subscribed is going to be the capital with which the business began the period plus any equity additions (a line item in the cash flow statement).

Thus, the process of finalising a projected set of balance sheets is a matter of what one might call 'bridging'. It is building a bridge between the figures we have already projected in our previous statements and the figures we need for the finished balance sheet layout. From time to time, there will be special bridging issues that might arise in a complex or large business but, when such circumstances arise, the entrepreneur will have the services of a corporate finance department, aided by the services of a major accounting firm if needs be, to decide what should be done in order to produce a sound set of projected balance sheets.

Using simulation to manage variance and change

The opening section of this chapter stressed that for each and every business there is and will always be an unlimited number of possible questions which prospective investors, whether lenders or potential equity participants, and practising managers involved in the day-to-day operation of the venture will want to ask. The entrepreneurial financial model has to be a living thing capable of answering those questions in currency terms. In general, a question will be put in the form: 'If we did this, what will be the financial consequences?'

The entrepreneurial financial model must be capable of coming up with the answers. That capability has several obvious technical implications and some that are less obvious.

One of the most important uses of the financial model comes immediately after a new product is launched and involves substituting actual sales and revenue for the projections. Month by month, or even week by week, a pattern of actual sales will develop that can be worked backwards into the market response model to refine it, which will immediately show the effect of any changes from the plan on the business's cash balances and net assets. If sales are too slow, then promotional expenditure can be boosted, staff hiring and equipment purchasing deferred and orders for materials and components cancelled. If sales are rising faster than the plan, the reverse set of actions can be put in train.

Keeping the financial plan updated has further benefits for a new enterprise; one is that the firm always has a mechanism for testing its ability to handle a large, unexpected order: not all orders are good news, particularly for a small and rapidly developing firm. Sometimes such orders must be declined or only accepted if accompanied by a deposit.

Before the venture is launched, the financial model can be used to test various scenarios, such as faster or slower sales, higher or lower costs or better or worse customer response to the product. A series of trials of this nature test the boundaries of stability for a firm; sometimes they show that a given iteration of a plan is vulnerable to a tiny change in circumstances, while a different approach can give the firm a margin of safety. Potential investors will want to know that this has been done and may wish to suggest some trials themselves.

One of the most important tests is that of the effect of different levels of capital: entrepreneurs cannot always raise all the capital they would like, and the financial model lets them rebuild the plan on a lower capital budget, rather than simply ploughing on with inadequate resources. If a new venture is successful in its first few years, it will receive many offers of additional capital: the model, if kept updated, will enable the entrepreneurial team to decide whether they will accept any of these offers and, if so, for how much.

As readers will recall from Chapter 7, directors of a company who permit it to trade when it is unable to pay its debts as they fall due are committing an offence. Directors who don't want to draw the 'go to gaol' card will make sure that the numbers in the line 'total current assets' are always bigger than those in the line 'total current liabilities' and that projected cash holdings will be sufficient to meet the business's projected liabilities in every future period.

CHECKPOINT

In this chapter we have described, in some detail, the construction of a set of pro forma accounts for a new venture, The approach we have chosen is eminently suitable for incorporating into an Excel® or other spreadsheet model, and the model, once created, can be used as a management tool by the new venture long after the launch is behind it.

You should be planning to take full advantage of the capabilities of a modern spreadsheet program in order to create a model you can use to justify and explain your projections to prospective lenders and investors and demonstrate the effect of suggestions they may make.

We pointed out in Chapter 6 that the ability to simulate alternative scenarios significantly increases the chances of a business plan gaining the support of investors; in this chapter we have described how you can build a spreadsheet model that will support such simulations. You will also use this model to generate the pro forma accounts you will include with your business plan.

Exercises

1 The traditional name for the statement of financial position is a balance sheet. Why? What balances?

2 Describe the relationship between the statements of financial position, financial performance, and cash flows.

3 If you are developing a business plan, whether as a class exercise or with a view to creating an enterprise, you should now complete your pro forma accounts. Demonstrate the flexibility of your accounting model by testing some 'what if' conditions, such as raising material costs by 10 per cent.

4 Take the model as developed in response to Exercise 3 and conduct some parametric ranging, that is, vary some parameters to find how far that they can change before your minimum cash balance falls to zero and your business is on the verge of (simulated) failure. How improbable are these variances?

5 If you are using Excel® or a similar package, experiment with the Goal Seek tool to repeat Exercise 4. You will need to make some additions to your model.

6 Make further additions to the model completed as Exercise 3 to compute the net present value of the EBDIT and profit rows for various discount rates; if your model forecasts n periods insert an artificial $(n+1)^{th}$ period containing a parameter-driven multiple of the value in the nth period; initially use a multiplier of 4 for the EBDIT line and 6 for the profit line.

7 Make further additions to the model completed as Exercise 3 to compute the net present value to an investor who subscribes all the equity capital, receives all the dividends, and sells his interest in period $(n+1)$ for the retained profits plus a parameter-driven multiple of the profit in the nth period; initially use a multiplier of 6.

8 Repeat Exercise 7 but compute the internal rate of return earned by the investor.

Notes

1   In this chapter, there is nothing concerning the technical aspects of accountancy that is not dealt with in far greater depth in any established textbook on accountancy. The authors make the assumption that the reader either has studied, is studying or will study both accounting fundamentals and the basic operation of an electronic spreadsheet package. What the chapter supplies is some 'value-added' for those who have a good grasp of accounting and spreadsheet basics. The philosophy, perspective and design principles result directly from the paradigm of entrepreneurial business planning presented in Chapter 6.

2   People on entrepreneurial and management teams who don't understand basic accounting tend to get bullied by those who do.

3   Firms using *kanban* or just-in-time purchasing are the main exception, and even there the main benefit is that materials are held, by suppliers at each level of the value chain, in the least transformed and therefore lowest cost form possible.

11 Preparing the business plan

This chapter

■ There are at least 50 books in print telling their readers how to write a business plan and probably hundreds. There are several excellent packages available on the Internet and no doubt more will appear in due course. In Chapter 6, we set out the essential properties of a quality business plan and any structure that meets those requirements is, under our definition, satisfactory. What we provide here is a structure that will, as long as the individual sections are well-researched and well-presented, lead to the assembly of a complete and convincing plan.

■ You don't have to use this structure but if you invent your own or base your plan on a different book or package, it becomes your responsibility to review the alternative against Chapter 6 and assure yourself that you are going to achieve a satisfactory result.

The entrepreneurial business plan paradigm

There are a large number of books in print setting out rules for writing a successful business plan.[1] With so much advice, not all of it entirely consistent, which entrepreneurial business planning guide should you follow?

The best answer may be that most of these guides miss one of the central points: formal excellence in plan presentation is neither a necessary nor a sufficient condition for a plan to be successful. A business plan is a documentary record of certain analyses and the conclusions and recommendations drawn from them, and if the preparatory work has been done correctly, presenting the results in a different order will not detract from the validity of the conclusions and recommendations.

In Chapter 6 we described the essential characteristics of an entrepreneurial business plan. We developed a general template for the production of entrepreneurial business plans. A successful plan must cover four key areas:

1. it must be a communication with a well-defined sender and receiver:
   ■ the sender must be a competent entrepreneurial team inviting the receivers to join the project, as financial investors or participants in some other form
   ■ the receiver(s) must be people who could reasonably respond positively to this invitation
2. it must convey a clear proposal for an entrepreneurial act of venture creation with well-defined objectives
3. it must be useful as a simulation device, to answer potential investors' questions

about the likely outcome and possible tactical options under various changes in external circumstances or internal capabilities

4. it must include two particular elements:
   - a well-written document as we describe in this chapter
   - a fully functional financial model as described in Chapter 10.

To summarise the success rules developed in Chapter 6:

- adapt the length of the plan and the depth of its detail to the interests and circumstances of the target audience
- empower the plan reader
- adapt the plan to meet the specific interests of particular investors
- anticipate and address the target audience's 'due diligence' requirements
- structure the 'deal' such that each investor is offered a reward appropriate to the level of their investment and the degree of risk assumed
- present a 'base case' scenario that is clearly:
  - practical
  - at least locally optimal (such that no single parameter or timing change can improve the expected outcome significantly)
  - soundly based.

Structuring the written plan

The rules set out in Chapter 6 and summarised above set out necessary and sufficient conditions for a plan to be successful, at least to the extent that it is read and understood by its target audience. If you have appreciated the lessons in Chapters 4 and 5, the members of the target audience should feel favourably disposed to the proposal; if the legal issues as outlined in Chapter 7 have been dealt with correctly, the members of the audience won't feel their consciences or security threatened; following the precepts in Chapter 8 you will have lined up such government support and endorsement as is available; and if you are working within a large corporation or seeking such a corporation's involvement in your proposed enterprise, Chapter 9 should have guided you past some of the potential pitfalls. Students seeking high marks and entrepreneurs preparing their first plan should review Chapters 4, 5 and 7–9 before putting the finishing touches to their venture proposal.

A venture proposal has two key elements: one is the active financial model described in Chapter 10 and the other is the written plan; here we set out a proven set of recommendations for producing an intelligible and attractive plan document. This is not the only possible structure: many of the popular business planning guides include valid structures that differ in detail from this one; but it is a structure that we are comfortable with. Entrepreneurs and planners who invent their own plan structure as distinct from adapting one of the established ones may be, in our opinion, adding an unnecessary layer of complexity and risk to their task.

We have learned from long and sometimes bitter experience that, whatever the exact format, two constraints should be observed if the plan is ever to be read by someone important enough to authorise it:

- A plan must start with an executive summary, which must be brief, readable and to the point. Plan writers whose executive summary exceeds two A4 pages or 700 words should examine it carefully to make sure that they have not been verbose or included extraneous material.
- The master plan, including the executive summary, should contain the minimum amount of material needed by a plan reviewer to make an initial judgement. Plans that exceed 40 A4 pages of text and five A4 pages of red tape, headings, titles, indices and so on are extremely difficult to read as well as difficult to appreciate as a whole.

The second constraint will generally mean that much material a careful reviewer needs to examine will be left out of the master plan. This material should be prepared and either supplied as separately bound appendices to the master plan or provided on demand, according to the reviewer's wishes. It will generally be much more detailed than the equivalent section of the master plan and it need only be friendly to specialist readers. The master plan might, for example, state that a key invention was protected by a number of patents: an appendix might contain the full patent specifications.

The reason for setting upper limits on the size of the plan and the executive summary is found in the nature of the review process. Senior executives in major companies spend, according to Gary Hamel,[2] a little over an hour a week thinking about the future of their corporation; they recognise that this is too little, but it is all the time they can spare from current pressing matters and they are not going to waste it if they can help it. Professional venture capitalists spend more time considering the future, but they have more proposals to consider: a professional first stage review of a business plan can take two or more days and a successful venture capitalist could be asked to support 20 or more projects every week.

The first paragraph of the executive summary tells the reviewer whether she should read the rest of it, pass the plan to someone else or forget it, and the rest of the executive summary tells the reader whether the rest of the plan is likely to repay the effort of reading it. The body of the plan must be flexibly bound and easy to handle because, among those plans and proposals piled into the 'to read' stack, those that can be read on an aeroplane or added to an overfull briefcase to be taken home are those that are actually likely to be read by the targeted receiver.

A: The executive summary

The executive summary must be structured, from its first paragraph, to capture the attention of the manager or venture capitalist for whom it has been prepared. At the same time, it must be an accurate overview of the plan as a whole. Certain points as listed below must be covered in the summary. The order given is not mandatory, but it makes a certain sort of sense:

- Who wrote this plan and (if the writer is not the entrepreneur) on whose authority?
- Who is the target reader (venture capitalist, banker, colleagues, superior manager in the same company, partners to a collaboration, partners to a new venture)?

- What does the plan writer want the plan reader to do?
- What is the principal benefit that the reader can expect, if she takes the recommended action and the plan is then carried out successfully?
- What is the most significant and collateral (non-cash) benefit offered to the plan reader?
- What is the project described by the plan intended to achieve? What is the objective measure of success and when will it be reached?
- What is the maximum cash exposure as far as the reader is concerned? What is the planned investment, over what period is it to be drawn down and what is the internal rate of return (IRR)?
- If the aim of the project is to introduce a new product, describe it in one sentence. What, in one more sentence, is its state of development?
- If it is a new product (a good or a service), will it be pioneering a new market, an early entrant in a developing market or a new product challenging for a share of an established market?
- What is the projected time to positive cash flow and a positive cash balance?

Further material is optional: if the executive summary can be kept to a single page, so much the better. If you are going to include additional material, then it must be material that the reviewing manager or investor needs to know. Such material might indicate who, if anybody, is going to be adversely affected by the new product. When a plan is being prepared for an existing business, an opportunity to punish a trade rival or put some pressure on an overbearing supplier may be regarded more favourably than a less aggressive plan with a slightly higher IRR.

A number of boxes in this chapter will be based upon the hypothetical – and inconsistent – UMB Ltd. The imaginary facts are not always going to be the same.

This plan has been prepared for evaluation by professional venture investors. We are seeking a lead investor who will head a syndicate that will raise a total of £2.5 million to enable the early success of the Ultimate Metal Bashing Company (UMB Ltd) to be built on.

UMB has just completed its second year of trading, turning over £2 million and showing a trading profit before abnormal items. We need extra capital to expand our facilities in order to fill a contract with a major multinational company. We hold a letter of intent covering sales to this customer of £8 million over the next three years. Other opportunities worth three times this are on hold until we are equipped to meet them.

Our plans show that UMB can be made ready for a stock market flotation, either on the London Stock Exchange or NASDAQ, in no more than five years, at which time it will have annual sales of over £35 million and still be growing strongly. EBDIT will be over £7 million.

UMB have designed and now manufacture a critical part of the catalytic converter used in motor vehicles. Cars incorporating our patented design weigh 750g less and use 0.5g less platinum than cars using older technology. These are important benefits for both fleet fuel economy and total manufacturing cost, and all the major motor manufacturers have shown a strong interest in our product.

We will look to the lead investor for advice on the most appropriate structure of the investment, but the example shown here suggests that the investing syndicate should receive an effective annual ROI of no less than 55 per cent.

B: The opportunity statement

B1: The value statement

Before describing the opportunity in any detail, summarise it in general terms, first from the users' and then from the supplier's viewpoint. State whether the product is bought by consumers or businesses, whether it is consumed, what the repurchase interval or frequency is and what is the nature of the benefit the user anticipates. If the product is to be bought by businesses, state how it fits into these customer businesses' value chain. If the product is to be bought by consumers, state the key valuable properties.

By taking the purchaser's viewpoint, it becomes possible to determine where the supplier is in the delivery chain, what proportion of the final value results from the supplier's activities and what factors assure the supplier of a continuing business. A firm's managers are also better placed to consider strategic options, such as downstream integration or alternate channel strategies, when they lift their focus from the cash they receive for their products to look at what their customers are doing with these products.

This section might reasonably conclude with a summary of the basic value proposition. If the product is to be marketed to other businesses, include a short description of how the product is to be put into use and an indication as to whether the primary advantages are received as cost reductions or revenue increases. Some indication of the absolute value a typical user might receive from using the product could fit in here. Any assumption about the size of a typical business user or the demographic characteristics of a typical consumer should be stated and not left to the reader's imagination.

Motor vehicle suppliers in most countries are obliged to observe strict pollution standards, including limits on nitrogen oxide and carbon monoxide emission. In the US they are also required to achieve certain fuel efficiency targets. Most petrol-engined vehicles are equipped with a catalytic converter in the exhaust system, which accelerates the conversion of nitrogen oxides and carbon monoxide to harmless nitrogen and carbon dioxide. The catalyst used is platinum or some other rare and precious metal.

UMB supply metal matrices to catalyst manufacturers, who add the platinum and sell converters to exhaust manufacturers, who build up complete exhaust systems, which they deliver to motor manufacturers for assembly into complete vehicles and eventual sale to the public.

UMB matrices are lighter than those now generally used, which helps manufacturers to improve the fuel economy of their cars, and the superior airflow characteristics means that less platinum is required, reducing the cost of the completed converter.

There are 30 million cars produced annually and nearly 400 million in service worldwide; if all of them used the lighter weight catalytic converters incorporating UMB's patented design, annual oil demand would fall by about 1.5 million barrels, worth £30 million. The saving in platinum is worth, at current prices, approximately £40 million a year.

B2: The gap

An opportunity consists of the combination of a product and the existence of a latent or unsatisfied demand for that product. A cautious reviewing manager must ask the questions: Why this product? Why this time? Very few ideas are wholly original. Most have been thought of before, but either no venture was launched or a venture was launched and failed. Very few opportunities go begging indefinitely, so the circumstances that make the new opportunity feasible must be relatively recent.

If some apparent demand has been unsatisfied for a long time, then there is an automatic doubt going to be raised about its urgency. The most attractive conditions for launching a new venture are when some recent and continuing change in the physical, technological, economic or social environment is activating the latent demand. If there is some proprietary technology that makes the venturer uniquely positioned to satisfy this demand, so much the better.

The nature of the changes creating a new set of opportunities should be explained and quantified. If, for example, a new set of environmental standards is about to be adopted, there will be a market in products that assist and test conformance. How long will it be before the demand for these products will become significant? How long will it take to be satisfied? What follow-on opportunities may there be?

> Catalytic converters were first fitted to cars in the late 1970s in response to environmental concerns and considerable effort was expended in optimising their design over the next few years. In recent years relatively little effort has gone into improving the performance or reducing the cost of these devices.
>
> UMB have secured the services of Dr Olga Petropavloska, whose previous credits include the design of the airspeed measuring assembly on the MiG 31 fighter aircraft. Dr Petropavloska applied advanced mathematical methods to the fluid mechanics of catalytic converters and was able to show that a revised design could achieve a significantly more uniform exposure of the exhaust gases to the catalyst. She was also able to develop a practical way of manufacturing the new core matrix.

B3: The industry, product and market

If the history of the market, previous products offered in it or previous versions of the product of which this plan is the subject will assist the plan reviewer to understand the scale and urgency of the opportunity described, then a brief description of the history and current state of the relevant industries and markets should be included here. This may be vital if the project involves a resurrection of some previous failure, particularly if the failure was notorious. If the reviewer needs to know something about the industry, and probably doesn't know enough, then it should also be included in this subsection.

If a reviewer needs some essential technical background information to make a proper judgement, this material should be provided here. This heading should not provide an excuse for the plan writer to show off, nor should it stray too far from the relevant products and markets. This is not the place to correct the shortcomings in the reviewer's education in economics, politics or modern history. If an employee of a computer company is directed to prepare a business case for a new software product, she may not enhance her career prospects by starting her plan with a 20-page dissertation on Babbage, Turing and Ada Lovelace. If a former employee of a computer company sets out to write a business plan for anyone else, she should make a conscious effort to avoid the liberal helpings of alphabet soup in which the computer industry is prone to float its output.

B4: Product definition

At the risk of being obvious, include a dispassionate and reasonably complete description of the actual product, including its name, principal components and how it is produced and used. Do not assume that the target readers have any technical knowledge whatsoever or, indeed, any specialist knowledge of any sort at this point.

If technical phraseology is avoided, then a statement of the totally obvious should not cause offence and it may save the plan from being rejected by someone who does not understand something that most people would find perfectly obvious. An English training establishment was thrown into confusion when a noble lord, enrolled on one of its courses, complained that there was something wrong with the water because his toothbrush would not foam. It was eventually discovered that this was the first occasion in the noble lord's life that he had not been attended by a nurse or valet and had therefore been expected to put toothpaste on the brush himself. Do not assume that the readers of the plan can drive a car, cook, sew, sweep floors or explain the operation of a nuclear reactor.

The complete product definition includes all the associated services, whether being offered under this business plan or not, the physical delivery system and the principle marketing messages. The relationship between the typical buyer, the user and the end user must be stated, possibly in general terms.

UMB manufacture catalyst matrices, fabricated metal objects about 250 mm long and 120 mm in diameter, which are then supplied to Johnson Mathey Ltd or other catalyst suppliers for the addition of catalytic material before onselling to manufacturers of exhaust systems.

The catalytic converters are placed where the exhaust gases from the motorcar's engine must pass through them. They are required to slow down and diffuse the exhaust gases so that at least 99 per cent of the nitrogen oxides and 80 per cent of the carbon monoxide is catalysed to harmless byproducts; at the same time, they are required to allow the exhaust gases to flow freely, so that back-pressure does not reduce the efficiency of the car's engine.

The exhaust gases are hot and somewhat corrosive as they arrive at the converter, and the matrix has to be able to function for at least the design life of the exhaust system without losing its structural integrity or efficiency.

B5: Pre-launch product development

There should be a clear and unambiguous statement of the state of development of the product (concept, prototype, ready for market, on market for x years with sales of y euros) and if the product is not ready for market, there should be a clear statement of the time and money expected to be involved in getting it ready for market. This must include any regulatory permissions and certifications required.

If the product is not already on the market, it is useful, at this point, to include a short summary of the track record and qualifications of the staff responsible for completing the development and gaining the regulatory approvals and test certificates. Examiners and plan evaluators are aware that nearly-ready and nearly-approved products can easily become massive financial liabilities.

UMB have been shipping Petropavloska-designed matrices for performance and accelerated life cycle testing for the past two years. No serious problems have been discovered and the minor ones have been completely rectified. Once the needed production equipment is in place, deliveries of the first model can start without further development.

Each different make and model of car will require a new design, but this is a routine process, which Dr Petropavloska has largely automated.

B6: Product security

What factors prevent or inhibit an imitator from replicating the product and initiating a price war? Outline the key patents, registered designs, copyrights, business names and trademarks that provide legal protection for the product. Describe other product security aspects if necessary: trade secrets, unique skills, pre-emptive marketing and/or production strategies or any other means proposed to avoid excessive, or excessively early, competition.

Any given model of matrix can be reverse-engineered fairly easily and we expect the after-market business to be substantially penetrated by such 'clones', in spite of our strong patents.

Each new geometry of matrix needs to be recalculated and, without access to Dr Petropavloska or the computer programs that she has written, this will prove exceedingly difficult. There are only six other mathematicians of Dr Petropavloska's eminence specialising in flow problems of this type in the world, and it is unlikely that any of them will give up their current positions to go into competition with her.

The circumstances that led to a world-class mathematician starting work at a small, regionally based metal fabricator are not likely to be repeated. Dr Petropavloska will leave us shortly to take up a senior position at a leading university, but she has signed an agreement with us that ensures that it is not in her interest to become our competitor.

B7: Product risks

Without turning the prospective investor's hair white too rapidly, summarise the major risks to the successful exploitation of the opportunity and the risks consequential on success. If the opportunity is to supply a safety-critical component for a range of passenger aircraft, product failure may have greater consequences and the possible legal liability may extend further than would be the case with a proposal for marketing pre-loved pet rocks.

This subsection of the plan should convey a justified confidence that the risks and possible liabilities have been properly analysed and that the risks are minimised and the liabilities quarantined. In some cases a full failure mode analysis will have been carried out and the results supplied as an appendix. Note that product liability is a developing area of the law and intuitive conclusions may lack legal support. It has been claimed, for example, that potatoes are only tolerated by long familiarity. A new product with the same level of oxalic acid and propensity to produce the poison solanine would be banned or supplied on prescription only.

B8: Development plans

A successful new product inevitably attracts imitators, and familiarity with the product almost equally inevitably reduces the perceived fair price of each unit of the product over time. If unchecked, these two factors will lead to the stunting or failure of the innovator's business.

A continued development plan is needed to anticipate and avert this cause of premature business failure. This plan will provide for the progressive addition of features to the product or introduction of complementary products. This in turn will maintain the innovator's market share and ensure that the innovator's business continues to grow with the market when it is no longer possible to grow faster than it. While the forward plans need not be stated in detail, they must be outlined and their probable cost set out. It will be useful to show what the development programme will cost as a fraction of revenue, but some definite number, either of staff or dollars, should also be shown.

If the plan is truly for a one-shot opportunity, with no intention of building an ongoing business, this should be stated clearly and early in the plan, since the absence of a long-term revenue stream will have a significant effect on the present value of the opportunity. If the plan is for a continuing business, but no long-term development plans are outlined, investors may evaluate it as if it was a simple market raid.

C: Market overview

C1: Summary

The critical facts to be brought out in the marketing overview, and worth summarising at the start of it, include: the number of potential customers; their annual value, in aggregate; the current and prospective intensity of the competition; the current sales channel and the proposed channel, if different; the typical bases of decision; and the diffusion parameters where relevant.

All these are important, but even more important is the confidence the reviewer will take away from reading the plan that these statements are the result of diligent research, not just wishful thinking.

C2: State of the market

This subsection should provide an analysis of the current market state and in what direction or directions it is heading. If the current proposal involves creating a new market, explain how the relevant needs are currently being satisfied – or frustrated. Explain how the market would develop if this proposal did not proceed. Describe the established firms most likely to identify the opportunity and fill the gap.

If the new product is to be launched into an existing market, describe the state of development of the market with as much precision as possible: how long since the first product into this market was launched, the fraction of potential users who are now actual users, the growth in the market in each of the last three years if known. Name the largest supplier to the existing market and estimate their market share. Provide an estimate of how this share has been changing in recent years. Estimate the number of suppliers in total and how many of them have a market share above 1 per cent.

The world market for cars, and therefore catalytic converter core matrices, is relatively stable at around 30 million per year and the typical buy-in price is £15. The demand for Petropavloska cores is new and the product very exciting to specialists, but adoption will be limited, partly by the rate at which new models are introduced and partly by UMB's capacity. Motor vehicle manufacturers do not like cutting in a new part of the emission control system during a model's life, because of the large cost of recertification, and UMB has made a strategic decision to be a manufacturer in order to avoid making life too easy for imitators.

C3: Buyer behaviour

In Chapter 4 we set out various market parameters, such as the cost of securing a trial, the probability of a trial creating a customer and the degree of internal influence (the effectiveness of 'word of mouth' recommendation).

At this point in the plan there should be estimates of all the relevant parameters, supported as necessary by a narrative account of typical initial and repeat purchases. If the product is potato crisps in single-serve bags, then displaying it behind bars in public houses and at child's eye level in supermarkets may be sufficient to generate a trial; but for a major capital item, such as a new aeroplane for an airline or a new weapon systems for a national defence establishment, the selling process may extend over a period of years. The narrative supports the estimate and will build a degree of comfort among the plan readers that the authors understand the basic sales and marketing process.

For infrequently purchased products, internal influence is critical to the products' eventual success and there should be at least anecdotal evidence of the importance that buyers, in the relevant market, place on recommendations from users. When a market is well established or the buyers in a new market are also buyers in an older one, it may be possible to use statistical tools to estimate the relative importance of recommendation and promotion (that is, internal and external influence).

C4: Prove it ...

There are two levels of consequences of serious errors in the estimate of these parameters: at the first level, marketing expense will rise as a proportion of sales, leading to disappointing returns; while if the errors are serious enough, a venture that appeared, in the business plan, to be attractive may turn out to be a black hole in which the entrepreneur's hopes and the investors' money will vanish without trace. It is all very well to feed parameters into a model, but a well-built model positively invites its users to fiddle the parameters in order to achieve a particular result. Microsoft Excel® includes the handy 'Goal Seek' tool to make such manipulation easier.

The ultimate test of any business plan comes in the marketplace, if it gets that far, and history is well stocked with accounts of marketing research making predictions, both favourable and damning, that the market utterly confounded. Tales of the Ford Edsel and Post-it Notes® obscure the fact that a lot of marketing research does produce tolerably accurate results; and some marketing parameters can be estimated almost exactly by recourse to statistical data collected by national statistical authorities and trade associations. There is simply no acceptable excuse for using incorrect numbers for a national population, the number of households whose income exceeds some threshold or the number of business establishments larger than a certain size.[3]

This section of the plan does not have to be excessively technical, but it must show the sources of the information used in making revenue projections and indicate those for which the information can be considered accurate and those where additional research might usefully be applied to refining the estimated parameter values and improving the projections. Some indication of what sort of research would be most effective could be included, together with confirmation that the research will (or won't) be conducted early in the life of the planned venture.

D: Marketing plan overview

An overview of the marketing plan must be included in the completed plan. It is not always necessary to bind the complete marketing plan with the business plan, but a complete plan should normally be prepared and can then be referenced by the marketing statement.

D1: Summary

Reviewers will know that overestimating or incorrectly specifying the market can easily prove fatal to an otherwise promising venture. They will want to know that the entrepreneurial team have taken active steps to establish the size of the potential market and to predict the likely user response to their new product.

The marketing statement should commence with a summary (which should normally fit onto a single page) in which the following points must be covered:

- the unit volume and the gross revenue for the product launch year and the last year of the business plan

- an indication of the early market research results and a consequent estimate of the marketing risk associated with the launch
- the geographic extent of marketing and distribution in the product launch year and the last year of the business plan
- the main and supplementary distribution channels to be used in the product launch year and the last year of the business plan
- the primary promotional messages (unique selling propositions) and vehicles to be used at product launch and at the end of the plan period.

D2: Volume and revenue projections

There should be a projection of sales to final purchasers for the whole of the plan period. The projections can be based on quarterly or annual periods; products with high margins sold in low volumes are best projected on an annual basis, while a quarterly projection suits faster moving products. The projections should show the average price and the final purchaser revenue for each period. Depending on the proposed distribution arrangements, these figures may need some manipulation in order to predict periodic cash receipts and periodic accounts payable for the new venture.

In 1995 UMB shipped 110,000 standard model core matrices at an average price of £12, as well as 5000 Petropavloska cores for testing at £15. Approximately 90 per cent of these cores were eventually fitted to EU manufactured vehicles. In 2002 we expect to ship 70,000 Petropavloska cores and 90,000 standard models, with 60,000 units exported. By 2004 we hope to ship 1 million cores, all Petropavloska models, and approaching 90 per cent exported.

We expect to be able to maintain current prices, giving a revenue forecast of £1.5 million, rising to £20 million in 2007.

We will continue to act as a core supplier to catalyst manufacturers; we have no plans to go into catalyst manufacture or direct sales to vehicle assemblers.

The methodology for developing the sales forecast should be stated but not necessarily explained in detail in the main body of the plan. If a computer model has been used, the model should be made available to the examiners or reviewing managers, and the main parameters and assumptions set out in the plan. We generally recommend the use of a computable model along the lines described in Chapter 4, but other methods of projection, to the extent that they have been proved in practice, can be used if they are believed to be more suitable.

Not every business plan will be improved by the use of a computable adoption and sales model. This is particularly so in the case where the major product is an expensive item with a small number of potential users. Model results, for plans involving less than four sales per period, are little better than guesses.[4] For this style of product, the computable model could be profitably replaced by a list of the prospective customers and a sample account sales plan.

D3: Distribution channels

The whole route from the planned venture to the end user should be mapped out, and where the venture is itself critically reliant on one or more suppliers, partners or distributors, the relationship between these suppliers and the venture must be shown.

Note that there are a number of information and possibly material flows that may need to be described:

- Product information, both current and planned, must reach potential buyers and users. Retailers, dealers, agents, franchisees and so on may also require it. How is it going to get to them, how much is it going to cost and who is going to pay?

- Orders must be taken from buyers and processed in some way. Who takes these orders at each stage in the distribution channel and how are they motivated and paid?
- Who arranges physical delivery or service application? What are the quality controls and how is customer satisfaction measured?
- What are the after-sales service requirements and how are they satisfied? What are they projected to cost and how are they to be paid for?
- Who collects the user's money, how does it find its way back to the supplier, what commissions and charges are taken off it in transit and how long will the journey take?
- How does legal liability flow up and down the channel? Can this supplier be put in jeopardy by the actions of an indirect agent or retailer? How is this risk controlled?

D4: Promotional strategy

The business plan does not have to include the complete promotional plan, but it should include an overview of the proposed launch and follow-on promotional strategy. Matters that should be covered include answers to the following:

- What is the planned launch budget and what are the principal launch events?
- What are the key promotional messages that will be used? How do they relate to the principal value proposition?
- What is the total promotional budget in the first and last year of the plan, expressed both as a pound amount and as a percentage of budgeted retail sales?
- What is the approximate division of the proposed expenditure between above the line (advertising) and below the line (focused promotion)? What sponsorships or other high-profile activities are planned?
- What media split is foreshadowed (trade press, general press, radio, television, billboards and so on)?
- When the downstream distribution system involves retailers, dealers or other third party distributors, who pays for the advertising and point-of-sale promotion material? Who designs it? Who determines (or strongly recommends) the expenditure level?
- What are the metrics and targets of the promotional campaign, in particular, the target levels of name recognition and brand/product approval among potential purchasers?

D5: Price management

The proposed launch price or price structure should be set out, together with an indication of the post-launch pricing strategy. Where there are competitors already established in the market, their pricing policies should be summarised here, together with an account of these suppliers' reactions to previous attempts to break into their markets. Some indication should be given as to the scale of volume and ad hoc discounts that are likely to be encountered.

If the product and the market are both new, an account of the price-setting process should be included here, including a reasonably detailed account of the current costs borne by a typical user in satisfying or suppressing the needs that the new venture's products address. When the product is offered to business users or confers some prestige or exclusivity benefits on early consumers, some account must be provided as to how the price structure will be managed after the early user benefits are exhausted and the perceived fair price falls.

> Core matrices have traditionally been sold by weight, and we shall continue to do so, although our price per kilogram for Petropavloska cores will be higher than that for standard cores, reflecting their increased sophistication and higher performance. The price to the catalyst manufacturers will typically be 5 per cent higher for a Petropavloska core than for a standard one, while the catalyst manufacturers can sell the completed catalytic converter at 3 per cent less while increasing their own margins.

E: Key actions and events

E1: Summary

For some plans, a complete project plan covering thousands of events and actions might be appropriate, and if such a plan exists, a one- or two-page summary could be included in the business plan at this point. In any case, a product launch will involve numerous events connected by time-consuming activities and a reviewing manager might like to see that these have been allowed for.

Similarly, when venture capitalists and reviewing managers permit projects to proceed, they have a natural curiosity about the results. This section of the plan tells them how long they will have to control themselves before demanding to see what has been done with their money. The primary purpose of the action plan is, however, a way of formalising the risks, in terms of both time and function that run between 'time now' and the time that net cash becomes positive.

E2: Operations

A business plan is a plan for doing things and this section of the plan is a suitable place to describe what is going to be done, and when. If the product(s) to be marketed have a tangible component or components, these must be manufactured, packed and distributed, with a provision for handling returns, providing warranty service and the like. If the plan is primarily concerned with a service opportunity, there will be training and documentation requirements for the service delivery personnel and provision for quality control and performance feedback.

Premises will be needed: Are they to be built or are existing premises suitable? Are they to be bought or leased? What are the possibilities for expansion or contraction? There may be vehicles, plant or tools to be acquired: What will the terms be and what contingent liabilities are going to be incurred?

E3: Milestones

Many venture capitalists and reviewing managers may be unfamiliar with fully developed PERT[5] diagrams and Gantt charts, but they will generally understand a milestone list. A list suitable for inclusion in the main business plan should be no more than one or two pages long and the number of levels of significance should be selected accordingly.

Care should be taken to include the milestones of particular interest to the reviewer, especially those that should be achieved before major capital drawdowns or the incurring of serious commitments. Events such as 'sign contract for new factory' should take place after events such as 'secure regulatory approval to market new gadget', unless the approval is known to be a formality.

Where the proposed product is at a prototype or earlier stage at the time the plan is being written, plans must include a detailed account of the stages that the product must go through before it can be put into production or released to the service delivery staff and start generating cash. This must be synchronised with the pre-launch marketing activities. Very few new ventures are sufficiently well funded to recover from a launch aborted in mid-flight because the product was undeliverable.

F: The management team

F1: Summary

There is no project so divinely blessed that no one can mess it up and few proposals beyond hope of rescue if the right combination of talent and determination can be found to manage them. Errors in the presentation of the rest of the business plan can often be corrected, but if the management team does not inspire confidence, the plan, as a proposal, must fail.

In the particular case of plans seeking funding for new ventures, the initial entrepreneurial team is unlikely to be a wholly balanced management group and a reasonable investor would not expect it to be. The team may lack anyone with manufacturing or sales experience, or be unfamiliar with the duties of company directors or accountants. This section of the plan should show that the entrepreneurial team has recognised their own limitations and made plans to recruit and reward a person or a small group of people to complement the team's talent.

Strong feedback applies at this point. The management team listed here will have, implicitly or explicitly, accepted responsibility for the construction of this plan. If the reviewing manager or prospective investor has any grounds to suspect the competence, accuracy or dedication of the management team, then this suspicion will spread, like a dull grey cloud, over that manager's perception of the entire plan. If, on the other hand, the reviewing manager has great confidence in the management team proposed, then any minor doubts the reviewer has about other aspects of the plan may be passed over in silence.

This, in turn, can become a serious threat to the project, particularly if the leading lights in the management team are believed to be unapproachable as well as infallible. To minimise this risk, the plan, and the management section in particular, must make it clear that the reviewing manager or venture capitalist or their trusted representative is being sincerely invited to become an essential, trusted and respected member of their team.

F2: Individual résumés

A curriculum vitae (CV) is (literally) a life story, and while preparing such a document (or book) is a valuable activity, including it at this point of the business plan is not obligatory. A résumé, a focused précis of the full CV, is more appropriate. If a full CV exists, it may be referenced as an optional appendix. Each résumé should include the subject's major relevant educational and career highlights, a list of the most significant achievements and the names of two or three suitable career referees if appropriate. One page, or about 350 words, is usually a reasonable target length: too much, particularly if some of the entries look like padding, is much worse than too little.

A short personal selling statement may also be appropriate. Such a statement should impress the reviewing manager or venture capitalist with the commitment of the member of the proposed management team to the new project and the ample alternative opportunities for less stressful or more pleasurable occupations that the team member is passing up.

F3: Descriptions of the missing people

Very few entrepreneurial teams will include in their number people with all the different varieties of experience and talent needed to staff an operating business: a project that was so blessed would be automatically suspected of either triviality or reckless indifference to resource consumption. It is more common to find an entrepreneurial team with some glaring holes: brilliant technicians with the sketchiest idea of accounting and no knowledge at all of sales or marketing; a marketing genius with an incomplete prototype and no idea of how to get it ready for economical manufacturing; or a brilliant development, sales and marketing team with no idea at all of how to move into routine production.

Reviewers will be looking for the quality of self-knowledge that enables the entrepreneurial team to identify those necessary tasks for which they are not fitted and then identify, recruit and reward the appropriate people. A new venture that needs a first rate sales executive, or a high-profile chairman, must be prepared to make an attractive offer to get the right person, even when the necessary enticement may appear to dilute the entrepreneurs' rewards significantly.

F4: Understudies and succession planning

It will be generally recognised that the members of the initial team will play a key and possibly a unique role in bringing the venture from birth to a successful growth business. This introduces two controllable risks. First, the growth of the business may place increasing and eventually impossible demands on the key person's time. Second, an accident (in the general sense of an unplanned event) may temporarily or permanently deprive the venture of the contribution of a key person.

The first of these circumstances leads to insidious damage to the venture, as critical work is skimped or omitted. The second may prove catastrophic. 'Key person' insurance sounds like a good idea, but it is unlikely to provide enough cover to compensate the venturers for the complete failure of their business and the consequent loss of the opportunity that the business represented.

Dependence on a few key staff creates a further risk to the value of the business: if the investors wish to harvest the growth in their investment, or the venturers wish to take up a new opportunity, the market value of a business that depends on a key person is going to be considerably lower than that of a similar business where the loss of any single individual will not be crippling.

The succession planning section of the plan will illustrate how understudies will be developed, initially to secure the business against the loss of a key person and eventually to facilitate her departure.

G: The organisation plan

G1: The organisation

We dealt with organisational issues in Chapter 5 and suggested how certain information should be captured. That information should be presented in this section of the written plan. Plan reviewers will look to this section in order to assure themselves that the plan objectives are going to be achievable with the proposed staff numbers and organisational structure. The staff numbers will then give credibility to the cost lines in the financial operating plans. Most plans will describe a changing organisation as the venture grows towards its various objectives, so the organisation and staff levels should be described at various key points in the projected development of the venture.

The numbers in this section will be compared to the phased revenue targets in order to arrive at a number of key indices, such as revenue and profit per head, sales per salesperson and average number of positions reporting to each manager. When a plan proposes numbers that lead to unusual values for any of these indices, these numbers should be explicitly justified, either in this subsection or later subsections of this section.

G2: Staffing requirements

As a new business grows, there will be more work to be done, which will generate a higher management and staff workload. Although a part-time book-keeper may suffice to get the project off the ground, the cash flow will hopefully grow rapidly to the point that a full-time accountant is needed. Stores may once have been kept in a heap at the back of a garage: soon a storeman may be needed to keep track of what is in stock and where it is.

Many growing businesses fail to anticipate these needs and get plunged into unnecessary cash or stock crises just at the point where the business appears to be about to take off. There is a double potential for error in this part of the plan: failure to recruit the necessary staff in time may cause an unpleasant glitch at a delicate time, and failure to put these staff into the operating plan will make it look suspiciously optimistic.

G3: Off-payroll staff

Some new ventures are proposed on the assumption that manufacture, distribution and delivery, as well as staff functions like accounting and marketing, can be delegated to contractors. This often makes the operating plan look better than it might otherwise be but is seldom a basis for long-term viability.

If the project becomes a success, the various contractors and contract staff will be eager to reap where they have but lightly sown and there may be little left over for the venturers. The extent to which it is proposed to use off-payroll staff for both line and staff functions should be stated, as should the mechanism proposed to keep their hands out of the till once the business prospers. A clear indication of how much value is going to be added by off-payroll workers will also suggest the level of risk that will be involved in continuing with them.

G4: Key skills and key personnel

It is a rare new venture where all the skills required in the first few years of its existence can be found among the founding entrepreneurs. Even if the requisite skill types and attainment levels were present at the founding of the venture, its success would soon stretch the founders to breaking point unless assistance was found for them.

Both time and money may need to be allocated in order to establish the venture staffing levels as required from time to time by other aspects of the plan. When the venture opportunity involves a new product and/or a new technology, it may be impossible to recruit suitably skilled staff and provision must be made for staff training. The training provision may involve more than money: a trainer must be recruited or someone transferred to training duties.

This subsection may need to be cross-referenced to the failure mode analysis referred to in section B7. Often the best or only way to control risks is to control the quality of the manufacturing, delivery and service processes. This in turn comes back to recruiting and motivating a suitable member or a group of members of staff. The need for a training and succession plan follows as a logical consequence.

H: Financial projections

H1: Summary

We discussed the essential elements of the financial statements in Chapter 10, where we emphasised both the production of certain statements and a spreadsheet model. The statements are included in the master plan; when the reviewers get to the 'due diligence' stage of their examination, they will almost certainly want a copy of the spreadsheet model on disk.

All the main revenue and expenditure headings must be present on the profit and loss forecast and the balance sheet and cash flow statements must be complete. Some care is required in preparing the chart of accounts, in order to ensure that significant numbers are not lost in aggregates, while the clarity of the plan is not destroyed by trivia.

Spreadsheets should be allowed to talk: they should not drivel or shout. A well-laid out plan should require no more than a single page, or at most a double-page spread, for each of the main statements. This may require putting the complete quarterly or monthly spreadsheets into an appendix and only reproducing annual summaries, or annual summaries after the first year, in the body of the plan. There should be plenty of explanatory notes: one for every line in the chart of accounts would not be excessive.

H2: Statements

A properly laid out set of pro forma profit and loss statements, balance sheets and cash flow projections should be prepared covering the whole of the plan period. Attention should be paid to the phasing of revenue and expenses and the proper accrual of taxation reserves and utilisation of early tax losses. Interest should be shown, whether earned on funds on deposit or due on overdrafts or other borrowing instruments. Care should be taken to ensure that interest is paid and credited in the correct periods.

Revenue should usually be shown as the recommended final purchaser price, and standard commissions and promotional offers should be shown as separate lines. (Recall that the 'final purchaser' is the last buyer who recognises a discrete product, and the term includes a purchaser who incorporates supplied components or materials into a product for subsequent sale.)

The balance sheets should balance and link the profit and loss and cash flow statements. Funds must be available to cover all payments, with a reasonable contingency to allow for slow sales or even slower creditors. Numerical accuracy is critical: this section of a business plan will frequently be reviewed by an accountant, and reviewing accountants are congenitally incapable of approving statements incorporating errors, no matter how trivial.

H3: Graphs

Well-prepared graphs can add significantly to a reviewer's understanding of the financial implications of a proposal and, at a minimum the value of various critical indicators such as the breakeven points should be presented graphically. Further graphs are a matter for judgement and, to some extent, the skill of the people preparing the plan. If extra graphs are prepared, there must be a clear rationale for presenting them and the presentation must clarify rather than obscure the plan.

J: The investment opportunity

J1: Deal structure – the financial proposition

This part of the plan is going to be scrutinised with a great deal of care before senior managers or venture capital providers authorise the project or commit funds. At the same time, it is where senior managers and venture capital providers will look to decide whether the proposition that they are being offered is worth their further consideration.

Senior managers and venture capital providers are acutely aware of the tendency among innovators, particularly high-tech ones, to regard the people who provide the money as intellectual inferiors, whose only mission in life is to obstruct the advance of technology. It is a short step from this attitude to a deliberate attempt to secure, by trickery, the financial support needed for a promising project. It is extremely important that nothing in this section of the plan, and particularly the summary to this section of the plan, arouses the slightest suspicion. One technique that is often successfully used to allay suspicion is to be honest, lucid and unambiguous in the presentation of the financial proposal.

A financial proposition for a new enterprise includes a statement of the equity and debt capital required, the security offered and the proposed repayment schedule in the case of debt capital; the internal rate of return (that is, the annual interest rate at which the net present value of the investment, on the day in which the investment is made, would be zero) and the proposed harvest method (public float, trade sale, capital return or dividend stream) for equity. When there are different classes of equity investors, the returns each can expect should be shown separately. Where the founders propose to hold shares issued at a lower price than the first venture investor is being asked to pay, this should be justified by their prior contribution to the venture, and 'we had the idea in the first place' may not, from the investor's viewpoint, seem a sound argument.

A proposal from within an established enterprise should indicate the maximum cash expenditure required to complete the project and the cash exposure, the maximum loss the company could sustain if the project was abandoned. To the

---

UMB currently has tangible assets worth approximately £1.1 million, which are sufficient to support its current standard model business which earns £110,000 before taxes and dividends – £1.5 million is needed to meet the orders now in hand and reasonably anticipated for the Petropavloska cores. Of this £1 million will be spent on plant and equipment and £0.5 million will be needed to finance materials and debtors.

We suggest that the investor should subscribe £0.8 million in new equity and will then hold 40 per cent of the common stock on issue, and provide a further £0.7 million as a convertible note, to be converted not earlier than December 2006 for shares of an equivalent value, discounted 10 per cent.

Assuming no dividends are paid before a stock market flotation in June 2007, and the stock sells at a p/e of 6.5, the investor's return will be 57.5 per cent effective annual rate before personal tax but with all company taxes paid.

extent possible within the firm's accounting and overhead allocation system, the internal rate of return of the project or the net present value should be stated. When key staff or key facilities will be required by the proposed project, this should be stated here as well.

J2: The new asset

The ethical and financial justification of a new venture requires that the result of undertaking the proposed enterprise will be the creation of something that is worth more than the value of the resources (including people's time) consumed to create it. A venture can be a financial success without being ethical, as when the value in the resulting enterprise was not created, but simply transferred from a dupe – or the unsuspecting public. It is unlikely to be an ethical success without being a financial one: there is nothing particularly praiseworthy about failure and the dissipation of resources.

The pro forma balance sheet for June 2007, at which time the market value of UMB is expected to be £45 million, shows tangible assets and cash worth $38 million. The major intangible asset will, at this stage, be our continued exclusive rights to the Petropavloska designs, but we will also expect to have a highly skilled and motivated workforce, such that cash flows could be maintained even if other manufacturers started matching the technical performance of the Petropavloska design.

A firm's capacity to add value to the fixed assets that it controls can be measured by the market-to-book ratio (M/B) – the difference between the price of the assets and the value of the firm as a going concern. Firms where the M/B ratio is less than one are destroying value: the assets in these firms would be more valuable outside the firm than inside it. When the M/B ratio is greater than one, the firm contains 'something' that makes the whole worth more than the parts. One way to boost the apparent M/B ratio is to understate B, the book value of the assets. After a period of inflation, as in the 1970s and 80s, many firms had assets, particularly property, in their books at its original purchase price. Raiders bought many such firms and sold the assets at market price, sometimes recovering the whole purchase price in this way.

Successful entrepreneurial firms have a high M/B ratio, but there are seldom any undervalued assets available to attract a corporate raider. The difference between the market and the book value of such firms represents invisible assets, assets that are only valuable as long as the firm is a going concern, and which would have little or no value if it was broken up. Some of these invisible and 'off-balance sheet' assets are:

- the embodied 'know-how' of the firm, an ability to get things done when the task lies outside the capacity of any single employee or manager
- the human capital of the firm, its ability to attract and retain people with unique skills and knowledge
- the firm's 'brand equity', the revealed preference of consumers for products bearing that firm's brands and trademarks
- the firm's reputation, as revealed by the preference towards the firm shown by industrial buyers and the preferential treatment it receives from its suppliers and distributors.

It is well worth the effort to set out, in a few paragraphs, just what invisible assets will be created if this business plan is put into effect successfully. Such a statement will lay the basis of a defence against market raiders if the venture should be listed: an American wheeler-dealer is said to have made a successful hostile takeover bid for a software firm. As he moved into his new conquest the staff moved out, and he learned that he had paid many millions of dollars for a few old desks, some worn out computers and a large amount of unfinished, and now worthless, computer code. An understanding of the true asset base of a firm can be a guide to the appropriate conduct of the firm under stress: if the basic invisible asset is brand equity, a firm might settle consumer complaints even when the law might not be on the consumer's side. Firms whose human capital is vital should be careful about enforcing punctuality rules or dress codes.

J3: Risks and opportunities

Real life seldom follows a plan exactly but a clear discontinuity is relatively rare. Plans involving innovations are almost always based upon exploiting a change: numerically, an opportunity is often the difference between two very large numbers. Quite small changes in either of these numbers can cause a dramatic change in the scale of a particular opportunity. This is emphatically true when the opportunity is created by changes in the broader social and economic environment.

When the product is its own agent of change, as for example when the proposed new venture offers a product that is superior, but equivalent, to a product already on the market, there is a different but no less serious set of risks. The suppliers of the established products may launch their own improved versions or respond to a new entrant with deep price cuts. Either action will have an effect on the eventual outcome of a new venture. Changes in this area affect the market assumptions underlying the plan.

J4: Environmental dependencies

This section of the plan should set out the assumptions made by the plan writers about the physical, political and economic environment. It must state clearly what both the base and trend assumptions were and show what the effects of possible changes in these assumptions would be on the plan outcome. It is worth taking some trouble to explore the longer range causes and effects: examine the likely reaction of the new venture's customers to various environmental changes and explain how these reactions will translate into positive or negative influences on the plan outcome.

Where possible, there should be some attempt to derive a metric linking the scale and direction of environmental change to the revenue projections for the business and provide a probability scale. A new lawn-watering system, for example, would be harder to sell if a drought resulted in a ban on lawn-watering from the public supply. The probability of such a drought can be established: this is a risk which should be acknowledged in the plan. Purchases of such systems are likely to be tied to demographic and economic factors: an improvement in the economic growth rate or a successful satellite city development could both increase demand for lawn-watering systems. Economics and politics are even more unpredictable than the weather, but they should still be listed as influences on the plan outcome. In particular, an opportunity for rapid growth may be inaccessible unless there is access to additional capital. If the possibility is foreshadowed in the plan, and the conditions demonstrably exist, the additional capital is likely to be made available promptly.

J5: Internal or market factors

When the venture proposes to launch a new or redeveloped product into an established market, the launch of the new product will almost certainly lead to a response from the established suppliers. When the venture is launched from within a division of a company that already supplies the target market, there will be an effect on the firm's established products. The plan must have assumed a certain scale and direction of the competitors' responses and the cannibalistic impact. Variation in these effects will represent risks or create new opportunities.

Research, or even anecdotal evidence, of how these suppliers responded to previous challenges will help the plan reviewer in estimating the risks and opportunities.

K: Appendices

K1: Appendices and supporting material

This section should list each appendix and other supporting documents, together with 10–50 words of description. The information provided must be sufficient to enable the reviewing manager or venture capitalist to decide whether to call for it herself, have it sent for separate review (and in such cases, what class of professional should review it) or pass up the opportunity of examining it.

K2: Research sources and tools

The major research sources used should be listed and the information gained from them summarised. Often this will involve a cross-reference to an appendix. When there has been a significant amount of market research undertaken, the tools used to analyse it should be listed and the confidence in the research results indicated.

K3: Reference books and papers

All the published books and papers that were relied on in constructing the plan should be listed in a standard reference format. Where the significance or importance of the reference cited is not obvious, a 10–50-word paragraph could be added to explain these points. An explanation should always be provided when the reference is apparently out of date, as is often the case when using census or yearbook data.

CHECKPOINT

A business plan must serve several purposes, but there are some common themes required by all of them:

- the plan must be written with its intended audience in mind, it must address their concerns and provide the information that they need before they can decide to support the proposal contained in it
- the plan's target audience must find it easy to read and unambiguous and the format of the plan, both structure and layout, must support this; adherence to, or departure from, any given structure is acceptable as long as it progresses this objective and unacceptable otherwise
- all claims and statements made in the plan, apart from those which will be regarded as common knowledge by the planner and the plan's audience, must be capable of independent verification, but the plan itself need not be cluttered by such verification as long as it includes appropriate references to publicly available material and specific supporting documentation.

Exercises

By far the most important exercise arising from this chapter is the construction of a complete business plan. Before showing your plan to someone else, reread it yourself and answer the following questions:

1 Is it perfectly clear who wrote this plan and on whose authority? Is the target audience clearly identified and the action expected from them clearly set out?

2 Is the prospective return of the investment requested clearly and unambiguously set out? Will the target audience find the justification for the action that they are asked to take a reasonable return on the risks and costs (including opportunity costs) involved?

3 If you are making a proposal to venture capitalists, have you set out a clear harvest strategy for them? If it is for a corporate venture, will your plan's completion deliver a lasting benefit and, if so, is it well described?

4 Does your plan describe what you are proposing to do in sufficient detail for the audience to understand it, without burying them in unnecessary detail or bombarding them with irrelevant facts?

5 Does your marketing research and the conclusions that you draw from it inspire confidence? Will an unbiased reader consider your revenue and marketing cost projections soundly based? Have you pro-

vided an indication of the confidence with which your projections should be treated?

6 If your plan involves a significant training and education load for your staff or those of your users, have you made a realistic, properly funded proposal for addressing this requirement?

7 Is your plan an element in a well-articulated strategy (or for a corporate venture, clearly consistent with the official corporate strategy)?

8 Have you provided a clear staffing plan, setting out starting (and where required by the plan, termination) dates, qualifications, outline training plans and remuneration proposals for each class of employee?

9 Does the venture management team command respect? If there are clear skill or experience gaps, does the plan set out well-thought-out, properly funded proposals to address them?

10 Is there a clearly set out remuneration proposal for the management team? Does it strike a proper balance between offering an incentive to the managers and protecting the interests of the other stakeholders?

11 Are the pro forma accounts clearly set out and easily appreciated? For a corporate venture, do they conform to corporate standards?

12 Does the plan include an adequate level of financial analysis, with cash balance and breakeven projections, an estimate of the target and worst case rate of return and a discussion of the risks and the planned responses to them?

Notes

1   Professor Karl Vesper (1993), one of the pioneers of American entrepreneurship scholarship, called them 'countless'. See for example: Abrams (1991); Banfe (1991); Bangs and Schaper (2001); Bell and McNamara (1991); Berle (1989); Blechman and Levinson (1991); Brandt (1982); Cohen (1990); Crego et al. (1986); Day (1991); Eckert et al. (1985); Fry (1993); Golis (1998); Kuratko and Hodgetts (2004); Longenecker and Moore (1991); Lynn (1989); McLaughlin (1987); McQuown (1992); Nesheim (1992); Osgood and Curtin (1984); Osgood et al. (1986); Rice (1990); Rich and Peters (1989); Rich and Gumpert (1985b); Richardson and Richardson (1992); Roberts (1983); Ronstadt (1989); Ryan (1985); Sahlman and Stevenson (1992); Samson (1988); Schillit (1990); Siegel et al. (1988); Stevenson et al. (1999); Taylor (1986); Timmons (1990); Vesper (1993); Vogelaar (1991a, 1991b); Welsh and White (1983).

2   Based on remarks made by Hamel at a seminar in Melbourne in 1995.

3   Students may have a little trouble getting at national statistics, apart from those of the USA, which are available to all on the Internet. Their own national statistics may be accessible through their university library, as may some European statistics for students in the EU. Other statistical information may have to be paid for.

4   For example, if a model based on essentially correct assumptions predicted 50 sales in a given year, the rules from Chapter 4 suggest that the annual sales will most likely fall between 45 and 55 units. In any one month, the expected value is 4.5 and any outcome between 2 and 7 is consistent with the model.

5   PERT = programme evaluation and review technique.

12 Investment and investors

This chapter

- In this chapter we will outline the various sources of finance available to a new enterprise. We will outline the financing stage model, as a convenient way to indicate who not to approach at various points in a business's development. We will also, for each class of investor, provide a thumbnail sketch indicating how their motivation will interact with that of the entrepreneur, how much money they may be able to provide and what they expect in return.

- Readers will gain an appreciation of the various sources of capital an entrepreneurial venture might draw on, and should be able to determine which finance sources should, and which should not, be approached as a venture develops.

- Venture financing is the subject of many substantial textbooks and is taught as a full-semester unit in entrepreneurship courses and entrepreneurship majors in well-structured MBA programmes. This chapter may serve as an introduction to such texts and courses, but not as a substitute for them.

Raising finance

Corporate entrepreneurs struggle round bureaucrats, dodge sniping from their rivals and shrug off carping from their critics, get stuck in an apparently endless cycle of proposal reworking to placate this or that department and continually rebuild their spreadsheets to adjust to the latest edict from the controller's office. They must sometimes envy the individual, creating his own proposal, answering to nobody. The corporate entrepreneur enjoys one magic moment that the individual cannot hope for: when the memo from the controller's office arrives, saying:

> The board has approved your proposal of ... date. Your account number is ... and your attention is drawn to the financial accountability section of the corporate procedures manual. Fred Charisma is your project accountant responsible for preparing monthly progress reports on your project; he must countersign all orders and cheque requisitions in excess of £5000. Please note that the board must approve all contracts involving more than £100,000 per month or capital sums in excess of £1 million.

For the individual entrepreneur and the start-up team, there is no controller's office to play either the wicked or the good fairy. As soon as the team members' per-

Basic research
Funding
  Government grants,
  pro bono foundations and
  institutions,
  personal resources
Return expected
  Public benefit,
  satisfied curiosity

Development/seed
Funding
  Special budget,
  government grant,
  angel or lead customer,
  specialist investor syndicate
  personal resources

Return expected
  Public benefit or
  100% pa return expected or
  corporate portfolio build

Seed/venture
Funding
  Special budget,
  government grant,
  'angel' or lead customer,
  venture capital,
  personal resources

Return expected
  75%+ pa

Venture
Funding
  Venture capital,
  operating budget,
  bank facility

Return expected
  45%+ pa

Maturing
Funding
  Self financing:
  excess cash generated

Return expected
  20%+ pa

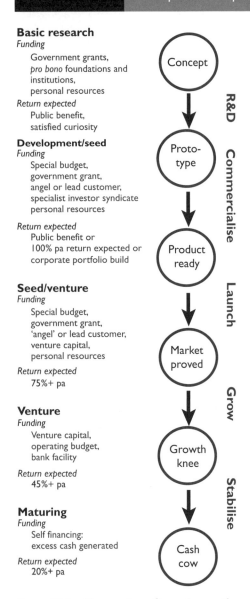

Figure 12.1 **The venture financing path**

sonal financial capacity is fully committed, the rest of the finance for the venture must come from relative strangers, people who start with no particular reason to regard the venture or the entrepreneurial team in a favourable light. The business plan, completed as we described in Chapter 11, provides the essential information that investors will need to review before deciding to support a venture. However, merely preparing a plan does nothing: the right investors must be approached and they must be made an offer that they will find worth considering. (If they accept it at once, it is probably too generous!)

This chapter is organised into two main sections: we follow a venture through its product life cycle and discuss the funding requirements and suppliers of funds at each stage; and we discuss each of the different classes of investor separately.[1]

Figure 12.1 links these together and brings out the point that new venture financing is a continuous process, which parallels the product life cycle. At no stage is financing an action that is completed, banked and forgotten. Even within stages, there may be successive financing steps. In the early stages of a project, the only finance sources for new ventures are informal ones supplemented by government schemes and corporate innovation policies, while once the venture has become an established, profitable and cash-positive business, the successful entrepreneurs will have little trouble securing finance, although there will always be arguments about the terms. Venture capital funds service the gap between the exhaustion of the various informal sources and government subsidies and the arrival of conventional financiers.

Figure 12.1 has been drawn as an open loop, but obviously the cash needed to finance R&D and the early stages of commercialisation must come from somewhere, and most of it comes from the value-added in normal operations during the normal trading activities of established businesses. The value-added in business operations is partly paid out in salaries and senior executives may earn enough to become 'business angels' upon their retirement; part of the value-added is paid as dividends, much of it to investment funds who must then reinvest most of what they get; some of it is paid as taxation, both as income and payroll taxes on employee salaries and as corporate income and other taxes, and this funds the government, which pays some of it out as various forms of R&D support; and some of it is retained within major corporations, where it could be, and sometimes is, spent on early stage development projects.

Listed corporations must keep their share price up and this means not only being profitable and paying dividends, but giving investors confidence that future profits and dividends will be higher than the current ones. Firms whose products have reached the mature stage of their life cycle find it difficult to generate increasing revenue, although a sufficiently ruthless attack on costs can make profits grow for a while and taking over other firms can give the illusion of revenue growth and an opportunity to increase margins. Corporations with no easy takeover targets, whose managers don't want to find themselves a target for some other predator, need a steady supply of products in the growth phase, generating growing revenue and 'new' profits, in order to support their share price.

Corporations can add growth products to their portfolio by buying promising new companies whose products have passed the growth knee but have not yet matured into cash cows. Rapidly growing businesses need cash (which major corporations generally have plenty of) but also generate growing profits, a task which major corporations often find difficult. Alternatively, corporations can 'grow their own growth', providing funds for speculative research and concept development, and bringing the risk back to acceptable levels by spreading it over a sufficient number of projects.[2] Once a sufficient number of unrelated projects are started, even if the expectation of success for any one of them is low, the group as a whole has a defined variance and can be judged on normal financial criteria.

In general terms, single products in the stage labelled 'R&D' in Figure 12.1 are hard to justify on financial grounds for technology-based projects, because the likelihood that a discovery can be turned into a product is low and the chance of it being commercialised before any applicable patents expire is lower still. Some large corporations do support fundamental research, for a mix of reasons. One is the sense of obligation to the community that 20 years of propaganda from 'shareholder value' fanatics has not entirely extinguished. Two further reasons have more private justification: the conduct of (relatively) basic research builds a firm's competencies in the relevant field, making it better able to integrate research results from internal and external sources into its product lines; and the 'lottery' argument: if a firm runs enough projects, even if the probability of any one of them generating lucrative returns is low, the probability that at least one lucrative invention may emerge is rather higher.

Only large firms are able to support large-scale research laboratories and even they are concerned not to spend a higher proportion of their revenue on early stage research than their rivals. There are two main arguments for this caution: one is that R&D expense is generally a charge against profits, and a company that spent an 'excessive' amount on R&D would be seen as a poor performer by the stock markets; and the other is that the boundaries between one firm's R&D facility and another's are anything but leak-proof, and a firm that outspends its rivals may be subsidising rather than gaining a competitive advantage over them.

To the extent that economists have studied R&D, one of the major continuing themes has been 'patent races' and the 'search for rents'. Such studies are predicated on the assumption that there is likely to be too much R&D activity and society as a whole would be better off if there were less. As we mentioned in Chapter 2, Romer and others argue that there is likely to be too little rather than too much R&D in a market economy. Relatively fragmented businesses, like farming, are also unlikely to overinvest in R&D because few individual farmers could afford to operate a research laboratory. For these and other reasons, much pre-commercial research is publicly funded, in universities or other public research institutions.

Very early stage activities present less of a funding problem in consumer products companies and service businesses, since there is, in general, little technology risk and the concept can be elaborated on paper in spare or otherwise unallocated time and so it will appear, at least in the formal accounts of a business, costless. Consumer product and service companies do not face the long delays between prototype and launch that sap the returns of high-tech and metal manufacturing industry companies and often enjoy substantial first-mover advantages once their product is launched, restricting their spillover losses.

Intellectual property protection, such as patents, do not solve the spillover problem facing technology-based products at the concept stage, in part because scientific principles can't be patented, and an otherwise undeveloped concept does not consist of much more than that, but also because a patent granted at the concept stage would often have expired before any cash could have been generated. These rights are not really strong enough to justify a socially desirable level of investment in development and it has been argued with considerable force that in industries such as pharmaceuticals, where most commercially funded development is under patent protection, the outcomes are far from socially optimum.[3]

Finance and project stages

Research stage: Concept to prototype

A concept is an idea: 'wouldn't it be nice to have ..., I wonder why no one makes/does it ...'. Sometimes the idea is well advanced, as when Ray Kroc saw the original McDonald's hamburger restaurant and wondered why people had to drive halfway across America to get a properly prepared hamburger at a fair price in clean surroundings. Sometimes it is little more than a glint in the eye, as when Fleming (later Sir Alexander) looked at a Petri dish and wondered why there were no bacteria inside a little ring around each of a few spots of penicillium mould. Fleming and Kroc lived to see their concepts become real products and realised their respective ambitions: Fleming died at a ripe old age, loaded with honours; while Kroc made a great deal of money and could, at the end of his life, reflect that it had been made honourably. To this day the McDonald's group returns something to the community, including the relatively lavish provision and endowment of apartments near major children's hospitals to allow parents to stay near seriously ill children.

By contrast with the twentieth-century work of Fleming and penicillin, the idea of powered flight is over 2000 years old, and although in 1903 the Wright Brothers built the first heavier-than-air machine to actually get a person off the ground and then safely back to it, very few of the concepts they employed were their own. Even being the successful constructors of the first prototype aircraft did not lead the Wrights into a major position in the aircraft business: it was not until the First World War was well advanced (or well bogged down) 13 years after the Wrights' first flight that aircraft came into serious use as weapons. It was not until 50 years after the Wrights' first flight that civil air transport began to displace trains and ships as the dominant international and intercity passenger transport mode.

Finance

Broadly, a concept will not, in most industries, attract finance from even the most generous venture capitalist. The term 'concept' is used in the film and musical comedy industries to describe what in technology would be called a 'prototype', a plot outline together with the provisional agreement of key people to participate: such concepts do get financed, but by specialists, and the returns to any one project are usually poor to zero, just occasionally remarkable. Films are legally counted as artistic works, with the strong protection against direct imitation provided by copyright, and so the spillover or externality problem can be controlled but, with the development of digital technology and the widening accessibility of the Internet, not eliminated.[4] Service and packaged consumer goods industries take concepts seriously, but don't generally pay outsiders for them; large companies in these fields employ staff whose job it is to think up new products and new ways to present and market established ones, and if they get suggestions from the public they may consider them, but they won't pay for them.

Firms with a technology-based concept can apply for a grant under one of the various government R&D schemes, or form an alliance with a researcher in a university department or other research organisation, and try to prove the concept to prototype stage. People who want to be involved in advanced technology, but don't have a fully worked out concept, can approach a university department or a research institution working in their field of interest and ask if they have any research ready for commercialising. They will often be offered their choice of a large number of promising projects: one reason why it is hard to sell a concept is that there are so many of them around.

People and firms whose concept is essentially a service or software one should start building an informal team to elaborate it, at least to prototype and possibly to market testing stage, before they make any attempt to approach any unrelated person for support. There are a number of government-aided centres in many countries where such firms and entrepreneurs can get introductions to potential partners. British examples include the London Innovation Centre (http://www.london-innovation.org.uk/), or other programmes run by the Department of Trade and Industry (http://www.innovation.gov.uk/). Australian examples include the Victorian Innovation Centre (iNNOVIC http://www.innovic.com.au) in Melbourne and the Australian Graduate School of Engineering Innovation (http://www.agsei.edu.au/) in Sydney.

Development stage: Prototype to product

A prototype is a realised concept, built to prove technical feasibility. It must work, although it does not have to work well, and it need not look exactly like a finished product. If it is a physical object, it may have been handcrafted at vast expense; if it is a piece of software, it might run incredibly slowly and be subject to various glitches; if it a new musical, the score may be sketched out on a piano and the author may stand in for the chorus line; but whatever it is, the prototype will be seen as proof that the concept 'works'.

A great deal of effort needs to be applied to turn a prototype into a marketable product: the mechanical prototype must become a smoothly operating and well-presented device suitable for volume production, and the production details such as bills of materials, operations plans and the like must all be complete; the software must work reasonably reliably and rapidly, be in a form suitable for installation and have complete documentation ready for the printer or CD-ROM publisher; the musical must have a full score and complete choreography, actors, singers and chorus fully rehearsed, the scenery built and every other detail of the production finished.

While it is rare for an unsurmountable problem to occur during the commercialisation process, the process is often subject to delay. Delays may be due to individuals: development of a musical show might have been started in the expectation that a particular star would be available to open it, and any number of things can delay this; or a product might have to meet stringent certification conditions, and minor issues force one or more sets of trials to be resubmitted. Plans for the development phase of a new product should not assume that 'it will all be right on the night'; such an attitude almost guarantees that it won't. Two useful proverbs that an entrepreneur undertaking product development should recite regularly are: 'more haste, less speed', and 'better late than never'. One of the worst things that can happen to a development project is that a salesperson takes charge of it: enthusiasm and determination are great attributes in a salesperson, but in a development manager they encourage short cuts and expedients that often lead to unnecessary delays in bringing the product to market. Short cuts almost inevitably insert hidden flaws which will cause trouble once the product has reached customers; if the managers in Exicom (liquidated in 1996) who decided to skip humidity testing in their telephone development project[5] could turn back the clock, a different decision would be taken the second time around.

The Boeing 777

The Boeing Commercial Aircraft Company abandoned many traditional practices when developing the B777. New aircraft development had traditionally been carried out in great secrecy, so as to keep the new ideas away from possible competitors; but this also kept them away from potential customers and the certification authorities.

Boeing, on the B777 project, gave several major airlines and the US Civil Aviation Authority (CAA) general read access to its design databases, so that they could make suggestions and start planning their tests

long before anything capable of flying was built.

Previous Boeing aircraft had had to undergo up to two years of testing after the first aircraft was completed, while sales negotiations got bogged down in trivia such as the location of lavatories and the size of the galleys. The B777 completed its CAA testing in months, rather than years, and the airlines had all their small requests catered for while it was a matter of changing a database, not cutting aluminium, and so deliveries could start almost the day certification was complete.

Finance

Professional investors are extremely unlikely to agree to back even the most promising development projects without some special encouragement, not only because the hurdle rates they would apply would make it difficult to come to an agreement with the entrepreneurs, but also because of the large amount of management time a development project requires. Most product development in technology and technology-dependent industries takes place within corporations or is organised by members of fairly tight groups of specialist financiers.

When corporations undertake product development, they rely on their combined corporate competencies in applying the relevant technology, managing related development projects and selling the result into a reasonably well-defined group of markets. Corporate entrepreneurs are involved in the selection, management and marketing of these projects and financial criteria are used to choose between them, but the finance is often treated as a normal expense of doing business in the relevant industry rather than a freestanding investment. When a 'paper entrepreneur' or asset-stripper gets hold of a company, one of the first things to get slashed is the development budget: the result is a major boost to short-term profits and the share price, bought at the cost of long-term corporate decline and ultimate failure.

Many entrepreneurs complete their development stage without any formal financing, running up bills on their credit cards, borrowing from friends or relatives and drawing down their savings. Entrepreneurs may keep their day job, working on development part time or at weekends, or taking contract jobs to build up their finances between bursts of work on their project. Entrepreneurs with life partners may live off their partner's income while they work on product development.

Other entrepreneurs raise what they need in relatively small sums from their friends and acquaintances:[6] with an average of 110 people in each person's 'chatter group', no single acquaintance need put up very much in order to get a tidy amount of money together. Such payments are more in the nature of gifts than investments: the people who subscribe should treat the money as spent, be grateful if they ever get any of it back and ecstatic if they get a positive return. Language fails to express the appropriate response if they find they have backed the next *Crocodile Dundee*,[7] but astonishment is a good start.

The reason professional investors avoid development projects is that the major risk to every venture, that of rejection by potential customers, is only tested once development is complete. Some entrepreneurs have been able to short-circuit both the risk and the professional investors by selling their concept, supported by a real or virtual[8] prototype, directly to its probable customers and taking deposits against future deliveries. Property developers do this when they sell 'off the plan' and home building firms do it when they demand a deposit and progress payments from their customers. There are, of course, plenty of opportunities for fraud in such arrangements and both parties would be well advised to get their lawyers to check any related agreements, but the elements of a win–win coalition are still there: the customers get exactly what they want and the entrepreneurs gain access to the finance needed to give it to them.

Suppliers are sometimes willing to back a venture in its fairly early stages, not so much for the direct financial benefits from the investment as much as the possibility that the venture, if successful, will attract many imitators and the final outcome will be a substantially increased demand for the supplier's product. Often such support is channelled through industry associations.

The term 'angels' came from Broadway, the centre of American commercial theatre. 'Angel' was the somewhat cynical term applied to investors who could be encouraged to finance new stage productions with uncertain financial prospects; the investor's return came, in part, from the opportunity to associate with the stars and participate in the general theatrical glamour. The modern business angel is a little more prosaic, providing a financial injection in return for an opportunity for personal participation in a development or early stage marketing project. Business angels are often retired executives who want an opportunity to use the skills that they spent their working lifetime developing; they anticipate a reasonable return on their investment and certainly don't expect to lose their money, but much of their return comes from the pleasure they get from being active and involved for a few hours per week, without the stresses of personal entrepreneurship or full-time employment.

Launch stage: Market proving

We use the term 'launch stage' to cover the period immediately following the first time a new product is offered for sale; others call it the 'early growth' phase. As we explain here, the reasons why there is a distinction between a launch/early growth phase and a growth/fast growth phase are financial, not market-based. If a venture's or new product's marketing campaign is optimally funded on the day of the launch, and the product is destined for success, the growth/fast growth stage starts immediately and this stage is skipped.

A product can only be destined for success when a sufficiently large number of people want it badly enough to pay for it. There is only one real way to discover if potential purchasers want a product: it is to offer the product to them at an economically viable price and see if they buy it. Even this immediate response does not guarantee the success of an enterprise: early customers must repurchase and/or recommend it if sales are to grow faster than marketing expenditure and the product is to deliver a satisfactory profit on its investment.

Some products have very high margins. Such products may only need market development finance during the months surrounding the launch, when marketing expenditure is going out and revenue from sales is yet to flow in, and growth beyond this stage can be financed directly from revenue. The only costs beyond marketing expenditure incurred by the producer of a successful film after opening night are the trivial ones of reproducing and transporting copies of the film to the many cinemas eager to show it. The same applies to a new computer software package. By contrast, a new manufactured product may earn gross margins of 20–30 per cent, and for each pound of new sales in a month, financing is required for 70–80 pence worth of inventory, work in progress and debtors for the three or more months between the time when suppliers must be paid and the manufacturer's share of the retail or user dollar finally filters back.

The marketing expense can, of itself, be a major item, even for high margin products. The major film production companies limit the risk of wasting marketing expenditure on a flop by showing a film to preview audiences. They do not commit to the expense of a full launch until the response of the trial audiences convinces them that early audiences will recommend the film to the extent needed, at least, to comfortably cover their marketing expenditure.

A small-scale film producer must bear the expense of early marketing and possibly even the rental costs of a few cinemas in order to carry out a market test, and only when the test is successful are they likely to get the money they need for a full-scale launch from a major distributor or production company. Independent film producers are just one example of an entrepreneur without the support of a major, cash-rich company. Such entrepreneurs need money to distribute and promote their product in order to prove that the market will accept it, but conventional financial sources are extremely reluctant to provide finance for a new enterprise until they can see proof that the market has, in fact, accepted its products.

Entrepreneurs with strictly limited ambitions may not find the absence of external finance a major problem. If they had set out to create a new small business, they need sufficient money to live and pay any fixed expenses of the business for a couple of years, but at the end of that time either the business is capable of surviving and paying wages or a little more or they have learned the lessons taught by failure and either started again or gone back to work for someone else. It might be an idea with tremendous potential, but without sufficient finance to launch a major marketing effort the potential will not be realised. If the idea is a good one and a more ambitious entrepreneur picks it up, the idea's original creators may or may not get something out of it. Ray Kroc paid the McDonald brothers for the use of their name and their concept as, for a while, the KFC Company did when it paid Colonel Saunders for the use of his face in its advertising and his recipe in its kitchens.

Entrepreneurs with more general ambitions need to keep their business, and its business plan, alive while they prove that their product can not only gain sales from new customers, but satisfy them to the point that they will return for more and tell their friends and acquaintances about it. At some point they will find a venture capital supplier of some type ready to open negotiations with them and they are ready to drive their business into its growth phase.

Corporate entrepreneurs should also prove that their product will be acceptable to the market before they call for a full-scale launch. This may take the form of extensive research, test marketing or even a significant production and marketing effort: Sony Corporation made a million Walkman cassette player-radios for their market trial. If such a trial is successful, very few major corporations will be unwilling to finance a proper launch, at least in the corporation's domestic market.

Finance

There are very few grants available for market proving of new products, but some countries offer export facilitation schemes for particular product classes.

Distributors, assemblers and major retailers can sometimes be approached successfully for assistance at the market proving stage; not usually with an equity investment; but a firm order or, even better, a firm order accompanied by a deposit will have a marvellous effect on the willingness of venture capital funds to support the new enterprise. By and large venture capitalists avoid firms without a sales record, counting the market risk as too high, but an order from a major name in the appropriate industry can change their view of that. The major names are not, in general, looking for a specific return on an investment, but for products that leverage their entire product line. When a supermarket chain like Sainsbury's or Safeway lists

A small suburban plant nursery near Melbourne developed a line of inexpensive, but attractive orchids and approached Woolworth Ltd (trading as Safeway in Victoria). Woolworth saw that the orchids were decorative and would attract customers with discretionary income who might go on to buy other relatively high-margin lines.

Woolworth waived all their listing, slotting and co-promotion fees and placed the orchids in a number of Melbourne supermarkets, where the sales did not disappoint Woolworth and were a major boost to the nursery. It applied the substantial margins it earned on sales through Woolworth in order to expand its growing facilities and increase its product range.

a new product, it will be one of the 200,000 or more in their computers; good, bad or indifferent, its performance won't perceptibly alter their bottom line. If, however, the product attracts more customers to their stores, who then add the product to a trolley-load of groceries that they might otherwise have bought at a rival store, the retailer will find the listing decision more than justified.

Many entrepreneurs look to their family and friends to continue supporting them into the market proving phase; it is important that entrepreneurs who rely on this support during the development phase do not exhaust it then, because it will still be needed when the development is completed and market proving has begun.

The growth stage

As we explained earlier, the period we call the 'growth stage' is called the 'fast growth stage' by some writers, but if growth is faster in this stage than during the previous one, it is because the marketing of the new product is better financed.

'New name' marketing involves a large expense for little immediate net return; firms, as we explained in Chapter 4, should not plan on earning a positive contribution margin from early sales to first time users after meeting sales and marketing expenses. The profits, if any, come from the early users' repurchasing and recommendations. If most early users are extremely satisfied, practically all of them will repurchase the product. If the product is in a category where recommendation is important, satisfied users' recommendations can be so effective that one new user enters the market spontaneously every year for every two such users. Depending on the frequency with which users return to the market, it takes between three months and two years to build up enough data to establish the recommendation and repurchase rates by statistical analysis.

Packaged consumer goods companies don't wait that long: they send market researchers to the supermarkets a month after the launch and ask people with the new product in their trolley whether this is their first or subsequent time of purchase. Many supermarket chains have introduced loyalty schemes where a customer presents a personalised card when checking out: these cards, combined with the scanner data and a certain amount of computer processing, enable the repurchase rate for new products to be estimated quite accurately.

The successful introduction of a new packaged consumer good can be extraordinarily remunerative if the churn rate of the customer base remains relatively low, such that the average customer continues to repurchase the product for at least two years. The major consumer product companies know this, which is why they are prepared to launch new lines with as little as a 10 per cent chance of surviving a year on the supermarket shelves.

Successful new consumer and intermediate durable products aren't as instantly lucrative as successful consumption products and so, with a few exceptions such as motorcars and advanced computing equipment, there are no giant corporations blazing away at the market with what resembles a bombardment[9] of new products. Even in the motorcar and computing equipment industries, the major companies control a relatively small fraction of the total value-added, and there are many openings for new entrants to supply components or complementary products. Occasionally, as with Microsoft, the component supply business may demonstrate extraordinary growth and profit.

Venture capitalists are attracted by new, market proved products because of the relatively high returns for relatively moderate risk. They offer to manage the entrepreneur's capital-raising and offer other management assistance in return for a share of the business. The venture capitalist's eyes are not on the profits made by the business during the growth phase as much as what happens when growth starts to slow down, the point at which approximately half the potential customers have been reached. At this point the enterprise still has substantial growth prospects and is both profitable and cash positive: it is the sort of business that a major corporation would like to have as a division or it may be suitable for a stock market flotation. A successful sale to a corporation can be quite lucrative: the venture capitalist firm Advent Corporation turned a $5 million investment in the 'bionic ear' firm Cochlear to $20 million in three years when they sold the business to Pacific Dunlop (who floated it separately three years further down the track for double the purchase price). Three years later Cochlear's market capitalisation had doubled again. The stock market flotation is the prospect that every venture capitalist dreams about.

Finance

During the whole of the five- to seven-year growth phase, a growing business may require new capital to finance its debtors ledger, cover material and equipment costs, throw a defensive ring of product variants around its core product and keep driving the market. As a very rough rule of thumb, each financing round needs to raise twice as much as the preceding one and the financiers are allocated the same fraction of the shares. The founding entrepreneurs have no spare cash (if they had they would not have invited venture capitalists to their party) and the firm is not in a position to pay them substantial dividends. For this reason they won't be able to buy shares in the various new issues and they will rapidly find themselves minority investors in 'their' enterprise.

Table 12.1 shows how the equity-financing process works in an idealised case: although the venture's founders become paper multimillionaires, and real ones if they sell their interests after a successful stock market float or if their firm gets absorbed by a major corporation at a fair price, their formal control of the venture falls quite dramatically. The way in which venture financing through equity extrudes the entrepreneur from control of the enterprise has led to the tag 'vulture capitalists'

Table 12.1 **Stylised venture investment pattern (observe the dilution of the founder's equity)**

Finance stage	Nominal share price	Shares issued (000s)	Shares on issue (000s)	Founders' holding (%)	Founders' value (000s)
0			600	100	
1	2.50	400	1000	60	1500
2	5.00	400	1400	43	3000
3	10.00	400	1800	33	6000
4	20.00	400	2200	27	12,000
5	40.00	400	2600	23	24,000
6	80.00	400	3000	20	48,000

First venture capitalist pays 1 million for 40 per cent of the venture being applied to venture capital firms, and there are many examples of venture capitalists removing the founding entrepreneur from the chief executive's position once the firm starts to grow.

Such extruded entrepreneurs may denounce the venture capitalists as vultures; they may even (misguidedly) demand to be bought out of the enterprise. The supposed vultures have their own story to tell: phrases such as 'pig-headed', 'erratic' and 'no sense of running a business' will generally occur frequently.

Sometimes an entrepreneur retains full control in spite of the selling-down process; the two essential ingredients are managerial competence and a sound understanding of the financing process. In the mid 1990s the Toyota Company broke with a long tradition and appointed a chief executive who was not from the Toyoda family. At the time the last Toyoda was appointed, the family's entire shareholding accounted for about 1 per cent of the voting capital; the financial institutions and individuals who owned the rest of the Toyota stock would not have wanted to hurt the feelings of the founder's family unnecessarily, but if the members of the Toyoda family had not been competent managers, the shareholders would have overcome their sense of deference rapidly enough.

Founders who want to retain control do not always have to rely on the sensitivity of their major shareholders. Golis (1998) describes a meeting with an American entrepreneur who was in rock-solid control of his fully financed enterprise: this entrepreneur had taken charge of the capital-raising from the beginning, and placed every tranche with a different syndicate so successfully that the second largest holding on the register, after the entrepreneur's, was only 5 per cent of the voting stock. Where the founders are personally important to the ongoing success of the venture, they may be able to negotiate arrangements involving options and partly-paid shares that strengthen their control, but such arrangements must make the venture less attractive to other equity investors and, where such arrangements exist, new investors may wish to pay less for shares than they otherwise would.

Exit and harvest	No market is infinite and a stage will be reached when the only people to whom satisfied users can recommend the product will be each other. If there has been sufficient continuing expenditure on enhancing the product and maintaining its market position, the strong preference its users have for it will not be challenged by the firm's competitors. Mature products can earn good margins; the revenue they generate will not, however, be capable of being grown much faster than the economy. Fast growth typically ends well before the market is actually saturated, usually when the market has reached about half its ultimate penetration.

In a market, even one with several active competitors, it doesn't make financial sense for any one competitor to detach satisfied customers from the others: the cost, in sales effort and marketing expense, simply exceeds the value of the revenue stream that such detached customers provide. Two factors are at work to limit the financial rewards to competitive capture programmes:

- among the people who switch suppliers in response to a special promotion, there will be a high proportion of people who form weak product loyalties and are therefore likely to switch to yet another supplier if offered a promotional incentive

■ many of the people who buy the attacking product while the incentives are on offer will return to their original choice as soon as the incentives are removed.

Firms operating in relatively mature markets cannot rely totally on the rationality of their competitors, and from time to time one firm may launch a major promotion aimed at gaining market share without any way to retain the customers gained. More dangerously for the complacent, an attack may be launched on the back of an innovation that does make the aggressor's product more desirable, so a significant proportion of those users who trial the attacking product stay with it. Sporadic promotional wars and occasional innovations mean that the cash flow from products in a mature market is not perfectly stable but it tends to be consistently positive, so the shares in companies marketing such products are attractive to those financial institutions whose own businesses involve paying out money as pensions or insurance claims.

Life assurance and superannuation funds expect their investments to yield stable cash flows to meet their pension and annuity commitments; to have high liquidity so as to be able to pay insurance claims on demand; and command steadily rising share prices in order to make their funds attractive to prospective policy buyers and superannuation contributors. New venture investments, no matter how socially desirable or valuable in the long term, fail on all three of the criteria used by life assurance and superannuation fund managers. By contrast, firms with a portfolio of products with substantial market shares in mature markets are very attractive to these financial institutions.

Finance Financial institutions are continually looking for suitable new investments; simply buying shares in established companies pushes the price up without increasing the dividends that the funds receive. Although the funds won't back new ventures, they rely on entrepreneurs to generate a steady supply of new enterprises that meet their particular requirements:

■ most financial institutions have a small pot of 'funny money' which they will put into syndicates providing third or fourth round finance to growing ventures
■ large corporations are placed under pressure by demands from their institutional shareholders for high dividends as well as steady growth – this discourages corporations from investing in their own new products and encourages them to buy firms whenever the cost of the cash flow is lower than their own average price/earnings ratio
■ if a new enterprise has grown to noticeable size, the managers of some of the smaller, more specialised funds will be willing to participate in a syndicate that underwrites a public flotation of it.

Small is a relative term; a start-up entrepreneur would not consider a million dollars as trivial, but to the managers of major superannuation and life insurance funds, a million pounds is an irritation, a nuisance if it gets mislaid and the auditors complain, and nice if a few extra ones turn up as the result of some long-forgotten investment, but of no real significance to their business.

In America, but not, so far, in most other countries, there is a high-volume market for corporate debt and so the major investment funds can secure the stable cash flow they crave by buying interest-bearing corporate securities and corporations can, at least in theory, provide capital for their stable lines from debt and apply their shareholders' funds to product and market development. This may be one of the reasons why share prices in the US rose steadily through the first half of the 1990s while those in many other countries grew slowly, if at all.

Investors and their criteria

People who support a new enterprise with money or other assets are investors, but the term covers many different classes of people and firms, each of which will have its own special considerations, both for investing in the first place and the type of returns they expect. Below, we provide thumbnail sketches of the various classes of investor that an entrepreneur might deal with, what they expect for their participation and the areas where they are likely to show particular concern. Table 12.2 provides a summary of this information.

Personal resources

Personal resources must be considered first, for the simple reason that an entrepreneur will have a great deal of trouble persuading people to invest in an enterprise which the entrepreneur is not personally prepared to support. In Table 12.2 we suggest that £4000 is a reasonable level of personal commitment; even entrepreneurs who do not have that much cash in their purse or wallet can usually raise it from a bank as a personal loan or a credit card limit. A failed venture's creditors will pursue the entrepreneur's home and any other personal assets, so a decision to become an entrepreneur means putting these assets at risk.

Any competent accountant or lawyer can draw up a scheme of trusts and gifts which places an entrepreneur's personal assets far out of the reach of the entrepreneur's creditors; any responsible bank manager or venture fund manager will look for such arrangements and, if they are found, will treat any proposal from such an entrepreneur with deep suspicion. Modern bankruptcy laws are far less severe than those of Elizabethan or even Victorian England, and in most developed countries bankrupts (and their families) are allowed to keep the tools of their trade, their personal clothing, certain jewellery such as wedding rings, a sound second-hand car and retain enough of their income to provide food and rent a modest house.

Bankrupts are not generally able to retain their houses, pay private school fees or excessive health insurance, keep a fleet of luxury cars or even take an overseas holiday without permission from their trustee. People for whom the prospect of enduring such privations for three years or more is intolerable should not set out to found a new venture.

Life partner

Many people are blessed with the loving companionship of another person and many successful entrepreneurs have relied on their life partner to provide food and shelter during the early years of an enterprise. Before an entrepreneur with such a partner runs up any substantial debts, the two need to agree about a number of issues; they may even be well advised to have a lawyer draw up an appropriate agreement.

Table 12.2 **Venture investors' summary**

Source	Amount	Will support if ...	Won't support if ...
Personal resources	£4,000 plus assets	Serious about venture	
Life partner	Living expenses; permission to mortgage family home	Trust in relationship	
Family and friends	£5,000–£100,000+	Minimal belief in venture; confidence in entrepreneur	No belief in venture
Government	Varies	Scheme conditions met (refer to Chapter 8 and individual scheme guidelines)	■ Proper forms not followed ■ Procedural error ■ Budget allocation exhausted
Business angel	'Cherubs' to £10,000; 'Seraphim' to £200,000	■ Reasonable prospects for venture ■ Opportunity for involvement in management and planning	'You want my money but you don't want me'
Customers, suppliers	Orders, letters of comfort, deposits, facilities, extended credit	Strong possibility of leverage; alliance may increase partner's throughput and/or margins	No apparent benefit from adopting new product
Venture capitalist	£1 million–£5 million	■ High confidence in market acceptance of product ■ High confidence in integrity and capability of management team ■ Strong business plan ■ Clean exit and harvest probable ■ Reassuring cash flow and breakeven analysis	■ Product not ready for market ■ Any doubts about integrity or commitment of venture team ■ Failure to agree on key performance indicators and/or action if they are not met ■ Demand by entrepreneurs for permanent control ■ Mark of the 'living dead'
Lease finance	Up to £5 million; more possible	Credible promise to pay lease charges	Any doubt about recourse to leased property or equipment
Bank	Varies with security and general economic conditions	Credible promise to pay interest and agreed repayments	Doubt about security
Corporate bond	Units of US$50 million	(Market US-based, but developing in other countries.) Firm rated by recognised credit agency	Wrong part of economic cycle
Private share investor(s)	£1000–£50,000 each	■ Investors understand industry and/or product ■ Prospect of substantial capital gain or secure income stream ■ Prospect of shareholder benefits	Other individuals not willing to invest
Institutional share investor	No limit	■ Secure and stable or growing cash flows ■ Reasonably liquid market in shares	■ Other institutions not willing to invest ■ Due diligence criteria not met

> He that hath wife and children hath given hostages to fortune; for they are impediments to great enterprises, either of virtue or mischief.
>
> *Francis Bacon, first Baron Verulam and Viscount St Albans (1625),*
> *'Of Marriage and the Single Life', Essays*

There are upsides and downsides to look out for. If the enterprise fails and ravenous creditors start hammering on the front door, the life partner may wish to say: 'Be off! This house is mine, as are all the cars in the garage, the jewels in the safe and the shares in my thick portfolio. My unfortunate lover owns nothing but the clothes he stands up in.' If this statement is backed by a properly drawn up legal agreement, the baffled bailiffs must withdraw, snarling to their kennels.

Should unhappy differences arise between the parties, the supporting partner can of course pull the agreement out of the drawer, push the ex-lover out the front door, and declaim: 'Be off! This house is mine' and so on. If the differences arise after the enterprise has become wildly successful, the entrepreneurial partner may use the agreement as an excuse to leave the ex-lover in charge of the house, jewels and so on while keeping sole ownership of the founder's share of the venture. If the dispute finds its way into the courts, the house, clothes, share portfolio and the founder's shares in the venture may all be sacrificed to keep a number of lawyers employed.

Successful business partnerships are not based on lust or a superior capacity for browbeating. An entrepreneur who relies on a life partner for support is morally and prudentially obliged to explain the risks and options to that partner, and if they can't agree on the appropriate sharing of risks and obligations, either to abandon the relationship or the enterprise. If a couple want to draw up a legal agreement during the period while a new venture is being founded, they also need to agree to update it regularly. They can, of course, dispense with the legal agreement altogether and take their chances together, as joint venturers, joint guarantors of the venture's debts and joint participants in the eventual rewards for success.

Family and friends

A person's family and friends form a network of mutual obligation and respect, and friends who will not help each other out to the extent of a few hundred or even a thousand pounds are poor friends indeed. As long as such arrangements stay informal, with a verbal agreement to repay the money when it is possible, the friendship is not being abused.

The two deep traps are the de facto partnership and the loan guarantee. If the written or other understandings between the entrepreneur and the entrepreneur's friends and obliging relatives take certain forms, it may be possible, in law, to infer that a partnership agreement existed and the friends, as partners, would in consequence become 'jointly and severally' liable for the venture's debts. This means that the creditors can pursue the friends on the basis of their ability to pay, not the size of their contribution: friends may legitimately be asked for a few hundred pounds to help one another, but they should not be entrapped into pledging their house to the success of their friend's venture.

The loan guarantee is a harmless looking explosive device: a lender promises to cover the entrepreneur's financial needs if someone, usually a parent, affluent sibling or close friend, will guarantee it. The standard guarantee contract that the parent, sibling or friend will be asked to sign is unlimited. Although the loan may be for £5000 or £10,000, the guarantee document pledges the guarantor's entire wealth: house, car, savings – the lot. If the venture fails, the guarantor may be pursued for sums far greater than the original loan, with the costs of the pursuit added like arsenic-green icing on a poisoned cake. The courts have repeatedly upheld such guarantees and their consequences.

Loan guarantees are superficially attractive, and slightly more so when the lender will agree to limit the guarantor's liability in default to the principal amount of the loan, but the entrepreneur is still obliged to pay interest at a time when the venture is unlikely to be generating a positive cash flow, and may have no sales at all. The interest simply compounds, eventually forcing the lender to seize the venture and/or the security so as to recover the principal and the accrued interest.

Government schemes

The bases for government support schemes available are described in Chapter 8; the details vary from time to time and country to country, and entrepreneurs should make a serious effort to ensure that their applications for government support, if any, are directed to schemes currently operating and that the applications meet the specific requirements of that scheme. The public servants and quasi-voluntary committees administering these schemes are almost all perfectly sincere in their desire to help new and growing ventures, and their duties include spending their budget allocation; they get no praise for spending too little. They are, however, tightly bound by the auditing rules of their respective public services, and shouting at them will not overcome the problems they will have in responding favourably to a partial, inconsistent or misdirected application.

Customers and suppliers

Potential customers and suppliers are often an important source of support for a new enterprise, but they are only rarely prepared to become formal investors. Requests for money do not always get a good reception, however they are phrased. Customers and suppliers look for leverage possibilities, the chance that, if the venture is successful, their own throughput and/or margins will rise substantially. When they see such possibilities, they will look for opportunities to support the venture by means short of direct investment.

Customers may give conditional orders; they may also assist with marketing research and may even provide introductions to the purchasing executives in their rivals' organisations. If they have technical facilities, they may give the venture access to them or even lend expensive equipment to the venture. If the product is one that needs better testing, a partner-customer may arrange it. Suppliers will often assist with materials; they too may offer help with marketing research and introductions.

Most of all, suppliers and customers offer credibility: not only every venture capital fund manager but every bank manager has heard of Tesco and Ford. If firms as important as this take the new venture seriously, the bank or fund manager must do so too.

Business angels

The model business angel is a retired executive, 55 years or older, living on generous superannuation or other investment income, who does not want to return to full-time employment but still wishes to make use of the skills developed over a working career. Angels, in the conventional model, are not usually expected to put up large sums of money; £10,000 would be a lot but they do expect to contribute their time and knowledge to the venture.

Because angels are private, they are not always easy to identify and such research as has been done casts some doubt on the model in the previous paragraph. Wenban et al. (1996) reported on a research project that was completed in 1995. The project managed to find and get information from approximately 40 Australian angels, and the results, in brief, are:

- they were largely male – it appears that women prefer to be partners or proprietors rather than informal venture investors
- they could be divided into two distinct groups, based on the size of their preferred investment tranche:
  - part of the group, called 'cherubs' in the paper, invest in amounts around A$25,000 (£10,000)
  - the 'seraphim' invest $500,000 (£200,000) or more in a single enterprise
- their backgrounds were also diverse:
  - some were well-educated professionals, with undergraduate degrees and sometimes postgraduate qualifications, in the age group 35–45
  - others were older 'battlers', who may not even have completed secondary education but had built a substantial asset base through operating their own business
- their main financial criteria for selecting investee firms were, first, the prospect of effective annual rates of return of 30 per cent or higher, and, second, the strength of the prospective cash flows the investee firms could generate
- the dominating non-financial factor in choosing investee firms was the angel's evaluation of the management team, and they also placed significant weight on the market growth potential.

In America, research has found that 'informal' finance plays a far greater role in new enterprise formation than does formal venture capital and may retain its importance even into the growth phase. New entrepreneurial ventures often seek such informal finance, but it is often also sought by the proprietors of established firms trying to grow. The respondents to the survey reported on by Wenban et al. regarded both classes of business as entrepreneurial and there was no unambiguous indication that they preferred one to the other. The importance that they placed on the strength of the management team is a hint that an established firm seeking funds for a growth project might have an edge over a start-up team.

Angels can be found by trawling the entrepreneurial team's friends and acquaintances, asking their lawyers and accountants or participating in one or more of the match-making schemes now available in many countries (a Google search for 'angel matching service' returned 63,800 web references, only a few of which offered to complete sets of ceramic angels). The combination of rapid economic growth and light or variable taxation systems in Southeast Asia has built up a substantial population of potential angels prepared to put £200,000 or more into a venture in a developed western country; they are best approached through mutual friends and we do not suggest that entrepreneurs should buttonhole passers-by in Singapore or Kuala Lumpur.

Venture capitalists

There is a pervasive myth about venture capitalists, to the effect that they are a group of dedicated men and women roving the world looking for promising ideas to back with millions of dollars. George Doriot, an American venture capitalist, did a great deal to set the myth going when, in 1957, his venture capital firm backed the young Ken Olsen with US$77,000 to buy soldering irons and other toys. Olsen and friends founded Digital Equipment Corporation[10] and invented and then innovated the minicomputer. Digital Equipment went from negligible sales in 1957 to US$11 billion in 1989, and George Doriot's venture capital fund ARD got fifty times its money back when Digital was floated on the New York Stock Exchange.

Doriot, in modern parlance, was a particularly blessed angel, not a venture capitalist at all, at least in his relationship with Ken Olsen. Modern venture capitalists do not enter the picture at the soldering iron stage and seldom as early as the launch: they want to see that the venture that they are being asked to back has a product with genuine, sales proven, market appeal. They also tend to focus on 'fashionable' industries and markets, with a view to their eventual harvest by initial public offering (IPO) or trade sale. Reasonably or not, they hope that the market will still be 'hot' when they come to sell their stake, since the price may well be higher under such conditions.

The managers of venture capital funds are intensely suspicious (those that were only moderately suspicious have all been fired) and besieged with proposals. Professional venture capitalists may fund as few as one in every hundred proposals that crosses their desks. Any suspicion about the integrity and commitment of the entrepreneurial team means sudden death to the proposal. If the actual and pro forma accounts are not transparently clear and clearly honest, the fund manager knows that he will have to rebuild the accounts in order to evaluate the proposal, so he will almost always go straight to the next proposal instead. Proposals from technical enthusiasts may get short shrift: at the point that the venture capital fund first invests, the major problem the venture faces is building profitable market share for the products it has, not creating new ones. Proposals that are too long, bound in stiff

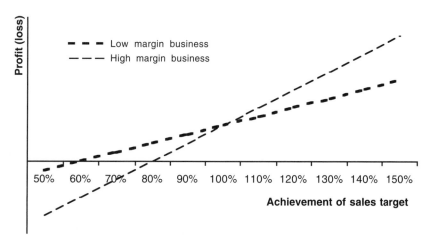

Figure 12.2 **A simple breakeven chart showing the profit impact of various levels of sales achievement**

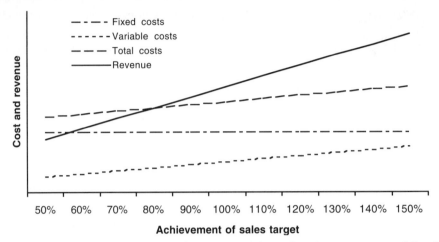

Figure 12.3 **A more conventional breakeven chart showing revenue and fixed and variable costs**

covers or presented with spelling and grammatical errors are begging to be passed over; their wish is usually granted.

Most venture fund managers will look to find some fairly simple ratios and indices when they examine the historic and projected accounts. They will look for a breakeven chart, as in Figure 12.2 or Figure 12.3 and a cash balance projection, as in Figure 12.4. When examining a breakeven chart, the venture fund manager will use the chart to estimate both the upside and downside potential of the business. Obviously if actual sales turn out to be somewhere to the left of the breakeven point, the business will not be able to cover its fixed expenses. For businesses where the variable cost is a high fraction of the price (that is, low contribution margins, as in mass market retail), sales will have to be a long way to the right of the breakeven point in

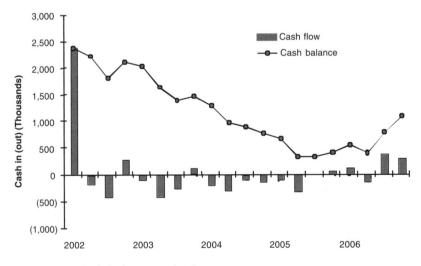

Figure 12.4 **Cash balance projection**

order to generate a decent profit, but from there they are fairly safe from slipping all the way back to a loss. By contrast, with high-margin products such as software and professional services, a business can look very profitable with sales just above the breakeven level, but only a relatively small fall in sales can leave the business making an equally large loss.

A cash balance or cumulative cash flow chart, such as Figure 12.4 (based on ExampleCo from Chapter 10), gives the reviewing manager two vital pieces of information. The first is the low point: in the example shown, the business starts with a cash balance of £2.5 million which falls to just over £300,000 during the fourth year before turning upwards. It could, and probably would, be argued that this is not a particularly attractive pattern from a venture investor's point of view, and so the second point is that examining it suggests ways of improving the outcome. For example, an investor might only inject £1 million at the beginning and only put more in if the actual performance of the firm justifies it. The investment plans might be scrutinised carefully, to see if some purchases could be converted to leases or deferred, while the staff schedule might offer further opportunities for tuning the proposal.

> The dominant question is not 'How will the fund put money in?' but 'How can the fund get it out again?'

Golis (1998) provides a list of indices that he checks when reviewing business plans: these are summarised in Table 12.3. While Chris Golis operates primarily in Australia, he is one of the most thoughtful, and successful, venture capital fund managers outside the USA; his opinions are worth taking seriously.

Once the venture fund manager has found reasons to reject the majority of proposals in front of him, he will start looking for reasons to support some or all of the remainder. The principle behind hurdle rates was explained in Chapter 4: an example, intended to be typical, of a product with two years of sales history, sug-

Table 12.3 **Golis's ratios**

Ratio	Calculation	Expected ranges		
Net margin	Post-tax profits divided by sales revenue (as received, not as at retail)	5%–10%		
Gearing	Ratio of total debt to shareholders' funds	Less than 100%		
Stock, creditors and debtors	Value of stock, debtors and creditors respectively, multiplied by 365 and divided by annual sales gross revenue	Stock greater than 60	Debtors greater than 50	Creditors less than 40
Return on equity	Profits after tax and interest divided by shareholders funds	Greater than 15% at maturity		
Interest cover	Pre-interest cash flow divided by interest payments	Greater than 2		
Annual sales/employee	Recalculate monthly based on planned figure workforce growth but presented as an annualised figure	Not less than £80,000	Not greater than £200,000	
Contribution margin	Recalculate monthly	Industry-dependent		
Breakeven sales	Recalculate monthly	Less than forecast sales		
Manufacturing cost analysis	Specialised figures	To survive examination by independent expert		

Source: Based on Golis 1998

gested that the minimum risk-weighted rate of return acceptable to a venture fund should be about 31 per cent. Venture fund managers, probably suspecting that even the most conscientious entrepreneur cannot resist polishing the financial projections a little, tend to look for 35 per cent or even 40 per cent on the plan, in the hope that they will get at least the 31 per cent minimum in reality. If a firm without any sales can get venture capital support, the hurdle rate used to evaluate its business plan will be closer to 70 per cent.

Since a new venture needs all its cash to grow, the venture fund cannot get any money out as dividends, and when the growth knee is reached, perhaps five years from the date the venture fund invests, and the firm stops growing rapidly, it will have only just started to produce a positive net cash flow. At this point, the venture fund, having put (say) £1 million in, wants between £3.9 million and £5.4 million out. The venture hasn't got it, the entrepreneur hasn't got it, so where is it coming from?

There are really only two possible sources:

- the business can be sold to the public through a float on a national stock exchange or possibly the US electronic market NASDAQ
- the business can be sold to a larger company which sees the venture's products as complementary to its own, and where the venture's profit stream will assist its adoptive parent to report improved earnings.

Successful stock exchange floats are very rewarding for the venture capital funds and the founding entrepreneurs. To be sure of being successful, the float must be underwritten, and underwriters want 5 per cent of the subscriptions plus their considerable expenses; they are not very interested in floats raising small sums. Every stock exchange has its own listing rules, but for the 'main board' on leading exchanges there will be a number of rules and regulations. As an example, the London Stock Exchange expects:

- proper incorporation as a public company (a plc in the UK)
- three years trading history verified by audited accounts
- working capital to sustain 12 month's operations
- no shareholder with more than 30 per cent of the post-listing shares
- at least 25 per cent of the post-listing shares must be with parties totally unrelated to the management
- the market capitalisation must be adequate: as at April 2002 the minimum was £700,000, but this is something of an historic relic and a much higher post-listing capitalisation is expected.

Firms that do not meet the 'main board' requirements may be able to list on a secondary market, such as the London Stock Exchange's AiM or NASDAQ in the US, where the rules are significantly more flexible. Issues on these markets are not usually underwritten and firms down to £10 million capitalisation can get traded, but they must show high margins and high growth to excite traders and buyers in secondary markets.

A sale to a larger company does not need underwriters but it does need a large company that wants to buy the venture. Consumer brands are usually easy to sell: new wine labels, new retail chains, new fast-food concepts (once proven and franchised), but some very profitable ventures are not. High technology, particularly medical high technology, gives the boards of many major corporations palpitations at the thought of the possible negligence suits from dissatisfied users. The major assets of some firms, including software companies, advertising agencies and many forms of brokerage are 'liveware'. A buyer may get nothing but a heap of resignations and some worn desks.

Venture capital fund managers have a rather unkind term, the 'living dead', for firms that don't get quite big enough to float and don't get fashionable enough to find a corporate buyer. Such firms can be vibrant and successful, as far as their employees, customers and founders are concerned, and yet with no buyer the venture fund is 'locked in', drawing dividends but unable to extract its capital. Firms can also become 'living dead' by executive action. If the entrepreneur(s) discover(s) the effect of second and later stage financing, as shown in Table 12.1, they may refuse to allow their shareholding to be diluted any further. Subsequent growth will be slowed or stifled by a lack of capital and, although the venture fund's money is safe, it will be stuck for an extended period of time.

Searchuno (www.serchuno.co.uk) provides a list of venture capital firms in the UK; as at early 2003 there were approximately 60 entries, but this is probably only a sample of the total activity. Australian venture capital funds are listed in the *Venture Capital Guide*, issued regularly by the publishers of the *Venture Capital Journal*; in the 2003 edition there are 143 venture capital firms listed but the guide must be purchased, it is not a free web resource.

Leasing

In general terms, when a new venture requires an item of equipment or access to premises, it will be possible to buy it, using up scarce capital, or arrange to lease it for a regular, usually monthly, payment. Leases come in a rich variety of shapes and sizes, but the basic premise in every case is the equipment is safe from the venture's creditors: if the venture fails, the lessor gets the equipment or the premises back. Since the value of the returned equipment or premises should be positive, the lease company may be able to work on a lower rate of return than the venture: if a venture's natural hurdle rate is 35 per cent, leasing, even at effective interest rates of up to 25 per cent, may be the correct decision.

Entrepreneurs should shop around for their lease finance, remembering that it is a crime in most developed countries to tie the sale of goods to a particular leasing company: a firm that sells them equipment cannot require them to use a particular finance provider. Huge differences in the effective interest rates charged by different leasing companies, and by the same leasing companies at different times, are common, and the other clauses, particularly those covering security deposits and penalties for early termination, will also vary dramatically between lease financiers.

Leasing deals will be killed stone dead by any suspicion concerning the lessor's security of title. If leased equipment is 'sold', either by a corrupt entrepreneur or by bailiffs on behalf of creditors, the lease company faces a long and tortuous legal route to recovering its property, while in the event of a venture's bankruptcy, the lessors of the missing equipment are unsecured creditors without much hope of recovering their money.

Banks create money (see box below) but the machine can run in reverse and destroy money as well. Banks are required to maintain certain prudential ratios, ensuring that depositors' money is not at serious risk. Banks usually stay a little bit on the safe side of the minimum level so as to be able to absorb minor write-offs without triggering a crisis.

If a bank does find its reserves close to the prudential minimum, the consequences of a further loan default are extremely serious. A major bank with €10 billion in equity on the balance sheet and lent 'on the limit' would, in the event of a €100 million bad debt:

- report a capital loss of €100 million, or about 1 per cent of shareholders' funds
- recall or sell to another bank €1.1 billion of loans
- report an earnings reduction of about €110 million until it can dislodge the excess deposits and reduce its recurrent expenses by €50 million or so.

Events such as these would knock the share price down by 10 per cent or more, causing outrage among the major shareholders. Several senior managers might join the many employees who would be shown the door in an attempt to bring expenses back into line with the reduced level of business.

These facts of banking life make banks extremely unwilling to lend money where they might be forced to write it off and they will go to considerable, sometimes ludicrous, lengths to protect themselves. They may ask for personal guarantees for sums that vastly exceed the guarantor's resources; they will try to extend their security over property worth far more than the amount of the loan, if they can get away with it; and they will reject, at least when in an insecure mood, propositions that ordinary people might regard as cast-iron.

When a bank does get into trouble, the process of cutting down the loan book can get ugly and extremely arbitrary. Profitable businesses with ample assets and a perfect payment record have been ordered to return half, or all, of their overdraft at one month's notice and have been forced into receivership, involving a wipeout of the shareholders and substantial losses to the bank, if they could not comply. Other businesses have had their overdraft interest rates pushed to usurious levels on specious 'risk' grounds as a troubled bank desperately tries to rebuild its balance sheet.

During the 1991–92 recession at least one medium-sized business's managers were astounded to be told that a signed, unconditional order from one of the world's richest non-finance companies could not be accepted as security at its face value. In a different case a successful restaurant business with a 15-year trading history and a perfect credit record was given 30 days, starting on Christmas Eve 1991, to reduce its substantial overdraft to zero or see the bank seize the business and the owner's house as well; even in the midst of a recession, this security was conservatively valued at several times the overdraft.[11]

Banks are fair-weather friends, and overdrafts, which may be the only form of finance offered to a small but growing business, are short-term debt and can be

---

Bankers' magic

Banks take deposits from investors and depositors, set a proportion aside as reserves, and then lend the rest. Borrowers use the advance to pay bills, and the people who get paid deposit their cheques in the bank, which then sets aside a fraction as reserves and lends the rest.

Each bank's shareholders' funds act as an insurance for the depositors. If a borrower defaults, shareholders' funds are drawn down, which is bad enough, but the reduced shareholders' funds can now only insure a smaller deposit base, which is worse.

A bank's margin is the difference between the interest it pays depositors and receives from borrowers;

the profit is the margin less expenses – €1 of shareholders funds can support about €12 of lending, and at a typical net margin of 1 per cent, generate €0.12 of profit, or a 12 per cent return on capital.

If a bad debt of €1 has to be written off, the bank must not only report a €1 loss but its lending limit will contract by a further €11. This can leave it overdeposited, with up to €12 of deposits that it can't lend but on which it must pay interest. At 5 per cent interest rates the €1 loss then leads to an annual reduction in margins of up to €0.60 as well excessive fixed costs until the bank can reinstate its capital or persuade €12 worth of depositors to take their money elsewhere.

---

recalled at any time. Even specific, secured term loans often have a clause allowing the bank to recall them or seize the security more or less at will. Listed companies are sometimes able to raise debt finance through fixed interest notes, often 'convertible' notes where the lender can, at its option, be repaid by the issue of a preset number of shares. New ventures may include convertible notes in a venture investment package organised by a venture capital fund, but they are unlikely to find banks among buyers of such securities.

Corporate bonds

In the US there is a large, active market in corporate bonds, usually fixed interest, fixed-term securities. Each lender is graded and regularly rerated by the ratings agencies, so the buyers of these bonds can choose from a range, with government-guaranteed debt at one end and 'junk bonds' at the other. Borrowers from outside the US can tap this market with two provisos: the instruments are written in US dollars, so the enterprise carries an exchange risk; and the minimum issue unit on the bond market is US$50 million, putting US-issued corporate bonds out of the reach of most new ventures.

There are less active bond markets in other countries, although various national stock exchanges are promoting them vigorously, and financial engineers of various degrees of integrity may offer to raise fixed interest capital for a new business, but in general terms, the fixed interest markets are 'out of the new venture's league'.

Share market investors

New ventures in unfashionable industries cannot rely on being bought by a major corporation, so they must look to the stock market to reward the venturers and supply additional capital once the fast growth phase is over. Investors are either institutional, representing superannuation and life insurance funds, or individuals of moderate to high net worth.

Institutional investors in English-speaking countries have, since 1987, come to demand large and rising dividends as their price for supporting a firm's shares. Since the dividends come from money that would otherwise have been retained within the business, hopefully to develop it, large firms with institutions dominating their share registers have tended not to grow very rapidly. If a growing firm sees its ultimate owners as large, managed funds, it should plan to dress itself so as to appeal to them. This requires a solidly defensible market share, minimal exposure to either commodity prices or changes in fashion and the ability to grow steadily, probably by mergers and acquisitions and line extensions rather than by developing radical new products.

Individual investors have a less calculating approach to their portfolio and they tend to take a longer term perspective than the institutions, looking to growth and to some extent emotional satisfaction as well as dividend flows. Small investors cannot afford to be as fickle as large ones, simply because of the transaction costs involved in buying and selling their shares, and the small shareholders' habit of holding on to their shares has helped many managements threatened by a hostile takeover. While it is neither legal nor ethical to overstate the immediate prospects of a venture in order to entrap investors, large or small, a firm whose revenues are intrinsically volatile would do well to attract individual investors, who are much less likely than the institutions to dump their shares or accept an undervalued takeover bid on the basis of a single setback.

CHECKPOINT   In this chapter you learned that there are various sources of finance available to new ventures, but at any one time in a venture's life most of these will be inaccessible. Each class of investor will have different priorities and, within each class of investor, individual investors will have their own specific expectations of the returns on their investment, both financial and other. For a venture to progress it must obtain investor support at every stage of its development until its growth knee is reached and it becomes self-funding. This will require a specific approach to specific investors, generally supported by an updated business plan to meet the venture's demands for cash.

You will *not* have learned any details of the techniques involved in structuring an investor–investee relationship: you may choose to study this subject, or read suitable books on it; or you may expect your investors and their advisers to set out a deal structure. In the latter case, this chapter should have helped you to understand the motivation that leads investors to propose such structures.

This is the last 'business planning' chapter in this book, and while the previous chapters have focused on how you research and develop your business plan, this chapter has discussed who you should present it to.

Exercises

1 Note down the stages in the venture stage model. Check you answer by reviewing it against Figure 12.1.
2 If you have been producing a business plan as you worked through this book, you should now be able to decide which class of investors you should present it to. Reread your executive summary and decide whether it will appeal to your target investors.
3 The box earlier in the chapter describes how Boeing approached the certification and early marketing of

the B777 aircraft. Explain the financial benefits to Boeing of this innovation.
4 An acquaintance needs £10,000 to complete the prototype of his invention, and has already exhausted his own resources. Who would you advise him to approach for further support?
5 A different acquaintance shows you his (generally convincing) business plan for growing his established small business, which shows a need for a cash injection of €600,000. He proposes to raise the money by

tapping the US junk bond market: do you foresee any problems?

6 A wealthy retired executive wishes to get involved with an entrepreneurial business on a part-time basis. How do you suggest he goes about it?

7 How does a successful test-marketing exercise change the attitude of investors and why?

8 Some notably successful entrepreneurs, including Sir Richard Branson and Mr Richard Pratt, have avoided bringing outside investors into their core business (although they have formed joint ventures with others: Virgin Atlantic is a joint venture between Virgin Ltd and Singapore Airlines, for example). What do you see as the advantages and disadvantages of their reluctance to introduce independent investors?

Notes

1   The treatment provided in this chapter is designed to provide a general overview of the types of funds and fund providers appropriate to various stages of financing a growing entrepreneurial venture. For greater detail on both the technicalities of finance provision and the specific availability of funds, we suggest the following references: McMahon et al. (1993) – a useful work for the student of entrepreneurial finance. By exploring the small business and entrepreneurship finance literature, this work raises all the issues relevant to financial management of small and growing ventures. However, it presumes that the reader possesses the financial skills acquired after doing a university finance course. It is a suitable companion to Weston and Brigham (1993) – a highly respected and frequently recommended finance textbook. Phillips (1986) provides a study of financial markets from an entrepreneurship perspective. Golis (1998) – this very readable work explains the financial aspects of business planning and new venture management requirements in a practical and thorough way. Other interesting scholarly and reference works include: Bygrave and Timmons (1992) – an important work on the modern venture capital industry. Some popular accounts of recent history in the financial markets can provide insights not always found in text and reference works: Bruck (1989) – an excellent account of the Michael Milken story. Burroughs and Helyar (1990) – relates the story of the biggest leveraged buyout in history and presents an indictment of the 1980s philosophy that 'greed is good'. Lewis (1990) – called by Tom Wolfe: 'the funniest book about Wall Street I have ever read'. Marsh (1992) – this institution affects the life of everyone on the planet. Marsh tells its story well. Wilson (1988) is a history of the family that dominated European finance from 1560 to the 1980s.

2   Since only a minority of early stage research projects lead to products that get to market, and an even smaller minority lead to profitable products, it is impossible to provide financial justification for any single early stage research project, but such a justification can be developed for running a portfolio of such projects. Major pharmaceutical companies are acutely aware of this problem, as are oil and mineral exploration companies, whose wildcat drilling programmes, taken individually, have a less than 50 per cent chance of success. For pharmaceutical companies, their laboratories and, for oil and mineral companies, their exploration programmes, are accepted as part of the cost of being in their business. Most other industries do not undertake any form of early stage research, either because they cannot afford to run multiple projects, or because they don't understand the potential benefits. During much of the twentieth century companies such as AT&T, Xerox and IBM maintained research laboratories where much early stage research was conducted, often to the benefit of the firm's rivals as much as themselves. As the dogma of 'shareholder value' spread across the English-speaking world at the end of the twentieth century, these laboratories and research centres were largely closed or redirected to work on immediate practical problems.

3   Many public health specialists believe that far too much money is spent on developing ethical preparations offering trivial advantages over those already on the market, while the development of vaccines and treatments for infectious diseases is relatively neglected.

4   Governments in most countries of the world support 'non-commercial' theatre and other forms of artistic expression, suggesting that, as with pharmaceuticals, a commercial system supported by intellectual property protection does not fully satisfy community needs.

5   Exicom Ltd held a major contract to supply telephone handsets in Australia. Their early products failed in tropical conditions, and the cost of recalling and replacing several hundred thousand handsets crippled the company.

6   This can take an entrepreneur close to the edge of the laws governing prospectuses and capital-raising by companies; once individuals are asked to contribute serious sums of money (in their context, not that of the City), a consultation with a lawyer is essential.

7   The actor-producer Paul Hogan raised most of the finance needed for the film *Crocodile Dundee* from private investors, many of them friends and many more fans of his TV persona. When the film became a major hit, the investors received several times their money back. Many of them subscribed for shares in the sequel and lost their investment.

8   Architectural drawings supported by engineering calculations are a prototype in the sense used here, as was Boeing's B777 database. Virtual reality preceded the computer industry, although technology makes virtual prototypes more fun to examine.

9   The analogy is not very far-fetched: US consumer products companies launch twenty thousand or more new products a year; on an eight-hour day/five-day week basis, this is a little more than a product every two minutes. During the attack on Iraq in 2002, the US used about five thousand 'smart' bombs and cruise missiles over twenty days, about one every five minutes.

10 Often referred to as 'DEC' (pronounced 'deck') by outsiders, but always Digital, or Digital Equipment, by the people who worked for it; now sadly gone from the scene, initially swallowed by Compaq which in turn vanished into Hewlett-Packard.

11 The National Australia Bank (NAB) agreed to refinance the business with five days to spare and the business continued to trade successfully until the owners retired and sold it as a going concern in 2002. Needless to say, the NAB received all the owners' business and that of their family over the whole of this period.

13 Beyond 'how to': key issues in understanding entrepreneurship

The previous chapters have followed a well-defined educational programme intended to help readers gain both an understanding of the place of ethical entrepreneurship in a liberally organised society and guide them towards the skills needed to prepare a convincing business plan ready for presentation to investors. For some readers this may be quite enough. Others may wish to learn more about entrepreneurship or consider its application under particular social or economic conditions.

In this chapter we will be more discursive, offering you more questions than answers, signposts rather than destinations. We will convey an overview of three areas not covered in any of the previous chapters:

- the vigorous academic discipline of entrepreneurship studies

- the GEM project, an international comparison of the role of and attitudes to entrepreneurship in different countries

- indigenous entrepreneurship, the attempt to use our developing knowledge of entrepreneurship to help deprived indigenous communities to take control of their own future

Research into entrepreneurship

The major emphasis of this book is to convey a collection of principles and techniques that will prove useful to people intending to create and manage a new organisation committed to the ethical exploitation of a new product and/or market opportunity. This involves some intensely practical skills, including:

- How do you evaluate an opportunity?
- How do you assess resource requirements?
- How do you write a convincing and compelling business plan?
- Who do you approach for the finance needed to make the plan a reality?

In terms of providing people with practical entrepreneurial skills, this 'how to' emphasis is logical and necessary. In terms of providing people with a satisfying intellectual understanding of a complex phenomenon, it has some shortcomings that we have only partly addressed in the earlier chapters of this book. There are some larger issues.

To begin with, a practical emphasis implies that the question, 'What is entrepreneurship?' is either irrelevant or completely defined in functional terms. This is not so. Asking 'what' immediately raises important issues and problems. Is entrepreneurship a field of study in its own right or just a jumbled collection of bits and pieces of knowledge from other disciplines? We do not have much difficulty distinguishing physics from biology, but can we distinguish entrepreneurship from economics, marketing, sociology, psychology and a host of other disciplines? If we can distinguish it, is entrepreneurship best defined from a practitioner perspective or the researcher's point of view?

Questions about who, where and when are just as challenging and interesting. Can anyone be an entrepreneur or does it require special characteristics? Are entrepreneurs 'born' or 'made'? Do entrepreneurs think differently from 'normal' managers and, if so, what is the nature of this different thinking? How many entrepreneurs are there? Are there differences in entrepreneurial propensity between countries; between men and women; between people without jobs and motivated by survival as distinct from those with jobs and motivated by desire for improvement? Who can and should teach entrepreneurship: successful business people or scholars with specialist academic qualifications in the subject, or both?

'Where' questions pose serious challenges to the fundamental situational assumptions inherent in most instructional books. General discussions of entrepreneurship usually assume that it concerns the creation of an 'independent' start-up venture by a profit-motivated entrepreneur (or team) operating in an environment possessing diversified capital markets. As is often the case, such received wisdom is partially true at best: the most successful entrepreneurs pursue a non-financial objective and see high financial returns as a proof of their success and a resource to support their further efforts. But entrepreneurship covers a far wider range of circumstances than this. Over the last few years, the importance and increasing prevalence of social entrepreneurship has become evident. For social entrepreneurs, creating new organisational approaches to problem-solving is vital but profit is not the motive. And corporate entrepreneurship is a field in its own right. Here, profit is part of the motive but the setting is far from independent. The crux of a corporate entrepreneurship decision may be whether it is better to retain a new initiative 'in-house' (intrapreneurship) or create a 'spin-off' (corporate venturing). Moving to the public sector, it must be asked whether governments or subsets of them can be locations for entrepreneurial activity? At the level of different peoples' value systems, one needs to ask what place does culture play in distinguishing various forms and levels of entrepreneurship? For instance, is entrepreneurship understood and performed differently by French men and English women? Or, in a state with a colonial or invader history, does indigenous entrepreneurship involve values, motives and performance evaluations that differ from non-indigenous entrepreneurship?

'When' questions are critical because timing is vital in the study of entrepreneurship. At the firm level, there are many theories about the life cycles of typical and atypical entrepreneurial ventures. Different stages of an entrepreneurial process require different skills and emphases. At the individual level, people often oscillate between being and not-being entrepreneurs. Indeed, if the ideal is to grow from a small, improvisational venture to become a large, established venture, success may demand that entrepreneurial founders make significant behavioural transitions. The early stage entrepreneur may well become the late stage technical manager. After selling out of successful ventures, some entrepreneurs do it all again (serial entrepreneurship) or become angel investors in others' new businesses. And some just retire to live on their capital.

Finally, there is a battery of questions associated with the great issue of 'why?'. Why do some people and not others discover and chose to exploit different entrepreneurial opportunities? When it comes to entrepreneurial motivation, what differences are there between businesses founded on necessity (by people without any employment alternatives) and those opportunity-oriented businesses created by people with a range of alternative employment options? Why are some people only entrepreneurial for a short period in a single venture, yet others become 'serial entrepreneurs', founding or participating in many ventures?

We would like to conclude this book, not with a series of prefabricated answers to these large and important questions, but with a brief coverage of some of the most important issues affecting the contribution that entrepreneurship can make to economic and social development.

The 'what' questions – defining a field of action and a field of study

Common ingredients but different recipes

It has always been a challenging endeavour to try to answer the fundamental question: what is entrepreneurship? The sheer fluidity and multitasking nature of entrepreneurship ensure that there will always be debate about the precise wording of any attempt at summary. One definition that the authors of this book sometimes employ because it combines comprehensiveness with brevity is: 'entrepreneurship is an organised effort designed to pursue a unique, innovative opportunity and achieve rapid, profitable growth.'

More important than the precise wording of any summary definition is its intent to convey entrepreneurship as a complex, plural and interactive network of behaviours comporting with established scholarship (Jennings 1994). It would be nice to have permission to limit the definition of entrepreneurship to one area such as 'the act of new entry' (Lumpkin and Dess 1996), 'the creation of a new organization' (Gartner 1989a)[1] or the act of 'creative destruction' (Schumpeter [1942] 1967) but the complexity of the phenomenon will not allow it. The field is obliged to consider entrepreneurial thinking wherever it occurs: prior to start-up, during start-up and for as long as the organisational environment is characterised by innovation and growth. Fortunately, the expanding quantum of entrepreneurship research provides considerable consensus on the importance of many pertinent definitional ingredients. These include:

- alertness to opportunity (leading to arbitrage) (Kirzner 1973; Shane and Venkataraman 2000)
- decision making in an uncertain environment (Knight 1921)
- innovation management (Schumpeter [1942] 1967);
- speculation and risk-bearing (Cantillon 1775 – quoted by Jennings 1994)

- coordination of disparate elements (Say 1828 – cited by Koolman 1971)
- leadership (Marshall [1920] 1949)
- product development and ownership (Hawley – discussed in Jennings 1994)
- creation of a new organisation to pursue an opportunity (Bygrave and Hofer 1991; Gartner 1989a)
- a focus on managing rapid growth in a volatile environment (Legge and Hindle 1997)
- ambition – distinguishing between 'real entrepreneurs', who are opportunity-evaluating, growth-oriented risk managers, and 'just SME owners' (Katz and Peters 2001).

Entrepreneurs have been seen as participating in a complex, plural and interactive network (Jennings 1994), embracing all or most[2] of the above concepts in a complex interaction. The proportions of these ingredients will vary from case to case and context to context. One entrepreneurial situation may, for instance, involve a high level of risk management and a low degree of organisation building. Another may involve high levels of leadership and low levels of arbitrage. And so on. The same fundamental ingredients, mixed according to different recipes, can be used to bake many dishes.

An activity focused perspective: the Penrosian view

There is one definition in the literature that, although it is not brief, possesses triple virtue. First, it has proven longevity (nearly 50 years' provenance). Second, it is comprehensive. Third, it was written by a genius in a book of seminal importance to many disciplines. In *The Theory of the Growth of the Firm*, Edith Penrose wrote that the term 'entrepreneur' referred:

> to individuals or groups within the firm providing entrepreneurial services, whatever their position or occupational classification may be. Entrepreneurial services are those contributions to the operations of a firm which relate to the introduction and acceptance on behalf of the firm of new ideas, particularly with respect to products, location, and significant changes in technology, to the acquisition of new managerial personnel, to fundamental changes in the administrative organisation of the firm, to the raising of capital, and to the making of plans for expansion, including the choice of method for expansion. Entrepreneurial services are contrasted with managerial services, which relate to the execution of entrepreneurial ideas and proposals and to the supervision of existing operations. The same individuals may, and more often than not probably do, provide both types of services to the firm. (Penrose [1959] 1995: 31–2)

To adopt Penrose's definition wholeheartedly, one need only note that it has two further virtues. First, it is not restricted to existing firms as a superficial reading may indicate. It encompasses organisational emergence (Gartner 1985; Katz and Gartner 1988) – that is, the creation of new firms – as a particular case of the general proposition. In a volume devoted to multiple scrutiny of the importance of Penrose's theoretical work (Pitelis 2002), Elizabeth Garnsey (2002) has discussed the application of Penrosian ideas to new venture creation. Second, there is a nice irony that the best argument for the worthiness of the socially entailed *individual* to serve as a unit of analysis in social science should come from someone writing an economic theory of the *firm*.

The Penrosian definition of entrepreneurship has stood the test of time, common sense and uncommon research.

A research focused perspective: the Shane and Venkataraman view

Mention the word 'research' and you soon face the issue of moving from definition (which can be complex and embracing) to the need to simplify. Social researchers need to develop simplifying frameworks or they could not hope to operationalise concepts in the form of testable propositions. Shane and Venkataraman (2000) have sought to develop a framework for distinguishing entrepreneurship research – and therefore the field of entrepreneurship – from all other fields of social inquiry. The essential predicate to Shane and Venkataramen's development of a framework for understanding entrepreneurship is a focus on entrepreneurial opportunities, as defined by Casson:

> Entrepreneurial opportunities are those situations in which new goods, services, raw materials, and organising methods can be introduced and sold at greater than their cost of production. (Casson 1982, quoted in Shane and Venkataraman 2000)

It is not hard to extend Casson's definition logically to the non-profit area of government and social entrepreneurship by thinking in terms of radical improvements (usually measurable in terms of lower cost or greater efficiency) to existing methods of service delivery. Throughout this chapter, our specific focus will be most often on for-profit enterprise but our implicit intent is always to embrace the non-profit applications of entrepreneurship as well.

There is an essential distinction between entrepreneurial opportunities and the larger set of all opportunities for profit – especially those concerned with enhancing the efficiency of existing goods, services, raw materials and organising methods. Entrepreneurial opportunities require the discovery of new means–ends relationships, not optimisation within existing means–ends frameworks

On this opportunity-based platform, Shane and Venkataraman build their brief definition:

> We define the field of entrepreneurship as the scholarly examination of how, by whom and with what effects opportunities to create future goods and services are discovered, evaluated and exploited. (p. 218)

This definition means that the field involves the study of:

- *existence* of entrepreneurial opportunities
- the processes of *discovery*
- the processes of *evaluation*
- the processes of *exploitation*
- the set of individuals who discover, evaluate and exploit opportunities.

Shane and Venkataraman used only words to describe the framework they produced. To aid description and discussion, we prefer to depict their framework for understanding entrepreneurship as a diagram linking four core attributes of entrepreneurial opportunities.

The *existence* of entrepreneurial opportunities depends on constant economic disequilibrium and asymmetries of information. Different uses (and accordingly different values of resources) are constantly being conceived. For instance, silicon is a fairly prevalent chemical element. It is, literally, as common as sand. During the phenomenal growth of 'the computer age', silicon embodied in an integrated circuit chip has come to be worth a lot more than silicon embodied in a glass bottle. At the outset of the era of the integrated circuit, only a very few people had the knowledge and insight required to envisage the revolutionary potential of a new technology based on an old raw material.

The *discovery* of entrepreneurial opportunities is centred on a key question. Why do some people and not others discover particular entrepreneurial opportunities?

Shane and Venkataraman argue that two factors influence the probability:

1. Information corridors – possession of prior knowledge
2. Cognitive properties – the thinking capacity needed to value it.

There is now a rapidly growing field of study called entrepreneurial cognition. We will discuss it in the next section ('who?') because what and how people think is such a big part of who they are. Discovery of an opportunity is a necessary but not sufficient condition for entrepreneurship to occur. *Evaluation*, in the form of a *decision to exploit* the entrepreneurial opportunity is required. The evaluation process used in this decision depends on two things: the nature of the opportunity and individual differences between evaluators. Established research has produced some worthwhile but fairly broad generalisations about the nature of opportunities. In general, higher expected value is likely to be perceived when:

- Expected demand is large
- Industry profit margins are high
- The technology life cycle is young
- Competition density is neither too high nor too low
- Population level learning from other entrants is available.

Individual preference (as distinct from cognitive process) is also an extremely important variable influencing the process of opportunity evaluation. For instance, some people may value their leisure time more highly than others. For them, the opportunity costs (measured with respect to foregone leisure) will be higher than for others for whom 'work is play'. Research has indicated a high measure of individual difference (in assessing the same opportunity) with respect to six variables: cost assessments; possession of greater financial capital; stronger social ties to resource providers; useful information stemming from previous employment; the degree of transferability of that information and prior entrepreneurial experience.

Finally, in the Shane and Venkataraman framework (Figure 13.1), if the opportunity is not rejected, the mode of exploitation may take two forms: new venturing (which they categorise as a 'markets' approach) or through existing entities (which they categorise as a 'hierarchies' approach). There are two circumstances where an opportunity can be exploited via existing entities. The sale process utilises other

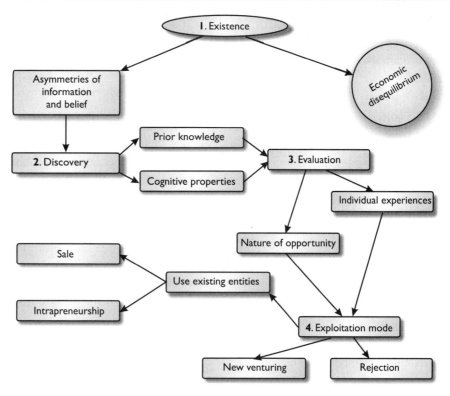

Source: Adapted from Shane and Venkataraman (2000)

Figure 13.1 **The four core attributes of entrepreneurial opportunities: flow-charting the argument of Shane and Venkataraman**

organisations in the marketplace. Or a firm can exploit the new opportunity under the auspices of its own established organisation. Many have called this latter process 'intrapreneurship' and distinguish it from 'corporate venturing' where a new organisation is created to pursue the opportunity.

There is a key virtue of the Shane and Venkataraman framework for understanding entrepreneurship. It permits researchers possessing different emphases to gain access to a wide range of questions without losing focus on the essential distinctiveness of entrepreneurship as a unique field of inquiry. For instance Shane and Venkataraman suggest that organisational scholars will be concerned with three sets of research questions. Why, when and how:

(a) opportunities for the creation of goods and services come into existence
(b) some people and not others discover and exploit these opportunities
(c) different modes of action are used to exploit these opportunities.

They provide, as one example of a different emphasis, economists' interest in the distribution of entrepreneurial talent across productive and unproductive activities – an interest pioneered in the work of William Baumol (1996). You can, no doubt, think of many other research emphases that can be accommodated without jeopardising the distinctiveness of entrepreneurship as a field in its own right.

Who, where, when – cognition, counting and cycles

Does who matter? From personality to cognition

William Gartner famously titled one of the most frequently cited entrepreneurship journal articles of all time: 'Who is an entrepreneur? is the wrong question' (Gartner 1989b). He argued that the search for personality characteristics – deep-seated, durable traits that distinguish different types of personality – had proved unfruitful as a focus for entrepreneurship research. What mattered, Gartner argued, was not who people intrinsically were but what they objectively did. And what an entrepreneur did, he claimed, was to create a new organisation to pursue an opportunity. Accordingly, in his view, the essence of entrepreneurship was 'organisational emergence' (Gartner 1988). Many scholars (including Shane and Venkataraman, whose research framework we have just explored) were unsatisfied with so unidimensional an emphasis. But there is no doubt that, in most publications in the mainstream of formal entrepreneurship research, the predominant unit of analysis has changed since Gartner's paper. Since Gartner, the majority of entrepreneurship researchers have chosen a variety of units of analysis, other than the individual, as the focus of study. These include: the firm, the industry, the nation, accounting performance data, disembodied 'decision-making', an amorphous surveyed sample, aspects of managerial behaviour – anything but the individual entrepreneur (or, collectively, a team of entrepreneurs).

Of course, there have always been exceptions and that is just as well. A rift has developed between the concerns of formal entrepreneurship research and the 'rusted on' beliefs of practitioners. Practitioners remain convinced that the role of key individuals is absolutely essential to successful entrepreneurship. So, if professional researchers choose to ignore the role of the individual, professional practitioners will be unconvinced by their work. Fortunately (roughly since the emergence of a seminal paper by Shaver and Scott in 1991), a field of study called 'entrepreneurial cognition' has emerged. It seeks to bring the individual back to the centre stage of entrepreneurship research. The emphasis is not upon immutable sets of personality traits (the emphasis pioneered by McClelland and criticised by William Gartner) but upon cognition. Entrepreneurial cognition is the way that entrepreneurs think in the context of the situations in which they find themselves.

The essential difference between entrepreneurial cognition and managerial cognition concerns boundaries. Managerial thinking tends to be constrained by accepted norms in a well-defined environment (Stevenson et al. 1999). The domain of entrepreneurial cognition focuses on unbounded thinking in uncertain environments (Mitchell et al. 2002). Entrepreneurial cognition has its antecedents in the more general managerial and organisational cognition literatures, which were systematically reviewed by Walsh (1995). He found an eclectic field populated by many significant constructs but the most important was 'knowledge structure or schema':

> A knowledge structure is a mental template that individuals impose on an information environment to give it form and meaning (Walsh 1995: 280)

Walsh developed an organising framework for classifying and commenting upon the various strands of the disparate knowledge structure research literature. It is

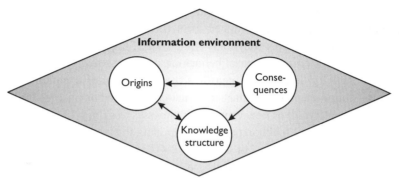

Source: Adapted from Walsh 1995

Figure 13.2   **Walsh's model of knowledge structure research: an organising framework**

reproduced here as Figure 13.2. The essential feature is the interaction between individuals' knowledge structures and the information environment. The domain of any cognition – social, organisational or entrepreneurial – does not lie simply between some individual's ears. Thinking always has a social context.

While the synthesising work of Walsh (1995) – and others such as Hodgkinson (1997) and Huff (1997) – provides vital background to the entrepreneurial cognition field, Daniel Forbes (1999) highlighted the foreground with his detailed review of cognitive approaches to new venture creation. He reviewed, dissected and arranged 34 studies, which may be regarded as the entrepreneurial cognition canon up to 1999. His classification mechanism made good use of an organisational sense-making model whose three prime components are scanning, interpreting and action. This sense-making model has its most direct pedigree with respect to three papers (Daft and Weick 1984; Milliken 1990; Thomas et al. 1993) but the common ancestor of most variants of sense-making models in the organisation literature is the genuinely seminal book by Weick (1979). Since Forbes arranged his conclusions according to a time-based framework, we will look more closely at them presently, under the heading of 'when'.

Post-1999 development of the field of entrepreneurial cognition is summarised in a 2002 special issue of *Entrepreneurship: Theory & Practice*, edited by Ron Mitchell. In that issue, Mitchell et al. (2002) explain that entrepreneurial cognition (singular) is the overarching process that encompasses a range of particular mental processes, called entrepreneurial cognitions (plural):

> Entrepreneurial cognitions are the knowledge structures that people use to make assessments, judgments, or decisions involving opportunity evaluation, venture creation and growth. In other words, research in entrepreneurial cognition is about understanding how entrepreneurs use simplifying mental models to piece together previously unconnected information that helps them to identify and invent new products or services, and to assemble the necessary resources to start and grow the business (Mitchell et al. 2002: 97)

So, 'who is an entrepreneur?' has once again become an acceptable question. And the answer seems to be that an entrepreneur is a person with the cognitive capacity to think through all the situational variables pertaining to opportunity discovery, evaluation and exploitation.

A lot of people are engaged in entrepreneurship. *How many?*

Table 13.1, reproduced from the *Global Entrepreneurship Monitor (GEM) 2002 Executive Report* (Reynolds et al. 2002: 7), is indicative of the worldwide pervasiveness of entrepreneurial behaviour, as represented by the TEA (total entrepreneurial activity) index. This measures the proportion of a nation's population engaged, as founders, in either start-ups (just-commenced or nascent businesses less than three months old) or new ventures (businesses less than 42 months old).

Of the 2.4 billion persons comprising the labour force represented in the 27 countries participating in the GEM 2002 study, 12 per cent (286 million) were either actively involved in starting a business or were the owner/manager of a business that was less than 42 months old. The total population is provided in the first

Table 13.1 **Total entrepreneurial activity (TEA) index and estimated counts by country**

Country	Population	Labour force	TEA Index	TEA participants	Participation 1999	2000	2001
India	1,046,000,000	591,466,000	17.9	105,872,000	x	x	
China	1,284,000,000	814,470,000	12.3	100,179,000			
United States	280,000,000	173,911,000	10.5	18,260,000	x	x	x
Brazil	176,029,000	106,442,000	13.5	14,369,000	x	x	
Thailand	62,354,000	40,435,000	18.9	7,642,000			
Mexico	103,400,000	58,331,000	12.4	7,233,000	x		
Korea	48,324,000	32,117,000	14.5	4,656,000	x	x	
Argentina	37,812,000	21,987,000	14.2	3,122,000	x	x	
Germany	83,251,000	53,458,000	5.2	2,779,000	x	x	x
Russia	144,978,000	94,330,000	2.5	2,358,000	x		
Italy	57,715,000	37,102,000	5.9	2,189,000	x	x	x
United Kingdom	59,778,000	36,927,000	5.4	1,994,000	x	x	x
Canada	31,902,000	20,565,000	8.8	1,809,000	x	x	x
South Africa	43,647,000	24,886,000	6.5	1,617,000	x		
Chile	15,498,000	9,388,000	15.7	1,473,000			
Japan	126,974,000	81,290,000	1.8	1,463,000	x	x	x
Spain	40,077,000	25,886,000	4.6	1,190,000	x		
France	59,765,000	36,682,000	3.2	1,173,000	x	x	x
Poland	38,625,000	24,899,000	4.4	1,095,000	x		
Australia	19,546,000	12,273,000	8.7	1,067,000	x	x	
Chinese Taipei (Taiwan)	22,548,000	14,708,000	4.3	632,000			
The Netherlands	16,067,000	10,348,000	4.6	476,000	x		
Hungary	10,075,000	6,557,000	6.6	432,000	x		
New Zealand	3,908,000	2,432,000	14	340,000	x		
Switzerland	7,301,000	4,696,000	7.1	333,000			
Israel	6,029,000	3,485,000	7.1	247,000	x	x	x
Norway	4,525,000	2,781,000	8.7	241,000	x	x	
Denmark	5,368,000	3,397,000	6.5	220,000	x	x	x
Sweden	8,876,000	5,433,000	4	215,000	x	x	
Ireland	3,883,000	2,289,000	9.1	208,000	x	x	
Belgium	10,274,000	6,376,000	3	191,000	x	x	
Singapore	4,452,000	3,191,000	5.9	188,000	x	x	
Hong Kong	7,303,000	4,955,000	3.4	168,000			
Finland	5,183,000	3,274,000	4.6	150,000	x	x	x
Croatia	4,390,000	2,739,000	3.6	98,000			
Slovenia	1,932,000	1,278,000	4.6	58,000			
Iceland	279,000	172,000	11.3	19,000			
Sum	3,882,068,000	2,374,956,000		285,756,000			
Country average			8				
Total population average			12				

Source: Reynolds et al. (2002); gemconsortium.org

column, the number of 'labour force' individuals (18 to 64 years of age) in the second and the TEA rate in the third. The fourth column is an estimate of the entrepreneurially active members of the population based on the sample percentages.

The study that produced these figures produces many more. The GEM project is worthy of the attention of anyone seriously interested in entrepreneurship.

The GEM project originated in September 1997 as a bold research initiative by Babson College (USA) and the London Business School. It brings together the world's best scholars in entrepreneurship, in a consortium, to study the complex relationship between entrepreneurship and economic prosperity. From the outset, the project was designed to be a long-term multinational enterprise, with a growing number of partner institutions. GEM was launched in 1999 with 10 countries. The project expanded to 21 countries in 2000, 29 in 2001 and over 30 in 2002 and 2003.

GEM refers to both a set of linked, international research projects and a set of documents that report project results. Each country produces an independent, national report (GEM UK, GEM USA, GEM Japan and so on) that explores in detail the nature, extent and effects of entrepreneurship within the individual country, including selected comparisons with other nations. Some participant countries – including the UK and Germany – also provide detailed regional studies. There are GEM Wales and GEM Scotland studies for every year of the project. At the international level, a coordinating document (the *GEM Executive Report*) is produced, presenting major findings across all participating countries, describing any emerging patterns and providing analysis and interpretation of these figures.

GEM explores three fundamental questions:

1. Does the level of entrepreneurial activity vary between countries, and, if so, to what extent?
2. Does the level of entrepreneurial activity affect a country's rate of economic growth and prosperity?
3. What makes a country entrepreneurial?

These questions are explored in the context of a theoretical model illustrated in Figure 13.3.

Before GEM, most studies of economic performance focused on established enterprises – the status sector of the economy. The value of emerging (as distinct from established) enterprises was missing from most attempts to measure economic performance. GEM focuses its attention on a set of factors that specifically influences the entrepreneurial sector. These are termed the 'entrepreneurial framework conditions'. These nine conditions (labelled in the diagram) are held to be the main determinants of the entrepreneurial environment. They achieve their influence in combination with entrepreneurial opportunity and entrepreneurial capacity. These factors – environment, opportunity and capacity (which includes both skills and motivation to capitalise on opportunity) – act together. Their combination determines the rate of a firm's birth, death and growth (business churning), which in turn contributes to economic growth and prosperity.

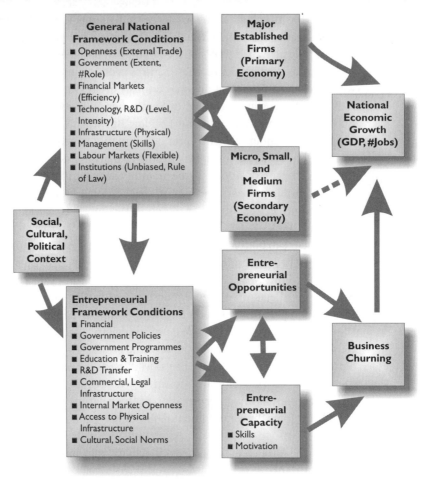

Source: Adapted from gemconsortium.org

Figure 13.3 **The GEM theoretical model**

Three main data collection methods are used for GEM research:

1. An adult population survey, randomly sampling a minimum of 2,000 typical adults per country.
2. Face-to-face 'open-ended' interviews with at least 36 experts (called 'key informants') on various aspects of entrepreneurship. These experts also complete a detailed, structured questionnaire.
3. The use of selected national economic data, measured in standard units, from credible international sources including the Organisation for Economic Cooperation and Development (OECD) and the World Bank.

Anyone can gain instant free access to all *GEM Global Executive Reports* (for years both past and present) and all published GEM reports of each participant country from the website www.gemconsortium.org.

The four years of GEM research, 1999–2002, demonstrate that a variety of important factors have a big influence on who becomes an entrepreneur. After four iterations of this international project, the GEM database now contains thousands of in-depth interviews with a wide variety of international experts in the framework conditions that are vital to a country's entrepreneurial capacity and achievement. A constant theme featuring strongly in all countries and all years of the GEM project is the importance of education – particularly education focused specifically upon the direct teaching of entrepreneurial skills to would-be practitioners.

This leads to a crucial 'who' question. Who can and should teach entrepreneurship?

Do you want to become a professor of entre-preneurship?

Many universities now offer PhD programmes in entrepreneurship; those who complete such programmes are eligible for appointment to the teaching staff of their own or another university. They will join a cadre of professional entrepreneurship educators – most particularly in the USA, where formal entrepreneurship PhD programmes are most heavily institutionalised – many of whom have not had and may never get much direct involvement in business. The distinction between *pouvoir* and *savoir* is an ancient one, but there are many respected fields in which teachers are not expected to have had extensive practical experience. For instance, most teachers of criminology have no criminal record. Both society and their students regard this as a good thing. Most coaches of elite sportspeople can no longer perform at the level of those they instruct. So it is with tutors of opera singers, actors and performing artists of all kinds. No recognised authority on Julius Caesar has ever visited ancient Rome.

Yet, in many quarters, there is a substantial belief that only those forged in the fire of practical experience have a 'right' to teach entrepreneurship. Both authors of this book have attended a great many entrepreneurship seminars, meetings and events involving mixed participants: entrepreneurship practitioners with entrepreneurship students, educators and researchers. We have never attended such an event at which the following scenario failed to occur. At the conclusion of an address by an entrepreneurship academic comes a time for questions and discussion. There will always be a question from the floor (usually from an established entrepreneur) that goes something like:

And how much shareholder value have you created in the last 18 months?

Or

Are you a millionaire? If you're not, how do you expect to train any?

These kinds of questions are representative of the extremity of what may be called the 'pro-practitioner' view concerning entrepreneurship educators.

In sharp contrast, Professor Ed McMullan of the University of Calgary expresses a strongly pro-academic view. He has over 30 years experience as an entrepreneurship educator and researcher. In June 2002 he spoke at a seminar, held in the University of Saskatchewan, designed to confront that institution with a range of issues germane to its proposed establishment of a new entrepreneurship programme. McMullan (2003) confronted the university with his view of the state of the art of entrepreneurship education.

He argued that entrepreneurship is a field characterised by 'missing educators'. He claimed that figures in his possession demonstrate that only 11 per cent of all registered US university faculty members involved in teaching entrepreneurship courses actually have a PhD in the subject. Most instruction is conducted by ad hoc 'adjuncts' – practitioners contracted to give 'one-off' elective subjects in undergraduate or MBA programmes. Moreover, most full-time, PhD-qualified faculty allegedly specialising in entrepreneurship he calls 'retreads'. These are people whose 'mother' discipline is not entrepreneurship but accounting, marketing or organisational behaviour or psychology; anything but entrepreneurship. With respect to entrepreneurship, McMullan claims these people are, effectively, self-educated scholars switching fields. McMullan argues that nowhere else in the university would formally unqualified instructors be so widely accepted as the norm. For instance, most chemistry academics are expected to have qualifications in chemistry as distinct from, say, physics or biology. He believes the problem is particularly acute at professorial level. Many chairs of entrepreneurship fall 'captive' to people qualified in a discipline other than entrepreneurship and many are awarded to practitioners fêted for their business acumen or their prominence in a network that may result in access to potential sources of financial support for the institution and its programmes.

Between these extremes – experienced practitioners or highly trained, educational specialists – one can fantasise about the 'ideal' person to teach entrepreneurship. She would be a serial entrepreneur of international prominence whose several failures led only to renewed determination and ultimate success as the leader of several highly ethical high-growth ventures. Somewhere along the line, she would have had time to complete an award-winning PhD thesis specifically in an entrepreneurship programme at an acclaimed, probably American, university. Several years teaching experience – not as an adjunct but as a full faculty member – complemented by a strong publications record exclusively in A-grade, highly focused, peer-reviewed journals would be desirable. The skills package would be rounded out by a track record of successful consulting assignments and possession of a powerful media persona and the gift of natural persuasion – particularly as it affected the attraction of sponsorship and research grants. She would be so wealthy, so public-spirited and so passionate about entrepreneurship education that a salary package would not be required and all funds from her endowed chair could be directed to dispassionate entrepreneurship research. Of course, we cannot have myths. So, what is feasible?

Entrepreneurship is a relatively new discipline (formally gaining its own distinct divisional status within the US Academy of Management in 1987). Demand for qualified teachers outstrips supply. It is also quite an eclectic field. So, the fact that academics come to it from a variety of perspectives may have some positive benefits – so long as the commitment to master the new field (rather than rehash the shibboleths of the old field in a new place) is genuine. The aim should be a well-balanced, well-mixed programme team – not a search for universal perfection in every single teacher. This may mean a higher proportion of team-teaching and multiple presenters within the one subject. Students could greatly benefit from a sprinkling of well-chosen adjuncts whose presentations are based on commitment to balanced education, not mortgaged to an egocentric perspective based on unanalysed personal experience. In a very different way, they would undoubtedly benefit from exposure to someone who 'really knows the literature'. Through provision of multiple perspectives – the differing strengths of differing people – it ought to be possible to avoid the worst excesses of inadequately prepared faculty. Plurality of perspective is likely to be the best safeguard against both the adjunct practitioner on an ego trip and the 'unworldly' academic lacking in business acumen and empathy.

Nationality

As already indicated, the GEM study reveals substantial variation between countries. Figure 13.4 is a portrait of total entrepreneurial activity by global region as measured by GEM national surveys in the year 2002.

In 2002 less than 3 per cent of adults 18–64 years of age were involved in entrepreneurial endeavours in Japan, Russia and Belgium, but more than 18 per cent were so engaged in Thailand. Entrepreneurial activity levels were lowest in the developed Asian countries (Japan, Hong Kong, Chinese Taipei and Singapore) and Central Europe (Russia, Croatia, Poland, Slovenia and Hungary). Participation rates in 2002 were slightly higher in the EU and Israel. They were substantially higher in Australia, Canada, New Zealand, South Africa and the US. They were higher still in Latin America and highest in the developing Asian countries (China, Korea, India and Thailand).

So, we know that 'where' matters in a national sense. But there is no reason yet to suspect that the pattern evident in Figure 13.4 will display any stability over time. On the contrary, 2002 demonstrated substantial movement from previous years in the relative positions of countries with respect to entrepreneurial activity. For instance, between 2001 and 2002, Australia fell from being the fourth most entrepreneurially

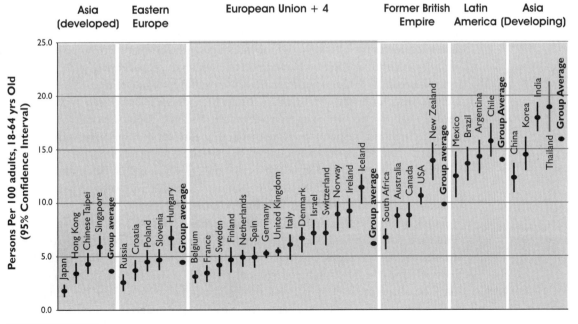

Source: gemconsortium.org

Figure 13.4 **Total entrepreneurial activity (TEA) by global region, 2002**

active country (with 15.5 per cent of the population engaged in new venturing) to sixteenth position (with only 8.68 per cent of the population engaged). In the same period in the UK, total entrepreneurial activity participation rates also fell (from 7.8 to 5.37 per cent). Entrepreneurship is a volatile phenomenon.

Culture, ethnicity, indigenous status and values

One needs to ask what place do culture, ethnicity, indigenous status and differing value systems play in distinguishing various forms and levels of entrepreneurship?

The term 'culture' is used ambiguously in the management literature. It is most commonly used to describe the shared beliefs held by the employees of a firm and in a context that implies that management may improve firm performance by adjusting its culture. Here we are referring to national or regional culture, beliefs shared by the employees and customers of a firm, but over which management has very little control. The literature discussing the impact of national and regional culture on management performance and entrepreneurial proclivity is less extensive; the Dutch scholar Geert Hofstede is associated with much of the leading research in this area. We have already introduced Putnam's concept of social capital in Chapter 1, where we included a disposition to trust others as one of the preconditions for entrepreneurship. People of a common ethnic background may share a distinctive culture leading to a level of entrepreneurial proclivity different from that of the wider society in which they are embedded; but research and even discussion of this area is inhibited by the ease with which it may be misused to reinforce racial stereotyping and the oppression and denigration of minorities.

We also introduced the concept of 'economic freedom' in Chapter 1; and there we described it as a precondition of entrepreneurship. In Chapter 1 we considered the legal position; but it is possible that cultural constraints might be equally inhibiting to potential entrepreneurs. This is implicit in the discussion of entrepreneurial morality as initiated by Jacobs and summarised in Chapter 2. In a culture where respect for tradition dominates the toleration of innovation, potential entrepreneurs may make little progress. A cultural tradition of common ownership of property may make it difficult for entrepreneurs to claim and keep the rewards that motivate many of them in more individualistic cultures; it may make it difficult to assemble the seed capital that is needed to support ventures in their very earliest stages. A culture that values social solidarity may not respond to entrepreneurship education or entrepreneurial incentives predicated on radical individualism as advocated by the followers of Ayn Rand.

There is a specific question of great relevance to states with a colonial or invader history. Does indigenous entrepreneurship involve values, motives and performance evaluations that differ from non-indigenous entrepreneurship?

In all nations with significant indigenous minorities, the economic and social deprivation of indigenous peoples has long been of deep concern to some and various policies have been put in place to address these issues. For most of the twentieth century the Australian government pursued policies of assimilation – essentially, an attempt to eliminate cultural differences by absorbing the indigenous population into the white majority. The cupidity and bigotry of those who implemented this policy overwhelmed any good intentions held by those who initiated it, and during the last quarter of the twentieth century the policy of assimilation was abandoned and the legal disabilities affecting indigenous Australians were removed. indigenous Australians were allowed to access the social security system and funds were allocated to improve their health, housing and educational achievement.

The debate and administration of indigenous issues – particularly the welfare issue – have not been in indigenous control. Whether the intentions of non-indigenous governance and aid agencies have been malicious or benign, the result of taking responsibility out of indigenous hands has resulted in a 'handout' culture (Pearson 2000). Stimulation of indigenous entrepreneurship has the potential to repair much of the damage through creation of an enterprise culture, which fully respects indigenous traditions but empowers indigenous people as economic agents in a globally competitive modern world. There is growing worldwide awareness that policies directed to developing indigenous entrepreneurship have the 'win–win' potential of enhancing indigenous self-determination while eliminating much of the waste endemic to passive social welfare programmes.

Hindle and Lansdowne (2002) provide a definition of indigenous entrepreneurship:

> Indigenous entrepreneurship is the creation, management and development of new ventures by Indigenous people for the benefit of Indigenous people. The organisations thus created can pertain to either the private, public or non-profit sectors. The desired and achieved benefits of venturing can range from the narrow view of economic profit for a single individual to the broad view of multiple, social and economic advantages for entire communities. Outcomes and entitlements derived from indigenous entrepreneurship may extend to enterprise partners and stakeholders who may be non-indigenous.

Globally, reconciliation of all kinds is a major theme in the relationship between the dominant state and indigenous peoples. A review of extant literature and policy implementations shows that reconciliation is at the heart of the two related themes that dominate the emerging field of indigenous entrepreneurship (Hindle and Lansdowne 2002). Those themes are:

- How do we reconcile tradition with innovation?
- How do we employ mutual cultural understanding to blend the best of both worlds?

The globally relevant answer to both questions is: 'hard work based on structured understanding'. Establishing empathy between mainstream and indigenous cultures requires great efforts based on sensitivity to indigenous heritage. It is much easier to set out a list of 'must nots' than to create a positive agenda: the majority must not turn their indigenous fellow citizens into museum exhibits; the majority must not expect the indigenous minority to act in a way that outrages their cultural traditions; the rogue element among the majority must not be permitted to stigmatise the indigenous minority as welfare cheats or the recipients of special privileges; above all, the majority must not tell the indigenous minority what to do.

Perhaps the one unequivocal 'must' is that the majority must welcome diversity and respect the right of the indigenous minority to make its own decisions, subject only to the broadest public policy considerations.

Corporate entrepreneurship

Corporate entrepreneurship is becoming a field of study in its own right. Here, achievement is the motive and profit is the justification but the setting is far from independent. Returning to the argument of Shane and Venkataraman, summarised above in Figure 13.2, it may be argued that the crux of a corporate entrepreneurship decision is whether it is better to retain a new initiative 'in-house' (intrapreneurship) or create a 'spin-off' (corporate venturing).

The overwhelming fact about large corporations is their size. According to the 2002 GEM report (Reynolds et al. 2002), in 2001 18,247 companies across the 34 GEM reporting countries shared $US59 billion in venture capital, or about $US3.2 million each. By contrast, Pilkington plc, the respected glass manufacturer but by no means the largest company in Britain, invested £170 million (about $US240 million) on the acquisition of new fixed assets in 2001–02; the very large corporation General Motors invested $US7 billion in this period, or as much as over 2000 new ventures. These numbers understate the total investment in innovation by Pilkington and GM, since both of them treat R&D and new product marketing activities as a current expense.

Innovations requiring investments on a scale exceeding $50 million, or smaller innovations with a time to harvest of more than five to seven years, will be undertaken by a corporation or not attempted at all; only corporations have the money and the patience to support such investments and the patience is by no means guaranteed.

When a group within a corporation come up with an innovative concept, there will be, in most well-run companies, a process by which they can apply for support to develop it to the point where further development may require serious money. At this point further support may be denied; but if the concept is considered valuable, the corporation needs to consider whether to continue the development using project funding, with a view to incorporating the development into its operations and/or sales portfolio eventually; or whether to set up a subsidiary company with a view to eventually disposing of its interest by a sale or a flotation.

Extreme cases present no problem: if a Ford employee suggest a way of improving production of motorcars, the innovation will have to be carried out in-house or not at all; while if a Pilkington employee came up with a similar proposal, there would be few good reasons for keeping the idea to themselves. Difficulties, both in practice and in theory, occur in the messy middle and how such dilemmas are resolved changes with time and place. There is plenty of scope for research, both into the theoretically correct way such decisions should be approached and to expose temporal and spatial patterns of behaviour when such decisions are required.

Beyond the profit motive – government and social entrepreneurship

There is a role for entrepreneurship within government. We will not dwell on this beyond the point of saying that analogy is the relevant guide. Many of the principles informing the practice of entrepreneurship in the private sector are relevant. The key difference is that 'greater efficiency' and 'faster, better, more abundant service' or a similar constructs can replace 'profit' and 'growth', respectively, as the measures of entrepreneurial outcome.

Table 13. 2 **The entrepreneurship policy framework**

	Individuals at large	Firms in general	Industry in general	Government sector	Society at large
Individual entrepreneurs	Role models	Challenge	Leadership	Taxes	Inspiration
Entrepreneurial firms	Employment	Role models	Renaissance	Taxes	Applied innovation
Entrepreneurial industries	Affiliation	Networks	Role models	Strategy	Feasibility
Entrepreneurial governments	Capacity: Education	Capacity: Infrastructure	Capacity: Horizon	Capacity: Role models	Value
The entrepreneurial society	Motivation	Choice	Challenge	Priorities	Diversity

Source: Hindle and Rushworth 2000: 41

One can distinguish creative endeavour within government from its role as a stimulator of enterprise. The government, as a maker and implementer of entrepreneurship policy, can help a nation to a more entrepreneurial future. Hindle and Rushworth (2000) developed a 'policy matrix' which is helpful for understanding the role of government in fostering entrepreneurship. Table 13.2 provides a representation of their conclusions.

The total area of the matrix may be thought of as the nation's 'entrepreneurship opportunity space'. Entrepreneurship is based on the availability, perception and conversion of opportunity. Entrepreneurship is opportunity-driven management. The five rows of the framework represent five levels of stakeholders who have the capacity to influence entrepreneurial activity in a nation. They are the 'actors' in the opportunity space. The five columns represent the level at which an entrepreneurial impact (given by an actor) is received.

This is an impact model designed to help stakeholders see where and how they can have impact in the 'entrepreneurial opportunity space'. The word or phrase in each cell of the matrix (the 'cell word') summarises the type of impact each type of stakeholder can have on each type of audience. Each cell word is designed to summarise an 'impact relationship'. For instance, ask the question: 'What impact can entrepreneurial firms provide to individuals at large?' Scanning the matrix gives the answer: 'employment'.

The impact model is a way to bring specific policy problems and issues into sharp focus without losing sight of the total context. Thus this simple matrix can be a useful tool. because it defines a role for all stakeholders, not just government policy-makers. Clearly, government has a vital role to play in creating a supportive environment for entrepreneurship to flourish, but the other stakeholders in an entrepreneurial country must play their part too. The media, being the interpreter of the actions of the various stakeholders, has a part to play throughout the entire matrix.

Suggested policy directions are given for key stakeholders in each key issue area, but all stakeholders are encouraged to identify where they might make a contribution. Where specific suggestions are made, they were contributed by the expert interviewees.

Government's educational role is to provide the capacity for individuals to acquire the education and skills they need by making available adequate funding to educa-

tion and ensuring it is appropriately directed. This may include government programmes to deliver specialist skills training. Government can assist the provision of
capital by programmes aimed at stimulating investment in early stage ventures and
programmes aimed at directing more of the overall investment funds in an economy
towards the entrepreneurial sector. Regulation and taxation is clearly in the purview
of government. Although regulatory complexity is a factor inhibiting innovation, it
is not easy to change quickly and reforms often create as many new regulations as
they abolish old ones.

Government is the major driver of a nation's short-term collective outlook and
one of the most important influences on national long-term horizons. The 'entrepreneurial government' row of the entrepreneurship policy matrix is dominated by the
word 'capacity'. Addressing the short-term outlook issue is about providing capacity
in the long term and making this commitment publicly so that other stakeholders
can rely on it. Expenditure on education, R&D and information distribution infrastructure should be seen as an investment in 'knowledge capital' – not as a cost.

Finally, if government initiatives are to be really valuable they should be predomi-
nantly bipartisan, giving following governments of different political persuasion no
incentive to change, but only to improve the specific shape and direction of well-
founded policies in the national interest. An entrepreneurial government will create
really good programmes, which will facilitate a creative combination of consistency
and flexibility to its successors.

Moving from government to the non-profit volunteer component of society, one
can observe the importance and increasing prevalence of social entrepreneurship.
For social entrepreneurs, creating a new organisation is vital but profit is no part of
the motive.

Our great and small social institutions and not-for-profit social enterprises owe
their existence and development to a largely unknown and unsung group of heroes.
In recent times, they are coming to be recognised as social entrepreneurs. It is now
becoming increasingly common in the US to think of 'philanthropy' as 'social
venture capital'. The context in which social entrepreneurs operate and the environment which is conducive to the development of such other-directed enterprises, we
can think of as social entrepreneurship. The contribution of the social sector to the
quality of life enjoyed by citizens of countries such as the UK and other established
democracies is often taken for granted but its immense value can be readily seen by
looking at less fortunate countries which do not enjoy such a community-based
infrastructure.

Social entrepreneurs have much in common with their better known friends, the
business entrepreneurs, who are the creators and developers of the business enterprise sector. Indeed, successful business entrepreneurs often change themselves into
social entrepreneurs as they mature and broaden their understanding of the larger
community of which they are a part. Many now famous social institutions owe their
existence and growth to the generous contributions of business entrepreneurs and
the foundations they have set up and left behind.

Yet, while a highly developed education and research infrastructure richly supports the business sector and its entrepreneurs, this is not the case for social entre-

preneurs and social entrepreneurship. The need for this is now urgent and growing in importance. In the UK and many countries, the distribution of wealth has been steadily polarising over the last couple of generations. The impact of this process on the poorer segments of society is now a major issue. Our social sector needs a major infusion of new talent and new initiatives. The old strategies are no longer sufficient. Nations need social entrepreneurs as much as they need new captains of industry and dynamic civil servants.

The 'when' questions – temporality issues

Stage models and life cycles

At the firm level, there are many theories about the life cycles of typical and atypical entrepreneurial ventures. Different stages of an entrepreneurial process require different skills and emphases. One of the most often-cited and author-modified 'stage models' of the entrepreneurial process was introduced by Moore in 1986. A modified depiction of it is reproduced as Figure 13.5.

In a previous section, we introduced Daniel Forbes' (1999) work in which he synthesised the 34-work 'canon' of works devoted to entrepreneurial cognition written up to 1999. His analysis resulted in a summarising framework reproduced as Figure 13.6.

The importance of temporality is represented by a 'timeline dichotomy': prefounding and post-founding. In the pre-founding stage, the emphasis is on organisational *intentions* represented by two key concepts: perceived feasibility and perceived desirability. In the post-founding stage, an organisational sense-making framework proceeds from *scanning* (where the conceptual emphasis is upon aspects of infor-

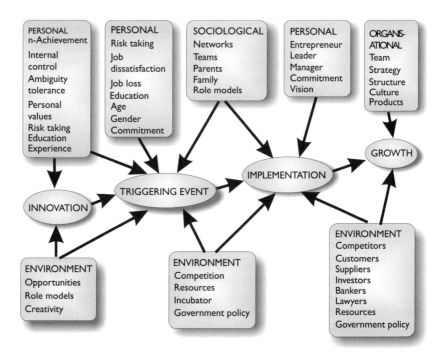

Sources: Adapted from Moore (1986); Bygrave (1989a); Bygrave and Churchill (1989b)

Figure 13.5 **Moore's framework of the influences on entrepreneurial process through time**

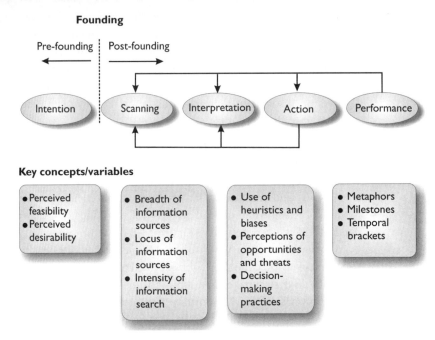

Source: Adapted from Forbes (1999)

Figure 13.6   **Forbes' cognitive stages in the development of new ventures**

mation sources), through *interpretation* (where the conceptual emphasis is upon the uses of heuristics and biases, perceptions of opportunities and threats and decision-making practices) through to *action*. The action phase places conceptual emphasis upon metaphors, milestones and temporal brackets. The final result is *performance*.

There is one dominant and simple implication to emerge from all the complexity inherent in the many forms of 'stage model' so popular in the entrepreneurship literature. Time and context are the essential factors for strategy development. There can be no non-contingent, all-embracing strategy for the entrepreneurial firm.

It's not a job for life

At the individual level, people often oscillate between being and not-being entrepreneurs. Indeed, if the ideal is to grow from small, improvisational venture to large, established corporation, success may demand that entrepreneurial founders make significant behavioural transitions. The early stage entrepreneur may well become the late stage technical manager. After selling out of successful ventures, some entrepreneurs do it all again (serial entrepreneurship) or become angel investors in others' new businesses. And some just retire and live on their capital.

Why do it, why study it?

Why be an entrepreneur?

The GEM studies have indicated that there are two fundamentally distinct motivations for being an entrepreneur: opportunity and necessity.

Opportunity entrepreneurs elect to start a business as one of several possible career options. Necessity entrepreneurs regard entrepreneurship as their last resort:

they feel compelled to start their own business because all other options for work are either absent or unsatisfactory. Using this categorisation in the 2002 *GEM Executive Report* (Reynolds et al. 2002), it was possible to label more than 97 per cent of those who were entrepreneurially active as either 'opportunity' or 'necessity' entrepreneurs. Indeed, according to the GEM 2002 research, three in five (61 per cent) of those involved in entrepreneurial endeavours across the world indicated that they were attempting to take advantage of a business opportunity, while 2 in 5 (37 per cent) stated that they were doing so because they had no other viable option. Still, great variability existed between GEM 2002's 37 countries in terms of the mix of the two motivations. For example, only about 1 per cent of Japan's labour force was currently pursuing opportunity-based endeavours, while in India and Thailand, 12 and 15 per cent, respectively, were so engaged.

The distribution of necessity entrepreneurship demonstrated even greater variation. For instance, there were virtually no necessity entrepreneurs in either France or Spain, while up to 7 per cent of the labour force was pursuing necessity entrepreneurship in Chile, China, Brazil and Argentina. In 17 of 37 countries the level of participation in necessity entrepreneurship was below 1 per cent, and in six it was below 0.5 per cent. In other words, in the nations ranking lower on entrepreneurial participation, less than 1 in 200 persons in the labour force participated 'involuntarily' in entrepreneurship.

There is an important issue as to whether the potential for a business to provide a major contribution to the economy is affected by the entrepreneur's motivation for initiating that business in the first place. Are necessity entrepreneurs, for example, only associated with small-scale, unsophisticated efforts that provide little more than self-employment for the founder-owner? Are opportunity entrepreneurs, therefore, the sole source of innovative, 'high impact' ventures? In order to address this important subject, the GEM 2002 research team compared the two motivations to each other along four dimensions widely presumed to contribute to national economic vitality:

1. expectations of job creation
2. projections for out-of-country exports
3. intention to replicate existing business activity or create a new niche
4. participation in one of four business sectors.

It is clear from this study that the motivation of the entrepreneur does in fact influence the direction and nature of the existing or proposed business entity. But further study will be required before we are ready to pontificate too vigorously about the relative 'merits' of necessity and opportunity entrepreneurship.

In relatively affluent countries where people have a definite choice, the reasons for choosing entrepreneurship will be as varied as the people who make the choice. It is likely that future research will confirm that desire for greater workplace autonomy ('being my own boss'), greater personal wealth ('you don't get rich working for somebody else') and a desire to make an impact on the world will remain as important as anecdote has always held them to be.

Why study entrepreneurship?

It is not well known in most parts of the world that entrepreneurship has been for many years a formal, academic discipline in its own right. In the US Academy of Management an interest group on entrepreneurship was formed in 1974. In 1987, it achieved the status of a division within the academy. Entrepreneurship is thus a distinct, established field of management science, possessing the same status as such other established managerial disciplines as marketing, organisational behaviour and finance. It is not legitimate for non-specialists to comment on, for argument's sake, physics if they have never heard of the theory of relativity. Is it any more legitimate for a commentator, no matter how well motivated, to enter the entrepreneurship debate without having read at least some of the relevant literature at the leading edge of world research in a vibrant and well-established scholarly field? We think not. There is a lot of knowledge already in the entrepreneurship scholarship box. Articulate members of a vibrant nation should use it. Why?

The first short answer – stemming from the discussion in the previous section – is 'jobs'. Anyone interested in the dynamism of an economy and a society should study entrepreneurship. Entrepreneurship is the engine of employment growth. It is the pacemaker implanted in any nation's economic heart. The electric jolts it gives to the economy are at once staccato and rhythmic. Without the shock of the new, old economies would wheeze, lumber and stall. Large, established corporations are always looking to reduce jobs in an effort to reduce costs. In developed nations, the majority of employment growth comes from a minority of high-growth, small and medium-sized entrepreneurial firms as they expand on their path to becoming the large corporations of tomorrow. Over the 30 years it took Richard Branson's Virgin Group to grow from nothing to 25,000 employees, GEC (now Marconi plc) headed in the opposite direction.

The entrepreneurially active respondents to the GEM 2002 survey were asked about their expectations for job creation. If they were in the process of starting a business, they were asked to project how many jobs they will have created five years after their start-up. If they were the owner/manager of a business less than 42 months old, they were asked to project how many jobs their venture will have created in the next five years. Worldwide, about 1 in 5 (20 per cent) reported that they expect to provide no jobs, and about 53 per cent of these individuals were necessity entrepreneurs. On the other hand, more than 1 in 4 entrepreneurially active adults expected to provide more than 20 jobs in five years, and about 70 per cent of these persons were motivated by opportunity. Figure 13.7 is a table of the distribution of job projections taken from answers provided in the UK 2002 GEM survey.

Now there is nothing bad and much good about a well-managed lifestyle business, so long as it creates value for its customers and joy for its owners. The great value of the small business sector lies in its variety. For many people, growth is an option they choose not to take. It is their right and their privilege. Well-managed, small-scale ventures are a cultural and economic necessity and just as deserving of policy initiatives and government support as any other sector of the nation.

But policies aimed at the majority of small businesses, which do not have high-growth aspirations, are unlikely to be of much assistance to the entrepreneurial firms. Therefore, it cannot be assumed that, because a government has developed a

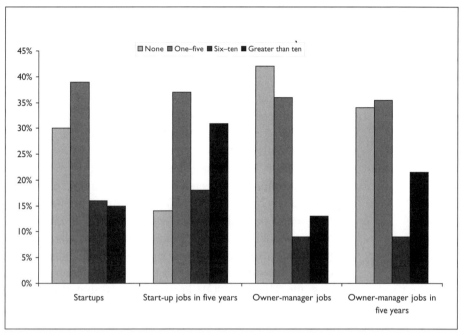

Figure 13.7 **Distribution of job projections**

small business policy, it has, in the process, addressed the needs of the minority of entrepreneurial businesses within that sector. Entrepreneurial businesses – the ones that achieve rapid growth and make disproportionate contributions to employment growth and tax revenues are a small minority – between 4 and 7 per cent of all small businesses (McMahon 2001).

Entrepreneurial enterprises therefore require special study on grounds of their difference from – not similarity to – the majority of small businesses. Focus on developing entrepreneurial enterprises needs to become a distinct element of national policy.

Since only a small minority of businesses will achieve substantial growth, it is tempting to try to identify those businesses before they grow and develop policy to assist them. This is easier said than done. In 1991, Turok asked the question – Which small firms grow? He tried to answer it with an empirical study of 166 firms among a population of small firms in West Lothian, a large district between Edinburgh and Glasgow in the UK (Turok 1991). He failed to find any simple, useful indicators of which firms would go on to achieve substantial growth.

Fortunately, policy-makers and those who help to provide them with guidance do not have to 'pick winners'. There is a whole industry, which exists solely to pick the growth venture winners. It is called venture capital. Many of the policy-makers' problems may possibly be resolved by focusing direct programmes on the general act of enriching the entrepreneurial environment – particularly the financial environment and, more particularly, the venture capital environment – than by attempts at direct intervention at the firm level. In either case, more detailed study of entrepreneurship is unarguably in the national interest. And it is not just of interest to would-be entrepreneurs but to society at large.

Entrepreneurship is not a solo endeavour. The old theme of 'the lone crusader versus the world' always was a myth and is now a dangerous one. So-called 'independent' entrepreneurship means 'different from corporate' entrepreneurship, not 'going it alone'. The first thing venture capitalists look at when an entrepreneur seeks funding is the quality of the management team. We need not forget the luminous examples of exceptional individuals as we seek a more plural basis for our study of the entrepreneurial phenomenon. There is a strong need for more studies which focus on the plurality and diversity of a society truly capable of fostering socially beneficial wealth creation.

In all this, we need to remember what entrepreneurship is not: it is not a panacea; it is not for everyone; it is likely to remain a minority employment choice; it is not the best path to all destinations. In summary, entrepreneurship is not the sole answer to achieving economic growth. Entrepreneurship can be a very inefficient process. Robert Cringely, Silicon Valley journalist, suffers no romantic notions about either entrepreneurship or venture capital and is very critical of the wastage involved in the start-win-or-crash nature of the game (Cringely 1992: 314). Wennekers and Thurik (2000) argue cogently that the economy needs a sensible balance of what McMahon (2001) would call the low-growth, capped-growth and high-growth firms.

Moreover, as we have discussed, being an entrepreneur is seldom a 'job for life'. The whole process is transitional. Yesterday's start-up team member of a dynamic, growth company may be today's technical director of a division of the large corporation that did the buy-out. That is good. That is success.

But the hard fact remains. On the critical issue of employment, entrepreneurship policy is far more important than small business policy and probably almost every other traditional policy heading usually associated with the attempt to ensure citizens have real, viable, valuable jobs. Unless policy-makers have the courage to face that fact and therefore make policy in the name of entrepreneurship (even though it is a 'minority' activity), they will be shirking the issue.

Good policy demands good research. The study of entrepreneurship is vital to a nation's economic and social destiny. And we still have a vast amount to learn. As Jay Barney says:

> Despite the early efforts of scholars like Schumpeter and Kirzner, and empirical efforts to describe the attributes of entrepreneurs that took place for over a decade, the field of entrepreneurship is still largely atheoretical. (Barney, in Fiet 2002: xiv)

From the point of view of economic and social potential, the key to dynamic and productive study of entrepreneurship will be a focus on what entrepreneurs can do rather than what they have done. Entrepreneurs can be fundamental and instrumental in building a better world. That is reason enough to study them with both diligence and fascination.

CHECKPOINT   You will almost certainly have read this book because of a practical interest in entrepreneurship, either as a student in a post-secondary education programme or as someone planning an entrepreneurial venture of some kind.

In this chapter we have endeavoured to expand our readers' horizons, both to see ways in which entrepreneurship skills may be applied to social problems and to outline some possibilities for research and teaching entrepreneurship. We haven't provided conclusions or recommendations for this chapter, or any revision questions. If you are interested, you may propose your own questions; and you may well find they are ones for which no one yet knows the answers and the way is clear for you to lead the way.

We know that this has not been an easy book to read, and if you have completed a business planning subject with this book as a text, you may find that you put in more effort than any of your other subjects demanded. We did not want to give you the impression that entrepreneurship was easy, or a matter of carrying out a set of precise instructions; but we do want you to feel that entrepreneurship can be an exceptionally rewarding activity, and not just financially.

Notes

1 This seminal article by Gartner is an often confused citation because the same paper appeared in two separate journals.

2 The area of highest consensus among entrepreneurship scholars is that 'newness' – in the sense of founding and developing a new organisation – is at the heart of the matter. The area of least consensus concerns the issue of growth. There remains considerable disagreement about the need for a founder of a new organisation to have conscious intentions in favour of high growth in order to qualify entrepreneurship as a category distinct from mere new business ownership. The would-be designer of a generic methodological framework must, of necessity, accommodate the full range of views on the growth issue, irrespective of personal belief as to whether growth or growth intention is a necessary condition of entrepreneurship.

Bibliography

Our sources

In this book we have attempted to set out a minimum of theory, very little of that in the form of a standard scientific argument, and we have tried to provide an essentially practical view of the problems and opportunities presented to an entrepreneur. The book is our original work, but we do not claim to be the originators of all the ideas in it. We have, throughout the text, used notes and references to identify those authors whose work most influenced our thinking. Undoubtedly we have failed to acknowledge all the writers who deserved it: to those we have slighted in this way we sincerely and humbly apologise.

There are two main strands in the references used in this book and in particular the works discussed in this bibliography. There are works originating in the study of entrepreneurship and management, essentially pragmatic discussions of relevant aspects of the real world: in general terms, such works introduce very little pure theory and may be based more on experience than on formal field research or the rigorous development of the consequence of stated postulates. Other works come from people who use much more rigorous approaches to analysis and the collection and reduction of data from field research: these people are often economists, by training who have chosen to step beyond the boundaries of the pure a priori model of economics.

Occasionally (not nearly often enough) there are cross-references: a management or entrepreneurship writer will quote an economist or (even more rarely) an economist will quote a management writer. Those economists who do deign to notice writers from outside their discipline often do so with a display of condescension straight from Jane Austen's Lady Catherine de Burgh. Non-economists, such as Kirchhoff (1991), reviewing the work of economists, tend to remark on the poverty of their models and show very little sympathy for the rigour needed before a true scientist can make an unequivocal statement.

Economics

Some of our readers may wish to move beyond the practical scenario set out in this book, and conduct research into those individual and environmental factors and techniques that promote or retard successful entrepreneurship. Others may wish to participate in debates about public policy insofar as they affect entrepreneurship and innovation; some will, of course, do both. The language of the public policy debate is that of economics, the queen or wicked witch (depending on one's perspective) of the social sciences, and participants need to be familiar with the main concepts and terms, at least.

It is not possible to even discuss entrepreneurship with economists from the modern neoclassical school, because recognisable entrepreneurs do not exist in their models (Baumol 1968). Barreto (1989), in a short, tightly argued monograph, explains why the entrepreneur is missing from contemporary economic orthodoxy and explains some alternative views such as the 'Austrian' description of entrepreneurship elaborated by Kirzner. To the extent that Barreto's argument can be summarised in a few words, it is that the centrality of the concept of general equilibrium to the neoclassical model, and its near centrality in the Austrian view, exclude the disequilibrating, innovating entrepreneur from serious consideration.

Freeman (1994) provides a survey of work by economists on growth and technological change, including a 22-page bibliography. Freeman and Soete (1997) provide a historical account of various epoch-making innovations going back to the middle of the eighteenth century before setting out some of the key conclusions of many years research at the Science Research Policy Unit (SPRU)[1] of the University of Sussex, where Freeman is an emeritus professor and former director. In this section we discuss a few of the major contributions to the theory of innovation-driven economic development.

Entrepreneurship

Ever since Newton's *Principia* set mathematical models at the pinnacle of a scientific paradigm, scientists of all disciplines – not just the physical sciences – have striven to express their theories mathematically. In the social sciences, mathematical models are more often than not a little more than a Laplacian[2] fantasy. Nevertheless, mathematics is being used more and more extensively by social scientists – none more so than economists and business researchers. Bygrave (1992) focuses on one area of social science, entrepreneurship, and examines the difficulties of trying to use mathematics to model entrepreneurship processes.

The entrepreneurship process involves a discontinuous change of state. It involves numerous antecedent variables. It is extremely sensitive to the initial value of these variables. To build an algorithm for a physical system with these characteristics would be daunting to the most gifted applied mathematician. Bygrave suggests that each instance of the entrepreneurship process is initiated by the volition of a unique human being, and for this reason mathematical modelling may be impossible, because there is an 'essential non-algorithmic aspect to conscious human action'. He argues that today's most prominent mathematical representation of entrepreneurship, population ecology, falls far short of Penrose's specification for a 'useful theory'.

Some observers believe that the answer to entrepreneurship theory may be found in chaos theory – a relatively new science popularised by Gleick (1987). Bygrave (1992) explores the chaotic zones of several algorithms that provide alluringly simple representations for the entrepreneurial process. One of them is the fundamental equation of population ecology theory. It shows how under some conditions that equation exhibits some wild, chaotic behaviour that gives an observer the feel of entrepreneurship. But it is no more than a mathematical metaphor because the accuracy of measurements that are needed to observe true scientific chaos in the entrepreneurial process are unattainable in practice.

Jennings (1994) provides an excellent treatment of the many ways that entrepreneurship can be – and is – perceived and explained. This book goes a little deeper into theoretical issues than is usual with entrepreneurship and management texts, and includes a short but lucid discussion of the relationship between economics and entrepreneurship. We can confidently recommend Jennings' book as a complementary text to this one, with some excellent cases and expositions. Papers by several of the authors listed below are also published in Jennings (1994).

A philologically precise definition of entrepreneurship will reveal a close link to the term 'enterprise' and in some senses at least an entrepreneur is one who creates and direct an enterprise, irrespective of its purpose. Baumol (1990) suggests that much the same talents will be required whatever the objectives of the enterprise. An entrepreneur may be ethical in the sense set out in Chapter 2, promoting an innovation that will have positive social and economic effects. Similar organisational and planning skills will be required to create an organisation devoted to extracting rents from society without contributing anything in return, or even after inflicting substantial costs on those outside the enterprise. While we prefer not to dignify the directors of unproductive and destructive enterprises with the epithet 'entrepreneur', we recognise that others are less fussy.

Notes

1 http://www.sussex.ac.uk/spru/index.html.
2 Pierre Simon, Marquis de Laplace (1749–1827) was a French mathematician and astronomer who completed Newton's work on the solar system. He came to believe that the universe could be completely explained by a system of equations to the point that, if some super- intelligent being knew the position and velocity of every particle in the universe at a particular time, that being would also know the entire history and future of the universe. Later mathematicians have proved that a Laplacian being, if it were to exist, must be infinitely more complex than the universe itself.

References

Abrams, Rhonda M. (1991), *The Successful Business Plan: Secrets and Strategies*, Oregon: Oasis Press.

Akerlof, George A. (1970), 'The Market for Lemons: Quality Uncertainty and the Market Mechanism,' *Quarterly Journal of Economics* (August), pp. 488–500.

Amis, D. and Stevenson, H. (2001), *Winning Angels: the 7 Fundamentals of Early-Stage Investing*, Harlow: Pearson Education.

Andersen, E. S. (1999), 'Railroadization as Schumpeter's Standard Example of Capitalist Evolution: An Evolutionary–Ecological Interpretation', *Paper for the workshop on Evolutionary Thought in Economics* (26–28 August), Jena: Max Planck Institute.

Ansoff, I. (1991), 'Critique of Henry Mintzberg's "The Design School: Reconsidering the Basic Premises of Strategic Management"', *Strategic Management Journal* **12**: pp. 449–461.

Arthur, W. Brian (1989), 'Competing Technologies, Increasing Returns, and Lock-in by Historical Small Events', *Economic Journal* **99**, pp. 11–31.

Arthur, W. Brian (1994), *Increasing Returns and Path Dependence in the Economy*, Ann Arbor: University of Michigan Press.

Atiyah, P. S. (1979), *The Rise and Fall of Freedom of Contract*, Oxford: Clarendon Press.

Axelrod, Robert (1984), *The Evolution of Cooperation*, New York: Basic Books.

Bacon, Francis (2003), *Novum Organum*: Preface [Webpage] [cited 7 May 2003]. Available from http://fly. hiwaay.net/~paul/bacon/organum/preface.html.

Banfe, Charles (1991), *Entrepreneur: From Zero To Hero:*

How to be a blockbuster entrepreneur, New York: Van Nostrand Reinhold.

Bangs, David, H. and Schaper, Michael (2001), *The Australian business planning guide: creating a plan for success in your own business*, 2nd edn, Warriewood, NSW: Business and Professional Publishing.

Barreto, Humberto (1989), *The Entrepreneur in Micro-economic Theory: Disappearance and explanation*, London: Routledge.

Bass, Frank M. (1969) 'A New Product Growth Model for Consumer Durables', *Management Science*, **15**(5), pp. 215–27.

Bass, Frank M., Krishnan, Trichy V. and Jain, Dipak C. (1994), 'Why the bass model fits without decision variables', *Marketing Science*, Linthicum: Summer **13**(3), pp. 203–23.

Baumol, William J. (1968), 'Entrepreneurship in Economic Theory', *American Economic Review*, Papers and Proceedings, **58**.

Baumol, William J. (1990), 'Entrepreneurship: Productive, Unproductive, and Destructive', *Journal of Political Economy* **98**(5, pt 1), pp. 893–921.

Baumol, William J. (1996), 'Entrepreneurship: Productive, Unproductive, and Destructive', *Journal of Business Venturing* **11**(1), pp. 3–22.

Bell, C. Gordon and McNamara, John E. (1991), *High-Tech Ventures: The guide for entrepreneurial success*, Reading, MA: Addison-Wesley.

Berle, Gustave (1989), *The Do-It-Yourself Business Book*, New York: John Wiley.

Bernanke, Ben S. (1983), 'Irreversibility, Uncertainty, and Cyclical Investment', *Quarterly Journal of Economics* **98**(February), pp. 85–106.

Bers, J. A., Lynn, S. A. and Spurling, C. (1997), 'Scenario Analysis: A Venerable Tool in a New Application: Strategy Formulation for Emerging Technologies in Emerging Markets', *Engineering Management Journal* **9**(2), pp. 33-40.

Blechman, Bruce and Levinson, Conrad (1991), *Guerilla Financing: Alternative techniques to finance any small business*, Boston, MA: Houghton Miflin.

Block, Z. and MacMillan, I. C. (1982), 'Can Corporate Venturing Succeed', *The Journal of Business Strategy* **3**(2), pp. 21–33.

Block, Z. and MacMillan, I. C. (1985), 'Milestones for successful venture planning', *Harvard Business Review* (September–October).

Block, Z. and MacMillan, I. C. (1993), *Corporate Venturing*, Boston, MA: Harvard Business School Press.

Bloom, Nick; Griffith, Rachel and Van Reenen, John (2002), 'Do R&D Tax Credits Work? Evidence from a panel of countries 1979-97', *Journal of Public Economics* **85**(1), pp. 1–31.

Boswell, James ([1791] 1896), Boswell's Life of Johnson (ed. Augustine Birrel) Vol. 1, Westminster: Archibald Constable & Co.

Boyd, Colin (1996), 'Case Studies in Corporate Social Policy' in Post, Frederick, *Business and Society*, New York: Lawrence and Weber.

Brandt, Steven C. (1982), *Entrepreneuring – The Ten Commandments for building a growth company*, New York: Nal Penguin.

Braudel, Fernand (1981), *Civilisation and Capitalism 15th–18th Century* (3 vols) (transl. Miriam Kochan, rev. Sién Reynolds), London: Collins/Fontana, originally published Paris: Library Armand Colin, 1979.

Bruck, Connie (1989), *The Predator's Ball: the junk-bond raiders and the man who staked them*, Melbourne: Information Australia Group.

Burroughs, Bryan and Helyar, John (1990), *Barbarians at the Gate – the fall of RJR Nabisco*, London: Arrow Books.

Bygrave, W. D. (1989), 'The entrepreneurship paradigm (I): a philosophical look at its research methodologies', *Entrepreneurship: Theory and Practice* **14**(20): pp. 7ff.

Bygrave, W. D. (1992), 'Theory building in the entrepreneurship paradigm', *Journal of Business Venturing* **8**, pp. 255–80.

Bygrave, W. D. and Churchill, Neil C. (1989), 'The entrepreneurship paradigm (II): chaos and catastrophes among quantum jumps?', *Entrepreneurship: Theory and Practice* **14**(2): pp. 7ff.

Bygrave, W. D., and Hofer, Charles W. (1991), 'Theorizing About Entrepreneurship', *Entrepreneurship Theory and Practice* **6**: pp. 13–22.

Bygrave, W. D. and Timmons, J. A. (1992), *Venture Capital at the Crossroads*, Boston, MA: Harvard University Press.

Bylinsky, Gene (1989), 'Where Japan Will Strike Next', *Fortune* **120**(7), pp. 42–9.

Card, David and Krueger, Alan B. (1994), 'Minimum wages and employment: A case study of the fast-food industry in New Jersey and Pennsylvania', *The American Economic Review* **84**(4), pp. 772–93.

Card, David and Krueger, Alan B. (1997), *Myth and Measurement: The New Economics of the Minimum Wage*, Princeton: Princeton University Press.

Card, David and Krueger, Alan B. (2000), 'Minimum wages and employment: A case study of the fast-food industry in New Jersey and Pennsylvania: A Reply', *The American Economic Review* **90**(5), pp. 1397–420.

Casson, Mark (1982), *The Entrepreneur*, Totowa, NJ: Barnes and Noble.

Chamberlin, E. H. ([1933] 1960), *The Theory of Monopolistic*

Competition, Cambridge, MA: Harvard University Press.

Cohen, Stephen S. and Fields, Gary (1999), 'Social Capital and Capital Gains: an examination of social capital in Silicon Valley', in Martine Kenney (ed.) *Understanding Silicon Valley*, Stanford: Stanford University Press, pp. 190–217.

Cohen, Stephen S. and Fields, Gary (2000), 'Social Capital and Capital Gains in Silicon Valley', *California Management Review* **41**(2), pp. 108–30.

Cohen, William A. (1990), *The Entrepreneur and Small Business Problem Solver: An encyclopaedic reference and guide*, 2nd edn, New York: John Wiley.

Cooper, Lee G. and Nakanishi, Masao (1988) *Market-Share Analysis: Evaluating Competitive Marketing Effectiveness*, Boston: Kluwer Academic Publishers [Internet publication (1999) http://164. 67. 164. 88/MCI_Book/new_page_2. htm]

Cornford, F. M. (transl.) (1966), *The Republic of Plato*, Oxford: Clarendon Press (first published 1941).

Coveney, Peter V. and Highfield, Roger (1995), *Frontiers of Complexity: The search for order in a chaotic world*, New York: Fawcett Columbine.

Crego, Edwin T. Jr, Deaton, Brian and Schiffrin, Peter D. (1986), *How to Write a Business Plan*, Melbourne: Centre for Professional Development.

Cringely, Robert X. (1992), *Accidental empires: how the boys of Silicon Valley make their millions, battle foreign competition, and still can't get a date.* London: Viking.

Currie, Wendy (1992), 'The Strategic Management of AMT in Japan, the USA, the UK and West Germany Part 1: Developing a Performance Measurement System for CAD in a US Manufacturing Company', *Management Accounting* **70**(10), pp. 32–41.

Daft, Richard L., and Weick, Karl E. (1984), 'Toward a Model of Organizations as Interpretation Systems', *Academy of Management Review* **9**(2): pp. 284ff.

Dawkins, Richard (1989), *The Selfish Gene*, new edn, Oxford: Oxford University Press.

Day, John (1991), *Small Business in Tough Times*, Melbourne: Lothian Publishing.

Deweerd, H. A. (1967), *Political-Military Scenarios*, Santa Monica, CA: Rand Corporation.

Dixit, Avinash K. (1992), 'Investment and Hysteresis', *Journal of Economic Perspectives*, **6**(1), pp. 107–32.

Dixit, Avinash K. and Pindyck, Robert S. (1994), *Investment under Uncertainty*, Princeton, NJ: Princeton University Press.

Dockner, Englebert and Jorgenson, Steffen (1988), 'Optimal Advertising Policies for Diffusion Models of New Product Innovation in Monopolistic Situations', *Management Science*, **34**(1), pp. 119–30.

Dodson, Joe A. and Muller, Eitan (1978), 'Models of New Product Diffusion Through Advertising and Word-of-Mouth', *Management Science*, **24**(15), November, pp. 1568–78.

Drucker, P. F. (1985), *Innovation and Entrepreneurship: Practice and principles*, New York: Harper & Row.

Eckert, Lee A., Ryan, J. D. and Ray, Robert J. (1985), *An Entrepreneur's Plan*, New York: Harcourt Brace Jovanovich.

Empson, John (1996), 'The History of the Milk Marketing Board 1933–1994: British Farmers' Greatest Commercial Enterprise', *Journal of the Royal Agricultural Society* **157**, pp. 21–36.

Fiet, James O. (2002), *The Systematic Search for Entrepreneurial Discoveries*, Westport, CT: Quorum Books.

Forbes, Daniel P. (1999). 'Cognitive approaches to new venture creation', *International Journal of Management Reviews* **1**(4): pp. 415ff.

Foster, Richard N. (1987), *Innovation: The Attacker's Advantage*, London: Pan Books.

Foxall, Gordon R. (1988), 'Marketing New Technology: Markets, Hierarchies, and User-initiated Innovation', *Managerial and Decision Economics*, **9**, pp. 237–50.

Freeman, Chris (1994), 'The economics of technical change (Critical survey)', *Cambridge Journal of Economics*, **18**, pp. 463–514.

Freeman, Chris and Soete, Luc (1997), *The Economics of Industrial Innovation* 3rd edn, London: Pinter.

Fry, F. L. (1993), *Entrepreneurship: A Planning Approach*, Minneapolis: West Publishing.

Fry, F. L. and Stoner, C. R. (1985), 'Business Plans: Two Major Types', *Journal of Small Business Management* **23**(1), pp. 1–6.

Fukuyama, Francis (1992), *The end of history and the last man*, London: Hamish Hamilton.

Fukuyama, Francis (1995), *Trust: the social virtues and the creation of prosperity*, New York: Free Press.

Galbraith, James K. (1998), *Created Unequal: the crisis in American pay*, New York: The Free Press.

Garnsey, E. (2002), 'The Growth of New Ventures: Analysis after Penrose', in C. Pitelis (ed.) *The Growth of the Firm – The Legacy of Edith Penrose*, Oxford: Oxford University Press.

Gartner, W. B. (1985), 'A Conceptual Framework for Describing the Phenomenon of New Venture Creation', *Academy of Management Review*, **10**(4), pp. 696–706.

Gartner, W. B. (1988), '"Who is an entrepreneur?" is the wrong question'. *American Journal of Small Business*, **13**, pp. 11–32.

Gartner, W. B. (1989a), 'Some Suggestions for Research on Entrepreneurial Traits and Characteristics', *Entrepreneurship: Theory and Practice* **14**(1): pp. 27ff.

Gartner, W. B. (1989b), '"Who is an entrepreneur?" is

the wrong question', *Entrepreneurship Theory and Practice*, **13**: pp. 47–64.

Gartner, W. B. (1993), 'Words Lead to Deeds: Towards an Organisational Emergence Vocabulary', *Entrepreneurship Theory and Practice*, **8**(3), pp. 231–40.

Gartner, W. B., Bird, Barbara and Starr, Jennifer (1992), 'Acting As If: Differentiating Entrepreneurial from Organisational Behavior', *Entrepreneurship: Theory And Practice*, **16**(3), pp. 13–32.

Geroski Paul A. (1999), 'A Review of *Evolutionary Economics and Creative Destruction* by J. Stanley Metcalfe', *Economic Journal*, **109**(453) pp. F256–8.

Gill, Alec (1994), 'All at Sea? The Survival of Superstition', *History Today*, **44**(12).

Gleick, James (1987), *Chaos: making a new science*, London: Heinemann.

Goldratt, Eliyahu M. and Cox, Jeff (1993), *The Goal. A Process of Ongoing Improvement*, Aldershot: Gower Publishing.

Golis, G. C. (1998), *Enterprise and Venture Capital: a business builders' and investors' handbook*, 3rd edn, Sydney: Allen and Unwin.

Greiner, L. E. (1972), 'Evolution and revolution as organizations grow', *Harvard Business Review* **50**(3), pp. 37–46.

Guttman, Joel M. (2003), 'Repeated Interaction and the Evolution of Preferences for Reciprocicity', *Economic Journal* **113**(July), pp. 631–56.

Hafsi, T. and Thomas, H. (1985), 'Planning under certain conditions: the case of Air France', Working Paper, Chicago: Graduate School of Business, University of Illinois.

Hamel, Gary and Prahalad, C. K. (1994), *Competing for the Future*, Boston MA: Harvard Business School Press.

Harberger, Arnold C. (1954), 'Monopoly and Resource Allocation', *American Economic Review Proceedings*, **44**(May), pp. 77–87.

Hartnett, Sir Laurence (1973), *Big Wheels and Little Wheels* (2nd edn), Melbourne: Gold Star Publications.

Heilbroner, R. (1986), *The Worldly Philosophers: The lives, times and ideas of the great economic thinkers*, New York: Simon and Schuster.

Hills, G. E. (1985), 'Market Analysis In The Business Plan: Venture Capitalists' Perceptions', *Journal of Small Business Management* **23**(1), pp. 38–46.

Hindle, K. (1997), 'An Enhanced Paradigm of Entrepreneurial Business Planning: Development, Case Applications and General Implications', Dissertation, Melbourne: Swinburne University of Technology.

Hindle, K. and Lansdowne, M. (2002), 'Brave Spirits on New Paths: Toward a globally relevant paradigm of indigenous entreprenuriship research', *Proceedings,*

Babson College Kauffman Foundation Entrepreneurship Research Conference, Boulder: University of Colorado.

Hindle, K. and Mainprize, B. (2003), 'A systematic approach to writing and rating entrepreneurial business plans', *Proceedings of the ASAC Conference 2003*, Halifax Nova Scotia: St Mary's University.

Hindle, K. and Rushworth, S. M. (2000), *Yellow Pages® Global Entrepreneurship Monitor Australia 2000*, Melbourne, Australia: Swinburne University of Technology.

Hindle, K. and Wenban, R. (1999), 'Australia's Informal Venture Capitalists: an exploratory profile', *Venture Capital* **1**(2), pp. 169–89.

Hodges, Andrew (1983), *Alan Turing – The Enigma of Intelligence*, London: Unwin Paperbacks.

Hodgkinson, Gerard P. (1997), 'The cognitive analysis of competitive structures: A review and critique', *Human Relations* **40**(6): pp. 625ff.

Hseih, Tsun-yan and Barton, Dominic (1995), 'Young Lions, High Priests and Old Warriors', *McKinsey Quarterly*, (2), pp. 62–74.

Huff, Anne Sigismund (1997), 'A current and future agenda for cognitive research on organizations', *Journal of Management Studies* **34**(6): pp. 947ff.

Ishihara, Shintaro (1991), *The Japan That Can Say No*, New York: Simon and Schuster.

Jacobs, Jane (1993) *Systems of Survival: a dialogue on the moral foundations of commerce and politics*, London: Hodder and Stoughton.

Jennings, Daniel F. (1994), *Multiple perspectives of entrepreneurship: text, readings and cases*, Cincinnati: South-Western Publishing.

Jennings, Daniel F. and Lumkin, J. L. (1989), 'Functionally Modelling Corporate Entrepreneurship: An Empirical Integrative Analysis', *Journal of Management*, **15**(3), pp. 485–503.

Jennings, Daniel F. and Munn, Joseph R. (1994), 'Firm Size and Entrepreneurial Activity: Schumpeter's Hypothesis Revisited', Conference Paper, Waco, TX: Hankamer School of Management, Baylor University.

Jones, Archer (1987), *The Art of War in the Western World*, London: Harrap.

Judge, Stephen (1999), *Business Law* (2nd edn), London: Macmillan – now Palgrave Macmillan.

Kanter, R. M. (1989), *When Giants Learn to Dance*, New York: Simon and Schuster.

Katz, J. A. and Gartner, W. B. (1988), 'Properties of emerging organizations', *Academy of Management Review* **13**(3): pp. 429–41.

Katz, J. A. and Peters, S. (2001), 'Understanding the entrepreneur in the growth process: a review and theory', *The International Journal of Entrepreneurship and Innovation Management* **1**(3/4).

Katz, R. L. (1970), *Cases and Concepts in Corporate Strategy*, Englewood Cliffs, NJ: Prentice-Hall.

Kauffman, Stuart A. (1993), *The Origins of Order: self-organisation and selection in evolution*, New York: Oxford University Press.

Kauffman, Stuart A. (1995), *At home in the universe: the search for laws of self-organization and complexity*, New York: Oxford University Press.

Kay, John A. (1993), *Foundations of Corporate Success: How business strategies add value*, Oxford: Oxford University Press.

Kay, John A. (1996), *The Business of Economics*, Oxford: Oxford University Press.

Kay, John A. (1998), 'Good Business', *Prospect* (March) http://www.prospect-magazine.co.uk.

Kay, John A. and Silberston, Aubrey (1995), 'Corporate Governance', *National Institute Economic Review*, **153**, August, pp. 84–97.

Keynes, J. M. (1936), *The General Theory of Employment, Interest and Money*, Cambridge: Cambridge University Press.

Kirchhoff, Bruce A. (1991), 'Entrepreneurship's Contribution to Economics', *Entrepreneurship: Theory and Practice*, **16**(2), pp. 93–112.

Kirzner, I. M. (1973), *Entrepreneurship and Economic Development*, New York: Free Press.

Knight, F. H. (1921), *Risk, Uncertainty and Profit*, Boston: Houghton-Mifflin.

Koolman, G. (1971), 'Say's conception of the role of the entrepreneur', *Economica* **38**: pp. 269–86.

Krugman, Paul (1996), *The Self-Organizing Economy*, Cambridge, MA: Blackwell.

Kuratko, Donald F. and Hodgetts, Richard M. (2004), *Entrepreneurship: Theory, Process and Practice* (6th edn), Mason, OH: Thomson/South-Western.

Langlois, Richard N. and Robertson, Paul L. (1994), 'An Evolutionary Approach to the Theory of the Firm', Conference paper, Canberra: Australian National University.

Lazonick, William (1991), *Business Organization and the Myth of the Market Economy*, Cambridge and New York: Cambridge University Press.

Legge, John M. (2002), 'Adapting and Extending the Bass Model to Forecast Sales of Frequently Repurchased Products', *Proceedings of the 16th ANZAM Conference*, Melbourne: La Trobe University.

Legge, John M. and Hindle, Kevin (1997), *Entrepreneurship: How Innovators Create the Future*, Melbourne: Macmillan Education.

Levitt, Theodore (1965), 'Exploit the Product Life Cycle', *Harvard Business Review*, November–December, pp. 81–94.

Lewis, Michael (1990), *Liar's Poker – two cities, true greed*, London: Coronet Books.

Longenecker, Justin G. and Moore, Carlos W. (1991), *Small Business Management: An entrepreneurial emphasis*, 8th edn, Cincinnati: South Western.

Longford, Elizabeth (1969), *Wellington, Years of the Sword*, London: Weidenfeld and Nicholson.

Longford, Elizabeth (1972), *Wellington, Pillar of State*, London: Weidenfeld and Nicholson.

Lumpkin, G. T. and Dess, G. G. (1996), 'Clarifying the entrepreneurial orientation construct and linking it to performance', *Academy of Management Review* **21**(1): pp. 135–72.

Lynn, Gary S. (1989), *From Concept To Market*, New York: John Wiley and Sons.

McGrath, R. G. and MacMillan, I. C. (1995) 'Discovery-driven Planning', *Harvard Business Review* **73**(4), pp. 44–54.

McLaughlin, Harold J. (1987), *Building Your Business Plan*, New York: John Wiley and Sons.

McMahon, Richard G. P. (2001), 'Deriving an empirical development taxonomy for manufacturing SMEs using data from Australia's business longitudinal survey', Dordrecht: *Small Business Economics*, **17**(3), pp. 197–212.

McMahon, Richard G. P., Holmes, S., Hutchinson, P. J. and Forsaith, D. M. (1993), *Small Enterprise Financial Management Theory and Practice*, Sydney: Harcourt Brace.

MacMillan, I. C. (1983), 'The Politics of New Venture Management', *Harvard Business Review*, November–December, pp. 8–16.

McMullan, Ed (2003), 'The Problems and Pitfalls of Creating an Entrepreneurship Program', *Proceedings of the Fostering Entrepreneurship: Building Better Entrepreneurs Conference*, Calgary: University of Saskatchewan.

McQuown, Judith H. (1992), *Inc Yourself*, New York: HarperCollins.

Mahajan, Vijay, Muller, Eitan and Bass, Frank M. (1990), 'New Product Diffusion Models in Marketing: A Review and Directions for Research', *Journal of Marketing*, **54**(1), pp. 1–26.

Main, Jeremy (1990), 'Manufacturing the right way', *Fortune* **121**(11), pp. 54–9.

Mainprize, B. and Hindle, K. (2003), 'Is The Quality of Entrepreneurial Business Plans Related to the Funding Decision?', *Paper Delivered to the Refereed Stream of the Babson-Kaufman Frontiers of Entrepreneurship research Conference*, Wellesley, MA: Babson College.

Mancuso, J. R. (1974), 'How a Business Plan is Read', *Business Horizons* (August).

Mansfield, Edward (1988), 'The Speed and Cost of Industrial Innovation in Japan and the United States: External vs Internal Technology', *Management Science* **34**(10), pp. 1157–68.

Marsh, David (1992), *The Bundesbank: the bank that rules Europe*, London: Heineman.

Marshall, Alfred (1920 [1949]), *Principles of Economics*, 8th edn, London: Macmillan – now Palgrave Macmillan.

Midgley, David F. (1977), *Innovation and new product marketing*, London: Croom Helm.

Milliken, Frances J. (1990), 'Perceiving and Interpreting Environmental Change: An Examination of College Administrators' Interpretation of Changing Demographics', *Academy of Management Journal* **33**(1): pp. 42ff.

Mintzberg, H. (1994), *The Rise and Fall of Strategic Planning*. New York: The Free Press.

Mintzberg, H. and Waters, J. A. (1982), 'Tracking Strategy in an Entrepreneurial Firm', *Academy of Management Journal*, **25**(3), pp. 469–99.

Mitchell, Ronald K., Busenitz, Lowell, Lant, Theresa and McDougall, Patricia P. (2002), 'Toward a theory of entrepreneurial cognition: Rethinking the people side of entrepreneurship research'. *Entrepreneurship: Theory and Practice* **27**(2): pp. 93ff.

Modis, Theodore (1992), *Predictions*, New York: Simon and Schuster.

Monod, Jacques (1971), *Chance and Necessity* (transl. A. Wainhouse), New York: Knopf.

Moore, C. F. (1986), 'Understanding entrepreneurial behaviour', in J. A. Pearce and R. B. Robinson Jr (eds) *Academy of Management Best Papers Proceeding, Forty-sixth Annual Meeting of The Academy of Management*, Chicago: Academy of Management.

Muzyka, D. F. (2000), 'Marking the key points on the opportunity map' in Birley, Sue and Muzyka, Dan (2000), *Mastering Entrepreneurship*, London: Financial Times/Prentice Hall.

Nelson, Richard R. and Winter, Sidney G. (1982) *An Evolutionary Theory of Economic Change*, Cambridge, MA: Belknap Press of Harvard University Press.

Nesheim, John L. (1992), *High Tech Start Up*, Saratoga, CA: Electronic Trend Publications.

Osgood, William R. and Curtin, Dennis P. (1984), *Preparing Your Business Plan With Lotus 1-2-3*, Englewood Cliffs, NJ: Prentice Hall.

Osgood, William R., Fletcher, William and Curtin, Dennis P. (1986), *Preparing Your Business Plan with Excel*, Berkeley, CA: Osborne/McGraw-Hill.

Paine, Lynn Sharp (1994), 'Managing for organizational integrity', *Harvard Business Review* **72** (March–April), pp. 106–17.

Paine, Lynn Sharp (1996), 'Moral thinking in management: An essential capability', *Business Ethics Quarterly* **6**(4), pp. 477–92.

Pearce, J. A. II, Freeman, E. B. and Robinson, R. B. Jr (1987) 'The Tenuous Link Between Formal Strategic Planning and Financial Performance', *Academy of Management Journal* **12**(4), pp. 658–75.

Pearson, N. (2000), *Our Right to Take Responsibility*, Cairns: Noel Pearson.

Penrose, E. ([1959] 1995), *The Theory of the Growth of the Firm*, Oxford: Basil Blackwell.

Pentony, B., Graw, S., Lennard, J. and Parker, D. (1999), *Understanding Business Law* (2nd edn), Sydney: Butterworths.

Peterson, R. A. (1982), *Marketing Research*, Plano, TX: Business Publications.

Phillips, A. (1986), 'Theory and the Analysis of Financial Markets', in G. Libecap (ed.), *Advances in the Study of Entrepreneurship, Innovation and Economic Growth*, Greenwich, CT: JAI Press.

Pitelis, Christos, (ed.) (2002), *The growth of the firm: the legacy of Edith Penrose*, Oxford: Oxford University Press.

Porter, Michael E. (1980), *Competitive Strategy: Techniques for analysing industries and competitors*, New York: The Free Press.

Porter, Michael E. (1985), *Competitive Advantage: Creating and sustaining superior performance*, New York: The Free Press.

Porter, Michael E. (1990), *The Competitive Advantage of Nations*, New York: The Free Press.

Prahalad, C. K. and Hamel, Gary (1990), 'The Core Competence of the Corporation', *Harvard Business Review*, May–June.

Putnam, Robert D. (1993a), *Making Democracy Work: Civic Traditions in Modern Italy*, Princeton: Princeton University Press.

Putnam, Robert D. (1993b), 'The Prosperous Community: Social capital and public life', *The American Prospect* **4**(13).

Rand, Ayn (1985), *Atlas Shrugged*, New York: Signet.

Reichheld, Frederic F. (1996), *The Loyalty Effect*, Boston, MA: Harvard Business School Press.

Reichheld, Frederic F. (2001), *Building Loyalty in the Age of the Internet*, Boston, MA: Harvard Business School Press.

Reynolds, Paul, Bygrave, W. D., Autio, Erkko and Hay, Michael (2002), *GEM Global Entrepreneurship Monitor 2002 Executive Report*, Boston and London: Babson College and London Business School.

Rice, Craig S. (1990), *Strategic Planning for the Small Business*, Holbrook, MA: Bob Adams.

Rich, Robert D. and Peters, Michael P. (1989), *Entrepre-*

neurship – *Starting, developing and managing a new enterprise*, Homewood, IL: Richard D. Irwin.

Rich, S. R. and Gumpert, D. E. (1985a), 'How to write a winning business plan', *Harvard Business Review* **63**(3), pp. 156–61.

Rich, S. R. and Gumpert, D. E. (1985b), *Business Plans That Win*, New York: Harper and Row.

Richardson, Bill and Richardson, Roy (1992), *Business Planning: An approach to strategic management*, London: Pitman.

Ridley, Jasper (1972), *Lord Palmerston*, London: Constable.

Roberts, Edward B. (1983), 'Business Planning in the Start-Up High Technology Enterprise' in Hornaday et al., *Frontiers of Entrepreneurship Research*, Wellesley, MA: Babson College.

Robinson, Joan (1969), *The Economics of Imperfect Competition*, 2nd edn, Cambridge: Cambridge University Press.

Romer, Paul M. (1986), 'Increasing Returns and Long Run Growth', *Journal of Political Economy*, **94**.

Romer, Paul M. (1994), 'The Origins of Endogenous Growth', *Journal of Economic Perspectives*, **8**(1), pp. 3–22.

Ronstadt, Robert (1989), *Entrepreneurial Financials*, Natick, MA: Lord Publishing.

Ropp, Theodore (1959), *War in the Modern World*, Durham, NC: Duke University Press.

Rosser, J. Barkley Jr (1991), *From catastrophe to chaos: a general theory of economic discontinuities*, Boston, MA: Kluwer Academic.

Rothschild, Michael L. (1992), *Bionomics: the inevitability of capitalism*, London: Futura.

Ruppel, Cynthia P. and Harrington, Susan J. (2000), 'The Relationship of Communication, Ethical Work Climate, and Trust to Commitment and Innovation', *Journal of Business Ethics* **25**(4) pt. 2, pp. 313–28.

Ryan, Fergus (1989), *Report Of Inquiry – Victorian Economic Development Corporation*, Melbourne: Government Printer.

Ryan, Graeme (1985), *Business Planning – How to kiss a princess*, Chatswood, NSW: G&S Ryan.

Sahlman, W. A. (1997), 'How to write a great business plan', *Harvard Business Review* (July–August), pp. 99–108.

Sahlman, William A. and Stevenson, Howard H. (1992), *The Entrepreneurial Venture*, Boston, MA: Harvard Business School Publications.

Sakiya, Tetsuo (1987), *Honda Motor: The Men, the Management, the Machines* (transl. Kiyoshi Ikemi, adapted Timothy Porter), Tokyo: Kodansha International.

Samson, Danny (1988), *Preparing a Business Plan*, Canberra: AGPS.

Sandy, W. (1990), 'Link Your Business Plan to a Perfor-

mance Plan', *The Journal of Business Strategy* (Nov/Dec), pp. 4–8.

Schillit, W. Keith (1990), *Entrepreneur's Guide to Preparing a Winning Business Plan*, Englewood Cliffs, NJ: Prentice Hall.

Schumpeter, J. A. (1933), 'The Analysis of Economic Change', *The Review of Economic Statistics*, **XVII**(4), pp. 2–10.

Schumpeter, J. A. (1934), *The Theory of Economic Development, An Inquiry into Profits, Capital, Credit, Interest and the Business Cycle* (transl. R. Opie), Cambridge, MA: Harvard University Press.

Schumpeter, J. A. (1939), *Business Cycles: A Theoretical, Historical, and Statistical Analysis of the Capitalist Process*, New York: McGraw-Hill, reprinted 1982, Philadelphia: Porcupine Press.

Schumpeter, J. A. ([1942]1967), *Capitalism, Socialism and Democracy*, London: Routledge.

Schwartz, P. (1991), *The Art of the Long View*, New York: Doubleday.

Schwenk, C. R. and Shrader, C. B. (1993), 'Effects of Formal Strategic Planning on Financial Performance in Small Firms: A Meta-Analysis', *Entrepreneurship: Theory and Practice* **17**(3), pp. 53–64.

Serle, Geoffrey (1982), *John Monash: A biography*, Melbourne: Melbourne University Press.

Shane, S. and Venkataraman, S. (2000), 'The promise of entrepreneurship as a field of research', *The Academy of Management Review* **25**(1), pp. 217–26.

Shaver, Kelly G. and Scott, Linda R. (1991), 'Person, process, choice; The psychology of new venture creation', *Entrepreneurship: Theory and Practice* **16**(2): pp. 23ff.

Sheridan, John H. (1990), 'World-class Manufacturing: Lessons from the Gurus', *Industry Week* **239**(15), pp. 35–41.

Siegel, Eric S., Schultz, Lauren A. and Ford, Brian R. (1988), *The Arthur Young Business Plan Guide*, Chichester: John Wiley.

Smith, Adam ([1759]1853), *The theory of moral sentiments: or, An essay towards an analysis of the principles by which men naturally judge concerning the conduct and character, first of the neighbours, and afterwards of themselves. To which is added a dissertation on the origin of languages.* (New edn with a biographical and critical memoir of the author, by Dugald Stewart), London: H. G. Bohn.

Smith, Adam ([1776]1835), *An Inquiry into the Nature and Causes of the Wealth of Nations*, Edinburgh: Nelson & Brown.

Solow, Robert M. (1956), 'Technical Change and the Aggregate Production Function', *Review of Economics and Statistics* **39**: pp. 65–94.

Stevens, Kathy C. and Martin, Linda R. (1989) 'The decline of US competitiveness: could internal decision models be to blame?', *S.A.M. Advanced Management Journal* **54**(1), pp. 32–6.

Stevenson, Howard H., Roberts, Michael J., Grousbeck, H. Irving and Bhide, Amar V. (1999), *New Business Ventures and the Entrepreneur*, 5th edn, Burr Ridge, IL: Irwin/McGraw Hill.

Sultan, Fareena, Farley, John U. and Lehmann, Donald R. (1990), 'A Meta-Analysis of Applications of Diffusion Models', *Journal of Marketing Research* **XXVII** (February), pp. 70–7.

Sykes, H. B. (1995), 'Critical assumption planning: a practical tool for managing business development risk', *Journal of Business Venturing* **10**(6), pp. 413–24.

Talbot, David (2003), 'Save the Earth – Dump Bush', *Salon* 19 November.

Taylor, James W. (1986), *How to Create A Winning Business Plan*, New York: Modern Business Reports.

Thomas, J., Clark, S. and Gioia, D. (1993), 'Strategic sensemaking and organizational performance: linkages among scanning, interpretation, action and outcomes', *Academy of Management Journal* **36**: pp. 239–70.

Timmons, J. A. (1980), 'A business plan is more than a financing device', *Harvard Business Review* **58**(2), p. 28ff.

Timmons, J. A. (1990), *New Venture Creation: Entrepreneurship in the 1990s*, 3rd edn, Homewood, IL: Irwin.

Timmons, J. A. (1994), *New venture creation: Entrepreneurship for the 21st century*, Homewood, IL: Irwin.

Tolkein, J. R. R. (1966), *The Lord of the Rings*, London: George Allen and Unwin.

Townsend, Robert (1970), *Up the Organisation*, London: Coronet.

Turok, Ivan (1991), 'Which small firms grow?' in Davies L. G. and A. A. Gibbs (eds), *Recent Research in Entrepreneurship*. Avebury, England, pp. 29–44.

Vesper, Karl H. (1993), *New Venture Mechanics*, Englewood Cliffs, NJ: Prentice Hall.

Vogelaar, Donald H. (1991a), *How To Write a Business Plan*, Melbourne: Information Australia Group.

Vogelaar, Donald H. (1991b), *How To Write Your Business Plan – Workbook*, Sydney: Prentice Hall.

Wade, R. (1990), *Governing the Market: Economic Theory and the Role of Government in East Asian Industrialisation*, Princeton, NJ: Princeton University Press.

Waldrop, M. Mitchell (1992), *Complexity: The Emerging Science at the Edge of Order and Chaos*, New York: Simon and Schuster.

Walsh, James P. (1995), 'Managerial and Organizational Cognition: Notes from a Trip Down Memory Lane', *Organization Science: A Journal of the Institute of Management Sciences* **6**(3): pp. 280ff.

Watson, Thomas J. Jr and Petre, P. (1990), *Father, Son and Co*, New York: Bantam Books.

Webster, F. A. and Ellis, J. (1976), 'The Very First Business Plan.' *Journal of Small Business Management* **14**(1), pp. 46–50.

Weick, Karl E. (1979), *The social psychology of organizing*, 2nd edn, New York: McGraw-Hill.

Welsh, John A. and White, Jerry F. (1983), *The Entrepreneur's Master Planning Guide*, Englewood Cliffs, NJ: Prentice Hall.

Weltman, J. C. (1995/1996), 'Using Consensus Forecasts in Business Planning', *The Journal of Business Forecasting* **14**(4), pp. 13–16.

Wenban, R., Hindle, K. G. and Jennings, D. F. (1996), 'How to Catch an Angel: a survey of profiles and perspectives in Australia's private equity market', *School of Management Working Papers*, Melbourne: Swinburne University of Technology.

Wennekers, Sander and Thurik, Roy (2000), 'Linking entrepreneurship and economic growth', *Small Business Economics* **13**, pp. 27–55.

Weston, J. F. and Brigham, E. F. (1993), *Essentials of Managerial Finance*, 11th edn, Fort Worth: The Dryden Press Harcourt Brace Jovanovich International edition.

Wilson, Derek (1988), *Rothschild: a story of wealth and power*, London: Mandarin Paperbacks.

Wyckham, R. G. and Wedley W. C. (1990), 'Factors related to venture feasibility analysis and business plan preparation', *Journal of Small Business Management* **28**(4), pp. 48–59.

Zhukov, Georgi K. (1969), *Marshal Zhukov's Greatest Battles* (ed. Harrison Salisbury), London: Macdonald.

Index